This book is based on some 1,400 individuals who lived in three northern English towns during the later middle ages. It analyses the many aspects of merchant society visible to the historian: achievements in politics, attitudes towards religion, the family, wider circles of friends and business acquaintances, and the nature and conduct of trade at every level.

Merchants were at the core of urban society, accumulating more wealth than most other townsfolk and developing a distinctive outlook and entrepreneurship in response to the opportunities and pressures of long-distance trade. They played a central role in the development of urban *mentalité*, using political rhetoric to promote a corporatist view of urban society, while their spending on charity, on public works and on religious observance shaped social attitudes.

JENNY KERMODE is Senior Lecturer in History, University of Liverpool

Cambridge Studies in Medieval Life and Thought

MEDIEVAL MERCHANTS

Cambridge Studies in Medieval Life and Thought
Fourth Series

General Editor:

D. E. LUSCOMBE

Leverhulme Personal Research Professor of Medieval History, University of Sheffield

Advisory Editors:

R. B. DOBSON

Professor of Medieval History, University of Cambridge, and Fellow of Christ's College

ROSAMOND McKITTERICK

Professor of Early Medieval European History, University of Cambridge,
and Fellow of Newnham College

The series Cambridge Studies in Medieval Life and Thought was inaugurated by G. G. Coulton in 1921; Professor D. E. Luscombe now acts as General Editor of the Fourth Series, with Professors R. B. Dobson and Rosamond McKitterick as Advisory Editors. The series brings together outstanding work by medieval scholars over a wide range of human endeavour extending from political economy to the history of ideas.

For a list of titles in the series, see end of book.

MEDIEVAL MERCHANTS

York, Beverley and Hull in the Later Middle Ages

JENNY KERMODE

CAMBRIDGE UNIVERSITY PRESS

PUBLISHED BY THE PRESS SYNDICATE OF THE UNIVERSITY OF CAMBRIDGE
The Pitt Building, Trumpington Street, Cambridge, United Kingdom

CAMBRIDGE UNIVERSITY PRESS
The Edinburgh Building, Cambridge CB2 2RU, UK   http://www.cup.cam.ac.uk
40 West 20th Street, New York, NY 10011–4211, USA   http://www.cup.org
10 Stamford Road, Oakleigh, Melbourne 3166, Australia

First published 1998
Reprinted 1999

Printed and bound in the United Kingdom at the University Press, Cambridge

Typeset in 11/12pt Monotype Bembo   [SE]

A catalogue record for this book is available from the British Library

Library of Congress Cataloguing in Publication data
Kermode, Jennifer
Medieval merchants: York, Beverley, and Hull in the later
Middle Ages / Jenny Kermode.
p.   cm. – (Cambridge studies in medieval life and thought)
Includes bibliographical references.
ISBN 0 521 49737 x (hardback)
1. Merchants – England – History.   2. England – Commerce – History.
3. Woolen goods industry – England – History.   4. England – Economic
conditions – 1066–1485.   5. England – Social conditions – 1066–1485.
6. Middle Ages.   I. Title.   II. Series.
HF3505.15K47   1998
381′.0942′09023–dc21   97–52953 CIP

ISBN 0 521 49737 x hardback

To
Mary and Michael,
Susan and Michael
and Michael

CONTENTS

Contents

ACKNOWLEDGEMENTS

This book has been a long time in gestation and its appearance in print is due to the interest and encouragement of many friends and colleagues. The longest serving and most important is Barrie Dobson who has observed the process from my student efforts in his Special Subject seminars at York to the final labour of publication. Richard Britnell, Ann Kettle and David Palliser read earlier versions of the manuscript, giving their advice and support when both were sorely needed. Christopher Allmand and Peter Hennock exerted firm pressure. Wendy Childs and Maryanne Kowaleski have generously shared suggestions and material with me, and, at different times over many years, Nick Alldridge, Caroline Barron, Judith Bennett, Bruce Campbell, Martha Carlin, Pat Cullum, Jeremy Goldberg, Alan Harding, Vanessa Harding, Derek Keene, Paul Laxton, Edward Miller, John Munro, Pamela Nightingale, John Oxley, Colin Phillips, Tony Pollard, Ben Power, Steve Rigby, Gervase Rosser, Heather Swanson and my siblings have made me reconsider some of my interpretations. I thank them all.

There have been many changes in the staff managing the archives at Beverley, Kingston upon Hull, York Borthwick Institute, York Minster Library and York City Record Office, but I especially want to thank Rita Freedman and Chris Webb for their help and patience over many years.

Domestic life can be undermined by the obsession demanded in writing a book but families often prove more resilient than the author. Helen and Richard Kermode have each been a distraction but always of the best sort and their encouraging tolerance was the greatest help of all.

I am at a loss quite what to say as thanks to my partner, Michael Power. He has been a pillar of strength: unstintingly supportive in practical matters and always able to refresh the formulation of this book with new approaches and ideas. It simply would not have been accomplished without him.

FIGURES

TABLES

List of tables

ABBREVIATIONS

See also manuscript sources in the Select bibliography, p. 354.

Arch. Reg.	Archbishops' Registers, Borthwick Institute of Historical Research, York
B C I–III	Beverley Borough Records, Humberside RO, Beverley
Beverlac	G. Poulson, *Bervelac, or the Antiquities and History of the Town of Beverley* (London, 1892)
Bev. Town Docs.	A. F. Leach, ed., *Beverley Town Documents*, Selden Society, 14 (1900)
BIHR	*Bulletin of the Institute of Historical Research*
BL	British Library
B R G I, B R E I and 2, B R B I	Hull Bench Books
Bronnen	H. J. Smit, ed., *Bronnen tot de Geschiedenis van den Handel met Engeland, Schotland, en Ierland, 1150–1485*, 2 vols. (The Hague, 1928)
Cal. Plea & Mem. Rolls City of London	A. H. Thomas *et al.*, eds., *Calendar of the Plea and Memoranda Rolls of the City of London, 1323–1482*, 6 vols. (Cambridge 1926–61)
CChR	*Calendar of Charter Rolls preserved in the Public Record Office, 1257–1516* (HMSO, 1906–27)
CCR	*Calendar of Close Rolls preserved in the Public Record Office, 1272–1509* (HMSO, 1900–63)
CFR	*Calendar of Fine Rolls preserved in the Public Record Office, 1272–1509* (HMSO, 1911–63)

C. Inq. Misc.	*Calendar of Inquisitions Miscellaneous preserved in the Public Record Office, Henry III–Henry V* (HMSO, 1916–69)
Corpus Christi Guild or CCG	R. H. Skaife, ed., *The Register of the Guild of Corpus Christi in the City of York*, Surtees Society, 57 (1872)
CPR	*Calendar of Patent Rolls preserved in the Public Record Office, 1272–1509* (HMSO, 1901–16)
Dec. & Cap.	Dean and Chapter Probate Register, Borthwick Institute of Historical Research, York
Durham Acct Rolls	J. T. Fowler, ed., *Extracts from the Account Rolls of the Abbey of Durham*, I, Surtees Soc., 99 (1898); II, 100 (1899); III, 103 (1901)
EETS	Early English Text Society
EcHR	*Economic History Review*
EHR	*English Historical Review*
Feodora	A. Clarke *et al.*, eds., *Rymer's Feodora, Conventions, Litterae, etc.*, 4 vols. (HMSO, 1816–69)
Hanseakten	K. Kunze, ed., *Hanseakten aus England, 1275–1412* (Halle, 1891).
Hanserecesse	C. Koppman, G. G. von de Ropp and D. Schafer, eds., *Die Recesse und andere Akten der Hansetage, 1256–1530*, 17 vols. (Leipzig, 1870–97)
House Book	York House Book, York RO
M&MA	M. Sellers, ed., *The York Mercers and Merchant Adventurers Company*, Surtees Society, 129 (1918)
MB	M. Sellers, ed., *York Memorandum Book*, I and II, Surtees Society, 120 (1911), 125 (1914); J. W. Percy, ed., *York Memorandum Book, B/Y*, III, 186 (1973)
Mem. Fountains	J. T. Fowler, ed., *Memorials of the Abbey of St Mary of Fountains*, III, Surtees Soc., 130 (1918)
PRO	Public Record Office
Prob. Reg.	Probate Registers, Borthwick Institute of Historical Research, York

RCHM	Royal Commission on Historical Monuments
RCHMS	Royal Commission on Historical Manuscripts
RO	Record Office: Chester, Humberside, Hull City, York City
Rot. Parl.	*Rotuli Parliamentum*, 6 vols. (London, 1783)
Test. Ebor.	J. Raine, snr and jnr, eds., *Testamenta Eboracensia*, I, Surtees Society, 4 (1836); II, 30 (1855); III, 45 (1865); IV, 53 (1869)
TRHS	*Transactions of the Royal Historical Society*
YAS	Yorkshire Archaeological Society
UHY	*Urban History Yearbook*
Urkundenbuch	K. Hohlbaum, K. Kunze and W. Stein, eds., *Hansisches Urkundenbuch*, 10 vols. (Halle and Leipzig, 1876–1907)
VCH Beverley	K. J. Allison, ed., *Victoria History of the County of York. East Riding*, VI (1989).
VCH Hull	K. J. Allison, ed., *Victoria History of the County of York. East Riding*, I (1969)
VCH York	P. M. Tillot, ed., *Victoria History of the County of York. City of York* (1961)
YCR	A. Raine, ed., *York Civic Records*, I, YAS, Record Series, 98 (1939); II, 103 (1941); III, 106 (1942)
Yorks Deeds	W. Brown *et al.*, eds., *Yorkshire Deeds*, I, YAS, Record Series, 39 (1909); II, 51 (1914); III, 63 (1922); IV, 65 (1924); V, 69 (1926); VI, 76 (1930); VII, 83 (1932); VIII, 102 (1940); IX, 111 (1948); X, 120 (1955)
Yorks Fines	W. P. Baildon, ed., *Feet of Fines for the County of York, 1327–47*, YAS, Record Series, 42 (1910); *1347–77*, 52 (1915)
York Freemen	F. Collins, ed., *Index of the Freemen of the City of York*, I, Surtees Society, 96 (1896)

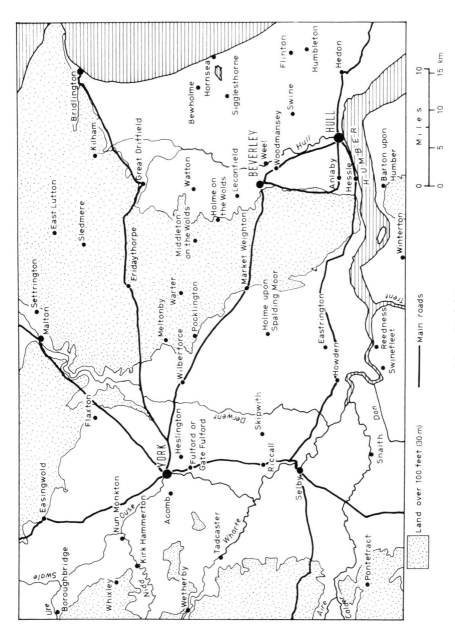

Map 1 Yorkshire

Land over 100 feet (30 m)

—— Main roads

0   5   10   Miles
0   5   10   15 km

INTRODUCTION

Medieval towns have been hailed as the cradle of modern society, places where flexible attitudes developed as a consequence of new forms of association: the partnerships, guilds and companies which economic activity particularly encouraged.[1] Many towns developed an environment which especially favoured entrepreneurs, and in the most successful of all, the commercial sector was more significant than even the most flourishing of specialised crafts.[2] York, Beverley and Hull were certainly places of innovation but also of conservatism as a result of the constant inflow of newcomers engaging with traditions and customs which were themselves subject to change.[3] Although many townsfolk had their own, sometimes recent, experience of rural communities, life in a town was very different from that in country villages.[4] Continued contact with rural birthplaces,[5] trade, the purchase of manors, intermarriage and polit-

[1] In Max Weber's view, these networks undermined the influence of family, kin and religion, creating fertile conditions for individualism to flourish: *Wirtschaft und Gesellschaft*, ed. J. Winkelmann (Tubingen, 1972), pp. 788, 815, 818, cited in J-P. Genet and N. Bulst, eds., *La ville, la bourgeoisie et la genèse de l'état moderne (XIIᵉ–XVIIIᵉ siècles)* (Paris, 1988), pp. 7–8. See also P. M. Hohenberg and L. H. Lees, *The Making of Urban Europe 1000–1950* (Cambridge MA, 1985), pp. 22, 36.

[2] It was a developed commercial sector which distinguished the medium and larger towns in western Europe from their smaller and less successful competitors: N. G. Pounds, *An Economic History of Medieval Europe* (2nd edn, London, 1994), pp. 227–8, 255–61.

[3] P. J. P. Goldberg, *Women, Work, and Life Cycle in a Medieval Economy. Women in York and Yorkshire c. 1300–1520* (Oxford, 1992), pp. 76–7, 280–304, 338; D. M. Palliser, 'A Regional Capital as Magnet: Immigrants to York, 1477–1566', *Yorks Arch. Jnl*, 57 (1985), pp. 111–23; *VCH Beverley*, p. 57; *VCH Hull*, p. 80; *VCH York*, pp. 108–9. For urban migration elsewhere see: P. McLure, 'Patterns of Migration in the Late Middle Ages: The Evidence of English Place-Name Surnames', *EcHR*, 2nd ser., 32 (1979), pp. 167–82; D. G. Shaw, *The Creation of a Community. The City of Wells in the Middle Ages* (Oxford, 1993), p. 59.

[4] For a discussion of some specific urban characteristics, see P. J. P. Goldberg, 'Urban Identity and the Poll Taxes of 1377, 1379, and 1381', *EcHR*, 2nd ser., 43 (1990), pp. 194–216 at p. 212; D. M. Palliser, 'Urban Society', in R. Horrox, ed., *Fifteenth-Century Attitudes. Perceptions of Society in Late Medieval England* (Cambridge, 1994), pp. 132–49 at p. 145.

[5] Some townsfolk could, for instance, refer to rural vicars by name. See, for example, *Test. Ebor.* I, p. 119 (Richard Ferriby) and for wider rural contacts see Prob. Reg. II, f. 243v. (Richard Patrington).

ical association with country families helped to blur the borders for a minority, but for the majority, urban living was a distinctive experience. Daily life in a densely populated town required a higher level of regulation and control but also offered a greater range of cultural and economic opportunities than was available in the countryside. In common with many of the larger English centres, York, Beverley and Hull had diverse occupational and social structures, aspects which have been the subject of much recent historical research.[6] However, comprehending the dynamics of urban society remains a daunting task and historians continue to disagree about the nature of relationships within towns and about the degree of consensus townsfolk shared.[7]

This study focuses on one urban group, the merchants: men, and very occasionally, women, whose livelihood largely depended on investments in wholesale trade and commerce.[8] They were at the core of urban society, accumulating more wealth than most. Through their spending on charity, on public works and on religious observance, they played an important part in shaping attitudes and in establishing collective objectives. This is not to claim that other groups were not also influential but the combination of commercial and secular power gave merchants a disproportionate prominence in urban affairs. In government, the political rhetoric of merchant oligarchs promoted a narrowly corporatist view of urban society, defining citizenship as part of the process of legitimising their own position. Merchant rulers thus had a central role in the development and management of urban *mentalité*, whether reflecting and responding to popular needs or imposing their own.

At a time when the social and geographical awareness of most Yorkshire urban migrants probably ended at their home village, usually only some fifteen to twenty miles distant from any of the three towns,[9] men whose knowledge extended beyond even London to continental Europe had a different perspective and outlook from most of their neighbours. The commercial world of late medieval Yorkshire merchants could extend from Iceland to North Africa and the Middle East.[10]

---

[6] In York, for example, Barrie Dobson has discussed one group of religious in 'The Residentiary Canons of York in the Fifteenth Century', *Jnl Eccl. Hist.*, 30 (1979), pp. 145–74, and 'Mendicant Ideal and Practice in Late Medieval York', in P. V. Addyman and V. E. Black, eds., *Archaeological Papers Presented to M.W. Barley* (York, 1984), pp. 109–22; Jeremy Goldberg, women, *Women, Work, and Life Cycle*; and Heather Swanson, craftsmen, *Medieval Artisans. An Urban Class in Late Medieval England* (Oxford, 1989).   [7] See below, pp. 11–14.

[8] See N. S. B. Gras, *Business and Capitalism* (Harvard, 1939), pp. 67–92 for a discussion which was perhaps too limited by the desire to locate different types of merchant within categories.

[9] See above, note 3.

[10] J. L. Bolton, *The Medieval English Economy 1150–1500* (London, 1980), pp. 287–319. Coins and precious metals travelled even further than goods. For the geographical extent of the interconnected and separate monetary systems functioning at this time, which took English coins to present-day Vietnam, see J. F. Richards, ed., *Precious Metals in the Later Medieval and Early Modern*

Overseas traders became geographically mobile and acquainted with all types and conditions of people from chancery clerks to Dutch porters, English abbesses and Baltic fur traders. They acquired a wide political awareness and expertise in foreign courts and cultures, as well as a knowledge of exotic commodities and currency exchange rates.[11]

Historians have generally concentrated their investigations of English medieval merchants on outstanding individuals such as Alice Claver, William de la Pole, Richard Whittington and the Cely family.[12] These studies have provided invaluable insights into the complex world of late medieval trade and finance but raise difficulties in assessing how typical such individuals were of the merchant class as a whole. Moreover, some historians have confined their discussions to probate records, evidence mainly of wealth and piety;[13] others have analysed mercantile business but paid little attention to political or personal matters.[14] It has therefore been difficult to establish a broader impression of both the social and political characteristics of the merchant community, and of the pattern of trading activity at every level within it.

The notable exceptions are the broader studies of Eleanora Carus-Wilson, Sylvia Thrupp and Pamela Nightingale.[15] All three explore inte-

---

Worlds (North Carolina, 1983), pp. 3–26; E. B. Fryde, 'Italian Maritime Trade with Medieval England (*c.* 1270–*c.* 1530)', *Recueils de la Société Jean Bodin*, 32 (1974).

[11] Such experience could be acquired rapidly. Just a year after becoming a freeman of York in 1471 and when 'about 23 years old', John Hagg of York was acting as a witness in a dispute in Bergen-op-Zoom, *Bronnen*, II, pp. 1056–7.

[12] C. M. Barron, 'Richard Whittington: The Man Behind the Myth', in A. E. J. Hollaender and W. Kellaway, eds., *Studies in London History Presented to Philip Edmund Jones* (London, 1969), pp. 197–248; A. Sutton, 'Alice Claver, Silkwoman', in C. M. Barron and A. F. Sutton, eds., *Medieval London Widows 1300–1500* (London, 1994), pp. 129–42; E. B. Fryde, *William de la Pole. Merchant and King's Banker* (London, 1988); Alison Hanham, *The Celys and Their World. An English Merchant Family of the Fifteenth Century* (Cambridge, 1985); R. Horrox, *The de la Poles of Hull*, East Yorkshire Local History Series, no. 38 (Hull, 1983); M. K. James, 'A London Merchant in the Fourteenth Century', *EcHR*, 2nd ser., 8 (1955–6), pp. 364–76 (Gilbert Maghfeld); E. Power, 'Thomas Betson, a Merchant of the Staple in the Fifteenth Century', and 'Thomas Paycocke of Coggeshall, an Essex Clothier in the Days of Henry VII', in her *Medieval People* (1924; 10 edn, London and New York, 1963), pp. 116–69.

[13] P. V. McGrath, 'The Wills of Bristol Merchants in the Great Orphan Books', *Trans: Bristol & Glos. Arch. Soc.*, 68 (1951) (seventeenth-century merchants); G. H. Nicholson, 'Bristol Merchants and their Wills in the Later Middle Ages' (Univ. of Birmingham MA thesis, 1970).

[14] E.g. Gilbert Maghfeld and see E. B. Fryde, *Some Business Transactions of York Merchants: John Goldbeter, William Acastre and Partners, 1336–1349*, Borthwick Paper No. 29 (York, 1966).

[15] P. Nightingale, *A Medieval Mercantile Community. The Grocers' Company and the Politics and Trade of London, 1000–1485* (Yale, 1995); S. L. Thrupp, *The Merchant Class of Medieval London* (Ann Arbor, 1948), and 'The Grocers of London, a Study of Distributive Trade', in E. Power and M. M. Postan, eds., *Studies in English Trade in the Fifteenth Century* (Cambridge, 1933), pp. 247–92; E. M. Carus-Wilson, 'The Merchant Adventurers of Bristol in the Fifteenth Century', *TRHS* 4th ser., 11 (1928). For a later period, see W. G. Hoskins, 'The Elizabethan Merchants of Exeter', in S. T. Bindoff, J. Hurstfield and C. H. Williams, eds., *Elizabethan Government and Society* (London, 1961), pp. 163–87; D. H. Sacks, *The Widening Gate. Bristol and the Atlantic Economy 1450–1700* (Berkeley and London, 1991).

grated aspects of the merchant community: its wealth, politics and social status. Eleanora Carus-Wilson was less interested in Bristol merchants as a social and political group than in their overseas trade. Sylvia Thrupp presented a virtual *histoire totale* of London merchants, discussing social attitudes, life expectancy, literacy, social cohesion and politics but largely ignoring their commercial ventures overseas. Her work on the London Grocers' Company, in contrast, was an assessment of their distributive trade within England, accompanied by an outline of their political development. The most recent study of the Grocers' Company, by Pamela Nightingale, traces its commercial and constitutional history, as part of a wider narrative of the interplay between traders and metropolitan and national politics.

This book is more inclusive and attempts to analyse all levels of merchant society by considering some 1,400 individual merchants who lived in York, Beverley and Hull during the fourteenth and fifteenth centuries.[16] The intention is to look at merchants' lives in as many aspects as are visible to the historian: their ambitions and achievements in politics, their attitudes towards religion, their family and extended circles of friends and business acquaintances, the nature and conduct of their trade at every level, and the impact such a significant group had upon their town communities.

In many respects the picture of Yorkshire merchants which emerges is similar to that of their London contemporaries. Both comprised a mobile and fluid class of people who quickly accumulated wealth within a single lifetime, only to see it as rapidly dispersed. Each generation largely made its own fortunes, earning a livelihood by developing distinctively flexible entrepreneurship in response to the peculiar opportunities and pressures exerted by long-distance trade. Merchants in Yorkshire exercised considerable influence on cultural and political life, and in some respects, like their London counterparts, may well have had more in common with merchants from other towns than they had with their fellow burgesses. However, it is difficult to identify a merchant class drawing apart from the rest of urban society, as Sylvia Thrupp did in the case of London. What was apparent in York, Beverley and Hull, however, was shared attitudes and ambitions, shaped by the distinctive experience of commerce and the exercise of political authority into an evolving class-consciousness.

---

[16] Neville Bartlett compiled biographies of York citizens, including merchants, but did not cover as many aspects as this present study or analyse them as a group: J. N. Bartlett, 'Some Aspects of the Economy of York in the Later Middle Ages, 1300–1550' (Univ. of London PhD thesis, 1958).

METHODOLOGY

In 1924, in her preface to *Medieval People*, subtitled *A Study of Communal Psychology*, Eileen Power argued for the value of reconstructing single lives as an antidote to learned treatises on economic developments. Twenty-four years later, Sylvia Thrupp adopted a more prosopographical approach to the London merchant class, commenting on the difficulty of constructing a 'type biography, a silhouette portrait that is a composite of many profiles and coincides with none'.[17] Both approaches have much to commend them, although biographies are probably more successful in overcoming some of the difficulties historians face in consolidating the separately recorded activities of an individual into a rounded portrait.[18] In this study, a middle way is taken. Thus, the variety of individual experiences is described but against a background of common characteristics.

Whether the following pages engage with all the merchants, however defined, of late medieval York, Beverley and Hull is another issue. It is more than likely that many have slipped through the net of this study (over 100 became freemen of York alone each year in the 1360s); but it does include those for whom probate records survive,[19] whose trading and commercial activities can be tracked in customs records and published sources,[20] and those whose political careers can be described from town and national records. The nature of particular sources and the interpretive problems associated with them are discussed in the appropriate chapters below. Occupational ascriptions provided the initial identification of individuals,[21] but the merchant group is defined in this study as including those who described themselves or were described as *mercator* or *mercer*, as well as anyone else who is recorded as active in regional or overseas trade and can be identified as of York, Beverley or Hull. A key

---

[17] Power, *Medieval People*, p. vii; Thrupp, *London Merchant Class*, p. xii.

[18] For an excellent collection of biographies see Barron and Sutton, *Medieval London Widows*; cf. J. I. Kermode, 'The Merchants of York, Beverley and Hull in the 14th and 15th centuries' (Univ. of Sheffield PhD thesis, 1990), appendix 4.

[19] J. Charlesworth and A. V. Hudson, eds., *Index of Wills and Administrations entered in the Registers of the Archbishops at York, 1316–1822*, YAS Rec. Ser., 93 (1937); F. Collins, ed., *Index of Wills from the Dean and Chapter's Court at York, 1321–1636*, YAS Rec. Ser., 38 (1907); *Index of Wills in the York Registry, 1389–1514, 1514–1553*, YAS Rec. Ser., 6 (1889), 11 (1891).

[20] K. Hohlbaum, K. Kunze and W. Stein, eds., *Hansisches Urkundenbuch*, 10 vols. (Halle and Leipzig, 1876–1907); C. Koppman G. F. von der Ropp and D. Schafer, eds., *Die Recesse und andere Akten der Hansetage, 1256–1530*, 17 vols. (Leipzig, 1870–91); H. J. Smit, ed., *Bronnen tot de Geschiedenis van den Handel met Engeland, Schotland, en Ireland, 1150–1485*, 2 vols. (The Hague, 1928); W. S. Unger, ed., *Bronnen tot de Geschiedenis van Middelburg in den landsheerlikjen Tijt*, 2 vols. (The Hague, 1923–6); J. Lister, ed., *The Early Yorkshire Woollen Trade*, YAS Rec. Ser., 64 (1924).

[21] Hard and fast divisions were probably only relevant for guild or company membership and some men embraced a wide description of their activities. John Richmond of York described himself in 1442 as chapman, alias shipman, alias mariner and finally as merchant: *CPR 1441–68*, p. 35.

criterion for inclusion in the analysis of trade below, therefore, is the identification of wholesale traders as opposed to retailers. This two-pronged approach, definition by function as well as by description, proved to be reasonably satisfactory, even though there were self-styled merchants, making wills, but not apparently engaged in local or distant trade, and other merchants active in trade and claiming residence in one of the three towns, but for whom no other corroborative evidence has survived.[22] The difficulties in describing regional and local trade are discussed in chapter 8.

The group under detailed discussion constitutes a cross-section of merchants, a mixture of elite and lesser merchants more representative than the top 1 or 2 per cent usually assumed to be typical. It will become apparent that not every merchant can be included in every analysis, a point starkly emphasised when quantifying the data. The quantification of inconsistent data is controversial but it overcomes some of the problems raised by relying on illustrative anecdotes drawn from exceptional but richly detailed documents. It is tempting to pick out the 'plums' as universally representative, but it is important that these are tested against a broader sample to establish just how far they do reflect widely shared attitudes. A context has been created here by combining as wide a range of evidence as possible, and revealing the unusual examples as atypical instances of many aspects of personal and business life.[23] Basic, less detailed but more numerous documents should not be ignored but taken as a complete record and aggregated to establish a balanced context.[24] Care has also been taken to include only those records which contain appropriate material for each analysis. Thus, although the probate records for 658 individuals have been consulted, the statistical analysis of religious expenditure was based on 412, and of cash estates on 425. The statistical discussion of overseas trade is based on 695 individuals who were active during three periods: 1306–36, 1378–1408 and 1460–1500. The overlap in sources for individuals is not large: information on both trading activities and estates at death was found for 225 merchants.

---

[22] The repeated trawling of documents is an essential process in compiling cumulative lists. Once the search of the Customs Account Rolls had begun, it became clear that identifying the home base of some of the merchants was a problem and so the names of those regularly listed alongside known York, Beverley or Hull merchants were noted, and checked in other sources.

[23] For an example of the anecdotal approach, see Eamon Duffy who argues that unusual and full preambles to wills are 'important indicators of the theology concealed under the simpler' preambles: E. Duffy, *The Stripping of the Altars. Traditional Religion in England 1400–1580* (New Haven and London, 1992), p. 326. See below, chapter 4.

[24] For a provocative discussion of the 'new social history', see J. A. Henratta, 'Social History as Lived and Written', *Am. Hist. Rev.*, 84 (1979), pp. 1293–333.

Introduction

YORK, BEVERLEY AND HULL

These three towns provide a good basis for comparison, located within forty miles of each other in south-east Yorkshire, on the lowland plain between the River Ouse and the uplands of the Yorkshire Wolds. The great north road linking southern England to the Scottish borders and the extensive Ouse/Humber river system were the keys to the region's development (see map 1). The Ouse was a great commercial highway, navigable up to Boroughbridge on the Ure. Its Yorkshire tributaries carried wool, and later cloth and lead, into the Humber and thence overseas through Hull. Timber was carried from Hull to Lincolnshire via the Trent and Foss Dike, and wool from the Lincolnshire Wolds back to Hull. Lead from Derbyshire and the south Pennines came down the Rivers Don and Trent, and wine returned to the north midlands by the same route. The Humber was the gateway to the North Sea fisheries and served all three towns. York enjoyed a strategic position, dominating regional road and river networks and the fertile Vale of York. Beverley, however, was not on any major road or waterway, and without the improved Beck would have been entirely land-locked. Edward I's new town of Hull, standing at the confluence of the River Humber and its tributary, the River Hull, had the advantage of a natural harbour and dominance of the Humber estuary.

Strategically adjacent to an extensive wool producing region, each of the three towns could readily engage in England's growing overseas trade. Perhaps more than any other factor, investment in North European markets accounted for the economic success of one urban centre over another during this period. Within the region, York, Beverley and Hull outran smaller rivals such as Hedon, Scarborough, Whitby and Yarm so that, by *c.* 1300, those ports had to be content with a limited role in coastal trade and a marginal involvement with international markets.[25] One important consequence was the absence of a sizeable merchant class in any other Yorkshire town in the later middle ages: a circumstance which afforded the merchants of York, Beverley, and Hull considerable influence beyond the immediate environs of their own towns. Even so, only Hull survived the international recession of the fifteenth century with some shreds of its overseas trade intact. By 1500, York and Beverley had fewer merchants actively engaged in trade beyond the region and, instead, came to rely on a mixture of traditional urban functions.

---

[25] For a fuller discussion of the region's development, see D. Hey, *Yorkshire from AD 1000* (London, 1986), pp. 1–118; Goldberg, *Women, Work and Life Cycle*, ch. 1. For a discussion of the region's urban development, see J. I. Kermode, 'Northern Towns' in *The Cambridge Urban History of Britain*, 1 (Cambridge, forthcoming).

York, with a population of probably some 14–15,000 in 1377, was a large and imposing city by English standards: capital of the north and second only to London in importance.[26] The city's forty-one or so parishes created an impressive array of spires and towers alongside those of fifteen religious foundations and the Minster itself. The panorama, from any direction, confirmed York's regional pre-eminence through the size and grandeur of its public buildings and the prevalence of stone and stained glass. York's strategic location guaranteed it regular royal visits and constant attention, drawing the city into national and county politics. The government lodged there in the early fourteenth century when the king was campaigning in the north. Parliament met in York thirteen times. In addition Richard II removed his household and government to York in 1392, but the city played no formal role in royal government until Richard III established the future Council in the North there in 1484.

Over the centuries, successive kings had demanded loyalty, cash, troops, hospitality and sanctuary and in return York had steadily acquired constitutional privileges until royal charters of 1393 and 1396 gave it the status of an independent incorporate county.[27] York was beholden to no-one except the king, from whom the city was held at farm: set at £100 since 1086. Its two MPs attended parliament regularly, paid by a council which was strongly committed to maintaining its national and regional presence. As home to the Minster, diocese and archbishopric of York, the city acquired an ecclesiastical importance which extended throughout the north of England. Archdeacons of Richmond and other officials of the archbishop routinely set out from York on their visitations into the northern counties and over the Pennines, drawing laymen back into the city to attend to church matters.

More mundanely, the presence of so many clerks, ecclesiastical offices and religious institutions created one of the largest, and perhaps most self-indulgent, consumer populations in the north. An unusually large conglomeration of highly specialised craftsmen resulted, with at least fifty craft guilds active in the fourteenth and fifteenth centuries. York combined an extensive industrial sector with its service role and had been a centre for textile and leather workers since the early thirteenth century at least; it was also the principal bell-foundry in the north. The city's thrice-weekly general markets, its fish, corn and cattle markets, and three annual fairs, attracted visitors from across the region.[28] They came to buy

---

[26] Pounds, *Economic History of Medieval Europe*, pp. 227–8, 255–61. For all that follows on York, see *VCH York*, pp. 25–116.

[27] See S. Rees-Jones, ed., *York 600: The Government of Medieval York. Essays in Commemoration of the 1396 Royal Charter*, Borthwick Studies in History, 3 (York, 1997).

[28] *VCH York*, pp. 484–91.

essential goods, imported dyestuffs, teasels and wine, alongside more exotic continental luxuries: almonds and liquorice, Mediterranean fruit and spices, silks and brocades. Performances of the Mystery Plays probably brought in countless more visitors as did royal dispensations of charity to the poor in the late fourteenth century.[29]

What distinguished York from other northern towns, apart from its size, was its complex combination of functions and its unique social and cultural ambience. However, even a varied economic base was not proof against shifts in England's trade and successive visitations of plague. From the prosperous heights of the 1370s and '80s, the city began to slide into recession. By 1524–5, its population had fallen to around 6–8,000, its investment in overseas trade had all but disappeared and its textile industry had severely contracted.

Beverley was originally an almost entirely ecclesiastical creation.[30] The town had grown around the Minster, under the lordship of archbishops of York. Pilgrims were attracted to St John's shrine from the eighth century, and by the 1120s, Beverley had become a borough with its own hansehus and annual fair. By 1377 it had a population of some 5–6,000. Like York, Beverley was an early textile centre, manufacturing a distinctive Beverley 'blue' cloth for export. Its proximity to the Yorkshire Wolds was an advantage to the town's merchants collecting wool and grain, giving them a significant edge over rivals in the early fourteenth century. A fairly diverse economy developed in the town and there were at least thirty-nine craft guilds active in the 1390s. The Beverley Mystery Play cycle may have attracted large crowds, as in neighbouring York, but performances became less frequent in the 1430s, suggesting that any economic advantages were insufficient to overcome the reluctance of the craftsmen to perform them. Two weekly markets and four annual fairs maintained Beverley's place as the largest market town in the East Riding: some compensation for being overwhelmed by the rise of Hull in international trade. By 1524–5, Beverley had disappeared from the ranks of major provincial towns and its population had shrunk by maybe a third to around 2,000.

The town remained subordinate to its seigneur, the archbishop of York, and was governed by twelve keepers under the supervision of his steward, not achieving independence until the 1545 charter of incorporation. MPs had represented the town between 1295 and 1306, but not again in the middle ages. Beverley never developed an expensive commitment to civic display, perhaps because its seigneur, the archbishop, and

---

[29] J. H. Harvey, 'Richard II and York', in C. M. Barron and F. R. H. Du Boulay, *The Reign of Richard II: Essays in Honour of May McKisack* (London, 1971), p. 210.

[30] For most of what follows, see *VCH Beverley*, pp. 2–47, 218–22.

local patrons, the Percy family, kept civic ambition in check.[31] Maybe their proprietorial attitude discouraged religious orders since only two friaries and the preceptory of the Knights Hospitallers were established in the town. The Minster canons may have been equally discouraging since they retained control over the two parishes which had been detached from their prebendaries in the thirteenth century.[32]

In a number of important respects, Hull was quite unlike either York or Beverley.[33] It did not share their antiquity, had little industry and was almost entirely engaged with port activities. When Edward purchased Wyke on Hull from Meaux Abbey in 1293, the small port was already well established: sixth in England in the value of its trade in 1203–5. Edward enlarged the quay, built a new water-mill and improved the roads from York, Beverley and Hessle. He extended the duration of the two weekly markets and annual fair, built a ditch around the town and in 1297 designated Hull as one of the nine English ports through which wool and leather could be traded. Two years later Hull was granted borough status, and in 1440 could afford to buy its independence as an incorporate county.

From the outset, the new borough concentrated on trade and exploited its position at the mouth of the Humber to control shipping. It remained a small town with a population of about 3,000 in 1377 which had scarcely changed by 1524–5. In 1401 contemporaries acknowledged that Hull was the 'key to the adjoining country and whole county of York'.[34] Manufacturing developed slowly and there is no record of craft guilds until the early fifteenth century: four or five by the 1470s including weavers, tilers and tipplers.[35] The town church, Holy Trinity, was dependent on the nearby parish of Hessle, although acquiring some parochial rights. Apart from two, possibly three friaries, and the Charterhouse founded in 1378, no other religious orders settled in Hull.

Developments within medieval English boroughs were also reflected in increasing record keeping. This was as much an expression of constitutional achievements as a consequence of bureaucratic necessity.[36] Borough archives usually contain copies of charters, milestones on their road to autonomy, financial records and some form of precedence book. Of the three towns considered here, York's records are the most plentiful and well organised.[37] The main categories consulted in this study were

---

[31] *Bev. Town Docs.*, p. 33; *VCH Beverley*, pp. 28, 34–42.   [32] *VCH Beverley.*, p. 162.

[33] For most of what follows, see *VCH Hull*, pp. 1–89, 407–12.

[34] *C. Inq. Misc., 1399–1422*, pp. 92–3.

[35] *VCH Hull*, pp. 56, 58; Hull RO, BRE I, pp. 16v., 17, 23v.; BRB I, ff. 39(2), 105, 120; M 479/356.

[36] Rees-Jones, 'York's Civic Administration 1354–1464', in her *York 600*, pp. 109–12.

[37] For extracts and discussion of all the York records, see A. F. Johnston and M. Rogerson, eds., *Records of Early English Drama: York*, 2 vols. (Toronto and London, 1979).

the freemen's rolls; the memorandum books[38] and their successors, the house books;[39] and the fourteen surviving chamberlains' account rolls.[40] Beverley has no separate record of freemen's entries but lists were recorded from time to time on the dorse of several of the sixteen account rolls which have survived between 1344 and 1502. The paper cartulary, great guild book and governors' minute book are Beverley's books of record and there is a small collection of borough deeds.[41] Like Beverley, Hull has no separate freemen's rolls, but a few lists have survived in three of the bench books,[42] Hull's books of precedent and record. Fifty-six chamberlains' rolls are extant and the city has a good collection of deeds.[43]

URBAN SOCIETY

The influx of migrants, attracted by opportunities for personal betterment, created problems as did the diverse occupational and social structure which characterised urban society.[44] Increased specialisation in the larger towns was matched by an increase in the numbers of semi- and unskilled and non-franchised people living at the margins, magnifying the distance between the top and bottom of urban society.[45] For some recent commentators, that very diversity generated such tension and conflict that the constant challenge was to find ways of keeping the townsfolk together.[46]

---

[38] M. Sellers, ed., *York Memorandum Book*, I and II, Surtees Soc., 120 (1911), 125 (1914); J. W. Percy, ed., *York Memorandum Book B/Y*, III, Surtees Soc., 186 (1973).

[39] First edited by A. Raine, *York Civic Records*, I–III, YAS Rec. Ser., 98 (1939), 103 (1941), 106 (1942), and partly replaced by a complete edition of books 1–6; L. C. Attreed, ed., *York House Books 1461–90*, 2 vols. (Stroud, 1991).

[40] R. B. Dobson, ed., *York City Chamberlains' Account Rolls 1396–1500*, Surtees Soc., 192 (1980).

[41] Extracts from all the Beverley sources appear in A. F. Leach, ed., *Beverley Town Documents*, Selden Soc., 14 (1900), and *Report on the Manuscripts of the Corporation of Beverley*, RCHMSS (1900); M. Bateson, ed., *Borough Customs*, 2 vols., Selden Soc., 18 (1904), 21 (1906).

[42] Hull RO, BRG 1; BRE 1; BRE 2; BRB 1.

[43] K. M. Stanewell, *Calendar of the Ancient Deeds, Letters, Miscellaneous Old Documents etc. in the Archives of the Corporation* (Hull, 1951). The account rolls for 1321–34 and 1464–65 have been edited, together with a selection of rentals, in R. Horrox, ed., *Selected Rentals and Accounts of Medieval Hull, 1293–1528*, YAS Rec. Ser., 141 (1983).

[44] R. H. Hilton, ' The Small Town as Part of Peasant Society', in his *The English Peasantry in the Later Middle Ages* (Oxford, 1975), pp. 76–94; R. Holt and G. Rosser, *The Medieval Town. A Reader in English Urban History 1200–1450* (London, 1990), p. 4; G. Rosser, *Medieval Westminster 1200–1540* (Oxford, 1989), p. 120; D. G. Shaw, *The Creation of a Community. The City of Wells in the Middle Ages* (Oxford, 1993), pp. 64–5.

[45] See Rosser, *Medieval Westminster*, pp. 217–25 for an interesting discussion of the inequalities of wealth distribution and of a specific group of marginal people, those seeking sanctuary at Westminster.

[46] Discussed in S. H. Rigby, *English Society in the Later Middle Ages. Class, Status and Gender* (London, 1995), pp. 169–77. As evidence for social cohesion, historians have highlighted instances of collective action as strategies for containment, whether the refurbishing of a church or street cleaning. See Rosser, *Medieval Westminster*, p. 3; Shaw, *Wells*, p. 132.

The development of urban government can therefore be seen either as a mediating process which diminished tension between the individual and society, or as the imposition of the ruling merchant oligarchy's ethos, proclaiming corporate values. If political and social cohesion was achieved, perhaps it emerged more naturally within the simpler structures of small towns. Large towns, like York, Beverley and Hull, were comprised of many groups of varying complexity and durability: families and households, workshops, parish congregations, fraternities and guilds.[47] It was probably the latter which eased the induction of migrants into urban life and gave them a sense of belonging, rather than the exhortations of merchant rulers to accept their idea of the 'community'.

Urban society was unquestionably hierarchic and, even though rank may have been perceived in material rather than occupational terms,[48] some occupations, such as commerce and trade, became synonymous with wealth. Contemporaries were sharply aware of distinctions between one group and another: most obviously that between the privileged burgesses and non-burgess residents. Surviving records abound with terms such as *inferiores*, *mediocres*, *probi homines* and so forth.[49] Hierarchy was routinely visible in the conduct of civic affairs and emphatically so in the blending of religious and civic ceremonials.[50] It extended from the mayor, alderman and council officials, to the craft and religious guilds with their own hierarchy of aldermen and wardens, subordinate searchers, masters and journeymen, and ultimately down to the faceless, statusless majority. Such organisations might have inculcated deference but, as we shall see, tensions erupted into violence in all three towns, most frequently in York where the mercantile oligarchy worked hard to impose its corporatist view.

Historians have to describe urban dwellers collectively, and acknowledge the divisions of hierarchy and of social and economic ranking. The

[47] See, for example, Charles Phythian-Adams' reconstruction of the subtleties and minor scale of personal and neighbourhood networks in Coventry: *Desolation of a City. Coventry and the Urban Crisis of the Late Middle Ages* (Cambridge, 1979), pp. 69–184.

[48] D. M. Palliser, 'Urban Society', in R. Horrox, ed., *Fifteenth-Century Attitudes. Perceptions of Society in Late Medieval England* (Cambridge, 1994), p. 141. In Coventry, even the distribution of holy bread was by rank and social degree: Phythian-Adams, *Desolation of a City*, p. 137.

[49] Hohenberg and Lees, *Urban Europe*, pp. 43–6. See below, p. 27, for political ranking.

[50] C. Phythian-Adams, 'Ceremony and the Citizen: The Communal Year at Coventry 1450–1550', in P. Clark and P. Slack, eds., *Crisis and Order in English Towns 1500–1700* (London, 1972), reprinted in Holt and Rosser, *The Medieval Town*, pp. 238–64; Phytian-Adams, *Desolation of a City*, pp. 170–9; M. K. James, 'Ritual, Drama, and Social Body in the Late Medieval English Town', *Past & Present*, 98 (1983), pp. 3–29; S. H. Rigby, 'Urban "Oligarchy" in Late Medieval England', in J. A. F. Thomson, ed., *Towns and Townspeople in the Fifteenth Century* (Gloucester, 1988), pp. 74–7; David Mills, 'Chester Ceremonial: Re-creation and Recreation in the English "Medieval" Town', *UHY* (1991), pp. 4–5. In the absence of formal local government, Gervase Rosser focuses on parish ceremonial, *Medieval Westminster*, pp. 271–4.

process has become complicated since the term 'community' has been corrupted by the cultural filters of the late twentieth century.[51] The current use of 'community' has implications of comprehensiveness and neighbourliness whereas the medieval understanding was often of a different phenomenon, a selective, exclusive minority.[52] Thus contemporary documents make it clear that the generality of townsfolk or commonalty (the non-burgesses) were outside the corporate body although ruled by it. Several meanings of community can be employed, sometimes simultaneously. Thus we talk of a city as a single community, of the parish community, neighbourhood and street communities. 'Community of interest' might be the controlling perspective of rulers, the economic interdependence of craftsmen and traders, or collective religious beliefs.

The idea that there was such a phenomenon as a town community is difficult to sustain, except perhaps in the widest possible sense of everyone living in a given area, and it is probably more meaningful to talk of the freemen community or, indeed, of the merchant community. 'Community' can also be an evaluative term to indicate the quality of relationships – invariably the positive quality of those relationships seen as a form of constructive neighbourliness or the compromises negotiated between individual aspirations and collective tolerance. The latter suggests a recognition of shared goals and values, collective philosophies articulated within such groups as religious fraternities, civic and guild oligarchies. However, we cannot know how widespread support for any of these notions may have been and to identify anything more coherent and durable is difficult, even in the case of merchants.[53]

More generally, there is no way of measuring the level and quality of townspeople's commitment to a consensus, except when participation fell short of prescribed requirements and the miscreant was punished. It is probable that the more closely group aspirations matched those of an individual, the more positively he or she engaged with that group, but it is also clear that the commitment of medieval townsfolk to collective goals was not constant and was often qualified. Not every householder willingly fulfilled ward duties or attended church. The extent to which urban populations participated in church life for instance, is itself open

---

[51] For the accumulation of definitions, see M. Stacey, 'The Myth of Community Studies', *British Jnl of Sociology*, 20 (1969), pp. 134–47.

[52] For a discussion of the medieval understanding of the term *communitas*, see S. Reynolds, 'Medieval Urban History and the History of Political Thought', *UHY* (1982), pp. 14–23.

[53] Some scholars regard community as a transient experience: 'not a continuous state, but [something] realised momentarily at particular conjunctures': Rosser, *Medieval Westminster*, p. 248; M. Taylor, *Community, Anarchy and Liberty* (Cambridge, 1982).

to question.[54] The relative importance of the parish church *vis-à-vis* the ward must have varied from town to town. York for instance had six wards and some forty-one parish churches, whereas Beverley had fourteen wards and only two parishes.[55] Not everyone opted into formal, hierarchic associations. We do not know for sure, but it seems likely that as many as 30 to 50 per cent of male poll tax payers in the late fourteenth century chose not to or could not become freemen and thereby participants in the formal political process.[56] Sometimes qualified craftsmen preferred to remain as journeymen and not progress into their guild establishment as masters.[57] Abusing civic officials was common and was countered with regular propagandist displays to encourage a more 'corporate' view.

In any case, as recent work on Wells has made clear, 'community' implying a collective philosophy can only be applied to a defined group, the burgesses, who are equated with the most active and aspirant part of the lay community – shapers and custodians of the town's *mentalité* and institutions.[58] The body of freemen was an exclusive group: the privileged townsfolk who paid to enjoy all the commercial and legal advantages conferred to their town by charter. They dominated the political institutions and urban records, making the history of medieval boroughs largely their history. However, we should not assume that they represented all townsfolk.[59]

Contemporary records offer many perspectives which reflected

---

[54] Contemporaries commented on popular irreligion: people 'come to matins no more than three times a year . . . they chatter, they lark about, [and] mock the priest', P. Hodgson, '*Ignorantia Sacerdotum*: A Fifteenth Century Discourse on the Lambeth Constitutions', *R. of English Studies*, 24 (1948), p. 11. Quoted in R. N. Swanson, *Church and Society in Late Medieval England* (Oxford, 1989), p. 253.

[55] *VCH York*, pp. 314–15, 365–6; *VCH Beverley*, p. 162. For a fuller discussion from the extensive metropolitan evidence for later centuries, see J. Boulton, *Neighbourhood and Society. A London Suburb in the Seventeenth Century* (Cambridge, 1987), especially chapter 10, and S. Rappaport, *Worlds within Worlds: Structures of Life in Sixteenth-Century London* (Cambridge, 1989).

[56] This was in the late 1370s at a time when towns were seeking immigrants to replace the high rate of population loss: R. B. Dobson, 'Admissions to the Freedom of the City of York in the Later Middle Ages', *EcHR*, 2nd ser., 26 (1973), pp. 17–18; Goldberg, *Women, Work, and Life Cycle*, pp. 52–4. For similar proportions see Phythian-Adams, *Desolation of a City*, p. 132; Shaw, *Wells*, pp. 140, 142–3.

[57] *VCH Hull*, p. 56; *VCH York*, p. 95. In fifteenth-century Canterbury there was a separate category of 'intrants', paying an annual fine to work and trade in the city: A. F. Butcher, 'Freemen Admissions and Urban Occupations', unpublished paper, Urban History Conference, Canterbury (1983).

[58] Shaw, *Wells*, pp. 7–8. See also F. Tonnies, *Community and Society*, translated by C. P. Loomis, 2nd edn (New Brunswick, 1988), pp. 64–7.

[59] Phythian-Adams describes the 'artificial construction' of a corporate image of Coventry and the dominance of the elite voice which led to society seeing itself as a 'community' even though one fifth of the townsfolk were excluded from burgess rights: *Desolation of a City*, pp. 170–80.

different levels of social and political interaction and the existence of several 'communities' within a single urban area. Some were shaped by ideology, others by material needs. It is likely that the more dependent, the poor, the very young and elderly people had stronger neighbourhood needs.[60] An occupation that was not geographically constrained, as well as wealth, helped people to transcend narrow local networks so that their personal links extended beyond the immediate vicinity of their homes and workplaces.[61] The degree of control a person exercised over his or her livelihood largely determined the structure of their personal network of relationships: that of a merchant or skilled artisan for instance, would differ greatly from that of an unskilled labourer. Each though, would recognise some links as strong, others as weak and their relative significances changed according to circumstances. Weak links such as those between the unfranchised and town rulers might strengthen during times of external threat and slacken during an economic recession. Whether or not individual networks ever coalesced into an overarching sense of urban community remains an open question, but was perhaps more likely within a sub-group such as merchants.

MERCHANTS

Merchants, it has been observed, were just one amongst many groups living in towns.[62] They were a sub-section of urban society defined by occupation. In terms of their shared economic base, access to power and inter-dependence, they reflected degrees of mutuality suggestive of a class in the process of formation. As it evolved, the merchant class covered a wider spectrum than might be supposed. It was socially fluid and probably encompassed a greater range of wealth than any other occupationally defined group. The core was readily identifiable and, to an extent, helped to define those on the periphery. At the bottom were men who infrequently engaged in wholesale trade and barely scraped a living. Their disposable surplus was meagre and their political achievements modest. At the top were men possessed of considerable commercial skill, great wealth and power. They mingled with members of the gentry and royal household within the region, and as MPs a few occasionally moved into metropolitan life at parliament. Some were taken into the ecclesiastical as well as the lay establishment. Thomas Carre of York sat as a member of

---

[60] It is though too early to talk of 'urban villages'. Palliser, 'Urban Society', p. 142.

[61] See W. K. D. Davies and D. T. Herbert, *Communities Within Cities. An Urban Social Geography* (London, 1993), pp. 63–85 for an enlightening spatial approach.

[62] M. Kowaleski, 'The History of Urban Families in Medieval England', *Jnl Med. Hist.*, 14 (1988), p. 48.

the archbishop of York's Court of Convocation on at least one occasion.[63]

In many respects, merchants were on a par with rural gentlemen: not all county gentlemen accepted those 'comen up lightly' but marriages between gentry and mercantile families were not unusual.[64] However, the ambition of the majority was focused on becoming prosperous and influential within their own towns.[65] Although some may have nurtured the ambition to become country gentlemen, few succeeded. Examples of a three-generational progression from rural beginnings, via urban commerce and back to country gentleman are hard to find: given the poor prospect of succession through male heirs and the inevitable dispersal of wealth, these are likely to be rare. Even within a single lifetime, only a tiny minority accumulated sufficient land to contemplate a life dependent on rents. As in so many aspects of his life, William de la Pole was the exception, and built up considerable holdings throughout northern England, in part through taking land as redemption for debts owed to him as well as by deliberately purchasing manors and estates.[66]

Occupation, wealth and status were visibly manifest in apparel and even within a large town such as York, the prominent would soon get to know the advancing successful men. Such was the finesse with which contemporaries could assess each other that in Hull in 1462, and in York in 1495, it was possible for the council to identify 'those likely to become sheriff'.[67] In contemporary terms, to be a successful merchant and civic dignitary was to be at the apex of society. Titles identified status at each level. 'Master' might be used out of respect for a particularly prominent merchant. Thus Richard Russell and John Thirsk were both called *magister*, perhaps in deference to their having served as mayor of the Calais Staple. It became increasingly the practice to refer to the recorder and aldermen as master from the 1490s.[68] In the late fifteenth century in York, the title of 'lord' mayor was used with greater frequency, and the wives of former mayors were accorded the title of 'dame' or 'lady'.[69] Within the city at any rate, those who completed the *cursus honorum* and achieved

---

[63] In 1426 he was involved in judging the case of a disobedient Franciscan: G. W. Kitchin, ed., *The Records of the Northern Convocation*, Surtees Soc., 113 (1907), pp. 146–7.

[64] *YCR*, II, p. 156; D. M. Palliser, *Tudor York* (Oxford, 1979), pp. 94, 100–1; *VCH York*, p. 112. See below, p. 111.   [65] For London examples, see S. O'Connor, 'Adam Fraunceys and John Pyel: Perceptions of Status Among Merchants in Fourteenth-Century London', in D. J. Clayton, R. G. Davies and P. McNiven, eds., *Trade, Devotion and Governance. Papers in Later Medieval History* (Stroud, 1994), pp. 17–35.

[66] Horrox, *The de la Poles of Hull*, p. 26; see below, chapter 9.

[67] Hull RO, BRB I, f. 77v., *YCR*, II, p. 121. See also Phythian-Adams, *Desolation of a City*, p. 128.

[68] *VCH York*, p. 104; Palliser, *Tudor York*, p. 100; York RO, House Books, *passim*.

[69] E.g. John Stockdale, d. 1506, made bequests to Lady Hancock and Lady Kirk, wives of former mayors Robert Hancock and George Kirk: Prob. Reg. VI, f. 185.

the higher reaches of civic government claimed the titles of gentility.[70]

Few merchants adopted the style 'gentleman' and when they did so it is difficult to establish if it reflected anything of significance.[71] John, son of Simon Grimsby of Hull, styled himself gentleman, whereas his father, who was twice mayor, had been content with the description of merchant.[72] Given that some commentators elevated merchants above gentlemen in the social hierarchy,[73] or at the very least, equated the two,[74] it may be a mistake to dwell on such designations. The Coppendale family of merchants had prospered in Beverley since the early fourteenth century, owned armour, were licensed to crenellate in 1366,[75] but it was not until the late fifteenth century[76] that they claimed to be armigerous in the person of Stephen Coppendale.[77] Members of another Beverley family called themselves esquires after several generations. Thomas Frost, who died in 1496, was the first Beverley Frost to do so.[78]

The small number of merchants who were knights were recipients of royal favour. There were three and all were York citizens: John Gilyot (1501), William Todd and Richard York (1497). The ascent of the de la Pole family of Hull to the peerage in 1385 was atypical of mercantile social achievement, and perhaps was only possible in the context of mid-fourteenth-century wool fortunes. The prestige of joining a national elite was a mixed blessing and Todd and York were granted annuities of £20 and £40 respectively from the Hull customs to ease the burden.[79] Neither was impoverished when they died, although they left more land than cash.[80] Thomas Neleson (then mayor) and John Gilyot preferred to pay

---

[70] R. Horrox, 'The Urban Gentry in the Fifteenth Century', in Thomson, *Towns and Townspeople*, pp. 32–3.

[71] See O'Connor, 'Adam Fraunceys and John Pyel', pp. 17–20 for a discussion of some of the criteria for claiming gentility.   [72] Prob. Reg. III, ff. 471v.; 398v.

[73] Chris Given-Wilson has argued that gentle birth was as important as land-ownership and that 'gentlemen' who possessed no land but lived in service or from trade were not regarded as the social inferiors of land-owning merchants: *The Nobility of Later Medieval England: The Fourteenth-Century Political Community* (London, 1988), p. 72.

[74] Horrox has drawn attention to Hull's reply to the enquiry for gentry eligible for military service in *c.* 1420, wherein the council pointed out that merchants had already supplied ships to the Crown. The implication was that merchants and gentry were the same, for practical purposes at least: Horrox, 'Urban Gentry', p. 33; A. E. Goodman, 'Responses to Requests in Yorkshire for Military Service under Henry V', *Northern History*, 17 (1981), p. 242.

[75] John Thornton Coppendale of Beverley, d. 1343, left all his armour to his son Adam: Arch. Reg. x, f. 310. It was he or his cousin whose house was crenellated: *CPR 1364–6*, p. 352.

[76] Even though, in *c.* 1420, Thomas Coppendale had responded to Henry V's enquiry for gentry eligible for military service: Goodman, 'Responses to Requests', p. 242. He had already served the Crown, in 1415 administering a grant to Beverley: *CPR 1413–16*, p. 275.

[77] He died in 1485. Prob. Reg. v, f. 486v.; Arch. Reg. v, f. 419.

[78] Prob. Reg. v, f. 486v. His great-uncle Walter Frost of Hull had done so in 1425.

[79] *YCR*, II, p. 28; *CPR 1485–94*, pp. 256–7, 303; *CCR 1485–1500*, p. 97.

[80] Prob. Reg. VI, f. 59v. (Todd); PRO, Prob. 11/11, f. 36 (York).

a fine in 1500 instead of accepting the honour. Neleson was obdurate and was fined again in 1504 but Gilyot succumbed in 1501.[81] The three urban knights of York remained citizens and continued to live in the city, even though they had extensive rural holdings. They did not discontinue their entrepreneurial activities, and Sir Richard York's grandson Bartholomew became free of the city as a merchant in 1526.[82]

There were other ways, perhaps more immediately effective than titles, by which merchants established their place in a superior social stratum. The Holy Trinity Guild in Hull, and the St Christopher and St George and Corpus Christi Guilds of York[83] transcended occupational distinctions. Although established primarily for religious purposes, the York Corpus Christi Guild, in particular, created a social network which included the upper lay and clerical echelons of York society, and indeed, of northern society.[84] As in Beverley,[85] the performance of the play cycles and associated Corpus Christi celebrations drew guild members and visitors into town. In the York Corpus Christi Guild, merchants played a prominent part in the more routine guild affairs, often serving as one of the six keepers. Three were recipients of Henry VI's charter of incorporation.[86] According to one historian: 'The membership of larger fraternities was so dominated by the local town oligarchy that they could well be described as the corporation at prayer',[87] but in York, merchants were only one amongst many categories in the Corpus Christi Guild, and of the cohort under review, 105 joined. The Guild drew in other members of merchant families: sixty-two of our cohort paid dues for their wives and merchant families and, amongst others, two widows, four sons, two daughters, one daughter-in-law and one mother joined on their own.[88]

In York, the Mercers and Merchant Adventurers' fraternity (later Company), developed to consolidate the mutual interests of men engaged in wholesale trade. It emerged from a fraternity supported by

[81] Palliser, *Tudor York*, p. 101; W. J. Kaye, 'Yorkshiremen who Declined to take up their Knighthood', *Yorks Arch. Jnl*, 31 (1932–4), pp. 362, 364.   [82] *York Freemen*, p. 248.

[83] L. Toulmin-Smith, *English Guilds*, EETS, OS, 40 (1870), pp. 160–1; R. Horrox, 'Urban Patronage and Patrons in the Fifteenth Century', in R. A. Griffiths, ed., *Patronage, the Crown, and the Provinces in Later Medieval England* (Gloucester, 1981), p. 156; E. White, *The St Christopher and St George Guild of York*, Borthwick Paper No. 72 (York, 1987), pp. 14–15.

[84] Lords Clifford, Latimer and Scrope, Richard of Gloucester and his mother, justices of the King's Bench, the archbishop of York, bishops, abbots of the major northern houses plus sundry gentlemen were all members alongside the townsfolk: *Corpus Christi Guild*, p. xii.

[85] J. R. Witty, 'The Beverley Plays', *Trans. Yorks Dialect Society*, part 23, 4 (1922), pp. 18–37; A. F. Leach, 'Ordinances of the Beverley Corpus Christi Guild', *Proc. Soc. Antiq.*, 2nd ser., 15 (1894), pp. 203–8.   [86] *Corpus Christi Guild*, p. 255.

[87] J. J. Scarisbrick, *The Reformation and the English People* (Oxford, 1984), p. 22.

[88] *Corpus Christi Guild*, p. 10; *VCH York*, pp. 47, 96, 482.

merchants and dedicated to the Virgin Mary, and initially welcomed country members but gradually developed a more exclusive policy so that membership became increasingly city based. The Company combined business with social functions and there were practical advantages in terms of welfare as well as conviviality which encouraged wives to become members with their husbands. Of the merchant cohort reviewed here, 112 joined the Company, sixty-eight with their wives.[89]

Attending guild and company functions drew attention to differences between successful merchants and other townsfolk and, in more fundamental ways, so did the quality of their lifestyle. Their consumption of material goods was conspicuously greater than that of their craftsmen neighbours,[90] confirmed in the detailed lists drawn up in wills[91] by merchant testators and their widows. Valuable items were naturally more prominent than general household goods: silver bowls and spoons, silver-plated dishes with gilding, and pewterware. Items such as blankets, sheets, bolsters and particularly featherbeds were frequently disposed of in bequests, and (less often) valuable furnishings such as Arras tapestries, cloth of gold and bejewelled religious images were left to particular friends or members of the family.[92] Domestic comfort was matched by personal adornment. Yorkshire merchants and their families dressed to suit their wealth and position, and itemised scarlet, violet, blue and brown gowns, often furred, which they left to their friends. They bequeathed other personal valuables such as armour and weapons,[93] bracelets, rings and books. John Stockdale of York left an unusually elegant gown lined with Cyprus satin to Robert Plumpton, one of his executors.[94]

The intermingling of all classes, of domestic, commercial and manufacturing buildings, was common in medieval towns and there is little evidence of social zoning in York, Beverley or Hull, even though merchants tended to cluster in the expensive central streets, close to commercial activity.[95] From the evidence of burial places chosen by

---

[89] *M&MA*, pp. 16, 49, 51–4, 66–8; *VCH York*, pp. 422, 482.

[90] Swanson, *Medieval Artisans*, pp. 156–64. For London, see Thrupp, *London Merchant Class*, pp. 130–51; C. Dyer, *Standards of Living in the later Middle Ages. Social Change in England c. 1250–1520* (Cambridge, 1989), pp. 205–7.

[91] No Yorkshire merchant's will compares with the inventory of wealthy London merchant Richard Lyons, which details an extraordinary level of domestic opulence, as well as itemising his high-quality trade goods: A. R. Myers, 'The Wealth of Richard Lyons', in T. A. Sandquist and M. R. Powicke, eds., *Essays in Medieval History Presented to Bertie Wilkinson* (Toronto, 1969), pp. 301–29.

[92] E.g. Prob. Reg. II, ff. 86v.–90v.; 220–1v.; v, ff. 402v.–3.

[93] Prob. Reg. VII, f. 27 (Jameson). See also II, f. 570v. (Bowland); III, ff. 523 (Graye), 599 (Esingwold); VI, f. 213 (Potter); Arch. Reg. XVIII, f. 310 (Coppendale).

[94] E.g. Prob. Reg. v, ff. 250v.–1; VI, f. 185 (Stockdale).

[95] A pattern observed in other towns. See, for example, Coventry in W. B. Stephens, ed., *Victoria County History of Warwickshire*, VIII (1969) p. 209; D. Keene, *A Survey of Medieval Winchester*, 2 vols. (Oxford, 1985), I, pp. 167, 175–6; J. Langton, 'Late Medieval Gloucester: Some Data from a

merchants in York, the parishes of St Crux and All Saints, Pavement were twice as popular as any others.[96] Only one or two lived or were buried in the outlying suburban parishes such as St Lawrence, St Denis, Walmgate, St Cuthbert's, Peaseholme, and St Olave. Jeremy Goldberg has identified St Martin, Coney Street from poll tax evidence as York's mercantile parish.[97] Beverley and Hull were smaller, compact towns where clustering was less likely, but in the late fourteenth century merchants showed some preference for central streets: in Beverley it was Lairgate and the Beckside and in Hull, Hull Street.[98]

We have little idea of the scale of individual merchants' homes. The reconstruction of Barley Hall in York, assumed to have been the home of the merchant William Snawsell, had a hall, but fairly cramped living quarters.[99] The evidence from other towns suggests that merchant houses might comprise several ranges of domestic buildings, undercrofts, storerooms and warehouses, sometimes built around a courtyard.[100] In Hull the enormously wealthy de la Pole family was responsible for a Humberside *palazzo* which became known as Courthall. It was a capacious house which stood on a large site between Beverley Street and Marketgate, and may have been rebuilt by Michael de la Pole in the 1380s. Names suggest other substantial merchant properties in Hull, for example, Snayton Place and Hellward Place, but 'place' may have been a fashionable term.[101] There were domestic stone buildings in thirteenth-century York, but the majority of the medieval survivals are multi-storeyed timber houses, built in a traditional box frame with the minimum of decoration.[102] A similar style probably predominated in

Rental of 1455', *Trans. Institute British Geographers*, NS, 2 (1977), p. 265; C. Platt, *The English Medieval Town* (London, 1976), p. 105; C. Platt, *Medieval Southampton: The Port and Trading Community, A D 1000–1600* (London, 1973), p. 97.

[96] All the rest attracted roughly equivalent numbers: Holy Trinity, Goodramgate, Holy Trinity, King's Court, St John Evangelist, St Martin, Coneystreet, St Martin, Mickelgate, St Peter Little, St Sampson's and St Saviour's. South of the river the large parish of St Mary Bishophill Senior was chosen by eight or so, All Saints, Northstreet, six, and Holy Trinity Priory, three.

[97] Goldberg, 'Urban Identity and the Poll Taxes', p. 201.

[98] PRO E179/202/71 mm. 2–6v.; 206/45 mm. 1–2.

[99] http://www.demon.co.uk/tourism/jvc/barley.html for a tour of the house.

[100] See, for example, P. Carrington, *English Heritage. Book of Chester* (London, 1995), pp. 77–8; W. A. Pantin, ' The Merchants' Houses and Warehouses of King's Lynn', and 'Medieval English Town-house Plans', *Med.Arch.*, 6–7 (1962–3), pp. 173–81, 202–39; V. Parker, *The Making of King's Lynn* (Chichester, 1971), pp. 56–64, 196–210; A. N. Brown, J. C. Greville and R. C. Turner, *Watergate Street, The Rows Research Project* (Chester City Council, 1987).

[101] *VCH Hull*, pp. 77, 79. In 1388 it had twenty rooms in addition to a chapel, hall and tower. A print of *c.* 1541 shows two courtyards and a gatehouse.

[102] *RCHM York*, III (London, 1972), pp. lxi, lxiii; E. A. Gee, 'The Architecture of York', in A. Stacpoole *et al.*, eds., *The Noble City of York* (York, 1972), p. 368. One elaborate porch canopy of the late fifteenth–early sixteenth centuries is now at Jacob's Well, Trinity Lane: *RCHM York*, III, p. lxii; N. Pevsner, *The Buildings of England. Yorkshire: York and the East Riding* (London, 1972), p. 147.

Beverley and Hull,[103] suggesting that merchants' homes were not always readily distinguishable from their neighbours' except perhaps in the numbers of servants employed.[104] References to 'my capital messuage' in wills imply some merchants enjoyed sole occupation of a property and the surviving physical evidence suggests this was possible.[105]

Material comfort and superior living standards were visible reflections of commercial profit and distinguished wealthy merchants from their neighbours. There were other manifestations. Individual merchants had aspirations to pursue and many obligations; they also had more disposable income than most townsfolk to spend on meeting them. They transformed entrepreneurial success into political power, became social and cultural leaders within their own towns and extended their community of commercial interest into their private and public lives.

This study will follow those processes in Part I below, above all by exploring the expenditure of merchants on private and public benevolence, their attention to spiritual matters, the characteristics of their personal relationships and their role in local government. Part II will discuss the complexities of the commercial world created by merchants and the sophisticated entrepreneurship they employed in accumulating the wealth which made their social and political ambitions attainable.

---

[103] *Beverley. An Archaeological and Architectural Study*, RCHM, Supp. Ser., 4 (1982), pp. 62–3.

[104] See below, chapter 3.

[105] *RCHM York*, III, p. lxiii describes a large, three-storeyed, late-fifteenth-century/early-sixteenth-century house on Mickelgate, with an L-shaped extension, which was apparently a single tenement.

Part I

Merchant society and politics

2

MERCHANTS IN GOVERNMENT

The history of English medieval local government is of a process in flux. It emerges from the interaction between central and local authority, the creation of representative and executive institutions, re-definitions of the concept of public good, and political rivalries. Boroughs were at the fore-front of these changes. Devolved judicial and administrative authority came to them through the acquisition of charters, enabling the evolution of structures to regulate some of the consequences of growing numbers of townsfolk living in crowded proximity and dependent on outside food supplies. As every aspect of their economies, of society and individual expectations became more sophisticated, so did public institutions.[1]

Urban political culture altered in the course of the fourteenth and fif-teenth centuries in response to the pressures of economic change but in ways which defy a single explanation.[2] In York, the rapid commercial successes of a rising merchant group brought about the overthrow of 'rentier patricians' by the 1360s, whereas during the 1380s, factional divi-sions were more apparent. In Beverley it was a mixture of lesser mer-chants and craftsmen who were challenging the established oligarchy in the 1380s.[3] Decline creates different pressures and social fractures, so that

---

[1] For a discussion of urban institutions, power and authority, see S. H. Rigby, *English Society in the Later Middle Ages. Class, Status and Gender* (London, 1995), pp. 158–77, and 'Power and Authority', chapter 12 in D. M. Palliser, ed., *The Cambridge Urban History of Britain*, 1 (Cambridge, forth-coming).

[2] See R. A. Rotz, 'Investigating Urban Uprisings with Examples from Hanseatic Towns, 1374–1416', in W. J. Jordan, B. McNab and T. F. Ruiz, eds., *Order and Innovation in the Middle Ages. Essays in Honor of Joseph R. Strayer* (Princeton, 1976), pp. 215–33. For a recent discussion in England see R. H. Hilton and T. S. Aston, *The English Rising of 1381* (Cambridge, 1984) and R. H. Hilton, 'Popular Movements in England at the End of the Fourteenth Century', in his *Class Conflict and the Crisis of Feudalism* (London, 1985), pp. 79–91.

[3] By the late fourteenth century, Beverley had already suffered a contraction in its former textile manufacturing and was losing ground in international trade. It is perhaps significant, therefore, that fullers, tailors and a draper were amongst the 1381 rebels: C. T. Flower, 'The Beverley Town Riots, 1381–2', *TRHS*, NS, 19 (1905), pp. 80–1.

those institutions and social processes which may once have relieved tensions become inadequate.[4] In late medieval towns, outsiders, foreign merchants and even beggars became scapegoats on occasion, though discontent was more often directed at the urban governors as in Beverley in the 1380s and York in the fifteenth century. The emergence of superior religious guilds and the multiplication of rites and feasts for different groups might be taken as a further indication of urban society not melding into a neighbourly community.[5]

The political system in some towns became more firmly set through the tighter definition of the *cursus honorum* and the creation of a hierarchy of councils. We can also see a more elaborate formulation of ideology, especially of the borough as an exclusive body, whose members had to fulfil specific conditions for admission.[6] Being 'in scot and lot' brought responsibility and privilege as the oaths of freemen and borough officials alike made clear. Thus the York mayor swore to 'maintendray et avanceray . . . les fraunchises, droites, loyes, usuaiges et custumes' of the city, and the Beverley keepers to 'keep the town of Beverley . . . with all their ability, not to spare any man unjustly because of friendship or consanguinity, nor to treat any man unfairly because of enmity or hatred'. The burgess oaths of all three towns pledged obedience to their rulers and, as the Hull oath made clear, a man 'had to work for the common good and not for singular profit'. It cost Beverley burgesses a £10 fine to become free of their oath of obedience.[7] The growing emphasis on public definitions of individual and collective privileges and responsibilities meant that towns began to retain legal counsel. This became a common feature of fifteenth-century town government, and one which excited criticism from the lower classes.[8]

Economic change brought other consequences. As their position was rendered increasingly vulnerable in the course of the late middle ages,

[4] For instance, even in one small town, according to Christopher Dyer, social mechanisms and institutional regulations for cohesion were just papering over the cracks: 'Small-Town Conflict in the Later Middle Ages: Events at Shipston-on-Stour', *Urban History*, 19 (1992), pp. 183–210 at p. 184.

[5] Rigby, 'Urban "Oligarchy"', pp. 74–7. For the opposing view, based on functional mutuality, see S. Reynolds, *An Introduction to the History of English Medieval Towns* (Oxford, 1977), pp. 135–6, 171; Thrupp, *London Merchant Class*, pp. 14–27; Shaw, *Wells*, pp. 4–6, 178–97, 202, 289.

[6] A. Ballard and J. Tait, *British Borough Charters, 1216–1307* (Cambridge, 1923), pp. 132–44; Reynolds, *English Medieval Towns*, pp. 123–6; Shaw, *Wells*, pp. 149–50.

[7] *York Freemen*, p. xiv; *MB*, II, p. 256, and for the oaths of other York officials, see pp. 257–8; for Beverley, Humberside RO, BC II/7/1, ff. 6v., 7v., 11v., 21, 26; for Hull, Hull RO BRG 1, ff. 12–14. See also Rigby, 'Urban "Oligarchy"', p. 64.

[8] E.g. *VCH Beverley*, p. 28; *VCH Hull*, p. 34; *YCR*, I, p. 178; II, pp. 54–5; York RO, House Book I, ff. 31v., 32v., 67, 94, 97v., 116; II, ff. 4, 8, 31v., 51; VII, f. 22v. and *passim* to IX, f. 35; Dobson, *York City Chamberlains' Account Rolls*, p. xxxiv. Compare the possible four lawyers retained in 1396–7 with the ten in 1486–7, pp. 2, 184. See also Shaw, *Wells*, p. 203.

town governors deployed more verbal and visible rhetoric to consolidate their rule. The corporation emerged as an organising concept, made visible in the building of town and guild halls,[9] official livery,[10] borough seals[11] and formal processions. As a unifying ideology, it was firmly the creature of the wealthy minority and its appeal was to establish an exclusive association as the *entrée* for the ambitious.[12] The nature of urban society itself was a major factor in challenging the elite, in that the ladders of economic opportunity and social advancement which had helped one group to political dominance, remained in place for other aspiring burgesses to ascend. Late medieval oligarchs, anxious to retain the power they had secured, created more and more elaborate layers of pseudo-representation in the form of extra councils. But power remained where it always had been: in the hands of a small group who controlled the nomination to the key offices. In York and Hull these were the *probi homines*, later aldermen, and in Beverley they were a less institutionally defined core, but still referred to as the *bones gentez* or *potentiores*.[13]

For the most part, it is the oligarchy's account of urban affairs which survives in the form of borough archives: court rolls, administrative records, council 'minutes' and memoranda of council business. Other voices, those 'of no power',[14] had no equivalent outlet but do occasionally emerge through the official narratives.

---

[9] R. B. Dobson, 'Urban Decline in Late Medieval England', in Holt and Rosser, *The Medieval Town*, p. 272; Reynolds, *English Medieval Towns*, pp. 179–80.

[10] Borough liveries were a natural development from royal and noble households. Craft guilds often wore the same livery and in Beverley were ordered to do so by the keepers: *Bev. Town Docs.*, pp. 31–2, 59, 94. See also Shaw, *Wells*, pp. 203–4; B. R. McRee, 'Unity or Division? The Social Meaning of Guild Ceremony in Urban Communities', in B. A. Hanawalt and K. L. Reyerson, eds., *City and Spectacle in Medieval Europe* (Minnesota, 1994), p. 192. Liveries could be provocative. For example, in July 1381, the ousted John Gisburn distributed liveries in York: PRO, c47/86/31/830. External liveries were even more challenging. In 1442, the Hull council forbade civic officials to accept clothes from outsiders, and during the Wars of the Roses, the York council ordered citizens not to use the livery of any lord, knight or gentlemen: Hull RO, BRE 2, f. 32v.; *VCH York*, pp. 50, 64–5.

[11] Seals had a different potency and the Beverley oligarchs seized the borough seal during the rebellion of April 1381: R. B. Dobson, 'The Risings in York, Beverley and Scarborough, 1380–1381', in Hilton and Aston, *The English Rising*, p. 127.

[12] Many civic and occupational corporations created rituals to affirm the sense of belonging which included oath-taking by new freemen, commensality in civic and guild feasts and drinking to mark major events such as elections. See, for example, L. C. Attreed, 'The Politics of Welcome: Ceremonies and Constitutional Development in Later Medieval English Towns', in Hanawalt and Reyerson, *City and Spectacle*, pp. 209–10; G. Rosser, 'Going to the Fraternity Feast: Commensality and Social Relations in Late Medieval England', *Jnl British Studies*, 33 (1994), pp. 430–66; Shaw, *Wells*, pp. 198–9; Thrupp, *London Merchant Class*, pp. 12–13, 19.

[13] Humberside RO, BC II/3, f. 12v.; *Bev. Town Docs.*, p. 34. In Wells, where new councils were created in 1384 and 1408, the inner core comprised the master, constables and former masters: Shaw, *Wells*, pp. 159, 167.

[14] In the preparations for Henry VII's visit to York, the council differentiated between the civic officials and other dignataries, and those 'who may not ride or be of no power': *YCR*, I, p. 156.

There was an uneven pattern of change in the structures and processes of town government during the late middle ages. The process of defining and establishing the liberties, privileges and responsibilities of town governments was neither automatic nor painless and was often achieved through sharp rivalry with local ecclesiastical institutions.[15] Acquiring and maintaining borough status depended upon the determined persistence of a group of aspiring townsfolk, and subsequent conflicts over the right to hold a market or fair, or over areas of borough court jurisdiction, provided a stage on which these town rulers could demonstrate their fitness to govern while strengthening the privileges of their fellow burgesses.[16] While some important towns developed no urban institutions whatsoever, for instance Westminster,[17] others moved at different speeds towards the relative independence of a corporate borough. By 1500, only a few towns had reached the apex of constitutional autonomy, that of a county, and York and Hull were amongst them. As a seignorial borough of the archbishop of York, Beverley remained subject to his authority until 1573.[18]

Government can be discussed simply in terms of a growth in regulation and public services, but the ability to raise taxes and to authorise their expenditure is only one aspect of the way in which towns conduct their affairs. Political systems develop alongside administrative institutions to control access to power as well as determining fiscal and regulatory policies. By the late middle ages, most English boroughs were governed by one of two systems: either by a hierarchy of elected officials, a mayor, or equivalent, sheriff or bailiff, and chamberlain or treasurer, plus one or more councils; or by a council of twelve keepers or wardens who collectively fulfilled the functions of the elected officials plus outer councils. Some were governed by a fusion of the two systems.[19] In Hull and York government was by hierarchy plus councils, whereas Beverley was governed by twelve keepers (later governors) and the archbishop's bailiff.[20]

---

[15] See L. Attreed, 'Arbitration and the Growth of Urban Liberties in Late Medieval England', *Jnl British Studies*, 31 (1992), pp. 205–35, for a detailed study of Exeter and some York comparisons.

[16] See, for example, Shaw, *Wells*, p. 122.

[17] G. Rosser, 'The Essence of Medieval Urban Communities: The Vill of Westminster, 1200–1540', *TRHS*, 5th ser., 34 (1984), pp. 92–3.

[18] The most visible constitutional limitation was the confrontation over the archbishop's assize of bread and ale and of the role of his bailiff: *VCH Beverley*, pp. 28–30, 65.

[19] A. S. Green, *Town Life in the Fifteenth Century* (London and New York, 1894), II, chs. 8–16; Platt, *English Medieval Town*, pp. 119–22; Reynolds, *English Medieval Towns*, p. 173. For single town studies see D. R. Carr, 'The Problem of Urban Patriciates: Office Holders in Fifteenth-Century Salisbury', *Wilts Arch. & Natural Hist. Magazine*, 83 (1990), pp. 118–35; A. Rogers, 'Late Medieval Stamford: A Study of the Town Council, 1465–92', in A. Everitt, ed., *Perspectives in English Urban History* (London, 1973); B. Wilkinson, *The Medieval Council of Exeter*, History of Exeter Research Group, Monograph No. 4 (Manchester, n.d.).

[20] *VCH Hull*, pp. 29–37; *VCH York*, pp. 70–2, 74, 77–8; *Bev. Town Docs.*, pp. xxi, xxiii.

Hierarchic administrative structures encourage oligarchy, a system readily identified in many medieval boroughs. Many of the latter were plutocratic, some mercantile and the majority were probably self-perpetuating. Within the modern pluralist state, universal suffrage and public accountability moderate the autocratic tendency of oligarchies, but such formal checks were generally absent in medieval towns. The outer councils were rarely summoned: the York forty-eight[21] and the Beverley thirty-six and forty-eight (there was no outer council recorded in Hull), appear fleetingly in the records as spectators to the inner councils' actions. In the late fifteenth century, although the ruling groups in Beverley and York began to involve more people in the process of electing officials,[22] no more were drawn into the heart of government. The role of the commonalty, that is the non-office-holding burgesses, was confined to approving the oligarchs' decisions, and the non-burgess majority had no formal role at all, but were subject to council authority.

In York, Beverley and Hull, oligarchies dominated: a form of government universal at this time and not automatically regarded as inimical or corrupt by contemporaries. Indeed, the notion that the rich should rule was accepted, as were inequalities of wealth.[23] To an extent, government was based on a consensus, perhaps no more than a 'tacit acceptance',[24] underpinned by three principles: governors were to be 'good', 'worshipful', 'sad' and 'discreet' men, ruling according to custom and with the assent of the people. The oaths of office holders emphasised their subordination to custom and duty to serve all burgesses.[25] The uneasy co-existence of these principles explains much of the tension in late medieval towns, and the sporadic outbursts of popular unrest in some.

Further pressure emerged from shifts of power within the ruling groups, reflecting economic advances and losses. Merchants were enabled by the nature of their occupation to accumulate wealth and to have time to spend on civic matters. 'Ability' to rule was in terms of financial ability,[26] and as 'able' was often coupled with other epithets such as 'discreet' and 'wise', material success implied other qualities. In some towns, the descendants of merchant families became a rentier patriciate, and had turned to investments in land, annuities and urban property without

[21] The record of one full council survives for York, at which the twelve, the twenty-four and the forty-eight were present in 1379 to discuss the problem of chamberlains who neglected their duties: *MB*, I, pp. x–xi, 33, 35.   [22] See appendix 1 for details of offices and elections.

[23] Reynolds, 'Medieval Urban History', pp. 14–23; and *English Medieval Towns* (1977), pp. 176–7. M. Kowaleski, 'The Commercial Dominance of a Medieval Provincial Oligarchy: Exeter in the Late Fourteenth Century', *Medieval Studies*, 46 (1984), pp. 368–9, observed an acceptance of the Exeter oligarchs' right to rule.   [24] Rigby, 'Urban "Oligarchy"', p. 66.

[25] See p. 26 above, note 7.

[26] In Coventry, oligarchy was justified by the need to have men 'able to bear the costs': Phythian-Adams, *Desolation of a City*, p. 137.

loosening their grip on town government. Even those actively engaged in trade and new to wealth may have been hostile to the economic and political ambitions of their artisan and craftsmen neighbours.[27] Irrespective of occupational dominance, it is debatable whether or not town governments reflected far beyond their own corporatist view, even though, as Sylvia Thrupp observed, 'it was convention to frame public policies in the name of general principles . . . the common profit, the honour of the city, justice or reason'.[28] This could, and did, encompass practical measures for the common good and public utility, but inevitably those were the measures approved by the council.

It is also a matter of debate whether or not councils were becoming more exclusive and less accountable.[29] In some towns, oligarchic power was modified through the competing ambitions of rival players: wealthy burgesses, the gentry and the non-franchised townsfolk. Large towns were likely to have a more pluralist character, with other institutions to challenge or support the judicial and political authority of the civic council. Craft guilds and the larger socio-religious guilds, for instance, which replicated the hierarchy of urban councils with their own aldermen and wardens, also provided both alternative and complementary political networks. In established towns, religious guilds offered shelter to, or perhaps even created, embryonic occupational guilds.[30] In York, for example, the Mercers and Merchant Adventurers' Company grew out of the Fraternity of Our Lady which had been licensed to own land in 1356, and in Hull, the Corpus Christi Guild (1358) and the Guild of the Virgin Mary which was founded by merchants in 1357, probably both financed commercial ventures.[31]

Elsewhere, large guilds were drawn into urban politics. In Coventry, membership of the Corpus Christi Guild was an important rung on the *cursus honorum* for younger men but did not have that role in York or Hull.[32] In York, the Mercers and Merchant Adventurers' Company might

---

[27] See Rotz, 'Investigating Urban Uprisings', pp. 231–2, where he discusses the tensions between upcoming merchants and artisans in Hanseatic towns.

[28] Thrupp, *London Merchant Class*, pp. 97–8.

[29] E. F. Jacob, *The Fifteenth Century* (Oxford, 1961), p. 385; C. J. Hammer, 'Anatomy of an Oligarchy: The Oxford Town Council in the Fifteenth and Sixteenth Centuries', *Jnl British Studies*, 18 (1979), pp. 1–27; Platt, *English Medieval Town*, pp. 119–24, 190; P. Clark and P. Slack, *English Towns in Transition, 1500–1700* (Oxford, 1976), pp. 128–9; Rigby, 'Urban "Oligarchy"', pp. 62–86.

[30] The role of the religious fraternity as a forum for non-religious activity is interesting. They may have taken the place of the guild merchant in the later middle ages: C. Gross, *The Gild Merchant. A Contribution to British Municipal History* (Oxford, 1890), I, pp. 83–4, note 11, 99, 159, or assumed a particular relevance in places faltering on the verge of becoming towns: Rosser, 'Vill of Westminster', p. 104.

[31] *VCH York*, p. 482; *M&MA*, pp. iii–xiii, 106, 111, 422; *VCH Hull*, p. 58; Toulmin-Smith, *English Guilds*, pp. 156–7, 160–1.

[32] Phythian-Adams, *Desolation of a City*, pp. 125–6. The Guild of St George was drawn directly into

have become part of the *cursus*, in so far as some of the men who served as Master of the company became mayor soon after, but this was by no means a routine pattern. The company itself was a powerful corporation within the civic body whose membership had become more tightly defined through occupation by the time it acquired its royal charter in 1430.[33] It was formed to protect the interests of its members overseas and attempted to establish a monopoly by ordering members to use the ships of other members.[34]

The urban political arena was even further complicated. Religious institutions claimed territorial independence of civic authority and in Beverley and York there were liberties where the council's writ did not run.[35] The presence of the Council in the North in York from the 1480s challenged the council's perspective of a burgess community as townsfolk took cases away from the civic courts to the alternative tribunal.[36] Constant vigilance was required to maintain the city's jurisdiction: an authority exercised over all townsfolk, including non-burgesses, without the reciprocal privileges of peer judgement. In addition to institutional rivals, other individual political 'players' were drawn into regional capitals on the occasions when Crown assizes, royal commissions or county courts were held there. A whole host of officials, lawyers, clerics, county yeomen and gentry, nobles, royal servants, estate stewards, foreign merchants and many others added to the tide of petitioners and patrons flowing through the city. Royal interests were never far away,[37] and in York, like other county capitals, the Crown retained a physical presence with its castle and precinct.[38]

government as a unifying forum and agency of mediation between factions, became the governing guild of 15th-century Norwich: B. McCree, 'Religious Gilds and Civic Order: The Case of Norwich in the Late Middle Ages', *Speculum*, 67 (1992), pp. 69–97.

[33] About 25 per cent of mayors, 1437–1510, had previously been master of the company: *M&MA*, pp. 322–3. Earlier members had included men from Hull, Newcastle and Whitby, as well as cooks, tanners and so forth: pp. xiii, 16.   [34] *M&MA*, pp. 64, 87.

[35] In York, St Mary's Abbey was the council's main protagonist amongst several institutions claiming exclusive jurisdiction within independent liberties which included St Leonard's Hospital and the Dean and Chapter: *VCH York*, pp. 38, 68; *YCR*, I, pp. 47, 64, 70–1, 100; II, pp. 147, 149–55, 157, 159, 161, 166, 169, 170–3; Dobson, 'Admissions to the Freedom of the City of York', pp. 12–13. In Beverley the Provost had his own peculiar and the Dean and Chapter their own liberties: *VCH Beverley*, pp. 16–18.

[36] York RO, House Book VIII, f. 129; IX, f. 28v.; F. W. Brooks, *The Council of the North*, Historical Association Pamphlet (1953), p. 21; R. R. Reid, *The King's Council in the North* (London, 1921), pp. 322–3.

[37] L. C. Attreed, ed., *York House Books 1461–90* (Stroud, 1991) and *YCR*, I–III, *passim*, for the regular exchange of letters between council and king. See also Attreed 'The King's Interest: York's Fee Farm and the Central Government 1482–92', *Northern History*, 17 (1981), pp. 24–43, and 'Medieval Bureaucracy in Fifteenth-Century York', *York Historian*, 6 (1985), pp. 24–31, for insights into this aspect of central and local relations.

[38] N. J. G. Pounds, *The Medieval Castle in England and Wales. A Social and Political History* (Cambridge, 1990), pp. 91–108.

Abbots, priors, bishops, minster dignitaries and especially archbishops[39] brought a combination of ecclesiastical authority, secular power, personal wealth and influence into urban life which have yet to be fully explored.[40] Although their direct involvement in urban politics was generally shadowy,[41] as ecclesiastical magnates individuals could excite loyalty or disaffection. The close relationship between Archbishop Scrope and the city eventually dragged York under direct royal supervision in 1405. However, such an outcome was unique in the city's history. As several archbishops combined national[42] with ecclesiastical office they were potentially important figures in northern politics and those with local connections played a pivotal role. For instance, in the charged atmosphere of the early 1380s, Archbishop Neville's infamous attack on the canons of Beverley Minster was undoubtedly a factor in the unrest of 1381–2.[43] A century later, Archbishop Thomas Savage, while president of the Council in the North in 1504, described himself as 'the Kings lieutenaunt and high commissionar withynne these North parties'. He may have seen himself as an 'especiall friende and loving ordinare', but his authority could not be ignored and both council and burgesses turned to him for advice and support during the riots of 1504. Gifts were made to him[44] and two years later he offered a loan to the city 'toward makyng of cloth' to assist the city to 'go forward'.[45]

Given the uncertainty of national and regional affairs, it was politic for civic rulers to spend some money and time nurturing useful patrons.[46]

[39] For the status and connections of some of the York ecclesiastics, see R. B. Dobson, 'The Later Middle Ages, 1215–1500', in G. E. Aylmer and R. Cant, eds., *A History of York Minster* (Oxford, 1977), pp. 62–81, 98.

[40] Jurisdictional disputes are the most visible. Hull, for example, had a lengthy dispute with the archbishop of York over prisage and over the coronership of the River Hull. Both were settled in the early fourteenth century but archbishops persisted with other claims in the town, to the prejudice of the town bailiffs, and these were finally settled in Hull's favour by royal charter in 1382: *VCH Hull*, pp. 14–15, 19–20, 49–50.

[41] Archbishops were asked for advice and support. For example, in the late fifteenth century, the council was soliciting advice on how to handle its early dealings with Henry VII, for support in its petition for the remission of the fee farm and a tax reduction, for help in disputes over common land and the lordship of Bootham: *YCR*, I, pp. 127, 133, 150, 166, 175; II, pp. 36, 154.

[42] The council was quick to exploit these connections. As archbishop of York and lord chancellor, John Kempe helped the York mercers and merchants to buy their own royal charter in 1430: *M&MA*, p. xv. The council gave claret and white wine to Thomas Scot, chancellor and archbishop, during the delicate negotiations with Henry VII in 1489, 'to thentent he to be gode and tender lord to this Cite': *YCR*, II, p. 49.

[43] A. F. Leach, 'A Clerical Strike at Beverley Minster in the Fourteenth Century', *Archaeologia*, 55 (1896), pp. 1–20. Alexander Neville came into conflict with the Hull council when he accused the mayor and bailiffs of unlawfully seizing one of his boats in 1383: Hull RO, BRE I, p. 281.

[44] The council had been advised by Henry VII to consult the archbishop, and the gift of bread, ten gallons of wine and three 'gret pykez' preceded their deputation: *YCR*, III, pp. 1–8; York RO, House Book VII, f. 85; IX, f. 19v.   [45] *YCR*, III, p. 18.

[46] *VCH York*, pp. 61–4; *VCH Hull*, pp. 24–5, 398; A. J. Pollard, 'The Tyranny of Richard III', *Jnl*

On one extraordinary occasion, during Richard III's visit to York in 1483, the mayor entertained 'iiij bishops, thre barons, the Cheff Justice of Yngland, with odir diwyrs, as wel jugs, sargaunts, knyghts, lerned men, esquiers, and odir of the Kings Counsell, at ij dyners with hym to hys greate charge and cost'. The unfortunate mayor, John Newton, had to foot the bill,[47] but such massive entertainments were rare. More common were gifts to influential individuals. These were an essential part of the process and indicate the continuing search by town rulers for 'good and tender' lordship. The Beverley keepers had been empowered as early as 1320 to make gifts on behalf of the commonalty; and by the late fifteenth century recorded such payments in a specific section of the borough accounts.[48] Other forms of 'sweetening' were employed. One of the clear objectives of the rulers of York and Beverley in developing the Corpus Christi play performance and procession was to enhance civic honour and dignity. The entertainment drew crowds from beyond the town and 'helped to extend and confirm the network of contacts with those whose wealth and power made them significant in the external relations of the community'.[49] Although mutual advantages were to be derived,[50] the commonalty harboured fears that their rulers were willing to abandon the common interest for noble goodwill.[51]

During the last half of the fifteenth century, the preliminary manoeuvrings and eventual outbreak of the Wars of the Roses entangled each of the three towns in magnate politics. The contracting economies of York and, to a lesser extent, of Beverley, were already creating their own pressures. Additionally, the Scottish and civil wars brought demands for men, money and ships, on a scale which had a deleterious impact on all three towns.[52] York's location made it inevitable that the city became the key

Med. Stud., 3 (1977), pp. 147–64; Horrox, 'Urban Patronage', pp. 145–66; Horrox, 'Richard III and the East Riding', in her *Richard III and the North* (Hull, 1986), pp. 89–93.

[47] *YCR*, I, p. 83.

[48] *VCH Beverley*, p. 28; *Yorks Deeds*, VII, p. 25.

[49] James, 'Ritual, Drama and Social Body', p. 12. Richard II was one of the York plays' eminent spectators: Dobson, *York City Chamberlains' Account Rolls*, pp. 4–5.

[50] York, for example, received a pension from the Hull customs from Edward IV, and derived some reductions in military demands in 1468: *CPR 1461–4*, p. 334; *VCH York*, p. 60; Attreed, *York House Books*, II, pp. 696–703, and promises to ease the fee farm: Attreed, 'The King's Interest', pp. 24–43, and 'Medieval Bureaucracy', pp. 24–31.

[51] The York commonalty were particularly suspicious of agreements between the council and outsiders over pasturage on the city commons. When Thomas Wrangwish, a servant of Richard III, was influential in the city in 1483, Richard's chamberlain, Lord Lovell, secured himself a favourable agreement to a disputed claim he first made in 1479. The October riots of 1484 were probably provoked by the council relinquishing its rights in a close belonging to St Nicholas' Hospital, at the behest of Richard III: Attreed, *York House Books*, I, pp. 193, 294, 303; II, pp. 439–41; *YCR*, I, pp. 102–5.

[52] For the impact on Hull see *VCH Hull*, pp. 23–6; A. Goodman, *The Wars of the Roses* (London,

to regional security[53] and the citizens had to accommodate kings, lords and their retinues, as well as physical attacks. The last decades of the century drew external rivalries into the city's affairs, and combined with the recession to create an unprecedented instability which the ruling oligarchy struggled to control.

This was an extraordinary phase in the nation's history which has been the subject of much investigation.[54] It is of relevance here in so far as the rulers of York, Beverley and Hull were drawn into the shifting world of national political patronage. The nature of the sources makes it difficult to establish how routinely magnate influence had been sought in less volatile times,[55] but certainly by the mid-fifteenth century all three town councils were making some effort to secure the positive support of influential men and, in particular, the Percy family, the dominant power in much of Yorkshire.[56] Beverley was barely six miles away from one of the Percy houses at Leconfield, and in addition to small gifts of bread and wine, the townsfolk occasionally entertained the earl and his family on Corpus Christi day.[57] The visible advantage was however one-sided as the Beverley keepers found themselves bowing to pressure to remit the fine due from a servant of Northumberland's son, Lord Egremont, for assaulting one of their number, and more often, contributing men and money to the earl's military expeditions.[58] Two Beverley oligarchs, Elias Casse and Thomas Bullock, were amongst the sixty-six indicted for the rising which resulted in the earl's murder in 1489, suggesting that perhaps their memory of his treachery at Bosworth was stronger than any recently won loyalty.[59]

Hull's relationship with the Percies and its other 'friend', the earl of Suffolk, were also mixed. Hull secured its charter of incorporation in

---

[53] C. D. Ross, *Richard III* (London, 1981), pp. 198–9; D. M. Palliser, 'Richard III and York', in Horrox, *Richard III and the North*, p. 55.

[54] For one of the most recent, see A. J. Pollard, *The Wars of the Roses* (London, 1988) and also his *North-Eastern England During the Wars of the Roses. Lay Society, War, and Politics 1450–1500* (Oxford, 1990) for an excellent regional study.

[55] Hull cultivated the descendants of its own de la Pole family, the earls of Suffolk, and to good effect since the securing of county status through its 1440 charter was achieved with the help of William de la Pole, earl of Suffolk: Horrox, *The de la Poles of Hull*, p. 39.

[56] The north had long been divided between the Neville and Percy families and their supporters. Their rivalry focused on York in the 1450s. For an excellent discussion of the region's power play, see M. Hicks, 'Dynastic Change and Northern Society: The Career of the 4th Earl of Northumberland', *Northern History*, 14 (1978), pp. 78–107 at p. 87.

[57] See, for example, the accounts for 1416; 1423 (£4 0s 4d for breakfast, dinner and supper in William Thixhill's house); 1433; 1450 (£3 to the earl's son at his first mass as a newly ordained priest): Humberside RO, BC II/6/7–9, 13; *Beverlac*, I, pp. 226–43; *VCH Beverley*, p. 28.

[58] See, for example, Humberside RO, BC II/7/1, ff. 92 (assault), 147, 161v., 163v., 165; BC II/6/7–9, 11–12: accounts for 1416, 1423, 1433, 1445, 1450.

[59] Hicks, 'Dynastic Change', p. 78; PRO, KB9/381.

1440 through the influence of the then earl, William de la Pole, but in return for a gift to himself of 200 marks and smaller gifts and dinners to his servants.[60] Gifts were given to the Percies regularly, as they were to a range of other lords, but the council did not hesitate to complain of the behaviour of Richard Percy and Lord Egremont in 1454, nor to defend staunchly its rights to the Court of the Admiralty in 1460, when they were threatened by Lord Egremont.[61] As in Beverley and York, the Hull council had to meet demands for men, money and ships, first from Henry VI and then from Edward IV. Money had to be spent on defending the town and port, and trade was interrupted by the fighting at some cost to the local merchants. In compensation, the town received a grant to trade custom free.[62] Unswerving loyalty was too costly to be sustained during such swiftly moving times. One mayor, Richard Anson, led a small contingent from Hull to support the Lancastrians, and was killed at the battle of Wakefield. Within six months the council was sending gifts of wine to Yorkists. Hull refused to admit Edward IV on his return in 1471, but the council eagerly sought the assistance of his lieutenant, Richard of Gloucester. Their relationship followed the predictable pattern of gifts of wine as well as contributions of men and money to Richard's campaigns against Scotland and Buckingham's rebellion. The reward was once again a grant to trade custom free.[63]

The earl of Northumberland was a constant presence for the York oligarchs as the council navigated between opposing sides, sending occasional gifts[64] and supplying him with men and money in his capacity as lieutenant to the king.[65] Lordship was a double-edged weapon though, and in 1485–6, the earl presumed too far in his relationship with the city by intervening on the king's behalf in the appointment of a new recorder to succeed the sick Miles Metcalfe. The council was obdurate and Northumberland failed.[66] However, when necessity demanded, the council willingly asked for the earl's advice: over the knotty problem of how to treat with Henry VII in the aftermath of Bosworth,[67] in a grazing

---

[60] Hull RO, BRE 2, ff. 12–12v.   [61] *VCH Hull*, pp. 53–4.

[62] One Hull brewer was paid £105 by Edward IV for supplying beer: *CPR 1461–7*, p. 272.

[63] *CPR 1461–7*, p. 289. See *VCH Hull*, pp. 23–6, for details of Hull's wartime role.

[64] See, for example, *YCR*, I, pp. 57, 72, 78.

[65] *YCR*, I, pp. 34–6, 58; II, p. 34. Attreed, *York House Books*, II, appendix II.

[66] *YCR*, I, pp. 131, 137, 141, 144–8. At one point, his countess arrived in the city and summoned the mayor and council to attend on her at the Augustinian Friary, where they were told to do nothing about the appointment until her next visit: *ibid.*, p. 151.

[67] *YCR*, I, pp. 119–20. Other lords found the council fiercely independent. Lord Clifford had written to offer his assistance with Henry VII, only to be told that 'the Mair of the said Citie is lieutenant, having full power and auctoritie under the King and . . . haveing knawlege by presidences remanyng of record in the Register of the said Citie, in what maner and forme thei shall recive the Kinge and how to deame theme to his highnesse in evere behalve': *ibid.*, pp. 154–5.

dispute with the Vicars Choral, and in defence of the city liberties against the sheriff of Yorkshire.[68] The earl could petulantly complain in 1484 that he had not been informed of riots in the city but then be generously hospitable three years later, in providing a banquet of venison and wine for the council and 600 of the commons, because of 'the love and affection' he held them in. York had recently stood firm against Lambert Simnel, in spite of rumours spread in the city that 'Northumberland doth little for us'.[69] The murder of the fourth earl in April 1489 redrew the political map in Yorkshire. It removed a major disruptive element, brought the Percy dominion to a temporary end and, for the first time in decades, left the north clear for the king.[70]

Much has been made of the special relationship between York and Richard III.[71] It seems to have been a classic instance of bastard feudalism, perhaps made possible by the city's economic plight, since it is clear that the council had seen the potential in Richard to become its ally in seeking remedies.[72] As patron to the city, Richard assisted in a number of local disputes, clearing fish-garths from the River Ouse, intervening with Edward IV when the city's common clerk was found guilty of fraud and so forth.[73] In return the city plied Richard with gifts, invited him and his wife to become members of the Corpus Christi Guild, entertained him in the city, loyally sent him men and money as required, and granted him rights over some of the city's fiercely defended common land.[74] This was an association engineered by the city rulers, or some of them, and was not to the liking of all the townsfolk.[75] In the gamesmanship of fifteenth-

[68] *YCR*, I, pp. 121–2, 133–4, 139, 178–80; II, pp. 42–4.

[69] *YCR*, II, pp. 4, 6, 20–3. The Guild of St Christopher and St George had to give him £6 because he was short of cash: *ibid.*, pp. 8–9.

[70] According to Michael Hicks, although the earl served Henry well, negotiating a truce with the Scots and dealing with Richard III's disaffected affinity, he remained ambivalent to the new king: 'Dynastic Change and Northern Society', pp. 97–8, 101. See J. Kirby, ed., *The Plumpton Letters and Papers*, Camden Soc., 5th ser., 8 (Cambridge, 1996), pp. 10–12.

[71] Richard's nephew John de la Pole, earl of Lincoln, also became involved in city business, largely through his association with Richard's Council in the North, and received gifts from the city council: *YCR*, I, pp. 103, 106–9, 111, 116.

[72] This is the tenor of its letter to Henry VII, pleading for a reduction in the city fee farm. See Attreed, *York House Books*, I, p. 390; *YCR*, I, p. 136.

[73] *YCR*, I, pp. 2–3, 9–11, 22–4, 82–4, 89; Attreed, *York House Books*, I, pp. 129–30.

[74] *VCH York*, pp. 61–2; *Corpus Christi Guild*, p. 101. See, for example, *YCR*, I, pp. 15–16, 41, 51–3, 56, 70, 77–8, 83, 89, 118; Attreed, *York House Books*, II, pp. 694–6, 699, 702–3, 713–14; Attreed, 'Politics of Welcome', pp. 208, 215–18. The visit of Richard and his queen in September 1483 prompted much discussion and a collection from the council to pay for their gifts. Most gave £8–£10 but John Gilyot contributed £30 and the recorder, Miles Metcalfe, £100: *YCR*, I, pp. 76–81.

[75] On two famous occasions, York men were hauled before the council to explain their alleged 'slander' of Richard. One had complained in 1482, 'What myght he do for the cite? Nothing bot gryn of us', and the other had claimed in 1483 that the commons would prefer not to have Richard's man, Thomas Wrangwish, as mayor: York RO A/Y, f. 23; E32, p. 49; *YCR*, I, pp.

century politics, even household servants could appear as welcome or threatening players in urban politics.[76] Some can be positively identified. John Marshall, a yeoman of the Percy household, was in York in 1478, but in the late '70s and '80s it was Gloucester's men who seemed to be filling the city.

Members of the affinity of Richard of Gloucester had steadily gained political positions in York: Thomas Wrangwish was Master of the Mercers and Merchant Adventurers' Company in 1471–3 and became mayor in 1484. Miles Metcalfe served as recorder in 1477–85, and Nicholas Lancaster as common clerk in 1476–9 and mayor in 1485 and 1493.[77] Their presence no doubt partly explains the stand-off which occurred between Henry VII and the York council in the uneasy after-math of Bosworth. Within weeks of lamenting the 'murder' of Richard, the council was quick to seek royal confirmation of city privileges in September 1485,[78] and in its subsequent dealings with Henry VII, spared no civic expense in presenting a proudly defiant image.[79]

In 1485 and 1486, during the illness and after the death of Metcalfe, Henry tried to get Richard Green appointed recorder of York. Metcalfe had been one of several who had loaned Richard III money to further his ambitions in April 1483. The council procrastinated and in March 1486 appointed another Richard supporter, John Vavasour, to the recordership. Henry persisted though, and following his carefully staged visit to the city in June, asked to appoint a new swordbearer. Once more the council stood firm, asserting its right to the 'ancheaunt liberties and costomes with free eleccion of all maner ther officers' and rejecting anyone who has served the king or other lord as a city official. However, circumstances changed and the council had to accept Henry's advice in the 1490s on law and order measures for the city.[80]

The final three decades of the fifteenth century were years of intensely partisan politics and so such transparent intervention in the northern capital's affairs was hardly surprising. At other times, patronage could be exercised as inconspicuously as lord and client chose and was, perhaps, solicited and exercised through association with the noble and gentry

vii–viii, 68–9; Attreed, *York House Books*, II, pp. 696, 707. Wrangwish attracted trouble, perhaps because of his association with Richard, and had been one of the candidates in the disrupted mayoral election of 1482 which attracted royal intervention: *VCH York*, p. 82. See also *YCR*, I, pp. 48–51, 69–70.

[76] The council ordered citizens not to use the livery of any lord, knight or gentlemen: *VCH York*, pp. 50, 64–5.

[77] Pollard, *North-Eastern England*, pp. 332, 354, 381; for Miles Metcalfe, pp. 357–8 and below, note 84. [78] *YCR*, I, p. 123. [79] *YCR*, I, pp. 152, 155–9.

[80] *VCH York*, pp. 61, 63, 75; *YCR*, I, pp. 48–9, 68–9, 141, 144–8, 151–2, 155–60. In 1476, a dismissed common clerk appealed to Percy for support, but the York council enlisted Richard of Gloucester's aid to maintain its right to elect its own officials freely; *ibid.*, I, pp. 8–11, 15–16.

members of royal commissions and the Corpus Christi Guild of York.[81] There is, though, little to suggest that outsiders routinely played an overt part in the final shaping of the membership of the government of any of the three towns. Even for that most visible of all political positions, that of MP, York and Hull were stoutly independent in their choice of representative.[82]

CIVIC OFFICE

On this crowded stage merchants emerged as the pre-eminent group in civic government, their political ambitions fuelled by commercial success. Merchant rulers in all three towns could find themselves dealing face to face or by letter with powerful individuals such as abbots of St Mary's, archbishops of York, the earls of Northumberland, the earl of Lincoln, the earl of Surrey and Sir Richard Tunstall.[83] There is little indication that they were intimidated by men of such elevated status, and indeed, a wealthy merchant might claim to have equal status to a gentleman by virtue of holding civic office. However, there was an often-cited incident in York, which neatly points up the different perceptions of contemporaries. In 1500 a local gentleman disparaged an alderman, John Metcalfe, calling him 'a carle . . . comen lightly up and of smale substance' and was rebutted by the mayor: 'I and my Brether and all this Citie knaweth that he wurshipfully hath been and born the charge as the Kynges lieutenant within this Citie.'[84] Treating with the high and mighty of the region was visibly elevating: as MPs, and as Crown-appointed commissioners, the most successful merchants moved amongst the region's landed gentry. Their political successes characterised the particular opportunities open to their class.

As with so much of their contribution to town life, the impact of merchant oligarchs was mixed. There is no doubt that merchant rulers played a key role in the development of urban government, as their quest for power brought constitutional gains for their own towns. However, the

---

[81] The Norwich St George's Guild brought town and country together in the same way: McRee, 'Religious Gilds and Civic Order', pp. 95–6. In Coventry, membership and office in the Corpus Christi Guild were part of the city's *cursus honorum*: Phythian-Adams, *Desolation of a City*, pp. 125–7.

[82] P. Jalland, 'Revolution in Northern Borough Representation', *Northern History*, 11 (1976), p. 50; J. S. Roskell, *The History of Parliament. The House of Commons 1386–1421* (Stroud, 1992), I, pp. 738, 750. [83] *YCR*, I–III *passim*.

[84] *YCR*, II, p. 156; House Book VIII, f. 89b. The gentleman was Sir William Conyers and, curiously, Metcalfe had served as a justice with Sir John Conyers in 1476. John Metcalfe had been appointed to several commissions in Durham by Richard III: Hicks, 'Dynastic Change', pp. 86–7. John Conyers was William's brother or great nephew: W. Hyton, ed., *Tonge's Visitation*, Surtees Soc., 41 (1863), p. 46.

majority of chartered privileges[85] brought advantages to traders and master craftsmen above all, while the less economically powerful burgesses were marginalised and 'foreigners' excluded completely. Only an exclusive minority of the townsfolk had a formal role in civic affairs or derived direct benefits from their borough's constitutional increments. If the burgesses comprised even as much as 25–30 per cent of the adult male townspeople, they were a group small enough to be individually recognised by the tellers at civic elections.[86]

Merchant domination can effectively be measured in terms of the proportion of merchants serving in single offices.[87] In York, of the 186 men who served as bailiff between 1300 and 1396, 34 per cent (sixty-three) were merchants. A further twenty-five were drapers, spicers or goldsmiths, and the next largest group were six butchers. From 1396 to 1509 there were 249 sheriffs, including those who died in office and their replacements. Of these, 48 per cent (119) were merchants but only 2 per cent (four) were butchers. Between 1300 and 1509, 122 men served as mayor and 79 per cent (ninety-six) were merchants. The pattern in Hull is less certain because of difficulties in identifying occupations from a scatter of freemen's lists. Of the 178 men who served as chamberlain between 1300 and 1509, 42 per cent (seventy-five) were merchants, whereas 37 per cent (fifty-seven) of the 153 bailiffs who served between 1300 and 1440 were merchants. Following the creation of the county in 1440, mercantile control may have increased: 49 per cent (thirty-five) of the seventy-one sheriffs between 1440 and 1509 were merchants. Of the ninety-eight mayors in office between 1332 and 1509, 72 per cent (seventy-one) were merchants, and a further dozen of unconfirmed occupations may also have been merchants. The extent of merchant engagement in Beverley's government is harder to gauge since there are few directly relevant sources. Only seventy-three keepers' occupations have been firmly identified during the period, of whom 77 per cent (fifty-six) were merchants, 9 per cent (seven) worked in textiles, and 8 per cent (six) were gentlemen.

As the *cursus honorum* became more formalised in the fifteenth century,

---

[85] Borough charters focused on the organisation of commerce, the exclusive rights of burgesses and the expansion of borough jurisdiction through local custom and burgess courts: Ballard and Tait, *British Borough Charters*, pp. xc–cii. See also Reynolds, *English Medieval Towns*, pp. 101–2, 109.

[86] In York, the sheriffs had to prick out individual votes in the mayoral elections, and in Hull, it was possible to identify 'those likely to serve as chamberlains'. See, for example, Hull RO, BRB 1, ff. 67, 77v., 81; J. I. Kermode, 'Obvious Observations on Oligarchies in Late Medieval English Towns', in Thomson, *Towns and Townspeople*, p. 92.

[87] Lists of councillors have not survived to enable an analysis of council membership. See Thrupp, *London Merchant Class*, p. 79, for an analysis of London's council in the fourteenth and fifteenth centuries. The following analysis is based on the lists in Kermode, 'Merchants of York, Beverley and Hull', appendix 1.

more merchant office-holders in York and Hull had complete careers, that is, served in all three senior offices. Thus in York, 44 per cent of fifteenth-century mayors had served both as chamberlain and sheriff, compared with only 12 per cent of their fourteenth-century predecessors, and in Hull, 65 per cent of mayors after 1440 had served as chamberlain and sheriff compared with some 7 per cent before 1400. The latter figure may be a gross misrepresentation given the patchy evidence.[88]

The overall pattern in all three towns then, is of merchants dominating the senior offices. Their closest rivals, wealthy craftsmen and gentlemen in the case of Beverley, were never so numerous as holders of senior offices. In fifteenth-century York there was a merchant mayor or sheriff virtually every year. Apparently any burgess could become a chamberlain, although previous service in the lesser office of bridgemaster was demanded in York from 1475.[89]

Apart from experience and wealth, were there other considerations? In York and Hull, certain occupations were considered to be *infra dignitatem*. Great emphasis was laid on the 'worship', the respectability and dignity of officials and council members, and extended beyond the prestigous symbol of the upturned sword and mace which the mayors of York and Hull were allowed to have carried before them in processions.[90] Each official was expected to conduct himself in the manner proper to his office; sheriffs were to be accompanied by their officers, aldermen were to wear correct gowns and to attend public processions.[91] The only recorded squabbles within the governing elite concerned financial dealings between officials and precedence in public processions.[92]

Councillors tried to ensure that men of common and vulgar occupations did not proceed high up the political ladder.[93] This was not explicitly stated, but was well understood. The keeping of an inn or hostelry seemed to be the most offensive occupation for a prospective officeholder.[94] John Petty was elected alderman in York in 1504, on condition

---

[88] Kermode, 'Merchants of York, Beverley and Hull', pp. 308–20.

[89] *MB*, II, p. 146. See also Chester where service in the lower office of levelooker became a prerequisite for service as chamberlain from 1541: Chester RO, Assembly Book 1, f. 79v.

[90] *VCH York*, p. 69; *CChR 1341–1417*, pp. 354–6, 358–60.

[91] In 1419 York sheriffs were ordered to walk about preceded by a servant, and were not to walk 'without dignity': *MB*, II, p. 86. Similarly, in 1490 aldermen were ordered to attend Minster processions, and in 1500 were ordered to wear their 'correct' scarlet robes: *YCR*, II, pp. 55, 145–6. For the behaviour proper for civic officers in Coventry, see Phythian-Adams, *Desolation of a City*, pp. 138–9. For a wider discussion see, Phythian-Adams, 'Ceremony and the Citizen', pp. 57–85.

[92] In 1485–6, John Harper and William Todd were arguing over precedence in the council: *YCR*, I, pp. 155, 170. See also *ibid.*, II, p. 148, for council orders about precedence.

[93] J. I. Kermode, 'Urban Decline? The Flight from Office in Late Medieval York', *EcHR*, 2nd ser., 35 (1982), pp. 193–5.

[94] There was antipathy towards innkeepers elsewhere. For example, a Norwich ordinance of 1415 forbade the mayor, sheriff or aldermen to keep a hostelry: F. Blomefield, *An Essay Towards a*

that he took down his sign and stopped keeping a hostelry, but by the mid-sixteenth century the prejudice against innkeepers and beer and wine retailers had faded.[95] In Hull, the mayor, sheriffs and aldermen could not sell ale in their houses, and the mayor was further forbidden to sell foodstuffs in the market.[96] In fifteenth-century York, a large proportion of chamberlains were butchers but very few served as sheriff and none has been traced in the aldermanic council.[97] The butchers' group is the only one out of the four largest occupational groups which did not produce a traceable alderman or mayor. The York butchers were articulate trouble-makers, probably excluded because of their dominant position in the food trades.[98] In Beverley the situation was rather different. A minority of the keepers was regularly recruited from the merchant group as well as from certain families, comprising an elite within the oligarchy[99] and making it possible for the remaining eight or nine keepers to be recruited from a variety of occupations as make-weights. Individuals with such occupations as butcher, baker, weaver, dyer and tailor held office as keeper from time to time. Whereas in York and Hull the sons of gentlemen generally became active merchants before embarking upon a career in local government,[100] gentlemen occasionally served as keeper in Beverley.

Repeated selection from the same families did not occur in York after 1364 or in Hull, and no dynastic pattern of office holding emerged as in Beverley. Relatively few sons followed their fathers into office, because relatively few officials had sons who survived long enough to hold office.[101] Of sixty-nine merchant office-holders with traceable sons in

Topographical History of the County of Norfolk (London, 1806), III, p. 129. I am grateful to David Palliser for this reference. As late as 1573 in Winchester a newly elected mayor was allowed to live in the east part of his house while his wife and servants ran his inn in the rest of the house! T. Atkinson, *Elizabethan Winchester* (London, 1963), p. 63.

95 *YCR*, III, p. 10; House Book IX, f. 20v.; Palliser, *Tudor York*, p. 107; W. G. Hoskins, *The Age of Plunder* (London, 1976), p. 100, observed that occupations that were socially unacceptable in one period became acceptable at a later date.

96 Hull RO, BRE 2, ff. 13, 21–2v., 77v.–8.

97 We can firmly identify the aldermen after 1476 through reasonably continuous documentation. Earlier identifications are more random.

98 *MB*, I, pp. 57–8, 121, 125, 132 and *passim*; *YCR*, I, p. 33. See also Norwich where in 1508 an alderman-elect had to renounce his butcher's trade: W. Hudson and J. C. Tingay, eds., *The Records of the City of Norwich* (Norwich, 1906–10), II, p. 107. The political fame of the London victuallers derived from their ability to exploit control over food supply: R. Bird, *The Turbulent London of Richard II* (London, 1949), pp. 63, 66–8; P. Nightingale, 'Capitalists, Crafts and Constitutional Change in Late Fourteenth-Century London', *Past & Present*, 124 (1989), pp. 3–35; G. Unwin, *The Gilds and Companies of London* (London, 1908), pp. 129–37.

99 For details see Kermode, 'Obvious Observations', pp. 95–6.

100 E.g. Brian Conyers of York, son of Christopher Conyers esq. of Hornby, became free as a merchant in 1473. See Kermode, 'Merchants of York, Beverley and Hull', appendix 4.

101 See below, p. 78, for the failure of the merchant group to produce male heirs.

late fourteenth- and fifteenth-century York, only twenty-eight had sons who held an office in their turn. In Hull, of twenty-seven merchant office-holders with sons, only eleven had sons who also held office. The majority of recruits into the ruling elites of York and Hull were first-generation immigrants, or the sons of non-office-holding small merchants and craftsmen. This pattern continued in York, and in the sixteenth century perhaps as many as four-fifths of the council were immigrants.[102]

It is possible to establish the intervals between offices held by York's merchant politicians.[103] Most became a chamberlain within six to ten years of becoming a freeman, a bailiff or sheriff two to three years after that, an alderman within six years and mayor within a further four years. If we assume men became burgesses at twenty-one,[104] then most York merchants would expect to set out on their political careers at between twenty-seven and thirty-six years old and to have served as mayor by the time they were forty-five.

Many careers in fourteenth-century York omitted lower offices, and culminated in several terms as mayor. Henry de Belton, free in 1323, went on to become a bailiff in six years and mayor five years later: the first of four consecutive years in that office. Roger de Moreton jnr, free in 1362, followed the same pattern, becoming a bailiff within six years and mayor five years later, but he was only mayor once. One of the rivals for power in the city in 1381, Simon de Quixlay, free in 1366, avoided serving as chamberlain and became a bailiff nine years later and served the first of his three consecutive terms as mayor in 1381.

Once service in urban government became more structured in the fifteenth century, fewer merchants omitted the lower offices before serving as mayor. Outstandingly successful local politicians can easily be identified. William Frost, who became free in 1395 and mayor a year later for the first of eight terms, was exceptional in many ways. His spectacular dominance of the mayoralty may have been due to the fact that he was already a well-established overseas merchant and a member of the prominent Frost family of Beverley and Hull. Nicholas Lancaster also served as mayor without previous experience of civic office, within thirteen years of becoming a freeman in 1472. The rise of Nicholas Blackburn jnr was even more rapid and he was elected mayor only seven years after becoming free in 1422. He had served as a chamberlain and a sheriff. Both Lancaster and Blackburn were sons of established York merchants, and may have owed their success to their fathers' reputations. Blackburn's

[102] Palliser, *Tudor York*, pp. 94–5.
[103] For all the examples cited below, see Kermode, 'Merchants of York, Beverley and Hull', appendix 4.   [104] See p. 44 below for a discussion of the likely age at entry.

father had served as mayor and died a very wealthy man.[105] Lancaster's father was engaged in overseas trade but did not hold office. Sons who survived and followed their fathers into local government were uncommon but John Gilyot jnr was another who had an exceptional political career, perhaps as a consequence of his parentage and of his own financial success. He became a chamberlain in 1482, within one year of his entry, sheriff two years later, and mayor for the first time within six years. He left at least £700 and a large urban estate. His son Peter looked as though he might follow an unusual family tradition when he became a chamberlain in 1522, one year after he had become a freeman, but he died three years later without holding another office.[106]

The reasons why other merchants were less successful are not so clear. The Brounfleet brothers, William and Thomas, waited thirty and twenty-six years respectively to be elected chamberlain. Thomas did become a sheriff the following year in 1457, but died a year later. Both were active in overseas trade and William's average annual trade was worth over £50. John Carter, free in 1469, was elected a chamberlain thirty-one years later and died in 1505 without holding another office. In some families one brother had a successful political career and another did not, maybe by agreement. Thomas Aldestonemore waited twenty years before he was elected to the only office he held, that of chamberlain, while his brother John, free in the same year, 1412, served as chamberlain in 1418, as sheriff in 1421 and as mayor in 1427.

The absence of reliable records of freeman entry into Hull and Beverley makes such a close analysis difficult, but the impression is that in Hull merchants were elected chamberlain within ten years of becoming free, but election as bailiff or sheriff did not follow as quickly as in York. The majority waited a further ten years but 46 per cent of the merchants traced became sheriff within five years. The mayoralty was achieved on average within ten years, but there was no pattern to their subsequent terms as mayor, which could occur between one and twenty years later. Robert Chapman's was a typical career. Free in 1464, he was a chamberlain in 1474, sheriff in 1478, and mayor in 1487 and again in 1493.[107] Many careers progressed in fits and starts but the high-flyers moved rapidly from office to office. In Hull, Edmund Coppendale, free in 1450, was elected chamberlain the following year, sheriff two years later, and mayor six years later in 1459. However, he was elected mayor for a second time in 1477, eighteen years after his first mayoralty. William Goodknappe was another high flyer. He was free in 1488, elected a chamberlain in 1490, sheriff in 1493 and mayor for the first time in 1497. He

---

[105] Prob. Reg. II, f. 605.   [106] Prob. Reg. IX, f. 324.
[107] Hull RO, BRG I, ff. 24, 26v., 27(a); BRB I, f. 118v.

43

was elected mayor for a second term in 1503, but was in Calais at the time and Robert Garner was elected in his place seven weeks later.[108]

The names of the Beverley keepers survive for consecutive years between 1436 and 1470.[109] Those who served several times could expect to hold office every four years or so until they died. Very few men were re-elected within three years of their preceding term, and given the collective nature of Beverley's government, long service with accumulated experience and consequent respect was the only goal. Since Beverley did not return MPs, there was not even the reward of jaunting up to London.

Why did men seek civic office? Was it because they had high ambitions or a strong sense of duty, a lust for 'worship' and respect?[110] It will be apparent that to get close to the heights of civic power in York and Hull, a man usually had to wait until he was fairly old, by contemporary standards, and indeed, merchants as a group may have had a long life expectancy. Two-thirds for whom entry dates and dates of death are known lived over thirty years after becoming free, that is to an average age of fifty-two, and one-fifth lived for over forty years. Death most commonly occurred between the ages of fifty and sixty.[111] What is not so obvious is whether or not there was a particular regard for age, since those rapidly promoted were not hindered by their youth. The aldermanic bench was undoubtedly a repository of wisdom and clear thinking, and in Beverley there was a group of *venerabiles*,[112] who were consulted from time to time like the Delphic oracle. Probably the twenty to twenty-five year wait to become mayor was inevitable, since most men would have to build up business to the state where only cursory supervision was required.

Aldermen held office until death or until they were incapable of attending meetings. There are several instances in York of men continuing as aldermen for another decade after serving as mayor. William Wells, Richard York, William Todd, William White, Michael White and George Kirk all sat as aldermen for at least a further ten years after their first mayoralties, and George Kirk and the two Whites served as mayor for a second term.[113] As aldermen they wielded great power in selecting

---

[108] Hull RO, BRG 1, ff. 18v., 21, 23, 25v., 27, 28, 29v.; BRB 1, f. 146; M479/2/27.

[109] Listed in *VCH Beverley*, pp. 198–200.

[110] In fourteenth-century Burgos, the ruling elite was allowed to wear and adopt an exclusive style of dress: T. F. Ruiz, 'The Transformation of the Castilian Municipalities: The Case of Burgos 1248–1350', *Past & Present*, 77 (1977), p. 19.

[111] This is based on the assumption that men became freemen at twenty-one to twenty-two. In London, the median age of death for a group of fifteenth-century merchants was forty-nine to fifty: Thrupp, *London Merchant Class*, p. 194. According to Hammer, it was the biologically successful who won the final prize, the alderman's scarlet: 'Anatomy of an Oligarchy', pp. 24–5.

[112] Humberside RO, BC II/2, f. 7v.

[113] See Kermode, 'Merchants of York, Beverley and Hull', appendix 4.

future mayors to join them from the twenty-four. For some who did achieve a place on the aldermanic bench, respect became less intoxicating and their duties became onerous and wearisome. Robert Hancock and John Harper retired for reasons of ill health in 1496, and in 1484 the council dismissed John Gilyot, William Marshall and William Neleson for the same reason. John Tong, on the other hand, had to ask the council several times to be dismissed because he was 'broken by great sickness' before his request was granted in 1490.[114] By then he had been absent from all council meetings for two years.[115] When William Snawsell was given leave to retire in 1492, because he was 'greatly diseased and vexed with many and diverse sicknesses', John Newton, another alderman, made the same request because he was 'so sick with the government that he might not come and show his mind'.[116] Was this due to the irascibility of age or increasing exasperation with colleagues of lengthy acquaintance?

Certainly in late fifteenth-century York, when records are reasonably full, it is clear that the council did not welcome individuals who did not take their aldermanic responsibilities seriously. Attendance and punctuality at council meetings was a constant problem and the regularity with which ordinances were passed, imposing fines on non-attenders and latecomers of the aldermen and twenty-four alike, suggests it was insoluble.[117] William Holbeck was persistently absent from meetings and was dismissed in 1476. His failings were compounded in the eyes of his fellow aldermen by his removing his household to live outside the city walls, to the Friars' Tofts.[118] In 1500 Thomas Scotton was similarly dismissed for absenteeism, but he had been reluctant to become an alderman in the first place, and refused to take his oath until he was threatened with a £40 fine.[119]

It has been suggested that there was a scarcity of willing and able citi-

---

[114] York RO, House Book VII, ff. 19, 19v., 117v.; VIII, f. 4v. William Todd retired through ill-health in 1503 and William White and John Elwald in 1506: *ibid.*, IX, ff. 9v., 27v.

[115] *Ibid.*, VI, ff. 133 et seq.

[116] *Ibid.*, VII, f. 60; IX, ff. 9v., 27v. William Chimney was summoned to take his annual oath in October 1503 and to bear the charges pertaining to an alderman, or else to pay a fine to be allowed not to attend council meetings. He was allowed to defer his decision until the next council meeting, and on 15 December 1503 he asked to be excused from serving as an alderman, because he was too old and too sick. The council agreed to discharge him, 'having tender consideration for his great age . . . he to take his ease and rest', on payment of £10: *ibid.*, IX, f. 9.

[117] E.g. *MB*, I, pp. 34, 49; II, p. 199; *YCR*, I, p. 8; II, p. 176. On the other hand, regular attendance did not aid promotion either, since there were men whose attendance at council meetings was exemplary but they never became aldermen. William Tate, a tailor and sheriff in 1478, attended almost every meeting of council until 1503 but was not favoured with a seat on the aldermanic bench. Likewise Thomas Allen, a baker and sheriff in 1470, attended regularly until he was too ill in 1500.   [118] York RO, House Book II, ff. 2v., 4; VIII, f. 99.   [119] *YCR*, II, p. 11.

zens to take on the burdens of office during the economic recession of the late fifteenth century.[120] At the very least, it has been argued, civic government came to reflect the diminution in the numbers of exceptionally wealthy and successful men in towns, and had to rely upon the next rank in society.[121] Clearly there were fewer very wealthy individuals in the older centres, and consequently fewer of them in local government, but it is debatable whether there was a dramatic resistance to civic duty amounting to a flight from office.

This issue has been discussed more fully elsewhere, but briefly it seems that, in York at least,[122] there always had been some men who avoided civic office, paying for exemptions and pardons.[123] The numbers of exemptions purchased did increase in the late fifteenth century, but in suspicious circumstances. Burgesses from a variety of occupations paid sums ranging from £6 paid by a cook in 1492 for exemption from the shrievalty for six years, to £2 paid by a goldsmith and a yeoman in 1499 for eight years.[124] It seems likely, however, that the council had a policy to compel men who were unlikely to be elected as sheriff to buy exemption from that office. In 1451 the council gained parliamentary cancellation of all previous royal exemptions from holding civic office.[125] In October 1495, it decided to raise the money required to pay off a specific debt of £62 14s by compelling men likely to be elected chamberlain or sheriff but unable to 'bear the office' to pay to be exempted.[126] The individuals purchasing council exemptions were generally retiring chamberlains who would not normally be expected to hold office as a sheriff for at least two years, and, in any case, were cooks, tapiters, fishmongers[127] – men unlikely to maintain the worship of the office. When a reason was given for such exemptions, it was usually that the individual concerned was 'not able to bear office'. John Reg, a fishmonger, was said to be 'a small person and not of sufficient stature to occupy the office of sheriff'. Thomas Chapman, a saddler, was similarly exempted 'unless he gain sufficient in years'.[128]

---

[120] Dobson, 'Urban Decline in Late Medieval England', p. 20.

[121] Hoskins, *The Age of Plunder*, p. 100.

[122] Kermode, 'Urban Decline?', pp. 179–98. Gary Shaw has concluded that there was no flight from office in Wells either, *Wells*, p. 172.

[123] As early as 1420 regulations were passed forbidding aldermen to leave the city on election day, on pain of a fine of £80. In 1445 John Thirsk, who had already served as mayor twice, acquired a royal exemption for life from holding any civic office: *CPR 1441–6*, p. 395.

[124] York RO, House Book VII, f. 85v.; VIII, f. 41v.

[125] The penalty for purchasing a royal exemption was a fine of £40: *Rot. Parl.*, v, p. 225. However, in 1501 Anthony Welbourn, who had purchased a royal exemption, was elected sheriff but did not serve: York RO, House Book VIII, f. 115v.   [126] *YCR*, II, p. 121.

[127] See, for example, York RO, House Book VIII, ff. 24v., 49, 136v.; IX, ff. 8v., 35v.

[128] House Book VI, f. 100; IX, f. 50.

Few merchants were recorded as buying or being granted exemptions from office with the exception of Thomas Catour and Thomas Hardsang, who paid 5 marks and £20 respectively in 1495. Hardsang was said to be 'insufficient in goods and discretion' but there is no clue as to why he paid over four times more than Catour. Some favoured merchants were allowed exemption without payment. Alan Staveley, who later served as sheriff and mayor, was exempted until he was 'able and sufficient in reason and discretion', whereas Brian Conyers was exempted until he had 'grown in goods and riches'.[129]

That 'riches' were essential for a man holding the highest offices is clear. Quite how much, is less so. It has been estimated that in early sixteenth-century York a man had to be worth about £80–£100 per year to be elected sheriff.[130] A man was expected to begin his year in office with a ceremonial 'riding' through the city and with a feast for the council; after which he took his oath.[131] He may also have had to pay £16 13s 4d or twice that on taking up his office as his contribution to the 'liflod' of the city, or as security against the expenses of his office.[132] Once in post, sheriffs had to maintain the dignity of the office by dressing correctly, wearing their fur tippets, and being accompanied by a serjeant in front and an honest servant behind, as required by a civic ordinance in 1419. Failure to observe these niceties could result in disgrace.[133] Hospitality and dignified conduct was expected of the mayor of York also, eased by his fee of £50 plus additional payments.[134] The sheriffs merely had their expenses covered, if that, from fines. Lavish expenses and excessive official fees aroused the hostility of the York commons as we shall see.

There are no hints in the Hull and Beverley records of expensive demands being made of office-holders. The Hull mayors and sheriffs were expected to proceed around the town with ceremony, like their York counterparts, but the Hull mayor's fee fluctuated; generally it was £20, but he and the sheriff also received extra income from fines.[135]

It may be that, just as older towns like York were encumbered with the complex guild and labour restrictions of the past, it was difficult to avoid expectations of civic behaviour which were equally financially draining.

[129] House Book VII, ff. 109, 138v.; *YCR*, I, p. 25.
[130] D. M. Palliser, 'Some Aspects of the Social and Economic History of York in the Sixteenth Century' (Univ. of Oxford DPhil thesis, 1968), p. 166.
[131] *YCR*, II, p. 179; York RO, House Book IX, ff. 9v., 20(ii)v.
[132] House Book VI, f. 29v. Bridgemasters also had to contribute to the 'liflod' on taking up office: *ibid.*, IX, f. 26, and chamberlains and aldermen had to make a payment when they took up office.
[133] *VCH York*, p. 72; *MB*, II, pp. 86–7. In 1500, for example, one of the sheriffs was fined for being in the street without a mace borne in front of him: *YCR*, II, p. 162.
[134] *VCH York*, pp. 70–1.   [135] *VCH Hull*, p. 31.

Alternatively, lavish public conduct may have been just another expression of rhetoric from an elite struggling to legitimise its position. The mayor's feast in Coventry, for example, was said to cost as much as half the yearly running expenses of his household.[136] Just the same, town government did not collapse during the worst years of economic decline; there were still men willing to serve. Local power and prestige were considerable and tempting: so maybe to some was the opportunity to serve in other capacities further afield. In York and Hull, election as an MP became the final rung of the civic ladder: 75 per cent of York MPs had served as mayor and 75 per cent of Hull MPs either had or would serve as mayor.

FURTHER HONOUR AND GLORY

Serving as an MP and on royal commissions could extend a merchant's political career on to a higher level. There were opportunities for public service beyond the boroughs for those who were so inclined and were deemed suitable. Once York and Hull had been granted their own commissions of the peace in 1396 and 1440 respectively, there was no longer the necessity for the Crown to appoint named commissioners. Local merchants had been involved on commissions of the peace to enforce the Statute of Labourers or to inquire into specific complaints of assault and breaches of the peace.[137] They continued to serve on county commissions.[138] Beverley never achieved its own commission of the peace and struggled to be free of the East Riding justices.[139] Merchants continued to serve on commissions of the peace from time to time,[140] and on their own town's pavage commissions.[141] Merchants from all three towns served on commissions of array, within their boroughs and in the county.[142] They also sat, apparently as equals with the gentry, on commissions of *wallibus et fossatis*, for weirs and obstructions in the Ouse,[143] and

---

[136] PRO, SP1/142, f. 66, cited in C. Phythian-Adams' 'Coventry and the Problem of Urban Decay in the Late Middle Ages', unpublished paper, Urban History Conference, London, 1977.

[137] *CPR 1313–17*, p. 415; *1317–21*, p. 85; *1350–4*, pp. 332, 449; *1354–8*, p. 497; *1364–70*, pp. 266, 434; *1370–4*, pp. 104, 355; *1374–7*, p. 554; *1377–81*, pp. 47, 503, 515, 518, 572; *1385–9*, p. 296; *1389–92*, p. 37; *1392–6*, p. 84.

[138] E.g. *CPR 1429–36*, p. 331; *1452–61*, p. 609; *1476–85*, p. 579; *1485–9*, p. 186.

[139] S. Walker, 'Yorkshire Justices of the Peace, 1389–1413', *EHR*, 427 (1993), pp. 296–7.

[140] *CPR 1350–4*, pp. 232, 391; *1367–70*, p. 418; *1429–36*, p. 628; *1467–77*, p. 637; *1476–85*, p. 579.

[141] *CPR 1385–9*, p. 518; *1401–5*, p. 227; *1405–8*, p. 284; *1413–18*, pp. 14, 275; *1436–41*, p. 488; Humberside RO, BC II/2, f. 24.

[142] *CPR 1364–7*, p. 432; *1370–4*, p. 101; *1374–7*, p. 502; *1377–81*, p. 37; *1429–36*, pp. 360, 470; *1461–7*, p. 31; *1467–77*, p. 407; *CCR 1476–85*, pp. 398, 484.

[143] *CPR 1330–4*, p. 131; *1338–40*, pp. 76, 144; *1350–3*, p. 542; *1358–61*, pp. 422, 583; *1377–81*, p. 471; *1385–9*, p. 471; *1396–8*, p. 101; *1407–17*, p. 427; *1461–7*, p. 206; *1467–77*, p. 354.

as royal subsidy collectors, mainly in Yorkshire.[144] Merchants were regularly appointed to serve as customs officials, generally as collectors or controllers in Hull, sometimes in Grimsby, Scarborough and Ravenser. Occasionally local merchants were appointed royal butler in Hull.[145] The Crown found their specialist knowledge useful, even though some merchants were guilty of smuggling, and appointed individuals as ulnager to commissions to enforce commercial regulations such as the collection of wool and cloth subsidies,[146] to enforce statutes against the export of bullion[147] and to fight piracy.[148]

During times of war, merchants from York, Beverley and Hull were appointed to collect money and suitable ships for the Crown,[149] and on one occasion in 1457, two Hull merchants were commissioned to press men into overseas service for the king.[150] Exceptionally, merchant burgesses were sent on diplomatic missions by the king: John de Ripon of York and Stephen de la Gard of Beverley were sent to Flanders in 1336, and Thomas Gra of York was one of three ambassadors sent to treat with the Hanse in Prussia in 1388.[151]

All of these appointments were additional to regular commissions given *ex officio* to the mayor and sheriffs of York and Hull and suggest a considerable range of devolved governmental responsibilities, beyond the purview of routine town government. They reflect the extent to which the Crown saw merchants as 'urban gentry' – men with the status to fulfil the duties they were given effectively[152] – and also the extent to which merchant burgesses were involved in the region around their urban strongholds. In this respect, the division between town and country[153] was not so very great in the devolving of administration from the centre

---

[144] *MB*, I, p. 131; II, p. 76; *CCR 1334–8*, p. 40; *1358–61*, p. 348; *1361–4*, pp. 302, 463; *1367–70*, p. 394; *1370–4*, p. 269; *CFR 1377–83*, p. 58; *CCR 1385–9*, p. 555; *1405–9*, p. 302; PRO, E179/217/42. Beverley men could only serve as tax collectors within the borough after 1401: Humberside RO, BC II/2, f. 2.

[145] *CPR 1334–8*, p. 166; *1345–8*, p. 277; *1350–4*, p. 658; *1401–5*, p. 383; *1413–18*, p. 10; *1418–22*, pp. 175, 392; *1446–52*, p. 60; *CFR 1327–37*, p. 211; *1377–83*, p. 169; *CCR 1330–3*, p. 257; *1346–9*, pp. 8, 219; *1389–92*, p. 122; Lister, *Early Yorks Woollen Trade*, appendices II, III; W. R. Childs, ed., *The Customs Accounts of Hull 1453–1490*, YAS Rec. Ser., 144 (1986), appendix A.

[146] *CCR 1339–41*, p. 590; *CPR 1338–40*, p. 393; *1350–4*, p. 28; *1358–61*, pp. 67, 162; *1377–81*, p. 438; *1381–5*, p. 244; PRO, C76/13.

[147] *CFR 1319–27*, p. 257; *CCR 1354–60*, p. 473; *CPR 1381–5*, p. 198; *1391–6*, p. 238.

[148] *CPR 1358–61*, p. 79; *1429–36*, p. 470; *1446–52*, p. 316.

[149] *CPR 1370–4*, pp. 227, 355; *1416–22*, p. 72; *1429–36*, pp. 334, 510; *1446–52*, p. 365.

[150] *CPR 1452–61*, pp. 172, 404.   [151] *CPR 1334–8*, p. 336; *1385–9*, p. 453.

[152] Other unusual commissions included merchants. In 1333 three Hull merchants were appointed to inquire into possible merchant collusion with the Scots: *CCR 1333–7*, p. 35. Robert del Gare of York was put on a commission inquiring into the debts of the late archbishop Alexander Neville in 1397: *CPR 1396–9*, p. 311. Two prominent York merchants were given responsibility for the inspection of the Castle Mills, Crown property, in 1401: *ibid. 1401–5*, p. 64.

[153] Horrox, 'Urban Patronage', pp. 155–6.

to the provinces, and maybe townsmen with the experience of local administration and commercial knowledge of distant markets stood out as men of distinction and ability. What we cannot know is how far merchants were inevitably the junior members of commissions with a mixed membership which included gentry and even local nobility.[154]

As with civic office, some merchants were uninterested in royal service, or became too old to continue to accept commissions. In 1383 for example, Adam Coppendale of Beverley was granted a royal exemption at the age of sixty-eight,[155] Nicholas Useflete and John Thirsk of York were exempted in 1437 and 1445 from serving on juries, as well as in civic office.[156] However, Thirsk went on to serve as mayor from 1456 and as treasurer of the Calais Staple from 1467 until his death in 1473.[157]

Although by no means typical, three York merchants will serve to illustrate the range of royal commissions to which individuals might be appointed. William Frost, the York merchant appointed keeper of the city in 1405, was an experienced royal commissioner, and his appointments provide a good example of the range of royal duties given to some merchants. He was appointed to several commissions to survey the weirs in Yorkshire waterways[158] and served as royal escheator in Yorkshire.[159] Twice he was appointed to commissions to inspect St Leonard's Hospital for the Crown. In 1400 he was asked to raise loans for the king's journey to Scotland[160] and in 1401 he was appointed with Thomas Gra to inspect the state of repair of the castle mills in York. Indeed he served the Crown so well that in 1404 he received a royal grant for life of two tuns of wine annually.[161] He was clearly a familiar and trusted servant of the Crown, an obvious choice for the difficult post of keeper in 1405, when the city paid the penalty for its support of Archbishop Scrope's rebellion against Henry IV.[162]

Thomas Gra was another York merchant much in demand for royal commissions. In 1371, 1379 and 1399 he was appointed to waterways commissions.[163] In 1377 he was appointed to a commission of *oyer et ter-*

---

[154] Since many of the borough appointees also served as MPs, they were men of calibre. Roskell, *House of Commons*, I, pp. 237–8.

[155] *CPR 1381–5*, p. 31. Thomas Holme and John Kelk, also of Beverley, were similarly granted exemptions in 1336 and 1390 respectively: *1334–8*, p. 318; *1388–92*, p. 205.

[156] *Ibid. 1436–41*, p. 126; *1441–6*, pp. 22, 395.

[157] Wedgwood, *Parliamentary Biographies*, pp. 845–6. Two other York merchants served as mayor of the Staple: Richard Russell in 1425 (*MB*, II, p. 159) and Richard York in 1466 (*Test. Ebor.* IV, p. 134n.). Hugh Clitheroe of Hull had occupied the lesser office of 'bocconer of all the wools' in Calais in 1396: PRO, SC8/179/8903.

[158] *CPR 1396–9*, p. 101; *1399–1401*, p. 124; *1401–5*, p. 273.

[159] *Ibid. 1388–92*, pp. 60, 104, 121, 209, 298, 376, 457; *1399–1401*, p. 450.

[160] *Ibid. 1391–6*, pp. 79, 131, 356.   [161] *CPR 1401–5*, pp. 64, 406.

[162] *VCH York*, p. 58.   [163] *CPR 1370–1*, p. 111; *1377–81*, p. 363; *1399–1401*, p. 124.

miner in a case of trespass, and he was appointed to at least eight commissions of the peace in the city[164] and made a JP in 1380.[165] He sat on inquiries into St Leonard's Hospital for the Crown[166] and was appointed to inquire into claims of destitution in Yorkshire occasioned by payment of parliamentary subsidies.[167] It is not surprising that when an embassy was sent to Prussia in 1388 to negotiate the return of arrested English shipping, Thomas Gra was chosen as one of the three ambassadors.[168]

Appointment to royal commissions occurred less frequently in the fifteenth century: Nicholas Blackburn snr, for example, was not as much in demand as Thomas Gra had been, although he was one of the more regularly appointed of his cohort. From his appointment as Admiral of the Seas north of the Thames in 1406, he was regularly appointed to commissions. In 1406 he was inquiring into forestallers in Yorkshire, and in the following year he was surveying the obstructions in the Ouse. In 1409 he was appointed to inquire into the illegal loading of boats by his fellow merchants, who were trying to avoid paying export subsidies, and in 1413 he was on a commission of *oyer et terminer* in Yorkshire.[169]

These were clearly exceptional men and their experience of royal service was unusual. The highest accolade for many no doubt was to be elected to represent their borough in parliament. Beverley was only twice represented in parliament between 1300 and 1509: in February 1304/5 when John le Porter and Stephen Rote sat and in January 1306/7 when Robert de Scarborough and Thomas le Hirde sat. Beverley merchants though were present at Edward's councils of merchants, whereas Hull men were not.[170]

Unlike Beverley, Hull did return members to parliament with increasing regularity from the 1330s. With the notable exception of William Eland, a lawyer and merchant, the majority of Hull's MPs already had or were to hold civic office and were merchants: 52 per cent in the fourteenth century and 75 per cent in the fifteenth. Several merchants were elected repeatedly: Adam Pund, William de la Pole, Walter Frost in the fourteenth century; Hugh Clitheroe, Robert Holme, John Fitling, Richard Anson, William Eland in the fifteenth.[171] Eland served thirteen

[164] *Ibid. 1377–81*, pp. 37, 572; *1381–5*, p. 137; *1385–9*, p. 254; *1388–92*, pp. 139, 219, 343, 524.

[165] *Ibid. 1377–81*, p. 503.   [166] *Ibid. 1377–81*, p. 465; *1399–1401*, pp. 270, 518.

[167] *Ibid. 1377–81*, p. 459.

[168] *Ibid. 1385–8*, p. 453. See also *ibid. 1334–8*, p. 336 for a similar mission by John de Ripon to Flanders. The Crown found merchants particularly useful in this capacity. In 1431 and 1434 Henry VI appointed a Lynn merchant as one of his ambassadors to Bruges. I am grateful to Mr E. C. Glover for this information. See also Thrupp, *London Merchant Class*, p. 56.

[169] *CPR 1405–8*, pp. 171, 236, 473; *1408–13*, p. 110; *1413–16*, p. 65.

[170] *Return of the Name of Every Member of the Lower House, 1213–1702.* Parliamentary Papers (1878).

[171] Kermode, 'Merchants of York, Beverley and Hull', appendix 1; *VCH Hull*, p. 39.

times between 1450 and 1484, and although never a city official, he was retained as counsel from 1447 to 1460 when he was made recorder. Uncertain political times may have encouraged the city to depart from its tradition in opting for Eland.[172] MPs were in effect chosen by the council which nominated four candidates from whom the commons chose two.[173]

In York, the process was less democratic with the aldermen and the twenty-four choosing two as MPs for ratification in the county court. The full council was rarely involved: attendance at the selection averaging twenty on ten occasions between 1419 and 1503.[174] As in Hull, the majority of York's MPs were drawn from the commercial elite of the city, and although in the early fourteenth century, many sat for the city several times, none dominated the city's representation on the same scale as the Gra family from 1344. William served at least fourteen times and his son Thomas at least twelve. They were quite exceptional and probably owed their frequent election to prominent royal service. No other MP served as often, though some merchants such as John de Acastre and William Helmesley were elected four or five times. After 1400, 75 per cent of MPs were elected only once.[175]

If there was direct external interference in urban politics, the selection of MPs would have been a prime target. There is no evidence that anyone other than the oligarchs of York and Hull was involved in elections,[176] though their choices may have been made with an awareness of the advantage to be gained from choosing men favoured by powerful nobles. Miles Metcalfe and Thomas Wrangwish were both in Richard of Gloucester's affinity and sat as MPs for York, in 1483 and 1484.[177] Richard Anson gained favour with the Duke of York, acquiring office in the forfeited Stafford estate in Holderness in 1460, but was beheaded for his disloyalty after capture at the battle of Wakefield. He sat as MP for Hull five times between 1439 and 1460 and it has been suggested that Yorkist favour helped his election.[178]

The advantages to individual boroughs in sending representatives to parliament are difficult to gauge. Their contribution to great matters must have been slight but on the other hand, MPs could perform some ser-

[172] Kermode, 'Merchants of York, Beverley and Hull', appendix 4 (Hull); Horrox, 'Urban Patronage', p. 159.   [173] *VCH York*, p. 39.   [174] *Ibid.*, p. 79.

[175] *VCH York*, p. 79; Roskell, *House of Commons*, I, p. 746; Kermode, 'Merchants of York, Beverley and Hull', appendices 1 and 4 (York).

[176] M. McKisack, *The Parliamentary Representation of English Boroughs during the Middle Ages* (Oxford, 1932), *passim*. See p. 38 above, note 82.

[177] Kermode, 'Merchants of York, Beverley and Hull', appendices 1 and 4; *VCH York*, pp. 62–3.

[178] Kermode, 'Merchants of York, Beverley and Hull', appendix 4; Wedgwood, *Parliamentary Biographies*, p. 13; Horrox, 'Urban Patronage', pp. 155, 159.

vices and gain knowledge and contacts useful to a provincial community. Thus Hull's MPs sought advice in London in 1430–1 on the difficulties of trading with Iceland under Danish rule and help in 1441–2 on paying poundage on cloth. York MPs complained in 1382 about a dearth of grain, won a decision in 1391 that cloth shipped to Berwick was not exported, and in 1451 obtained the cancellation of letters patent by which men could be exempted from civic office. Given that both York and Hull conscientiously paid their members 4s each day as well as expenses for attending parliament,[179] and that cumulatively this constituted a regular payment against each city's income,[180] then neither council was indifferent to the access to Westminster they bought.

POLITICAL EFFECTIVENESS

It may seem redundant to consider the political effectiveness of merchant oligarchs. Their dominance of the key urban offices and near monopoly of parliamentary representation testifies either to their accepted capabilities or to their effective manipulation of the electoral process which kept other occupational groups out of office. However, the aspirations of individuals, including newly wealthy merchants seeking access to political power, became an important and destabilising ingredient in urban politics. The persistence of more general unrest in medieval towns suggests an ongoing struggle between the priorities of the oligarchy and those of other townsfolk, as the former developed a view of its regulatory role at odds with the wider interests of society: descending versus ascending power.[181]

Political ambition though, was only one of several disruptive elements in late medieval towns, and, far from establishing a universal motivation or pattern of unrest, historians are increasingly aware of the diversity of rebellions and of the specific circumstances in each locality.[182] The status of rioters, causes and effects varied from town to town, as the evidence from York, Beverley and Hull demonstrates, but one thread linking all three was a belief in the possibility of change coupled with a confidence that existing institutions could accommodate and sustain reform once

---

[179] *VCH Hull*, pp. 39, 64; Hull RO, M479/13, 14; *VCH York*, p. 79.

[180] For instance, York paid £83 4s to its MPs in 1475 when the city's finances were in deficit: Dobson, *York City Chamberlains' Account Rolls*, pp. xxxv, 156. Hull, for some reason, only paid its MPs between £10 and £20 in most years throughout the fifteenth century: Hull RO, M479 *passim*. See Kermode, 'Merchants of York, Beverley and Hull', appendix 2.

[181] W. Ullman, *A History of Political Thought: The Middle Ages* (Harmondsworth, 1965), pp. 12–13, 159–61; S. H. Rigby, 'Power and Authority', in Palliser, *Cambridge Urban History of Britain*, I (forthcoming).

[182] One surveyor of urban unrest recently observed, 'the range of historical opinion on the subject is at least as wide as . . . [the late medieval crisis] itself': Rotz, 'Investigating Urban Uprisings', p. 215.

achieved.[183] Apart from the short-lived attempt to introduce a tri-umvirate in Beverley, there was no explicit rejection of existing structures but a continuous effort to ensure they worked through improving access to office. In the fourteenth century, the fighting was between 'ins' and 'outs'; in the fifteenth century it was more often about the conduct of the governors. Specific complaints usually centred on the conduct of government: corruption, incompetent financial management, lavish expenditure and the failure to support the common interest.

The government of early-fourteenth-century York, and probably of Beverley, was controlled by gentry rentiers: families such as the York Langtons, three of whom served as mayor thirty times between 1306 and 1363. Henry de Belton, wool merchant and royal purveyor,[184] was one of the first merchants successfully to challenge the landed interest in York, achieving the mayoralty in 1334. By 1364 that challenge had become overwhelming and non-merchants rarely became mayor thereafter. As the production and trading of cloth spread profits more widely, the merchant class itself spawned political rivals, but, more fundamentally, even though the complexion of the rulers changed, access to power did not. The political role of the commons remained limited, in spite of the increasing numbers of new freemen swelling the franchise. The council in all three towns controlled admissions to the freedom, and in York at least, also influenced the rate of setting-up fees for artisans.[185] Non-office-holding burgesses had formal but limited access to government and were probably the group referred to in records as the 'commonalty': always present to 'elect' officials from council nominees. Representatives of the commonalty may have comprised the outer councils of forty-eight in York and Beverley but they rarely met.[186] Although there were some changes in the political systems in the three towns, merchants remained the dominant group, controlling access to and up the *cursus honorum*.[187]

How acceptable that was to their fellow citizens is open to debate. Perceived from below, government was expected to be competent and to keep the civic budget balanced. Oligarchic government was supposed to be impartial, with a paramount duty to act for rich and poor alike, and most civic officials' oaths reflected that philosophy.[188] The Beverley

[183] Similar optimism was apparent in Europe: J. R. Strayer, 'The Fourth and Fourteenth Centuries', *Am. Hist. Rev.*, 77 (1972), pp. 1–14 at p. 10.

[184] *CPR 1321–4*, p. 342; *1334–8*, p. 486; *CCR 1337–9*, p. 430.

[185] Dobson, 'Admissions to the Freedom of the City of York', pp. 18, 20; Swanson, *Medieval Artisans*, p. 119.

[186] Kermode, 'Merchants of York, Beverley and Hull', pp. 285, 297. In 1379 the York forty-eight were referred to as the 'artificers': *MB*, I, p. 39. [187] See p. 39 above, note 86.

[188] Rigby, 'Urban "Oligarchy"', p. 64; *VCH York*, p. 30; *MB*, II, p. 246; *VCH Hull*, p. 30; Hull RO, BRG I, ff. 12–14; Humberside RO, BC II/3, f. 6v.

keepers also swore not to spare any man unjustly because of friendship or consanguinity.[189] Rulers were expected to rule according to the customs of the town, and this implied that action to curb those who ignored such constraints was justified. Some historians have adduced therefore, that a consensus existed with opposition only emerging when that consensus was violated.[190]

The evidence from York, Beverley and Hull suggests that a consensus model is inadequate. The burgesses were the most likely adherents to an ideology of community, but not inevitably so. Most visibly in York, but also in the other towns, there was repeated pressure from below to ensure a wider circulation of offices, even though most of the changes to election procedures had little impact upon the pool of candidates for the higher offices. The repetition of regulations implies that the effect of regulations was minimal.

The representation of every occupation in the unattractive office of chamberlain in York demonstrated a wider willingness to share administrative responsibility than occupational representation in the higher civic offices might suggest.[191] Access to power was jealously guarded by the elite, whether within the civic or, indeed, the guild hierarchy, and the notion of guilds as embryonic trade unions, defending their members against predatory councillors, has little to recommend it.[192] There is accumulating evidence of the extent to which civic and craft leaders encouraged the occupational labelling and gathering of individuals into guilds to facilitate their regulation. In York the guilds of the bowstringmakers and saucers were probably set up as vehicles for the searchers of those crafts.[193] Councils benefited financially and used guild searchers to supervise manufacturing and employment standards.[194]

---

[189] Humberside RO, BC II/3, ff. 7v., 26. This was impossible to police and rarely traceable in the records. In one example from York, an alderman, John Glasyn, stood as surety for his brother, Thomas, when he was elected sheriff in 1469: *Corpus Christi Guild*, p. 49.

[190] Reynolds, *English Medieval Towns*, pp. 135–6, 171, and 'Medieval Urban History', pp. 14–23; Rosser, *Medieval Westminster*, pp. 247–8.

[191] See Shaw, *Wells*, pp. 158–9, 162–3, for the argument that the acceptance of the corporatist ideology in Wells gave each office-holder, however tightly they were restricted to lowly tasks according to their occupation, a sense of fulfilled participation. He estimates that 25 per cent of all burgesses held some sort of office.

[192] R. H. Britnell, *The Commercialisation of English Society, 1000–1500* (Cambridge, 1993), p. 175.

[193] R. H. Hilton, 'Medieval Market Towns and Simple Commodity Production', *Past & Present*, 109 (1985), pp. 16–17; Swanson, *Medieval Artisans*, pp. 108–20. In contrast see Phythian-Adams, *Desolation of a City*, pp. 106–8.

[194] If the York oligarchs were reluctant to countenance any monopoly but their own, it could only have applied to wholesale trading, and the council acceded to what look like the wishes of individual craft guilds regarding entry requirements, employment practices and so forth: H. Swanson, 'The Illusion of Economic Structure: Craft Guilds in Late Medieval English Towns', *Past & Present*, 121 (1988) p. 47; *MB*, I and II passim.

Guilds were drawn into an auxiliary political role, very much as the subordinate parties. In Beverley by 1465, guild aldermen were members of the rarely summoned council of forty-eight. By 1464 a committee of guild searchers was playing a small role in mayoral elections in York and was being used in 1489 to police the city to encourage a peaceful election. They soon assumed a new role, as representatives of the wider community, presenting bills of complaint in 1505 and 1509. When the new Common Council was created in 1517, guild searchers were rewarded with significant electoral duties.[195] The restructured council effectively ended the wider involvement of the commonalty in civic elections; the 1517 settlement had excluded some key crafts entirely – the tanners and cordwainers – and had consigned the 'wealthy but unacceptable' butchers to a place amongst the minor crafts.[196] The manipulated consensus then, served to bolster guild oligarchy as much as it did civic oligarchy.

Cohesion within the ruling elite was not automatically achieved. Some of the violent outbursts in towns emanated from discontented groups within the merchant class and the wider body of freemen seeking access to power. This was a characteristic of the fourteenth-century conflicts in York which surfaced in 1357, 1364, 1371 and most dramatically in 1379–82.[197] The assault on the mayoralty in York in 1380–2 was one stage in the continuing jostling within the oligarchy and one element in the violent events which rocked the city between November 1380 and November 1382 and involved eight of the city's future MPs.[198] It began with the removal from office of the mayor, John Gisburn, in November 1380. He was an exceedingly wealthy overseas merchant who had served as mayor three times already, defeating John Langton in 1371. Their rivalry went back several years. In 1357 Langton, who was a survivor of the older rentier patriciate, had objected to the nomination of Gisburn as a bailiff, dismissing fourteen of the original nominating panel of twenty-four and appointing another merchant as bailiff instead. Langton failed to secure the mayoralty in 1365, losing to Richard Wateby, one of the dismissed nominating panel, and then to Gisburn six years later. The violence attending the election that year attracted royal attention, and within days of Gisburn taking up office, the council legislated to restrict tenure of the mayoralty to one year, forbidding re-election within eight years.[199]

[195] Kermode, 'Obvious Observations', p. 101; *VCH York*, p. 137; *CPR 1467–77*, pp. 328–9, 416; *YCR*, II, pp. 40, 43; III, pp. 17, 51–9; York RO, House Book XI, ff. 29v., 44v.; Humberside RO, BC II/7/1, f. 191v.   [196] York RO, A/33, 1547 Charter; Palliser, *Tudor York*, pp. 68–9.
[197] York RO, C/Y, f. 313v.; *VCH York*, pp. 80–2; *MB*, I, p. 16; *CPR 1364–7*, p. 208; *CCR 1369–74*, p. 275.   [198] Roskell, *House of Commons*, I, p. 745.
[199] York RO C/Y, f. 313v.; *CCR 1364–7*, p. 208; *CPR 1369–74*, p. 275.

Gisburn's 1380 mayoralty was associated with a number of scandals, including the imprisonment of a prominent citizen, John Savage, and embezzlement by the city's common clerk. His opponents recalled abuses from 1371, accusing him of irregularities at the royal mint and of harbouring criminals. The commonalty put another merchant, Simon de Quixlay, in Gisburn's place, but the respite was short lived as the local struggle became embroiled in the national conflagration when news of events in London reached the city in June 1381. The tangled narrative of gang warfare, attacks on the Dominican Friary and St Leonard's Hospital, crown intervention, claims and counter-claims, has been fully analysed elsewhere.[200] What emerged in those two momentous years was a physically violent hostility towards one man from many sections of society, including fellow aldermen, butchers, websters and other craftsmen. Gisburn did have some prominent supporters, including John Bolton jnr, a fellow overseas merchant of considerable wealth. A major cause of unrest was the commons' outrage at the corrupt conduct of government, which could only be expressed through physical action. As is the nature of violent disorder, other resentments were expressed in the street fighting and general mayhem and in attacks on religious houses in the city.[201] The local solution was to purge the existing system by imposing a truly 'worthy' man as mayor, a man from the same background as the disgraced Gisburn, and to confirm regulations preventing townsfolk seeking justice beyond the reach of the city courts. This was conservative consolidation and not radical reform.

Beverley also witnessed riotous scenes during 1381 when a group of butchers, fullers, tilers, tailors and other lesser craftsmen, possibly supported by Archbishop Neville, seized control of the town and imposed a totally different and new form of government: a triumvirate assisted by twenty-four guardians instead of the twelve keepers.[202] Serious opposition to the keepers had occurred at least once before, when in 1356 the 'good men' of the town claimed that the election had been stopped by the armed insurrection of 500 rioters.[203] Confusion surrounds the dramatic events of the 1380s, but the intention of the rebels was clearly to

---

[200] Dobson, 'The Risings', pp. 112–24, 138–43.

[201] St Leonard's had been a target for antagonism before, arising out of disputed areas of jurisdiction. On different occasions, the mayor and former mayors had been accused of attacking the hospital's privileges and of encouraging riotous behaviour towards the master. See, for example, *CPR 1307–13*, p. 129; *CCR 1374–7*, p. 433. In 1401 the mayor ordered the destruction of hedges and ditches erected by the hospital around common pasture near Heslington: *MB*, I, pp. 179–80. The Dominican precinct was attacked on 17 June and it is likely that the Franciscan Friary and St George's Chapel were attacked on the same day: *MB*, II, pp. 69–70.

[202] *VCH York*, pp. 80–2; Flower, 'The Beverley Town Riots', pp. 80–1; Dobson, 'The Risings', pp. 119–30, 139–42.

[203] *Bev. Town Docs.*, pp. xxv–xxviii; *Beverlac*, pp. 126–8; Dobson, 'The Risings', p. 126.

unseat the local establishment. Trouble was brewing in March 1380 when Robert Tirwhit, one of the long-established local merchant families, complained that his servant had been the victim of corruption amongst the jury hearing his case in the archbishop's local court. Simon Cartwright was one of the jurymen, and in his complaint Tirwhit claimed that Cartwright and others had 'often procured the commonalty of Beverley to . . . come to his house and those of Tirwhit's friends and would have slain him'.[204]

On 25 April, six weeks after the inquiry into Tirwhit's complaint, the Beverley commons refused to elect the usual twelve keepers and chose a triumvirate of their representatives instead: an alderman and two chamberlains. The following year, 1381, a second triumvirate was chosen: Thomas Manby, Simon Cartwright and William Ithun. Fifteen days later a commission of the peace was appointed until the dispute ongoing between the archbishop and the Minster canons was resolved, but the visible dispute was between the ousted establishment and the new men. Several former keepers, Thomas de Beverley, Adam and Stephen Coppendale, William Dudhill, John Gervays and others, were accused of raiding the Guildhall and stealing money and muniments, including the borough seal. News of these events reached Westminster on 25 May but the commonalty were already proceeding against the *probi homines*. John Bygod, commissioner of the peace in Ripon and Beverley, found against the Coppendales and the others, but Bygod's commission had been revoked on 13 April, presumably because he had been superseded by Robert Roos. Richard II repeated the revocation on 25 May, complaining of 'divers unlawful presentments' being made before the justices and ordering them before his court for 'mature deliberation'.

By departing from the strict letter of his commission, Bygod had materially helped the commonalty and he reappeared the following June to stand as mainpernor to four of the rebels.[205] During June 1381, gangs of 400 or more of the commons continued to terrorise the town and extracted bonds from the *probi homines*, conditional upon them accepting the judgement of Archbishop Neville later that summer. Adam Coppendale and others targeted by the commons' threats fled the town and waged a campaign through petitions to the king. One anxiety was that if any bonds were extorted under Statute Merchant, they would be impossible to counter, and on 26 September, the archbishop's bailiff was ordered to prevent further bonds being extorted.[206]

---

[204] *CPR 1377–81*, p. 469.
[205] *Ibid.*, p. 634; *CCR 1377–81*, pp. 511, 523; *1381–5*, p. 64; *Bev. Town Docs.*, pp. xxix–xxx; PRO, SC8/264/13178b; KB27/484 m. 25.
[206] PRO, SC8/266/13260, 13262; *CPR 1381–5*, pp. 66, 81, 87, 113; *CCR 1382–5*, p. 104. The saga

The restoration of order to the town became crucial as personal vendettas and violent assaults continued. As in York, the rebels attacked ecclesiastical lordship: the under-bailiff of the chapter and the steward of all three fees, the chapter, provost and archbishop.[207] Some sixty or so of the commons were said to have pursued the Coppendale group south to London, parading armed through the streets of the capital. Even as late as April 1382, the archbishop's bailiff dared not attempt the arrest of three commons' leaders for fear of his life. Stability was secured finally on 27 June, when the archbishop, his brother John, Lord Neville, the sheriff of Yorkshire and many other Yorkshire knights came to the town to receive the pledges of good behaviour from over 400 townsmen, including *probi homines* alongside *communes*. Royal letters of pardon cost the town 1,000 marks in October 1382, marking the end of serious disorder, although nine of the commons leaders were excluded. Reprisals continued however, certainly into 1385, and given the savagery of some of the incidents recorded, revenge was probably inevitable.[208]

Before government by twelve keepers was restored, as it certainly was by 1391, the establishment had already recovered its dominant position. At least two of the triumvirates of 1385 and 1386 were former keepers, John de Ake and Adam Coppendale, Thomas Gervays and John Tripock, and thereafter access to power was securely controlled by the merchant-dominated oligarchy. If the scale of the rebellion and the complaints against the keepers are to be believed, Beverley's government had been autocratic and corrupt for some considerable time. The 'many insolences, evils and dangers committed [had] more than usually happened in Beverley chiefly by default of good government', according to the king.[209] What gives these momentous events significance is the imposition of a different form of government and the entanglement with regional political cross-currents involving the archbishop and John Bygod. Their apparent support of the rebels is impossible to explain in terms other than self-interest.

Unfortunately the records are sparse for events in Hull during 1381 and few conclusions can be drawn about the impact of nearby revolt. Perhaps the introduction of a council in 1379 had helped to dilute tension. Several prominent merchants had to answer for various trespasses in late 1382,

---

of the writs was finally concluded when they were cancelled in April 1382, following the failure of Thomas Manby or Richard Middleton to present either themselves, the key to the chest where the bonds were secured or the bonds themselves to Chancery as ordered: *CCR 1381–5*, pp. 38, 43, 45–6, 52; *CPR 1381–5*, p. 493; PRO, SC8/225/11098.

[207] BL Add. MS 40008, f. 348; *VCH Beverley*, p. 23.

[208] *CPR 1381–5*, pp. 146, 210, 213, 493; *CCR 1381–5*, p. 53; *Rot. Parl.*, III, pp. 133, 397; PRO, SC8/225/11203; *VCH Beverley*, p. 23.

[209] Humberside RO, BC II/6/3; II/2, f. 18; *CCR 1381–5*, pp. 45–6.

including Walter Frost and Robert de Selby, but the record does not suggest any link with the wider revolt.[210]

Superficially, unity prevailed within the oligarchy of each town, since all decisions were made by 'all the keepers' or 'the mayor and his brethren', but it was fragile and disputes inevitably broke out. In Hull, the serjeants of the mayor and of the sheriff argued over their respective areas of jurisdiction mid-century,[211] and in 1467, the recorder and aldermen had to arbitrate in a dispute between the sheriff and the mayor.[212] Late-fifteenth-century York was in a constant state of unease. In the context of economic recession and with hostility towards the city rulers, nurtured by assumptions of their corrupt conduct, divisions within the oligarchy became the occasion for wider disorder. In 1471,[213] 1476,[214] 1482[215] and 1516/17[216] it was the personal rivalry of individuals which undermined the council's control. At other times, animosities festered but were contained by council action. Sometimes councillors barely concealed their dislike of each other, called each other names, and squabbled over precedence in processions. For instance, in 1483, the recorder Miles Metcalfe called the mayor John Newton 'a false harlot' and in 1486, John Harper and William Todd, two aldermen bickering over precedence, resorted to defamation and fighting.[217] The private and public were not separate domains and the overlap became clearly visible on one occasion in 1503 when the council tried to build on land which alderman William Neleson claimed to be his. Neleson responded by reminding the current mayor that he would get his own back if elected mayor himself the following year![218]

Local government was becoming more complex in many late-medieval towns and the responsibilities of their ruling oligarchies increased. Their perceptions of their duty widened from the maintenance of customs and defence of civic liberties to encompass a whole range of employment and commercial supervision as well as the regulation of public amenities. Popular expectations also changed and it is clear from the occasions of popular rebellion that councillors did not always match up to those expectations. The objections of the York commons can be deduced from petitions they presented to the mayor and council in 1475,[219] 1484[220] and 1490.[221] Their accusations were of venality, financial

---

[210] PRO, KB9/1069, m. 24; Dobson, 'The Risings', p. 117; E. Gillett and K. A. MacMahon, *A History of Hull* (Oxford, 1980), pp. 35, 47, 63.

[211] *VCH Hull*, pp. 32–3; Hull RO, BRB 1, ff. 13, 38(2)v., 83–v., 97; BRE 2, f. 95.

[212] Hull RO, BRB 1, ff. 109v.–10. [213] *VCH York*, p. 82; *CPR 1467–77*, p. 239.

[214] *VCH York*, p. 61; YCR, I, pp. 2–3, 11. [215] *VCH York*, p. 82; YCR, I, pp. 48–52, 69.

[216] *VCH York*, p. 137; YCR, III, pp. 51–9.

[217] *VCH York*, p. 90; YCR, I, pp. 153, 155, 170; *Test. Ebor.* IV, p. 212n.

[218] *VCH York*, p. 77; *MB*, II, p. 256; York RO, House Book IX, f. 12v.

[219] *MB*, II, pp. 245–7. [220] YCR, I, pp. 89, 104–5. [221] *Ibid.*, II, pp. 54–5.

mismanagement, lax regulation of the markets and inadequate street cleaning. Incompetence and corruption were implicitly acknowledged by the York council when it agreed in 1485 to a retrospective auditing of the accounts and to ensure better qualified men were elected chamberlains.[222]

Accusations of embezzlement surfaced periodically to tarnish claims of 'good government'. This was always an easy allegation to make since the duties of civic officers allowed considerable leeway, but when fiscal manipulation was added, the allegation became a powerful stimulant to action. As early as 1301, the York commons were complaining that they did not know how city taxes had been spent, and in 1311 and 1316, the tax collectors were accused of fraud.[223] In 1306, there was a complaint brought against a guild of 'wealthy burgesses' (which included several civic office-holders), led by Andrew de Bolingbroke. During his two mayoralites in 1305 and 1309 he was the victim of violent assaults. It was alleged that the guild was conspiring to avoid taxation by shifting the burden onto others, settling disputes outside the city courts, thereby undermining council authority and depriving it of judicial profits.[224] In 1476, the York common clerk was dismissed for dishonesty[225] and suspicions concerning the unfair skewing of taxation assessments persisted. In 1504, a merchant, Roger Whetely, prominent in the riot of that year, accosted the mayor, wanting to know 'how individuals in the city had been assessed for the levy'.[226]

York council's difficulties in balancing the city accounts in the fifteenth century are well known.[227] That failure and repeated pleas of poverty undoubtedly encouraged a pessimistic view of the city's plight which back-fired. Anxiety over financial excess and incompetence spurred the commonalty to rebellion and sometimes to propose constructive remedies. In 1475, reminding the council that 'for alsmuch we ben all one bodye corporate', they demanded that no-one be elected chamberlain unless they had previously served as a bridgemaster. In 1485 their petition was against the sale of offices[228] and in 1487 they wanted a committee to view the accounts from the previous fifteen years.[229] Two years later, they wanted the retrospective audit to extend to 1469, all legal counsel to be discharged, the mayor's fee

---

[222] *MB*, II, p. 246. [223] *CPR 1292–1301*, p. 624; *1307–13*, p. 418; *CFR 1307–19*, p. 300.

[224] G. Sayles, 'The Dissolution of a Guild at York in 1306', *EHR*, 55 (1940), pp. 85–6, 88, 92.

[225] *VCH York*, p. 75; *YCR*, I, pp. 8–11. [226] *YCR*, III, pp. 8–9.

[227] Dobson, *York City Chamberlains' Account Rolls*, pp. xxvi–xxvii; *VCH York*, pp. 65–6, 72–5.

[228] *MB*, II, p. 246; *YCR*, I, p. 113.

[229] The committee was to comprise two aldermen, two from the twenty-four, two auditors and four honest commoners: Attreed, *York House Books*, II, p. 563; York RO, House Book VI, f. 92.

to be reduced to £20, the recorder's to 20d.[230] Their demands were ignored.[231]

Complaints of financial corruption and incompetence also surfaced in Beverley. Accusations of extortion and the embezzling of borough income were thrown at individual keepers during 1381, and complaints made against local business taxes, *bustsilver* and *pundale*.[232] Another direct tax, collected in boxes,[233] aroused suspicion, and during election disturbances in 1457, the commonalty demanded that the annual contributions to the common box were to be accounted in the presence of the alderman and stewards of each craft, not later than two weeks after 24 June, under pain of a £10 fine. The ordinance was reiterated in 1460 and suggests that the keepers were often in arrears with their accounting. The incoming keepers had to accept the accounts of expenses given on oath by the retiring keepers without question, and as no one keeper was officially delegated to be responsible for the accounts, all twelve were equally responsible.[234]

By comparison, the Hull council was a model of probity. Its accounts had been subject to an annual audit since 1356, conducted by four auditors from at least 1452. Even though the accounts were regularly in deficit from 1442,[235] there were no specific complaints of mismanagement.

Common grazing was another sensitive issue in medieval towns.[236] The York council was caught between the crossfire of landowners competing with the citizens over common rights and the citizens' insistence that these be protected. Fuel was added to the conflict when the council, apparently favouring Richard III's clients, relinquished rights of common to Lord Lovel in 1483 and St Mary's Abbey in 1484. The latter concession provoked fierce riots.[237] Later incidents suggest, however, that in less

---

[230] *YCR*, II, pp. 54–5. The mayor's fee had been £20 in the fourteenth century, and he had received additional payments. The £20 fee was insisted upon in 1372, but had to be raised to £40 in 1385 and to £50 in 1388: *VCH York*, pp. 70–1. The recorder had been receiving £1 6s 8d plus extra expenses in the mid-fifteenth century: Dobson, *York City Chamberlains' Account Rolls*, pp. 31, 62, 73, 92, 108, 125, 151, 168, 184, 206.

[231] In 1499 the mayor received £50, the recorder £1 6s 8d in addition to a payment of £12 he received from the sheriffs. The first record we have of this extra £12 is to Miles Metcalfe, Richard of Gloucester's man, in 1478–9: Dobson, *York City Chamberlains' Account Rolls*, pp. 168, 184, 204, 206.

[232] Humberside RO, BC II/2, f. 19v.; *Bev. Town Docs.*, pp. xxix, xxxi–xxxii; *CPR 1381–5*, p. 213. *Bustsilver* was a charge of ½d on each victualler's shop, *pundale* a charge of ½d for every pound's worth of goods sold in the market. For a full description see *VCH Beverley*, pp. 30–1.

[233] The boxes (*pixedes*) were collected initially on a street by street basis, and on a craft basis by 1366–7.   [234] Humberside RO, BC II/2, f. 16; II/3, ff. 21–v.

[235] Kermode, 'Merchants of York, Beverley and Hull', appendix 2; Hull RO, BRE I, p. 173; BRB I, f. 23; BRG I, f. 14; M479; *VCH Hull*, p. 42.

[236] Reynolds, *English Medieval Towns*, pp. 176, 178. Riots over common lands occurred in Coventry at least five times in the fifteenth century: Phythian-Adams, *Desolation of a City*, p. 183.

[237] *YCR*, I, pp. viii, 30, 32–3; 81, 89, 100, 104–5.

partisan times the council did work to defend the city's grazing. Disputes arose with Sir James Danby, the Vicars' Choral, the prebendary of Fridaythorpe and others. Riots over the grazing issue flared again in 1492 and 1494, and on the latter occasion the council was warned by Henry VII·that he would put other rulers in their place if they could not uphold law and order.[238] A grazing dispute with the Vicars' Choral incurred legal costs which were passed on to the community. Four citizens were appointed in each parish to assess their fellows for a levy, on pain of forfeiting their freedom: an indication of their reluctance to carry out the duty in the teeth of intense animosity.[239]

There is evidence to suggest that resentment and distrust of rulers was prevalent and could be fanned into open resistance when an incident exacerbated tensions. Key officials such as the mayor and sheriffs of York and Hull were protected by at least one serjeant,[240] but hostility was never far below the surface and easily flared into verbal abuse and occasionally physical assaults.[241] Such behaviour was punishable by fine or imprisonment, and abuse hurled at the mayors of York[242] and Hull,[243] and the Beverley keepers, common clerk and common serjeant, were most severely dealt with.[244] Again the evidence for York is more abundant. The unpopular Andrew de Bolingbroke, mayor in 1305, was attacked by a man with a knife, and his second mayoralty in 1309 generated further incidents.[245] Roger de Selby was nearly killed performing his mayoral duty in 1369, and an ex-mayor, William Wells, was killed during the troubles of 1487, perhaps for being identified with a particular faction.[246] For all their claims to wisdom, gravity and discretion, the difference between the governing elite and those who assaulted them was not very great. Oligarchs also took the law into their own hands, physically assaulting persons and property to redress a grievance.[247]

Resentment against wealthy oligarchs was unambiguously explicit in several fifteenth-century incidents. Richard Wayte, a York vintner, complained in Chancery that he was unlikely to have a fair hearing in York, in a case of recovery of debt, because the other party, Thomas Neleson, was rich and 'of standing in the city'. A similar resentment was expressed

[238] *Ibid.*, I, p. 177; II, pp. 37–8, 50–1, 53, 61–2, 65, 83, 94, 105–7, 109–12.
[239] *Ibid.*, II, p. 118.   [240] *VCH York*, pp. 70, 72; *VCH Hull*, pp. 30, 32.
[241] E.g. *YCR*, II, p. 127; III, p. 38; *MB*, II, p. 289.
[242] *VCH York*, p. 70; *YCR*, I, p. 31; II, p. 148; III, pp. 14, 36.
[243] *VCH Hull*, p. 30; Hull RO, BRB 1, ff. 105–6.
[244] Humberside RO, BC II/2, ff. 7–v.; *VCH Beverley*, p. 22.
[245] *CPR 1301–7*, p. 541; *1307–13*, p. 39.   [246] *CCR 1369–74*, p. 59; *YCR*, II, p. 14.
[247] For example, three York office-holders, John and William de Acastre and John de Beverley, attacked and imprisoned a fourth, William Aton. A Beverley keeper, Thomas Coppendale, tried to murder fellow keeper Thomas Mayne: PRO, C1/6/216; *CPR 1343–5*, p. 589; *1345–8*, p. 80. See also *CPR 1317–21*, p. 375; *1338–40*, p. 780; *1350–4*, p. 79; *1364–7*, p. 146.

by a former chamberlain, William Scauceby, who also took a debt case to Chancery, because he claimed the other party, William Wells, would be believed in York 'because he was an alderman'.[248]

If the commons had political goals independent of merchant leaders, what were they? Craft guild regulations provide no clues since these were the product of guild oligarchs, themselves openly allied to the interests of civic governors,[249] and filling a similarly elitist role. For instance, in *c*. 1420–30, the master cordwainers had to act against irregular and seditious activities amongst their journeymen and apprentices. The latter were forbidden to make federations between themselves; to usurp the authority of the guild by making their own ordinances; or to form conventicles, insurrections, or popular movements against the king's peace in the city.[250] The tailors' servants also tried to form their own fraternity, but in vain.[251]

Discontent was most visible at election times since those were the occasions when the commonalty's limited constitutional role gave it potential leverage.[252] However, it is difficult to argue that the commons of all three towns consistently sought a more democratic system of government. In Beverley in 1457, the commons asked that elections be conducted according to the 'customs of the town',[253] an appeal to a principle which accepted their right to complain in such circumstances. Their demands were accepted but discontent persisted and in 1461 the keepers issued several law and order regulations prohibiting unauthorised meetings in the Guildhall or the friaries.[254] In the same year, the keepers decided to be called 'aldermen' or 'governors'. Rioting erupted during the 1465 election, but no reforms were introduced. Moves in York, Beverley and Hull to broaden electoral representation were probably done in response to commons' pressure, but only the York commons persistently agitated. Even so, it was not until 1504 that the records reveal an explicit demand for the York commons to be involved in the election to the key office of sheriff.[255]

Few instances of riots were recorded in Hull. A gang of shipmen went on a rampage to release some of their fellows from the gaol, shouting 'doune with the maire doune with hum'.[256] In 1442 the council declared that the sheriff's attendants were to carry weapons only when there were riots or disorder, and the following year the election procedure was reformed for 'the quietness of the town'.[257] In general, the Hull rulers

---

[248] PRO, C1/64/485; 67/53.

[249] Assisting in elections, for instance. See Kermode, 'Obvious Observations', p. 89, and York RO, House Book VII, f. 22v.; Swanson, *Medieval Artisans*, pp. 110–12.

[250] *MB*, I, p. 193.   [251] *Ibid.*, p. 191.   [252] Rigby, 'Power and Authority', pp. 29–30.

[253] Humberside RO, BC II/3, f. 7v   [254] Humberside RO, BC II/3, ff. 7v., 21.

[255] Kermode, 'Obvious Observations', pp. 89–93.   [256] *VCH Hull*, p. 30.

[257] *Ibid.*; *CPR 1441–6*, pp. 180–1.

attracted less hostility, maybe because their system of government appeared to be more efficient and transparent, maybe because there were no long-established guilds of specialist craftsmen with their own organisational and political experience.[258]

Law and order in medieval English towns was maintained by the perpetuation of the belief in the legitimacy of those ruling. It was for this reason that so much emphasis was placed upon the worthiness of prospective officials, upon the respect due to individual civic officials and to their collective superiority in civic processions and ceremonials.[259] In York at least, the council and officials paraded whenever possible. They were expected to proceed to service in the Minster on Sundays when summoned; officials were to conduct themselves in the proper manner especially with regard to dress and attendants; aldermen were to be attended by a servant bearing a torch at the Corpus Christi parade.[260] Such propagandist displays must be treated critically. They dramatically expressed a cohesive ideology,[261] but to see them as accurate reflections of reality is misleading.[262] Locating the plays, and the processions from which they became separated, within the evidence of resistance and conflict surrounding them, makes it difficult to see them as anything other than politicised rituals reflecting the interests of the ruling groups of both city government and craft guilds.

The use of religion to express a political aspiration did not always work and how deep acceptance went is a matter for conjecture. The play cycles and processions generated squabbles between guilds[263] and were occasions for fights and for making money.[264] Craftsmen in York and

---

[258] Kermode, 'Obvious Observations', pp. 93, 102.

[259] The council took care to decide exactly what colours citizens should wear to greet respected visitors. See, for example, *YCR*, I, pp. 52, 56 (aldermen in scarlet, the twenty-four in murray or crimson); p. 70 (aldermen in violet, twenty-four in blue); p. 120 (grey); p. 146 (aldermen in violet); pp. 152, 155–9 (for Henry VII's first visit: aldermen in scarlet, twenty-four in murray, Common Council in violet, commonalty in red).

[260] *VCH York*, p. 70; *MB*, II, pp. 86–7; *YCR*, I, pp. 2, 5–6; II, pp. 55, 59, 89, 145–6. For Hull see *VCH Hull*, pp. 30–2.

[261] Reynolds, *English Medieval Towns*, p. 180 argues that such pageantry engendered unity. See also Phythian-Adams, 'Ceremony and the Citizen', pp. 57–85; Palliser, 'Urban Society', pp. 147–8.

[262] The Corpus Christi pageants may indeed have provided 'a display of wholeness versus social differentiation', or even 'an opportunity to confront tension', but this is an optimistic reading of the events: James, 'Ritual, Drama and Social Body', pp. 9, 15.

[263] *MB*, II, pp. 79, 156–8. For regulation in response to disruption elsewhere, see W. H. Hudson and J. C. Tingay, eds., *The Records of the City of Norwich* (Norwich, 1910), II, p. 230; McRee, 'Unity or Division?', p. 189, note 3; M. Rubin, *Corpus Christi: The Eucharist in Late Medieval Culture* (Cambridge, 1991), pp. 261–3.

[264] *VCH York*, p. 96. There were complaints at a public meeting in 1416 that certain individuals were profiteering from the seat-charges paid at the pageant stations: *MB*, II, p. 64. Thereafter the council was to receive one third of the receipts. On a later occasion, in 1432, there were complaints that the crafts were using the plays as a means to advertise: *ibid.*, pp. 156–8, 172.

Beverley were compelled to support their pageants, sometimes to their financial detriment.[265] In Beverley the lesser crafts persistently rejected these demands from the late fourteenth century and the performance was only kept going through the efforts of the keepers. In 1411, they resorted to arranging a contribution from the 'worthier sort' to the 'lesser sort' to subsidise their pageants,[266] and by 1520 all support had disappeared.[267]

Temporal pageantry was another useful medium for political propaganda.[268] By the late fifteenth century at least, the York councillors made efforts to construct and convey a complex image of an ancient, learned city.[269] When it entertained the Papal Legate in 1486, the council greeted him 'with good wordes in Latyn' and a selection of wines. A similar combination of erudition and display was evident in the series of flamboyant events planned to greet Henry VII on his first visit to the city the same year. As ever, the occasion served several purposes. The evocation of the antiquity of the city's independent and proud spirit through the image of Ebrauk, was directed at the king, reinforcing the oligarchy's claim to govern. The 'spontaneous' acclamation from the populace was to confirm the image presented of the city united in its joyous loyalty. Aldermen and councillors from the twenty-four wore different coloured gowns appropriate to their different ranks, so the whole spectacle reinforced the dominance of the merchant oligarchy, benignly presiding over a harmonious community.[270] The most cursory glance through the city records reveals the fantasy behind this optimistic spectacle.

CONCLUSION

The three towns each offer very different experiences of government. These depended partly on their strategic importance and the extent to which they were caught up in regional and national politics. Towns of

[265] Swanson, 'Illusion of Economic Structure', p. 44, and *Medieval Artisans*, pp. 119–20.

[266] *Bev. Town Docs.*, pp. 33–6; James, 'Ritual, Drama and Social Body', pp. 13–14.

[267] James, 'Ritual, Drama and Social Body', p. 14; A. H. Nelson, *The Medieval English Stage: Corpus Christi Pageants and Plays* (Chicago, 1974), pp. 92, 94, 99; *RCHMSS Beverley*, pp. 171–2.

[268] See Nelson, *Medieval English Stage, passim*; M. Dorrell, 'The Mayor of York and the Coronation Pageant', *Leeds Studies in English*, NS, 5 (1971), pp. 34–45; M. Dorrell and F. Johnston, 'The Domesday Pageant of the York Mercers', *ibid.*, pp. 29–34; J. I. Kermode, 'The Merchants of Three Northern English Towns', in C. H. Clough, ed., *Profession, Vocation and Culture in Later Medieval England* (Liverpool, 1982), pp. 35–6.

[269] See Attreed, 'Politics of Welcome', pp. 216–18, 220–3 for full descriptions of the visits of Richard III and Henry VII to York.

[270] *YCR*, I, pp. 155–9; Attreed, *York House Books*, II, p. 470; Kermode, 'Merchants of Three Northern Towns', p. 36; A. H. Smith, 'A York Pageant, 1486', *London Medieval Studies*, I (1939), pp. 382–98. See also Palliser, 'Urban Society', p. 147 for other mythical evocations of urban identity.

self-conscious antiquity like York and Beverley had already developed
more complex administrative and political systems by 1300 than Hull had
a hundred years later. York and Beverley had both accommodated the rise
and fall of different social and occupational groups, whereas Hull was
experiencing the formation of a ruling class during the period under
consideration. The ruling class in most medieval English towns was composed of several groups: ambitious immigrants, younger sons of the
gentry, minor royal officials, established merchants and successful trades
and craftsmen. The political prospects of each group differed, but in
York, Beverley and Hull, as in other towns, merchants were dominant in
that even the most successful craftsman was less likely to become mayor
than was a merchant. Political success defined the merchant class to such
a degree that, it could be argued, merchants became synonymous with
urban privilege.[271]

There were noticeable differences between the three towns. Beverley's
governing elite included more gentlemen and successive members of
minor local 'dynasties'. In York and Hull the *cursus honorum* became more
tightly defined, and in fifteenth-century York, offices circulated more
widely through a larger group than had been so before the 1370s. Hull,
by contrast, accepted a higher degree of repeated office-holding and a
smaller oligarchy than either of the other two towns, perhaps because its
smaller population imposed unavoidable limits on the pool of candidates
for office.[272] Power remained with an inner core in all three towns,
although controlling merchant bias over the election process was most
visible in York.

York's oligarchy deployed more self-conscious rhetoric, perhaps
because the council came under such severe pressure from aspiring
newcomers, discontented craftsmen, secular and ecclesiastical magnates,
and indeed, successive kings. During the last quarter of the fifteenth
century, the council struggled to keep control as the dynastic struggles of
the Wars of the Roses threatened its autonomy and rebellious townsfolk
challenged its authority.

The violent disorder of York and Beverley contrasts sharply with the
relatively peaceful experience of Hull. One explanation might come
from the differences in government. Hull's was apparently more transparent: its elections more open and its financial administration more
accountable. Another might be the smallness of its population which pos-

---

[271] Cf. late medieval London where it has been claimed that the merchants drew apart as a superior
social class: Thrupp, *London Merchant Class*, p. 29.
[272] Kermode, 'Obvious Observations', pp. 88–106. In fourteenth-century Exeter the 'oligarchic
pool remained small but not stagnant': Kowaleski, 'A Medieval Provincial Oligarchy', pp. 379–80,
and for fourteenth-century Wells, see Shaw, *Wells*, p. 172.

sibly obscured differences in wealth and life-style,[273] and encouraged a tolerance of narrowly circulating offices. However, it is more likely that it was the youth of the town and the nature of Hull's economy which kept it free of major disturbances. Unlike York and Beverley, Hull had no tradition either of manufacturing or of a landed patriciate and therefore no strongly entrenched interests dictated the political scene. As a port, Hull weathered the economic recession better than either York or Beverley, and seemed not to perceive such a sharp contrast with earlier prosperity.

As to why men sought public office, one can only conclude it was a desire to be at the centre of things and to savour the consequent respect and status.[274] Hierarchic systems of government create oligarchy and stimulate ambition, particularly in fluid times. Urban government differed from its national equivalent in that the highest levels were accessible to all those burgesses who achieved the appropriate wealth and status, though not all sought public power. There is little direct evidence of personal self-interest, of individuals embezzling civic funds or abusing their responsibilities, although there are strong suggestions that people believed it was so.[275] It was, of course, very much in the interest of merchants to concern themselves with civic affairs. As individual members of an expanding commercial community they also prospered. Service in local government could and did bring a man respect and status. In appointing merchants to local commissions, the Crown accorded them respect as it did the local gentry, and was equally dependent upon both for the maintenance of law and order. Although most merchants had to be content with prominence in urban affairs, others could establish close links with the gentry through a common interest in local affairs as well as through business and marriage.

The government of medieval towns was increasingly complex, assuming responsibilities for many aspects of urban life, and there can be no doubt that the Crown depended upon the merchant groups in the three towns to fulfil a variety of local government duties. The two main responsibilities of medieval town councils, the privileges of their own burgesses and the keeping of the King's Peace, contributed to the quality of urban life. Although on occasions the councils of each of the three

---

[273] Reynolds, *English Medieval Towns*, p. 163.

[274] Freeman Foster concluded that in Elizabethan London, greed and gain were not the motivation. F. F. Foster, *The Politics of Stability: A Portrait of Rulers in Elizabethan London* (London, 1977), p. 6.

[275] In London, three aldermen were accused of exploitation in the Good Parliament: London Guildhall RO, Letter Book H, p. 11, cited in *MB*, I, p. xv.

towns were inept in their handling of financial affairs, or in their response to national crises, and although they were unresponsive to pressures for more accountable and competent government, they did maintain a surprising degree of stability and efficiency.

3

MERCHANT SOCIETY: FAMILIES, DEPENDANTS AND FRIENDS, THE EVIDENCE OF WILLS

Within the hurly-burly of the urban experience, individual merchants established many kinds of personal relationships, some to augment their political connections and others to retain accumulated profits within the merchant class. Travel and personal negotiations were integral to an entrepreneur's life in the immediate confines of his own town and region and often further afield. Business associations and partnerships often melded into friendships and in some instances led to the closer ties of marriage. A merchant's family and household thus became an integral part of his commercial and political world, making social networks an important element in the genesis of a powerful urban class.

The reconstruction of medieval English urban society is a particular challenge for historians.[1] We do not have the wealth of evidence created by Ghent's tightly regulated society, Florentine fiscal records or even the Bristol and London courts of orphans.[2] The evidence for York, Beverley and Hull has been sifted out of the probate records for some 650 testators: merchants and their stem family members.[3] The distribution of surviving wills is heavily biased towards the wealthier in an already socially select minority. Historical evidence has to be teased out of a document created for many purposes. For some scholars a 'will was, in principle, a religious document'.[4] This was certainly what lay behind the develop-

---

[1] M. Kowaleski, 'The History of Urban Families in Medieval England', *Jnl Med. Hist.*, 14 (1988), pp. 47–63. For an excellent sixteenth-century study, see Rappaport, *Worlds within Worlds*. Rural families have been reconstructed from the evidence of court rolls in J. M. Bennett, 'Spouses, Siblings and Surnames: Reconstructing Families from Medieval Village Court Rolls', *Jnl Brit. Stud.*, 23 (1983), pp. 26–46.

[2] C. Carlton, *The Court of Orphans* (Leicester, 1974); E. Clarke, 'City Orphans and Custody Law in Medieval England', *Am. Jnl. Legal Hist.*, 34 (1990), pp. 168–87; D. Herlihy and C. Klapisch-Zuber, *Tuscans and Their Families: A Study of the Florentine Catasto of 1427* (New Haven, 1985); D. Nicholas, *The Domestic Life of a Medieval City. Women, Children, and the Family in Fourteenth-Century Ghent* (Lincoln NE, 1985).

[3] See below, chapter 4, for a fuller discussion of the shortcomings of testamentary records in relation to religious observance.   [4] Duffy, *The Stripping of the Altars*, p. 355.

ment of the *ultima voluntas* and testament but, although religious provision remained the prime consideration for some testators, it was not always so for the majority by the early fifteenth century. Thomas Gra's use of the language of business to describe the chantry for his relatives, 'the souls for which I am bound or am debtor', demonstrates very neatly the multiple uses of a religious form.[5] We will never know how far a testator was trying to construct an image to redress the balance of his lifetime actions. The last will and testament presented a unique opportunity for individuals to settle a number of personal matters within a formal and legally enforceable document, however minimal its provisions.[6] Clearly the impulse to draw up a will was generated by several motives: the need to take stock, to identify executors, to provide for family and dependants, to settle unfinished personal and business matters, to make a social statement, to arrange the secular and spiritual future, and to organise the final rites attendant upon death. Whatever else they intended, the major consideration of the testators reviewed here, whose wills were made between 1380 and 1500, was to ensure their testacy and to confirm the identity of heirs and executors.

The context in which each will was written could be dramatically different from that of another. Where one man negotiated between his past and future on a sickbed, at home or abroad, flustered by anxious creditors and relations, another could review his own circumstances calmly, deliberating over the extent of his responsibilities, his resources and the optimum allocations to meet all his family, spiritual and business needs. We are observing a single statement, constructed at a particular time in a man's life when he was predisposed to turn his attention from the public arena to the personal. The testator was simultaneously defining his identity and reflecting his personality. We know little of his lifetime concerns, and even at the critical juncture of preparing *post mortem* provision, we often do not know his age or that of his dependants. Nor do we know who may have influenced the testator. Given that most wives were named as executors and widows were expected to supervise apprentices and a continuing business, it seems likely that they were consulted.

Ambiguities and omissions notwithstanding, wills remain the most numerous of extant personal medieval records. Careful analysis can elucidate attitudes towards religion and urban society, and can open up the personal, business and familial networks developed by merchants to strengthen their commercial activities. Using mainly the evidence of

---

[5] Prob. Reg. III, f. 235.

[6] Cf. P. Cullum and P. J. P. Goldberg, who regard such wills solely as expressions of faith: 'Charitable Provision in Late Medieval York: "To the Praise of God and the Use of the Poor"', *Northern History*, 29 (1993), pp. 24–39 at p. 25.

wills, we can suggest some of the networks of responsibility and of friendship that augmented and sometimes replaced families, and which together extended the influence of merchants throughout urban society.

The family was the pivotal unit in Western European society.[7] Evidence for Yorkshire suggests bilateral kinship based on strong nuclear families and indicates a relatively late age at marriage for both sexes after the Black Death, particularly in towns. Remarriage by both sexes was common, generally determined by employment opportunities and the economic status of the parties.[8] There were complicated family patterns as a consequence of remarriage, but the family remained important. It provided nurturing and training for children, reinforced public association, was a means of accumulating and transmitting wealth, and was an agency for social advancement.[9]

It is difficult to draw any precise conclusions as to the size of mercantile families. Testamentary evidence suggests an average family size of three or four children, but these cannot be regarded as complete families. Some children, older sons in particular, may already have been provided for and ignored in wills. Recorded urban families of six or more were not uncommon,[10] but we have no way of knowing how long children remained in the parental home either as unpaid domestics or as junior partners. In the buoyant labour market of the late fourteenth century, an exceptional time perhaps, very few tax-paying daughters were recorded although sons occasionally were.[11]

Households were as important as families as units of social organisation, certainly in terms of their immediate presence in a neighbourhood, but it is difficult to estimate their size. Stepchildren and other relations were beneficiaries in merchant wills, but no indication was given as to their place of abode. Many merchant households employed domestic ser-

---

[7] In most respects, the merchant families of the three towns were similar to those of fourteenth-century Ghent: Nicholas, *The Domestic Life of a Medieval City*, p. 8. See also Phythian-Adams, *Desolation of a City*, pp. 84, 95; Thrupp, *London Merchant Class*, pp. 28–9, 192–3, 196 n. 10.

[8] Goldberg, *Women, Work, and Life Cycle*, pp. 7–15, 204–17, 264–5, 272–9.

[9] These were some of the roles in Coventry: Phythian-Adams, *Desolation of a City*, pp. 150–2.

[10] In fifteenth-century Norwich, the average size of families was 2.24 children: N. Tanner, 'Popular Religion in Norwich with Special Reference to the Evidence of Wills, 1370–1552' (Univ. of Oxford DPhil thesis, 1973), p. 58. Thrupp found families which ranged from nineteen children down to one or two: *London Merchant Class*, pp. 198–9. In fourteenth-century Bishop's Lynn, the estimated average was 2.41: J. Beauroy, 'Family Patterns and Relations of Bishop's Lynn Will-makers in the Fourteenth Century', in L. Bonfield *et al.*, eds., *The World We Have Gained. Histories of Population and Social Structure* (London, 1986), pp. 23–42 at p. 27. For the wider discussion of urban household size see also S. L. Thrupp, 'The Problem of Replacement Rates in the Late Medieval English Population', *EcHR*, 2nd ser., 18 (1965); J. T. Krause, 'The Medieval Household – Large or Small?', *ibid.*, 9 (1956–7); P. Laslett and R. Wall, eds., *Household and Family in Past Time* (Cambridge, 1972), p. 197; Phythian-Adams, *Desolation of a City*, p. 246.

[11] For example, the sons of William Bate and Robert de Holme were both living in Hull with their parents in 1377: PRO, E179/206/45 m. 1. See below, p. 98.

vants as well as apprentices and some may have lived with their masters. Such estimates as we have suggest that the the average household in late-fourteenth-century York was probably between 3.91 and 4.58, those of poorer artisans being smaller.[12]

Migrants entered urban society at all levels and many preserved important links with the local region by maintaining connections with their rural birthplaces.[13] Following a well-established pattern of migration into the three towns, predominantly from the Vale of York and the East Riding,[14] the majority of merchants whose external origin can be traced came from villages in the three Ridings and north Lincolnshire. Nicholas Blackburn snr of York was exceptional in migrating as an established merchant from another town, Richmond (N.R.). Thomas Glasyn, although not definitely an established merchant, migrated from Ripon to York.[15]

Migrants did however come from further afield: Northumberland, Durham and, possibly, Cumberland.[16] Although increasingly trading in Yorkshire, few southerners seem to have settled there. John Thompson of Beverley may have originally come from Dunstable, Thomas Wood of Hull from Cambridgeshire, and John Bosewell and Henry Tutbak of York from Ipswich and Great Yarmouth, but if they did so they were rarities.[17] Some Yorkshire merchants moved south, notably to London. Examples are the sons of Thomas Bracebridge, and John Fisshwyke and Walter Pund's nephew.[18] Business contacts with southerners could also lead to marriage, and the departure of daughters.[19] Exceptionally an alien

---

[12] P. J. P. Goldberg, 'Female Labour, Service, and Marriage in Northern Towns during the Later Middle Ages,' *Northern History*, 22 (1986), pp. 18–38.

[13] Cf. A. F. Butcher, 'The Origins of Romney Freemen, 1433–1523', *EcHR*, 2nd ser., 27 (1974), pp. 25–6; Platt, *English Medieval Town*, pp. 96–8.

[14] *VCH Beverley*, p. 57; *VCH Hull*, p. 80; *VCH York*, pp. 40, 108–9; Palliser, 'A Regional Capital as Magnet', pp. 111–23. Similar patterns of local migration are found in other towns. See, for example, M. Bonney, *Lordship and the Urban Community. Durham and its Overlords, 1250–1540* (Cambridge, 1990), p. 179; McLure, 'Patterns of Migration', p. 177.

[15] *York Freemen*, p. 98; Prob. Reg. v, f. 139 (Glasyn).

[16] E.g. Robert Savage and Bertram Dawson to York from Northumberland, Patrick Lawe of York, Ralph Langton and John Swan of Hull from Durham/Northumberland, Richard Bagot from Teesside to York, Robert Collinson possibly from Cumberland to York. Prob. Reg. II, ff. 76 (Lawe), 378–80 (Collinson); III, f. 18 (Savage); v, f. 7 (Swan); VI, f. 22v. (Langton); IX, f. 96 (Dawson); Dec. & Cap. I, f. 332 (Bagot).

[17] Prob. Reg. III, f. 4 (Tutbak), f. 223 (Bosewell); v, f. 402v. (Wood); VI, f. 146 (Thompson).

[18] Bracebridge, *Yorks Deeds*, IV, p. 161; Pund, Hull RO, D427, 457; Fisshwyke, *Cal. Plea & Mem. Rolls City of London, 1413–37*, p. 148.

[19] E.g. Lawrence Swattock's daughter Agnes married and moved to London: Prob. Reg. v, f. 411.

merchant decided to settle in England and became naturalised: for example the Brabanters, Geoffrey and Peter Upstall in 1393 and 1416 respectively, and a German, Henry Market, in 1430. All three settled in York.[20]

From time to time the sons of country gentlemen moved into one of the three towns, entered the freedom as a merchant and emerged in the governing elite. In York, Thomas Danby, son of Robert Danby esq. of Farneley, became free in 1424, Brian Conyers, son of Christopher Conyers esq. of Hornby, became free in 1473, and Alan Staveley, son of Miles Staveley of Ripon Park, became free in 1489.[21] William Eland of Hull, free in 1450, may have been a member of the Eland family of Eland.[22]

Movement between the three towns was probably more common than the records reveal, although we cannot always be sure if a merchant was taking up multiple freedoms in several towns while continuing to reside elsewhere. Branches of Beverley mercantile families established themselves in Hull, for example the Coppendales, Bromptons and possibly Alcocks: the York Daltons were surely not the only family from their city to migrate to Hull. John Raghton of York appears to have been planning to move to Hull when he was admitted to the freedom in 1405 but he later withdrew.[23] There was a Hugh Clitheroe in York in 1398, perhaps the father or grandfather of Hugh Clitheroe, mayor of Hull in 1443, and Robert Chapman, once a York merchant, became a freeman of Hull in 1443–4. Common surnames derived from place-names make it impossible to decide whether individuals belonged to the same family or not. Robert Holme snr of York came originally from Holme-on-the-Moor and the contemporary Robert Holme and Thomas Holme of Beverley and Hull may well have come from the same village if not the same family, since Robert Holme of York took Thomas son of William Holme of Beverley as his apprentice.[24] It is likely that the famous Walter de Kelstern of York was related to the Kelsterns of Beverley.[25] The Beverley Frost family had a branch in York and certainly William Frost of Beverley was living in York in his old age.[26] In any event, merchants probably maintained connections in all three towns, and of course a dispersed

[20] *CPR 1391–6*, p. 285; *MB*, II, pp. 49–50, 185.
[21] *Test. Ebor.* II, p. 215n.; *Corpus Christi Guild*, pp. 90n., 122n.
[22] Hull RO, BRG I, f. 20v.; W. Longstaffe, ed., *Tonge's Visitation*, Surtees Soc., 41 (1863), p. 69; Horrox, 'Urban Patronage', pp. 159–60.
[23] Hull RO, BRE I, p. 244 (Raghton). See also BRE I, p. 265 (Spencer of Beverley); M479/22 (1443, Chapman of York); Prob. Reg. I, f. 69 (Aton of York buried in Hull).
[24] Prob. Reg. I, ff. 100v.–3v.
[25] *CPR 1396–9*, p. 363; Hull RO, M479/21; *Test. Ebor.* II, pp. 42n., 234n.
[26] *CCR 1405–9*, p. 316.

family could provide useful local contacts as well as the occasional bed for the night.

The problems of setting up in commercial business as a newcomer must have been daunting. Apart from the initial capital,[27] the goodwill and respect of the established merchants had to be acquired and contacts with suppliers created. Migrants like Robert Holme of York, who came from the Wolds, had an immediate advantage in their local knowledge of wool producers. Others became apprenticed to established merchants, and although not allowed to trade for their own profit while indentured,[28] they were introduced to valuable contacts[29] as well as being taught the rudiments of trade. This custom can be traced most easily in Hull, where merchants who later rose to high civic office had served apprenticeships with prominent merchants. Nicholas Ellis, John Liversege and John Ricard, later mayors of Hull, were all apprenticed to Robert Shackles, a former mayor, who in his turn had been a servant to Peter Stellar. Ralph Horne, later mayor, and Stephen Gildhouse, later sheriff, were both apprenticed to John Gregg, one of Hull's wealthiest early fifteenth-century merchants. Roger Bushell and Ralph Langton were typical of successful merchants who attracted, and doubtless needed, apprentices. They, like Shackles and John Gregg, each had at least four apprentices during their active lives.[30]

The help given by an established merchant to a newcomer from his home town or village must have been invaluable.[31] Edmund Coppendale, a migrant from Beverley to Hull, took on Thomas Brackenburgh, a fellow townsman from Beverley, as his apprentice.[32] The opportunities offered by a training with a prominent merchant were probably the same in Beverley and York but the records of apprenticeships in both towns are sparse. The recorded instances in York reflect the Hull pattern. For example, John Northeby was a 'servant' of William Vescy, a prosperous wool merchant. John Lincoln, sheriff in 1502 and Master of the Mercers

---

[27] We have no evidence from Yorkshire, but in London amounts ranged from £10 to £1,000 of stock: the majority had between £20 and £200: Thrupp, *London Merchant Class*, p. 103.

[28] *YCR*, I, pp. 163–4. Some London companies allowed apprentices to trade: Thrupp, *London Merchant Class*, p. 104.   [29] Hanham, *Celys and Their World*, p. 203.

[30] Hull RO, BRE, I pp. 246, 252, 254, 256, 258, 265; Prob. Reg. III, f. 267. Other examples were William Alcock to John Sanderson, Richard Scoles to William Pund, John Snayton and John de Holm to John Tutbury, BRE I, pp. 241, 244–5, John Dalton to John Swan, James Thomlinson to William Eland, BRG I, ff. 20v., 24.

[31] Geographical connections were exploited by migrants to London. Derbyshire was the shared birthplace of William Shore and his apprentice John Hawe: A. Sutton, 'William Shore, Merchant of London and Derby', *Derby Arch. Jnl*, 106 (1986), pp. 127–39 at p. 128. See also J. M. Imray, '"Les bones gentes de la mercerye de Londres": A Study of the Membership of the Medieval Mercers' Company', in A. E. J. Hollaender and W. Kellaway, eds., *Studies in London History Presented to Philip Edmund Jones* (London, 1969), p. 169.

[32] Hull RO, BRG I, ff. 23–6v.; Prob. Reg. V, f. 383v.

and Merchant Adventurers' Company in 1507, entered his freedom as an apprentice to John Ferriby, a former mayor. John Beseby jnr, sheriff in 1506, was an apprentice of Thomas Beverley, a former mayor,[33] and further examples could be cited.[34]

References to benefactors appear regularly in merchants' wills, and reflect the importance of good early contacts. William Frost, several times mayor of York, remembered two established merchants as his benefactors, Roger de Moreton and Roger Hovingham, and endowed a joint chantry in his own and their memory. Such was Robert Hancock of York's great affection for his master Thomas Barton that he wanted to be buried next to him.[35] Attachments to other members of a master's household could develop, and the advancement of an apprentice through marriage to his master's daughter or even to his widow was a possibility.[36] Only one example of such a marriage has been discovered in the three towns. Robert Harrison of Hull, an apprentice of John Dalton, married Dalton's widow Katherine after his death in 1496. Harrison had also enjoyed the encouragement of Ralph Langton, a successful merchant mayor, and wanted to be buried at Langton's feet in Holy Trinity, Hull.[37] A similar relationship may have existed between Thomas Aldestonemore and fellow York merchant John Gare, since Aldestonemore wished to be buried next to Gare if he died while in Calais.[38]

Friendly advice and introductions were of great advantage, but the major obstacle to most ambitious young merchants was their initial capital. For some their inheritance was sufficient; others sold rural property to raise cash or borrowed from established merchants or elsewhere.[39] As a group, merchants could provide the necessary financial support for their successors, and as members of the governing elite they occasionally showed sympathy for a young merchant by helping him to avoid the financial drain of civic office. Brian Conyers of York was excused from

---

[33] *York Freemen*, p. 206; *M&MA*, p. 323; Prob. Reg. v, f. 434.

[34] John Yarum was servant to Thomas Siggeston, Robert Ward to Robert Holme, John Kent to Thomas Kirkham, John Langton to William Chimney. See Kermode, 'Merchants of York, Beverley and Hull', appendix 4.

[35] *CPR 1391–6*, p. 711; Prob. Reg. v, f. 473.

[36] Rich widows were not uncommon in sixteenth-century Exeter: W. G. Hoskins, 'The Elizabethan Merchants of Exeter', in S. T. Bindoff, J. Hurstfield and C. H. Williams, eds., *Elizabethan Government and Society* (London, 1961), p. 167. See below, note 69, for the preponderance of widows relative to widowers in Yorkshire towns.

[37] Hull RO, BRG I, f. 29; Prob. Reg. v, ff. 483v.–5; IX, f. 112; XIII, f. 32a.

[38] Prob. Reg. III, f. 413.

[39] E.g. John Romondby sold the manor of Romondby after he became a York freeman: *Yorks Deeds*, I, p. 146. The London mercers' and grocers' companies assumed that new shopholders would obtain their initial stock on credit. The grocers' company provided loans for that purpose from its funds. Londoners could also borrow from the Court of Orphans: Thrupp, *London Merchant Class*, pp. 107–8 and 'The Grocers of London', p. 253.

further office-holding after his term as a chamberlain, until he was better established.[40]

In York it is possible to trace the emergence of several merchant families from other occupations. William Brereton became a freeman as a cook in 1396; one of his sons, Robert, remained in the same occupation, but another, John, became free as a merchant in 1430. John's son, Thomas, became a freeman in his turn as a clerk. The Jameson family also moved into the merchant group from another occupation. William Jameson had become free as a yeoman in 1456 and his son Thomas, and grandsons, John, Thomas and Michael, all became merchants. In 1433 William Lancaster became a freeman as a clerk, his son John became a merchant, and his two sons Nicholas and Richard became a lawyer and a clerk respectively in the 1470s although Nicholas was described as a merchant and clerk.[41] Dual occupation was not uncommon: George Essex of York was a merchant and apothecary, as was Lawrence Swattock of Hull. Moving in the reverse direction, Thomas Brounfleet of York became a merchant although his father John had been an apothecary.

In Hull the distinctions between seafaring and trading were blurred. Robert Michelson, for instance, became free as a mariner in 1466 but had been trading on his own account for at least two years. Similarly, William Bank was a mariner who came to own a ship. He traded in his own right and as a partner in a collective venture with several Hull merchants, but described himself as mariner in his will in 1505. Why he preferred the identity of 'mariner' is not at all clear. Perhaps nomenclature was only of consequence for the socially aware. It did apparently matter to Robert Bennington, who became a freeman of Hull as a mariner in 1445 and described himself in his will in 1460 as a merchant, after a life in overseas trade.[42]

FAMILIES

Heirs, family survival and class formation

One major difference in the life of the three towns was the political longevity of families in Beverley. The Coppendales, Holmes and Tirwhits were outstandingly successful in providing men to serve as keeper.[43] If they all came from the same family, their experience was uncommon by any English standards; but unfortunately we cannot do

[40] *YCR*, I, p. 25. [41] *York Freemen*, pp. 97, 143, 144, 175, 178, 200, 205, 211, 232, 237, 244.
[42] Prob. Reg. IV, f. 181 (Bennington); VI, f. 214 (Bank); Hull RO, BRG I, f. 23v. (Michelson).
[43] *VCH Beverley*, pp. 198–200.

much beyond remark the persistence of their surnames. The Coppendales of successive generations may have been members of the urban stem family or of a rural branch, or indeed of rural stem or urban branch. More often surnames disappeared with childless male heirs.

The survival of male heirs was not to be taken for granted. According to their biographer, the Celys 'did well to raise three sons to maturity',[44] and few families survived more than one or two generations in the male line. This was a common pattern. It is claimed that in Bury St Edmunds, 75 per cent of all families failed to produce male heirs for more than two successive generations.[45] In London, between 16 and 49 per cent of the orphans left by merchants in the period 1318–1497 died before reaching twenty-one. Allowing for the probability of wills excluding eldest sons, it is remarkable, not that there were few male heirs, but how rarely families survived into a second generation through direct male issue.[46] Of course it is impossible to discover conclusively if or why a male stem had disappeared, but if a merchant's grandson was active in trade, local government, or had moved out of town within the see of York, it would be surprising if his name did not occur in any of the sources checked. Sons have been firmly identified for 311 merchants: and circumstantially for a further seventy. Of the 311 merchants from all three towns, only forty-two had grandsons by male descent, five had great-grandsons, and one had great-great-grandsons. Several families such as the Beverley Coppendales, Tirwhits, Ryses and Holmes, and the York Holmes, probably survived into four or more generations but that assumption is based on the continuing appearance of men of wealth and status with those names and not on testamentary evidence. The numbers of sons a merchant had does not seem to have had any direct bearing on the numbers of generations his family survived. Robert Louth of York had six sons living in 1407, one of whom married twice, but no grandson has been traced to the family. William Bowes of York had only one son but four grandsons by 1439, and Thomas Neleson of York, with two sons and two daughters, had eight grandsons through his eldest son William by 1484.[47]

It was not unusual for two sons to be given the same name, in anticipation that one would die young, and to ensure that a traditional family name survived. Robert Fisher of Beverley and Robert Fisher of Hull

---

[44] Hanham, *Celys and Their World*, p. 17. For similar succession problems, see J. T. Rosenthal, 'Heirs' Ages and Family Succession in Yorkshire, 1399–1422', *Yorks Arch. Jnl*, 56 (1984), pp. 87–94.

[45] R. S. Gottfried, *Bury St Edmunds and the Urban Crisis 1290–1539* (Princeton, 1982), p. 248.

[46] A similar situation obtained in London: Thrupp, *London Merchant Class*, pp. 200–4. In contrast, see sixteenth-century Exeter where successive generations of families held office: W. T. McCaffrey, *Exeter 1540–1640: The Growth of an English Town* (London, 1958), p. 36.

[47] Prob. Reg. III, ff. 265 (Louth), 580–3 (Bowes); v, ff. 212–13 (Neleson); IX, f. 203 (Neleson).

were brothers, as were John Carleton snr and John jnr of Beverley.[48] Explicit references to the death of heirs appears in several wills. John Aldestonemore of York who died in 1434, a plague year, prefaced almost every bequest in his will with the phrase 'if he/she should live'.[49] Many merchants had grandsons through female heirs, but on that basis their families were absorbed into another, and did not carry forward the family name.[50]

Medieval society accepted illegitimacy as a commonplace,[51] and although many merchants acknowledged their bastard offspring, for example John Stockdale of York had one of each sex by 1506, such children were normally excluded from any inheritance beyond a small cash bequest. The case of Robert Holme snr of York was exceptional, and his bastard son Robert inherited because he had no surviving legitimate child. Accepting an inherited family responsibility, William Girlington of York left £4 in 1444 to the two bastard sons of his uncle John. Others acknowledged the mothers of their bastard children: John Goddysbuk of York for instance left £1 to Emmota by whom he had had a daughter, and John Selby left a bowl to the mother of his bastard son.[52]

In the absence of a son, nephews often became their uncle's heir. Henry Pollington of Beverley left the bulk of his estate to his nephew Robert since he had no son of his own to inherit in 1479. Similarly, in 1406 Thomas Holme of York made a nephew, Thomas, his heir.[53] Several families failed in the male line for reasons other than infertility. Entrance into holy orders could end the legitimate male line after one generation. Stephen Tilson of Beverley's only son Thomas became a priest. Two of Thomas Bracebridge of York's sons became priests; one predeceased him and the other migrated to London.[54]

The failure of male heirs had a profound impact on the merchant group in each town. Above all, it prevented the formation of a dynastic oligarchy based on inherited wealth. Instead there was a steady flow of newcomers into the merchant group and thence into the governing elite.

---

[48] Prob. Reg. I, f. 38v. (Carleton); V, f. 8 (Fisher).

[49] Bartlett, 'Aspects of the Economy of York', p. 193; Prob. Reg. II, ff. 406–8.

[50] Richard de Acastre of York died in 1401, predeceased by his son John whose heir was his niece Agnes Selby: Prob. Reg. III, ff. 56, 65v.–6 (John).

[51] According to David Nicholas, 'bastardy carried more legal than emotional disabilities': *Domestic Life of a Medieval City*, pp. 149, 154–72.

[52] Prob. Reg. II, f. 84 (Girlington); I, ff. 11v. (Selby), 100v.–3v. (Holme); III, ff. 276 (Goddysbuk), 365 (Holme). See also III, 406 (Aldestonemore).

[53] Prob. Reg. III, ff. 255–5v. (Holme); v, f. 147 (Pollington). Richard Russell of York dispersed his estate amongst his siblings, nephews and nieces. His daughter Ellen was well provided for through her marriage to John Thirsk: *ibid.*, III, ff. 339–441.

[54] Prob. Reg. III, ff. 487–90 (Bracebridge); V, f. 138 (Tilson). See below, note 236, for other merchants with sons who took holy orders.

Even in Beverley the long-established families provided only a small, if powerful, minority of the keepers. On average mercantile businesses survived two generations at the most and the wealth of individuals was continually redistributed amongst other members of the merchant group in bequests and through marriage. The merchant group accordingly could not depend upon the survival of individual families, but only upon the collective strength of each generation. An important effect of marriage between merchant families was to retain capital, investments, real estate and business goodwill within the group. Marriage was also a means whereby newcomers were absorbed into the group and assisted in their careers.

An astute marriage could rapidly advance the fortunes of an ambitious merchant.[55] For example, William Stockton of York married the widow of Robert Collinson, Richard Wartre married John Moreton's daughter Alice, John Metcalfe married John Ferriby's daughter, and as Metcalfe was said to be 'comen lightly up' his marriage at least was clearly advantageous. Each of these marriages were into successful merchant families, and each man in turn obtained thereby a thriving business in trade.[56]

The network of marriages which linked contemporary merchant families was extensive and complex and could draw in many families. Thus Adam Baker of Beverley, a merchant keeper active in the early fifteenth century, married Elene, the sister-in-law of another merchant keeper, William Rolleston, and their daughter married a third merchant keeper, John Brompton. William Bowes snr of York married both his daughters Katherine and Joan to other York merchants, Robert Louth and John Blackburn respectively. His son William married the daughter of a third merchant, Robert de Kirkeby. Hugh Clitheroe of Hull married Joan, the daughter of Robert Holme, another Hull merchant, and his sister Mary married two Hull merchants, John Thwayt and then John Scales.[57] Thomas Beverley snr of York married Alice, daughter of a fellow merchant Henry Market, and their son John married Anne, daughter of John Ferriby also a merchant of York. Anne's sister Ellen married John Metcalfe of York, thus linking together four of York's mercantile families through the marriage of three merchant mayors and two merchant sheriffs.[58]

The appended family trees detail the even more extensive connections which could be achieved. Through the marriages of their children, six

---

[55] On advantageous marriages, see Thrupp, *London Merchant Class*, pp. 28–9, 106–7; Sutton, 'William Shore', p. 128; Power, *Medieval People*, p. 126 for an arranged business marriage.

[56] *Corpus Christi Guild*, p. 29n.; YCR, II, p. 156; Prob. Reg. IV, f. 115 (Wartre); V, f. 417 (Ferriby).

[57] Prob. Reg. III, ff. 71v. (Baker), 580 (Bowes); Hull RO, D342; *CCR 1435–41*, p. 40.

[58] Prob. Reg. II, f. 70; V, ff. 184, 417.

contemporary and prominent York merchants came together and through the marriages of their grandchildren, three more merchant families became part of this extended family (see figure 1). Thus two generations of the Aldestonemore, Blackburn, Bolton, Bowes, Gascoigne, Holbeck, Kirkeby, Louth and Ormeshead families were united in a wide family circle. This circle consolidated political and commercial associations: most of the merchants held civic office, John Aldestonemore and John Bolton were MPs together in 1429, William Bowes in 1426 and William Ormeshead in 1430. John Aldestonemore and Nicholas Blackburn snr traded together, Thomas Aldestonemore and Blackburn traded with Thomas Gare and Richard Russell, Russell with John Bolton. Even more extensive were the connections between Richard Thornton and two other York contemporaries, which extended to include three more mercantile families through the marriage of their grandchildren (see figure 2). When Richard Thornton's great-granddaughter Catherine married Bartholomew York, Thornton's group of relationships was added to those of the Yorks. The York family connections were not so extensive but were with a number of lesser gentry families. Marriage could bring families within unacceptable degrees of consanguinity. John Beverley of York had to obtain a papal dispensation to marry John Ferriby's daughter Anne, to whom he was related in the third degree, although no marriage between the two families had recently taken place.[59] Marriage also united families from the three towns. For example Ralph Langton of Hull married his daughter Ellen to John Middleton of Beverley; John Bedford of Hull's daughter Ellen was married to Thomas Gare of York.[60]

The life expectancy of merchants in this period is difficult to calculate since dates of birth rarely survive. Instead, the date at which a man became a freeman must be used to estimate age, but this also presents difficulties. Of the three methods of entry, by fine, patrimony, and through a completed apprenticeship, only the last was well documented. In Beverley the merchant guild insisted on a seven-year apprenticeship in 1446, and in the first ordinances of Hull guilds, recorded in the late fifteenth century, seven-year apprenticeships were the rule.[61] In York most apprenticeships were for at least seven years by the fifteenth century,[62] although the curriers and pinners required at least six years, and the scriveners, five years. Only the scriveners' ordinances recorded the age at which an apprentice should take up his indenture, and they insisted that a boy should be at least fifteen.[63] The minimum five years'

---

[59] *Test. Ebor.* III, p. 196 n.   [60] Prob. Reg. IV, f. 96v.; II, f. 220; *Corpus Christi Guild*, p. 11n.
[61] *Bev. Town Docs.*, p. 92; Hull RO, M478/1–4.   [62] *MB*, I, pp. 54, 59, 71, 77, 80, 83, 89, 181.
[63] *Ibid.*, pp. 56, 87; II, p. 167.

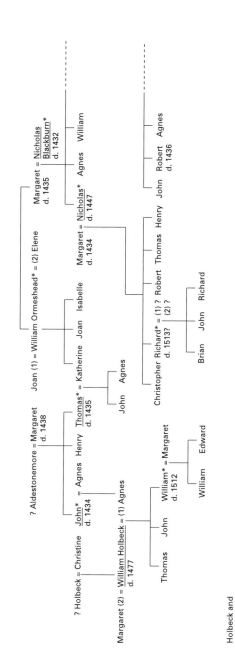

Holbeck and
Aldestonemore

Prob. Reg. III f. 406
Prob. Reg. V f. 22
Prob. Reg. VIII f. 96

Ormeshead

Prob. Reg. III ff. 406, 413, 503

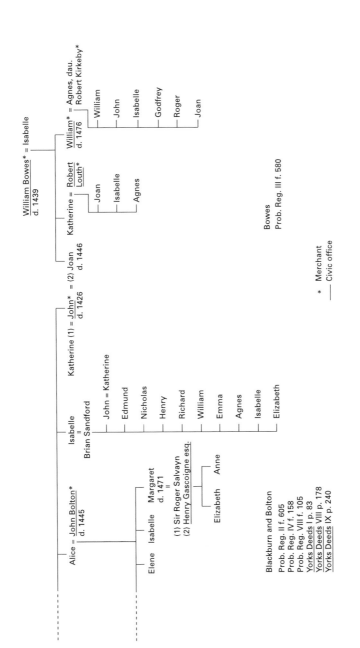

Figure 1 The Aldestonemore, Blackburn, Bolton, Bowes, Holbeck and Ormeshead families

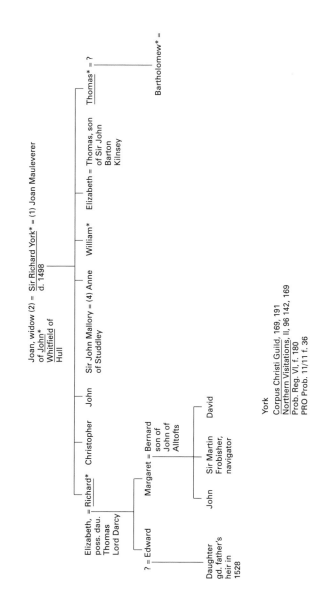

Joan, widow (2) = Sir Richard York* = (1) Joan Mauleverer
of John* .... d. 1498
Whitfield of
Hull

Elizabeth, = Richard* Christopher John Sir John Mallory = (4) Anne William* Elizabeth = Thomas, son Thomas* = ?
poss. dau. of Studdley of Sir John
Thomas Barton
Lord Darcy Kilnsey

? = Edward Margaret = Bernard Bartholomew* =
son of
John of
Alltofts

Daughter John Sir Martin David
gd. father's Frobisher,
heir in navigator
1528

York
Corpus Christi Guild, 169, 191
Northern Visitations, II, 96 142, 169
Prob. Reg. VI, f. 180
PRO Prob. 11/11 f. 36

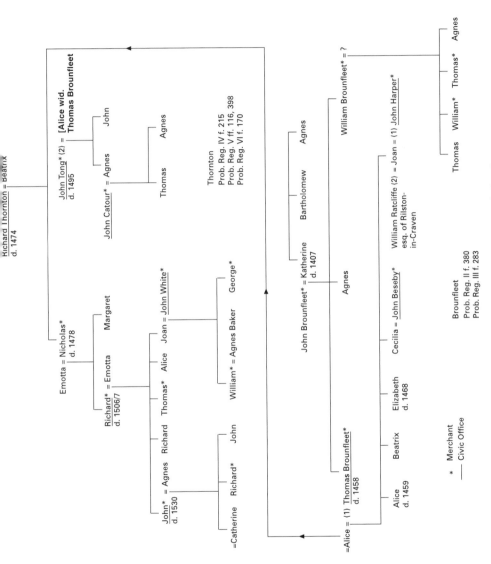

Figure 2 The Brounfleet, Thornton and York families

service meant that scriveners completed their apprenticeship by twenty at the earliest.

It has been calculated that in late fifteenth- and early sixteenth-century London,[64] the average age of entry was twenty-two or twenty-three; and that in sixteenth-century York[65] it was at any age between twenty-one and twenty-six, and could be as late as thirty-five. There is a piece of evidence which supports the argument for an average age of twenty-two. John Hagg of York became a freeman in 1471 and was said to be 'about 23 years old' when he served as a witness in a dispute in Bergen-op-Zoom that same year.[66] On balance then, it seems reasonable to take twenty-two as the average age for entry to the freedom.

On that basis, the merchants of York and Hull, like those of London,[67] were reasonably long lived. (There are too few entry dates to make any equivalent calculations for Beverley merchants.) Up to 1410, 70 per cent of those for whom entry dates and dates of death are known lived to an age of forty-five or over. In the fifteenth century where both dates are known for more merchants, 67 per cent lived to forty-five or over and 20 per cent to over sixty. Death most commonly occurred between thirty and forty years after entry, that is between the ages of fifty and sixty. Compared to their fellow townsfolk, York merchants enjoyed better health and longevity. Evidence from the cemetery of St Helen-on-the-Walls, used from the tenth to the sixteenth century, suggests that of the men and women reaching adulthood, 36 and 56 per cent respectively died before they reached thirty-five years of age, and that only 9 per cent survived to sixty or beyond.[68]

In spite of the apparent longevity of Yorkshire merchants, the majority, 79 per cent, left a widow.[69] Of 442 merchants with named wives, only ninety-one (21 per cent) survived their wives,[70] and of these fifty-three were known to have had more than one wife. Those with more than two wives were exceptional: forty-four were married twice and nine three

---

[64] The ages of mercers' and grocers' apprentices when they became freemen ranged from twenty-one to twenty-six between 1463 and 1493. In 1491 the London grocers ruled that their apprentices could not become freemen until they were twenty-five or twenty-six. Sylvia Thrupp has calculated that the average age at entry was twenty-two or twenty-three: *London Merchant Class*, pp. 11, 93, 194. [65] Palliser, *TudorYork*, pp. 194–5. [66] *Bronnen*, II, pp. 1056–7.

[67] By way of comparison, the median age of death for a group of fifteenth-century London merchants has been estimated at forty-nine or fifty: Thrupp, *London Merchant Class*, p. 194.

[68] J. D. Dawes, and J. R. Magilton, 'The Cemetery of St Helen-on-the-Walles, Aldwark', in *The Archaeology of York* (York, 1980).

[69] Cf. 82 per cent of all male testators in Bristol left widows, 1382–1405: Kowaleski, 'Urban Families', p. 55; and 61 per cent of Londoners, 1258–1500: B. A. Hanawalt, 'Re-marriage as an Option for Urban and Rural Widows in Late Medieval England', in S. S. Walker, ed., *Wife and Widow in Medieval England* (Ann Arbor, 1993), p. 146.

[70] Ten out of sixty (17 per cent) of London aldermen outlived their wives, 1448–1520: Thrupp, *London Merchant Class*, p. 197.

times. These are conservative figures, derived from references to chantries or obits for previous wives and from strong references in other merchants' wills.[71] Twelve wives are known to have been widows on their marriages to the merchants studied, and ten others are known to have remarried after their merchant husbands' deaths. The remarriage of widows is difficult to trace and the numbers were probably higher. The evidence suggests either that female life expectancy was much higher than that of men, or that men generally did not marry until some time after becoming free and after they had become established, and that when they did marry, their wives were younger than they.[72]

The patterns of remarriage of merchant widowers and widows reinforced the cohesive nature of the merchant group. John Stockdale of York's wife Ellen had previously been married to William Hancock and Robert Johnson, both York merchants. Isabella, wife of Robert Gaunt of York, had four husbands, three of them merchants. Katherine Stellar of Hull, widow of Peter Stellar, a merchant mayor, remarried one of her husband's former associates, John Tutbury, who was also a merchant mayor.[73] A consequence of such marriages was that some of the working capital and assets of a merchant's business were retained in the merchant group, since wives traditionally inherited one-third of their husbands' estates. However, as we shall see below, some merchants tried to discourage their widows from taking another husband, by imposing conditions on their inheritance. Remarriage within the merchant group was common, not only in each town but between the three towns. For instance, Thomas Gra of York married the widow of John de Colthorp of Hull and became a co-executor of her first husband's will. Thomas Helmesley of York married the widow of another Hull merchant, Richard Bille.[74]

One interesting familial network which illustrates several of the features discussed above was created through the marriages of one woman to three established merchants. Joan (maiden name unknown) first married John Dalton, a merchant mayor of Hull, and their son John's marriage united the families of Alcock and Dalton. After Dalton's death she married another Hull merchant mayor, John Whitfield, and their daughter married Henry Mindram, also a wealthy merchant mayor of Hull. Joan's two groups of children, three by her marriage with John

[71] The pattern in late sixteenth-century York was similar: Palliser, *Tudor York*, p. 122.
[72] This concurs with Goldberg's analysis: *Women, Work and Life Cycle*, pp. 225–32. In London, merchants were generally between twenty-one and twenty-six and their wives seventeen or over when they married: Thrupp, *London Merchant Class*, pp. 192–3, 196.
[73] *Test. Ebor.* IV, p. 121n.; *Corpus Christi Guild*, p. 18n.; Arch. Reg. XVIII, f. 357.
[74] *CPR 1401–5*, p. 74; *1452–61*, p. 181.

Dalton, and four by her marriage with John Whitfield, were united into one family of step-brothers and sisters. Finally she became the third wife of Sir Richard York, a merchant mayor of York, whose grandson Bartholomew married into the Thornton group of families.

Marriages between widows and widowers could produce complicated new family units. The children usually followed their widowed mother to a new step-father's family,[75] but combining two families in this way might generate tensions. When John Bedford of Hull married Agnes, widow of Richard Dalton of Hull, her son John became co-heir with Bedford's children by his first wife. Bedford made John Dalton's inheritance conditional upon him not 'molesting' his mother Agnes, and imposed the same condition on his own son Nicholas Bedford.[76]

The complexities of several sets of children being merged into one family, through successive marriages, did not inevitably lead to hostility. Merchants like William Tele and Robert Johnson of York were careful to make bequests to their step-children, although Johnson discriminated by giving his two daughters £5 each and making them the residuary heirs to his land, whereas his five step-daughters were to receive £2 each and no land.[77] Some sense of family survived multiple relationships and was reflected in bequests. John Dalton for instance, the son of his mother's first marriage, made bequests to her second and third families, the Yorks and Whitfields, and his step-father John Whitfield, made John and Thomas Dalton his residuary heirs[78] (see figure 3). John Tanfield of York gave his widowed step-mother a belt he had inherited from his own mother.

Second marriages brought a new set of responsibilities. The surviving partner commonly included dead spouses when they subsequently arranged obits for themselves, but adding several partners in one set of prayers suggests a generous willingness to fulfil obligations. John Northeby of York wanted land sold to pay for masses for the souls of his wife and her first husband. Henry de Yarom, also of York, left his widow property, specifically to be sold for masses for her and her first husband's souls.[79] Requests to be buried close to dead spouses reflect similar sentiments.[80]

A woman might thus find herself playing a complex family role,

---

[75] It was quite the opposite in some European cities where the rights of the father and his family took precedence. In Ghent, for example, it was assumed that children would go back to their dead father's family and widows could become the legal guardians of their children only with the authorisation of their dead husband's family: Nicholas, *Domestic Life of a Medieval City*, p. 121.

[76] Prob. Reg. II, ff. 220–1v. For similar warnings, see Prob. Reg. III, ff. 223v. (Cottesbroke), 365 (Holme).   [77] Prob. Reg. IV, ff. 162–v. (Tele); v, ff. 510v.–11 (Johnson).

[78] Prob. Reg. v, ff. 148v., 483v.–5.   [79] Prob. Reg. I, f. 57v. (Yarom); II, f. 620 (Northeby).

[80] Those who had had more than one spouse had to decide near which to be buried. Joan, who outlived her third husband, Sir Richard York, chose to be buried next to her second husband in

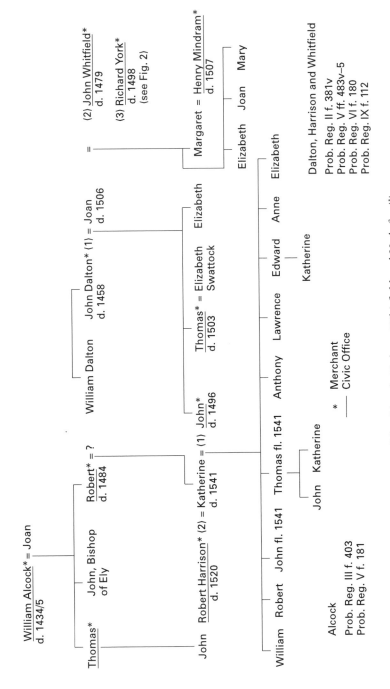

Figure 3 The Alcock, Dalton, Whitfield and York families

balancing the demands of her several sets of children. Ellen Stockdale was successively the widow of William Hancock, Robert Johnson and John Stockdale. Four of her five daughters by Hancock were still alive in 1507 and received girdles as bequests, including her own mother's girdle of blue silk and gold, and one of silver and red silk she wore on her first wedding day. Her two daughters by Robert Johnson, Maud and Jennet were due their child's part (presumably from their father according to the custom of legitim),[81] and their whole part, which was to be made up from their father's remaining goods (worth £13) and their mother's 'own part' after debts had been paid, to make the sum of £100. They were only to receive both parts if they agreed to accept the counsel of their mother's executors concerning their marriages.[82]

Wives and widows

The role of women in urban families and households is well attested, though women remained relatively shadowy figures until widowhood gave them a legal identity.[83] Whether or not a widow chose independence or remarriage depended on the state of the economy as well as on her individual circumstances.[84] It has been suggested that while the employment situation in York was buoyant after the Black Death, many young women preferred to remain independent and to delay marriage.[85] More

---

Holy Trinity, Hull. William Burgh of Hull predeceased his third wife and wanted to be buried next to both his previous wives: Prob. Reg. II, f. 423v. (Burgh); XI, f. 57 (York). For some merchants their place of burial reflected the warmth as well as the formality of lifetime relationships. Thomas Bracebridge of York wanted to be buried in St Saviour's next to his wife and children who had predeceased him, and John Esingwold wanted to be buried in the Austin Friary next to his brothers: Prob. Reg. III, ff. 487 (Bracebridge), 599 (Esingwold). Some merchants wished to prolong a master–apprentice relationship. Robert Hancock of York asked to be buried next to his former master, Thomas Barton, and similarly Robert Harrison of Hull wanted to be buried at Ralph Langton's feet, and Henry Mindram of Hull next to John Whitfield: Prob. Reg. V, f. 473 (Hancock); VII, f. 25v. (Mindram); IX, f. 112 (Harrison).

[81] On legitim and the division of estates, see p. 293 below, note 105.

[82] Prob. Reg. VI, f. 227 (Stockdale). See also III, f. 502v. (Tanfield)

[83] For a clear account of women's legal status, see A. J. Kettle, '"My Wife Shall Have It": Marriage and Property in the Wills and Testaments of Later Medieval England', in E. M. Craik, ed., *Marriage and Property* (Aberdeen, 1984), pp. 89–103.

[84] In seventeenth-century Salisbury, widows chose to remain unmarried when they could survive independently: B. J. Todd, 'The Remarrying Widow: A Stereotype Reconsidered', in M. Prior, ed., *Women in English Society 1500–1800* (London, 1985), pp. 54–93, esp. pp. 78–9; P. J. P. Goldberg, 'Female Labour, Service, and Marriage in Northern Towns during the Later Middle Ages', *Northern History*, 22 (1986), pp. 18–38, esp. pp. 52–3, and 'Marriage, Migration, Servanthood and Life-cycle in Yorkshire Towns in the Later Middle Ages: Some York Cause Paper Evidence', *Continuity and Change*, 1 (1986), pp. 141–63, esp. pp. 158–9. For a general discussion, see Barron and Sutton, *Medieval London Widows*, pp. xxiii–xxvii.

[85] Goldberg, 'Marriage, Migration, Servanthood', pp. 141–69, and *Women, Work, and Life Cycle*, pp. 270–3. For remarriage patterns in Coventry, see Phythian-Adams, *Desolation of a City*, pp. 91–2.

usually, young widows with children were under pressure to remarry.[86] Indeed, it might have been that wealthy widows were pestered by unwelcome suitors. Isabel Green, widow of John Green of Hull, was harassed by one Robert Daveson whom she claimed had long wished to marry her. His unwelcome attention degenerated into actions of debt and of trespass against her and in 1470 Isabel finally took out a writ against him.[87]

The majority of merchants left their widows at least a life-interest in the matrimonial home.[88] Edmund Cottesbroke was exceptional, allowing his widow to remain in his house for one year only, and the tone of his will of 1405 suggests that he expected her to challenge his arrangements.[89] A widow's right to dower in property was fixed at one-third of all the lands of which her husband had been solely seised at his death.[90] A husband could not deprive his wife of her dower unless she agreed to a conveyance by fine in a court (as John Goldberg's wife Ellen did in York in 1331), or unless he settled the land to his own use, thereby creating an equitable estate.[91]

In boroughs, the right to devise freely, which was the main characteristic of burgage tenure, was in conflict with the common law as it was developing in relation to married women, and their position in boroughs varied from place to place according to local custom.[92] Dower rights in real estate were certainly respected in York, and thus in 1432 Robert Holme of York left his wife Margaret one-third of all his lands and tenements 'for her dower, as her accustomed right'.[93] Women could and did inherit and dispose of real estate. Joan, widow of Robert Louth of York, retained a property she had inherited from her father to dispose of herself, as did another widow, Anne Beverley of York, in 1492.[94] Women were well aware of their role as agents for transmission through their own blood-line and Katherine Levesham of York stipulated that her children should inherit 'whatever my father left to my children'. Since her husband survived her, she was reliant upon his co-operation to carry out

---

[86] Barron and Sutton, *Medieval London Widows*, p. xxv.   [87] PRO, C1/46/171.

[88] See, for example, Prob. Reg. I, f. 55v. (Burton). Under common law, widows had the right (freebench) to remain in the family home for forty days after their husband's death, and in some boroughs this was extended to life so long as they did not remarry: Bateson, *Borough Customs*, I, p. cx; Kettle, '"My Wife Shall Have It"', p. 92. In London widows had residence for life: Barron and Sutton, *Medieval London Widows*, p. xxviii.

[89] Prob. Reg. III, f. 223v. (Cottesbroke).

[90] W. S. Holdsworth, *A History of English Law*, 4th edn (London, 1935), III, pp. 189–93.

[91] *Ibid.*, p. 196; A. W. B. Simpson, *An Introduction to the History of the Land Law* (Oxford, 1961), p. 66; Bateson, *Borough Customs*, I, p. 277. Ellen Goldberg released her right to dower in only one property, a house in Mickelgate: *Yorks Deeds*, VII, pp. 197–8.

[92] Bateson, *Borough Customs*, I, p. 277; II, pp. civ–cv.   [93] Prob. Reg. III, f. 365 (Holme).

[94] Prob. Reg. III, f. 450 (Louth); v, ff. 419–v. (Beverley). In some boroughs, husbands could not sell their wife's inherited property without her permission, and this may have been the case in York: Bateson, *Borough Customs*, II, p. 115.

her wishes. However, a married woman could not act as plaintiff or recover without her husband and so Thomas Glasyn of York had to sue for his wife's inherited estate in Poppleton.[95]

Transmission of inherited property was not always straightforward and John Lofthouse of York had to sue for his wife Katherine's inheritance from her first husband, who had enfeoffed four friends with property worth 40 marks. The trustees were reluctant to re-enfeoff Katherine.[96] Problems of a different kind confronted William de Barneby's widow Joan in 1409. She was violently evicted from a tenement in Walmegate and a garden in Paynelathes in the suburbs by his son John, who caused 20s worth of damage. The court found in her favour.[97]

In the absence of male heirs, some women became heiresses to several estates. John Swynfleet of Hull, who died in 1426, had inherited his mother's inheritance which came to her as niece of Geoffrey and Hugh Hanby of Hull, as heiress of Thomas Longspey of Brompton (N.R.), and as wife of Thomas Swynfleet, son and heir of John Hanby of Yafford.[98] Expectations such as these were not routine, but the ramifications of successive marriages could result in unanticipated cumulative windfalls.

The regular income for widows was another matter altogether. Most seem to have been expected to survive on vague cash bequests subsumed in the 'residue' of their husband's estate, or on their own resources unless an earlier settlement had been arranged. Some merchants did anticipate how their widows could derive a regular income. Thomas Scauceby of York, for example, left his wife £2 annual rent income in 1471,[99] and widows may have sub-let accommodation in the family home. John Bedford of Hull gave his son Richard 'a place' in Hull in 1344, so that he could pay John's widow £2 a year. Businesslike terms were drawn up by another Hull man, John Harrison, in 1525 to guarantee that his widow received 26s 8d annually from their son.[100]

Chattels were treated differently from real estate in law, and a married woman's rights were the subject of contradictory views. Canon lawyers argued that a married woman had a right to dower in chattels and, as she could dispose of these, she had the capacity to make a testament. However, from the mid-fourteenth century, common lawyers insisted that married women could not make testaments as they owned no property. A woman's chattels became her husband's at their marriage and so a married woman could make a testament only with her husband's consent.

[95] Prob. Reg. I, f. 94 (Levesham); PRO, C1/203/41 (Glasyn).
[96] PRO, C1/61/39. In his will Thomas Manby disposed of two tenements which had belonged to his first wife, for her soul and those of her dead parents: Prob. Reg. III, f. 75.
[97] *MB*, I, pp. 140–1.   [98] Hull RO, BRE I, p. 271.
[99] Prob. Reg. VI, f. 169. In 1443, Thomas Caldbeck of Beverley left his wife and children 12d weekly: *ibid.*, II, f.76.   [100] Hull RO, BRE I, p. 24; Prob. Reg. IX, f. 328 (Harrison).

Common law allowed that her personal ornaments and clothes, her para-
phernalia, could come to her on her husband's death, unless he had previously alienated them.[101] Although even their personal belongings
belonged to their husbands,[102] in practice married women did dispose of
personal possessions. As in the case of their husbands, their wills dealt
with personal belongings, bedclothes, domestic utensils and small
amounts of cash bequeathed to family, friends and relations.[103] Care was
taken to differentiate the best from the second-best gown or girdle, and
presumably the best from the second-best friend![104]

There was a reduction in the number of wills made by married women
in the fifteenth century: 50 per cent of the 136 wills made by women
between 1398 and 1408 in York were those of wives, whereas only two
of the eighty-nine made between 1470 and 1500 were.[105] In York,
Beverley and Hull, ninety-four wills made by merchants' widows and
wives have been found;[106] one-third were made by wives. Several
deferred to their husbands whose consent was required. Margaret, wife
of Adam Baker of Beverley, made her will in 1401 'through the assent
and licence of her husband' and Emma Preston used the same phrase in
her will, coincidentally in the same year.[107] Ivetta, wife of William de
Burton of York, peppered her will with the remark 'if my husband
wishes', while in 1400, Margaret Besyngby of York left the choice of her
burial place to her husband John. The reverse consideration was not
legally required, so that Robert Poppilton of York was demonstrating
quite unusual public sensitivity in 1414, when he made some of his
bequests conditional upon his wife's agreement.[108]

It was customary in the York diocese for a man to divide his estate into
three portions: one for his wife, one for his children and one for himself
to dispose of as he wished. In 1334, Richard de Huntingdon of York left
his wife cash as 'her just and right portion', and in 1405 Thomas Gra of

---

[101] Holdsworth, *A History of English Law*, 5th edn (1942), III, pp. 543–4.

[102] I have found only one instance of a husband specifically bequeathing his wife's clothes to her,
William de Rumlay of York in 1391: Prob. Reg. I, f. 37.

[103] E.g. Prob. Reg. I, ff. 88 (Burton), 89–90 (Ireby), 96v. (Crome); II, ff. 121 (Kirk), 584v.
(Grantham), 640 (Upstall); III, ff. 227 (Lokton), 423v. (Thirsk).

[104] Men invariably left their 'best gown' for their mortuary payment but less often ranked their other
bequests. Anthony Potter of Hull distinguished between his best and second best damask dublets,
his horses and their trappings: Prob. Reg. VI, f. 213.

[105] P. J. P. Goldberg, 'Women in Fifteenth-Century Town Life', in Thomson, *Towns and Townspeople*,
p. 115.

[106] Elsewhere relatively few women made wills: only two or three survive in the London
Archdeacon's Register between 1380 and 1415: R. A. Wood, 'London and Bury St Edmunds: A
Comparative Study of Urban Piety *c.* 1380–*c.* 1415' (unpublished paper circulated to the
Fifteenth-Century Colloquium at Winchester in 1987), p. 26 n. 17.

[107] Prob. Reg. III, ff. 60v.–1 (Preston); 71v. (Baker). See also Kettle, '"My Wife Shall Have It"', p.
95.   [108] Prob. Reg. I, f. 88 (Burton); Dec. & Cap. I, ff. 129 (Besyngby), 166 (Poppilton).

York gave his wife Alice £10 out of his goods above 'the ascertained portion belonging to her by right', and many other references make it clear that this custom was commonly observed in the three towns.[109] Nicholas Blackburn, who planned to spend £200 on public works in York, asked his wife to draw on her portion if his bequest was insufficient. We do not know if she carried out any of his wishes, but when she died four years later her testamentary provision came to over £500. If a wife predeceased her husband or there were no children of the marriage, the custom was for his estate to be divided into two and occasionally a merchant might anticipate his widow's death by arranging such a division. Thus Thomas Wells of Hull stipulated in his will in 1429 that, after his widow's death, his eldest son should receive one-half of her property and the other three children were to share the remaining half in equal portions.[110]

Restrictions on widows inheriting freely if they remarried were not uncommon. The opinion of one sixteenth-century Londoner neatly sums up what were evidently common considerations: 'She will marrie and enrich some other with the fruites of my travaille. Wherefore I think it necessarie to abridge her of that liberty which the custom [of the city of London] doth extende.'[111] Elias Casse of Beverley insisted in 1501 that his widow should 'take vows' before she could inherit his land,[112] and in 1507 John Stockdale left property to his wife, who had been married twice before, on condition that she did not marry again.[113] If Richard Ayley of Beverley's wife remarried, she would receive an annuity of 26s 8d instead of his chief messuage at Crossbridge. Thomas Spicer of York stipulated in 1505 that if his wife were to remarry, she was to receive only her part (portion), and a piece of silverware: the implication being that she would otherwise receive some of his own third.[114]

Not all merchants died wealthy and many widows must have faced the prospect of seeking another husband, not inevitably a preferred choice, or employment.[115] As we shall see, a few merchants' widows continued

---

[109] Prob. Reg. III, f. 235 (Gra) and see also, for example, Dec. & Cap. I, f. 14 (Huntingdon); Prob. Reg. I, f. 34v. (Cleveland); II, ff. 108v. (Procter), 110v.–11v. (Gare), 423 (Burgh); III, f. 504v., (Ormeshead); v, ff. 7 (Swan), 13 (Fisher), 425 (Marshall).

[110] Prob. Reg. II, ff. 605 (Nicholas Blackburn jnr), 555 (Wells); III, ff. 415v.–16 (Margaret Blackburn). Robert Flinton of Hull made a similar two-part division, v, f. 401.

[111] Quoted in Susan Staves, *Married Women's Property 1660–1833* (Cambridge MA, 1990), pp. 34–6.

[112] Prob. Reg. VI, f. 12a (Casse). Two other Beverley merchants imposed as condition that their widows should pray for their souls and support obits: Prob. Reg. II, f. 243v. (Patrington); IV, f. 148 (Ashton). See also Kettle, '"My Wife Shall Have It"', p. 99.

[113] Prob. Reg. VII, f. 30 (Stockdale). See also Dec. & Cap. II, f. 43 (Elwald).

[114] Prob. Reg. III, f. 105 (Ayley); VI, f. 208v. (Spicer).

[115] No general pattern has emerged and remarriage rates amongst widows vary: 45 per cent of 162 aristocratic widows in the fifteenth century: J. T. Rosenthal, 'Aristocratic Widows in Fifteenth-

in trade following their husbands' deaths and Marion Kent even became a member of the council of the Mercers and Merchant Adventurers' Company.[116] Such women were unusual in Yorkshire however,[117] and most widows seeking work would have found that their opportunities depended very much on the overall employment situation.

Living in a large borough such as York brought considerable advantages. A married woman trading apart from her husband might claim the legal independence of a *femme sole*,[118] and many guilds included women in their regulations. Women in York could work as barber surgeons, cappers, chapwomen, clothsellers, cooks, freshwater fishers, fishmongers, ironmongers, litsters, parchmentmakers, stringers and vintners amongst other occupations. They rented shops from the city council and conducted their own commercial affairs.[119] The opportunities were there at different times and, from the evidence of guild regulations, women could still find employment in specialist crafts late in the fifteenth century. There is no reason to suppose that women in Hull or Beverley were worse off,[120] and indeed the brewsters of Beverley had formed their own guild by 1364.[121]

Some married women left considerable sums of money at their deaths, but the source of their disposable wealth is not clear. Isolde de Acastre of York was still married when she died in 1395, disposing of at least £264 and real estate. Another York wife, Anne Beverley, left £8, a quantity of wool and real estate in 1492.[122] Some widows died extremely wealthy: Ellen Gisburn left £142 in 1408, Alice Cateryk £40 in 1440, Alice

---

Century England', in B. J. Harris and J. K. McNamara, eds., *Women and the Structure of Society* (Durham NC, 1984), p. 40, 50 per cent in late sixteenth-century Abingdon and 25 per cent a century later: Todd, 'Remarrying Widow', pp. 54–92. See above, note 84.

[116] *M&MA*, p. 64.

[117] London women engaged in international trade, buying and selling and lending money: K. Lacey, 'Women and Work in 14th and 15th-Century London', in L. Charles and L. Duffin, eds., *Women and Work in Pre-Industrial England* (London, 1985), pp. 24–82, esp. pp. 53–4. For examples of working widows, see Barron and Sutton, *Medieval London Widows*, pp. 1–29, 47–54, 99–164.

[118] *MB*, II, pp. 144–5. This was possible elsewhere: Bateson, *Borough Customs*, I, pp. 185–6; Barron and Sutton, *Medieval London Widows*, pp. xxviii–xxix.

[119] *MB*, I, pp. 6, 7, 82, 198, 201, 209, 221; II, p. lxi.

[120] For a discussion of the variety of women's employment in towns, see Goldberg, 'Women in Fifteenth-Century Town Life', pp. 116–21; D. Hutton, 'Women in Fourteenth Century Shrewsbury', in Charles and Duffin, *Women and Work*, pp. 83–99; M. Kowaleski, 'Women's Work in a Market Town: Exeter in the late Fourteenth Century', in B. A. Hanawalt, ed., *Women and Work in Pre-Industrial England* (Bloomington, 1986), pp. 145–64; M. Kowaleski and J. M. Bennett, 'Crafts, Gilds and Women in the Middle Ages', *Signs*, 14, no. 2 (1989), pp. 474–88; Lacey, 'Women and Work', pp. 24–82.

[121] *Bev. Town Docs.*, p. 41. Brewing was commonly an occupation for country women: J. M. Bennett, *Women in the Medieval English Countryside. Gender and Household in Brigstock Before the Plague* (Oxford, 1987), esp. pp. 120–9, 160–2.

[122] Prob. Reg. I, f. 81 (Acastre); V, ff. 419–v. (Beverley).

Beverley £137 in 1485.[123] Margaret Blackburn, dying only three years after her husband Nicholas in 1435, made bequests totalling over £520.[124] Although the size and composition of a woman's initial inheritance from her spouse affected the size of her own estate, the length of time she had spent living independently might also have been important. Jane Neleson had inherited property from her husband Thomas when he died in 1484. When she died forty-nine years later, she disposed of only 15s in her will.[125] However, Isabelle Hamerton, who died in 1433, twenty-seven years after her husband, left £106 and some exotic items including a spice box, an enamelled cross, a veronica from Rome, an alabaster head of St John the Baptist, as well as quantities of sea-coal, wool and cloth.[126] John Stockdale left £44 in February 1507, and just over three weeks later his widow Ellen left over £111.[127] She may of course have drawn up her will anticipating a larger legacy from her husband, but had not lived long enough to discover just how much he actually had. There are too many hidden factors to suggest even the most general of observations about widows' estates. Some were large, some small and each was affected by individual circumstances.

The majority of married merchant testators, over 90 per cent, anticipated that their widows would execute their wills, relying on them to see their wishes fulfilled.[128] Some merchants, however, doubted their wives' ability to cope alone at a time of profound disruption and asked friends to step into the breach. In 1459 John Hanson of Hull's friends were to help his widow 'in necessities and negotiations'. Another Hull merchant, John Gyll, wanted a friend to keep an eye on his widow and to ensure that 'no man do her wrong' in 1506, while in 1497 Edward Grenely wanted friends to 'strengthen his widow in her necessity'.[129] However, in 1406, Alan Hamerton of York rather less optimistically paid his servant Richard Grunnays £10 a year to stay with his wife for two years to 'diligently recoup debts'. Grunnays served his master well and Isabelle Hamerton died a wealthy woman in 1433, remitting Grunnays' debts to her. George Birkbeck of York arranged for his father 'to protect' his wife, and although William Hedon of Hull was confident that his widow

---

[123] Prob. Reg. III, ff. 283v. (Gisburn), 600–1 (Cateryk); v, ff. 28–9 (Beverley).

[124] *Ibid.*, II, f. 605 (Nicholas); III, ff. 415v.–16 (Margaret).

[125] *Ibid.*, v, ff. 212–13 (Thomas); xI, f. 57 (Jane).   [126] *Ibid.*, III, ff. 345 (Isabelle), 244 (Alan).

[127] *Ibid.*, VI, ff. 185 (John), 227 (Ellen).

[128] This corresponds to the average of about 80 per cent of male testators naming wives as executors: Kettle, '"My Wife Shall Have It"', pp. 100–1.

[129] Prob. Reg. II, f. 393 (Hanson); VI, f. 107 (Gyll); v, f. 501 (Grenely). Circumstances could work against a widow's prospects. For instance, one Colchester woman, Alicia Haynes, claimed to have been so alone and without help during her widowhood that she had been unable to execute her husband's will properly: J. C. Ward, 'Wealth and Family in Early Sixteenth Century Colchester', *Essex Archaeology and History*, 21 (1990), pp. 110–17 at p. 113.

would cope as sole executrix, he asked two merchant friends to supervise the sale of his real estate.[130]

It is difficult to generalise about women within the merchant group, given such a small sample, but there is no doubt that many were capable of the sort of independent and active engagement in public affairs witnessed in other studies. As crucial perhaps was their less obvious and more passive role as key figures in passing on land, cash estates and even working businesses, to other merchant families within their own and later generations. As important of course, but less easy to explore, was the place that mothering played in developing and transmitting the familial and religious attitudes of merchant society.

Dependants

Women had no legal right of custody of their children.[131] In 1482 John Hapsam of York expressly wished his widow 'to bring up his children',[132] and some merchants explicitly made their wives *tutrix* to their children by leaving them under their wives' tutelage.[133] John Kent required his widow Anne to give up the guardianship of their children if she remarried.[134] This was in accordance with canon law. Nicholas Strensale's widow was removed as *tutrix testamentaria* by the York ecclesiastical court when she did marry again. In her place, the court appointed a man designated by Strensale in his will for such an eventuality.[135] Such was William Kyam's opinion of his wife in 1446 that, whether or not she remarried, he wanted his children under the tutelage of his kinsman, and specifically not of his wife.[136]

Children who were still minors[137] at the time of a parent's death generated particular anxiety. Of those York merchants with traceable heirs, 10 per cent left under-age children,[138] but in reality the numbers must have

---

[130] Prob. Reg. II, f. 523 (Hedon, 1427); III, ff. 245v., 345; IV, f. 158v. (Birkbeck, 1471).

[131] For a comprehensive discussion of the practice in fourteenth-century Ghent, with particular regard for the problems of safeguarding children's rights when a parent remarried, see Nicholas, *The Domestic Life of a Medieval City*, pp. 112–22.

[132] Prob. Reg. v, f. 59 (Hapsam).   [133] E.g. *ibid.*, II, f. 127v. (Kyam); III, f. 523 (Graye).

[134] *Ibid.*, VIII, f. 59 (Kent, 1510).

[135] York Borthwick Institute, Act Book M2(1)c, f. 8v. Discussed in R. H. Helmholz, 'Roman Law and Guardianship, 1300–1600', *Tulane Law Rev.*, 52 (1978), p. 224.

[136] Prob. Reg. II, ff. 127–v. (Kyam).

[137] In medieval Ghent, appointing guardians for orphans was the responsibility of the civil magistrates: Nicholas, *The Domestic Life of a Medieval City*, p. 111. In London and Bristol, orphans came under the civic courts: Clarke, 'City Orphans', pp. 168–87. For a fuller discussion, see Carlton, *Court of Orphans*.

[138] Professor Palliser has calculated that 27 per cent of male heirs in York in the first half of the sixteenth century were orphaned under age: *Tudor York*, p. 97. It is impossible to work out a directly equivalent figure for the fourteenth and fifteenth centuries.

been higher. Women dying after their second marriage had to entrust their children to the stepfather and, in the majority of cases for which there is clear evidence, merchant widowers were conscientious in this respect. Henry Market of York took the occasion of drawing up his own will to fulfil two small bequests made by his dead wife. Joan, wife of Peter Stellar of Hull, left £10 in 1383 to her son Thomas White when he came of age. When Stellar made his will in 1395, he had remarried, but he honoured his stepson's legacy.[139] Robert Graye of York married for a second time, but in 1437 sensitively left silver spoons which had belonged to their mother to his sons by his first wife. He also entrusted one of those sons to his second wife's tutelage.[140]

It was customary for even wealthy parents to send their offspring into another household for service,[141] and appointing guardians or godparents was an extension of that process of seeking support beyond the stem family. Choosing guardians allayed a common fear that an inheritance would be dissipated before minors were old enough to claim it. Given that common law, under the system of primogeniture, supplied a guardian for the eldest son only, and that most infants were left to 'shift for themselves and to get guardians as best they might from time to time for the purpose of litigation',[142] it is not surprising that merchants appointed guardians for their under-age children, even though their mother or stepmother might still be alive.[143] Such arrangements came within the jurisdiction of the ecclesiastical courts. The process was not inevitably without compassion and in 1371, when the York consistory court had to name a guardian[144] for the children of a York merchant Roger Hovingham, the judge asked all their relatives to be present and

---

[139] Prob. Reg. I, f. 98 (Stellar); II, ff. 69–70 (Market); Arch. Reg. XII, f. 64 (Joan Stellar).

[140] Prob. Reg. III, f. 523. Personal possessions retained sentimental value recognised by several merchant testators. William Bank of Hull and George Essex of York both left silver spoons which had belonged to a dead parent: Bank to his daughter and Essex to his step-daughter. John Petty of York left his daughter coral beads and jewellery which had been her mother's. He had subsequently remarried: Prob. Reg. VI, f. 214 (Bank); VIII, f. 51 (Essex); Dec. & Cap. II, f. 76v. (Petty).

[141] Thus Robert Gare's daughter was servant to Margaret Marshall and Paul Gillow spoke of his daughter Agnes 'serving out her indentures with Mistress Atkinson': *Test. Ebor.* I, p. 27 (Gare); V, p. 150 (Gillow).

[142] F. Pollock and F. W. Maitland, *The History of English Law Before the Time of Edward I*, 2nd edn (1911), II, p. 444.

[143] E.g. Ralph Close of York named Robert Wilde to be tutor to his son, even though his wife was still alive: Prob. Reg. VIII, f. 117.

[144] There was a legal distinction made between acting as a *tutor* and as a *curator* in that the former acted for the child until it reached puberty and the latter from puberty until it came of age. In practice, if no-one had been named in the will, judges often appointed a *tutor dativus* as guardian.

chose two to act as guardians. In another case the judge made his appointment with the agreement of the children concerned.[145]

The majority of merchants, when considering the situation of their under-age children, seem to have left them in the care of their mothers and/or guardians. Thomas Kirkham of York gave fellow merchant John Warde sole responsibility, whereas John Gilyot jnr left each of his three children to the protection of three separate merchant friends. Nicholas Rumlay of York, however, left his daughter Joan her portion in 1442, to have without governance or tutelage.[146] A case involving the children of William Goodknappe of Hull reveals the York consistory court at work. Goodknappe died in 1504 and was survived by his second wife. He wished his brother John 'to tend to my soul, my wife and my children'. By 1509 the court was dealing with the problem of the children's guardianship, so presumably Goodknappe's widow and brother John had died in the interim. Roger Bushell, a fellow Hull merchant, was named *tutor et curator legitimus* to Goodknappe's children after he had proved he was their uncle.[147] The prospects for minor heirs were not inevitably bleak. William, Thomas Neleson's son, did not reach maturity until four years after his father's death in 1484, yet thirty-seven years later he was able to transmit to his son the estate he himself had inherited virtually intact.[148]

Some merchants clearly did not trust their wives to safeguard the interests of their children. Richard Bille of Hull made provision that if his wife remarried, Richard Anson, Nicholas Stubbs, John Green and three other Hull merchants were to have the safekeeping of his sons' portions until they came of age. William Tailor, also of Hull, wanted his curate and the mayor to receive 'good and sufficient surety in the town' from any proposed husband of his widow, that he could 'well and truly' pay Tailor's daughter 100 marks when she came of age or married. She was also to receive any interest accrued in the mean time.[149] In 1405 the cautious Edmund Cottesbroke chose a trustee to manage his estate until his son was of age, additionally arranging for one of his executors to audit

---

[145] York Borthwick Institute, Act Book M2(1)c, f. 7. Discussed in Helmholz, 'Roman Law and Guardianship', p. 226.

[146] Prob. Reg. II, f. 42 (Rumlay); III, f. 487 (Kirkham); VIII, f. 34 (Gilyot). See also II, f. 127v. (Kyam); III, ff. 223v. (Cottesbroke), 523 (Graye), 567–8v. (Clynt).

[147] Prob. Reg. VI, f. 107 (Goodknappe); York Borthwick Institute, Act Book Cons. AB6, f. 14v.; Helmholz, 'Roman Law and Guardianship', p. 225.

[148] Prob. Reg. V, ff. 212–13v. (Thomas); IX, f. 203 (William).

[149] Prob. Reg. II, f. 233v. (Bille, 1451); VIII, f. 31 (Tailor, 1509). From the step-father's point of view, marrying a widow with children could provide the capital necessary to establish a business if he exploited his step-children's inheritance: Thrupp, *London Merchant Class*, pp. 106–7.

the trustee's accounts annually. As a final precaution, he forbade his son to marry without his executors' consent.[150]

The choice of a marriage partner[151] was more usually a problem associated with daughters, but there is little direct evidence to suggest parental intrusion. One York merchant, William Shirwood, objected to his daughter leaving home to marry, on the grounds that she did not have his consent. Of more concern was the need to ensure a daughter would not be destitute, and William Goodknappe of Hull attached to his daughter's inheritance in 1504 the condition that she would only receive her £30 legacy if her father-in-law made a satisfactory property settlement upon her and her husband. If Goodknappe's brother and widow thought that the property was inadequate, then the £30 was not to be paid. A fellow Hull merchant, Robert Alcock, arranged for the payment of £69 promised to his son-in-law at the time of the marriage of his daughter Katherine, but only on condition that she should be enfeoffed of any property purchased during her lifetime. The £69 was made up of three debts outstanding to Alcock![152]

If daughters were not married at the time of a merchant's death, he might provide a sum of money *ad maritagium*, in addition to any other share in the estate. John Crull of York regarded such a provision as obligatory. He left goods to his daughter in full payment of £4 13s 4d, 'which I owe her for her marriage'. Sums varied according to parental wealth. Thomas Brounfleet of York left his daughter Alice 10 marks in 1458, in addition to a silver bowl. John Gilyot jnr of York left his two daughters £20 each in 1509,[153] and Stephen Coppendale of Beverley left his two daughters £100 each in 1485. Marriage portions could vary within one family. Thomas Frost of Beverley left his daughter Margaret £40, £30 of that in uncollected debts, her sister Joan £30 and his stepdaughter £20.[154]

From time to time a merchant would leave cash toward the marriage portion of a friend's daughter. John Gilyot jnr left £2 to Kate Anlaghby in this way.[155] A general condition attached to marriage portions, and to the legacies of minors, was that if the beneficiary died before marriage or reaching maturity, that portion would revert to the estate. The daughters of one or two merchants became nuns, but this did not prevent them from inheriting. Roger de Moreton jnr of York had a daughter at St

[150] Prob. Reg. III, f. 223v.
[151] See Jeremy Goldberg's discussion of the choice of marriage partners amongst the non-landed classes: Goldberg, 'Women in Fifteenth-Century Town Life', pp. 114–15. For an arranged marriage to a younger wife, see Sutton, 'William Shore', p. 129.
[152] Prob. Reg. v, ff. 84 (Shirwood), 229 (Alcock); vi, f. 107 (Goodknappe).
[153] Prob. Reg. II, f. 386 (Brounfleet); v, f. 29v. (Crull); VIII, ff. 32–4 (Gilyot).
[154] Prob. Reg. v, f. 271v. (Coppendale); Arch. Reg. XVIII, ff. 384v.–5 (Frost).
[155] Prob. Reg. VIII, ff. 32–4.

Clement's priory, and Adam Coppendale of Beverley had a daughter at Watton, and both were beneficiaries under their fathers' wills.[156] For those unmarried daughters not safely lodged in a convent, a merchant father sometimes provided accommodation. John Gregg of Hull installed his daughter Agnes in a house in Marketgate, at a fixed rent for forty-eight years, presumably the expected duration of her life.[157]

Beyond the immediate family, merchant testators acknowledged a wider network of responsibility which might range from step-grandparent or great nieces to cousins. John Asseby of York included the five children of his dead son Thomas in his dispositions in 1459.[158] Although a merchant's extended family network might include his or his wife's parents, aunts, uncles, brothers or sisters, it is not clear if they were included in the resident household. Thomas Clyff of York, whose parents and brother survived him, simply recorded bequests to them in 1483 but gave no other details.[159] However, Richard Sawer of York left 2s a year to his sister Katherine Robinson towards her rent, so she was clearly living elsewhere, as was Richard Bagot's father, who had remained in Yarm when his son migrated south. Richard left him a life-interest in the house he was occupying at his son's death in 1476.[160]

Studies of sixteenth- and seventeenth-century society have suggested that urban dwellers were more 'kin conscious' than their rural cousins. My analysis suggests that, of those testators making personal bequests, between 35 and 50 per cent included non-stem family members, with the lowest incidence amongst Hull testators. Bequests to nephews and nieces ranged from 14 to 31 per cent in York, 16 to 25 per cent in Beverley, and 15 per cent in Hull: figures close to Vann's 16 per cent for Banbury between 1550 and 1800, but higher than Cressy's figures for country yeomen of the 1680s.[161] Nephews sometimes became heir to a merchant estate in the absence of sons, another strategy for retaining wealth within the merchant class.[162]

In a society which regarded a man as 'venerable' once he was over forty years old,[163] but in which merchants regularly lived to over fifty, the care

---

[156] Prob. Reg. I, f. 14 (Moreton); Arch. Reg. x, f. 310 (Coppendale).
[157] Hull RO, BRE I p. 283.   [158] Prob. Reg. II, ff. 396v.–7v. (Asseby).
[159] Prob. Reg. III, f. 350 (Clyff).   [160] Prob. Reg. v, f. 190 (Sawer); Dec. & Cap. I, f. 322 (Bagot).
[161] D. Cressy, 'Kinship and Kin Interaction in Early Modern England', *Past & Present*, 113 (1986), pp. 38–69 at p. 59; R. T. Vann, 'Wills and the Family in an English Town: Banbury, 1550–1800', *Jnl Family Hist.*, 4 (1979), pp. 346–67. See also C. Howell, *Land, Family and Inheritance in Transition: Kibworth Harcourt, 1280–1700* (Cambridge, 1983), pp. 255–7.
[162] Prob. Reg. III, ff. 255–v. (Holme); v, f. 147 (Pollington).
[163] Thomas Phillips and Roger Bushell of Hull were described as 'venerable' in 1479 when they were forty-two and fifty-two respectively: Prob. Reg. v, f. 167v. Robert Hancock was so described in 1489 when he was forty-nine: *ibid.*, v, f. 355.

of 'elderly' parents was accepted as a responsibility by some merchants,[164] but in different ways. The wealthy Thomas Clynt of York left his father only a gown in 1439, 'for his sustenance', but a century earlier, Gilbert Bedford of Hull had given his parents a life-interest in two shops in Hull.[165] The dozen or so testators with parents still alive simply left them sums of money as John de Acastre did in 1401. It is less common to find a parent made an executor as John Tykhill of York did in 1395.[166] Some parents, like Margaret, Nicholas Blackburn jnr's mother, were well able to survive financially[167] and would have made no claims on their children's estates.

Siblings, including step-siblings, were mentioned in about 25 per cent of wills and, in Hull at least, families often lived next door to each other. Thomas and John Tutbury lived together, next to Roger Tutbury who lived next to Adam.[168] Some merchants' sisters were nuns: John Beseby's was prioress of Stanfield, Lincs, William de Clyveland's was said to be 'living with the nuns' at Clementhorpe.[169] Thomas Horneby of York left £5 to his widow in 1426, to ensure his brother Edmund was kept in food and clothing for the rest of his life. Thomas Doncaster, anxious about his sister's future, arranged for Richard Russell to supervise a cash pension of £2 for her over five years. John Thompson of York was more interventionist and left his sister £2 but only if she accepted his wife's counsel 'towards her marriage'.[170]

Institutional care was available to those who could afford the subscriptions to be members of social and religious guilds. Many York merchants paid for their wives to become 'sisters' of the Merchant Adventurers' Company for such benefits, and William Fox left money to the son and daughter of his friend Thomas Hessill in 1393, so that they might become a brother and sister of the Company's hospital. Long-lived merchants faced the problem of supporting themselves when they could no longer earn a living. In 1444 Robert de Yarom was admitted to the almshouse of the Merchant Adventurers' Company with a weekly pension of 9d,

---

[164] In a Coventry will dated 1558, the testator exhorted his son 'that he lyke a good and obedyent chylde to se hys mother, beyng an old woman, wych is not able to help hyr selfe well, kept wyll she lyvythe': M. Hulton, '"Company and Fellowship": The Medieval Weavers of Coventry', Dugdale Soc. Occasional Papers, No. 31 (1987), p. 18.

[165] Prob. Reg. III, ff. 567–8v. (Clynt); BRE I, p. 23.

[166] Prob. Reg. I, f. 76v. (Tykhill); III, f. 65v. (Acastre). John Aldestonemore left his mother £20 in 1435 and when she died three years later, she left a mere £3 4s: *ibid.*, III, ff. 406 (John), 554 (Margaret).

[167] Prob. Reg. III, ff. 415v.–16. In fourteenth-century Ghent various solutions to providing care for elderly parents were tried and brothers were expected to provide for their unmarried sisters: Nicholas, *Domestic Life of a Medieval City*, pp. 177–81.

[168] Further up Hull Street, John and Richard de Hanby lived next to Hugh Hanby's large household: PRO, E179/206/45 m. 1   [169] Prob. Reg. I, f. 34v. (Clveland); XI, f. 148 (Beseby).

[170] Prob. Reg. II, ff. 506 (Horneby), 603 (Doncaster); Dec. & Cap. II, f. 123v. (Thompson).

and when he died the following year, the Company paid 8s 9d to have him buried.[171] Thomas del Gare of York's solution was to transfer extensive property to his son, in return for an annual pension of £13 14s 8d, in 1427.[172]

Servants

From the evidence of the late-fourteenth century lay poll tax returns, it is clear that one characteristic of urban society was the high number of domestic servants. Of all the households recorded in 1377, one third of those in York and one sixth of those in Hull included servants. In the central streets of Hull and York, those dominated by merchants, some 50 to 55 per cent of household heads were married and about 30 per cent of the unmarried population was in service. Most merchant households had servants, in addition to their immediate family and apprentices. In York in 1377, the mercantile trades accounted for over 50 per cent of all servants, employing an average of two per household.[173] Hull merchant households were comparatively better staffed, if the tax returns are to be believed, and individual merchants might employ as many as eight or nine live-in servants, all named. Walter Frost, for instance, paid tax for nine resident servants, including a married couple, while Roger, his married *famulus*, paid tax on his own household, twenty-one properties further along Hull Street from his master.[174] Beverley displays the patterns of a less urbanised society, with a higher proportion of married household heads and a smaller servant population.[175] Some 15 per cent of Beverley and Hull merchants' wills mention servants or *famuli* receiving small gifts of cash or bolsters and bedding, 24 to 46 per cent in York, and these make it very clear that servants were regarded as an extension of the household, even after they had left its service.[176]

Servants were regularly remembered in wills with small gifts of cash, clothing or bedding. Substantial gifts were less common: like the clock Anthony Potter of Hull left his servant in 1505 or the four dozen bonnets

---

[171] *Corpus Christi Guild*, p. 25.   [172] Prob. Reg. I, f. 54v. (Fox); Dec. & Cap. II, f. 47 (Gare).

[173] Goldberg, 'Urban Identity and the Poll Taxes', pp. 199, 201, and *Women, Work, and Life Cycle*, pp. 187–9; J. I. Leggett, ed., 'The 1377 Lay Poll Tax Return for the City of York', *Yorks Arch. Jnl*, 43 (1971), pp. 128–46.

[174] The widow Elena Box's household comprised a married couple and nine other servants. See also Robert Crosse, William Snayton: PRO, E179/217/16; 202/75.

[175] The 1381 collectors recorded servants separately from households in Beverley and the data may under-record the numbers of servants and unmarried individuals: Goldberg, 'Urban Identity and the Poll Taxes', pp. 204–5, and *Women, Work, and Life Cycle*, p. 373.

[176] See below, note 179; Goldberg, 'Women in Fifteenth-Century Town Life', p. 113.

Richard Sawer of York left his servant in 1477.[177] Sometimes a merchant left money towards the marriage portion of his female servants, as he did for his daughters.[178] Servants who had married and moved away were not forgotten and the phrase 'once my servant' often appears in wills. Agnes Stockton, prompted by practical considerations as well as affection, left her servant Matilda to a friend to complete her training until she reached twenty.[179] Edmund Cottesbroke took over his servant Isabelle from his father-in-law William Fysshe. Some members of the household had an ambiguous position and, although they were clearly not members of the immediate family, they were either distant relatives or particularly favoured.[180] *Cognati* and *famuli* were frequent recipients of specific bequests,[181] and gifts to the servants of fellow merchants were not uncommon.[182]

For servants resident in the household the death of their master had serious implications. Servants were often allowed to stay on for a period following their master's death. Edmund Portington of Beverley, who was apparently unmarried, allowed most of his servants to remain in his house for four months following his death in 1463 but gave two a life-interest in a house each.[183] If he had been leaving his property to a wife or family some of his servants would have stayed on in their service in any case, but his forethought reveals the degree of dependence of servant upon master. Cash was sometimes added to a free life tenancy, though rarely as much as the £40 John Northeby gave his servant Emma Kirkeby. John Garton of Hull left one of his servants a featherbed and bedding, but only a year's free residence, whereas John Coppendale expected prayers from his servant Alice in return for a life 'habitation in four houses . . . next to St Mary's church'.[184]

Apprentices, however, were less often beneficiaries, being recorded in 5 to 15 per cent of all the Yorkshire merchants' wills which mention servants or *famuli* receiving small gifts of cash or bolsters and bedding. John

---

[177] Prob. Reg. v, f. 190 (Sawer); vi, f. 213 (Potter).

[178] John Russell of York, for example, Prob. Reg. ii, f. 68.

[179] Dec. & Cap. i, f. 171. John Craven left £1 to his former servant Joan, newly married to Robert Parchiminer: Prob. Reg. iii, f. 607 (Craven).

[180] Prob. Reg. i, f. 47 (Fysshe). William Scorburgh, for example, described one of his beneficiaries, William Sallay, as *consanguineous* and servant: Prob. Reg. ii, f. 601v.

[181] John Russell of York left 13s 4d and clothes and his best horse to his *famulus* John Turner, £2 13s 4d to his *famula* Joan Chester for her marriage, and 3s 4d to each of his other servants. He also left £1 to John Brandesby, *famulus* of John Bolton, a fellow merchant: Prob. Reg. v, f. 68 (Russell).   [182] E.g. Prob. Reg. iii, f. 508.   [183] Prob. Reg. ii, f. 595.

[184] Prob. Reg. ii, ff. 327v. (Garton), 620 (Northeby); v, f. 21 (Coppendale). For other examples, see Prob. Reg. iii, ff. 74v. (Manby), 384v. (Fitling).

Whitfield of Hull exceptionally left 6s 8d to each of his apprentices in 1479.[185] Apprentices enjoyed a different status, closer to their master's own. After all, most masters had served their time in someone else's household.[186]

Taking on an apprentice brought particular responsibilities which focused on the necessity for the term of apprenticeship to be successfully completed.[187] Richard Chase of York, who died in 1402, wished his apprentice to serve out his indenture with his wife and, although most guilds accepted widows as successors to their husbands' businesses, some demanded heavy fines should a non-guildsman marry into an occupation by marrying a widow.[188] Apprentices and servants could enjoy the close confidence and respect of their master during his lifetime, going on to act as executor or even as supervisor of his will.[189] Robert Holme charged his servant John de Derfield 'to execute his negotiations faithfully', Alan Hamerton's apprentice was to serve his master's widow well for two years, and Joan, widow of John Gregg, gave two of his former apprentices, Stephen Gildhouse and William Arnold, a thirty-second share in a boat and enlisted them as her executors.[190] The mutual regard and affection between master and servant could run deep. Robert Hancock served his master Thomas Barton as an executor in 1461 and, anticipating his own death in 1495, asked to be buried next to Barton's grave.[191]

Executors

Perhaps the most important figures at the end of a merchant's life were the relatives and friends he chose as executors. All a merchant's last wishes, his pious hopes for the future of his soul, his plans for the care of his children and wife, his support of the church, benevolence to the poor and generosity to his friends, would not become possible without reliable executors. The majority appointed their surviving spouse and

---

[185] Prob. Reg. v, f. 148v.

[186] See above, p. 75.

[187] One Londoner was exonerated from his apprenticeship to a tailor, because his master left the city without making any arrangements for him to complete his apprenticeship: *Cal. Plea & Mem. Rolls City of London, 1413–37*, p. 148.

[188] Prob. Reg. III, f. 76; *M&MA*, p. lxi.

[189] See, for example, Prob. Reg. II, ff. 243 (Patrington), 570v. (Bowland); III, f. 331 (Catlynson).

[190] Prob. Reg. I, f. 101v. (Holme); III, ff. 244 (Hamerton), 555v.–6v. (Gregg). Perhaps less welcome were the two books Lawrence Swattock of Hull left his servant, to be 'of good and loving disposition to Janet my wife after my death': *ibid.*, v, ff. 410v.–11 (Swattock).

[191] Prob. Reg. II, f. 451 (Barton); v, f. 473v. (Hancock).

then a combination of son or daughter, friends and associates, and very occasionally, a priest.[192] Associated status might be sought in choosing prominent men to act as executors, supervisors of wills and as god parents.[193]

At this juncture the strength of personal and business networks was tested as well as the probity of individual executors. Executing a will was a profoundly serious duty which could require protracted attention and last for years.[194] Such a responsibility might be handed on through a succession of friends,[195] or an executor's imminent death might overtake the completion of his duties. In just that situation in 1437, William Ormeshead asked fellow merchant Nicholas Wyspington to take his place as an executor of Nicholas Blackburn, who had died five years earlier.[196] The choice of executors might affirm a testator's status as well as a desire for competence, and fellow merchants fulfilled both requirements. John Tutbury of Hull's wife Agnes named as her executors John Bedford, John Snayton and John Steton, all merchants and sometime mayors like her husband. The resources of the merchant class were thus mobilised to extend support beyond the immediate family. Adam Pund of Hull assumed responsibility for the wife and children and all the debts of John Fox, who left him an income for the purpose.[197] Sometimes a merchant would be asked to act for several members of the same family. Thus John Ferriby of York acted as executor for Thomas Beverley and for Thomas' widow Alice.[198] William Stockton and William Holbeck were named as executors by both John Aldestonemore of York and his mother. His

---

[192] This was a fairly standard practice. See, for example, J. Murray, 'Kinship and Friendship: The Perception of Family by Clergy and Laity in Late Medieval London', *Albion*, 20 (1988), pp. 376–7, where 75 per cent of male testators named their wife as sole executor, 4 per cent wife and friends; Beauroy, 'Bishop's Lynn Will-makers', p. 30, where 30 per cent of executors were wives of the testator.

[193] For the spiritual responsibilities of godparents, see R. Dinn, 'Baptism, Spiritual Kinship, and Popular Religion in Late Medieval Bury St Edmunds', *Bull. John Rylands Library*, 72 (1990), pp. 93–106.

[194] See pp. 149–50 below for long-term charitable arrangements. William Vescy of York's will was one of the more demanding, especially in his requirement in 1407 that 2s 6d be given to each of the four orders of friars, every Thursday for a year: Prob. Reg. III, f. 267.

[195] Thomas Aldestonemore, dying within months of his brother John, passed on his executor's responsibility for John's chantry: Prob. Reg. III, ff. 408 (John), 413v.–14 (Thomas).

[196] Prob. Reg. II, f. 605 (Blackburn); III, f. 504 (Ormeshead). The execution of Nicholas jnr's will generated problems. The two friends appointed executors in 1447 would not take the administration and left his widow, Margaret, the third executor, to deal with it alone. Nicholas had left property to be sold and the proceeds divided between Margaret and his soul. She failed to sell the land and instructed her executor to make the division. However, Nicholas' uncooperative executors now refused to allow the sale and division and kept the property for themselves: Prob. Reg. II, ff. 168v.–9; PRO, C1/71/10.

[197] Prob. Reg. II, f. 667v. (Tutbury); Hull RO, D126 (Pund).

[198] Prob. Reg. v, ff. 28 (Alice), 184 (Thomas).

brother Thomas only used them as witnesses to his will, and as John's heirs were defrauded by Messrs Holbeck and Stockton, Thomas acted wisely.[199]

Friendships cemented between families, acting as executors for each other, could last for generations: Roger Bushell of Hull (d. 1483) appointed Richard Doughty snr of Hull (d. 1488) as one of his executors; Doughty's son Richard (d. 1521) in his turn made Bushell's son Roger (d. 1538) one of his.[200] Sometimes a merchant's choice implied a confidence based on previous business dealings. John Day of Hull named as one of his executors John Middleton of Beverley, with whom he had had property dealings in Beverley.[201]

The ramifications involved in executing a will could be a sore trial of friendship and patience. It was common practice to leave executors a gift, 'to bear the burden of administering my will', as William Helmesley of York put it, leaving each of his executors 20s.[202] The administrative expenses were another item of course, and one we know little about. Thomas Wilton of Beverley thought his executors' expenses might cost 25 marks in 1454, but Thomas Vicar's executors spent only 20s on tracing and collecting his debts, and a further 20s riding around to settle everything in 1451.[203] Some odd bequests must have taxed the patience and ingenuity of executors. How did the executors of William Procter deal with his wish that £5 be taken to purchase cloth for a convent in Iceland; or of Richard Bille's bequest to his servant of two lasts of stockfish owed to him and to be collected in Iceland; or of Thomas Beverley's bequest of 6s 8d to support the Papal War against the Turks?[204]

Administering a will could involve giving support and solace to the bereaved, pursuing debtors, defying creditors, selling real estate, applying to the royal courts for writs and handling family feuds. John Spicer of Hull made it clear that if either of his sons disputed their legacies, they were to get nothing at all. Thomas Cottesbroke was not to molest his father Edmund's executors and his mother was not to impede them. William Neleson's irritation with his greedy and parasitical son-in-law William Gascoigne was eloquently expressed in 1525. Gascoigne was not

---

[199] Prob. Reg. III, ff. 406–8 (John), 413 (Thomas), 554 (Margaret).

[200] Prob. Reg. v, ff. 87v. (Bushell), 350v. (Doughty snr); IX, f. 17b (Doughty jnr); XI, f. 352 (Bushell jnr).   [201] Prob. Reg. IV, f. 79; *CCR 1466–76*, p. 44.

[202] Prob. Reg. III, f. 215 (Helmesley); v, ff. 22v.–3v. (Holbeck).

[203] Prob. Reg. II, f. 309 (Wilton). In *c*. 1415 it cost John Talkan of York's executors £8 6s 8d to collect his debts and settle his estate: total value about £104: *Test. Ebor.* III, pp. 87–9, 120–2. Cf. Bristol merchant Philip Vale, whose executors' expenses for settling debts and selling property in 1393 came to £7: *Cal. Plea & Mem. Rolls City of London 1381–1412*, pp. 208–15. See p. 129 below.

[204] Prob. Reg. II, ff. 108v. (Procter), 233v. (Bille); v, f. 184v. (Beverley).

to intercept the small cash bequests made to his children because he had already 'had of me above reason in money, raiment and dinners'. Elizabeth, widow of Robert Garner of Hull, stipulated in her will in 1513 that, if her son Peter tried to defraud his two brothers, he was to be removed from the position of executor. Not all sons paid heed to the monitions of the dead. William de Barneby's widow was forcibly evicted by her son John and had to take legal action to get her house back, but by then the family feud was beyond the competence of her husband's executors.[205]

Debts could comprise a large or a small proportion of a merchant's estate, but they had to be recovered. Bad debts were particularly difficult when a joint venture was involved. John Russell and John Bolton of York, for example, bought two quantities of wool and shipped them under Bolton's name to Calais, where they were sold. Both partners died before the transaction had been completed in 1443 and 1445 respectively, and Russell's widow Joan, and her co-executors, had to take Bolton's widow Alice to Chancery for restitution of one third of the proceeds of the sale. Alice had bound the only two witnesses (there was no written agreement) in 700 marks not to testify, thus confusing the case even further.[206]

Even if an estate was not lost in bad debts, fragmented into worthless portions or diverted to the church for prayers, it was by no means certain that the rightful heirs would inherit. Complaints by heirs dispossessed of their inheritance by dishonest executors flooded the royal Chancery,[207] and merchant testators were keenly aware of the temptation for executors to abuse their trust. John Dalton of Hull, doubtless with such possibilities in mind as he drew up his will in 1496, exhorted his executors 'to do their duty as they will answer at the dreadful day of Doom . . . and to do for me as they would I did for them'. Nicholas Molde of Hull urged his wife in 1474 to 'dispose for me as I would for her'.[208]

Just as merchants manoeuvred to safeguard investments and maximise profits, so they schemed to protect their *post mortem* dispositions. In 1465 Richard Wartre of York required all his obligations, deeds and silver to be locked up in a strong chest after his death, and to be kept in the Minster until all his executors were present. In 1431, Thomas Doncaster of York insisted that none of his other executors should act without the consent of the supervising executor, Richard Russell.[209]

[205] Prob. Reg. III, f. 223 (Cottesbroke); V, ff. 450–1v. (Spicer); VIII, f. 105 (Garner); IX, f. 203 (Neleson); *MB*, I, p. 140 (Barneby).

[206] Prob. Reg. II, ff. 68 (Russell), 107 (Bolton); PRO, C1/16/592.

[207] Eg PRO, C1/22/154a, 61/58, 32/170.

[208] Prob. Reg. IV, f. 127 (Molde); V, f. 484 (Dalton). See also *CPR 1401–5*, p. 74 (Colthorpe of Hull).

[209] Prob. Reg. II, f. 603 (Doncaster); IV, f. 116 (Wartre).

In *c.* 1486, Richard Thornton of York found himself in an extraordinary position with one of his executors and possibly his uncle, John Tong. Tong had either been given or had acquired the deeds and other evidence of Thornton's possession of a certain property in York, and he refused to return the documents to Thornton. Thornton took the case to Chancery because he feared that Tong would try to dispossess his heirs. In another case, the heirs of John Aldestonemore claimed that some of his goods worth £1,600 had been maliciously seized by two of his executors, his son-in-law William Holbeck and William Stockton, both merchants and sometime mayors of York. That left only £100 to settle Aldestonemore's debts and to execute his will, and the complaining heir had to abide by the arbitration of four other merchants. Holbeck and Stockton also twice dispossessed Aldestonemore's niece, contrary to the provisions of the will they were supposed to be executing.[210]

Even when a merchant chose respectable citizens as his feoffees to use, the action was not without risks, and there was no guarantee that they would re-enfeoff his heirs after his death. John Thirsk[211] of York found that his trustees refused to allow him to use the property during the remainder of his life, and the trustees presumably enjoyed the income until Thirsk died, when they were expected to reconvey the property to his heirs. Enfeoffment to use in this manner was particularly unreliable, and some merchants with adult sons avoided problems by enfeoffing their heirs themselves. John Kelk of Beverley, for example, enfeoffed his son William of property in Bainton (E.R.) and Appleby (Lincs) in 1403, three years before his death.[212]

William Ormeshead of York tried another solution: distrusting his executors, he took the precaution of asking the archbishop of York to supervise the sale of his property after his death.[213] Perhaps he feared that his executors would undersell to themselves. William Burgh of Hull was left three tenements in Hull by Thomas Diconson in 1447 to establish a chantry for a certain John Bilton. By the time of his own death in 1460, Burgh seemed to have forgotten about Diconson's wishes, and left the properties to be sold to pay off his own debts.[214] Even when executors were not downright dishonest,[215] some seem to have been dilatory and unduly slow. The notorious William Holbeck apparently did nothing to put into effect John Aldestonemore's 1435 wishes for *post mortem* masses until drawing up his own will in 1477.

[210] *MB*, II, pp. 296–7; PRO, C1/58/125 (Thornton), 10/296, 14/25, 15/86.
[211] Prob. Reg. V, f. 484; PRO, C1/270/28.
[212] *CPR 1374–7*, p. 369; *1403–5*, p. 233; Prob. Reg. III, f. 263.   [213] Prob. Reg. III, f. 504.
[214] Prob. Reg. II, f. 258 (Diconson); f. 423v. (Burgh).
[215] One London mercer's daughter claimed that her father's executors had embezzled the will and forged another! *Cal. Plea & Mem. Rolls City of London, 1381–1412*, p. 263.

Acting as guardian to a friend's under-age children[216] and administering their portions of their father's estate could be an arduous and long-term commitment which was not completed until the executors accepted the heirs had come of age.[217] This may have been one of the expected roles of godparents. The guardian had to provide for and to educate or train the children until they reached puberty. He had to act as their legal representative and was expected to keep personal items and cash to hand over when each child came of age. Administering real estate was more complex and the expectations less clear.[218] The last act required of the guardian was to make a formal account of his guardianship.[219] These burdens were to an extent eased by an awareness of reciprocity between families, acknowledged by gifts. Within York for example, Richard Russell left William Birkhead's widow £2 in 1435, and in 1468, John Skipwith left five marks to Richard Wilde's daughter Agnes, adding that she should be under his own wife's guidance until she reached twenty.[220]

Social mobility

Few merchants acquired sufficient rural property to remove themselves from urban life,[221] but they did associate with the county gentry and nobility through government, business and social contacts. The will of John Brompton of Beverley encapsulated something of the range achievable, bequeathing cash to his cousin Thomas, husbandman of Langetoft, and appointing the countess of Northumberland an executor. She was one of John's debtors.[222] Out of town membership of such guilds as the Corpus Christi and St Christopher and St George's Guild of York, drew merchants into association with the rural and urban gentry.[223] Although the sons of several gentry families became freemen of York and Hull[224] there was not the same degree of close interplay between town and country families as perhaps there was in some other English towns in the sixteenth century.[225]

---

[216] See *Cal. Plea & Mem. Rolls City of London, 1381–1412*, pp. 208–17, for the scale of the task confronting the executors of Richard Toky, a London mercer who left five minors, and for the complaints of incompetence levelled at them by one of Toky's heirs!

[217] *MB*, I, p. 247.   [218] Helmholz, 'Roman Law and Guardianship', pp. 233, 235–7, 239–40.

[219] See above, note 216.

[220] Prob. Reg. III, f. 439 (Russell); IV, f. 145 (Skipwith). See also *ibid.*, III, f. 268 (Vescy).

[221] Raine believed that John Dalton of Hull founded a family seated in Richmond: *Test. Ebor.* IV, pp. 21–2.   [222] Prob. Reg. II, ff. 86v.–90v.

[223] Horrox, 'Urban Patronage', p. 156; White, *St Christophr and St George Guild*, pp. 14–15.

[224] E.g. Guy Fairfax, son of Richard Fairfax esq. of Walton, became recorder of the city; Robert Plumpton, common clerk of York in 1490, was a bastard son of Sir William Plumpton. *York Freemen*, p. 193; *VCH York*, p. 74; *Corpus Christi Guild*, pp. 56, 125.

[225] Cf. Chester, where members of the local gentry were active in trade and in local politics, while

However, there was a tradition of merchant and gentry association through marriage, and such marriages must often have been to the advantage of both parties. They were generally between county esquires and prominent York merchant families and occurred throughout the period. In the late fourteenth century John Barden married his daughter Ellen to John, son of Thomas Dauney of Escrick, and his granddaughter Joan made an exceptionally good marriage to Sir William Gascoigne of Gawsthorpe, the eldest son of the Lord Chief Justice. John Gisburn's daughter Alice married Sir William Plumpton and in the following century John Glasyn married Joan, daughter of William Neville esq. of Thornton Bridge.[226] It was possible for a merchant family to acquire wide gentry connections through several marriages. In the mid-fifteenth century, Thomas Neleson married his daughter Elizabeth first to Brian, younger brother of Sir John Conyers, and second to Robert Wassnes esq. of Heydon, Notts.[227] His son William married Joan, daughter of John North esq. of Bilton and their daughter Catherine married William, son of Ralph Gascoigne esq. of Bundy.[228] Another merchant's daughter married into the Gascoigne family at around this time: Margaret Bolton. Her first husband was Roger Salvayn esq. and her second was Henry Gascoigne of Harswell (d. 1457), great-grandson of John Barden.[229]

The merchant knights of late fifteenth-century York were perhaps in a better position to marry into the more prominent Yorkshire families. Sir John Gilyot jnr married Elizabeth, daughter of Sir Henry Vavasour of Haslewood,[230] and Sir Richard York married into a famous Yorkshire family on his marriage to Joan Mauleverer. His daughters Anne and Elizabeth married Sir Thomas Mallory of Studdley, and Thomas, son of Sir John Barton of Kilnsey, respectively. His son Richard married Elizabeth, possibly daughter of Thomas, Lord Darcy, and their grandson was Sir Martin Frobisher, the famous navigator.[231]

Even though ingress to gentry society was achieved by very few merchants, advancement through education was a more likely possibility. Long-distance commerce encouraged basic literacy as well as numeracy,[232]

retaining and visiting their country estates. Horrox, however, argues that there was not such a sharp division between rural and urban: 'Urban Patronage', *passim*.

[226] *Corpus Christi Guild*, pp. 49n., 239–40n.; *Test. Ebor.* I, p. 387.

[227] *Corpus Christi Guild*, p. 90n.; W. Longstaffe, ed., *Tonge's Visitation*, Surtees Soc., 41 (1863), p. 8.

[228] *Test. Ebor.* II, pp. 15n., 92n.

[229] *Yorks Deeds*, IX, p. 241; *Corpus Christi Guild*, p. 38n. See also Prob. Reg. II, f. 169: John Raghton's widowed mother married Sir Edmund de la Pole, son of the Newburgh de la Poles.

[230] C. H. Hunter-Blair, ed., *Northern Visitations*, III, Surtees Soc., 144 (1930), p. 61.

[231] See figure 2 on p. 84.

[232] Not enough for a York goldsmith who required in 1374 that his son should be *in bona conversatione ad discendum ad scolas et ad artem aurifabri*: *Test. Ebor.* I, p. 92. I am grateful to Edward Miller for this reference.

and York and Beverley, and, to a lesser extent, Hull, boasted good educational opportunities.[233] In addition, merchants provided legacies to support young men studying away from home.[234] Some decided to move out of trade and into a career in the church, or eventually in the law courts or royal administration. Merchant families had intimate and personal associations with the church,[235] through sons, daughters and other relatives who took holy orders.[236] Advancement from the Yorkshire merchant class was not as high as in Norwich, where some 10 per cent of all testators' sons became clerics.[237]

There were some notable achievements amongst merchant sons. Adam, probably a son of John Coppendale of Beverley, was a doctor of laws and prebendary of Beverley Minster at the time of his death in 1481–2.[238] John Lancaster's son Nicholas qualified as a doctor of laws and became common clerk to the city of York.[239] Robert Rolleston, d. 1450, was the son of William Rolleston, a merchant of Beverley, and became provost of St John of Beverley, while his brother Roger became armigerous.[240] Probably the most successful and famous merchant son from the three towns was John, son of William Alcock of Hull, who became bishop of Ely yet maintained close relations with Hull.[241]

---

[233] Ecclesiastical centres such as York and Beverley had many educated clerics who could tutor children, and all three towns had some provision for organised teaching: H. M. Jewell, 'The Bringing up of Children in Good Learning and Manners: A Survey of the Secular Educational Provision in the North of England, *c.* 1350–1550', *Northern History*, 18 (1982), pp. 1–25; J. Moran, *Education and Learning in the City of York, 1300–1560*, Borthwick Paper No. 55 (York, 1979); *VCH Yorkshire*, I, p. 348; A. F. Leach, ed., *Early Yorkshire Schools*, I, YAS Rec. Ser., 27 (1899), pp. vii, xxiv–xxxix; *VCH Beverley*, pp. 250, 253.

[234] John Stockdale of York left £1 to his nephew in 1506, who was attending Eton College. In 1435 Richard Russell of York left £30 to his nephew Robert to enable him to go to Oxford, and John Brompton of Beverley and John Day of Hull left rents and £20 respectively for their sons' exhibitions, presumably to Oxford. Prob. Reg. II, ff. 87v. (Brompton), 439 (Russell); IV, f. 79 (Day); VI, f. 185 (Stockdale). For further educational bequests, see *ibid.*, I, ff. 47–v. (Fysshe); II, ff. 10 (More), 58–9 (Useflete), 243v. (Patrington), 640 (Alice Upstall); IV, ff. 93 (Burdall), 140 (Gyll).

[235] A York merchant, Richard Russell, was brought up by the monks of Durham, but opted instead for the world of commerce: R. B. Dobson, *Durham Priory 1400–1450* (Cambridge, 1973), p. 60. In 1435 he left an unusually extensive library and £30 for his nephew's education at Oxford: Prob. Reg. III, f. 425.

[236] E.g. Prob. Reg. II, ff. 21 (Stockton), 397v. (Asseby), 439 (Curtas), 531 (Esingwold); III, ff. 17 (Savage), 487 (Bracebridge), 495 (Tanfield); IV, f. 185 (Grene); V, ff. 310 (Odlow), 402v. (Wood); VI, f. 185 (Stockdale); Arch. Reg. XVIII, f. 384v. (Frost); Hull RO BRE 1, p. 209; *Corpus Christi Guild*, pp. 25n. (Bawtre), 42n. (Barton); Dobson, *Durham Priory*, p. 58 (Nesbitt).

[237] If 10–11 per cent of all testators' sons in late-medieval Norwich became clerics, the scale of recruitment from the Yorkshire merchants was below average: Tanner, 'Popular Religion in Norwich', p. 58.   [238] Prob. Reg. V, f. 21; *Test. Ebor.* IV, p. 8n.

[239] *York Freemen*, pp. 192, 208.   [240] Prob. Reg. II, ff. 370–v.; Humberside RO, BC II/6/6.

[241] *Test. Ebor.* III, p. 42n. Other merchants whose sons entered holy orders were William de Appilby, Thomas Bracebridge and John Tanfield of York, Stephen Tilson of Beverley and Thomas Gare of Hull.

CONCLUSION

no personal bequests . . . no person, whether a member of his family, a friend, an ex-apprentice or a member of his household, is remembered individually with affection or care. No shafts of gratitude, love or solicitude lighten the cold and formal document . . .

Thus Richard Whittington's biographer hauntingly describes a man whose lifetime was one of social isolation – according to the evidence of his will alone. We do know however, that, in spite of his apparently friendless state, Whittington did provide for his servants during the year following his death; like many wealthy burgesses, he accepted some responsibility for their continued well-being.[242] There were no compelling social or religious pressures to encourage a testator to mention family or friends so we cannot assume that the omission of children or of named beneficiaries always indicates a limited circle of friends. *Inter vivos* settlements on children, most likely as they reached maturity, can sometimes distort our impressions.[243] However, family priorities and networks of friendship and responsibility beyond the immediate family can be uncovered in testamentary sources. The generosity to individual beneficiaries reflects a testator's living world and can identify interconnecting and overlapping groups of associates encircling individual merchants.[244]

The family undoubtedly played a central role in mercantile society. For those testators making personal bequests, their immediate concern was with their stem family – wives, children, grand and godchildren, siblings and parents. Household servants, apprentices and former employees made up a second group, while friends, business and religious contacts made up a third. Within all categories, there is evidence that bequests sprang from emotional as well as pragmatic considerations. Even the more ostentatious spreading of gifts throughout the region, in the style of Richard Russell of York for example,[245] speaks of both warm sentiment and long commercial association.

Naming individual beneficiaries affirmed their significance to the testator. The fifty-six or so people Richard Russell of York chose as his beneficiaries were a mixture of family, friends, servants, named friars, a nun, chaplain and business associates: confirming his position as a successful

---

[242] Barron, 'Richard Whittington', p. 233.

[243] John Gregg of Hull, for instance, gave his daughter cash, silverware and the lease on a house as her portion in 1431, but did not mention her in his will six years later: Hull RO, BRE 1, p. 263; Prob. Reg. III, ff. 507v.–8.

[244] Subjecting this aspect of will-making to quantification can be a precarious exercise and has not been attempted here. Some recent studies have produced tables of affective and associative relationships. See, for example, Beauroy, 'Bishop's Lynn Will-makers', pp. 27–35.

[245] Prob. Reg. II, f. 441, and see pp. 124–5 above for other widely scattered bequests.

and widely travelled merchant. Extensive circles of named beneficiaries were common amongst York merchant testators,[246] less so for Hull,[247] and uncommon for Beverley.[248] Comprehensively listing beneficiaries was a self-conscious act and widely dispersed gifts suggest an understanding of the power of acknowledging public association as well as personal affection. Thus wills could be effective vehicles for statements about status as well as legal devices to ensure family survival.

Whatever an individual's religious intentions in drawing up a last will and testament, there is no doubt that many found the process invaluable for more worldly purposes. The historian can see in them an acknowledgement of familial and social responsibilities. From such self-conscious statements, it would seem that thought was given to wives and children and to a wider network of kinship, friends and acquaintances. In spite of kaleidoscopic family patterns, bonds of affection and duty developed between stepchildren, parents and siblings, between first, second and even third families, and between present and past spouses. The frequency of half-siblings and stepchildren meant that people felt kinship with a far greater number of individuals than we commonly do today. Even a relatively uncomplicated family could generate multiple links. For instance, William Yarom of York's will of 1436 mentions his wife, sons and daughters, father, stepmother, sister, brother, nieces, nephews, uncle, cousins, godsons and their children, a consanguine, domestic servants, friends and their children.[249]

Mutual interdependence, especially amongst the middling to top-ranking merchants, is well illustrated by their reliance upon each other to act as guardians to children, advisors to widows and executors of wills. Merchants were accustomed to enjoying a degree of autonomy and economic opportunism during their lifetimes and inevitably sought to exercise control over their wealth and families after death. As the group within the merchant class with the greatest material gains, their accumulated wealth also generated high expectations of its *post mortem* disposal. Whatever the discrepancy between an individual's actual estate and his testamentary aspirations, wills record some of the testator's familial and

---

[246] Prob. Reg. III, ff. 439–40. For those naming over twenty individuals see, for example, John Aldestonemore (III, ff. 406–8), William Bolton (II, f. 564v.), Thomas Carre (II, f. 79v.), Edmund Cottesbroke (III, f. 223v.), Thomas Curtas (II, ff. 438–9), Robert Holme (I, ff. 100v.–3v.) and John Duffield (III, f. 35), thirty or more, Thomas Esingwold (II, ff. 531–2), Henry Market (II, ff. 69–70), William Vescy (III, ff. 266v.–8v.) and William Yarum (II, ff. 466v.–7); forty or more, Thomas Bracebridge (III, ff. 487–90) and Robert Louth (III, f. 265).

[247] Only John Tutbury named over twenty individuals (Prob. Reg. II, ff. 371v.–2v.), but several others named over fifteen: e.g. Richard Bille (II, f. 233v.), William Procter (II, f. 108) and Robert Shackles (II, f. 119v.).

[248] Only John Ake named over fifteen beneficiaries: Humberside RO, BC III (Ake's will).

[249] Prob. Reg. III, ff. 466v.–7v.

wider priorities, and overall they do provide convincing evidence of a class creating interdependent networks which strongly underpinned its commercial and political successes.

Marriage played a key role in the cohesion of the merchant group and might have been the culmination of many forms of association. It created mutual opportunities for the groom and in-laws alike: the acquisition of a business associate, cash and property for investment, and the possibility of heirs. Inter-marriage reinforced political connections[250] and retained wealth and commercial expertise within the merchant class.

The mingling of private and public relationships was clearly announced by merchants rich enough to pay for an obit or chantry. William Frost, several times mayor of York, endowed a chantry in his own name and those of his two benefactors, the prominent merchants Roger de Moreton and Roger Hovingham. John Radclyffe of York spread his net even wider and paid for prayers for himself, his parents, two wives, three sons, two daughters-in-law, five daughters, his brother and wife, as well as Nicholas Blackburn snr and other friends and associates.[251] Social and religious concerns were effectively combined in a single process and, whatever the spiritual intentions of prayers, this form of collective remembrance also satisfied a wider social purpose. It announced the individual merchant's material successes, confirmed his acceptance of familial responsibilities and established his status. Although few merchant families from York, Beverley or Hull established intimate connections with the gentry, they could confidently claim their place at the apex of urban society.

---

[250] See Roskell, *House of Commons*, I, p. 747 for the marriage networks of York MPs, for instance.

[251] *CPR 1391–6*, p. 711; Prob. Reg. II, ff. 90v.–1 (Radclyffe). See also *ibid.*, III, ff. 10 (More), 92v. (Derfield); VIII, f. 105 (Garner); *CPR 1377–81*, p. 550 (Brigenhall).

4

MERCHANTS AND RELIGION,
THE EVIDENCE OF WILLS

The extent and depth of religious belief and observance amongst the late medieval English laity is a perplexing and controversial topic. Religion is a social phenomenon; it has fashions and conventions as well as an inner and spiritual importance.[1] Lay piety[2] has excited much interest in recent years as the debate over the impact of religious changes of the 1530s and 1540s draws on the experiences of the late middle ages[3] to test the depth and rigour of faith amongst the populace at large.[4] Such an endeavour is beset by every conceivable pitfall, generated as much by the nature of the records themselves as by the objectives and methodology of historians. Acknowledging the 'particularism' of regional and local religious practice has created difficulties of synthesis which are compounded by the limited range of sources within which local studies are confined. At first

---

[1] M. Keen, *English Society in the Later Middle Ages 1348–1500* (London, 1990), pp. 271–2.

[2] For local studies, see C. M. Barron, 'The Parish Fraternities of Medieval London', in Barron and C. Harper-Bill, eds., *The Church in Pre-Reformation Society. Essays in Honour of F. R. H. Du Boulay* (London, 1985), pp. 13–37; A. D. Brown, *Popular Piety in Late Medieval England. The Diocese of Salisbury 1250–1550* (Oxford, 1995); Dinn, 'Baptism, Spiritual Kinship, and Popular Religion', pp. 93–106, and his, 'Death and Rebirth in Late Medieval Bury St Edmunds', in S. Bassett, ed., *Death in Towns. Urban Responses to the Dying and the Dead, 100–1600* (Leicester, 1992), pp. 151–69; R. B. Dobson, 'Citizens and Chantries in Late Medieval York', in D. Abulafia, M. Franklin and M. Rubin, eds., *Church and City 1000–1500* (Cambridge, 1992), pp. 311–32; P. Heath, 'Urban Piety in the Later Middle Ages: The Evidence of Hull Wills', in R. B. Dobson, ed., *The Church, Politics and Patronage in the Fifteenth Century* (Gloucester, 1984); N. Tanner, *The Church in Late Medieval Norwich 1370–1532* (Toronto, 1984); J. A. F. Thomson, 'Piety and Charity in Late Medieval London', *Jnl Eccl. Hist.*, 16 (1965), pp. 178–95; K. Wood-Legh, *Perpetual Chantries in Britain* (London, 1965).

[3] J. Bossy, *Christianity in the West 1400–1700* (Oxford, 1985); Duffy, *The Stripping of the Altars*; C. Haigh, ed., *The English Reformation Revised* (Cambridge, 1987); A. Kreider, *English Chantries, the Road to Dissolution* (Cambridge MA, 1979); Scarisbrick, *The Reformation*; Swanson, *Church and Society*.

[4] According to Euan Cameron, the priorities and preferences of elite religion were very different from those of popular religion: *The European Reformation* (Oxford, 1991), pp. 10–12. For a wider discussion, see Bob Scribner's review of Bossy, *Christianity in the West*, in *EHR*, 101 (1986), pp. 683–6.

sight, testamentary evidence offers us a source, extant in many regions, likely to answer universal questions within a local context; a source at once tantalisingly intimate and conventionally standardised. Yet as a source, wills have come to enjoy an almost unrivalled notoriety which derives from serious interpretive problems,[5] some of which have been discussed.[6] They cannot be ignored though, especially where they are numerous, and we are surely right to persist in refining and modifying our use of them, however many qualifications we have to make.

This study of one provincial social class[7] can offer, at best, a limited perspective on a national phenomenon. The intention here is to explore the attitudes of merchants through one aspect of urban life. It will become readily apparent that, whatever the depth of individual belief, religion was a vehicle for expressing many social concerns and for making personal statements. As the wealthiest and most numerous group of testators,[8] the merchants of York, Beverley and Hull were in a better position than most townsfolk to express whatever religious beliefs they held, to order their spiritual priorities as they had their secular responsibilities, and to exploit the ambiguous potential of religious display for self-advertisement. The extent to which others emulated or aspired to the same pattern of religious investment remains unknown. Doubtless the presence of a wealthy merchant was welcomed within a parish congregation in the expectation of generous embellishments to the church fabric and funerary largesse, though some hopeful congregations were very likely disappointed.

[5] For recent discussions of these problems, see C. Burgess, 'Late Medieval Wills and Pious Convention: Testamentary Evidence Reconsidered', in M. A. Hicks, ed., *Profit, Piety and the Professions in Later Medieval England* (Gloucester, 1990), pp. 14–33; J. Chiffoleau, 'Les testaments provençaux et comtadins à la fin du moyen âge: richesse documentaire et problèmes d'exploitation', in P. Brezzi and E. Lee, eds., *Sources of Social History: Private Acts of the Late Middle Ages*, Papers in Medieval Studies, 5 (Toronto, 1984), pp. 131–51; Swanson, *Church and Society*, pp. 265–8.

[6] See p. 71 above.

[7] With the exception of Thrupp's *London Merchant Class*, the gentry have received the most attention as a social group. See, for example, C. Carpenter, 'The Religion of the Gentry of Fifteenth-Century England', in D. Williams, ed., *England in the Fifteenth Century. The Proceedings of the 1986 Harlaxton Symposium* (Woodbridge, 1987), pp. 53–74; P. W. Fleming, 'Charity, Faith and the Gentry of Kent, 1422–1529', in A. J. Pollard, ed., *Property and Politics. Essays in Later Medieval English History* (Gloucester, 1984), pp. 36–58; C. Richmond, 'The English Gentry and Religion c. 1500', in C. Harper-Bill, ed., *Religious Belief and Ecclesiastical Careers in Late Medieval England* (Woodbridge, 1991), pp. 121–50; N. Saul, 'The Religious Sympathies of the Gentry in Gloucestershire, 1200–1500', *Trans. Bristol and Glos. Arch. Soc.*, 98 (1980), pp. 99–112; M. G. A. Vale, *Piety, Charity and Literacy Among the Yorkshire Gentry, 1370–1480*, Borthwick Paper No. 50 (York, 1976).

[8] Even allowing for the vagaries of registration, the 434 wills and letters of administration extant for merchants, 1370–1510, far exceed those for any other group in York. The next most numerous were the wills of seventy tailors/hosiers and the fifty-five cordwainers, 1370–1510. Very few craftsmen left estates amounting to over £20: Swanson, *Medieval Artisans*, pp. 156–7. For merchant estates see below, table 9.1 (p. 297).

Two matters deserve comment before we can discuss the pattern of testamentary religious provision in the three towns: these are the quality of the evidence and the nature of this enquiry. Wills remain the most numerous extant medieval record of individual expression if not of individualism. They do require cautious evaluation but, to a considerable extent, historians have problematised the interpretation of wills by imposing an ambitious agenda. Authorship, for instance, has implications for the ascription of theological changes yet there is direct evidence of only a few testators writing their own wills. The way in which the much-cited preamble of John Dalton's 1487 will was repeated by his brother in his own will of 1497, repeated again by a former apprentice Robert Harrison in 1520, and once more by another merchant Robert Walker in 1521, suggests that individual authorship was no guarantee of individual expression.[9] The standardised format of most wills suggests that clerks may have been responsible for much,[10] even though they read back the document to the testator in some instances.[11] Given such circumstances and the sparsity of idiosyncratic comments,[12] it is unlikely that we can do much more than survey the range of possibilities of devotional expression.[13] However, in their search for the fullest understanding of lay piety, historians naturally highlight the most richly detailed and eloquent testaments,[14] disregarding the more numerous, cursory statements, because those do after all make extremely short and dull reading.

Perhaps it is unrealistic to attempt more than a reconstitution of a composite impression of the pious testator, a figure pulled together to accom-

---

[9]   Heath, 'Urban Piety in the Later Middle Ages', pp. 212–14; Prob. Reg. v, ff. 483v.–5 (John Dalton); vi, ff. 51–2 (Thomas Dalton); ix, ff. 112 (Harrison), 160 (Walker).

[10] For bequests to scribes who composed wills, see Dec. & Cap. i, ff. 145 (Cottesbroke), 76v. (Petty). Alan Hamerton served at least two merchant testators as scribe: Prob. Reg. iii, ff. 265 (Louth), 607 (Craven). In smaller communities it is easier to identify scribes: M. Spufford, 'The Scribes of Villagers' Wills in the Sixteenth and Seventeenth Centuries', *Local Population Studies*, No. 7 (autumn 1971), pp. 28–43.

[11] Richard York's codicil was read to him 'at 10 o'clock' and it was agreed, by him, to be his last will and testament and he added his name: PRO, Prob. 11/11, f. 36.

[12] Cf. Dobson, 'Residentiary Canons of York', pp. 159–60, where the individual phraseology of their religious preambles is discussed. Eamon Duffy argues that the unconventional preambles are 'important indicators of the theology concealed under the simpler' preambles: *The Stripping of the Altars*, p. 326 See also M. L. Zell, 'The Use of Religious Preambles as a Measure of Religious Belief in the Sixteenth Century', *BIHR*, 50 (1977), pp. 246–9.

[13] Norman Tanner's scrupulous and 'holistic' study of Norwich, based on 1,804 wills, unravels the form and extent of lay piety in late medieval Norwich: *Church in Norwich*. See also John Thomson's pioneering analysis of Londoner's wills, 'Clergy and Laity in London, 1376–1531' (Univ. of Oxford DPhil thesis, 1960), in part published as Thomson, 'Piety and Charity in London', pp. 178–95.

[14] To the extent that the same unusual religious preamble to Dalton's Hull is quoted repeatedly as though it represented many others: Heath, 'Urban Piety', pp. 213–14; Duffy, *The Stripping of the Altars*, p. 324; J. A. F. Thomson, *The Early Tudor Church and Society* (London, 1993), p. 320.

modate every possible variety of bequest and religious intention. But using the 'best bits' of wills, extracted from many scattered over time and place, to create a single 'typical' testator is misleading. We must handle our evidence with more circumspection.

Just as Part II of this book will attempt to establish a broad context against which to measure the achievements of the highly successful entrepreneur, so we need to establish a similarly broad context from every level of testamentary provision within which to set the unusually specific and reflective testator. We can allow for many of the obvious shortcomings of wills by asking modest questions and by looking at the extent of religious observance rather than at the degree of individual intensity. For instance, instead of being distracted by their possible influence, we can accept that scribes and clerics may have tempered individualistic, pious phrases by reducing them to a neutralised form. Equally they may have encouraged a false impression of orthodoxy by leading testators through a standardised format. Enough 'Lollard' phrases crept through,[15] as well as variations in giving to different parts of the church, to suggest that testators with particular concerns could and did express them. For the rest, a casual conventionality sufficed, whether of their own or the scribe's creation.

Some intractable problems remain. What is to be done with 'empty' wills which have little to say about pious intent? Should we assume that the testator wasted little space on providing for his soul because he had made adequate arrangements during his lifetime or because his widow or his executors[16] knew how they were expected to dispose of the 'residue' of the estate, in the light of established local custom?[17] Undoubtedly this was the case in many instances, but we cannot know how many could afford an earlier investment, how many intended no further donations because they accepted the precept that lifetime charity was all that was

---

[15] These were only hints when testators referred to their 'creator/saviour/redeemer': thus William Belford of York in 1433 (Prob. Reg. III, f. 392v.), Alan del Hill in 1438 (III, f. 540), William White in 1479 (V, f. 161), Robert Johnson in 1498 (V, f. 510v.) and Elizabeth Garner of Hull in 1513 (VIII, f. 105). Some were slightly ambivalent: Thomas Carre of York left his soul to the creator as well as a full set of masses and an amulet for the image of the virgin in St Peters (II, f. 79v.), and Ralph Close, in 1512, included 'the glorious mother Our Lady' (VIII, f. 117).

[16] No doubt many testators had no choice but to ignore the evidence of corrupt executors and to rely on local custom. For complaints about executors, see K. L. Wood-Legh, ed., *Kentish Visitations of Archbishop William Warham and his Deputies, 1511–1512*, Kent Records, 24 (1984), pp. 160, 162, 170–1, 238, 288. See also Swanson's discussion of misleading 'shallow spirituality', *Church and Society*, pp. 266–8.

[17] This is one of the points made by Clive Burgess in, '"By Quick and by Dead": Wills and Pious Provision in Late Medieval Bristol', *EHR*, 102 (1987), pp. 855–6. However, in one example cited on p. 842, the testator does in fact make provision for a chantry but with no detailed instructions. In that instance we can accept the evidence of his intention as it stands without further qualification. See also Burgess, 'Wills and Pious Convention', p. 16.

required, nor for how many others, 'testamentary silence' did indeed reflect the testator's indifference. As it became the custom to link a *post mortem* gift to the choice of burial place, intestacy could deprive the church of income. Wilful intestacy could be seen as 'tantamount to rejecting the ministry of the church' and might result in exclusion from consecrated ground. If this notion was widely accepted, it gave those who could afford it a strong motive for drawing up a will of the most basic kind.[18]

Another controversial issue is the relationship between living and 'death-bed' giving. Wills are our major source for death-bed giving, bede rolls and churchwardens accounts for lifetime donations. Explicit references to a lifetime's benevolence were not made in wills[19] even though day-to-day benevolence did play an important part in the church's life as we can see from other parish sources. For instance, gifts of goods and money, recorded in the bede roll of donors at All Saints, Bristol, filled 150 folios by the late fifteenth century, too much for a single reading.[20] Ideally one would want both types of evidence for one person, but there are no complementary parish records available for this Yorkshire group,[21] and the following discussion is based entirely on testamentary sources.[22]

Although some 26 to 50 per cent of the wills in this study were proved within one month of being written,[23] not all testators were physically or

---

[18] M. M. Sheehan, *The Medieval Will* (Toronto, 1963), pp. 141–2, 232; R. C. Finucane, 'Sacred Corpse, Profane Carrion: Social Ideals and Death Rituals in the Late Middle Ages', in J. Whalley, ed., *Mirrors of Mortality. Studies in the Social History of Death* (London, 1981) pp. 40–60 at pp. 43, 56.

[19] Clive Burgess has argued that wills are also misleading on the extent of *post mortem* chantry foundations and that, together, these limitations render wills a 'treacherous source': '"For the Increase of Divine Service": Chantries in the Parish in Late Medieval Bristol', *Jnl Eccl. Hist.*, 36 (1985), p. 46; '"By Quick and by Dead"', p. 840.

[20] Duffy, *The Stripping of the Altars*, p. 335; Bristol All Saints churchwardens' accounts in E. G. C. F. Atchley, ed., 'Some More Bristol Inventories', *Trans. of the St Paul's Ecclesiological Society*, 9 (London, 1922–8), pp. 1–50.

[21] The only surviving pre-reformation churchwardens' accounts in York are those for 1518–28 from St Michael Spurriergate. York Minster Library MS Add. 220/2. Even in Bristol, where there is a greater range of extant evidence, Dr Burgess has been able to associate wills with other records for only a few benefactors. For his examples, see 'Wills and Pious Convention', pp. 19–25; '"By Quick and by Dead"', pp. 842–4.

[22] For the variety of pious giving elucidated from wills, see Tanner, *Church in Norwich*, chapters 2 and 3.

[23] The percentages are of those wills which give dates of writing and probate:

	No. of wills	months			
		<1	<6	6–12	12+
York	264	46%	82%	8%	10%
Beverley	46	48%	80%	9%	11%
Hull	79	26%	77%	15%	8%

mentally incapacitated. Perhaps not many could be as confident as William Clitheroe of Hull who claimed to be 'mighty of mynd and of hayll witt' but some very detailed and lengthy wills were drawn up days before the testator died.[24] Contemplating death assuredly prompted those who wished to do so to make a gesture towards the range of penitential actions encouraged by the church and it is unlikely that anyone who fulfilled their parochial obligations and who gave alms regularly during their lifetime would neglect to do so in preparing for death.[25] Whereas a series of complicated donations might have exhausted the strength of a sick or dying testator, a minimal gesture towards the poor would not, and the absence of such gestures is indicative of a degree of casualness at the very least, which should not be discounted entirely.

However we approach testamentary evidence, the exercise raises as many doubts as certainties, an appropriate mirroring of the dying testator's own experience. We do need to remember Peter Heath's sage advice: 'The historian who exploits wills must evade the dangers of being deluded on the one hand by statistics and on the other by impressions.'[26] The discussion which follows deploys both approaches and is based on an analysis of 412 wills,[27] through a number of basic questions intended to elucidate those aspects of merchants' belief which are visible: the belief in purgatory, in the power of intercession, in the mitigation of charitable acts, and the place of the parish church. There seems little to gain from attempting to put a monetary value on spiritual spending. Aspirations may have outstripped a testator's resources and the amount included in the residue of estates remains unknown for the most part. As only a minority of testators disposed of real estate as primary bequests[28]

The percentage of York wills proved within one month increased during the period 1420–60 to 60 per cent compared with 34–7 per cent in the late fourteenth and early fifteenth century, reflecting the impact of plague in the city. In Norwich four-fifths of all wills were proved within one year: Tanner, 'Popular Religion in Norwich', p. 224.

[24] Prob. Reg. II, f. 295 (Clitheroe). E.g. Robert Holtby of York, who drew up his will less than twenty days before his death in September 1438, but could describe the complicated devise of his property amongst six beneficiaries, or John Brompton of Beverley, who could specify over 100 bequests and the exact weight of gold items in ounces in his will drawn up less than twenty-two days before he died in July 1444: Prob. Reg. III, f. 542v. (Holtby), II, ff. 86–90v. (Brompton).

[25] It is not clear from Burgess's published papers whether or not any of the Bristol testators, identifiable as benefactors during their lives, then made no mention of charitable donations in their wills.

[26] Heath, 'Urban Piety', p. 212.

[27] This present discussion qualifies some of the general conclusions in my earlier paper which relied on a more anecdotal approach, bearing out my contention that aggregation can help to establish a broader perspective: Kermode, 'Merchants of Three Northern Towns', pp. 7–50.

[28] The situation in London was different. From the 1,753 extant testaments of London merchants, 1400–1450, 35.6 per cent of their primary bequests of real estate was for religious purposes, the proportion rising between 1421 and 1425 and from 1431 to 1450: J. M. Jennings, 'The Distribution of Landed Wealth in the Wills of London Merchants 1400–1450', *Medieval Studies*, 39 (1977), pp. 261–80.

Table 4.1. *Testamentary expenditure: religious and charitable bequests*

(The distribution is expressed as a percentage of the wills analysed for each town. Bold figures indicate the average percentage for the three towns combined.)

	1370–1420				1420–60				1460–1500				1500–10[a]		
	Y	B	H	Av.	Y	B	H	Av.	Y	B	H	Av.	Y	H	Av.
Religious expenditure															
Friars	62	71	81	**71**	87	74	74	**78**	52	78	50	**60**	49	75	**62**
Parish	62	43	55	**53**	62	61	52	**58**	66	61	59	**62**	56	75	**66**
Mortuary gown[b]	27	0	9	**12**	23	0	9	**11**	30	0	18	**16**	22	25	**24**
Tithes/fabric	49	21	81	**50**	61	65	71	**66**	71	83	57	**70**	87	83	**85**
Wax/candles	60	0	36	**32**	53	8	9	**23**	52	0	0	**17**	22	0	**11**
Total[c]	92	86	98	**92**	92	96	97	**95**	98	88	98	**95**	91	98	**95**
Expenditure on charity															
Funeral doles	46	43	45	**45**	26	35	32	**31**	56	17	1	**25**	35	0	**18**
Institutions[d]	45	57	9	**37**	44	48	10	**34**	45	55	2	**34**	28	58	**43**
Total	52	64	45	**54**	53	70	45	**56**	56	67	18	**47**	39	58	**49**
Number of wills examined[e]	73	14	11		101	23	31		62	18	44		23	12	

Total number of wills analysed: 412

Notes:

[a] Only four possible merchant wills were found for Beverley in this decade and hence were not included here.

[b] Includes only those wills specifying a gown. Bequests for forgotten tithes and fabric sometimes implied these were to cover mortuary costs.

[c] Includes each will which contained bequests for one or all of the items listed above in addition to donations to recluses, anchorites, hermits and religious houses.

[d] Includes hospitals, leper houses, almshouses, prisons.

[e] Includes all wills which specified bequests in cash or kind.

to fund their pious intentions, this analysis has concentrated upon the dis-position of moveables in wills.

Table 4.1 gathers together the crude evidence in those wills, grouped by towns into four periods.[29] It is intended to provide a straightforward overview of the evidence by grouping associated categories of donations. Bequests specifically requesting prayers, before, during and after the funeral, short and long term, have been grouped together so that a testa-

[29] This table is not intended to suggest changes in levels of spirituality, although grouping types of provision does get around the problem of changing customs over time to an extent. See also Chiffoleau, 'Les testaments provençaux', p. 143.

tor paying for an elaborate funeral, interment, monthly and annual obits, and perpetual chantry is counted as one event, just like the testator paying for a single chaplain. This has obvious drawbacks but it allows us to count the number of testators, though not the depth or monetary value of their spiritual provision. By this minimalist measure, as illustrated in table 4.1, *post mortem* provision remained consistently afforded by over 90 per cent of all merchant testators from 1370 to 1510. A similar grouping includes all acts of benevolence, whether a single donation or a series of complicated bequests to every conceivable institution in the north-east. The pattern suggested in table 4.1 suggests a slight diminution of charitable giving from over 50 per cent to under 50 per cent, after 1460. The trends suggested by the larger cohort of York wills are probably more reliable as indicators than those of the smaller Beverley cohort.

It should be remembered that quantifying such variable data is merely a way of indicating the extent of testamentary attention to religion and of presenting both the negative as well as positive evidence. We do have to allow for gradations in belief from outright hypocritical observance of the forms to profoundly committed devotion,[30] and to allow that cursory provision may have been intentional.

PURGATORY, PRAYERS AND DYING

It was a fundamental tenet of church doctrine, emphasised by the friars in particular, that most souls entered purgatory. Prayers for the dead had a redemptive value, and the benefit which the living and the dead received varied in direct proportion to the number of masses said, and the amount of offering made.[31] The laity was taught that even small-scale benevolence would profit the giver and speed the souls of their dead loved ones towards salvation.[32] Thus in a faith which regarded the visible and invisible, the dead and the living, as a single church, all benefited from charitable acts.

Jean le Goff's recent elaboration of this philosophy has encouraged younger scholars to take up many of his ideas.[33] Le Goff suggests that the

---

[30] See Susan Reynolds' comments on the diversity of beliefs and social mentalities which suggest that many medieval people were sophisticated sceptics: 'Social Mentalities and the Case of Medieval Scepticism', *TRHS*, 6th ser., 1 (1990), pp. 21–41, esp. pp. 21–6, and her *Ideas and Solidarities of the Medieval Laity. England and West Europe: Social Mentality and the Case of Medieval Scepticism* (Aldershot, 1995)

[31] B. L. Manning, *The People's Faith in the Time of Wycliff* (Cambridge, 1919), p. 73; J. T. Rosenthal, *The Purchase of Paradise* (London, 1972), p. 11.

[32] J. Le Goff, *The Birth of Purgatory* (translated in 1984 from the French 1981 edition), pp. 237–8.

[33] In particular by C. Burgess, '"A Fond Thing Vainly Invented": An Essay on Purgatory and Pious Motive in Later Medieval England', in S. J. Wright, ed., *Parish Church and People* (London, 1988), pp. 56–84.

combination of a belief in purgatory, the notion of Christian altruism which gave redemption through good works and charity, and the greater merit achieved in assisting others' souls became fundamental to the way ordinary men and women expressed their faith. What le Goff calls the 'solidarity between the living and the dead'[34] was reinforced as they were united in the *post mortem* provisions of individuals. The executors and heirs gained merit from carrying out instructions, and the testator's soul[35] and those of predeceased spouses, parents and friends also benefited from a fresh injection of masses.

Virtually every merchant testator left money to the church[36] and we can probably assume that it was for reciprocal prayer even when this was not specifically requested. Interesting qualifications begin to emerge though when specific destinations of donations are examined, and these have been gathered into appropriate associative groups aggregated in table 4.1.

Mendicants and other religious

All the mendicant orders consistently attracted modest donations from within their own towns:[37] some 75 per cent of all merchant testators made bequests, generally gifts of between 2d and 6s 8d to each order. John Gregg of Hull departed from the usual pattern by leaving money in instalments to the Carmelite and Augustinian friars of Hull so that they should receive 6d per week for five years.[38] Merchants in Beverley and Hull as often remembered their neighbouring friaries as their own. Donations to the York friars began to contract in the later fifteenth century but, even so, half the merchant testators continued to remember their 'four orders'.[39]

Few other religious houses drew in bequests as consistently. An occasional testator scattered bequests to houses throughout the north: William Goodknappe of Hull left money to the abbeys of Freyn, Greenfield (Lincs), Harfordlithe/Staxton (E.R.), Hornby (Lancs), Ledburn, North

---

[34] Le Goff, *Purgatory*, p. 357.

[35] *Ibid.*, pp. 356–7; Burgess, '"A Fond Thing Vainly Invented"', p. 67.

[36] A handful merely stipulated their burial place and bequeathed the residue of their goods: Prob. Reg. I, ff. 3 (Romondby), 97v. (Middleton); II, ff. 117v. (Lyllyng), 157v. (Blawfront); IV, f. 181 (Benington); VI, ff. 60 (Barley), 74 (Jackson); VII, f. 56v. (Lincoln).

[37] In Norwich 44–7 per cent, and in London 36 per cent of all testators left money to the friars: Tanner, *Church in Norwich*, p. 119; Thomson, 'Piety and Charity in London', p. 189. For the continued popularity of the friars in this context, see Dobson, 'Mendicant Ideal', pp. 116–17.

[38] Prob. Reg. III, f. 507v.

[39] During the prologue to Dissolution in York, bequests to the friars rose by some 40 per cent between 1531 and 1538: D. M. Palliser, *The Reformation in York, 1534–53*, Borthwick Paper No 40 (York, 1971), p. 2.

Ferriby (E.R.) and Nun Cotham (Lincs), and to the churches of Harfordlithe, Drypool, Benbroke, Barton, Grimsby and Sutton, all thereby delineating his business zone.[40] Nicholas Useflete of York left £1 each to the convent of Rievaulx and its abbot, William Spencer, with the request that they settle their debts with his executors![41] Even in York, St Mary's Abbey, St Leonard's Hospital and the Priories of Holy Trinity and Clementhorpe only very occasionally attracted a merchant benefactor. St Peter's, on the other hand, derived considerable benefit as the north's metropolitan cathedral and over 30 per cent of Beverley, 30 per cent of York and 25 per cent of Hull merchants left sums to its fabric fund. There were fewer merchant donors from York and Hull in the late fifteenth century.

Pilgrimages

It was not uncommon in the middle ages for benefactors to pay for a pilgrimage to be made by a proxy, though very few did so because of the expense and difficulty in finding a reliable deputy. Accordingly, this seems to have been more of a feature of the fourteenth- and early fifteenth-century Yorkshire wills, and some were very elaborate. William Vescy of York left elaborate provision in 1407 for at least nine separate pilgrimages to be made on his behalf to such English holy places as Walsingham, Bury St Edmunds and Canterbury. The fee to be paid for each journey was carefully worked out and varied from 2d for the journey to St Paul's, London, to 5d for the journey to Walsingham.[42] Rome attracted several testators, as pilgrims themselves, for proxy pilgrims or simply for masses.[43] John Radclyffe was more particular and in 1444 left £10 for a chaplain to journey to Rome and to celebrate mass there for himself, his two wives both called Katherine, his nine children, parents, brother and sister-in-law.[44] In 1387 John de Bilby chose a more exotic destination for his proxy:

---

[40] Prob. Reg. VI, f. 107 (Goodknappe). See also Robert Collinson, II, ff. 378–80 and below, pp. 205–6. For the identified houses, see D. Knowles and N. Hadcock, eds., *Medieval Religious Houses in England and Wales* (London, 1953), pp. 148, 166, 223, 225, 275.

[41] Prob. Reg. II, f. 59.

[42] Prob. Reg. III, f. 268 (Vescy). For a general discussion of pilgrimages and the shifting fortunes of shrines, see J. Sumption, *Pilgrimages. An Image of Medieval Religion* (London, 1975) and R. C. Finucane, *Miracles and Pilgrims. Popular Beliefs in Medieval England* (London, 1977). On the strong appeal of English shrines see Thomson, *Early Tudor Church*, p. 327, and for more general discussion see Duffy, *The Stripping of the Altars*, pp. 190–250.

[43] Alice and William Durem of York were planning a joint journey to Rome in 1391. William Kyam, 1446, and John Radclyffe of York left cash, 3s 4d and 10s to the hospital of St Thomas of Canterbury at Rome. In 1395, Isolde de Acastre left 6s 8d for masses in Rome and 10s to pilgrims: Prob. Reg. I, ff. 20 (Durem), 81 (Acastre); II, ff. 91 (Radclyffe), 127 (Kyam). See also Tanner, *Church in Norwich*, p. 125.

[44] Prob. Reg. II, f. 91 (Radclyffe). See also Humberside RO, BC III (Ake's will, in which he left 6s 8d for Thomas Ellerton to make a pilgrimage to Rome).

St James in Galatia.[45] Two fourteenth-century Hull merchants, Geoffrey Hanby and Thomas de Santon, acquired licences for themselves to travel abroad as pilgrims in 1350, but it is not known if they went.[46] This form of distant expenditure was unusual and its rare appearance in wills does not warrant the assumption that Hull burgesses were unadventurous because only two fifteenth-century testators funded pilgrims.[47] Even Londoners rarely indulged in *post mortem* pilgrimages.[48]

Parish prayers

The parish church was the natural focus for lay piety.[49] Each person belonged to a specific parish where she or he was expected to attend regularly and to pay to maintain the living, materials for service and the fabric of the church building through tithes.[50] The most formidable challenge had come from the mendicant friars, and although we have no means of knowing how many lay people attended services or made regular offerings in the friaries of York, Beverley or Hull, the evidence from wills demonstrates convincingly that merchants maintained a strong formal association with their parish, alongside an attachment to their local friars. Between 80 and 90 per cent of merchants left money for parish prayers.[51] Payments for forgotten tithes to the parish clergy and so on were part of a wider expenditure on what the Elizabethan puritan Philip Stubbes called 'masses, diriges, trentals, de profundis . . . and such pelting trash'.[52] For some a broad gesture was adequate, and prayers before and at interment were expected in response to oblations (general cash gifts) and to specific small gifts made to any permutation of the rector, parish priest, parish chaplain, parish clerk, sub-clerk and every chantry priest in the town. Richard Russell of York left 3s 4d to a former clerk of his parish and even extended the payments to be made to those

---

[45] Dec. & Cap. I, f. 87.   [46] *CCR 1349–54*, p. 272.

[47] Heath, 'Urban Piety', p. 224. These were both merchants, John Wells (1405) and Richard Bille (1451): Prob. Reg. II, ff. 115v. (Wells), 233 (Bille).

[48] C. Gittings, *Death, Burial and the Individual in Early Modern England* (London, 1984), p. 33; Wood, 'London and Bury St Edmunds', pp. 19–20.

[49] In both Norwich and London, 'the parish . . . seems to have been the most important context within which the majority of the laity . . . lived the religious aspect of their lives': Tanner, 'Popular Religion in Norwich', p. 44; Thomson, 'Clergy and Laity in London, 1376–1531', pp. 18–19.

[50] G. Rosser, 'Parochial Conformity and Voluntary Religion in Late-Medieval England', *TRHS*, 6th ser., 1 (1991), p. 174.

[51] Most testators in late medieval Bristol simply requested a service and left cash but no particular instructions: Burgess, '"By Quick and by Dead"', p. 853. York testators retained this association with over 75 per cent making donations to their parish churches well into the later sixteenth century. See L. C. Attreed, 'Preparation for Death in Sixteenth-Century Northern England', *The Sixteenth-Century Journal*, 13 (1982), pp. 37–66 at p. 47.

[52] Quoted in Gittings, *Death, Burial and the Individual*, p. 39.

priests attending his funeral to include their parish clerks and sub-clerks.[53] For others, the majority, it was important to choose a longer-term *post mortem* provision, either an anniversary obit or a chantry priest celebrating throughout the year following the testator's death, annually for one or more years, or in perpetuity.

Chantries and obits

There was a preference in all three towns to establish chantries and to pay for obits in parish churches.[54] There were exceptions in York, possibly rare documented examples of a wider phenomenon. Nicholas Blackburn snr endowed a double chantry in the Dominican friary, alderman Thomas Neleson funded an obit and reglazed the east window in the Augustinian priory in Micklegate, and John Gilyot jnr paid for an obit in the Carmelite friary.[55] Perpetual chantries were either endowed with specific rents or with a cash lump sum to be invested in property. A licence to alienate the necessary property had to be purchased from the crown either by the benefactor before his death or by his executors.[56] The total number of licences declined in the fifteenth century for the country as a whole,[57] and in York it has been estimated that most of the perpetual chantries were established by citizens before 1400. More bequests were made to augment existing chantries than to establish new ones. Some new chantries were founded in the fifteenth century however, and John Gilyot's of 1501 was the last established before the suppression. The pattern was of single chantries scattered among the large number of parish churches in the city and in the chapels on Ousebridge and Fossbridge.[58] No merchant managed to secure a perpetual chantry in the Minster, although the wealthy Robert Holme

---

[53] Prob. Reg. III, ff. 439–41; *Test Ebor.* II, p. 55. Oblations were customarily made in London, associated with the costs of burial: V. Harding, 'Burial Choice and Burial Location in Later Medieval London', in S. Bassett, ed., *Death in Towns: Urban Responses to the Dying and the Dead, 100–1600* (Leicester, 1992), pp. 119–35, esp. p. 125. See p. 141 below.

[54] The preference for chantries in parish churches rather than in cathedrals is discussed in R. B. Dobson, 'The Foundation of Perpetual Chantries by the Citizens of Medieval York', in G. J. Cuming, ed., *Studies in Church History*, IV (Leiden, 1967), pp. 22–38. See also G. Rosser, *Medieval Westminster 1200–1540* (Oxford, 1989), p. 260; Tanner, *Church in Norwich*, pp. 222–3; M. A. Hicks, 'Chantries, Obits and Almshouses: The Hungerford Foundations, 1325–1478', in Barron and Harper-Bill, *Church in Pre-Reformation Society*, pp. 123–42.

[55] Dobson, 'Citizens and Chantries', pp. 316–17, 322, York RO, G70, nos. 36–7, 39.

[56] T. F. T. Plucknett, *The Legislation of Edward I* (London, 1949), pp. 94–102, 109; S. Raban, 'Mortmain in England', *Past & Present*, 62 (1974), pp. 3–26.

[57] Rosenthal, *Purchase of Paradise*, p. 128.

[58] Dobson, 'Citizens and Chantries', pp. 322–3, and 'Perpetual Chantries', pp. 30, 32. Cf. London 1380–1415 where perpetual chantries were rare and Bury St Edmunds where there were none at all: Wood, 'London and Bury St Edmunds', p. 15.

aspired to do so.[59] Roger de Moreton jnr exceptionally endowed a chantry outside York at Rievaulx Abbey. The wish of John Carre of York to found a chantry in the church of St Leonard's Hospital was also unusual.[60] In Beverley and Hull too few perpetual chantries were endowed for there to be any discernible fluctuation, and the small number of churches available, two in Hull and two and a chapel in Beverley, meant that chantries were more concentrated than in York. In all three towns the few citizens who endowed perpetual chantries were nearly all members of the merchant group. In Hull there was a marked tendency for merchants to endow a combined hospital or almshouse with their chantries. Beverley's biggest chantry, that of John de Ake on the Crossbridge, was of this type.[61] In York citizens preferred either to endow a chantry or an almshouse, but the two were not often combined.

The size of the initial endowment of perpetual chantries varied, although the average annual salary for a chantry priest in the late fourteenth and fifteenth centuries was 7 marks ($£4$ 13s 4d).[62] In 1370–1 the executors of William Grantham and William de Santon, both merchants of York, alienated rents worth $£5$ per annum but had to pay $£20$ for the licence.[63] Richard Thoresby of York's endowment in 1405 was $£30$ and Thomas Rolleston of Beverley's, $£66$ 13s 4d ten years later.[64] There seems to have been no preference for a direct property endowment instead of cash or vice versa as land values fluctuated. The wealthiest merchants of York left enormous sums for chantry foundations from the late fourteenth to the early sixteenth century: Robert Holme $£400$ in 1396, Richard Wartre $£336$ 6s 8d in 1465, and John Gilyot jnr $£400$ in 1509, each wishing to endow single chantries.[65] Yet the intention must have been to buy property or rent charges to provide an income in perpetuity.[66] Such was the policy of the York council when it was entrusted with large cash sums to endow chantries. In 1428 Robert Holme jnr left 500 marks for a chantry in St Anne's chapel on Foss Bridge, of which the

[59] He left $£400$ for the purpose, at 12 marks yearly. He also left $£500$ to endow a chantry in Holy Trinity, Goodramgate, for twenty-five chaplains for four years, or, if they could not be found, for ten chaplains: Prob. Reg. I, ff. 101–2; Dobson, 'Perpetual Chantries', p. 26.

[60] *CPR 1377–81*, p. 458; York RO B/Y, f. 106. Carre's chantry was eventually established in St Saviour's church in 1489, the year after his death: *Test. Ebor.* IV, pp. 26–7.

[61] Humberside RO, BC III (Ake's will). For almshouses and hospitals see below, p. 147.

[62] This does not support the suggestion that testators were stingier in the north: Thomson, *Early Tudor Church*, p. 179. In Bristol chantry priests were paid $£5$ to $£5$ 6s 8d in the early fifteenth century and $£6$ by the late fifteenth century: Burgess, '"Increase of Divine Service"', p. 50. In the 1320s York chantry priests were paid 5 marks: Dec. & Cap. I, f. 3v. (Dene).

[63] *CPR 1370–4*, pp. 41–2.

[64] Prob. Reg. III, f. 245 (Thoresby); Arch. Reg. XVIII, f. 34v. (Rolleston).

[65] Prob. Reg. I, f. 102 (Holme); IV, f. 116 (Wartre); VIII, f. 33 (Gilyot).

[66] Cf. Thomas Bataill, a London merchant, who left 100 marks in 1445 to purchase an annual rent charge of 4 marks: Thrupp, *London Merchant Class*, p. 123.

council invested 100 marks to buy a tenement in Coney Street to produce an annual rent of 6 marks.[67]

Richard Russell of York left both specified properties and instructions to acquire property to endow his chantry at his death in 1435. In addition to a perpetual chantry, he left extensive bequests for short-term prayers and further property for a thirty–year chantry. His executors took twenty-five years after his death to obtain an alienation licence, and possibly would not have bothered had not one of them, John Thirsk, wanted to share the chantry.[68] Occasionally executors would find that the testator's endowment was inadequate for the scale of his proposed chantry. John Gisburn of York left £40 for two chantry priests in 1390 but his executors had to reduce the establishment to one.[69]

In Hull, four of the five chantries established in the fourteenth century were endowed by merchants, and ten of the possible eleven, established in the fifteenth century. As with burials, the parish church, Holy Trinity, attracted the most and, from at least 1409, had twelve chantry priests organised in a college known as the Priests of the Table.[70] John Gregg left them twelve houses to live in at the west end of the churchyard. Their appointment was in the gift of the mayor of Hull and vicar of Hessle.[71] Exercising patronage over a chantry was a direct form of lay control[72] and it may be that some benefactors used the establishment of a chantry for that purpose. References in wills to priests by name make it clear that some merchants had close and friendly relations on an individual basis with priests or retained their own chaplains. Establishing a chantry was one way to provide for them.[73] Thus Richard Russell of York named John Turner as priest of his chantry while John Gilyot jnr left the patronage of his chantry to each of his sons in succession, probably hoping that his family would look after the chantry and that it would not revert to the care of the York council.[74] John Carre's chantry involved four parishioners acting with Mount Grace Priory as patrons, a powerful demonstration of lay power.[75]

---

[67] Dobson, 'Citizens and Chantries', p. 326.
[68] Prob. Reg. III, ff. 439–40 (Russell); *CPR 1452–5*, p. 632.
[69] Prob. Reg. I, ff. 15v.–16 (Gisburn); *CPR 1401–5*, p. 496.
[70] *VCH Hull*, p. 287.   [71] *VCH Hull*, pp. 287–9; Heath, 'Urban Piety', pp. 210, 219–20.
[72] See Swanson, *Church and Society*, pp. 255–7 for a discussion of lay control.
[73] Dobson, 'Perpetual Chantries', pp. 36–7. Named clergy appeared in the following examples: Prob. Reg. I, ff. 47 (Fysshe, 1391), 50 (friars: Bridsall, 1392), 88 (Burton, 1395); II, ff. 91 (Radclyffe, 1444), 121 (Kirk, 1446); III, ff. 223v. (Cottesbroke, 1404), 331 (Catlynson, 1498); IV, ff. 93 (Burdall, 1476), 142 (Clitheroe, 1468); V, f. 336v. (friars: Gaunt, 1488).
[74] Prob. Reg. III, f. 439 (Russell); VIII, f. 34 (Gilyot). Joan Gregg of Hull named John Wilde as the first priest of her chantry, III, f. 556v. See also Vale, *Piety, Charity and Literacy Among the Yorkshire Gentry*, pp. 18–19.
[75] *Test. Ebor.* IV, pp. 26–7; Thomson, *Early Tudor Church*, pp. 349–50.

Ensuring the provision of continuous prayers particularly beset founders of chantries, since these could fail as rent income fell. In 1451, Agnes Bedford, John's widow, left 8s rent in Newcastle for an annual obit, but wanted her heirs to use a property in Hull should the Newcastle rent decay.[76] Once established a chantry could attract fresh investment from succeeding generations of townsfolk but the management of the income as well as the patronage of the chantry required continuity. In all three towns, the council was the only secular institution likely to survive in perpetuity and consequently became the residuary legatee and thus trustee for several chantries.[77] More proactively, the York council created an 'equipe for spiritual welfare', a permanent group of chaplains serving the chantries in what were, in effect, the civic chapels of St William's, Ousebridge and St Anne's, Fossbridge. Exercising their patronage of chantries, mostly established by former mayors and aldermen, offered the councillors of the day considerable scope for lay control.[78] Eventually the York city council found that its responsibilities as trustee incurred the city in considerable expense. In 1528 it was claimed that this expenditure was an important factor behind the city's inability to pay the fee farm. By act of parliament in 1536, the city was released from its maintenance of chantries.[79] In Hull the Priests of the Table often served with the councillors as trustees and, even before the elevation of Hull to a corporation in 1440, merchants had used the council in that capacity.[80] It may have been, as has been argued, that the creation of the corporation in 1440 encouraged more foundations but this is difficult to confirm. Indeed one proposed chantry, that of Robert Holme, provided for in his will in 1449, never came to fruition.[81]

As with so many religious rituals, establishing a chantry was a way of uniting the living with the dead, linking parents, siblings, in-laws, business partners and benefactors. Composite chantries were an efficient way of maximising an endowment. Thomas Rolleston's included his parents, two wives and one set of in-laws, Henry Wyman's his wife and parents, two fellow merchants and their wives, John Bedford's his two wives, his benefactor John Tutbury and John, duke of Bedford for extra kudos.[82]

---

[76] Prob. Reg. II, f. 418 (Bedford).

[77] See Wood-Legh, *Perpetual Chantries*, chapter 7 for civic authorities as guarantors of chantries.

[78] The Beverley keepers claimed similar authority: Humberside RO, BC II/7/1, f. 89; Swanson, *Church and Society*, p. 257; *VCH Beverley*, pp. 25, 32. Detailed prescription was a characteristic of other York chantry foundations, part of an 'almost obsessive lay control': see Dobson, 'Citizens and Chantries', pp. 321–5.

[79] A. G. Dickens, 'A Municipal Dissolution of Chantries at York, 1536', *Yorks Arch. Jnl*, 36 (1944–7), pp. 164–73; *VCH York*, p. 123.

[80] See, for example, Arch. Reg. X, f. 322 v. (Preston, 1347); Prob. Reg. III, ff. 371–2 (Tutbury, 1432); 507v.–8 (John Gregg, 1437).   [81] Prob. Reg. II, f. 211 (Holme); III, f. 507 (Gregg).

[82] Arch. Reg. XVIII, f. 34v. (Rolleston, 1415); Prob. Reg. II, ff. 69 (Market, 1443), 221 (Bedford, 1451).

One York merchant, William Vescy, left ornaments, silverware including a chalice, and linen cloth in 1407, as though he regarded his chantry as an extension of his home. At the very least his soul would be commemorated in style.[83]

Injections of religious capital in the form of chantry endowments guaranteed the presence of a cantarist in a church and gave all parishioners the opportunity to buy prayers.[84] Some were associated with specific altars:[85] in Beverley merchants paid for prayers in the charnel chapel of St Mary's.[86] All chantry priests made their living by singing as many masses as time allowed. One cantarist in Hull was permitted to absent himself from Holy Trinity in 1486 because his income did not provide a livelihood.[87]

Merchants preferred a one-, three- or seven-year endowment for anniversary masses[88] and endowments for periods over ten years were unusual. William Bowes and John Gilyot snr of York left money for chantry priests to sing masses for twenty years, but these were exceptional as short-term chantries were usually endowed with a lump sum from which the yearly salary was to be paid. John Northeby of York's arrangement for his twenty-year obit was quite unusual, providing £20 to be divided into three equal payments of 6s 8d to pay for six chaplains, for bread, and for the poor. If priests were paid to sing for many souls at varying times, it is not surprising that Richard Wartre of York was anxious to ensure that the prayers for which he donated £50 were not misdirected. His solution was to have his name and those of his parents and two wives written down on 'bills' so that all the chaplains could have the names in front of them as they sang.[89] Detailing the form of an obit was uncommon. John Radclyffe wanted two chaplains to sing daily

---

[83] Prob. Reg. III, ff. 226v.–8.

[84] There may have been as many as 300 parish clergy in York in the 1430s. Thomas Bracebridge estimated that £5 would pay each one 4d in 1436: Prob. Reg. III, f. 488; Dobson, 'Perpetual Chantries', pp. 37–8.

[85] In addition to founding a new chantry for himself in 1509, John Gilyot jnr left property worth 4 marks a year to the chantry priest of St Thomas' altar in All Saints, Pavement: Prob. Reg. VIII, f. 34 (Gilyot). See Burgess, '"Increase of Divine Service",' pp. 46–65 for comments on the number and role of chantry priests.

[86] E.g. Prob. Reg. II, ff. 86v. (Brompton, 1444), 283 (Cockerham, 1453), 342 (Bridekirk, 1457), 535 (Tirwhit, 1428); IV, f. 93 (Burdall, 1476); V, f. 309 i (Malyerd, 1487).

[87] John Thomson suggests that this might have been because northern benefactors were stingy, but the average annual fee for priests remained at £4 13s 4d: *Early Tudor Church*, p. 179; see above, p. 128 (note 62).

[88] Anniversary masses were generally popular, and in London and Bury St Edmunds, 1380–1415, were common: Wood, 'London and Bury St Edmunds', p. 14. See also C. R. Burgess, 'A Service for the Dead: The Anniversary in Late Medieval Bristol', *Trans. Bristol, & Glos. Arch. Soc.*, 105 (1987), pp. 168–96.

[89] Prob. Reg. II, f. 619 (Northeby, 1432); III, ff. 580–3 (Bowes, 1439); V, f. 237 (Gilyot, 1484); VI, f. 116 (Wartre, 1466).

vespers and *Salve Regina* for his soul and all other faithful souls.[90] Alice Esingwold, Thomas's widow, gave £20 to St Leonard's hospital in York to perform an elaborate annual obit to be 'with *Placebo* and *Dirige*, the mass of the dead and ringing of great bells; in the daily Mass of Requiem, to remember Alice and Thomas in the prayer *Incline Domina*. Each year the 10s 10d to the brothers saying the mass was to be divided equally immediately after the offertory of the said Mass, as is the custom . . .'[91]

To gather in as many prayers as possible, the town crier could be paid 'to proclaim' the obit or mass. Thomas Esingwold, John Hagg and William de Helmesley, all of York, paid the 'crier for ringing the bell through the city, as the maner is, to excite the people to pray . . .'.[92] Thomas Phillips of Hull wanted his memory revived annually through a mass, said 'with the great bell ringing'. He had the foresight to leave £1 to Holy Trinity's bells.[93] Two York merchants asked for holy water to be sprinkled on their graves: John Beseby after daily mass for one year and John Hagg quarterly and accompanied by the *de profundis*.[94]

The preceding discussion has ranged over a rich diversity of provision but, amongst the merchant testators overall, a surprising number did not specify what form their intercessionary prayers should take. If we exclude those simply leaving an umbrella donation to the fabric and/or for tithes, the percentage falls to about 60 per cent of all testators buying parish prayers. This perhaps represented the pious core.[95]

Payments to the church fabric and for tithes comprised as little as 21 per cent of Beverley gifts in 1370–1420 and as much as 87 per cent of York gifts in 1500–10.[96] This may reflect encouragement by the busier and more experienced York scribes. Testators did not always distinguish gifts to the fabric from those for tithes or from those for mortuary pay-

---

[90] He directed 140 marks to be spent over ten years for the purpose. It looks as though this was to be paid from his property in Fulford, enforced through an indenture with two other York merchants, though the indenture might have referred to another arrangement for masses: Prob. Reg. II, ff. 90v.–1.

[91] *MB*, II, pp. 222–3. In 1444, John Radclyffe of York wanted daily vespers and *Salve Regina*, leaving 140 marks for two chaplains to celebrate for ten years: Prob. Reg. II, ff. 90v.–1.

[92] *MB*, II, pp. 37–8 (Helmesley), 222–3 (Esingwold); Prob. Reg. III, ff. 215 (Esingwold), 308 (Hagg). This practice was common in Bristol: Burgess, '"By Quick and by Dead"', p. 848. In Bury St Edmunds, bells were rung during the procession of the cortege from house to church: Dinn, 'Death and Rebirth', p. 155.   [93] Prob. Reg. V, f. 493 (Philips).

[94] Prob. Reg. III, ff. 307–8 (Hagg); V, f. 434v. (Beseby).

[95] Both Burgess and Dinn believe that testators omitted such provision because customary practice would ensure prayers were purchased. But Dinn also argues that, increasingly after 1490, testators in Bury St Edmunds did become more prescriptive as they took more control: Dinn, 'Death and Rebirth', pp. 152–3.

[96] At least 95 per cent of testators who made any religious provision paid towards forgotten tithes. It was a routinely occurring item in the wills of London merchants: Thrupp, *London Merchant Class*, p. 185, and in medieval Norwich: Tanner, *Church in Norwich*, pp. 5–6. In Bury St Edmunds, 70 per cent of all testators made such a payment: Wood, 'London and Bury St Edmunds', p. 6.

ments.[97] The church was after all the sole agency for burial, and testators needed to ensure goodwill. No mortuary payments were specified in the Beverley wills and it may be that some other custom operated there or that *inter vivos* arrangements had been concluded. In York and Hull testators left a gown, often their best, for their mortuary and it is likely that this was a well-established custom. In 1509, Sir John Gilyot of York referred to his mortuary bequest as 'the custom of the city'.[98] The gown was not disposed of with the corpse and the priest presumably could dispose of it as he wished, perhaps selling it or giving it to a needy parishioner. John Bowland of York thoughtfully left his best gown, *after* his mortuary, to his friend Robert Ferriby in 1421.[99] Only one merchant, Robert de Preston of Hull, left his horse in 1347 for his mortuary, although this was a custom in the region.[100]

These formal payments represent an acknowledgement of the testator's obligations to his parish, obligations still to be met even when individuals chose to be buried elsewhere.[101] Only about 5 per cent of merchant testators chose to be buried in another parish and this was more common in York, with its more numerous parishes.[102] The reasons varied. Some testators had moved away from the parental home but wanted to be buried there, sometimes beside a relative. William Bolton wanted to buried under the same marble slab as his father in St Saviours and left 20s and six torches to his own parish church of St Cuthbert.[103] Donations to the fabric of their 'new' church recognised and fulfilled an important obligation. Merchants who settled or stayed for lengthy visits overseas anticipated being buried there and left money to their parish churches at home as well as in Calais, Danzig and Dordrecht. John Briscow left

---

[97] According to *Lyndwood's Provinciale*, eds. J. V. and H. C. Bell (London, 1929), p. 6, mortuary was to be paid by the testator 'for and in recompense and satisfaction of such tithes and offerings as he hath taken or kept from the parson'. In the Yorkshire wills, however, mortuary and tithe were often paid as two separate items. Cf. Norwich, where the incidence of tithe bequests increased after 1490: Tanner, *Church in Norwich*, p. 6. See also A. K. McHardy, 'Some Late-Medieval Eton College Wills', *Jnl Eccl. Hist.*, 27 (1977), p. 390, where she describes such payments as conscience money. In London payments to the church work or fabric were customary after 1420 and by the mid-fifteenth century, some churches had a fixed rate: Harding, 'Burial Choice', p. 130.

[98] Prob. Reg. VIII, f. 32.

[99] Together with his great kettle and a share of his arrows: Prob. Reg. II, f. 570v.

[100] Arch. Reg. X, f. 322. This custom was still active in Lincoln in 1521, whereas in Thirsk, the testator left sheep not horses: Thomson, *Early Tudor Church*, p. 290.

[101] E.g. John Spicer of Hull asked to be buried in the Austin Friary in 1494 and left tithes to Winterton church in Lincolnshire, presumably his birthplace, and to Holy Trinity, Hull, his 'new' parish church: Prob. Reg. V, ff. 450–1.

[102] Londoners could choose to be buried in any parish and of the 90–98 per cent of testators who specified, only one chose another parish church. Between 62 and 86 per cent chose their own parish: Harding, 'Burial Choice', p. 122.

[103] Prob. Reg. II, f. 564v. (Bolton). See also I, f. 99v. (Stillington); II, f. 536 (Winkburn); III, ff. 266v. (Vescy), 365 (Howme), 528 (Selby).

money in 1444 to the fabric of All Saints, Pavement, York and to the friars in Danzig for his burial there. John Carre expressed a fearful perception of foreign cultures in 1487 when he asked for a Christian burial, if he should die overseas.[104]

In addition to these familial payments, between 10 and 30 per cent of merchant testators made donations to other parish churches. For some, imminent death turned their thoughts back to the parish of their birth. Sir Richard York wanted a memorial to himself and his ancestors to be made in the chapel of St Catherine, Berwick, but most other memorials of this nature were less grandiose. Nicholas Blackburn snr[105] of York left £10 to the fabric of his parish church of Richmond. John Ferriby of York left £9 6s 8d for a priest for two years at Barton-on-Humber where his parents were buried. Bertram Dawson left money for a vestment for the church of his birthplace, at Bamburgh, Northumberland.[106]

Other bequests suggest that merchants made donations as a convenient and effective way of acknowledging family links, friendships and business associations. Bequests could be to the neighbouring parish, nearby as Hessle was to Hull, or at a considerable distance like Great Yarmouth, Skidbroke (Lincs) and Yarm (North Yorks).[107]

Guilds and fraternities

During the late fourteenth and fifteenth centuries the laity developed several complementary forms of worship, usually based within the parish church but not constrained by its parochial boundaries.[108] Sometimes these took the form of an expression of occupational solidarity, with craft guilds supporting an altar light or, as in the case of the Beverley butchers, annually celebrating a mass together.[109] The less wealthy, who could not afford an independent endowment, could share in an established collective chantry in the form of a religious guild or fraternity.[110] The largest

---

[104] Prob. Reg. II, ff. 72v.–3. See also John del Gare who left 10s to the Staple chaplain at Calais in 1393, I, ff. 58v., and 2v. (Dunnock); v, f. 327 (Carre); Dec. & Cap. I, f. 76v. (Helmesley).

[105] PRO, Prob. 11/11, f. 36 (York); Prob. Reg. II, f. 605 (Blackburn).

[106] Prob. Reg. v, f. 417 (Ferriby); IX, f. 39v. (Dawson).

[107] Prob. Reg. I, ff. 57v. (Yarom), 83v.–5 (Crosse); II, ff. 619 (Northeby), 393v. (Hanson); III, ff. 4 (Tutbak), 244 (Hamerton), 299v. (Riplingham); vi, f. 107 (Goodknappe); IX, f. 112 (Harrison). John Hanson of Hull made bequests to four Lincolnshire parishes in 1458: II, f. 393.

[108] Rosser, 'Parochial Conformity and Voluntary Religion', p. 188; Tanner, *Church in Norwich*, pp. 67–8.

[109] In 1426 their mass was at the Franciscan Friary and may have been there from the 1360s: *Bev. Town Docs.* p. 123.

[110] Women seem to have been particularly attracted to religious guilds and fraternities. For London see Barron, 'Parish Fraternities of London', pp. 30–1, and for York see Goldberg, 'Women in Fifteenth-Century Town Life', pp. 110–11.

were established by royal licence, and could own property for maintaining their religious services. They consisted of chaplains, paid by the guild, who regularly celebrated masses in a particular church for the members of the guild, who usually paid an annual subscription.[111] York had three large religious guilds, about ten smaller guilds in parish churches, and one or two in religious houses.[112] Hull had four or five large religious guilds which were for specific crafts, and about fourteen smaller guilds, of which at least twelve were in Holy Trinity. Beverley had three large religious guilds, and at least five small ones.[113]

Recent work on parish religious fraternities in London shows that there was a rapid acceleration in their foundation following the Black Death. Dr Barron[114] suggests that their primary purpose was to ensure a decent burial for members, with the full attendance of the fraternity, candles, prayers and singing. By the late fifteenth century, the emphasis had shifted as the plague-induced horror of mass graves receded in people's memories. Such fraternities and social guilds continued to be founded and to be popular. Some in part defined a social group, others a neighbourhood association. In London[115] they lost what appeared to be a continuing part of their function in York and Hull, namely the chance of sharing in collective masses or the maintenance of a light. Members of guilds in York continued to expect the brothers and sisters to be involved in funerals. William Denby left 6s 8d to the Guild of St Christopher on condition that it 'make a hearse around my corpse' in 1427.[116] Jane Neleson wanted the Master and aldermen of the Corpus Christi Guild to attend her funeral in 1533 'as is the custom', and in 1530 John Thornton wanted the keepers of the guild to be his pall-bearers.

---

[111] H. F. Westlake, *The Parish Gilds of Medieval England* (London, 1919) is still the fullest discussion. For a more recent summary see Scarisbrick, *The Reformation*, ch. 2.

[112] E.g. Robert Poppilton of York left money to the fraternities of St Christopher and Our Lady in the Carmelite friary in 1414, Dec. & Cap. I, f. 166v., and see Prob. Reg. II, f. 127 (Kyam). Nicholas Useflete left money to the guild of the Blessed Virgin Mary in St Mary's Abbey in 1443, III, f. 59, and there was a guild of St Helen in the Franciscan friary in Beverley in 1378: PRO, c47/46/446; *VCH York*, pp. 481–3. This contrasts with the pattern in Norwich where all seven craft guilds and eighteen religious fraternities met in religious houses: Tanner, 'Popular Religion in Norwich', pp. 138, 346–7.

[113] *VCH Hull*, pp. 58, 289, 295; *Beverlac*, pp. 612, 726; *RHMSSC Beverley*, p. 5.

[114] Barron, 'Parish Fraternities of London', pp. 14, 23–4. Gervase Rosser has argued more recently that the virtual cessation of new parochial creations after 1300 forced new and shifting communities to adopt the fraternity as an alternative framework: G. Rosser, 'Communities of Parish and Guild in the Late Middle Ages', in S. J. Wright, ed., *Parish, Church and People. Local Studies in Lay Religion 1350–1750* (London, 1988), p. 33.

[115] Barron, 'Parish Fraternities of London', p. 28, Rosser, 'Communities of Parish and Guild', pp. 37–8 discusses some of the social functions.

[116] Prob. Reg. II, f. 518v. (Denby). Both craft and religious guilds were important providers of funeral accoutrements and some London companies owned their own elaborate hearses in the early sixteenth century: Thomson, *Early Tudor Church*, p. 348.

Status-conscious John Ferriby, who died during his mayoralty in 1491, paid 13s 4d to four aldermen to attend his funeral as pall-bearers.[117]

From the evidence of guild regulations throughout the country,[118] it is clear that in addition to offering participation in collective prayers and some forms of welfare to the aged and infirm,[119] guilds and fraternities saw themselves as embodying ideal moral standards. The wardens of the York Paternoster Guild examined applicants for admission regarding their willingness 'to conform to the moral expectations of the brotherhood and urged members to shun unworthy activities and associations'. In Hull, the Guild of the Virgin Mary expelled convicted felons and members guilty of a string of misdemeanours including bullying, night-walking, lying, behaving as a harlot, being excommunicate or any other crime injurious to the good name of the guild. In Beverley only 'honest clerics and artisans' could become members of the Corpus Christi Guild. Members were self-selected, and these associations, whether based on locality or wealth, began with or developed firm ideas as to the sort of persons they wished to include.[120] The Hull Corpus Christi Guild was quite explicit and charged differential admission rates: more for those not related to existing members.[121]

Guilds and fraternities signalled group identities on a scale smaller than the entire town; they could gather in the *inferiores* excluded from the associations of the *superiores*. As their emphasis shifted to a concern with behaviour, they can be seen as agencies of social control,[122] encouraging a conformity to a generally Christian ideal. The involvement of some merchants in the creation of many of these guilds identifies their 'establishment' perspective. William Craven and John Kirkham, both York merchants, were recipients of the foundation licence for the St George's Guild of York in 1447. Thomas Crathorn, William Bell, Thomas Cotys

---

[117] Prob. Reg. v, ff. 417–18 (Ferriby); IX, f. 464 (Thornton); XI, f. 57 (Nelson). William Hagg paid 1d each for twenty-four torches of the four guilds of which he was a member, in addition to 4d each for the six keepers and 8d to the Master of the Corpus Christi Guild to attend his funeral: *ibid*. III, f. 307. In Bury St Edmunds, the presence of fraternity brethren similarly conferred status: Dinn, 'Death and Rebirth', p. 155.

[118] Toulmin-Smith, *English Gilds*, and for a more recent analysis see B. McRee, 'Charity and Gild Solidarity in Late Medieval England', *Jnl British Studies*, 32 (1993), pp. 195–225.

[119] M. Rubin, *Charity and Community in Medieval Cambridge* (Cambridge, 1987), pp. 251–9, 289; B. A. Hanawalt, 'Keepers of the Lights: Late Medieval English Parish Gilds', *Jnl. Med. & Ren. Studies*, 14 (1984), pp. 32–3; Wood, 'London and Bury St Edmunds', p. 18.

[120] W. R. Jones, 'English Religious Brotherhoods and Medieval Lay Piety: The Inquiry of 1388–9', *The Historian: A Journal of History*, 36 (1974), pp. 651–2.

[121] Toulmin-Smith, *English Gilds*, pp. 160–1.

[122] An idea more fully developed by B. McRee, 'Religious Gilds and the Regulation of Behavior in Late Medieval Towns', in J. Rosenthal and C. Richmond, eds., *People, Politics and Community in the Later Middle Ages* (London, 1987), pp. 108–22. See also Thomson, *Early Tudor Church*, p. 298.

and Richard Thornton, all merchants of York, were active in 1446, reforming the St Anthony's Guild as the St Martin's Guild.[123]

Testamentary evidence does not reflect the known scale of membership of, for instance, the York Corpus Christi Guild,[124] or mercantile involvement in foundations. Religious associations did not attract as many bequests from Beverley and Hull merchants as from York merchants, who continued the practice from the late fourteenth to the early sixteenth centuries, generally involving 15 per cent of testators.[125] Their popularity with York merchant testators jumped during and· after the mortality crisis of the 1430s when fifteen out of forty-four of those making religious bequests left money to religious associations, and eight out of twenty-three in the 1440s,[126] suggesting that they were indeed 'piously petrified'.[127] Thereafter bequests dwindled to the regular pattern of two or three per decade. Fewer merchants in the other two towns remembered guilds.

Membership of religious guilds and fraternities attracted the whole family. Not only were individual merchants supporters of such bodies, but so were their sons, daughters and wives. The social cachet of belonging to an association which included many of the city's ruling group might explain the popularity of the York Corpus Christi Guild whose members included clerics and gentry. In the 137 years of its life, between 16,000 and 17,000 individuals enrolled.[128] The benefits of welfare, spiritual comfort or social identity were such that many merchants' widows, wives and children joined. For instance, William Belford's widow Katherine became a member in 1441, eight years after his death.[129] Wives often became 'sisters' of the Merchant Adventurers' Company for the same reasons.[130]

---

[123] *CPR 1441–6*, p. 442; *1446–52*, p. 80.

[124] In Norwich the Corpus Christi Guild attracted more bequests from all testators than any other guild or religious fraternity: Tanner, *Church in Norwich*, p. 132.

[125] In London between 1393 and 1415, 8 per cent of the extant 1,383 wills included gifts to religious associations: Barron, 'Parish Fraternities of London', p. 25.

[126] Prob. Reg. II, ff. 42, 70, 79v., 90, 104v., 107, 127, 150, 153; III, ff. 406, 413, 428v., 438, 440, 486, 502, 503, 523, 530v., 533v., 540v., 542v. See also *VCH York*, p. 111; *VCH Hull*, p. 58. John Gregg of Hull left money to the guild of St Mary in St Brigid's church, London, and to six other guilds in Holy Trinity, Hull: Prob. Reg. III, f. 506v.

[127] Kreider, *English Chantries*, p. 86, argues that mortality crises did not encourage the growth of lay religious associations following the Black Death.

[128] *Corpus Christi Guild*; *VCH York*, p. 111; Thomson, *Early Tudor Church*, pp. 297–8; Keen, *English Society*, pp. 104–5.

[129] *Corpus Christi Guild*, p. 39. Prob. Reg. III, f. 392v. (Belford). Several merchant widows left money to the guild, suggesting that they had found it of particular benefit. E.g. Alice Brereton, Prob. Reg. II, f. 35; Katherine Radclyffe, II, ff. 375–6; Alice Upstall, II, f. 640; Marion Kent, III, f. 320; Joan Louthe, III, ff. 450–1; Margaret Aldestonemore, III, f. 554; Joan Ince v, f. 362.

[130] *M&MA*, pp. 44–9, 66–8.

Another form of lay worship, increasingly popular in some parts of England, was the maintenance of votive lights. Parish churches had altars dedicated to individual saints in addition to the high altar, and a light was kept burning over each. Groups and individuals could contribute to the upkeep[131] but very few merchants left money to maintain them.[132] Testators did leave cash or wax for funerary candles and torches, and invariably spent time elaborating on the weight and cost of each candle and torch. Some specified that the remains be placed on particular altars in one or more churches. Thomas Gra of York divided his 30lb of wax into five candles and eight torches, value 30s, between three different churches, spreading his investment in 1405 as he spread his goods between several ships. This was not an unusual request in York where over half the merchants left wax or cash for candles. This dropped to 22 per cent after 1500. There seems to have been a similar contraction in Hull where over one third of testators had been concerned with funerary lights in 1370–1420 but scarcely any thereafter.[133]

Individual merchants sometimes served as warden of the lights in their own church. This was a minor office, usually subordinate to that of the churchwarden who had overall responsibility for the fabric of the church, although John Beaume of Beverley served as warden of the fabric and lights in St Mary's chapel in Beverley Minster in 1392. His fellow merchants, William de Holm and Thomas Skipwith, both served in 1417 as churchwarden in the parish church of St Mary.[134]

Buildings and ornaments

A donation to the fabric of a church often represented a conventional gesture towards the costs of burial or the maintenance of the building,[135] but from the particularly detailed arrangements of some bequests, the testator's intimate concern and familiarity with his church emerges. Late medieval townscapes were dominated by ecclesiastical buildings. During the late fourteenth and fifteenth centuries, the laity funded the building of three churches in Beverley and Hull, of which Holy Trinity, Hull, is the largest parish church in England and St Mary's, Beverley, arguably the

---

[131] The goldsmiths guild of Beverley supported St Dunstan's light in St Mary's: *Bev. Town Docs.*, p. 40. See p. 134 above for proto-guilds and lights.

[132] Only twenty-eight out of 615 lay testators left money for votive lights in Norwich: Tanner, 'Popular Religion in Norwich', p. 359. See also McHardy, 'Eton College Wills', p. 391.

[133] Prob. Reg. III, ff. 235 (Gra), 415–16v. (Blackburn), 439–40 (Russell), 487v.–90 (Bracebridge), 606–7 (Craven); v, f. 327v. (Carre).   [134] *CPR 1391–6*, p. 150; *Yorks Deeds* VII, p. 34.

[135] Each year the masters of fabric of Lincoln Cathedral would send out nuncios to publicise the episcopal indulgences offered to benefactors of the fund: K. Edwards, *The English Secular Cathedrals in the Middle Ages*, 2nd ed. (Manchester, 1967), p. 231. Perhaps in response, Robert del Crosse of Hull left a silver chalice to Lincoln Cathedral: Prob. Reg. I, ff. 23v.–5.

most beautiful.[136] In York the appearance of most of the parish churches was changed in the course of the fifteenth century through lay bequests. At least seven churches were wholly or partly rebuilt: aisles widened, chancels extended and towers built. During the same period the York and Beverley minsters were completed.[137]

Richard Russell of York donated money for the completion of the belfry in St John, Hungate, which he had been funding during his lifetime. He also left money for the bell frame and ladder, the repair of three altars and the glazing of three windows. Bells and glazing attracted gifts.[138] William Goodknappe of Hull left £3 6s 8d in 1504 towards the building of a steeple on St Mary's, Hull, a church which used mercantile bequests to maintain its peal of bells for decades.[139] Windows enhanced the beauty of the recipient church and, apart from the famous Blackburn window in All Saints, North Street (not mentioned in the donor's will),[140] several other windows owed their existence to the gifts of merchants. John Swan left £11 for a window in Holy Trinity, Hull, and Robert Garner arranged for a window in memory of himself and his wife to be made in the cloister at Swine priory.[141] Memorial windows were not often recorded in wills and more may have been made before the death of the benefactor as in the case of Nicholas Blackburn.

More structural repairs were funded by the laity. In 1452 Richard Patrington of Beverley left £10 to repair the cross aisle in St Mary's providing that it was done within three years. Others preferred to supply the building materials: Guy Malyerd gave St Mary's, Beverley, thirty squared trees and wainscots to repair the choir stalls in 1457; Thomas Spicer gave ten trees and some stone to St John's, York, to build/repair an aisle in 1505.[142] Thomas Preston of Hull considerably left £33 6s 8d in 1451 to the Austin Friars for lead and carpentry to repair their church, and told them to keep whatever was left over for another time![143]

Maintaining a connection with a parish could also be achieved by

---

[136] *VCH Hull*, p. 76; Pevsner, *Yorkshire*, pp. 17, 180, 268–70.

[137] Gee, 'Architecture of York', pp. 178, 343–50; *VCH York*, p. 107; Pevsner, *Yorkshire*, p. 171. A similar rebuilding was underway in fifteenth-century Bristol, E. M. Carus-Wilson, 'Bristol', in M. D. Lobel, ed., *The Atlas of Historic Towns* (London, 1975), II, p. 11.

[138] This was a universally popular form of memorial: Wood, 'London and Bury St Edmunds', pp. 7–8; Tanner, *Church in Norwich*, pp. 128–9.

[139] Prob. Reg. v, f. 107 (Swan, 1476); VI, ff. 107 (Goodknappe), 393v. (Hanson, 1459).

[140] *VCH York*, p. 107.

[141] Prob. Reg. v, f. 7 (Swan); VI, f. 204v. (Garner). See also II, ff. 572–3 (Bawtre); III, ff. 439–40 (Russell). Merchants were, of course, not the sole source of gifts of windows. See P. E. S. Routh, 'A Gift and its Giver: John Walker and the East Window of Holy Trinity Goodramgate, York', *Yorks Arch. Jnl*, 58 (1986), pp. 109–22.

[142] Prob. Reg. II, f. 243v. (Patrington); v, f. 309b (Malyerd); VI, f. 208v. (Spicer).

[143] Prob. Reg. II, f. 225. See also II, f. 575v. (Wilcock).

donating an object or money to buy a specific item for regular use.[144] Usually the cost or value was precisely stated. John Gaunt of York left 20s to buy a silver cross for St Mary's, Castlegate. John Thompson of York wanted the new altar cloth for his church to be made from cloth at 6½d per yard.[145] William Goodknappe left £20 for the purchase of two altar tables, £2 for a new altar cloth and £6 for new vestments for St Mary's, Hull. As priests had to supply their own vestments, such gifts must have been welcomed, and William Baron's gift of a cope of 'red purple cloth of velvet with good great flowers of gold', and Thomas Barton of York's £26 for suits of white damask with gold fringes for the chaplains, deacons and choir especially so. No doubt the priest in St Saviour's, York, was grateful to Richard Wartre for a red velvet vestment, decorated with Wartre's insignia.[146]

'Signing' gifts in this way guaranteed remembrance but other gifts were less obviously self-advertisements. Richard Russell of York left books, altar cloths and chasubles to his parish church. William Ripplingham of Hull left books and ornaments, and Nicholas Vicars of York, 5 marks to repair several books, plus 4d 'and no more' to each parishioner.[147] Books were clearly an integral part of the provision of service in the view of several testators. Richard de Taunton asked that some of his silverware be sold to buy a missal for his wife's lifetime use and thereafter for the benefit of his parish church.[148]

Gifts of bed hangings were unusual amongst merchant testators and a curious custom is revealed in the will of Thomas Wood of Hull, who left his best Arras bed (hangings) to Holy Trinity, Hull, in 1491, 'to cover his grave at the anniversary of his death, and to be hung among other worshipful beds at the feast of St George'.[149] Status conscious to the last, his intention to store his earthly bedding until resurrection raises interesting theological questions. Other bequests of small and precious items hint at particular devotions. Alice Helmesley of York and Cecilia Malyerd of Beverley, for instance, both left jewelled necklets to be hung around statues of the Virgin.[150] A dramatic request was made by William Hedon,

---

[144] Duffy, *The Stripping of the Altars*, p. 330.

[145] Prob. Reg. v, ff. 336–v. (Gaunt); Dec. & Cap. II, f. 123v. (Thompson).

[146] Prob. Reg. II, f. 451 (Barton); IV, f. 116 (Wartre); v, f. 251 (Baron); VI, f. 107 (Goodknappe). John Petty of York left his church a velvet jacket to be altered into vestments: Dec. & Cap II, f. 77v. See also Prob. Reg. IV, f. 116 (Wartre). John Gilyot jnr supplied vestments to the Carmelites emblazoned with his monogrammed initials in gold: Dobson, 'Citizens and Chantries', p. 317.

[147] Prob. Reg. III, ff. 299v.(Ripplingham), 439 (Russell); v, f. 355 (Vicars).

[148] Prob. Reg. I, f. 63v. See also I, ff. 100v.–3v. (Holme); II, f. 2 (Robert Duffield).

[149] Prob. Reg. v, f. 403v. Cf. similar gifts of clothing and bed hangings in Wood, 'London and Bury St Edmunds', pp. 9–10.

[150] Prob. Reg. III, ff. 64v.–5, 1401 (Helmesley); v, f. 317, 1487 (Malyerd).

who wanted a house sold to pay for a new reredos in Holy Trinity, Hull, in 1427.[151]

Rehearsing examples of colourful and singular gifts might suggest that merchants were a deeply pious class, generously sharing their accumulated wealth to embellish the worship of their fellows. Lifetime gifts apart, however, it was only a minority of testators who donated ornaments and cash in such a specific manner: 4 per cent in Beverley, 14 per cent in York, and 23 per cent in Hull.[152]

Final rites

Concern for a decent burial was an important force behind the emergence of religious guilds in the fourteenth century, reflecting the belief in the continued association of the soul and body. A churchyard was preferred as a collective place where souls awaited judgement.[153] Burial inside the church was reserved for the elite[154] and 90 per cent of merchant testators asked to be buried in their own parish church,[155] sometimes in front of a specific altar. A dwindling percentage left their final resting place to 'wherever God wills'.[156] In Hull, between 65 per cent and 75 per cent chose Holy Trinity over the lesser chapel of St Mary's, and in Beverley 85 per cent chose St Mary's over St John's between 1370 and 1420. Thereafter choices between the two were more or less equal. In

---

[151] Prob. Reg. II, f. 523.

[152] Between 1380 and 1415, 4 per cent of London testators made such bequests: Wood, 'London and Bury St Edmunds', p. 7.

[153] Bossy, *Christianity in the West*, pp. 30–1. For a discussion of the church's evolving attitude towards the unity of corporeal remains and the soul, see E. A. R. Brown, 'Death and the Human Body in the Later Middle Ages: The Legislation of Boniface VIII on the Division of the Corpse', *Viator*, 12 (1981), pp. 221–70.

[154] Finucane, 'Sacred Corpse, Profane Carrion', pp. 43, 56; R. Dinn, '"Monuments Answerable to Men's Worth': Burial Patterns, Social Status and Gender in Late Medieval Bury St Edmunds', *Jnl Eccl. Hist.*, 46 (1996), p. 247.

[155] Heath, 'Urban Piety', p. 215. Prob. Reg. II, f. 494 (Petyclerk). In Norwich eight or nine out of ten sought burial in their own parish church: Tanner, *Church in Norwich*, pp. 11–12. The same pattern was observed in London and Bury St Edmunds: Wood, 'London and Bury St Edmunds', p. 4. In contrast, many of the nobility sought burial in a religious house: Rosenthal, *Purchase of Paradise*, pp. 82, 85, 92. The Yorkshire gentry on the other hand showed a marked preference for a parochial burial: Vale, *Piety, Charity and Literary Among the Yorkshire Gentry*, pp. 8–9.

[156] The percentages to be buried 'wherever' were:

	York	Beverley	Hull
1370–1420	15	7	0
1420–60	7	0	3
1460–1500	2	0	11

York, with a greater number of parishes, the pattern of burials reflected the pattern of residence, with most merchants living in the central parishes. Several expected to die while away from home. John Yarom and John Grantham, both of York, were taken ill in London and had to be buried there in 1347 and 1391 respectively. Alexander Wharton of Hull died in London in 1506 and wanted to be buried in St Mary Magdalen, Old Fish Street. John Aton of York, however, wanted to be buried in Holy Trinity, Hull, in 1394, for no apparent reason, and had perhaps been born in Hull.[157] Only 4 per cent sought burial in a friary compared to the 10 per cent of all testators in Norwich, whose preference for a mendicant burial created tension between the parish clergy and the friars.[158] Robert Goldyng of Hull's choice of the Charterhouse in 1453 was unusual, but his uncle was the prior. The Franciscans were marginally the most popular for burials in York and Beverley, the Austin friars in Hull.[159]

Families expected to be buried together in the same church. John de Acastre of York left 40s to the fabric of his church on condition that no-one else was buried in his tomb, but Robert Howell wanted to be buried as close as possible to his wife Margaret in Holy Trinity.[160] In death, all manner of relationships could be accommodated in the tomb as they were in combined chantries.

A minority of merchants addressed the matter of their tombs and, of those who did, few aspired to greater glory than a marble slab. Thomas Rolleston of Beverley left 10 marks for one in 1415,[161] John Braithwait of York, or maybe his widow on her own initiative, paid £20 in 1471 for a stone cross to his memory in Thursdaymarket.[162] Elias Casse of Beverley was a businessman to the last and he left 20s to St Mary's, Beverley, in 1501 for a 'proper' tombstone, but the money was to be halved if no tombstone were provided.[163]

It was not necessarily the burial itself which was significant in the

---

[157] Prob. Reg. I, ff. 69 (Aton), 45 (Grantham); VI, f. 216 (Wharton); Arch. Reg. X, f. 320 (Yarom).

[158] Tanner, *Church in Norwich*, pp. 11–13. Perhaps 3 per cent of the testators whose wills were enrolled in the London Court of Hustings requested burial in a friary: Harding, 'Burial Choice', p. 124.

[159] Prob. Reg. II, f. 285. See also, for instance, Thomas Preston with the Austin Friary in Hull (II, f. 225); Thomas Rolleston and Stephen Coppendale with the Franciscans in Beverley (Arch. Reg. XVIII, ff. 34v., 354); William Appilby with the Austin Friars in York (Prob. Reg. I, f. 3v.); John Wakeman with the Carmelites in York (II, f. 659); William Ireby with the Dominicans in York (I, f. 55v.). Their popularity did not apparently diminish: John Crull in 1482, John Skelton in 1487 and Thomas Scotton in 1503, still chose a mendicant burial: Prob. Reg. V, ff. 29v. (Crull), 298v. (Skelton); VI, f. 60 (Scotton).

[160] Prob. Reg. III, f. 65v. (Acastre, 1401); VIII, f. 109v. (Howell, written 1513). Cf. London: Harding, 'Burial Choice', p. 127.

[161] Arch. Reg. XVIII, f. 34v. Stephen Coppendale, an armigerous member of the extensive Beverley mercantile family, wanted a slab with his arms carved upon it in 1486: Prob. Reg. V, f. 271.

[162] *MB*, II, p. 100.   [163] Prob. Reg. VI, f. 12a (Casse).

middle ages but rather the funeral, the services and rituals which preceded the interment. The funeral incorporated the laying out of the corpse, the religious services, prayers of the mourners, carrying of candles and tapers, and distribution of doles to the poor. It 'provided multiple intercession for the testator's soul and a sharing of the burden of sorrow for the bereaved. The funeral harmonised these twin functions to provide comfort for the dying testator and his family.' Extending over the seven days following interment, the funeral encouraged the notion of death as a process.[164]

Funerals were usually conducted by the parish priest, but some testators did have their own familiar and favourite priests. Nicholas Blackburn snr wanted Sir Gilbert Gyghley to officiate at his funeral in 1432.[165] The proceedings were accompanied by as many intercessionary candles and prayers as possible. To that end it was a common practice to leave wax or cash to buy candles and torches[166] to burn during the funeral: that is throughout the whole period of mourning, the interment and until the 'eighten day'. This was a popular final day and might warrant fresh candles.[167] Those merchants who specified masses were content with one mass and, less commonly, one or two trentals: thirty requiem masses celebrated in quick succession.[168] William Clitheroe of Hull was exceptional in paying for nine, in groups of three, two groups dedicated to the Trinity and to the Virgin Mary, and the third to be requiem masses.[169]

It was especially meritorious to be associated with the poor and, for merchants wishing to maximise the impact of intercessionary prayers, poor men and women could be incorporated into the funeral as an appropriate backdrop. It was customary to select twelve or thirteen, an echo of the Last Supper, to serve as attendants or torchbearers. Detailed specifications were given: 4 yds of cloth per gown, russet and white gowns, black caps and so forth, to ensure that the spectacle expressed both

---

[164] Gittings, *Death, Burial and the Individual*, pp. 23–4. See also Dinn, 'Death and Rebirth', pp. 154–65 for an excellent description of funeral and burial rites.

[165] Gittings, *Death, Burial and the Individual*, p. 29; Prob. Reg. II, f. 605.

[166] There was no standard amount. E.g., William Winkburn left 90 lb in 1438 and Thomas Hykson 5 lb in 1503. Prob. Reg. II, f. 536 (Winkburn); VI, f. 76v. (Hykson).

[167] E.g. Prob. Reg. II, ff. 365 (Holme, 1433), 439 (Russell, 1435); III, ff. 503 (Ormeshead, 1437), 540 (Bedale, 1438); II, ff. 211–12 (Holme, 1448); V, f. 424v. (Marshall, 1492); Dec. & Cap. II, f. 43 (Elwald, 1505).

[168] St Gregory's mass was sometimes specified, perhaps because it was relatively cheap: Prob. Reg. II, ff. 34–5 (Kirke), 364 (Danby). It was popular elsewhere. See Wood, 'London and Bury St Edmunds', p. 13; Dinn, 'Death and Rebirth', p. 164. Duffy, *The Stripping of the Altars*, pp. 368–9 describes the order of service in detail.

[169] Prob. Reg. II, ff. 295–v. (Clitheroe). Cf. a John Derlyngton of London who wanted four trentals, a chantry priest for one year and 1,000 other masses! Wood, 'London and Bury St Edmunds', p. 12; London Guildhall Libr. MS 1403, ff. 5–v. For similar practices, see C. W. Foster, ed., *Lincoln Wills Registered in the District Probate Registry at Lincoln, I*, Lincoln Rec. Soc., 6 (1914), pp. 245–7.

the drama of the occasion and the quality of the testator.[170] They were sometimes paid with cash or food or by being allowed to keep the funeral garments provided. Handing out cash doles or food to all paupers praying for the testator or attending his funeral was another custom,[171] although it could not have been easy for executors to sort out the poor from the rest of the crowd. York merchants, in particular, left money to buy bread or cloth for a funeral distribution.[172] This was one way of enticing as many people as possible to attend and pray, and William de Helmesley left 100s to be distributed, 1d each, to all the paupers who attended his funeral. Another was to hand out cash to 'each priest celebrating', whether beside the hearse or in their own chapels was rarely specified.[173]

The details of garments, black, white and russet gowns and caps, to be worn by pauper attendants, suggest that some merchants had a clear vision of poor men, occasionally women and even children, decked out as actors in a dramatic setting.[174] One or two merchants had more elaborate funeral plans, a possibility positively rejected by many Londoners.[175] Thomas Wilton of Beverley wanted virtually all the members of St John's staff, the chancellor, sacrist, precentor, seven parsons, nine vicars, nine chaplains, eight clerks, the two treasurers and eight choristers to sing a mass for him at his funeral for 7s 8d divided between them. He also left 13s 4d for the bells to be rung.[176] Although such splendour was excep-

---

[170] Duffy, *The Stripping of the Altars*, pp. 361–2. Dinn, 'Death and Rebirth', pp. 155–6. For York examples, see Prob. Reg. II, ff. 79v. (Carre, 1444), 83–4 (Girlington, 1444), 451 (Barton, 1461), 494 (Petyclerk, 1426), 531–2 (Esingwold, 1428); III, ff. 406–8 (Aldestonemore, 1435), 487–90 (Bracebridge, 1437), 523 (Graye, 1438), 567 (Clynt, 1439), 580–3 (Bowes, 1439), 599v.–600 (Esingwold, 1440); IV, ff. 115–16 (Wartre, 1466), (Scauceby, 1471); V, ff. 328 (Carre, 1488), 473v. (Hancock, 1496); VIII, ff. 32–4 (Gilyot, 1510). For Beverley examples, see Humberside RO BC III (Ake, 1398); Prob. Reg. II, f. 76v. (Caldbeck, 1443); IV, f. 96v. (Middleton, 1475); V, f. 99 (Jackson, 1480). For a Hull example, see Prob. Reg. V, f. 383v. (Coppendale, 1490).

[171] This practice was extolled by one contemporary, who argued that the fashion for self-abasing funerals defrauded the poor of their rightful expectation of doles: P. H. Barnum, ed., *Dives and Pauper*, I, EETS OS, 275 (1976), pp. 213–17.

[172] See, for example, Prob. Reg. I, ff. 15v.–16 (Gisburn, 1390), 50 (Bridsall, 1393), 55v. (Burton, 1393); II, ff. 34–5 (Kirk, 1442), 378–80 (Collinson, 1458); III, ff. 439–40 (Russell); IV, f. 53 (Kent, 1468); V, ff. 310 (Odlow, 1487), 478 (Harper, 1496), 500v. (Scot, 1497); VIII, f. 32 (Gilyot); Dec. & Cap. II, f. 43 (Elwald, 1505).

[173] Gittings, *Death, Burial and the Individual*, pp. 26–9. In Richard Russell's will, he anticipated that each priest would be attended by his clerk and sub-clerk: *Test. Ebor.* II, p. 55. See also e.g. Prob. Reg. I, f. 96v. (Crome); III, ff. 92v. (Derfield), 215 (Helmesley).

[174] John Hagg paid 1d to five children to attend his corpse dressed in surplices: Prob. Reg. III, f. 307. Black, white and russet were universally popular colours: Dinn, 'Death and Rebirth', p. 155.

[175] This seems to have been a theme amongst a handful of London merchants, from the late fourteenth to the early sixteenth centuries, who preferred a modest display as a symbol of proper Christian humility: J. A. F. Thomson, 'Wealth, Poverty and Mercantile Ethics in Late Medieval London', in J-P. Genet and N. Bulst, eds., *La ville, la bourgeoisie et la genèse de l'état moderne (XIIᵉ–XVIIIᵉ siècles)* (Paris, 1988), p. 270. Wood, 'London and Bury St Edmunds', p. 5.

[176] Prob. Reg. II, f. 309 (Wilton). Elaborate funerals were more common amongst the nobility

tional, there is scant evidence of a self-conscious rejection of funerary excess. John Fitling is the only merchant testator found who asked his executors to eschew vainglory in his funeral arrangements, and to do only what was necessary for the praise of God.[177] The majority of Yorkshire merchants left their funeral arrangements to their executors with no hint of the tension 'between a strong sense of personal status and idealised humility'.[178]

An individual would be remembered after a dramatic funeral, and even more particularly if a funeral feast was provided. William Vescy, Bertram Dawson and John Beseby, all of York, left money for 'the calling of friends'.[179] Guy Malyerd and John Ashton of Beverley both left money for future memorial bibulation: Ashton, a mercer, left 6 gallons of wine in 1460 to his fellow mercers to drink on Rogation Day, and Malyerd 10s to the aldermen and fellows of his guild in 1486 for three similar occasions.[180]

CHARITY

No distinction was made in the middle ages between alms and gifts for prayers to religious institutions. The same outcome was anticipated.[181] The remarkable window depicting the Seven Corporeal Acts of Mercy and the adjacent 'Prick of Conscience' window in All Saints, North Street, York, provided a constant reminder of the works of mercy expected of the congregation and of the horrific inevitability of the day of judgement.[182] It was the act of giving that was thought to be important, engendered by a reciprocal acceptance that giving brought spiritual merit, and it has been argued recently that 'charity was a central preoccupation for medieval men and women'.[183] For the majority, that may

---

towards the end of the fifteenth century. In 1489, £1,038 was spent on the funeral of Henry, fourth earl of Northumberland: Gittings, *Death, Burial and the Individual*, pp. 25–6. See also Carpenter, 'Religion of the Gentry', p. 61.

[177] Prob. Reg. III, ff. 284v.–5.

[178] Thomson, 'Mercantile Ethics', p. 271. Robert Dinn noted a 'marked tendency' towards detailing the funeral arrangements in wills from the 1490s, suggesting a desire for greater personal control: 'Death and Rebirth', p. 153.

[179] Prob. Reg. III, f. 266v. (Vescy); IX, f. 39v. (Dawson); XI, f. 147 (Beseby). See also *ibid.*, I, f. 96v. (Eva Crome); II, f. 68 (Russell); III, ff. 72(i)v. (Chartres), 235 (Gra), 254v.–5v., 365 (Holme); VIII, f. 98 (Harper); and see Dinn, 'Death and Rebirth', p. 157.

[180] Prob. Reg. IV, f. 148 (Ashton); V, f. 309v. (Malyerd). Jayne Harper specified spices and ale to be served at her wake: *Test. Ebor.* V, pp. 36–7 (1513).

[181] Duffy, *The Stripping of the Altars*, pp. 357–68; Swanson, *Church and Society*, pp. 300–8; Thomson, *Early Tudor Church*, p. 334; Vale, *Piety, Charity and Literacy Among the Yorkshire Gentry*, p. 28.

[182] *RCHMYork*, III, p. 8, plates 103, 111–13; Duffy, *The Stripping of the Altars*, pp. 357–68; D. Pearsall, *Piers Plowman by William Langland: An Edition of the C Text* (London, 1978), p. 162.

[183] Rubin, *Charity and Community*, p. 1.

have been true at intervals during their lives, and should have been press-ingly so as they took stock of their life's endeavours and spritual future. It is surprising, therefore, how many merchants made no specific provi-sion for charitable donations in their wills, even though their accumu-lated wealth was routinely dispersed amongst family and friends. Mercantile benevolence has been seen as a manipulative tool, deployed to achieve selfish social and economic goals,[184] but the attitude of many merchants perhaps was rather one of indifference, and the pattern of their giving replicated that of other groups in society.[185] One might argue about the political construction of the ideal and the designation of appropriate forms of benevolence, but the main difference between mer-chants and other groups was one of scale. Merchants were more likely to spend more because they had more to spend.

Without lay donations, a range of charitable welfare would have been more difficult to sustain. The laity supported the guilds' care of the needy and individuals' direct gifts to the poor were considerable. Professor Jordan estimated that in early-modern London, the merchant group comprised 36 per cent of all charitable donors, but was responsible for over 56 per cent of all charitable donations.[186] No equivalent figures have been calculated for the three Yorkshire towns. Instead the numbers of individuals making such donations within specific categories have been aggregated (see table 4.1). Compared with the 75 per cent of all lay York testators who made no specific charitable bequests,[187] about 50 per cent of the merchant testators neglected to do so, unless such bequests were subsumed into the all-purpose phrase, 'funeral expenses at the discretion of my executors'.[188] The other half accounted for a steady and fairly con-stant flow of benevolence in the variety of ways briefly described below. Moreover, there is no indication that this flow was fundamentally affected by the state of the local economy: donations continued during periods

---

[184] G. R. Elton's review of Jordan in *Historical Jnl*, 3 (1960), pp. 89–92; Rubin, *Charity and Community*, p. 6.

[185] Tanner, *Church in Norwich*, pp. 113–40; Vale, *Piety, Charity and Literacy Among the Yorkshire Gentry*, pp. 23–8; Swanson, *Medieval Artisans*, pp. 155–7, based on some 850 wills; Cullum and Goldberg, 'Charitable Provision in Late Medieval York', pp. 24–39.

[186] W. K. Jordan, *The Charities of London, 1480–1660* (London, 1960), p. 48. In spite of criticism, his general thesis is supportable. See Thomson, 'Piety and Charity in London', p. 178. One major reservation lies with Jordan's contention that philanthropic spending increased from the late fif-teenth to the early seventeenth century. See, in particular, W. G. Bittle and R. T. Lane, 'Inflation and Philanthropy in England: A Reassessment of W. K. Jordan's Data', *EcHR*, 2nd ser., 29 (1976), pp. 203–10.

[187] This was 75 per cent of 2,286 testators whose wills were registered between 1321 and 1500: Cullum and Goldberg, 'Charitable Provision in Late Medieval York', p. 24.

[188] Burgess, '"By Quick and by Dead"', p. 845.

of recession. The claim that 'charity loomed large in towns in periods of prosperity' is not borne out in testamentary records.[189]

It may be that, as has been recently argued, the pattern of charitable bequests reflected the Seven Corporeal Acts of Mercy.[190] There was certainly a preference for the care of the sick and aged, the disabled most commonly endowed.[191] A necessary and effective form of lay charity was the foundation and maintenance of hospitals and maisonsdieu, usually a combination of almshouse and ward, irrespective of title. There were six main hospitals and about fifteen to twenty maisonsdieu in York; four small hospitals, the Charterhouse and at least nine maisonsdieu in Hull; and six hospitals and at least three maisonsdieu in Beverley.[192] In York the majority of these were established by 1400, during the prosperous decades following the Black Death, whereas most of the Hull maisons were creations of the mid-fifteenth century.[193] Maisonsdieu were rarely *post mortem* foundations and provided opportunities for lifetime charity from the founder and other beneficiaries.

Several of these institutions were founded by individual merchants, in anticipation that they would continue to attract gifts from others. They continued the functions of a chantry in so far as a chaplain was appointed and the inmates were expected to pray for the founder and subsequent benefactors.[194] Robert and Thomas Holme of York, for example, each established a maisondieu in the city in 1396 and 1406, and John Craven established another near Layerthorpe in 1415. The four small Hull hospitals were established by merchants: one in the fourteenth century by Robert Selby, and three in the fifteenth century by John Alcock, John Bedford and Joan Gregg.[195] John Ake, who died in 1398, left property to establish a twenty-four person almshouse at the Crossbridge in Beverley. Its first chaplain was not instituted until 1432, and it became known as Trinity Hospital.[196] John Armstrong of Beverley established a trust to administer £20 annual income from rents, to maintain the St John the

[189] Rubin, *Charity and Community*, p. 12.

[190] Cullum and Goldberg, 'Charitable Provision in Late Medieval York', p. 28.

[191] Cf. London where Thomson estimates that a quarter of its testators left money to hospitals and almshouses, 'Piety and Charity in London', p. 185. See also Tanner, *Church in Norwich*, pp. 132–4.

[192] *VCH York*, pp. 363–5; *VCH Hull*, pp. 333–5; *VCH Beverley*, pp. 182–3; Prob. Reg. I, f. 38v. (Carleton); II, f. 342(i)v. (Bridekirke).

[193] P. H. Cullum, ' "For Pore People Harberles": What was the Function of the Maisonsdieu?', in D. J. Clayton, R. G. Davies and P. McNiven, eds., *Trade, Devotion and Governance* (Stroud, 1994), pp. 36–54, esp. pp. 40, 43.

[194] Cullum and Goldberg, 'Charitable Provision in Late Medieval York', pp. 30–3; Cullum, 'Maisonsdieu', p. 50.

[195] Prob. Reg. I, ff. 16 (Gisburn), 103 (Robert Holme); III, ff. 254v. (Thomas Holme), f. 607 (Craven); *VCH Hull*, pp. 333–5.

[196] Humberside RO, BC III (Ake's will); *Yorks Deeds*, VII, pp. 26–33.

Baptist maisondieu and five others in Beverley, of which no other record has been found. Bequests to such institutions usually took the form of a small cash gift to each incumbent, or to each house. Although such gifts are difficult to estimate in total, some individuals' donations must have been considerable. More immediately practical was Richard Crull of York's gift in 1460 of 100 bundles of faggots to several York maisons-dieu.[197] Bequests to maisonsdieu and hospitals[198] were more frequently made in York and Beverley than in Hull: a steady 45 to 50 per cent compared with Hull's 10 per cent. Their popularity with merchant testators may well have reflected their own needs as much as a desire to help the totally destitute and needy.[199]

In York it was also customary to leave money to the main prisons, the Kidcotes, castle and archbishop's prisons: 15 to 20 per cent of merchant testators did so in different ways. For example, William Bowes left 5s to each prison, whereas William Chimney left 2d to each prisoner and John Carre, 40s to be spent on meat and drink shared amongst the prisoners.[200] Few such bequests occur in Beverley or Hull wills although there was a prison in each town. Occasionally the York prisons would be remembered by Beverley or Hull people. Joan Gregg of Hull, for example, left 6s 8d to the prisoners in the archbishop's prison in York.[201]

Bequests to institutions outnumber those directed to the poor in general in York and Beverley, even though doles handed out at funerals were probably the simplest form of charity. Without specific references it is difficult to address the contention that 'doles were invariably handed out at funerals' even though it was likely.[202] Although the 'deserving' were sometimes preferred by testators,[203] most bequests were simply to poor people and one can imagine the spirit of anticipation which must have followed news of a prominent merchant's demise, bringing hopeful paupers crowding around his house. That, of course, was one of the intentions behind such doles: the attraction of as many individuals and their prayers as possible.[204] Some merchants left very large sums for this

---

[197] Prob. Reg. II, f. 431v. (Crull); VI, f. 117 (Armstrong).

[198] Even when not identifying any institution, most testators making such bequests left money 'to the lepers', a preference shared by most York testators: Cullum, 'Maisonsdieu', p. 39.

[199] For merchant use of maisonsdieu, see p. 102, above.

[200] Prob. Reg. III, f. 581 (Bowes); V, f. 327 (Carre); VIII, f. 3 (Chimney); *VCH York*, pp. 491–7; Cullum and Goldberg found that prisoners were not prominent recipients in York: 'Charitable Provision in Late Medieval York', p. 34.   [201] Prob. Reg. III, f. 555v.

[202] Duffy, *The Stripping of the Altars*, p. 360.

[203] These were randomly chosen and the recipients were rarely categorised by anything other than domicile or occasionally by sex. This is contrary to John Thomson's view, *Early Tudor Church*, pp. 335–6. It may be that the growing belief (from about 1500) that, as the efficacy of such gifts depended on the state of grace of both donor and recipient, only 'deserving' paupers should be so advantaged. See Duffy, *The Stripping of the Altars*, p. 366.

[204] Gittings, *Death, Burial and the Individual*, pp. 26–8.

purpose. Richard Russell of York left £13 6s 8d for funeral distribution, the same sum for the most needy in three York parishes, and a further £20 for the poor in the rest of York and £10 for the sick. John Brompton of Beverley left £18 in cash for funeral distribution and £10 to buy bread for eighty paupers. Robert Holme of York chose to mark the stages of his funeral by leaving £20 for the poor on the day of his burial and a further £20 on the eighth day.[205] Not many could afford such munificence and the restriction of doles to the poor 'in my parish' was not uncommon. Charity began and ended even closer to home for some testators. John Goddysbuk of York left 4d to each pauper 'in the lane where I live', and Thomas Cliff 12d to the poor in North Street.[206]

Young women sometimes faced difficulties in attracting a husband without a dowry and testators occasionally left sums *ad maritagium*, ranging from £2 to £26.[207] Poor widows and 'other sinners' in St John's, Hungate, York, received 12d and 4d respectively from Richard Wartre while Roger de Burton included bedridden widows, unable to get out to obtain 'necessaries', in amongst his recipients. John Tutbury of Hull left 100s to be shared between honest virgins but 3s 4d to each baptised boy.[208]

Some merchants left money for distribution in instalments, maybe to prolong the period of prayers from grateful paupers. In 1437 John Gregg of Hull left £43 6s 8d for the poor of Hull at 20d per week for ten years, and £21 13s 4d for the poor of Beverley at the same rate for five years, in addition to a sizeable gift of land to maintain his wife's maisondieu. Gregg also made extraordinary bequests to the Austin and Carmelite houses in Hull: 20s each to buy grain and a further 6d per week to buy food for five years. The specific arrangements he made no doubt reflected the agrarian crisis within the region in the late 1430s.[209] In less severe economic circumstances, spreading out benevolence could only have been designed to extend the period of prayers. Another Hull merchant, Thomas Preston, left 1d in 1451, for three paupers, weekly, for ten years.[210] Long-term bequests must have been very difficult, if not impos-

---

[205] Prob. Reg. I, f. 100v. (Holme, 1396); II, f. 86v. (Brompton, 1444); III, f. 439 (Russell, 1435).

[206] Prob. Reg. III, ff. 276 (Goddysbuk, 1407), 530 (Clyff, 1438).

[207] Prob. Reg. II, f. 327v. (Garton); V, ff. 99 (Johnson), 212–13 (Nelson), 327 (Carre); VI, f. 130 (Middleton). In early-sixteenth-century Coventry, it was difficult for a young man at the poorer level of society to set up house without his wife's dowry: Phythian-Adams, *Desolation of a City*, pp. 84–5.

[208] Prob. Reg. I, f. 55v. (Burton, 1393); III, f. 371v. (Tutbury, 1433); IV, ff. 115–17 (Wartre, 1466).

[209] Prob. Reg. III, f. 507v. (Gregg). See Heath, 'Urban Piety', pp. 224–5, for details of the Greggs' charity, and Pollard, *North-Eastern England*, pp. 50–2, for years of dearth.

[210] Prob. Reg. II, f. 225 (Preston). Reinforcing gratitude may have been the intention of Nicholas Blackburn snr of York, even though he made his plans in 1432. He arranged for three large distributions in the year following his death: £100 at Easter, £100 at All Hallows and £60 at the feast of the Purification of the Virgin Mary: *ibid.*, II, f. 605 (Blackburn).

sible, to put into effect, and some executors must have blessed the dear departed many times.

One or two testators left money to buy clothes, food and other goods for the poor and it is apparent from the complexity of some of these bequests that thought had been given as to the most effective means of relief. Joan Gregg of Hull left £40 for wool and linen cloth for the poor of Hull, whereas Richard Wartre of York wanted his executors to have 100 gowns made and distributed together with bread. John Gilyot jnr left very precise instructions that fifty new beds each worth 10s and a new mattress and two new blankets and sheets per bed should be given to paupers in the city, that £10 should be given to the most needy married couples in the city, and that £10 6s 8d be given for dowries for forty poor maidens.[211] It has sometimes been assumed that the religious houses served as agencies for charity from donor to pauper but this was made explicit in only one instance. Thomas Curtas left cloth for clothes to be distributed *via* the Carmelite and Austin friars in York in 1461.[212]

Public amenities

Individual merchants who travelled to London and abroad had seen examples of civic improvements,[213] and visitors presumably drew loud and partisan comparisons with their own towns. Practical considerations led merchants to finance public works such as street paving, the provision of a water supply, bridge repairs and highway maintenance. These were popular projects in many late-medieval towns, a form of practical piety not readily differentiated from other forms of benevolence.[214] Thomas Gra of York left one rent to support his chantry *and* a light in the public latrine on Ousebridge.[215] Such purposeful benevolence should be seen as one, perhaps increasingly fashionable, form of charity and not as a reflection of protestant utilitarianism.[216]

---

[211] Prob. Reg. III, f. 556 (Gregg); VI, f. 116 (Wartre); VIII, f. 33 (Gilyot). John Carre of York also left money for fifty mattresses and stipulated two sheets, two blankets and a coverlet with each: *ibid.*, v, f. 327.   [212] Prob. Reg. II, ff. 438–9.

[213] In early fifteenth-century London, the public were accustomed to a certain standard of public hygiene, and it has been argued that there was in fact only a small minority of the citizens who did not co-operate: E. L. Sabine, 'City Cleaning in Medieval London', *Speculum*, 12 (1937), pp. 25–7.

[214] Amongst London merchants, 1400–50, only 1.8 per cent of 1,753 testators left real estate towards public works as a primary bequest: Jennings, 'The Distribution of Landed Wealth in the Wills of London Merchants', p. 264. Cash bequests were more common but still accounted for only a small proportion of all charitable bequests in late fifteenth-century and early sixteenth-century London: Jordan, *The Charities of London*, p. 21. John Thomson calculated they accounted for some 12 per cent: Thomson, 'Piety and Charity in London', pp. 179, 187–8. In Norwich, such civic projects were rare: Tanner, *Church in Norwich*, pp. 137, 223.

[215] *CPR 1377–81*, p. 435.   [216] Scarisbrick, *The Reformation*, pp. 4–5.

Good communications were close to commercial interests and the repair of roads and bridges regularly attracted donations from testators. Such benefactions had a double advantage, in that they also earned the approval of the Church. One version of a bidding prayer encouraged the congregations to pray for 'thaim that brigges and stretes makes and amendes that God grant us part of thare gode dedes and thaim of oures'.[217]

The majority of donations were towards the upkeep of roads and bridges close to a merchant's home. Richard Russell of York left money in 1435 for the repair of roads and bridges within a ten league radius of the city. Other merchants favoured the Hull–Beverley road, the Hull–Drypool road, Hull bridge in Beverley, or more distant roads and bridges which were regionally important, including the road across Hessay Moor, the bridge at Stamford Bridge, Caterick bridge and Frodsham bridge in Cheshire.[218] The repair of the internal roads and bridges was generally paid for from pavage grants and tolls. All the same, Thomas Neleson of York (d. 1484) felt that the provision was inadequate and left £10 for the purpose.[219]

Once in a while a merchant would take upon himself responsibility for a major public project. William Todd of York paid for work on a long stretch of the city walls near Fishergate Bar during his mayoralty in 1486–7. Robert Holme of Hull contributed the materials for the construction of a lead conduit in the city, and when it was pulled up and the lead sold in 1462, the council paid for a perpetual mass to be sung for him.[220] With some foresight, Nicholas Blackburn snr left £40 to York in 1432, towards the city's tax contribution,[221] but we do not know if the gratitude of the council extended to paying for a mass!

The late middle ages was a time when a collective sense of civic pride was increasingly manifested in the building of new guildhalls,[222] enterprises possible only through collective effort. Four substantial halls were built in York,[223] all to serve exclusive groups: the Merchant Adventurers'

---

[217] Quoted in T. P. Cooper, 'The Medieval Highways, Streets, Open Ditches and Sanitary Conditions of the City of York', *Yorks Arch. Jnl*, 28 (1913), pp. 280–1.

[218] Arch. Reg. X, ff. 309v.–10 (Coppendale); Prob. Reg. I, ff. 15v. (Gisburn), 100v.–3v. (Holme); II, ff. 327v. (Garton), 605 (Blackburn); III, ff. 263 (Kelk), 439v.–40 (Russell), 507v. (John Gregg), 555v.–6v. (Joan Gregg); V, ff. 308 (Ince), 327–9 (Carre).

[219] Prob. Reg. V, f. 212 (Neleson). According to Cooper, 'The Medieval Highways', pp. 270–86, York's streets were appalling and, in spite of personal donations and pavage grants, little improvement was made until Elizabeth's reign.

[220] *Test. Ebor.* IV, p. 213; Hull RO, BRE I, p. 95.   [221] Prob. Reg. II, f. 605.

[222] The London Guildhall was rebuilt in the first half of the fifteenth century: C. M. Barron, *The Medieval Guildhall of London* (London, 1974). See also V. Parker, *The Making of King's Lynn* (Chichester, 1971), p. 12; J. Campbell, 'Norwich', in Lobel *Atlas of Historic Towns*, II, p. 15.

[223] Two others existed, the butchers' and the shoemakers' halls. A. Raine, *Medieval York: A Topographical Survey Based on Original Sources* (London, 1955), pp. 65, 186–7.

Hall, built in the late fourteenth and early fifteenth centuries by the guild of Our Lord and the Blessed Virgin; Merchant Taylors' Hall built before 1400; and St Anthony's Hall built sometime between 1446 and 1453. The fourth or common hall, now the Guildhall, was originally built in the mid-fifteenth century by the guild of St Christopher and the corporation. It was largely destroyed in the 1939–45 war and subsequently restored.[224] All four halls attracted individual donations towards the initial building costs and upkeep.[225] York was unusual in having several large halls of this type and it was clearly important for a community to have the financial resources to indulge a taste for the fashionable. Council guildhalls were recorded in Beverley and Hull, and were probably of fourteenth-century origin, but we know little about them. Hull possibly had, in addition, two religious guildhalls: the famous Trinity guildhall was started in the 1460s and was probably a two-storied half-timbered building with some brickwork.[226]

CONCLUSION

It has not been argued that merchants were particularly pious or honourable, but that they followed the religious conventions and philanthropic fashions of their day. A minority were visibly members of a core of devout Christians whose faith and support of institutional worship allowed the majority the luxury of conventional orthodoxy without deep commitment. Their acceptance of orthodox doctrine is confirmed by the widespread consistency of religious provision in merchants' wills. The belief in purgatory and in the efficacy of prayers for the dead was universal.[227] We should hesitate before claiming that there is evidence for a profound piety in conventional testamentary expressions. We know that not all merchants drew up their own wills; even the literate may have thought that such an important document required a scribal expertise to match their own mercantile skills. Inevitably we are left with the conundrum as to whose pious sentiments we are reading: the scribe's or the testator's. This is not to argue that testators did not agree with the standard form or that those who wished, could and did diverge.

---

[224] *VCH York*, pp. 481–3, 543–4; Gee, 'Architecture of York', pp. 372–3.

[225] Thomas Barton and Richard Wartre, for example, left £1 in 1460 and £20 in 1465 respectively towards the York Guildhall: Prob. Reg. II, f. 451 (Barton); IV, f. 116 (Wartre). Similarly in London: Barron, *London Guildhall*, p. 36.

[226] *VCH Hull*, pp. 76, 398, 433; *Beverlac*, pp. 420–2.

[227] In this respect, merchants were as 'utterly conventional' as the contemporary gentry (Carpenter, 'Religion of the Gentry', p. 58) and the chaplains in the York diocese (P. MacKie, 'Chaplains in the Diocese of York, 1480–1530: The Testamentary Evidence', *Yorks Arch. Jnl*, 58 (1986), pp. 123–33).

However, there is unequivocal evidence of individual piety in the acquisition of private oratories by a few merchants and their wives,[228] suggesting a particular spiritual need.[229] Perhaps the most spectacular surviving object, testifying to one man's faith, is the Bolton Book of Hours (*c.* 1420–30), commissioned by John Bolton, a York merchant and sometime mayor of York. His wealth exceeded that of most of his contemporaries and his lavishly illustrated Book combined secular patrons with saints.[230] Although merchants left money to all the mendicant orders and to monastic houses within the region, most of their religious provision was directed towards their parish churches in which they wished to be buried. The continued and consistent support given to parish churches, albeit of a conventional form, confirms their dominant place in contemporary thinking, however sparse or numerous parishes were in different towns.[231] They were the mainstay of local religious practice and continued as such in spite of competition from newer organisations such as the mendicants and the religious guilds and fraternities.[232]

It is harder to assess the depth of religious sentiment as we must rely on relatively few wills for indicative detail. Moreover, it could be argued that the occasional munificence of mercantile charity and the elaborate arrangements made for a funeral or *post mortem* prayers were intended to confirm the superiority of the testator as much as to express a lifetime's devout belief. Demonstrations of piety and charity as display activities and funereal self-advertisement were an accepted part of medieval religious practice. Far from levelling society, death could be the opportunity for insisting on the differences of status. Names prominently displayed on windows and liturgical robes monogrammed with the donor's initials kept these gestures before the congregation's gaze.

Some status-conscious oligarchs carried civic pride to their funeral, John Ferriby paying for aldermen attendants and alderman Thomas Scauceby choosing his best scarlet gown for his mortuary.[233] Membership

---

[228] On private worship and oratories, see C. Richmond, 'Religion and the Fifteenth-Century Gentleman', in R. B. Dobson, ed., *The Church, Politics and Patronage in the Fifteenth Century* (London, 1984), p. 199.

[229] York, Borthwick Institute Prob. Reg. v, f. 229 (Alcock); Reg. Bothe, ff. 101 (Marion Kent), 167 (Gilyot); Reg. Rotherham, f. 25 (Lambe); *Cal. Papal Registers, 1427–47 (Letters)*, pp. 188 (Ormeshead), 395 (Barton). Beverley: *Test. Ebor.* II, p. 101 (Brompton); III, pp. 237n., 238 (Frost); *VCH Beverley*, p. 60.   [230] York Minster Library.

[231] York's forty-one or so parishes were probably as important a focus in this context as were Coventry's two: Phythian-Adams, *Desolation of a City*, p. 166.

[232] Tanner, *Church in Norwich*, p. 140.

[233] Prob. Reg. IV, f. 169 (Scauceby, 1471); v, f. 417 (Ferriby). Ferriby died during his mayoralty in 1491 and his corpse was accompanied by six aldermen and the city sword and mace: C. Kightly and R. Semlyen, *Lords of the City. The Lord Mayors of York and their Mansion House* (York, 1980), p. 10.

of an elitist association such as the Corpus Christi Guild could, at the very least, ensure social equals were in attendance at funerals, as well as the paupers waiting for doles.

Most merchants kept their expenditure within reasonable limits, although one or two may have jeopardised their social provisions by the amount of money or land they wished to divert into the Church. The amounts are only estimates of course, based on totals of all the sums listed by individuals in their wills for religious purposes.[234] John Aldwik of Hull, for example, left all his property to the city to maintain his chantry and his son Geoffrey received a life pension. John Gisburn specified £242 out of an estate of some £300 for spiritual investment in 1390.[235] In the late fifteenth century, both John Gilyots, father and son, committed large cash sums and real estate: Gilyot senior £143 out of some £155, and junior, £538 out of £722. Of this, £500 alone was to buy land to maintain a perpetual chantry.[236] Personal vagaries determined what percentage an individual spent. Robert Savage spent only £6 out of £106 in 1399, Richard Taunton, £66 out of £86 in 1394.[237]

Whatever the liturgical or theological sympathies of the testator, wills and testaments were seen as a way of meeting a lifetime's obligations and responsibilities and of ordering the future as best one could. John Dalton encapsulated a particularly mercantile concept, when he charged his executors to do their duty as they will 'answer affore god at the drefull day of Dome and specially to pay my debts chargyng thame an trust god in discharging me and my soule'.[238]

Friends and family gained spiritual as well as material benefit from implementing the wishes of the dead, while he (or she) derived reassurance from a knowledge that, at least in spiritual matters, the correct form of benevolence had been observed and the appropriate reward would be received. There was comfort in the reuniting and gathering of family and friends, the living and the dead, in prayers. William Marshall of York wanted those mourning him to pray also for his grandparents, parents, his brothers and sisters; John Thirsk for his three wives, daughter and son-in-law.[239] Affirming family identity through several generations was clearly important. In all these respects, merchants were united with their fellow townsmen. The differences were purely those of wealth. Since merchants generally enjoyed a greater disposable income than most craftsmen and artisans, they could spend more (if they so chose) on their souls.

---

[234] See pp. 291–5 below for discussion of using probate records to estimate cash estates.
[235] Prob. Reg. I, ff. 15v.–16 (Gisburn); II, f. 96 (Aldwick).
[236] Prob. Reg. V, f. 237; VIII, ff. 32–4. See also Holme of York, £963 out of £2,500, I, ff. 100v.–3v.
[237] Prob. Reg. I, f. 63 (Taunton); III, ff. 17–18 (Savage).   [238] Prob. Reg. V, f. 484.
[239] Prob. Reg. V, f. 424 (Marshall); IX, f. 112 (Harrison); *CPR 1461–7*, p. 541 (Thirsk).

Noteworthy individuals accepted responsibility for the churches with which they were associated and although it is clear that the intention of the donors was to purchase prayers, the careful thought that went into some of the bequests reflects a close involvement and pride in their parish churches. The relationship was reciprocal and just as lay society depended upon the Church in all its forms for salvation, so the Church was heavily subsidised by the laity and in particular by the wealthy laity. In York we can clearly see the impact of the trade recession, not only on the shrinking group of active overseas traders, but on the churches and chantries of the city. In the late fifteenth century, the council began to merge chantries because their incomes could no longer support their priests. By 1526 the city was complaining that the decayed endowments of many chantries had left the city with an annual deficit of £50, and in 1536 the council carried out its own dissolution of chantries.[240] In 1547 the city's inability to support its numerous parish churches was recognised, and permission was given to unite several of those most decayed.[241] This low point marked the end of an era.

[240] E.g., in 1477 the chantry to St Peter in St Martin's, Coneyst was merged with St Mary's chantry in St Helen's, Stonegate: *MB*, II, pp. 269–70. See also *YCR*, II, pp. 120, 123, 190–1 for mergers in 1495 and 1496, and Dickens, 'A Municipal Dissolution', pp. 164–73; Thomson, *Early Tudor Church*, p. 182.

[241] D. M. Palliser, 'The Union of Parishes at York, 1547–86', *Yorks Arch. Jnl*, 46 (1974), pp. 87–102; *VCH York*, pp. 117, 123, 143.

Part II

Entrepreneurship and capital accumulation

Map 2 Northern European ports

5

THE GEOGRAPHY AND COMPOSITION
OF TRADE

What distinguished merchants from others was their engagement in wholesale and long-distance trade. Moving out into different regions and countries away from the familiar environs of the local marketplace to negotiate contracts with strangers, set merchants apart from their fellows. Trading away from the security of familiar business contacts, local courts and habitual customs required a multiplicity of skills as well as courage. The material rewards could be enormous and optimism was an essential characteristic of every trader. A minority enjoyed great commercial success but all merchants were affected by fluctuations and changes in the pattern of overseas trade, even those whose business was primarily domestic.

The transformation of England's international trade in the fourteenth and fifteenth centuries is well known, but it is difficult to discuss the activities of a group of provincial merchants without setting the context as it bore directly upon Yorkshire. Discussion below will be confined to major overseas commodities: wool, cloth, wine, miscellaneous Atlantic coast and Baltic imports, and to domestic and coastal trade.

EXPORTS

Wool and the Low Countries

Without wool, it is difficult to conceive of any role for England in international trade. The dependence of the textile manufacturers in the Low Countries and Italy on English wool created conditions in which the country's export trade flourished. Wool became the staple produce in those regions where conditions favoured the development of sheep farming: inextricably linking the fortunes of individuals and communities to the fluctuations of international markets. In 1275, Hull was, after Boston and London, the third major wool port in England. Its exports were almost exclusively to Picardy, sometimes for return cargoes of woad for Yorkshire's textile industry, where the leading wool manufacturing centres were, in order of importance, Pontefract, York, Doncaster and Beverley. Hull merely served as the point of embarkation. Increasing quantities were destined for the Low Countries and Italy. Between 1297 and 1315 there were more alien merchants exporting through Hull than denizens, and although 2,100 individuals were involved, almost one quarter of the total wool exports were accounted for by a dozen merchants, eight German and four English. During the same period, Yorkshiremen constituted the largest group of English merchants: at least seventy from Beverley and fifty-six from York. The few Hull men associated with this trade were probably mariners, since their shipments were very small, irregular, and always in English ships.[1]

The first quarter of the fourteenth century was crucial for English merchants, notably those from Beverley, as they worked to reverse the dominance of the Flemish, Italian and Hanse merchants shipping wool through Hull.[2] As the Crown tightened its control over this lucrative trade, Yorkshire merchants were immediately involved. York was chosen as one of the eleven home staples set up in 1326, which were intended to exclude alien merchants from exporting wool.[3] York's superior strategic and administrative importance made the city a natural choice over Beverley. Practical and cost implications resulted from the requirement that all wool had to be transported to York, weighed and packed there before being shipped down the Ouse. The heated debate about the retention of home staples versus an overseas staple involved the king and merchants of towns beyond Yorkshire and reached a climax at a meeting in the Minster chapterhouse in York in January 1328.

Denizens naturally preferred the retention of home staples, but in the end the government abolished all staples in April 1328. An illegal staple was set up in Bruges by a confederation of merchants, seven of whom came from Yorkshire. In 1328 there had been a strong resistance to home staples by a group of merchants led by William de la Pole of Hull, but their opposition could not prevent the government ending the illegal

---

[1] T. H. Lloyd, *The English Wool Trade in the Middle Ages* (Cambridge, 1977), pp. 54, 65, 129; PRO, E122/55/5–57/6. The Bardi and Peruzzi of Florence and later the ubiquitous Lombards all shipped wool through Hull: *CPR 1301–7*, p. 538; *1313–17*, p. 169; *1338–40*, pp. 154, 331; *1340–3*, pp. 24, 85, 145; *1391–6*, p. 227.

[2] The Hanse accounted for 57 per cent of all the wool shipped through Hull in 1304–5 but by 1329–30 alien merchants then accounted for only 13 per cent of all wool exported. Three Beverley merchants (John de Cottingham, Richard Tirwhit, and Walter de Kelstern) and one Pontefract merchant (John Metal) each exported over 1,000 sacks between 1297 and 1315. See Lloyd, *English Wool Trade*, pp. 129–30; G. Unwin, ed., *Finance and Trade under Edward III* (London, 1918), pp. 93–135; E. M. Carus-Wilson and O. Coleman, *England's Export Trade 1275–1547* (Oxford, 1963), pp. 43, 122–3.   [3] Lloyd, *English Wool Trade*, p. 115.

Bruges staple and introducing home staples once more from April 1333 until March 1334.[4] Five Beverley and two York merchants were involved in the illegal staple at Bruges, out of a total of forty-two merchants who seized the goods of a merchant who would not comply with their attempted monopoly. They were therefore not 'the bulk of the confederation', as Dr Lloyd claimed, since seven men from Coventry, six from Northampton and four from Ludlow were also present.[5]

York was selected as the home staple once more, and this time royal customers collected export duties there and not at the port of loading. This posed a direct challenge to Hull where the customers usually operated, but was short-lived. From 1334, the staple moved to and fro between various towns in Europe, mostly in the Low Countries, and when home staples were introduced once more in 1353-4, Hull was selected as well as York.[6]

By the late 1330s the relative position of York and Beverley was changing, spurred on by Edward III's exploitative trading policies. The outbreak of war in 1337 made all trade more uncertain, but at the same time Edward III had begun to squeeze more money from the trade than was available to him from customs duties. The demands of his military ambitions in France, coupled with the monopolistic ambitions of some English merchants to exclude all alien merchants from the wool trade, led initially to the wool monopoly of 1337 and ultimately to the establishment of the Company of the Staple at Calais.[7]

This was an important sequence of events in which Yorkshire merchants played a major part. In May 1336 writs were sent to twenty-two towns summoning representatives to a meeting with the king at Oxford. Thus began a series of merchant assemblies through which Edward hoped to manipulate wool merchants into agreeing to a collective loan. Yorkshire merchants were summoned to almost all the subsequent assemblies. Four Beverley merchants and William de la Pole represented Yorkshire at the second assembly in June 1336; three Beverley and two York merchants with William and Richard de la Pole at the third in September.[8] Only two other northern towns, Newcastle and Pontefract,

---

[4] *Ibid.*, pp. 120-1.   [5] *CCR 1330-3*, pp. 466-7, 498, 519; Lloyd, *English Wool Trade*, p. 120.
[6] Lloyd, *English Wool Trade*, pp. 207-8; L. F. Salzman, *English Trade in the Later Middle Ages* (Oxford, 1931), pp. 293-4.
[7] Lloyd, *English Wool Trade*, pp. 144-92; J. L. Bolton, *The Medieval English Economy 1150-1500* (London, 1980), pp. 194-5.
[8] *Lords' Report on the Dignity of Peers*, IV, pp. 459, 464, 524, 560. There were few Hull merchants trading in wool in this period and the de la Poles were their only representatives until two others were summoned in August 1340. No other Hull merchants were summoned until two in 1343 and four in 1348. Until the council of 1340, there were usually more Beverley than York merchants summoned, but thereafter the York merchants outnumbered those from anywhere else in the north.

were represented.[9] In 1336–7 the Yorkshiremen constituted almost 20 per cent of the thirty-seven merchants summoned but, as Edward tried to broaden the basis of his negotiations, more merchants were summoned and the Yorkshire contingent was reduced to comprise some 5 per cent in 1337–8.[10] Not all were eager to give their advice and on 10 November 1342 Walter de Kelstern of York was peremptorily summoned to attend the council under threat of punishment.[11]

The details of the agreement concluded between Edward III and the company of merchants led by William de la Pole of Hull and Reginald Conduit of London are well known.[12] Merchants from the three towns, with their local knowledge and contacts, were vital to the success of the operation, and the certainty of profits attracted newcomers to the wool trade in Yorkshire. On 30 July 1337 eleven Beverley, four York and one Hull merchant were appointed deputy royal collectors of wool, and Henry de Belton and Henry Goldbeter of York were appointed soon after.[13] In addition, some forty-eight Yorkshire men made private contributions as independent collectors, many of them like John de Acomb of York appearing as wool merchants for the first time in the records.[14]

In the event the whole enterprise turned into something of a fiasco: a massive shortfall in the amount collected, wholesale smuggling and royal intervention meant that sales were made at a loss. Edward entered into 317 obligations for payment of each merchant's share of the profit, minus the £2 and the ancient custom of 6s 8d per sack which had not yet been paid. Many merchants suffered severe losses. They were faced with unpaid suppliers at home and had royal bonds in lieu of their profit. Small merchants, unable to survive long periods without cash, sold their bonds to wealthier merchants, no doubt discounted.[15] The Crown used every means known to it to redeem these bonds, the Dordrecht bonds, other than by direct cash redemption. The most common form of settlement was to allow merchants to export wool at half the official subsidy to the sum of the debt.

This was hardly a satisfactory alternative to direct payment as embargoes on wool exports frequently interrupted the course of trade and, in any case, further heavy investment in wool was required to finance new ventures to recover the debt. The experience of one Yorkshire group

[9] Lloyd, *English Wool Trade*, pp. 511, 514, 520, 524.
[10] *Ibid.*, pp. 464, 491–2, 555.   [11] *CPR 1341–3*, p. 700.
[12] Unwin, *Finance and Trade*, pp. 186–93; E. B. Fryde, 'Edward III's Wool Monopoly of 1337', *History*, NS, 37 (1952); Lloyd, *English Wool Trade*, pp. 147–8; Bolton, *Medieval English Economy*, pp. 196–7.   [13] *CPR 1334–8*, p. 485; *CCR 1337–9*, p. 148.
[14] The names of the merchants from York, Beverley and Hull can be found in appendix 2; *CCR 1337–9*, p. 430; Lloyd, *English Wool Trade*, p. 117.
[15] Lloyd, *English Wool Trade*, pp. 175, 182.

provides an apposite example. On 9 May 1338 Henry de Belton and other local merchants were assigned £6,000 from the subsidies of the tenth and fifteenth for the 1,000 sacks they had collected and shipped from Yorkshire, but on 22 May payment had still not been made and was to be recovered instead through a system of reduced customs payments on their exports. Many of them had still not been repaid in 1344.[16]

The ramifications of the collection and the arrangements for payment rumbled on for years. Not only did merchants suffer financially, but some of them bore the brunt of royal anger at the inefficiency of the collection. Richard Brigenhall of York was dismissed as a collector in December 1337, having been ordered in October to speed up the operation. Under this sort of pressure from the Crown and faced with possible financial losses, some merchants reacted violently. The sheriff of Yorkshire, sent to enquire into the wool collection in 1338, was assaulted by Thomas Holme, Adam Tirwhit and Thomas Waghen, all eminent merchants and keepers of Beverley.[17]

One of the curious features of this eventful and hectic period in the history of the wool trade was the emergence of merchants who had not been recorded previously in the customs records. At least eighteen merchants from York, Beverley and Hull were newcomers, and it may be that the urgency of the royal collections, or the temptation of possible profit, drew in men more usually engaged in local business.[18] They were partners in the syndicates headed by John Goldbeter, William Acastre and Thomas Lindsey who in turn were collaborating with Walter Chiriton and Co. Their activities have been described by Edmund Fryde[19] and it seems reasonable to suppose that some of the money they raised for Edward III was invested by a circle of lesser merchants who were drawn into the wool trade as the only means of recovering their loans.

The list of those trying to recover the repayment of bonds through export concessions also provides a brief view of the Yorkshire merchants: twenty-seven from Beverley accounted for £5,302 8s 4d; twenty from York accounted for £5,136 1s 4d; and three from Hull, including William de la Pole, accounted for £2,298 19s 5d. De la Pole alone claimed £2,039 12s 7d.[20] When Edward attempted to raise money again

---

[16] Appendix 2; *CCR 1337–9*, pp. 365, 429–31; *1343–6*, p. 402.

[17] *CCR 1337–9*, pp. 270, 271, 426; *CCR 1338–40*, p. 179.

[18] Appendix 2. Given the absence of customs rolls between 1343 and 1351, when the customs were farmed, and of the Particular Rolls for Hull from 1335 until 1346 and then until the end of the reign, it is difficult to dismiss them altogether as monopoly opportunists. See Kermode, 'Merchants of York, Beverley and Hull', appendix 4.

[19] E. B. Fryde, *Some Business Transactions of York Merchants: John Goldbeter, William Acastre and Partners, 1336–1349*, Borthwick Paper No. 29 (York, 1966).

[20] *CPR 1337–9*, pp. 424–34, and see appendix 2.

in 1340 and 1341, a number of Yorkshire merchants formed syndicates to take advantage of the parliamentary grants to the Crown of 20,000 and 30,000 sacks of wool. For some merchants it was probably the only course open to them in the hope of recouping some of their earlier losses. In 1340, for example, Thomas Tirwhit of Beverley and Hardelph Barton of Hull bought 500 sacks for the Crown in Nottinghamshire, and Walter de Kelstern and Henry Goldbeter of York and Walter Frost of Beverley contracted to buy 1,500 sacks in Yorkshire. In 1341 Nicholas Scoreby of York, Robert Stut of Hull and Thomas Berwick of Pocklington collected almost 500 sacks in June, and William Acastre, John Goldbeter and William Skelton, all of York, collected over 800 sacks in July.[21]

Henry Goldbeter, Walter de Kelstern, John Randman and William and John Luterington, all of York, lost wool to the value of £701 13s 4d at Dordrecht. On 2 June 1340 they agreed to pay a royal debt to John de Hanault, of a further £701 13s 4d, and to receive £3,218 13s 4d in repayment from the ninth to be collected in the Isle of Axholme and West Riding of Lincolnshire. By 14 January 1341 they had received only £66 6s 8d and the assessors of the subsidy were again ordered to pay them. They had still not been satisfied by July 1342[22] when the Crown ordered their repayment from the customs of London, Boston and Hull. Their experience was probably typical of many merchants. Henry Goldbeter was involved in at least five other syndicates and in another with Kelstern, Randman and Luterington, which purchased wool for the Crown in 1341.[23] His brother, John Goldbeter, was also involved in several syndicates, as were William Acastre, Thomas Gra and Thomas Lindsey.[24]

Whether any of the 'ordinary' merchants made a profit out of their dealings with Edward III is impossible to discover. Regular wool merchants could not have anticipated or avoided the morass. Above all, medieval merchants needed a constant flow of business and anyone not involved in the wool monopoly and loans would have been excluded from trading except under licence during the ban which lasted from August 1336 until 1342.[25] Even then, it was only possible to export wool to the staple at Antwerp.[26] Eventually Edward III and a representative group of merchants agreed that payment to the Dordrecht bondholders was to be by means of an allowance of 20s per sack exported during the

---

[21] *CPR 1340–3*, p. 103; PRO, c76/1/5, 16.
[22] *CPR 1338–40*, p. 542; *CCR 1339–41*, p. 601; *1343–4*, pp. 153–5.
[23] *CPR 1341–3*, pp. 256–9; Lloyd, *English Wool Trade*, p. 183. [24] See note 19 above.
[25] M. M. Postan, 'Credit in Medieval Trade', *EcHR*, 1 (1927–8), p. 261; Lloyd, *English Wool Trade*, pp. 179, 183. [26] Lifted for about five months in 1339, Lloyd, *English Wool Trade*, p. 180.

year following midsummer 1343 and an allowance of 6s 8d per sack exported during the following two years, 1344–6.[27]

This dubious chapter in royal finances brought some exceptional provincial entrepreneurs onto the national stage. One was William de la Pole, whose skilful financial footwork gained him a fortune. De la Pole was, however, atypical and few of his contemporaries had his nerve and skill to set up deal after deal, with scarcely any substantial collateral. He created a reputation which he successfully exploited for royal favour, amassing enormous wealth before he eventually fell into royal displeasure. De la Pole was an opportunist, a true capitalist who almost outwitted the wily Edward III.[28]

Whatever the short-term impact of royal policy on the wool trade, exports through Hull in the fourteenth century generally ran at an average of between 3,000 and 5,000 sacks a year, only exceeding 6,000 sacks in 1305–9, 1330–4, and 1355–9. After 1430, however, exports all but collapsed as a consequence of government policy to increase the supply of bullion. Successive governments tried to exploit the wool trade as a means of attracting coin into the country, while restricting the flow of English coins out. The Staple at Calais and its mint were used to attract bullion as a source of revenue to pay the garrison there. Following the Statute of Purveyors in 1352, English coins became popular because of their high specie content compared with continental currencies.[29] There was a continuous struggle for bullion in the late middle ages, and whereas the dukes of Burgundy pursued aggressive debasement policies from the 1380s up to the 1470s,[30] the English government tried to ensure new supplies of bullion by demanding it as part of the purchase price paid by aliens, especially for wool. A combination of a bullion shortage, government policy and rising demand for cloth squeezed the market so that traders most dependent on credit began to suffer. By 1405–6 London grocers were withdrawing from the wool trade but the pattern elsewhere remains obscure.[31]

In 1429 and 1430 the Bullion and Partition Ordinances were passed. Effectively these ended the extensive use of credit in the purchase of wool

[27] Lloyd, *English Wool Trade*, p. 194.
[28] E. B. Fryde, *The Wool Accounts of William de la Pole*, Borthwick Paper No. 25 (York, 1964), and 'The Last Trials of Sir William de la Pole', in *Studies in Medieval Trade and Finance* (London, 1993), XII; Horrox, *The de la Poles of Hull*.
[29] Bolton, *Medieval English Economy*, p. 298; Lloyd, *English Wool Trade*, p. 184; Salzman, *English Trade*, pp. 14–24, 99.
[30] J. H. Munro, *Wool, Cloth, and Gold. The Struggle for Bullion in Anglo-Burgundian Trade 1340–1478* (Toronto, 1972), *passim*.
[31] Nightingale, *Medieval Mercantile Community*, p. 351. There are insufficient customs records extant for Hull to identify a similar response.

at Calais and the buyer had to hand over the whole price in gold or silver. The seller was required to deliver one third of the price in bullion or foreign coins to the Calais mint.[32] Eileen Power described this as the killing of the goose that laid the golden egg, and indeed the effect was catastrophic. The smaller English merchants were ruined since they received proportionately less for their sales and could not afford to wait for payment. They lost the 'banking' facilities of the Staple and their main customers, Dutch and Flemish merchants, found it difficult to pay for wool outright rather than on credit, and the bullion requirement compounded their difficulties.[33]

The Ordinances were repealed in 1444, but the duke of Burgundy's angry reaction had halted trade for nearly four years before 1439. National wool exports fell from a decennial average of over 13,500 sacks to 7,377 in 1431–40, although there was a brief upsurge in 1439–40. Thereafter exports averaged 8,000–9,000 sacks per year, eventually tumbling to about 200 sacks at the beginning of the sixteenth century.[34] Efforts were made to strengthen the Ordinances in 1445 and 1463, provoking further protective embargoes by the duke of Burgundy between 1447–52 and 1464–7. These were ineffective because too many people were dependent on the shipping and handling of English cloth; but the Burgundian bans did account for sudden fluctuations in England's pattern of exports.[35]

The pattern of wool exports through Hull closely followed the national trend. (see table 5.1). From a peak of 6,471 sacks per annum in 1355–60, exports plummeted to an annual 2,379 in 1430–5 and fell again to 1,311 in 1435–40. In part, this may have been a consequence of losses in fleece weights due to a decade of hard winters, culminating in 1434–5, but the Ordinances hit trade harder.[36] Annual exports through Hull picked up again to 2,102 sacks in 1440–5 only to fall below 1,000 after 1455, where they remained thereafter.

---

[32] Lloyd, *English Wool Trade*, pp. 261, 270–1, 273; Bolton, *Medieval English Economy*, p. 298.

[33] E. Power, *The Wool Trade in English Medieval History* (Oxford, 1941), pp. 102; M. M. Postan, 'Private Financial Instruments in Medieval England', in *Medieval Trade and Finance* (Cambridge, 1933), pp. 49–51. Bolton, *Medieval English Economy*, p. 299.

[34] A. R. Bridbury, *Medieval English Clothmaking. An Economic Survey* (London, 1982), p. 116; Carus-Wilson and Coleman, *England's Export Trade*, pp. 59, 68–70.

[35] Bolton, *Medieval English Economy*, p. 299; J. H. Munro, 'An Economic Aspect of the Collapse of the Anglo-Burgundian Alliance, 1428–1442', *EHR*, 85 (1970); Munro, 'Industrial Protectionism in Medieval Flanders: Urban or National?', in H. A. Miskimin, ed., *The Medieval City* (Yale, 1977), pp. 247, 249.

[36] H. H. Lamb, *Climate, Past, Present and Future* (1977) II, pp. 564–5; Lloyd, *English Wool Trade*, pp. 260–4. M. J. Stephenson argues that fleeces were at their worst in terms of weight and quality, and in 1440 returned only a third of the 1250s yield: see 'Wool Yields in the Medieval Economy', *EcHR*, 2nd ser., 41 (1988), pp. 368–91 at pp. 383–4.

Table 5.1. *Hull wool exports, 1300–1510*

(number of sacks from Michaelmas to Michaelmas)

Period	Denizen	Alien	Total	Quinquennial averages
1300–5	20,959	6,611	27,570	5,514
1305–10	13,554	18,239	31,793	6,359
1310–15		2,638[a]	23,588	4,718
1315–20	Denizen and alien counted together		17,326	3,465
1320–5		1,990[b]	14,517	2,903
1325–30	13,574	4,415	17,989	3,598
1330–5	27,836	3,922	31,758	6,352
1335–40 [3]	16,529	2,389	18,918	6,306
1340–5 [3]	10,199	1,407	11,606	3,869
1345–50	Farmed 1343–50			
1350–5	10,810	14,508	25,318	5,064
1355–60	26,297	6,058[c]	32,355	6,471
1360–5	13,052	9,245[d]	22,297	4,459
1365–70	12,767	3,306	16,073	3,215
1370–5	21,556	2,492[e]	24,048	4,810
1375–80	15,549	485	16,034	3,207
1380–5	13,415	872	14,287	2,857
1385–90	17,974	2,048	20,022	4,004
1390–5	21,129	2,156	23,285	4,657
1395–1400	17,520	471	17,991	3,598
1400–5	15,248	12	15,260	3,052 (3,806)
1405–10	18,170	64	18,234	3,647 (5,039)
1410–15			16,313	3,263 (4,984)
1415–20			21,374	4,275 (5,434)
1420–5			22,398	4,480 (5,154)
1425–30	all denizen		18,070	3,614 (4,686)
1430–5			11,894	2,379 (3,199)
1435–40			6,555	1,311 (1,736)
1440–5			10,510	2,102 (2,212)
1445–50	8,261	30	8,291	1,658 (3,262)
1450–5			7,912	1,582 (2,314)
1455–60			2,075	415 (4,184)
1460–5			1,714	343 (2,421)
1465–70			3,443	689 (5,046)
1470–5	all denizen		2,392	478 (4,049)
1475–80			3,041	608 (5,554)
1480–5 [3]			1,215	405
1485–90			1,243	249
1490–5 [4]			798	200
1495–1500			1,600	320

Table 5.1 (*cont.*)

Period	Denizen	Alien	Total	Quinquennial averages
1500–5			1,863	373
1505–10			1,736	347

Notes:

[ ] Denotes number of years figures available if fewer than five.

( ) London quinquennial average.

a 1310–15 counted together, aliens separate 1310–11.

b 1320–5 counted together, aliens separate 1323–5.

c 1355–60 counted together, aliens separate 1355–6.

d 1360–5 counted together 1361–2, 11,183 sacks.

e 1370–5 counted together 1371–2.

Source: E. Carus-Wilson and O. Coleman, *England's Export Trade 1275–1547* (Oxford, 1963).

The 1420s and 1430s were critical for England's overseas trade. Exports fluctuated from year to year, but overall cloth sustained a steady growth against wool and, in spite of Burgundy's embargoes, exports between 1437 and 1467 rose to 60,000 cloths per year. As the sales of English cloth went up, so European demand for wool went down, even though the mid-century glut brought wool prices down: from an average of £5 10s per sack to £5.[37] The wool trade never recovered. Normal credit transactions were not allowed until the late 1470s, and although the remaining staplers could fix high prices to suit themselves, they ruined their main customers and opened up the European market still further for English cloth. Eventually, textile workers in the Low Countries found employment in finishing English cloth and re-exporting it to the Baltic.[38]

In mid fifteenth-century England, profits could still be made in wool (although the Celys thought Yorkshire wool was not worth exporting) and total exports through Hull were still more valuable than total cloth exports: £16,155 compared to £4,495 in 1430–1 and £3,330 compared to £1,260 in 1471–2.[39] After 1410 no aliens exported wool through Hull except for thirty sacks in 1447–8. Against a national measure, Londoners were the biggest investors in the wool trade, but northern merchants dominated those of 'middling stature', exporting from thirty to 100 sacks annually. A small number of York, Beverley and Hull merchants continued to invest in wool, about twelve in 1465, twenty-six in 1473, ten in

[37] Bolton, *Medieval English Economy*, pp. 293, 306; Carus-Wilson and Coleman, *England's Export Trade*, pp. 97–113; T. H. Lloyd, *The Movement of Wool Prices in Medieval England*, EcHR, supplement no. 6 (1973), p. 20.   [38] Bolton, *Medieval English Economy*, p. 300.

[39] Bartlett, 'Aspects of the Economy of York', p. 135.

1489–90.[40] It is also worth noting that of the shrinking band of wealthy Yorkshire merchants active in the second half of the fifteenth century, several were wool staplers. Their trade was not confined to wool however. John Thirsk and Richard York of York both imported wine and woad, and exported lead and cloth.[41] Access to Calais and its mints was an extremely important element in the credit options open to merchants and it could be argued that, without it, provincial credit was insufficient.[42] A diminishing band of staplers continued to be active in trade, and to some fell the ultimate honour of serving as Mayor of the Calais Staple: Richard Russell in 1425, John Thirsk between 1456 and 1473, and Richard York in 1466.[43]

The commitment of Yorkshire merchants to the wool trade is reflected in the steady stream of men who acquired property and other attachments in Calais. Richard Wood and John del Gare, both of York, anticipated dying in Calais and wished to be buried there in the 1390s.[44] Throughout the first half of the fifteenth century, merchants from York especially continued to own property in Calais and several bequeathed rents from Calais properties in their wills.[45] John Kelk of Beverley and his son William also owned rents there in 1407–8[46] and Thomas Brompton of Beverley owned a woolhouse there in 1436. John Aldestonemore of York left wool in Calais to be sold when he died in the same year,[47] and Robert Alcock of Hull, one of the few active wool merchants shipping through Hull in the later fifteenth century, left unspecified goods to be disposed of in Calais in 1484.[48] As late as 1520, Robert Harrison of Hull left £10 to St Mary's in Calais.[49] Virtually all the wool exported through Hull was destined for the cloth manufacturing towns of Artois, Brabant and Flanders, and it is evident from a scattering of references that several Yorkshire merchants were resident there, though fewer seem to have acquired property. John de Helmesley of York asked to be buried in Dordrecht in 1383; Henry Tutbak, also of York, left 6s 8d to St Mary's,

---

[40] Lloyd, *English Wool Trade*, pp. 266–7; PRO, E122/62/19; 63/8.

[41] PRO, E122/61/71; 62/1, 4, 5, 7, 9–11, 13, 16, 17, 19. See also Hanham, *Celys and Their World*, p. 246.

[42] Hanham, *Celys and Their World*, p. 112; Postan, 'Private Financial Instruments', pp. 49–51.

[43] Wedgwood, *Parliamentary Biographies*, pp. 846–8; *VCH York*, p. 104. In 1450, the Staplers' Company made one of several loans to the king, and those being repaid through reduced customs on their exports through Hull included Nicholas Bedford, Hugh Clitheroe and John Marshall of Hull, William Stockton, John Thirsk, William Bracebridge, Richard Lematon and Richard Wartre of York, and John Brompton and Edmund Coppendale of Beverley: *CPR 1446–52*, p. 323; *1452–61*, p. 211. [44] Prob. Reg. I, ff. 58v. (Gare), 61 (Wood).

[45] E.g. Thomas Holme, 1407, Prob. Reg. III, f. 255; Thomas del Gare, II, ff. 110v.–111.

[46] Kelks, Prob. Reg. III, f. 263; Arch. Reg. XVIII, f. 15.

[47] Prob. Reg. III, ff. 406–8, 475. [48] *Ibid.*, v, f. 229b. See also II, f. 68 (Russell in 1443).

[49] Power, *Wool Trade*, pp. 102–3; Prob. Reg. IX, f. 112.

Hareleve, in Brabant in 1398. Peter Upstall left property in Brabant in 1430.[50]

It is not possible to distinguish the types of wool, nor the precise area of its provenance once it had arrived at Hull to be shipped. The customs rolls do not contain those details.[51] A shipment of several sacks no doubt included many different qualities of wool.[52] Yorkshire merchants purchased wool from throughout Yorkshire:[53] a mixture of rough wool from Pennine and upland sheep, derived for the most part from Holderness; Craven, near Skipton; Spaldingmoor, to the south-west of Market Weighton; Cleveland; Richmond, and Blackmoor, in the southern part of the North Yorkshire moors. Better quality wools came from Sherburn-in-Elmet; Burghshire, a region west of the River Washburn; Ripon; Ryedale; 'Walde' which could refer to several parts of the Wolds;[54] and occasionally wool from the Lincolnshire Wolds.[55]

Cloth, the Hanse and the Low Countries

Yorkshire had been a textile manufacturing region long before the expansion of the mid-fourteenth century. Beverley 'blue' cloth had found a ready overseas market in the thirteenth century.[56] Production did not end in the early fourteenth century although the exported output fell.[57] Imported cloth was banned in 1337 and it is likely that exports had increased substantially within a decade to have attracted Edward III's fiscal attention with the imposition of a regular customs duty in 1347. England's recovery in cloth exports was generated by the production of

[50] Dec. & Cap. I, f. 76; Prob. Reg. II, f. 663v; III, f. 4.

[51] For differential Calais deposits reflecting the different regional values, see H. Hall, ed., *Select Cases Concerning the Law Merchant*, II, Selden Soc., 46 (London, 1929), p. 158.

[52] Hanham, *Celys and Their World*, pp. 111–47. On varieties of quality and price within one region, see J. H. Munro, 'The 1357 Wool-Price Schedule and the Decline of Yorkshire Wool Values', *Textile History*, 10 (1979), pp. 211–19; Bartlett, 'Aspects of the Economy of York', p. 160.

[53] See p. 201 below for personal networks which indicate places where wool was purchased.

[54] P. J. Bowden, *The Wool Trade in Tudor and Stuart England* (London, 1962), pp. 36–7; E. Kerridge, 'Wool Growing and Wool Textiles in Medieval and Early Modern Times', in J. G. Jenkins, ed., *The Wool Textile Industry in Britain* (London, 1962), pp. 19–20; Munro, '1357 Wool-Price Schedule', pp. 213–14.

[55] William de la Pole was exporting Lincolnshire wool: Fryde, *Wool Accounts of William de la Pole*, p. 9. Richard Russell of York was buying Lyndsey wool in the early fifteenth century, Prob. Reg. III, ff. 439–40. See also PRO, C1/16/592; *Bronnen*, II, p. 116.

[56] E. Miller, 'The Fortunes of the English Textile Industry in the Thirteenth Century', *EcHR*, 2nd ser., 18 (1965); H. Heaton, *The Yorkshire Woollen and Worsted Industries*, 2nd edn (Oxford, 1965), pp. 2–4.

[57] W. Childs, 'The English Export Trade in Cloth in the Fourteenth Century', in R. Britnell and J. Hatcher, eds., *Progress and Problems in Medieval England* (Cambridge, 1996), pp. 121–47; P. Chorley, 'English Cloth Exports During the Thirteenth and Early Fourteenth Centuries: The Continental Evidence', *Hist. Research*, 61 (1988), pp. 1–10.

cheaper fabrics and straits (narrow cloths). Subsequently, broadcloths did reappear so that, as the cloth industry recovered, it was more widely based to include a greater variety of cloths. By the mid-fourteenth century, 15 to 20 per cent of national exports were the medium-priced worsteds. However, the cloth shipped out through Hull was almost all unfinished: broadcloths and straits, which became most popular with the Hanse in the late fourteenth century.[58]

Between 1350 and 1368, cloth exports grew nationally at an annual average rate of 18 per cent. It was not simply that cloth was paying export duty at a lower rate than wool, nor that the wool trade was still reeling from the consequences of Edward III's woolmongering, as exports in 1353–4 reached 44,914 sacks.[59] In the aftermath of the Black Death in England as food prices began to fall, domestic consumption increased, so stimulating production.[60] If the figures recorded for cloth exports through Hull between 1350 and 1368 were indicative of hinterland production at this time, the expansion in textile manufacturing was four times the national rate (see table 5.2).

At the same time, wool was increasingly subject to control by a diminishing number of merchants determined to monopolise the trade, whereas the cloth trade remained accessible to a larger number of people. More people participated in the different stages of textile production. Investment in trading required relatively little outlay and could begin on a very small scale: John Brompton of Beverley, for instance, exported one half cloth worth 10s in 1391.[61] Textile production and trade offered an outlet for the increasing surplus in the growing prosperity of the mid-fourteenth century. Overseas, the Gascon economy began to recover, and provided a market for English cloth in return for wine and woad.[62] Whereas wool was more or less confined to those countries which had the skill to process it, cloth proved to be a mobile commodity which travelled easily into distant places.[63]

---

[58] Bolton, *Medieval English Economy*, pp. 199–200; Bridbury, *Medieval English Clothmaking*, pp. 86–91; Carus-Wilson and Coleman, *England's Export Trade*, pp. 11–13; N. S. B. Gras, *The Early English Customs* (Cambridge MA, 1918), pp. 66–73. According to Postan, straits were not included in the general cloth custom and so were more popular with the Hanse: 'The Economic and Political Relations of England and the Hanse from 1400 to 1475', in E. Power and M. M. Postan, *Studies in English Trade in the Fifteenth Century* (Cambridge, 1933), p. 145.

[59] Bolton, *Medieval English Economy*, pp. 292, 297; Carus-Wilson and Coleman, *England's Export Trade*, pp. 47, 75–8.

[60] J. Hatcher, *Plague, Population and the English Economy 1348–1530* (London, 1977), pp. 33–4, 50; H. Miskimin, *The Economy of Early Renaissance Europe, 1300–1460* (Cambridge, 1975), p. 135.

[61] PRO, E122/59/24; 58/14 (Hugh de Hanby of Hull). Half cloths were regularly brought to the aulnager for sealing: see e.g. Lister, *Early Yorks Woollen Trade*, pp. 66–8, 70.

[62] Bolton, *Medieval English Economy*, p. 290; P. Wolff, 'English Cloth in Toulouse, 1380–1450', *EcHR*, 2nd ser., 2 (1950), pp. 291–4.

[63] E.g. English cloth was traded into North Africa and the Levant by Italians. See Fryde, 'Italian Maritime Trade', reprinted in his *Studies in Medieval Trade and Finance*, pp. 291–337 at pp. 318–19.

Table 5.2. *Hull cloth exports, 1350–1510*

(numbers from Michaelmas to Michaelmas)

Period	Denizen	Hanse	Others	Total	Quinquennial averages
1350–5	87		168	255	51
1355–60	1,081		827	1,908	382
1360–5	2,456	688	395	3,539	708
1365–70	5,994	815	789	7,598	1,520
1370–5 [3]	2,485	400	189	3,074	1,025
1375–80	4,012	328	569	4,909	982
1380–5	15,913	1,693	284	17,890	3,578
1385–90	14,015	1,671	355	16,041	3,208
1390–5	15,966	1,534	215	17,715	3,543
1395–1400	15,665	1,543	209	17,417	3,483
1400–5	10,590	1,811	458	12,859	2,572 (11,351)
1405–10	6,396	2,567	460	9,423	1,885 (14,251)
1410–15	7,785	3,056	182	11,023	2,205 (14,493)
1415–20	7,931	3,418	250	11,599	2,320 (12,698)
1420–5	11,940	456	112	12,508	2,502 (16,812)
1425–30	17,860	205	43	18,108	3,622 (17,498)
1430–5	13,578	202	125	13,905	2,781 (17,069)
1435–40	13,387	1,392	428	15,207	3,041 (18,124)
1440–5	13,896	519	26	14,441	2,888 (23,938)
1445–50	15,377	97	57	15,531	3,106 (14,225)
1450–5	10,678	829	73	11,580	2,316 (15,393)
1455–60	7,701	636	11	8,348	1,670 (16,695)
1460–5	5,968	1,068	92	7,128	1,426 (16,538)
1465–70	3,118	391	50	3,559	712 (20,878)
1470–5	3,578	444	131	4,153	831 (23,239)
1475–80	10,861	2,104	315	13,280	2,656 (34,534)
1480–5	7,852	2,616	247	10,715	2,143
1485–90	3,477	669	49	4,195	839
1490–5	6,580	1,759	145	8,484	1,697
1495–1500	6,700	3,183	379	10,262	2,052
1500–5	11,778	3,539	660	15,977	3,195
1505–10	6,046	2,288	297	8,631	1,726

Notes:

[ ] Denotes number of years figures available if fewer than five.

( ) London quinquennial average.

Source: E. Carus-Wilson and O. Coleman, *England's Export Trade 1275–1547* (Oxford, 1963).

Clearly there is no single explanation for the way cloth replaced wool: even Edward III's attempts to lure Flemish textile workers to settle in England have to be taken into account.[64] By the mid-1360s, English cloth exports were posing a serious threat to Flemish textile towns and Flemish demand for wool began to fall. English textile producers benefited from a dip in wool prices in the 1380s, due to overproduction bringing additional cost benefits to textile producers. It is important though not to overemphasise the success of the cloth trade versus that in wool. Although it was growing more rapidly, and 40,000 cloths per annum were going to new overseas markets, sufficient wool was still being exported in 1400 to make the equivalent of 80,000 cloths.[65] The intrinsic value of the wool was of course less, but its transport overheads were higher. Such calculations lay at the heart of every commercial deal and the individual's finesse in estimating costs and profits determined his success or failure in a rapidly changing international market.

By 1400 the pattern of north European trade had become more complex and sophisticated. While English cloth was now handled throughout Europe, English merchants generally travelled no further than their traditional markets in the Low Countries and France. Nonetheless, the export of cloth facilitated a two-way trade with Europe, and the late fourteenth century witnessed the arrival in England of an enormous diversity of goods: raw materials, luxury foodstuffs and manufactured goods. These were the preliminary stages in the development of a multiple exchange trade in general merchandise, which advanced the role of brokers and other middlemen and an increasingly complicated manipulation of investment. These were, perhaps, the most fundamental and influential outcomes of the expansion of a large-scale cloth trade.

In Yorkshire, as in the rest of England, the expanding cloth trade attracted growing numbers of merchants from York, Beverley and Hull. Cloth exports through Hull rose from sixty cloths in 1352–3 to 1,396 in 1367–8: a growth rate for average annual exports of 74 per cent (see table 5.2). By 1385 exports were running at an annual average of 3,500 cloths. Why the Yorkshire region was able to respond so quickly to new market opportunities remains unclear. Growth in exports through Hull rapidly diminished, even though local manufacturing continued to expand. Hull lagged behind London and the south coast ports and exports remained at 2–3,000 cloths a year until the volume of trade began to fall off as rela-

---

[64] Bridbury, *Medieval English Clothmaking*, pp. 86–105; E. Lipson, *A Short History of Wool and its Manufacture* (London, 1953), p. 57; Gras, *Early English Customs*, p. 117.

[65] Miskimin, *Early Renaissance Europe*, p. 94; Bolton, *Medieval English Economy*, p. 199; Lloyd, *Movement of Wool Prices*, p. 20. Carus-Wilson and Coleman, *England's Export Trade*, p. 16, estimate that one sack of wool was sufficient to manufacture four to four-and-a-half cloths of assize.

tions with the Hanseatic League degenerated around the end of the four-teenth century. Following the fragile peace concluded with the League in 1408, national cloth exports maintained an uneven but overall rise, until they fell by one third in the 1450s and '60s. Trade picked up once more, averaging 60,000 cloths per year in 1489–90 and 90,000 in 1509–10.[66] The trend through Hull was similar: annual averages of 2–3,000 fell to 1,670 in the late '50s, dipping to just over 700 cloths between 1465 and 1470. The Treaty of Utrecht (1474) had an immedi-ate impact and exports climbed back to the levels of the 1410s, but over one sixth was shipped by Hanse merchants. The recovery was short-lived, and, along with other east coast ports, Hull's cloth exports lan-guished as London tightened its grip on yet another major commodity trade.

Most of the cloths exported through Hull were broadcloths and straits, a narrow cloth half the size of the broadcloth[67] and one which could be fulled in the traditional way. Since the customs officials calculated all cloths in terms of broadcloths, it is difficult to distinguish the straits. When the distinction was made, as in the Particular Roll covering December 1391–September 1392, the majority were broadcloths and less than one sixth of the cloth was described in ells or dozens of straits.[68] Of the cloth brought for aulnage in York in 1394–5, 90 per cent was broad-cloths.[69]

Worsteds were not recorded in all customs rolls and it has been argued, may have been underestimated as exports.[70] However, given the predominance of short staple wool in the region, it is doubtful if worsteds were manufactured locally in Yorkshire on a significant scale before the 1470s, and then they were most likely made from the long wool of Lincolnshire.[71] Equivalents, bed covers and hangings, were exported via Hull throughout the fifteenth century, but were always a small part of total textile exports. Even during the late-fourteenth-century boom, single and double beds exported might have been worth £60 per annum, compared to the average £4,800 worth of broadcloths. The stray references to York merchants exporting worsteds come from Hanse records and the origin of the cloth was not recorded. For example, Richard Bawtry and others exported twenty-five worsteds in 1404 as part of a largely broadcloth cargo, and Richard Fasset a further

[66] Carus-Wilson and Coleman, *England's Export Trade*, pp. 91–113; Bolton, *Medieval English Economy*, p. 292.   [67] I.e. 12 yds by 1 yd *Statutes of the Realm*, II, pp. 403–4.
[68] PRO, E122/59/23.   [69] Bartlett, 'Aspects of the Economy of York', pp. 72–3.
[70] Campbell, 'Norwich', p. 16.
[71] R. A. Pelham, 'Medieval Foreign Trade, Eastern Ports', in H. C. Darby, ed., *An Historical Geography of England Before 1800 AD* (Cambridge, 1936), p. 253; PRO, C. Inq. Misc. Chancery, 1307–49, no. 1628. See Prob. Reg. II, ff. 378–80 (Collinson) for Lincolnshire wools.

twenty pieces in 1407, again as part of a largely broadcloth consignment.[72]

Almost without exception, all cloths exported through Hull were described as *sine grano*, which implies that they were not finished, although not necessarily that they had not been dyed with grain.[73] These cloths were also being made by textile workers in the West Riding, in direct competition with workers in Beverley and York.[74] Production in the region continued to expand (see table 5.3). In the late fourteenth century, most was destined either for the Low Countries, Gascony or Hanseatic customers in the Baltic region, but it is not possible to estimate how much went where. Some was an essential component of the exchange trade with Gascony, especially useful when there was a shortage of currency, so that cloth was exchanged directly for woad or wine. Some cross-shipping of other commodities occurred probably for the same reasons: for instance Yorkshiremen carried Baltic corn and timber to Gascony and Portuguese figs to Normandy.[75]

Lead

Lead was well established as an export commodity by the mid-fourteenth century but quantities are difficult to measure before the fifteenth century. Overseas demand for lead stimulated production from a mid-fifteenth-century low,[76] and by 1471–2 constituted 74 per cent by value of all Hull exports excluding wool, cloth and hides. Joint ventures mounted by the Hull corporation accounted for most of the lead shipped in 1473, and Hull merchants routinely handled more than did the merchants from York, or indeed, Beverley. By the 1490s, however, the Hanse had come to dominate the trade: in 1492–3 they accounted for £585 worth of the total £1,342 of lead exported and in 1496–7 they shipped all £825 worth.[77]

[72] PRO, E122/59/2, 8, 23, 159/11; Bartlett, 'Aspects of the Economy of York', pp. 73–6; *Hanserecesse, 1256–1430*, V, pp. 331–2; *Hanseakten*, p. 236.

[73] J. H. Munro, 'The Medieval Scarlet and the Economics of Sartorial Splendour', in N. B. Harte and K. G. Ponting, eds., *Cloth and Clothing in Medieval Europe* (London, 1983), pp. 13–70.

[74] For detailed discussion, see pp. 316–17 below.

[75] *VCH Hull*, pp. 65–7; PRO, E101/128/31, E122/159/11, C1/19/43.

[76] *CPR 1350–4*, p. 129. Pollard, *North-Eastern England*, pp. 74–5; I. S W. Blanchard, 'Seigneurial Entrepreneurship and the Bishops of Durham and the Weardale Iron Industry, 1406–1529', *Business History*, 15 (1973), pp. 91–111 at pp. 100–1.

[77] *VCH Hull*, p. 67; PRO, E122/62/7, 19.

Table 5.3. *Yorkshire cloth production, estimated from aulnagers' accounts*

5.3.1 Cloth production by district

Period	Number of cloths	District
1378–9: Nov–Jan	504+	East Riding only
1394–5: July-Nov	1,253+	County only
1394–5: July-Nov	3,256+	City of York
1395–6: Nov–Nov	1,718+	County excl. York
1396–7: Nov–Nov	484	West Riding
1398–9: Apr–Oct	592	City of York
1469–70: Sep–Sep	2,586	West Riding
1471–3: Mar–Sep [2.5]	4,747+	Hull, West Riding
1473–5: Sep–Sep [2]	4,802+	Hull, York, County
1475–8: Sep–Mar [2.5]	7,128	Hull, York, County

5.3.2 Cloth production by major centre

Period	York	Hull	Halifax	Ripon
1394–5	3,256			
1395–6				168+
1396–7				177
1398–9	592			
1469–70			853+	889
1471–3		295	1,518+	1,597
1473–5	2,346+	426+	1,493+	1,396+
1475–8	2,288	426+	1,493+	1,385+

Notes:

[ ] = More than one year.

+ = Parts of a cloth of assize. All varieties of cloth were converted into an equivalent standard cloth of assize for the purposes of the subsidy.

These figures must be treated with caution and can only indicate trends. The identical figures for 1473–5 and 1475–8 suggest an *ad hoc* approach for those years at least.

Source: Aulnagers' Rolls transcribed in J. Lister, ed., *Early Yorkshire Woollen Trade*, YAS, Rec. Ser., 64 (Leeds, 1924).

The geography and composition of trade

Wine and the Atlantic ports

Before the preliminary skirmishes and then the Hundred Years War, Gascon ports had been exporting between 75 and 100,000 tuns of wine annually. The outbreak of war disrupted shipping to such an extent that exports fell by over 70 per cent in one year between 1335–6 and 1336–7; thereafter quantities fluctuated but never recovered pre-war tunnages. The share enjoyed by English consumers cannot be calculated precisely, but it was probably Gascony's principal market.[78] Between 1325 and 1350, Hull was ranked second or third in England as an entrepot for wine: all but a trickle coming from Gascony.[79] Wine was generally the return cargo in a two-way trade in cloth and food. During the mid-fourteenth century corn was the largest single English export to Gascony, with the addition of ale, peas and beans in years of bad harvest.[80] In the bullion-conscious 1360s, vintners exported cloth themselves for the express purpose of trading it for wine and woad in Gascony.[81] Cloth and re-exports of Baltic goods such as corn and timber became a major part of Hull's trade into Gascony.[82] One consequence of the disruptions of war was an increase in the numbers of French merchants actively engaged in the wine trade.[83] Some English merchants, including Yorkshire men, found the risks of wartime trade acceptable if commercial contacts were to survive. Encouraged by the government, Thomas de Santon and others of Hull exported grain under licence to Bordeaux in 1347, and Walter Box and other vintners of Hull, and Robert de Selby and others of York, were granted licences in 1364 to take £50 in cash to Gascony to buy wine.[84]

The scale of overseas trade into Hull is harder to estimate during the second half of the fourteenth century, but from records of alien shipments, wine imports seemed to be falling (see table 5.4). A certain urgency on the part of both producers and buyers was evident whenever

---

[78] M. K. James, *Studies in the Medieval Wine Trade* (London, 1971), pp. 9, 32–3.

[79] For individual Hull merchants see *CPR 1330–4*, pp. 414, 425, 432; *1345–8*, pp. 216, 281–3; *1350–4*, pp. 130, 384, 464, 467, 479; *1354–8*, pp. 43, 94, 285, 324, 346, 467, 471–2, 477, 518, 625.

[80] E.g. Roger Swerd and Walter Helleward of Hull, *CPR 1334–8*, p. 345. See also *1345–8*, p. 281; Y. Renouard, ed., *Bordeaux sous les rois d'Angleterre* (Bordeaux, 1965), p. 431.

[81] E.g. Richard Bate and Robert de Selby of Hull, *CPR 1361–4*, p. 496; *1364–7*, p. 522. In statutes of 1363, 1402 and 1403, the government tried in vain to achieve a perfect balance of trade by insisting on goods being purchased in England to the same value as imported wine: James, *Wine Trade*, p. 78; M. G. A. Vale, *English Gascony 1399–1453* (Oxford, 1970), p. 15.

[82] Wolff, 'English Cloth in Toulouse', pp. 290–4; T. H. Lloyd, *England and the German Hanse 1157–1611* (Cambridge, 1991), p. 89.   [83] James, *Wine Trade*, pp. 26–7.

[84] PRO, E101/25/20 (my thanks to Christian Liddy for this reference); *CPR 1345–8*, p. 281, *1364–7*, pp. 16–17. See also *1361–4*, pp. 491, 495–7, 500, 517, 522; *1364–7*, pp. 15, 32, 50, 59, 86; *1370–4*, p. 118.

Table 5.4. *Hull wine imports, 1323–1505*

(Michaelmas to Michaelmas)

Period	Quinquennial totals		Quinquennial averages
	Denizen ships	Alien tuns (new custom)	
1323–5 [2]	10	677	
1325–30 [1]	4	617	
1330–5 [4]	16	3,180	
1335–40 [4]	54	1,082	
1340–5 [3]	92	1,390	
1345–50 [4]	34	110	
1350–5		500	100
1355–60 [4]		455	114
1360–5 [4]		731	183
1365–70 [2]		132	66
1370–5		0	0
1375–80 [4]		154	39 .
1380–5		0	0
1385–90		0	0
1390–5 [3]		118	39
	Denizen + alien tuns		
1385–90 [2]	2,985		1,493
1390–5 [1]	803		803
1395–1400	not available		
1400–5 [2]	2,118		1,059 (3,853)
1405–10	5,352		1,070 (3,788)
1410–15	7,786		1,557 (5,646)
1415–20	5,719		1,144 (5,584)
1420–5 [2]	1,815		908 (3,635)
1425–30	3,104		621 (3,168)
1430–5	4,877		975 (3,541)
1435–40	3,310		662 (2,185)
1440–5	5,635		1,127 (4,135)
1445–50	5,736		1,147 (2,933)
1450–5	3,430		686 (2,520)
1455–60	1,033		207 (1,409)
1460–5	1,782		356 (2,013)
1465–70	1,876		375 (1,900)
1470–5	2,152		430 (1,824)
1475–80	2,989		598 (2,592)
1480–5	2,115		423 (3,328)
1485–90	1,458		292 (3,359)
1490–5	2,189		438 (3,567)
1495–1500	2,587		517 (3,621)
1500–5	2,447		489

Notes:
[ ] Denotes number of years figures available if fewer than five.
( ) London quinquennial average.
Source: M. K. James, *Studies in the Medieval Wine Trade* (London, 1971); *VCH Hull.*

a truce was declared during prolonged fighting, even though prices had risen as a consequence of the war. Heavy buying followed the truce of 1389; Hull and London imported 8,000 tuns – over half the total for the country. Denizens accounted for all wine imported through Hull by 1371–2 and for almost all cargoes in 1389–90.[85] French wine frequently made up the entire cargo of ships entering Hull: nine out of fifteen ships in 1391–6 and sixteen out of twenty-one in 1398–9. By the 1390s, imports from the Atlantic ports were becoming more varied. England had become an importer of salt mainly from the Bay of Bourgneuf in southern Brittany, although often transhipped via the Low Countries. In 1398–9, 723 quarters worth £132 were shipped into Hull, and whole shiploads occasionally arrived. Similarly, whole shiploads of woad arrived from Normandy and later from Brabant: about 400 tuns were imported in 1383–4 and 1391–2. Other items in their cargoes included Spanish iron, imported via Bayonne, and Portuguese cork, figs and raisins. Imports from the Baltic into Hull were transhipped on to Gascony and included timber, flax, herrings and corn.[86]

Between 1400 and 1450, Hull was once again the second or third largest port for French wine imports, accounting for close to 1,000 tuns annually. Some of this may have come from other sources because Bordeaux's exports fell severely in 1438–9, due to bad weather in 1437–8 and pillaging in the Bordelais the following year. Imports into Hull though, faltered only slightly, falling from 634 tuns in 1437–8 to 447 tuns in 1438–9 and up to 828 in 1439–40.[87] Following the truce of 1444, 136 ships carried wine from Bordeaux to Hull between September 1444 and February 1445.[88] Ships of varying sizes were used: for example, in 1435 two Hull ships, the *Petit Gabriel*, and the *Grand Gabriel*, carried 50 tuns and 133 tuns respectively, and in 1459, the *Anthony* of Hull carried 650 tuns.[89] A feature of the wine trade during the fifteenth century was the increasing capacity of ships, best exemplified by the huge Italian carracks and galleys trading out of Southampton. Eventually, of course, these economies of scale gave the Italians unbeatable advantages in their continuing preference for southern ports, to the detriment of the east coast ports.[90]

After the military defeat in Gascony in 1453, wine imports to Hull plunged to under 500 tuns a year, a possible cause of the sharp fall in

---

[85] James, *Wine Trade*, pp. 29–30; *VCH Hull*, p. 64.

[86] A. R. Bridbury, *England and the Salt Trade in the Later Middle Ages* (Oxford, 1955), pp. 124, 170–2; *VCH Hull*, pp. 40, 67–8.   [87] James, *Wine Trade*, pp. 40–1, 111.

[88] R. Boutruche claims that 13,000 tuns were imported in those months: *La crue d'une société: seigneurs et paysans de Bordelais pendant la guerre de cent ans* (Paris, 1947), p. 404. James, however, calculated a figure of only 1,278 tuns for the whole of 1444–5: *Wine Trade*, p. 111; BL Add. MS 15524.

[89] Renouard, *Bordeaux*, pp. 554, 556.   [90] Fryde, 'Italian Maritime Trade', pp. 308–13.

Hull's cloth exports in the late '50s. Wine imports recovered slightly after the Treaty of Piquigny was made in 1475–6, but languished thereafter (see table 5.4). Eight Yorkshire merchants, including one from Bridlington, were licensed to trade at Bordeaux in 1483, and although the tunnage of their ships ranged from 50 to 300 tuns, it is not possible to estimate the quantities of wine they imported.[91] It could not have been very great. French woad and other dyestuffs, salt and wine still came to Hull, but increasingly *via* the Low Countries.[92] Trade with northern France began to increase from about 1460: between 1460 and 1499, six ships from Dieppe and one from Rouen were recorded trading in Hull. Imports had become more varied and included canvas and fruit, and transhipped Baltic commodities such as wax, pitch, timber, fish and iron. Return cargoes were made up of cloth, lead and some coal.[93]

Spanish and Portuguese merchants rarely ventured up the east coast, although a Spaniard was buying corn in Hull in 1346 to ship to Bordeaux.[94] Some Yorkshiremen did trade directly with Spain and Portugal.[95] Hull merchants were active on the pilgrim run to Santiago via Corunna in the early fifteenth century.[96] Others exported corn and peas to Portugal in the 1340s and a Breton was licensed to carry corn from Hull to Portugal in 1485.[97] More often, Spanish iron and wine, and Portuguese cork, raisins, figs and oil were imported either via Bayonne in the fourteenth century or increasingly through the Low Countries in the fifteenth.[98] Castilian merchants traded directly with Hull in 1465, but the primary focus of their commerce was on London and the ports of the south and west. Few English merchants ventured beyond Gibraltar or

---

[91] F. Michel, *Histoire du commerce et de la navigation à Bordeaux*, I (Bordeaux, 1867); BL Harl. MS 1433, f. 78v.   [92] James, *Wine Trade*, p. 48; Bridbury, *England and the Salt Trade*, p. 124.

[93] PRO, E122/63/8 (Bay salt); M. Mollat, *Le commerce maritime normand à la fin du moyen âge* (Paris, 1952), pp. 97, 134–43, 145, 149–50, 160. Several merchants from Yorkshire were active in Rouen, 1419–22, including Richard Rolleston of Beverley, William Alkbarowe of York, John Bedford, John Fitling, John Tutbury, Robert Shackles, John Grimsby and William Malton of Hull. See ADSM Tabellionage de Rouen, ff. 214, 314, 336v., 438v. I am grateful to Robert Massey for these references.   [94] *CPR 1345–8*, p. 206; *VCH Hull*, pp. 64–5.

[95] In 1427 a group of Hull and Beverley merchants sought a safe-conduct for a Bilbao ship, laden with iron for Hull: PRO, Treaty Roll 5H VI m. 9. I am grateful to Wendy Childs for this reference. See also *CPR 1364–7*, p. 59 for Geoffrey Hanby of Hull importing Spanish wine; *CCR 1385–9*, p. 368 for York merchants importing figs, raisins and wine from Portugal via London; *1392–6*, p. 324 for Robert del Crosse of Hull and others in Algarve.

[96] Davy and Shackles of Hull: PRO, Treaty Roll 6H VI m. 16.

[97] PRO, E122/193/14; *CPR 1476–85*, p. 540.

[98] PRO, E122/59/23, 24 (1391–2); 159/11 (1398–9); 62/4 (1462–3); 62/17 (1471–2 imported from Liege); 63/8 (1489–90); Lloyd, *English Wool Trade*, p. 140; W. R. Childs, *Anglo-Castilian Trade in the Middle Ages* (Manchester, 1978), p. 179; *VCH Hull*, p. 65. Two Hull men made bequests of Spanish iron in their wills: Alan Wilcock in 1408, and Thomas Wood, draper, in 1490: Prob. Reg. II, f. 575v. (Wilcock); V, ff. 402v.–3v. (Wood).

shipped directly to Mediterranean ports, and John Taverner of Hull, who was granted a licence in 1449 to send goods to Italy, was unusual.[99]

Baltic trades

While the visits of traders from France, Portugal and Spain to Hull were rare, those of the Hanse merchants were all too frequent. They competed fiercely with east coast traders throughout the fourteenth and fifteenth centuries, using the political strength derived from their commercial confederation to manipulate international diplomacy.[100] Their eventual triumph and the failure of English merchants to develop alternative markets had disastrous consequences for the merchants of York and Beverley.

The English need for Baltic products, especially timber, fish and grain, was initially more important than the Baltic demand for cloth in generating commerce between the two regions and, indeed, the balance of trade through Hull suggests that English demand remained the determining factor there. As early as the first decades of the fourteenth century, when a dozen or more Baltic cargoes might reach Hull in a year, timber was inevitably one of the commodities. In 1304–5, over 25,000 boards and wainscots, about 600 empty barrels, over 4,500 troughs, bowls and boxes, 660 lances and 7,950 bowstaves were shipped into Hull. Timber and wooden items continued to be a regular and important commodity as can be seen from imports for 1401, when 18,000 wainscots and boards, 2,000 spars, 11 masts, 70 bowls, tables and boxes, 2,000 arrow-shafts and 7,680 bowstaves were imported.[101]

Just as other branches of international commerce became increasingly diversified during the late fourteenth century, so, along Hanseatic trading routes, came increasing quantities of copper and iron from Sweden, stockfish and cod from Norway, herrings from Skania and later Iceland, grain and timber from Prussia and Poland, minerals from Hungary, wine from southern Germany, salt from France and Portugal, fur from Lithuania, pitch, oil and tar from Russia. There was generally a deficit balance along this east–west axis, with the east providing more valuable raw materials and the west cheaper manufactured goods. Hull was the major east coast port for iron imports, especially high quality Swedish

[99] PRO, E122/62/7, 63/8; *Feodera*, V (2), p. 21; Childs, *Anglo-Castilian Trade*, pp. 178–9, 224.
[100] P. Dollinger, *The German Hansa* (1964, translated 1970), pp. xix–xx, 94; T. H. Lloyd, *Alien Merchants in England in the High Middle Ages* (Brighton, 1983), pp. 139–44; M. M. Postan, 'Relations of England and the Hanse', in Power and Postan, *Studies in English Trade*, pp. 131, 133; G. D. Ramsay, *English Overseas Trade during the Centuries of Emergence* (London, 1957), pp. 99–100.
[101] PRO, E122/55/20, 60/2.

osmunds, and although iron may have accounted for 7 per cent of Hull's imports by value in 1398–9,[102] fish were far more important. Herrings have been estimated to have been worth £1,237, over one third of Hull's imports, excluding wine, in 1389–9.[103]

The demand for and supply of fish was fundamental to Anglo-Baltic trade. English ships, carrying little or no freight, ventured into the Baltic and, in 1368, one third of the Danzig ships trading in the west returned home in ballast. However, cloth was becoming as important to Hanse merchants as fish and timber were to the English. By 1368, it comprised one third of all imports into Lubeck, for example, and one quarter of total trade.[104] Hanse demand for cloth remained high, but showed an increasing preference for kerseys in addition to traditional broadcloths by the 1390s.[105] Whatever Yorkshire cloth found its way into Hanse cargoes after 1420, very little was shipped through Hull. More likely it was carried overland for loading in London.

DOMESTIC TRADE

It has been inevitable that English historians have traditionally placed a greater emphasis on overseas rather than coastal and internal trade. Perceptions of England as a sea-trading nation with a seaborne empire encourage that view. More practically, the sources for domestic trade and commerce have survived more randomly, so that while one or two regional trading networks have been reconstructed,[106] most have remained obscure, and probably always will. Without appropriate sources such as accounts of local tolls, urban court records and local estate and household accounts, it is difficult to do more at present than to sketch in suggested probabilities. Much more will no doubt emerge as rural and urban historians bring their work together.

Redistribution

Hull was the major entrepot for much of the north and east of England, with excellent river connections facilitating waterborne carriage.

---

[102] *VCH Hull*, pp. 40, 67–8; W. R. Childs, 'England's Iron Trade in the Fifteenth Century', *EcHR*, 2nd ser., 34 (1981), pp. 25–47 at p. 37.

[103] Lloyd, *German Hanse*, p. 89; *VCH Hull*, p. 61; PRO, E122/55/20, 60/2.

[104] Dollinger, *Hansa*, pp. 213–15, 218; Miskimin, *Early Renaissance Europe*, pp. 123–4.

[105] Lloyd, *German Hanse*, p. 78.

[106] Two, based heavily on court rolls, are R. H. Britnell, *Growth and Decline in Colchester, 1300–1525* (Cambridge, 1986), pp. 80–5, 100–2, 107, 246–8, and M. Kowaleski, *Local Markets and Regional Trade in Medieval Exeter* (Cambridge, 1995), pp. 222–333. See also Britnell, 'Colchester Courts and Court Records, 1310–1525', *Trans. Essex Arch. Hist. Soc.*, 3rd ser., 17 (1986), pp. 133–40.

Redistribution became an important part of the general merchant's business. We know that the increasing variety of goods imported through Hull was destined for customers throughout the region, but we cannot identify many individually. In the early fourteenth century the royal butler was a regular customer, purchasing direct from importers and freighting wine on to a wide range of royal manors and castles: to the manors of Burstwick and Colwick via Torksey and deep into Nottinghamshire to Nottingham castle and thence to the manors of Clipston and Sherwood.

Several of the religious houses in the north of England used York and Hull as shopping centres, as well as making many purchases directly from merchants from all three towns.[107] Some purchased wine direct from the importers, mainly in Hull but sometimes in York.[108] Alan Staveley of York supplied the Minster[109] but most institutional purchases were made from several merchants and in varying quantities. For instance, in 1458–9 Fountains Abbey bought one hogshead from Thomas Brereton of York for £4 8s 4d; three hogsheads from William Wells of York for £4; and £2 14s worth from Thomas Hawthorn of Hull. Maybe it was policy to 'shop around', but the pattern is suggestive of sales at the quayside. Fountains also bought from Ripon merchants and borrowed money from them,[110] and Durham monks made purchases from Hartlepool and Newcastle merchants as often as they did from South Yorkshire men. Indeed, in the fourteenth and fifteenth centuries, Newcastle and Hartlepool merchants dominated the priory's supply of French wine. Although it has been argued that London supplied more exotic wines,[111] York merchants were also selling the priory malmsey in 1412–13 and Spanish wine in 1414–16.[112]

Wine was only one of many luxury items sold to the ecclesiastical corporations. Thomas Barton of York, for instance, supplied at least two canons in York Minster with spices, and their debts to him were listed in their wills. Another York spicer, Roger Belton, provided York canons

---

[107] E.g. Richard Allerton was selling corn to Bolton Priory in York in the 1320s: I. Kershaw, *Bolton Priory. The Economy of a Northern Monastery, 1286–1325* (Oxford, 1973), p. 93. A John Langton, probably of Hull, was supplying Archbishop Savage with large quantities of cloth for liveries in the late fifteenth century: J. Raine, ed., *The Historians of the Church of York and its Bishops*, III, Rolls Series (London, 1984), p. 370.   [108] James, *Wine Trade*, pp. 180–1.

[109] *Test. Ebor.* IV, p. 86; *VCH Hull*, p. 54; N. Morimoto, 'The English Wine Trade and Durham Cathedral Priory in the Fourteenth Century', *Nagoya Gakuin University Review*, 10 (1973), pp. 57–146.

[110] J. T. Fowler, ed., *Memorials of the Abbey of St Mary of Fountains*, III, Surtees Soc., 130 (1918), p. 88.   [111] Dobson, *Durham Priory*, pp. 14, 265; Morimoto, 'Durham Wine Trade', pp. 75–92.

[112] J. T. Fowler, ed., *Extracts from the Account Rolls of the Abbey of Durham*, I, Surtees Soc., 99 (1898); II, 100 (1899); III, 103 (1901) at pp. 609, 611. Indeed, Durham bought wine directly from Hull merchants at the port: *ibid.*, I, p. 151; II, pp. 488, 494, 516, 545; III, pp. 613, 619.

with medicines in the 1450s.[113] The account rolls of Fountains Abbey and Durham Priory reveal an extraordinary range of imported basic goods as well as luxuries bought throughout the fourteenth and fifteenth centuries, mainly in York. The list includes bitumen, wax, oil, iron, salt, vinegar, raisins, Cyprus sugar, ginger, aniseed, stockfish and, for feast days, eels, lampreys, perch, fresh salmon and swans.[114] Thomas Bracebridge and Thomas del More of York acted as purchasing agents for the archdeacon of Richmond.[115]

As far as general trade was concerned, both Durham Priory and Fountains Abbey used a variety of suppliers. In the first half of the fifteenth century, Durham Priory bought most of its cloth in York: in bulk if green, also a blue medley was favoured.[116] During the fourteenth and fifteenth centuries they purchased miscellaneous items in York and Hull,[117] but also bought goods at Boston's fair, wine and Spanish iron at Newcastle, fish, wax and oil at Scarborough, and spices, figs, raisins, fish and cloth from Ripon men.[118] The merchants from York, Beverley and Hull, then, never had a clear monopoly over general trade in the region, but did have advantages as the primary importers of many of these items.

Gentry households might be expected to have been important customers, but the evidence is scanty. Lady Elizabeth Clifford, who died in 1424, bought wine from John Pettyclerk of York, and owed John Souerby of York, another of her suppliers £6 (for what we do not know). Similarly the countess of Northumberland (so described) owed John Brompton of Beverley £104 6s 8d when he died in 1444.[119] In the fifteenth century there is some evidence that both gentry households and religious houses were finding it difficult to pay their bills in cash. Fountains Abbey was settling its accounts in a mixture of wool, lead and cash in the 1450s, whereas the chaplain of Lord Scrope of Bolton preferred to settle a £14 debt to John Metcalfe of York, with twelve fothers of lead.[120]

It is unlikely that merchants had any interests in local victualling but there was enough profit in bulk sales to attract them from time to time, especially when there were restrictions on the movement of grain. John

---

[113] *VCH York*, p. 99; *Test. Ebor.* III, pp. 114, 142–3.

[114] *Durham Acct Rolls*, II, pp. 516, 537, 551, 566; III, pp. 653, 655, 656; *Mem. Fountains*, III, pp. 11, 45–6, 70, 72, 89, 112.   [115] *Test. Ebor.* III, p. 20.

[116] Dobson, *Durham Priory*, pp. 62, 261; *Durham Acct Rolls*, III, pp. 616, 632, 636.

[117] *Durham Acct Rolls*, III, pp. 653, 655, 656, 658, 692; *Mem. Fountains*, III, pp. 10–11, 26–9, 45–6, 70–2, 88–9, 104, 110–12, 145, 147, 156.

[118] *Mem. Fountains*, III, pp. 111–12, 144, 150, 156, 196; Dobson, *Durham Priory*, p. 261; Morimoto, 'Durham Wine Trade', pp. 67–146, and 'Purchases of Cloth by Durham Cathedral Priory in the Fourteenth Century', *Nagoya Gakuin University Review*, 10 (1973), pp. 357–422.

[119] *Test. Ebor.* III, p. 87; IV, p. 298; Prob. Reg. II, f. 86v.

[120] *Mem. Fountains*, III, p. 76; PRO, C1/148/2.

de Ryse of Beverley had to obtain a licence to buy corn in 1356, Stephen and Adam Coppendale, also of Beverley, to buy corn to sell in London in 1371,[121] Robert de Selby of Hull, to carry 1,000 quarters of grain to Scotland in 1378–9.[122] It is difficult to estimate how unusual such a procedure was. John Toty, a baker of Penrith, owed William Ormeshead of York £23 in 1441, maybe for corn, anticipating York's development as a grain centre from the 1450s.[123] Grimsby was a rival entrepot for Yorkshire oats, wheat, beans and malt, regularly shipped to London, drawing men from York, Beverley and Hull to trade through Grimsby.[124]

Merchants also anticipated enough profit as victuallers to the army and royal household to mobilise their capital and local suppliers.[125] Merchants from all three towns worked in the Crown's service in this way. John and Walter Helleward were both victuallers for the Crown in York and Newcastle in 1321. Walter acted as a victualler in 1319 and again in 1322 together with Robert Upsale and Thomas de Yafford of Hull and Thomas Waghen of Beverley.[126] John Southcoup of Hull shipped sixty-three tuns of wine and ten tuns of flour from Bordeaux to Newcastle for the Crown in the early fourteenth century.[127] John Barton of Hull was procuring corn for the Crown in the East Riding in 1335–6 and was a royal purveyor in 1338–9.[128] In spite of the risk of being political scapegoats, as in 1343, when the dilatory payment of loans by northern merchants was used to explain Balliol's invasion,[129] royal purveyance still attracted individuals in the fifteenth century. Nicholas Blackburn of York and John Liversege of Hull were victualling Berwick in 1405, and in 1416 Blackburn and John Lofthouse of York undertook to supply the royal household with fish from their own deep-sea fishing boat. Thomas Barton of York was licensed to victual Berwick in 1448, and it would seem that the responsibility for supplying Berwick was transferred to Yorkshire merchants when Newcastle men were insufficient.[130]

The regular flow of lead to merchants for export probably also

---

[121] *CPR 1354–8*, p. 406; *1370–4*, p. 54.

[122] PRO, c76/61 m. 2; *Bronnen*, I, p. 755. Three Beverley men were licensed to ship 400 quarters of grain to Middleburgh in 1388, and Robert Shackles of Hull, to ship grain to Bordeaux: *Bronnen*, I, p. 479; PRO, sc8/179/8943.

[123] *CPR 1441–6*, p. 7; Bartlett, 'Aspects of the Economy of York', p. 50.

[124] PRO, e122/47/4; S. H. Rigby, *Medieval Grimsby: Growth and Decline* (Hull, 1993), p. 59; South Humberside RO, Grimsby Court Rolls, 18 rII October and May; 2 hvI April, May, November. I am grateful to Steve Rigby for these references.

[125] For more on victualling see *VCH York*, p. 100; C. J. Given-Wilson, 'Purveyance for the Royal Household, 1362–1413', *BIHR*, 56 (1983), pp. 145–63.

[126] *CPR 1317–21*, pp. 376, 597; *1321–4*, pp. 86, 109; *VCH York*, p. 100. See also *CPR 1313–17*, pp. 540–53.   [127] PRO, sc8/75/3702–4.

[128] *CCR 1333–7*, p. 543; *1337–9*, p. 91.   [129] *CCR 1343–6*, p. 87.

[130] *CPR 1405–8*, p. 30; *1416–22*, p. 52; *1446–52*, p. 150. Cf. Rigby, *Grimsby*, p. 58.

depended on contacts with suppliers. Marion, widow of John Kent of York, continued his business after his death and may have taken over his contract with a Miles Radcliff of Rilston, as she inherited Radcliff's debt to the business of £8 worth of lead. John Gisburn of York must have been sure of his suppliers when he agreed to obtain seventeen and a half fothers of lead for the roof of New Hall, Oxford, being built by William of Wykeham, bishop of Winchester.[131]

The broad pattern of inland trade can be inferred from the network of debts generated between Yorkshire merchants, their customers and associates. Indebtedness will be discussed more fully in chapter 7 and it will suffice here to note the pattern of distribution. Beverley merchants were owed money by men from Wakefield and Lincoln, and were dealing with London woolmongers.[132] Hull's debtors were more widespread, and came from Newcastle, Whitby, Grimsby, Lincoln, Chesterfield, Southampton, Cheshire and London, including a debt to Robert Holme acknowledged by Ubertinus de Bardes in 1424–5.[133] The debtors of the York merchants were equally widespread, and came from Whitby, Snaith, Hedon, Yarm, Bolton-on-Dearne, Doncaster, Pontefract and other places in Yorkshire;[134] and from Newcastle, Penrith, Lancaster, Coventry, Burton-on-Trent and Newark.[135] There is evidence of an increasing number of debts between York and London traders in the fifteenth century, a reflection of the growing interest of Londoners in northern trade.[136]

Coastal trade

Coastal trade accounted for a rarely measurable but crucial proportion of many ports' business.[137] Indeed it may have been the bulk of many merchants' trade. Hull was an established port of call for ships from Europe, London and other east coast ports, *en route* for Newcastle, Berwick and possibly Iceland. Ships from Hull carried wine, salt and other imported commodities along the coast. Durham Priory often purchased wine in

---

[131] *CPR 1381–5*, p. 50; *1476–85*, p. 84.

[132] *CCR 1330–3*, p. 606; *1333–7*, pp. 58, 728; *CPR 1385–9*, p. 573; *1452–61*, p. 185.

[133] *CPR 1358–61*, pp. 38, 112; *1388–92*, p. 259; *1408–13*, p. 341; *1418–22*, p. 95; *CCR 1405–9*, pp. 226, 487; *1429–35*, p. 371; Hull RO, D454. See also *Cheshire Sheaf*, 22 (1925), p. 76 for John Grene of Hull's debt of £225 to a Londoner and two Chester merchants in 1463.

[134] *CPR 1446–52*, p. 293; *1452–61*, pp. 384, 447, 456; *1461–7*, pp. 9, 410, 431.

[135] *CCR 1318–23*, pp. 106, 131, 133; *CPR 1436–41*, pp. 216, 457, 458; *1441–6*, pp. 7, 18; *1456–61*, p. 241; PRO, c47/86/21/538.

[136] *CCR 1447–54*, p. 352; *CPR 1436–41*, p. 322; *1452–61*, p. 132; *1461–7*, pp. 315, 322, 502. See below, chapter 8, for further discussion of competition with London.

[137] Kowaleski, *Medieval Exeter*, pp. 33–8, and 'Port Towns in Fourteenth-Century Devon', in M. Duffy, B. Greenhill, S. Fisher and J. Youings, eds., *A New Maritime History of Devon*, I (1992), pp. 62–72. See also Platt, *Medieval Southampton*, ch. 13.

Hull in the fourteenth century and had it shipped up to Newcastle and Hartlepool,[138] and in 1504–5 bought and shipped eels, wainscots and other items in the same way.[139] Ships from Grimsby, Lynn and Yarmouth carried grain and herrings to Newcastle[140] and Newcastle sent salt, salmon and coal down the coast to London. Coal was the mainstay of Newcastle's coastal trade, and quantities of coal were regularly exported from Hull, presumably having been offloaded from Newcastle ships. The amounts were usually small, but on occasions did exceed 100 chaldrons.[141] London's demand for grain was met in part by northern suppliers. One transaction of 1351 comprised 147 quarters of rye, 126 quarters of malt, 104 quarters of wheat and 75 quarters of oats, brought from the West Riding to Hull for shipment. Some was milled into flour and shipped by lighters to Grimsby and thence to London. The remainder was sent in four ships from Hull, taking thirty days.[142] Hull merchants carried large quantities of ale from Grimsby back home for local consumption.[143] Trade up and down the east coast slumped badly after 1450, and although Yarmouth was an exception, Hull was not. Later though, during Henry VII's reign, Hull and Lynn both made spectacular recoveries: there was an increase of 300 per cent in poundage collected in Hull between 1485 and 1505, and it was briefly the pre-eminent port on the east coast in terms of the value of shipping.[144]

Yorkshire merchants certainly took a share of this coastal trade. William Gaunt of York, for example, together with some Prussian merchants, was shipping goods from London to Hull when they were attacked by Newcastle men in 1453: in 1455 and 1459 he was trying to recover a debt of £80 from a Newcastle man.[145] In 1483, two York merchants were

---

[138] Although in 1380, when Robert de Selby of Hull sold the priory three tuns of wine, it was taken by water to York and thence by packhorse to Durham: Morimoto, 'Durham Wine Trade, pp. 67–146. [139] *Durham Account Rolls*, II, pp. 516, 545; III, p. 658.

[140] G. V. Scammell, 'English Merchant Shipping at the End of the Middle Ages: Some East Coast Evidence', *EcHR*, 2nd ser., 13 (1961), p. 229; Rigby, *Grimsby*, pp. 60–1.

[141] Scammell, 'English Merchant Shipping', p. 329; Bartlett, 'Aspects of the Economy of York', p. 139; PRO, E122/61/32, 64/10. Grimsby men shipped coal up to York as an offshoot of their main coastal coal trade: Rigby, *Grimsby*, p. 60. York men also exported coal via Scarborough: PRO, E122/134/7. [142] Salzman, *English Trade*, pp. 216–17.

[143] E.g. in 1377 Robert Hokenall was licensed to buy 1,000 barrels to sell in Hull, and double the quantity in 1378 with John Leget: *CPR 1377–81*, pp. 4, 145. See also *CPR 1381–5*, pp. 212, 241, 235; *1388–92*, p. 259; *1416–22*, p. 298; Rigby, *Grimsby*, p. 60.

[144] Scammell, 'English Merchant Shipping', pp. 329–30.

[145] *CPR 1452–61*, pp. 174, 264, 453. Links with Newcastle went back a long way. Newcastle men joined the York Fraternity of Our Lady in 1368: *M&MA*, p. 16. That year Geoffrey Hanby of Hull was owed £14 10s by a Newcastle man, and Nicholas Blackburn snr, who eventually settled in York, was exporting wool from there in 1396, with Thomas Gare and Richard Russell of York in 1399, and with John Aldestonemore and John Sampson of York in 1410–11: *CPR 1339–41*, p. 38; PRO, E122/106/26; *Bronnen*, I, pp. 503, 543. The wife of John de Bedford of Hull may have come originally from Newcastle as she left property there in 1459: Prob. Reg. II, f. 418.

licensed to carry 1,000 quarters of malt from Barton-on-Humber and Grimsby.[146] But even the transhipping of goods came to be dominated by Londoners, and by the mid-sixteenth century, wine, hops, prunes, woad, madder, iron and pitch were being carried to Hull in London ships.[147]

CONCLUSION

For most of the fourteenth century English overseas trade flourished and Yorkshire merchants enjoyed a parallel commercial success. By the 1390s, expansion was slowing down, and as the fifteenth century opened, it was already apparent that England was caught up in a wider recession.[148] Furthermore, between 1408 and 1460 the international situation changed to the detriment of the east coast ports: access to the Baltic became perilous and restricted and Burgundy was lost to the French. Merchants from each of the three towns reflected these developments in their trade, importing less wine and exporting less cloth and increasingly diversifying their commercial interests. English cloth still travelled well and held its value, and although few English merchants penetrated far into Europe, the demand for cloth stimulated investment in return cargoes of miscellaneous imports.

A striking feature of late fourteenth-century trade was the amazing variety of commodities imported back to England to supply the expanding consumer market. Whatever reached the Low Countries' international fairs, from the Far and Middle East or from the Mediterranean or the Baltic, found its way into cargoes shipped to Hull. The *Saint Maryship* of Middleburg docked in Hull on 16 August 1383 with a cargo of almonds, alum, canvas, caldrons, coarse soap, herrings, garlic, ginger, linen, madder, mirrors, paper, skins (lamb or buck), verdigris, wine and woad. She returned on 31 December with a new master, laden with a similar cargo and in addition argol (basis of cream of tartar), cloth (rays), coffers, copperas, dudgeons, girdles, iron (probably Hungarian or Pomeranian), kettles, oil, onion seed, soap, vermillion, walnuts and assorted small metal goods such as wool-cards, strainers and wire. Other vessels that year carried armour, bitumen, brimstone, combs, fustian, lace, liquorice, pepper, plate, purses, quills, 'redelaye', rye flour, saffron, swords, timber as boards, bowstaves and wainscots, wax and woad from Brabant, Picardy and Ripland.[149]

By the 1390s even conduct of the wool trade was becoming more flex-

---

[146] Rigby, *Grimsby*, p. 61.   [147] Bartlett, 'Aspects of the Economy of York', p. 178.

[148] Miskimin, *Early Renaissance Europe*, p. 96; Bolton, *Medieval English Economy*, pp. 294, 299.

[149] PRO, E122/59/8; *Bronnen*, I, pp. 354–5, 358–9. A similar variety of goods came into Hull in the fifteenth century: see Childs, *Hull Customs Accounts*, glossary, pp. 235–49.

ible as Yorkshire staplers increasingly recovered their profits by investing in cargoes of mixed import. The traditional direct exchange of wool for credit or cash apparently persisted in the south, although towards the end of the fifteenth century, the Celys were diversifying into miscellaneous imports.

In the course of the fifteenth century, the value of Hull's export trade plummeted dramatically from £400,000 between 1407 and 1417 to £270,000 in the decade 1427–37. The decline continued: reaching its lowest value of £100,000 in the decade 1457–67. Hull's trade barely recovered and between 1467 and 1487 was worth only about £120,000. The value of exports remained fairly constant thereafter: rising briefly to £200,000 in 1497–1507. Overall, trade through Hull declined by an estimated 75 per cent in the course of the fifteenth century, and, as we shall see in chapter 8, local investment shrank, allowing alien merchants to increase their share by over 50 per cent.[150]

The kind of overseas trader changed. Merchants trading in a wide variety of commodities became more numerous and the formal establishment of the York Merchant Adventurers' Company in 1430 perhaps confirms the growing confidence of the general merchants at this time.[151] Their investment was concentrated in cloth and lead exports and in importing wine and miscellaneous goods, but not exclusively so, and some occasionally exported wool. Thomas Neleson of York regularly invested in large import shipments, but did occasionally export wool.[152]

Wool traders, numerous and successful in the early fourteenth century, had almost disappeared from sight, except in Hull, by the late fifteenth century.[153] It seems that numerically staplers began to lose ground in the early decades of the fifteenth century but the absence of Hull's particular customs rolls for the 1410s and 1420s makes it difficult to establish the point of decline more exactly. However, several famous local staplers (for example, John Bolton, Richard Russell, John Thirsk and Richard York, all of York, Thomas and William Brompton of Beverley, and John Swan of Hull) kept alive the tradition of the powerful woolmen up to and beyond the end of the fifteenth century.[154] Investment in wool was their

---

[150] Bartlett, 'Expansion and Decline', p. 28; *VCH York*, p. 105.   [151] *M&MA*, pp. v–x.

[152] See his biography below in appendix 3. This was not uncommon and the division between staplers and merchant adventurers was quite flexible in practice. Hanham, *Celys and Their World*, pp. 246–7.

[153] The numbers of wool merchants in each town were: 1378–1408, York, twenty-two of the twenty-four A merchants and fifteen of the thirty-seven B merchants; Beverley, all seven of the A merchants and six of the ten B merchants; Hull, six of the thirteen A merchants and five of the thirteen B merchants. 1460–1500, York, three of the eight A merchants, three of the eleven B merchants; Beverley, the solitary A merchant; Hull, five out of the six A merchants.

[154] Cf. the ninety-four London staplers of whom 21 per cent were merchant adventurers in 1488: Hanham, *Celys and Their World*, p. 246.

priority, but even staplers increasingly diversified into exporting cloth, lead and leather. It has been argued that it may have been more profitable in the fifteenth century for a wool merchant to re-invest in the Calais Staple, recovering maybe a net profit of 20 per cent (38–43 per cent on the best wool),[155] but the Yorkshire staplers preferred to import not only wine, but dyestuffs and teasels for the new northern textile centres, linen cloth, cloth from Brabant, spices, fruit and manufactured domestic goods.[156]

The decline of the staplers had repercussions for the region which will be discussed later.[157] Staplers tended to deal on long credit, but for all merchants in the Low Countries within the regime of bullion control, the marts were the key point for exchanging goods or credit for imports and goods or credit for cash or transferable bonds and vice versa. The staplers retained access to the financial services of the Calais Staple, the advantages of regulated credit and the higher unit values of the wool trade. This meant that they generated large sums to be recovered overseas, thus pulling imports back into Yorkshire. Their withdrawal from the wool trade, accordingly, altered the nature of the region's link with the continent, ultimately to the region's detriment.

---

[155] Power, *Wool Trade*, p. 56; Hanham, *Celys and Their World*, pp. 245–7, 399–400.

[156] For Brabant cloth, see PRO, E122/61/32, 62/3, 4, and for linen see E122/59/23, 159/11, 63/8. Linen was also exported, e.g. E122/62/16.   [157] See pp. 310–12 below.

6

THE PRACTICE OF TRADE

As the expansion of international trade in the late middle ages presented increasing opportunities for individual profit, so the regulation of traders and the conduct of commerce attracted the attention of rulers. Commercial rivalries became one more source of conflict between countries, making it a difficult time for England's merchants.[1] Uneasy truces, rumbling hostility and outright war characterised international relations during the fourteenth and fifteenth centuries, while dynastic disputes and internal fighting distracted the home government from pursuing a coherent and pro-commerce foreign policy. The latter, in so far as it existed, preferred to use trade as a weapon so that for most of our period the North Sea and the Channel became uncomfortable and dangerous routes for traders. This was an era of casual piracy and government-sponsored privateering on an unprecedented scale, encouraged by intermittent war with France and her allies from the 1330s, and by diplomatic jostling and warfare with the Hanseatic towns. A relatively durable peace was negotiated with France and the Hanseatic towns in the mid-1470s, but before that all branches of trade had been directly affected. Government action, or inaction, probably accounted for the most wide-reaching impact on transaction costs.

The costs of trade included what Halyburton called 'oncostis'[2] and what twentieth-century historians have described as transaction costs: the costs which 'arise not from the production of goods but from the transfer of goods from one owner to another'.[3] They are not totally separate elements although Halyburton was primarily counting the visible over-

---

[1] See below, chapter 8.
[2] 'Oncostis' is a late fifteenth-century Scots term; see C. Innes, ed., *Ledger of Andrew Halyburton*, Scottish Record Publications (Edinburgh, 1867), p. 355 and *passim*.
[3] C. G. Reed, 'Transaction Costs and Differential Growth in Seventeenth Century Western Europe', *Jnl Econ. Hist.*, 32 (1973), pp. 177–90 at p. 181. See also D. C. North, 'Transaction Costs in History', *Jnl European Econ. Hist.*, 14 (1985), pp. 557–76.

heads of late medieval Scottish traders, those of which contemporaries took account: the cost of credit, transport costs and customs payments. North identifies a number of invisible costs: search and information costs, investment, contract enforcement and market regulation. Transaction as well as carriage costs and the peculiar circumstances of the wool monopoly accounted for the more than doubling of the purchase price of wool in Yorkshire of between £3 12s and £6 in 1337 to a selling price of over £11 in Flanders.[4] Variations in all costs bore down upon the competitive edge sought by every entrepreneur – some costs he could influence, others he could mitigate, but many were largely beyond his control. Allowance had to made for unanticipated expenditure and so, probably as a general rule, the costs of a venture were paid out of the profits after the cargo was discharged.[5]

All branches of international trade were vulnerable to the extra charges incurred due to regulation, and warfare became an important component of overall costs. Moreover, the conduct of trade in specific commodities differed, with significant repercussions on the choices facing individuals. Transaction costs varied between commodities and some costs affected only one commodity whereas others continued to be borne by every branch of trade. It was crucial for any trader and, indeed, for any region, to establish and maintain a reasonably continuous flow of trade. Failure to do so increased transaction costs to the extent that competitiveness was lost and access to some areas of overseas trade became impossible to regain without a major individual effort or dramatic change of circumstances.

Governments everywhere manipulated tariffs and imposed embargoes in an effort to maximise revenues and as part of their foreign policy. As well as exploiting overseas trade for fiscal purposes, the English Crown attempted to control the quality of domestic cloth production through the system of aulnage.[6] Local councils deployed similar policies: refining the imposition of tolls, the management of retail and wholesale business and policing the conduct of all traders. The regulated markets of larger towns provided legal and financial services, important in reducing debt and contract costs and in attracting traders and so reducing search and information costs. Market towns were a mixed blessing though, depending on an individual's status. Burgesses were privileged over all others in

---

[4] Fryde, *Wool Accounts of William de la Pole*, p. 9; J. H. Munro, 'Wool-Price Schedules and the Qualities of English Wools in the Later Middle Ages *c.* 1270–1499', *Textile History*, 9 (1978), p. 137; W. Cunningham, *The Growth of English Industry and Commerce During the Early and Middle Ages*, 5th edn (Cambridge, 1910), I, p. 636.

[5] Prob. Reg. II, f. 292v. (Thorn); IV, ff. 126v.–7 (Molde).

[6] Bridbury, *Medieval English Clothmaking*, pp. 47–55.

their own towns, but elsewhere could be at a disadvantage to Hanse merchants flourishing government-endorsed trading concessions.

COSTS ENGENDERED BY REGULATIONS

The most immediate visible costs imposed beyond the individual's political reach were the tolls, customs and subsidies paid on goods through the national and local customs systems. These comprised one element of the expanding regulation of trade, which raised costs for merchants while increasing government revenue. As regulation became more burdensome, charging denizens and aliens for exemptions from tariffs and for licences to trade in restricted areas became extremely lucrative for the government.[7] However, regulation also encouraged smuggling as individuals deployed all manner of tactics to evade imposts. Some reduced the costs and delay in obtaining a licence by trading without one.[8] Bypassing English port authorities was a common practice as was avoiding the staple and the high impost levied on wool.[9]

Smuggling was such a continuous activity that the Crown appointed searchers to every port of significance in England.[10] Even though it is not possible to calculate smuggled goods as a proportion in estimating export totals, numerous incidents illustrate how endemic it was, and the lengths to which merchants were prepared to go. Individual merchants could be in an ambiguous position. It was not uncommon for some to be accused of piracy one moment and to hold high civic office or a government appointment the next. Most immediately paradoxical was the propensity of merchants to smuggle and to serve as customs officials, charged with the regulation of trade.[11]

Nicholas Stubbs of Hull, who, like many other merchants, was caught smuggling in 1439[12] and served as a customs official, exemplified a difficulty facing the Crown. Local merchants had the necessary experience and local knowledge to administer the law effectively. They were often chosen by the Crown as commissioners and customs officials but

---

[7] The Italians in particular paid large sums for exemption licences: E. Power, 'The Wool Trade in the Reign of Edward IV', *Camb. Hist. Jnl*, 1 (1926–8), pp. 20–1.

[8] Licences to trade with Iceland were issued regularly in 1430–84: E. M. Carus-Wilson, 'Iceland Trade', in Power and Postan, *Studies in English Trade*, pp. 167–70; W. R. Childs, 'England's Icelandic Trade in the Fifteenth Century: The Role of the Port of Hull', *Northern Seas Yearbook*, 5(1995), pp. 11–31.

[9] See p. 195 below and *CCR 1343–6, p.* 402 (wool and false coins).

[10] J. B. Blake, 'Medieval Smuggling in the North East', *Arch. Aeliana*, 4th ser., 43 (1965); Childs, *Hull Customs Accounts*, pp. xvi–xvii.

[11] Their duties were not confined to routine customs posts. Merchants were appointed to scrutinise the coinage in 1358: *CCR 1354–60*, p. 473.

[12] *CPR 1436–41*, pp. 294–5. See also *Bronnen*, I, pp. 589, 604; II, pp. 689–90, 735, 868, 926.

were as often caught evading official regulation. Any perceived conflict of interest was not an obstacle. Walter Box of Hull was caught selling ungauged wine in 1353, the year after he had served as a customs collector,[13] while William Bell, a draper of York, took cloth to be sealed and served as deputy aulnager![14] Collusion may well explain the large number of 'Nil' returns from the Hull searchers. 'Experts' were required to value goods forfeited to the Crown by smugglers. Merchants often acted as valuers, with fellow merchants usually as the ultimate purchasers of such goods.[15] John de Acastre of York bought two 'little' ships and their cargoes of wool and lead, forfeit in 1342, and Robert Alcock of Hull acquired a Spanish ship by the same means in 1471.[16]

Avoiding the payment of customs and subsidies, or exporting wool to ports other than the staple, might have been a way of cutting costs during a depression but was not a temporary phenomenon. Merchants tried many tactics to avoid payments to the Crown throughout the period, perhaps regarding customs and subsidies as an unjust imposition by an unsympathetic government. Edward III's wool monopoly created particularly galling conditions for individual traders, even those party to the agreement.[17] A group of York merchants led by Henry and John Goldbeter, Thomas Gra, William Acastre and Walter de Kelstern and others involved in the wool collection were accused in their absence of illegal practices in 1340. Apparently they were too useful to the king in other respects for serious steps to be taken against them. Thus in September 1341 Walter de Kelstern was appointed to a commission to search all the shipping along the Humber coast for uncustomed goods, and in November of the same year Henry Goldbeter was similarly appointed to search specifically for uncustomed wool,[18] the commodity he may well have been smuggling! John Goldbeter was caught in the act, fined £200 and then pardoned in October 1338. In 1341 his wool was arrested by the collectors of York, and he claimed that although it was loaded in a small boat at Selby he was not trying to avoid customs payments. An inquiry was ordered but Goldbeter 'procured the men on it' so a new one was summoned.[19] John Goldbeter was accused of smug-

[13] *CCR 1349–54*, p. 346; *CPR 1350–4*, p. 479.
[14] *CPR 1377–81*, p. 438; Lister, *Early Yorks Woollen Trade*, pp. 85, 89, 96.
[15] PRO, E166/61/57; E122/61/57.   [16] *CCR 1341–3*, p. 426; *CPR 1467–77*, p. 267.
[17] During the agreements negotiated between Edward III and the wool merchants in 1337, 1340 and 1341, an embargo was placed on wool exports by anyone other than official collectors. Smuggling inevitably occurred as merchants tried to evade legal restrictions on their private exports. It has been calculated that about 2,500 sacks were illegally exported in 1337–8: Fryde, 'Edward III's Wool Monopoly', pp. 19–20.
[18] *CCR 1339–41*, p. 655; *CPR 1340–3*, p. 323; PRO, C76/16.
[19] *CPR 1338–40*, p. 191; *1340–3*, pp. 212, 303.

gling wool again in 1346 and 1363. His pardons were not automatic and he was in the Fleet prison in 1346.[20]

Smuggling continued throughout the late middle ages and all sorts of ploys were used to avoid discovery. In 1417 Beverley merchants disguised wool by storing it in barrels, and York merchants were accused of by-passing the customers at Hull and secretly loading wool at Ravenspur. Hull merchants were involved in smuggling as well, and in 1439 Robert Auncell used John Goldbeter's small boat technique to good effect at Patrington, downriver from Hull. Avoiding the staple was also a common practice. John Jackson of Hull, for example, shipped his wool straight to Veere from Hull and not to the Calais Staple in 1475.[21] Wool was the most commonly smuggled commodity, in spite of its bulk, but the additional staple costs made it worth the risk. However, other goods were sometimes shipped illegally. An entire cargo of the *Katherine*, destined for Iceland from Hull, was discovered to be uncustomed, and contained mainly beer, butter, barley and other victuals. At least half a dozen prominent Yorkshire merchants were involved.[22]

Opportunity and the existence of stretches of unguarded shore no doubt made smuggling hard to resist, but it may also have been the sort of challenge merchants relished.

Domestic regulation

Tariffs on domestic trade were almost entirely imposed in towns. The objective of urban trading regulation was to maintain the commercial advantages of burgesses, control quality, and to raise revenue.[23] Well-regulated markets could have lowered transaction costs, but, where there is evidence for other towns, regulation was not easily achieved. Burgesses were generally exempt from their own local tolls,[24] and although foreigners (non-burgesses) could trade under licence, they still did not enjoy the same trading advantages as burgesses. The advantages must have been considerable if John Lylling, a York mercer guilty of adulterating steel and alum and expelled from the city's freedom in 1428, was willing to pay 540 marks for readmission.[25] Retail markets were increasingly controlled, not just through the Crown's assizes of bread and ale, but through the authority of the 'clerk of the market' and borough by-laws. The presence of

[20] *CCR 1346–9*, pp. 187, 241; *CPR 1361–4*, p. 342; *1364–7*, p. 46.
[21] *Bronnen*, I, pp. 589–90, 753, 1116. For other examples, see II, pp. 543, 753, 884.
[22] *CPR 1436–41*, 294–5. See also *Bronnen*, I, pp. 589, 604; II, pp. 689–90, 735, 868, 926.
[23] See, for example, Coventry's wool market regulations: M. D. Harris, ed., *Coventry Leet Book*, I, EETS, OS, 134 (1907), pp. 192–3, 636, 787.   [24] See Kowaleski, *Medieval Exeter*, p. 191.
[25] A. Raine, ed., *Early English Miscellanies*, Surtees Soc., 85 (1888), pp. 1–10.

exempted liberties within towns created regulation problems for civic rulers and undercutting competition for burgess traders.[26]

Regional entrepots developed elaborate penalties and marketing arrangements for all manner of retail activities.[27] Wholesale trade excited particular interest and town authorities tried to restrict all such deals to their own burgesses and to keep them under immediate view within the town liberties. In any case, pledges were usually required from foreigners and aliens generally had to be hosted by a burgess as surety. Some borough councils tried to lengthen their regulating tentacles by claiming a regional monopoly over specific trades. York's council, for example, spent much of the fifteenth century protesting its right to have all the lead from Boroughbridge weighed on the city's crane.[28]

Towns negotiated the exemption of their burgesses from one another's tolls.[29] Hull had agreements with Blythburgh, Dunwich and Scarborough, down the east coast, but fought off claims for exemptions from men of the duchy of Lancaster. One indication of the intensification of competition over contracting overseas trade in fifteenth-century Yorkshire was Beverley's defence of its position against York in 1423 and Driffield five years later. In 1448, Beverley and Hull were disputing claims by Beverley merchants for passage into the Humber free of tolls. In 1463, there were fears in York that Hull was encouraging York merchants to complete transactions with strangers before goods were landed, to the disadvantage of York council. In 1508, the fear was that York merchants were not being allowed to deal direct with aliens and were subject to extra heavy local duties.[30]

Tolls and search costs were reduced for everyone during fair-time, and the emergence of specialist fairs in particular, eased transaction costs of all sorts. Freedom from local tolls, piepowder jurisdiction for quick justice, and a concentration of specific commodity traders to speed up price fixing explain their growing popularity. The advantages of reducing costs in this way were obvious, and York city tried to boost its flagging economy in 1502 by petitioning for two new fairs.[31]

---

[26] On regulation see Britnell, *Commercialisation*, pp. 155–78. On liberties see *VCH York*, pp. 68–9; Kowaleski, *Medieval Exeter*, pp. 198–200; S. Reynolds, *An Introduction to the History of English Medieval Towns* (Oxford, 1977), p. 116.

[27] *VCH Beverley*, pp. 218–22; *VCH Hull*, pp. 407–12; *VCH York*, pp. 484–91.

[28] *MB*, II, pp. 65, 81; *YCR*, II, pp. 142–4; III, p. 19. York council backed the girdlers' guild in its attempt to establish a monopoly within a thirty-two mile radius of the city: *MB*, I, p. 183.

[29] Thus in 1458 Dunwich signed an agreement with Hull: A. Suckling, *History and Antiquities of Suffolk* (London, 1848), II, p. 242; BL Add. Rolls 40739–40. See also O. Coleman, 'Trade and Prosperity in the Fifteenth Century: Some Aspects of the Trade of Southampton', *EcHR*, 2nd ser., 16 (1963–4), pp. 10, 13; Kowaleski, *Medieval Exeter*, pp. 196–8.

[30] BL Lans. MS 896; Pro, CI/17/111; *Beverlac*, pp. 197–9; *VCH Hull*, pp. 45–6; *M&MA*, pp. 119–20; Power and Postan, *Studies in English Trade*, p. 169.

[31] *YCR*, II, pp. 166, 172, 174; *CPR 1494–1509*, p. 257; *VCH York*, p. 490.

COMMODITY DIFFERENTIALS

It was difficult for an individual to reduce regulatory costs but a competitive advantage was possible through a combination of luck and entrepreneurship, depending on the commodity and state of the market. It is axiomatic that the higher its sale value, the better an item absorbs costs. Thus the more expensive cloths and wool varieties cost the same to transport, store and retail as did cheaper alternatives, but trading costs constituted a smaller proportion of the market value of the former. Medieval traders were aware of cost implications, as well as fluctuations in demand and supply, and increasingly diversified to spread risks and to keep costs down. The cost advantages in exporting cloth were significant. By the 1390s, wool exports had to accommodate heavy duties of up to 50 per cent of mean prices while cloth more easily absorbed the light impost of only 3 per cent.[32] By the late fourteenth century, few merchants traded in a single commodity and a minority in wool alone. Manufacturers were as aware of the narrowness of the competitive edge and there is evidence that some moved into manufacturing higher quality cloth to manoeuvre around crippling competition.[33]

Wool

Wool and cloth were Yorkshire's primary products. The production of each was not within coterminous areas. Sheep grazed throughout the northern region, textile production for the market began within the old urban centres, mainly Beverley and York, but in the course of the fourteenth and fifteenth centuries, all the primary processes and some finishing processes developed in the small towns and villages of the West Riding and North Yorkshire. Curiously though, significant cloth production never developed in Lindsey or the Lincolnshire or Yorkshire Wolds which produced the best quality wool.[34]

With production so scattered, the role of the trader was paramount in getting goods to market, whether he was a chapman, wool brogger, clothier, merchant or mercer. From the evidence, it seems that the organisation of the wool and cloth trades was very different. There was probably a critical volume of business in wool trading required to cover the

---

[32] J. H. Munro, 'Patterns of Trade, Money, and Credit', in T. A. Brady, H. A. Oberman amd J. D. Tracy, eds., *Handbook of European History 1400–1600: Late Middle Ages, Renaissance and Reformation*, I (Leiden, New York, 1994), p. 163.

[33] York weavers moved into linen in the 1470s: Swanson, *Medieval Artisans*, pp. 29–30. Colchester traders were trying to move away from russets in 1418 for similar reasons. Britnell, *Commercialisation*, p. 176.

[34] Still the best survey is Heaton, *Yorks Woollen and Worsted Industries*.

higher overheads, especially transport costs, and small quantities were very rarely traded. Wool was generally a less flexible commodity to trade, involving more expert judgement of quality and knowledge of growers. Buyers needed up-to-date market information and a sharper judgement of exchange rates.[35] They were selling into a much more tightly regulated and geographically restricted overseas market, via the staple, but their activities at home were largely conducted beyond the view of urban regulators.[36]

Wool merchants traded in futures as well as wool in hand and on credit. Evidence for the early stages of wool sales is richest for the late thirteenth and early fourteenth centuries when it was not uncommon for merchants to buy the anticipated wool clip for up to three years.[37] Credit could be extended over six months or more, and full settlement not concluded until the proceeds from sales overseas were recovered as bullion, in some form of credit or reinvested in imported goods. Payment to sellers might be in instalments: one third cash in hand and two stages of credit with payments at perhaps eight and twelve months.[38] The state of the Calais mint and availability of bullion directly affected the speed of recovering profits.[39] Full payment was not concluded until the proceeds from sales overseas were recovered either as bullion, credit, or reinvested in return cargoes. With such a reliance on credit, wool traders were, perhaps, particularly vulnerable to shortages of bullion. They had to pay the high wool subsidy in cash before embarking for Calais, and once there, had to meet their immediate duties in cash. Wool producers were unlikely to be in a situation where goods could be bartered in lieu, and, in the end, staplers had to pay them in cash.

Credit flowed from buyer to seller or vice versa, depending on the state of the market. Thus in the late thirteenth century, buyers bought futures but as prices fell in the mid-fifteenth century, growers allowed purchase on approval.[40] Italian merchants, in particular, enjoyed preferential credit terms from wool suppliers and long periods for repayment.[41] In the early fourteenth century, the buyer arranged and paid for the dressing and

---

[35] All these skills are described in Hall, *Select Cases*, II, pp. lxxxvi, 28–30; Hanham, *Celys and Their World*, pp. 114–15 (judgement), 122 (for a series of price shifts). See A. Hanham, 'Profits on English Wool Exports, 1472–1544', *BIHR*, 55 (1982), p. 146.

[36] Special commissioners and scrutineers were appointed from time to time, particularly to search for clacked and bearded wool. E.g. *CPR 1436–41*, pp. 265, 372, 373, 439–40, 554, 563; *1441–6*, pp. 52–3. [37] Power, *Wool Trade*, pp. 41–57.

[38] Hanham, *Celys and Their World*, pp. 1, 113–19.

[39] The Celys, for instance, experienced severe difficulties in getting their proceeds home when the Calais mint closed. Hanham, *Celys and Their World*, pp. 231, 235.

[40] Lloyd, *English Wool Trade*, pp. 295, 303, 313.

[41] W. Childs, 'To Oure Losse and Hindrance', in J. I. Kermode, ed., *Enterprise and Individuals in Fifteenth-Century England* (Stroud, 1991), pp. 76–7.

packing of wool but these costs were borne by the producer in the late fifteenth century. Packing was the critical stage in the sales process since it was at this point that the type and quality of the wool was attested. The producer also paid for carriage to the agreed rendezvous with the purchaser.[42]

What evidence there is from other regions suggests that a large part of the market was increasingly controlled by middlemen, buying from producers and selling on to textile craftsmen or export merchants.[43] William Pontefract, a draper of York who bought the Durham wool clip in 1395–6 for £41, might have been buying for himself or as intermediary.[44] In Yorkshire, religious houses like Bolton Priory, Byland, Durham, Fountains, Meaux and Rievaulx collected from smaller farmers as well as selling their own wool.[45] Economies of scale gave them some advantages over smaller competitors in pricing, which were passed on to the buyer. In regions where estates were the main growers, they might have acted as a cartel in determining regional prices, yet the variations in wool prices within Yorkshire alone suggest that fine and precise judgements were made on the basis of close physical examination of fleeces and fells.[46] It is impossible to estimate how much the smaller producers accounted for: farmers or gentry such as Philip Neville or Roger Bigod and William Playce who were active in Yorkshire in the 1330s and 1360s.[47] Where significant numbers of smaller growers supplied the market, purchasing wool could be more time-consuming, involving personal visits to the producers.[48]

Quality was everything in wool and an expert eye essential if losses were to be avoided in the contracting market of the early and mid-fifteenth century. Wool, either as fleeces or fells, deteriorates over time and can rot or lose volume and weight through drying.[49] In the depressed market of the mid-fifteenth century,[50] growers had to store wool for

---

[42] Hall, *Select Cases*, II, pp. 69–71; Hanham, *Celys and Their World*, p. 111; Lloyd, *English Wool Trade*, pp. 295–9, 304–6.

[43] Our best evidence is from the Celys. In the fifteenth century the family bought from middlemen but sorted and repacked the wool themselves, since their reputation depended on delivering what they promised. Hanham, *Celys and Their World*, pp. 1, 113–19.

[44] Morimoto, 'Durham Wine Trade', p. 126.

[45] *CPR 1307–13*, p. 210; *CCR 1307–13*, pp. 184, 195; E. A. Bond, ed., *Chronica Monasterii de Melsa*, Rolls Series, 43 (London, 1868), III, pp. 85, 144–5; Kershaw, *Bolton Priory*, pp. 85–94.

[46] Munro, '1357 Wool-Price Schedule', pp. 213–14.

[47] *C. Inq. Misc. 1307–49*, p. 399; B. Putnam, ed., *Yorkshire Sessions of the Peace, 1361–4*, YAS Rec. Ser., 100 (1939), p. 14.

[48] Hanham, *Celys and Their World*, p. 62. See also Power, *Medieval People*, pp. 132–3.

[49] Hanham, 'Profits on English Wool Exports', pp. 141–2.

[50] Prices were an average of 25 per cent lower after the 1450s than they were in the early fifteenth century: J. Hatcher, 'The Great Slump of the Mid-Fifteenth Century', in R. Britnell and J. Hatcher, eds., *Progress and Problems in Medieval England* (Cambridge, 1996), pp. 250–1.

longer and longer periods before sales,[51] buyers became more choosy, selecting the best clip, and some growers responded by classifying more of their wool as inferior or rubbish and selling it locally. According to the Cely evidence, once a buyer had agreed to a price, based on the samples seen, the seller was responsible for cleaning, packing and transporting the wool to an agreed location.[52] The woolpacker became an increasingly influential figure,[53] advising on prices as well as guaranteeing that the wool purchased was what was delivered.[54]

Fraud was not uncommon. The courts heard cases of all sorts of odds and ends being twined in with good wool: of inferior wool being passed as 'young' Cotswold wool and of the usual variety of nefarious and cunning schemes which characterised the world of commerce. A partnership of two York merchants, alderman John Moreton and John Coupland, Thomas Mayne of Beverley and two Leicestershire merchants sold wool to Genoese merchants, who took the Leicester agent to court in 1431 over the 'untrue and unjust packing' of eighty-six sarplars of wool they had agreed to buy. Given that the buyer had usually parted with at least one third of the price before taking delivery and may have incurred transport and shipping costs to Calais, before discovering the fraud, his losses amounted to more than just the difference in value.[55]

Pricing also became more difficult in the fluctuating market of the 1430s and '40s, and was compounded by the time-lag between purchase and sale. Wool of all sorts was still traded on a long credit chain in the mid-fifteenth century so that even by concentrating on the best quality clips, merchants who delayed could find prices falling to their advantage.[56] Matching quality and price was central to the wool trade and the deposits demanded in Calais against sales reflected the variable quality from different regions.[57] The best quality available in the north came from Lindsey, north Lincolnshire,[58] which Yorkshire mer-

---

[51] In one of the bishop of Winchester's stores at Wargrave, between 1423 and 1430, eight-year-old wool was common and the bishop resorted to exporting direct to Normandy to reduce his stock: Lloyd, *English Wool Trade*, p. 312.

[52] Hanham, *Celys and Their World*, p. 111; Lloyd, *English Wool Trade*, pp. 295–9, 304–6.

[53] A London fellowship of wool packers had emerged by the mid-fifteenth century: Power, 'Wool Trade in the Reign of Edward IV', p. 25. An all-female equivalent had formed in Southampton by the early sixteenth century: A. Ruddock, 'London Capitalists and the Decline of Southampton in the Early Tudor Period', *EcHR*, 2nd ser., 2 (1950), p. 143.

[54] Power and Postan, *Studies in English Trade*, p. 51, note 57.

[55] *Cal. Plea & Mem. Rolls City of London, 1413–37*, p. 249. See also Hall, *Select Cases*, II, pp. xxvii, 28, 69–70. Cases in Power, 'Wool Trade in the Reign of Edward IV', p. 25; Hanham, *Celys and Their World*, p. 111.

[56] For instance, a London merchant delayed so long in collecting his purchased wool from the Cotswold supplier, that the price fell by 4 marks per sack. Cited in Lloyd, *English Wool Trade*, p. 313.   [57] Hall, *Select Cases*, II, p. 158; Hanham, *Celys and Their World*, pp. 111–47.

[58] *Rot. Parl.*, IV, p. 126; *Bronnen*, I, pp. 93, 156 (Leyden ordinances).

chants sometimes purchased, along with a mixture of rough wool from upland farmers.[59] John Hanson of Hull included four Lincolnshire parishes in his will of 1458, suggesting a long-standing association.[60]

Some types of wool fared better than others in the market. Short-stapled fine wool from the Cotswolds was exported by Italians to the Mediterranean via Southampton and maintained its price well. Even the lesser quality northern wools from Craven, Holderness, Richmond and Spaldingmoor, for example, held their low prices from the mid-four-teenth to the mid-fifteenth century, while the better quality, higher-priced wools from Elmet, Fountains, Riponshire and the Yorkshire Wolds fell by as much as 50 per cent between 1357 and 1454.[61] Was this because the 'poorer' wools found immediate buyers in the expanding Yorkshire textile industry while the 'better' wools were more exposed to fluctuations in the overseas market and to government regulation in Calais? Whatever the explanation, exports through Hull fell, even after wool from the northern counties was exempted from the subsidy in 1423,[62] when northern wool was said to be too cheap to bear the costs of the Calais Staple.[63]

A network of well-nurtured contacts underpinned the wool mer-chant's business and was one of his most important assets. From the warm concern expressed in some wills, it seems as though more than a business relationship developed between individual merchants and their suppliers. Richard Allerton, a wool merchant of York, alienated some of his York property to Byland Abbey in 1327, presumably in return for prayers. More personal still, Robert Holme of York left 100 marks in 1396 to the heads of poor families in those parishes where he had purchased wool. Similarly, in 1435, Richard Russell of York left £20 to be distributed among the householders from whom he had bought wool on the Yorkshire Wolds and a further £10 for his Lindsey growers.[64] Robert Collinson, also of York, in his will of 1456 disarmingly asked the poor of

[59] PRO, c1/16/592; *Bronnen*, ii, p. 116 (Lincolnshire wool); Prob. Reg. iii, ff. 439–40 (Lyndsey). Bowden, *Wool Trade*, pp. 36–7; E. Kerridge, 'Wool Growing and Wool Textiles in Medieval and Early Modern Times', in J. G. Jenkins, ed., *The Wool Textile Industry in Britain* (London, 1962), pp. 19–20; Munro, '1357 Wool-Price Schedule', pp. 211–19.

[60] Prob. Reg. ii, f. 393.   [61] Munro, '1357 Wool-Price Schedule', p. 212.

[62] The four main northern counties were Cumberland, Durham, Northumberland and Westmorland. In 1463 the exemption was extended to wool from Northallerton and Richmond in Yorkshire. *Rot. Parl.*, iv, pp. 250–1, v, p. 503; Power and Postan, *Studies in English Trade*, p. 43.

[63] Wool incurred further handling costs on arrival at Calais, in addition to the deposits and fees required. Hanham, *Celys and Their World*, pp. 6 *et seq.*

[64] *CPR 1327–30*, p. 146; Prob. Reg. i, ff. 100v.–3v. (Holme); iii, f. 441 (Russell). Richard Russell's brother John continued to buy from Lindsey growers; PRO, c1/16/592. Cf. Thomas Betson's practice: Power, *Medieval People*, p. 138.

twenty-two West and North Riding parishes to forgive him if he had ever made a profit in his dealings with them. Collinson was a clothier and his dealings may have been in cloth as well as wool.[65]

This may have been one regional variable in costs: the pattern of suppliers. One might suppose that in upland areas, where flocks were small and scattered, merchants had to seek supplies from a wider network of growers so that not only was the quality of the fleece generally inferior but the range of choice was more limited compared with, say, Wiltshire or the Cotswolds where large-scale purchases involved fewer individual transactions. Brokers could reduce these information and search costs by buying across a region and storing the wool until a buyer was found,[66] but it is difficult to generalise about practice. Holme and Russell collected their own wool and exported it through Hull, but another York man, John de Appleton, who bought wool from Durham Priory, only exported cloth.[67] Wool broggers exploited a niche as smaller scale middlemen, and began to appear more frequently in the fifteenth century.[68] The York council tried to regulate their activities in 1428 and 1460,[69] but that may have been connected with a wish to control supply to local spinners and weavers. Another group who began taking up the freedom of York after 1413 was woolmen. This may have been a simple change in terminology, or a version of woolmonger. What is remarkable is that the activities of a group of wool middlemen started to become visible just when the overseas wool trade was entering a critical period.

Cloth

By contrast, cloth was a more flexible commodity than wool in international marts and was not subject to staple regulation. It could be sold on at any stage in the manufacturing process, in any quantity, by anyone, and to any overseas destination.[70] Cloth retained its value over time. Little, if any, venture capital was required, the credit chain was generally shorter and the returns should have been quicker at each point of sale. In practice, however, experience might prove otherwise. When Maud Denby (a

---

[65] See below, at note 95, for a list; Prob. Reg. ii, ff. 378–80, and *Test. Ebor.* ii, p. 217. See also Prob. Reg. iii, ff. 266v.–8 (Vescy) for a dozen named abbeys suggesting his circuit.

[66] Britnell, *Commercialisation*, p. 162.   [67] See their biographies below, appendix 3.

[68] In the Cotswolds, Wiltshire and elsewhere. Power and Postan, *Studies in English Trade*, p. 53 for woolmen alias clothmen alias merchants alias yeomen buying and selling wool in the Cotswolds.

[69] *MB*, ii, p. 55; Swanson, *Medieval Artisans*, pp. 140–2.

[70] The cloth which reached Toulouse in the 1430s was from Devon and Somerset via Bristol; Hampshire and Wiltshire via Southampton; East Anglia via Colchester and London. Cloth was being sold by butchers and an illuminator of manuscripts. Wolff, 'English Cloth in Toulouse', pp. 291, 293.

spinster?) sold £24 worth of cloth to a prominent York merchant, William Thorp, in the 1460s, she could not have anticipated that her executors would have to pursue him through the Chancery for payment.[71] Such exigencies aside, trading in cloth was less risky than trading in wool. Expert judgement was not essential and export duties were paid on the valuation of the customs officials at the quayside. National and local regulations provided some control over quality and government officials implemented statutes regulating size.[72] However, compared to wool, the domestic trade was more closely regulated by guilds and civic rulers.[73]

In the expanding textile trade of the late fourteenth and fifteenth centuries, one might suppose that competition became less intense and pricing less critical, but it is apparent from the fate of cloth traders in our three towns that even a strong and established share of the market could be undermined. Free of borough and guild taxes, and with easy access to cheap wool and a good water supply, rural cloth workers in Yorkshire increased production. As early as 1300, York and Beverley were facing competition from at least eight other centres.[74] Thereafter, and at an accelerating pace, the manufacturing and finishing, especially of the cheaper kerseys, was undertaken away from, and at the expense of, the older urban centres. By 1379, this transformation was well established in the West Riding, accelerating the growth of several emergent towns such as Barnsley, Bradford, Halifax, Leeds and Wakefield. There is no evidence however of traders based in the small towns, perhaps because at this stage in the expansion of rural production, borough-based merchants still dominated the trade in cloth or perhaps craftsmen doubled as wholesalers.[75]

Manufacturing was scattered throughout the region and all sorts of people took pieces to the aulnager to be sealed.[76] Spinsters, dyers, drapers, merchants, mercers, weavers and even occasionally butchers, were involved in this first stage in the process of marketing.[77] By 1469, at

---

[71] PRO, c1/390/28.   [72] Bridbury, *Medieval English Clothmaking*, appendix A.

[73] In 1432 and 1434 William Girlington of York was caught selling cloth in his shop which he had fraudulently stamped with his own seal. Bartlett, 'Aspects of the Economy of York', p. 416.

[74] Hedon, Leeds, Northallerton, Pickering, Pontefract, Selby, Whitby and Yarm: E. Miller and J. Hatcher, *Medieval England Towns, Commerce and Crafts 1086–1348* (London, 1995), pp. 100, 109–10; Hey, *Yorkshire from AD 1000*, p. 85; Heaton, *Yorks Woollen and Worsted Industries*, pp. 1–8; *VCH York*, p. 44.

[75] Miller and Hatcher, *Medieval England*, p. 113; Anon, 'The Rolls of the Collectors in the West Riding of the Lay Subsidy', *Yorks Arch. Jnl*, 5 (1879), 6 (1881), 7 (1882).

[76] Although the figures recorded in aulnagers' rolls might be suspect, the names of producers probably are not: see E. M. Carus-Wilson, 'The Aulnage Accounts: A Criticism', reprinted in her *Medieval Merchant Venturers* (pbk edn, London, 1967), pp. 279–92. A. R. Bridbury believes they at least suggest some broad patterns: *Medieval English Clothmaking*, pp. 48–9.

[77] *VCH York*, p. 88; Lister, *Early Yorks Woollen Trade*, pp. 47–95.

least ten West Riding towns and villages had emerged as foci for textiles, in addition to York and Hull,[78] and it is indicative of the rural workers' success that when a York tailor, John Carter, died in 1485, his shop was stocked with cloths produced in the West Riding.[79] It is possible that the process of administering government regulations in part created new centres and, more importantly, reduced search costs, making life easier for non-local traders. While Yorkshire textile production continued to grow, York city's share in production and trade fell (see table 5.3 p. 176). Production collapsed in the 1470s and weavers diversified into linen.[80]

This was not the consequence of a narrowly controlled cartel as some historians have argued,[81] but of relatively open commerce. There was no significant connection between production and exports to suggest merchants had complete control over supply and demand. By tracking individuals named in the Yorkshire aulnage rolls and the particular customs accounts for the 1390s, it seems clear that although 30 per cent of exporters were presenting cloth for sealing, the majority must have been buying in from small producers or from middlemen.

It is difficult to identify any pattern of specialisation in cloth trading. John Braithwait, a draper of York, had nineteen separate lots of cloth stamped between September 1394 and August 1395, but never shipped any cloth through Hull, whereas John Birkhead of York and Thomas Kelk of Beverley, for instance, took cloths to be sealed but only exported wool.[82] Thomas del Gare, however, regularly took cloths for sealing and exported at least 214 cloths in 1391–2.[83] Some 113 merchants from York shipped cloth through Hull during Richard II's reign, of whom, according to the aulnage rolls, only 29 per cent paid aulnage. The proportions for Beverley are similar: 31 per cent of a total of twenty-six cloth shippers.[84] The majority of cloth exporters were buying in from small producers, or from middlemen like the draper John Braithwait.

The later aulnage rolls do not permit such a detailed analysis, generally naming only a few individuals 'and others of' their town. Between 1473 and 1475, an unknown number of York merchants paid aulnage on 2,346½ cloths, and a group of Hull merchants paid aulnage on 295 cloths between 1471 and 1473.[85] The provenance of the cloth is unknown. In

---

[78] Lister, *Early Yorks Woollen Trade*, pp. 102–6. Hull paid aulnage on 295 cloths between 1471 and 1473. *Ibid.*, pp. 34, 35, 103.

[79] *Test. Ebor.* III, pp. 301–2. Rural manufacturing was expanding in other regions, e.g. Wiltshire. Bolton, *Medieval English Economy*, pp. 268–9.

[80] There had been 111 broadlooms operational in York in the 1450s: Swanson, *Medieval Artisans*, pp. 29–30. See below, chapter 10.   [81] Swanson, *Medieval Artisans*, pp. 131, 141–2.

[82] Lister, *Early Yorks Woollen Trade*, pp. 43, 51–2, 56, 58, 74–6, 81, 88, 91–2, 101.

[83] *Ibid.*; PRO, E122/59/19.   [84] Six of the forty-three Hull cloth exporters paid aulnage.

[85] Lister, *Early Yorks Woollen Trade*, pp. 34, 35, 103.

1432 and 1434 William Girlington of York was caught selling cloth in his shop which he had fraudulently stamped with his own seal, which suggests it had been made locally.[86]

Merchants were well placed to develop the role of middlemen, co-ordinating production between the wool grower, weaver, fuller and dyer.[87] This effectively displaced some of the investment risk onto artisans. In 1338 Walter de Kelstern bought ten sacks at Scotton and carried it to York, to make cloth 'as it is believed'.[88] Robert Ward of York, for example, had sixty-six dyed cloths stamped between October 1394 and August 1395.[89] York wool merchants made bequests to textile workers: Robert Holme to five dyers including one from Pontefract, Robert Collinson to each dyer, fuller, sherman and tailor who had worked for him. York middlemen took their business to the most profitable workers, irrespective of location. Thomas Clynt of York left money in 1439 to the fullers and dyers in Tadcaster who had worked for him, as well as others in the city and suburbs of York. Dyers in Stamford Bridge and York were remembered by York mercer Thomas Curtas in 1461,[90] and there is evidence that York merchants advanced credit to their outworkers. Dyers were indebted to John Bedale in 1427 and, more intriguingly, a dyer from Kingston-upon-Thames owed Thomas Holme money in 1381.[91] This is not substantial evidence but it does indicate the impact in one specific area, of inward investment from external trade, as Bedale, Collinson, Curtas and both Holmes traded overseas.

From the evidence of commercial networks, it is likely that information costs remained particularly high in the wool trade, because prices could change quickly.[92] We have only scattered evidence to suggest the nature and extent of a few individual merchants, but all reflects a wide geographical dispersal of contacts. One of the fullest sources is the will of Robert Holme snr of York, dated 1396,[93] in which he released four men from their debts, including a man from Grantham and another from Holme on the Wold. He left money to unnamed parishes where his servants had purchased wool, bequests to the nuns at Malton, Kirkham, Watton and Wartre, to the families of three Beverley merchants, a Londoner and a man from Wakefield. His extensive and varied connec-

---

[86] Bartlett, 'Aspects of the Economy of York', p. 416.
[87] Swanson, *Medieval Artisans*, pp. 144–5.   [88] *C. Inq. Misc. 1307–49*, p. 399.
[89] Lister, *Early Yorks Woollen Trade*, pp. 52, 75, 76, 88, 91.
[90] Prob. Reg. I, ff. 100v.–3v. (Holme); II, ff. 378–80 (Collinson), 438–9 (Curtas), 567–8v. (Clynt); *VCH York*, p. 88.   [91] *CCR 1377–81*, p. 523; *CPR 1422–9*, p. 366.
[92] Datini agents in London recorded a range of 9 marks in wool prices, 1395–1404, 50 per cent of the average value of a sack, a major consideration being the health of the flocks: H. Bradley, 'The Datini Factors in London, 1380–1410', in Clayton *et al.*, *Trade, Devotion and Governance*, pp. 60–1.
[93] Prob. Reg. I, ff. 100v.–3v.

tions reflected his large-scale cloth and wool exporting business. Although we might regard him first and foremost as an exporting merchant, Holme's inward investment did generate local employment and not just for his dyers.

Sixty years later, the will of York mercer Robert Collinson reveals a man cutting costs by extending direct control into manufacturing. He died in 1458, probably fifty-four years old, but his business career falls tantalisingly into one of the gaps in the Hull customs records. The only evidence we have of his trade is that he sold cushions and spices to Fountains Abbey in the 1450s and had a share in goods arrested in Danzig in 1440.[94] His will of 1450 suggests that he was a clothier, probably buying wool directly from rural producers, and certainly co-ordinating the finishing of cloth from dyeing to shearing. Bequests in his will were spread throughout Cumberland, Westmorland, North Yorkshire and the West Riding. Gifts to several churches and priories in and around Carlisle are as suggestive of his own origins as of his business connections. Some of his beneficiaries, religious houses like the priories of Bolton-in-Craven and Richmond, as well as unnamed individuals, may have been his wool suppliers, others spinners and weavers of cloth. Contributions to the repair of Catterick and Greteham bridges and to the road from Ferrybridge to York confirmed the necessity of maintaining reliable communications.[95]

The debts of another York merchant, Thomas Neleson, can be plotted within a slightly smaller radius between 1449 and 1481. Neleson was a large-scale general merchant, whose imports of general merchandise usually exceeded his mixed exports in value. His visible debtors owed sums of between £2 and £60 and lived in the north-east, which may reflect the distribution area for his imports.[96] When he died in 1484, his estate included an unusually wide distribution of properties throughout an almost identical area.[97]

---

[94] *Mem. Fountains*, III, pp. 45, 46, 104; *Hanserecesse, 1431–76*, II, p. 542.

[95] Prob. Reg. II, ff. 378–80 and *Test. Ebor.* II, p. 217. The locations of his institutional beneficiaries were: Appleby, Arthington, Bolton-in-Craven, Carlisle, Drissold, Knaresborough, Penrith, Nunmonkton, Northallerton, Sinningthwaite, Richmond, Ripon, Watton, Wetherall, York. The parishes were: Berwike-in-Elmet, Bramham, Brotherton, Dighton, Hamsthwait, Harwood, Kippax, Kirkby, Knaresborough, Ledesham, Nunmonkton, Pateley Bridge, Pontefract, Ripley, Ripon, Saxton, Sherburn, Spoforth, Stanlay, Swillington, Tadcaster, Whitekirk.

[96] *CPR 1446–52*, p. 198 (Snaith); *1452–61*, pp. 384 (Whitby), 456 (Hunmanby); *1467–77*, pp. 9 (Bolton-on-Dearne), 431 (Hedon); *MB*, II, p. 274 (five husbandmen and one gentleman from Alne, Rothwell and Tollerton).

[97] His will was drawn up six years earlier in 1478: Prob. Reg. v, ff. 212v.–13v.

Wine

In some respects, the wine trade was fairly uncomplicated. Imports were supervised by the king's butler and customs collectors, retail sales by local regulations. Buying wine called for expertise in tasting and blending and required merchants to travel to Bordeaux for the initial selection and price fixing, leaving a factor or apprentice to conclude the deal. Bordeaux and its region were hungry for foodstuffs and manufactures. Trading in wine thus often began with the gathering of a mixed cargo: fish, peas, grain, hides, wool and especially textiles. Bordeaux became something of a specialist market for English cloth, creating a significant reduction in transaction costs of all sorts. In such a well-established market it was possible to leave unsold goods with a French host while the return cargoes of wine were shipped home before they deteriorated.[98]

Wine involved a long-term investment, beginning with the initiating export cargo. The voyages were lengthy compared with the shorter distances covered by wool and cloth *en route* to Calais and the Low Countries. Ships hugged the coast and regularly put in to take on fresh provisions. The *Margaret Cely* took about five months to complete the round trip to Bordeaux in 1487.[99] Time was critical because wine was a perishable commodity and the major concern was to sell while the wine was still in good condition.[100] Dregs and sour wines were sometimes mixed in a barrel to dilute the wine but this seems to have been most commonly practised by smaller retailers.

The trade was conducted by a large number of small-scale merchants, acting both as importers and wholesale distributors and supplying both the large households and small consumers.[101] The latter bought small quantities locally on a day-to-day basis; the butlers and stewards of the former sometimes bought their wine abroad, from the importer or from middlemen, and purchased in bulk to ensure supplies for some six months or so.

AGENTS AND CONTRACTS

All commodities traded over long distances incurred further costs in the employment of agents. These men negotiated prices, credit, the terms of

---

[98] James, *Wine Trade*, pp. 161–66.
[99] She left London on 20 September, stayed for about one month in Bordeaux and returned the following March. James, *Wine Trade*, pp. 169–70; Hanham, *Celys and Their World*, pp. 369–71.
[100] See the case of John Green below, p. 243.
[101] Between 1478 and 1488, only six London traders imported over 100 tuns of wine in any one year: James, *Wine Trade*, pp. 160, 176–8.

partnerships, found suitable ships, handled the dispatch of goods, and paid the customs and subsidies. They found buyers for exports and put together return cargoes. It is worth reflecting on the skills and time necessary for negotiating the purchases which made up a cargo of mixed imports. Some agents were permanent employees of a trading house, apprentices or relatives, while others were hired under specific instructions to invest a given sum to venture for profit,[102] or to complete a specific task.

Perhaps only a minority of merchants travelled overseas, but the practice was not uncommon and several bought property and formed other attachments in distant ports.[103] William Palmer, John Sparwe and others of York and Hull were in Prussia long enough to be physically attacked in the early 1380s, and in 1420 there were sufficent Yorkshire merchants in Rouen to act as arbitrators for the local court in a dispute between William Alkbarow of York and Richard Rolleston of Beverley.[104] An alternative was to employ an agent, often another merchant, based in Calais or the Low Countries. Thomas Redmar of Hull offered the services of his servant in Holland to other local merchants in 1413, no doubt at a charge! This was an appropriate form of training and merchants sent their sons or young aspirants to act for them. William Northeby of Hull's son Peter was in charge of his affairs in Antwerp in 1422, whereas in 1410 William Newland of York sent his servant Thomas Vescy. Vescy became a burgess of the city in 1412, as a merchant in his own right.[105] Such arrangements occasioned their own problems, and in 1495 the York Merchant Adventurers' Company agreed to ensure that members' servants working overseas were supervised by someone from the Company.[106] Apprentices traded illegally for their own profit,[107] and

---

[102] Margaret Blackburn of York claimed that she was due a bond for £400, owed to her late husband by their son-in-law John Bolton and Alice his wife. Margaret left it with Bolton *ad mercandizand* for the two years following her death, after which he was to pay her heirs the £400. No more is heard of this bond, and her son and heir Nicholas left only £19 when he died thirteen years later: Prob. Reg. II, ff. 168v.–9 (Nicholas jnr), 605; III, ff. 415v.–416v. (Margaret).

[103] For overseas property see above, chapter 5. According to Wolff, English merchants very rarely went to Toulouse but conducted much of their trade through the merchants of neutral Bearn, 'English Cloth in Toulouse', p. 293.

[104] *Hanserecesse, 1256–1430*, III, p. 409; ADSM Tabellionage de Rouen, ff. 214, 314, 336v., 438v. See also PRO, SC8/26/1275 for Robert Holme of York, who was in Guienne in 1430, and who drew up his will on 15 March 1435 (Prob. Reg. III, f. 413), anticipating that he might be in Calais shortly. In the event he died at home by 18 April.

[105] *Bronnen*, I, pp. 545–6, 589, 604. See also *ibid.*, II, pp. 1056–7 and *CCR 1392–6*, p. 200.

[106] *M&MA*, p. 93.

[107] In 1486 William Hancock of York's apprentice was transacting business of his own with a Hanse merchant in Hull: *YCR*, I, p. 163. William Garnet's apprentice was merely careless and left 14s behind in Hull after concluding a deal. Prob. Reg. VIII, f. 102. William Randolph of York left his master 10 marks 'for his transgressions' in 1393: *ibid.*, I, f. 95v.

agents to whom a fixed sum was given to venture at an agreed percentage of any profit, defrauded their patrons. When the agent of John Box of Hull could account for only £77 of the £110 he had been sent, he was imprisoned in the Fleet prison in 1310–11. For non-staplers exporting wool, it was convenient to use the existing arrangements of a neighbour: thus in 1433 Nicholas Blackburn jnr of York used the Calais agent of York stapler William Marshall to sell £54 worth of wool for him.[108]

There were so many stages and different parties involved in ventures that it was important to establish clear liability. This was more easily desired than achieved in a process exposed to unexpected events. No party was beyond damage, however precisely terms had been laid down. The detailed accounts of two York disputes unravel the complicated milieu of long-distance trade. In December 1415 William Warde, a York spicer, authorised William Eseby to buy £68 worth of Flemish goods for Warde at 5 per cent commission. The agreement made it clear that the transaction was to be at Warde's own risk. Eseby bought the goods and duly shipped them in the *Hulke*, but *en route* from Zeeland to Hull the ship was wrecked. Warde would not reimburse Eseby for his labour or the capital he had expended, and Eseby brought an action which resulted in an inquisition being held in York in March 1416, by the order of the king. Apparently undaunted by his experience with Warde, Eseby continued to act as an overseas agent, and three years later appeared once more before the York council. This time he was trying to recover £23 2s from Richard Etton, agent of Robert Tup of Hull. Eseby had acted as Eton's pledge in a bond agreed with Jaques Weit, a burgess of Bruges: Weit, unable to find Eton, was demanding payment from Eseby.[109]

The second case, begun in York but eventually heard before the Exchequer, tells us much about the relationship between a merchant and his agents and the way business was conducted.[110] A stapler, John Bolton, engaged two other York merchants, John Brandesby and Simon Swan, to act for him in Calais, mainly handling wool exports but also dealing in cloth and herrings. Bolton disputed their accounts, accusing them of receiving monies not properly accounted for, of claiming fraudulent expenses during a twenty-one-month period and of owing him £489 6s 6d. Apart from the colossal amounts of wool handled, some £3,286 8s 2d worth from Bolton's store, what emerges is the liability of the agent for on-the-spot expenses. Brandesby could find neither bullion nor bills to pay the Calais mint against the sale of wool and became indebted to

---

[108] G. J. Turner, ed., *Year Book 4 Edward II*, Selden Soc., 26 (1911), p. 139; PRO, C1/44/277.

[109] *C. Inq.Misc., vii, 1399–1422*, pp. 302–3; *MB*, II, pp. xxiv–xxv, 55, 56, 87–9.

[110] Hall, *Select Cases*, II, pp. xxxvii, lxix, 106–9, 156–9. PRO, C1/16/592. The wealth of detail which emerged from this case is too engaging to omit, and Hall's précis has been copied in appendix 4.

some Flemish merchants for a loan. In order to gain possession of a house in which to store and display merchandise in Bruges, Brandesby paid out 30s additional to £6 13s 4d previously paid. He was also bound by an obligation to merchants from Lombardy and Picardy which he could not meet and was imprisoned. He could not attend to Bolton's business until he was bailed out of prison by Philip Cassel, to whom he was thereby indebted. Although several of these disputed payments were in further-ance of Bolton's business, many of them were disallowed by the auditors. Eventually Brandesby had to answer to a claim of £22, the balance of the arrears due to Bolton. One item disputed was Brandesby's fees. He claimed £13 6s 8d per annum for two years, Bolton an inclusive fee for the two years of £6 13s 4d plus two cloaks and hoods worth 40s. Mutual distrust would better describe this business arrangement; Bolton's con-stant fear that his agents would trade to their own advantage with his goods and money percolates throughout the record.

Not surprisingly, given the fragile line between friend, servant and sleeping partner, some merchants chose to settle overseas where they acted directly on their own behalf and for friends and associates. Some developed close ties with their temporary homes, even to the extent of marrying foreign nationals.[111] In the late fourteenth century, several York merchants died abroad, and were buried in Danzig, Calais and Dordrecht.[112] Death brought to light all sorts of assets accumulated by merchants active overseas – houses, land and stored goods – and, as ever, fellow merchants were relied upon to deal with them. Thus John Russell of York asked another York merchant, Richard Lematon, and Philip Best of Calais to sell off his goods in Calais in 1443. In 1484 Robert Alcock of Hull requested his son-in-law John Dalton to sell his goods and liquidate all his assets in Calais to the greatest profit.[113]

Every long-distance merchant's business was based on some form of contract: maybe a handshake in the churchyard of St Margaret's Walmegate, York[114] or a complicated series of agreements involving third parties. It was imperative that each party was confident that a contract was enforceable and legal practice evolved to meet the needs of com-merce. Whether battling for compensation in a foreign court or manoeu-vring to gain a hold on a defaulting debtor or embezzling partner, merchants were astute manipulators of legal processes. Their direct expe-

---

[111] John Milner alias Tutbag of York left money in 1438 to his sister's children 'overseas' as well as 6s 8d to an Antwerp man: Prob. Reg. III, f. 526 (Tutbag).

[112] See above, p. 134.

[113] Prob. Reg. II, f. 68 (Russell); III, ff. 36 (Spencer), f. 526 (Tutbag); v, f. 229b (Alcock).

[114] Or 'on the sands at Scarborough' in 1402: York Borthwick Institute, cause papers CP 4 F 23, 58. I am grateful to Jeremy Goldberg for these references.

rience contributed to the development of formal, legal procedures, particularly in making contracts, registering debts, guaranteeing the quality and measurement of commodities.[115] All of these could be seen as a way of reducing their transaction costs. Two aspects are of particular relevance here: the hierarchy of courts and jurisdiction (access, speed and costs), and the flexibility of legal actions (wager, evidence and security of judgement).[116]

At a practical level, we can see in the creation and refinement of financial instruments evidence of the overwhelming need to secure enforcement alongside the desire for a negotiable bond. Merchants might choose between local courts which could process bonds and sometimes statutory bonds, and the central courts in London which could enforce bills of exchange and other contracts under merchant law. Local courts provided adequate enforcement of locally based contracts, even those involving foreigners. In 1424, for example, Hull men took their cases against Dutch merchants before the Grimsby borough courts, even though one complaint dealt with a sale contracted in the Low Countries.[117] The impression is that when plaintiffs sought speedier remedies in one of the central courts it was for many reasons, including the suspicion that it was difficult to get a fair hearing in the courts of another town.[118]

The possibility of spending time and money to enforce a contract in a distant court was an important consideration for any merchant entering a partnership, securing credit or dealing with anyone outside his own region. Trade, however, is for optimists. Most merchants presumably hoped that they would not be shipwrecked or assaulted by pirates or have to pursue an erstwhile partner through the royal courts in London, or, even worse, through a court overseas.[119]

---

[115] In his introduction to *Select Cases*, II, pp. xl–li, Hubert Hall discusses these issues. The Court of the Admiralty developed its jurisdiction from the mid-fourteenth century in response to the failures of the common law to deal with piracy and pressure from merchants for enforceable reparations: R. G. Marsden, ed., *Select Pleas in the Court of the Admiralty*, I, Selden Soc., 6 (London, 1892), pp. xiv–xv, xix, xxii–xxvi.

[116] See S. F. C. Milsom, *Historical Foundations of the Common Law*, 2nd edn (London, 1981), pp. 243–85 for a discussion of different types of action. For developments see M. Hastings, *The Court of Common Pleas in the Fifteenth Century* (Ithaca, 1947); R. C. Palmer, *English Law in the Age of the Black Death* (Chapel Hill, 1993); A. W. B. Simpson, *A History of the Common Law of Contract. The Rise of the Action of Assumpsit* (Oxford, 1987), pp. 199–236.

[117] South Humberside RO, Grimsby Court Rolls, 2 HVI April, November. I am grateful to Steve Rigby for these references.

[118] See below, p. 236, note 73, and for a bias elsewhere, see Kowaleski, *Medieval Exeter*, pp. 113–14, 219; Platt, *Medieval Southampton*, p. 176.   [119] See below, pp. 221, 229.

CORPORATE STRATEGIES

One solution to reducing all transaction costs was to spread risks. Partnerships offered savings, so long as they worked, but the records inevitably tell us more about the failures than the successes. Partnerships extended to shipowning. Part shares in ships eased investment but also offset losses, an important advantage in times of volatile international relations. A share could be as small as a thirty-second part, but a quarter share was more common.[120] Business partnerships will be discussed as one of the many commercial options available to merchants in chapter 7.

Merchant companies could offer similar reduced costs, on an altogether different scale though. The Hanseatic towns had demonstrated just how successful collective action could be, and by 1407 an English merchant adventurers' company was holding assemblies and electing governors. The York mercers and merchants emerged from an earlier fraternity into an adventurers' company in 1430: a response to the challenges they faced, not just from the Hanse, but from London. Hostile competition at home and abroad characterised relations between northern and London merchants.[121] In contrast, English wine traders supported each other in Bordeaux irrespective of their home town and it has been claimed that individuals were so well known and trusted that the need to form a company to protect their interests did not arise.[122]

Cutting costs or at least achieving parity was critical and difficult to accomplish. The York Merchant Adventurers' Company lobbied against the imposition of poundage on cloth and to protect its interests against alien traders and wool staplers.[123] York merchants were still negotiating together in an attempt to establish a maximum for the fees to be charged to them in Bruges, Antwerp, Barow and Middleburg in 1495.[124]

The York Company recognised the importance of enforcement costs and agreed to hear debt cases of the fellowship in its own court. It is not clear how often the court was used. The Company also acted as a sort of shipping agent: it chartered ships to carry collective cargoes, fixed freight rates, arranged dates for convoys and the payment of protection money.

---

[120] Prob. Reg. III, f. 556 (Joan Gregg, 1438). In 1449, six Hull ships were owned by six different partnerships: Hull RO, D81; BRB I, f. 11.

[121] *M&MA*, pp. v–x, 65, 74–80; *VCH York*, pp. 103–4, 130; Heaton, *Yorks Woollen and Worsted Industries*, p. 155. See below, chapter 8.   [122] James, *Wine Trade*, p. 175.

[123] Bolton, *Medieval English Economy*, pp. 316–17; Carus-Wilson, *Medieval Merchant Venturers*, pp. 153–7.

[124] In 1497 Yorkshire merchants may have collaborated with other non-Londoners in petitioning against charges imposed on them overseas by the London adventurers: *M&MA*, p. 87; N. J. M. Kerling, *Commercial Relations of Holland and Zeeland with England from the Late Thirteenth Century to the Close of the Middle Ages* (Leiden, 1954), p. 155.

In return merchants paid an appropriate sum back to the Company, out of which overheads were then paid. The earliest record of the activities of freighting managers is from 1578, but there is no reason to suppose that the system which operated in the fifteenth century was very different. Several accounts of voyages have survived from the fifteenth century, including those for ventures to Iceland by William Todd and John Ferriby in 1475.[125] In Hull it was the Corpus Christi Guild, a religious guild for merchants, which made loans to members, but not for overseas ventures. The Guild of the Virgin Mary, on the other hand, was financing ventures to Iceland and the Low Countries in the mid-fifteenth century.[126] Hull city council facilitated collaboration in the 1460s by supporting several voyages.[127]

TRANSPORT COSTS

A major item in any venture was transport, and overseas traders faced the additional expense of shipping.[128] Although a large number of ships from the Low Countries, and a declining number of Hansard ships, plied for trade between Hull and the continent, local shipping competed successfully, accounting for between 30 to 40 per cent of shipping in the fourteenth and late fifteenth centuries. Of 138 sailings in 1398–9, forty-seven were Hull ships, with an occasional vessel from neighbouring places such as Beverley, Hedon, Grimsby or York, and of eighty-nine sailings in 1471–2, thirty-two were Hull ships.[129]

A ship was a useful source of income: a working outfit and an asset to set against loans. William Crathorn, of York, calculated in 1440 that the loss of his ship for seventeen months cost him £200 at least.[130] He was unusual among York and Beverley merchants, few of whom invested in ships during this period,[131] although a handful of ships were registered in both.[132] Merchants from those towns were therefore dependent upon others for the carriage of their goods and increasingly this meant Hull

---

[125] *M&MA*, pp. xlviii, 40, 68, 72–3, 195.

[126] *VCH Hull*, pp. 58–9; Toulmin-Smith, *English Guilds*, pp. 156–7, 160–1.

[127] See below p. 271.

[128] Losses of ships due to enemy action and impressment led to an acute shortage in the mid-fifteenth century. Most wine was carried in alien ships: James, *Wine Trade*, p. 171.

[129] PRO, E122/62/17.

[130] *Hanserecesse, 1431–76*, II, pp. 542–5. The Celys, however, regarded shipowning as a possible liability. Hanham, *Celys and Their World*, p. 397.

[131] Only John Brompton of Beverley, who owned a three-quarters share: Prob. Reg. II, f. 86v. See Power and Postan, *Studies in English Trade*, p. 237, for the emergence of such a group in Bristol. Even in the sixteenth century no Exeter merchant was wealthy enough to own a whole ship. Hoskins, 'Merchants of Exeter', p. 170.

[132] E.g. Childs, *Hull Customs Accounts*, pp. 58, 93, 101, 106, 110.

owners. Each owner of a share was expected to pay an equivalent share of the overheads. John Thom of Hull left his share in the *George* to his son Robert in 1453, on condition that Robert pay 'all the costs that belong to my part of the ship if it gets home safely'.[133]

Packing, storing and carriage were a further consideration. Goods had to be carted to ships at the port of embarkation, weighed once more and stored there. The process had to be repeated on arrival overseas and for inward cargoes. Recent research suggests that the inland costs of transporting grain in the mid-fourteenth century added only 0.4 per cent, but no figure for the fifteenth century has been proposed.[134] It is impossible to generalise since so many variables were involved: regional labour rates, size of cart, numbers of horses, the hiring of equipment for pack-horses and so on. One York mercer, John de More, owned his own pack-horses and cloths.[135] Specific references provide clues however, but these can only be illustrative. We do know, from the case of a greedy vintner who sold wine in Beverley in 1364 at 12d a gallon, that he should have allowed only ½d on his purchase price of 8d per gallon for transport from Hull.[136]

Wool had to be packed in canvas, to reduce spoiling and to ease handling of such a bulky commodity. Fleeces or fells were heavier and their carriage cost more. Wool incurred further costs on arrival at Calais. William de la Pole paid 6d per sack carriage from York to Hull in 1337 and 10d per sack from Nottingham to Hull in 1339. His total costs from Hull to Flanders were 6s per sack in 1337 and 5s in 1339. It has been estimated that the transport, packing and warehousing of wool purchased by him in Lincolnshire and shipped from Hull in 1336–7 comprised 9 per cent of the total cost, compared to some 14 per cent of the total cost of Shropshire wool shipped by him from London.[137] In the 1470s the average costs per sack incurred by the Celys were about 7s 2d in England and a further 9s in Calais: the cost of transporting wool from the Cotswolds to London adding about 2 per cent of the purchase price.[138] Agents' commission had to be added to these overheads. Geography was

---

[133] Prob. Reg. II, f. 292v.

[134] J. Masschaele, 'Transport Costs in Medieval England', *EcHR*, 2nd ser., 46 (1993), p. 274.

[135] Prob. Reg. III, f. 10 (1398), and see Alice Upstall, a widow who left cloths and saddles: II, f. 640. William Bedale of York may have owned equipment which he hired out. A Leicester carrier owed him 40s in 1432: *CPR 1429–36*, p. 176.

[136] James, *Wine Trade*, p. 147. In 1355 it had been agreed that vintners within twenty-five miles of a port should charge ½d per gallon, and those twenty-five to fifty miles away should charge 1d per gallon. *Foedera*, III, p. 294.

[137] Fryde, *Wool Accounts of William de la Pole*, pp. 10–14. The estimate of costs was kindly supplied by Edward Miller. De la Pole shipped 120 quarters of wheat to Flanders at a cost of £6 7s 6d: about 3d per ton mile: Masschaele, 'Transport Costs', p. 273.

[138] Hanham, *Celys and Their World*, pp. 119, 123–4. For a fuller discussion of all additional costs, see *ibid.*, pp. 116–33.

important too. By 1500, transport from Scotland to the Low Countries was adding an average 7 per cent to the final sale price of a large Scottish sack of wool.[139]

The bulk of Hull's imports consisted of non-sweet Gascon wines, which faced a hazardous voyage even in peace-time. Pilots were required and charges varied according to the type of ship, time of year, weather and distance. Thus, in the early 1330s, pilotage from the River Gironde to Hull cost between £1 and £1 6s 8d. During Edward II's reign pilotage to Hull cost 6s 8d and by Edward III's reign had risen to between 13s 4d and £1. If a ship stopped anywhere *en route*, local pilotage was charged. Freight costs also varied: from Bordeaux to Hull or London, wine cost 6s 8d, 8s and 10s a tun to ship in 1333–5; from Hull or London to Calais, 6s 8d in 1346–7; and from Bordeaux to Hull or London between 16s 8d and 22s in 1414. Costs increased markedly during war but also at other times.[140]

COSTS OF PIRACY AND WAR

Overseas enterprise, especially on a significant scale of investment, involved risks, and the hostile climate of late medieval international relations required a steady nerve. Conditions encouraged traders to take the law into their own hands. In 1343, Roger Swerd, later mayor of Hull, killed a man while engaged in a deliberate and criminal act of piracy against a foreign ship, but was pardoned by Edward III.[141] The constant stream of complaints in the diplomatic correspondence of the early fourteenth century led to the emergence of the Court of the Admiralty to deal with a problem beyond the competence of the common law.[142] Physical assaults, theft in all guises, piracy and licensed privateering were part of the merchant's world: a world of individual aspiration and uneasy collaboration when business demanded. When an English wine fleet was attacked by Genoese pirates in 1415, the unfortunate ship of Hull merchant John Tutbury was abandoned by the rest.[143] As we shall see, Tutbury was no stranger to piracy and was involved in a number of dubious events apparently without compunction.[144]

[139] A. W. K. Stevenson, 'Trade Between Scotland and the Low Countries in the Later Middle Ages' (Univ. of Aberdeen PhD thesis, 1982), p. 213.

[140] James, *Wine Trade*, pp. 25–7, 126, 140–5, 151–3, 155; *MB*, I, p. 172; *Rot. Parl.*, III, p. 283.

[141] *CPR 1343–5*, p. 214; *CCR 1343–6*, p. 349. Another instance of collective lawlessness occurred in 1375 when several Beverley keepers assaulted a justice *en route* to York to implement the Statute of Labourers: see *CPR 1374–7*, p. 146.

[142] Marsden, *Pleas in the Court of the Admiralty*, I, pp. xiv–xv. For the Admiral of the North, see *VCH Hull*, pp. 52–4.

[143] *Rot. Parl.* IV, pp. 85, 103. See also *CCR 1374–7*, p. 494; *1377–81*, p. 414; Salzman, *English Trade*, pp. 254–8.   [144] See below, p. 217.

Such attacks were not always simple acts of aggression, but should be seen as part of a repertoire of strategies to gain compensation for injuries and losses. Letters of marque were granted as a formal means of recovering goods from any merchant of the offending nation, but were not seen as essential.[145] Robert de Selby captured a ship in 1377, deliberately to recover some compensation for his own goods pirated at sea by Normandy merchants.[146] Given the protracted negotiations in which he might otherwise have become embroiled, Selby's action was perhaps understandable and others shared his views. In 1384 for instance, William Burton, William Holme, William Tickhill, William Fysshe, John Swan, John de Gisburgh, William Bell and others of York, John Arnald of Hull and Roger de Gouton of London freighted a ship with goods in York to the value of £1,000, which was seized off Great Yarmouth *en route* for London. The Dieppe and Crotay ships with the men involved took the ship and cargo back to Dieppe, leaving the Yorkshire merchants to obtain writs from the sheriffs of London, Southampton and Plymouth and the bailiff of the Thames to arrest the goods of Frenchmen to the equivalent value. A year later, in March 1385, they were still pursuing the action, having spent money on petitioning two parliaments and on negotiations at Calais in vain.[147]

During the fourteenth century the shifting alliances around the Anglo-French wars encouraged acts of piracy,[148] and from the late fourteenth century, Anglo-Hanseatic rivalry infected the entire North Sea region, as alliances and accords were negotiated and broken. 'Regrettable incidents' and savage mercantile reprisals had threatened trade for centuries,[149] but in the absence of a permanent navy, merchants found themselves deeply involved in warfare at sea[150] as open hostility flared between England and the Hanse. Quite blatant acts of piracy and privateering soon became a feature of North Sea relations, random action giving way to officially sanctioned opportunism. The Crown granted licences to fit out ships to 'defend the realm' on condition that any prize was shared three ways between the king, the soldiers on the ship and the licensed privateer.[151] Hull merchant

---

[145] Salzman, *English Trade*, p. 260.   [146] *CCR 1374–7*, p. 494; *1377–81*, p. 414.

[147] *CCR 1381–6*, pp. 366, 373, 536. See also the case of John Byston, a Lynn merchant who was still pursuing compensation in 1482, nine years after his losses at the hands of Veere merchants: *CPR 1474–85*, p. 321.

[148] In 1313 Flemings seized a cargo of Yorkshire wool, seeking refuge with English enemies in Aberdeen, before taking it back to Flanders: *CCR 1313–18*, p. 7. See also *Bronnen*, I, pp. 175–6 for the loss of Beverley goods *en route* from Middelburgh in 1320.

[149] Hall, *Select Cases*, II, p. xxxi; Salzman, *English Trade*, pp. 255–79 for examples.

[150] C. F. Richmond, 'The War at Sea', in K. Fowler, ed., *The Hundred Years War* (London, 1971), pp. 96–121; and 'English Naval Power in the Fifteenth Century', *History*, 52 (1967), pp. 1–15.

[151] PRO, sc8/254/12686. For example, William Pund and William Page of Hull received £20 as their share of a prize: *CPR 1385–9*, p. 412. In 1406 the merchant community was given tonnage

ship-owners, generally prominent citizens, seized the chance to take their commercial rivalry onto the high seas. In July 1387, William Terry, John Tutbury and Peter Stellar of Hull and Walter Were of Grimsby equipped a ship, ballinger and barge at their own expense, to arm themselves 'against the king's enemies'.[152] Further licences were granted with a broader remit to 'arrest the pirates who patrol the seas and attack merchants',[153] and the 'Hullers' seized Scots, Danes, Dutchmen and, of course, Hanse merchants.[154] Terry, Tutbury and others from Hull engaged in unlicensed piracy when friction with the Hanse intensified in the 1390s.[155]

The line between serving as the royal navy and acting as privateers was a fine one. William Terry of Hull was licensed in June 1400 to take his ship the *George* to sea, and again in March 1402 to take the *George* and the *Janet* with forty mariners to serve the king.[156] He and John Tutbury, several times mayor of Hull, illegally captured a vessel sailing to Berwick under a letter of protection.[157] John Tutbury was also 'defending the realm' in the English Channel when he helped to capture two enemy ships in 1412.[158]

The fifteenth century was a time of increasing difficulty and danger. Worsening relations between Norway and Denmark increased the risks to merchants, reflected in the succession of complaints, from all sides, of harassment, piracy and seizures.[159] Governments issued safe-conducts and licences to individual traders and negotiated short-term peace agreements; but they failed to establish trading conditions acceptable to all sides. From the merchant's viewpoint, irrespective of the national alliances all protagonists invoked to justify attacks on shipping, the hard reality was serious commercial loss. A few instances will serve as illustration.

In 1422, fifteen merchants from York, Beverley and Hull lost goods *en route* from Danzig. In 1426, John Bedford of Hull lost a ship[160] and two

---

and poundage and a grant from the subsidy on wool to maintain a body of soldiers. They could keep all the prizes captured, except ships of notables which had to be handed over to the king. *Rot. Parl.* III, p. 610.   [152] *CPR 1385–9*, p. 339.

[153] Danger did not only come from foreigners. William Gaunt, who was shipping goods from London to Hull, was pirated by Newcastle men in 1453: *CPR 1452–61*, p. 174.

[154] See, for example, *CCR 1377–81*, p. 414; *CPR 1399–1401*, p. 352; *CPR 1405–8*, p. 302; *CCR 1405–9*, p. 60; *CCR 1409–13*, pp. 291, 376.

[155] E.g. *Urkundenbuch*, V, p. 322, 483; VI, p. 360; *CPR 1405–8*, pp. 236, 304, 353, 416.

[156] *CPR 1385–9*, p. 339; *1399–1401*, p. 352; *1401–5*, p. 55; PRO, SC8/254/12688.

[157] *CCR 1402–5*, pp. 1–2, 42, 56, 256.   [158] *CCR 1409–23*, p. 376.

[159] *VCH Hull*, pp. 59–60, 62–3; *VCH York*, pp. 102–4; Carus-Wilson, 'Iceland Trade', pp. 163–7; *MB*, II, pp. xxi–xxvii. For example, *CPR 1413–16*, p. 19 (ship and cloth, 1417); *CCR 1446–52*, p. 41 (ship and goods, 1446); *Hanseakten*, pp. 236, 238 (Norwegian pirates, 1407); *Hanserecesse, 1431–76*, II, p. 542 (theft, 1440).

[160] *Hanserecesse, 1256–1430*, VII, pp. 398–9; *1431–76*; II, p. 65; *Urkundenbuch*, VI, pp. 305–86 (1424), 358 (1426).

separate groups of Yorkshire merchants lost cargoes: Robert Holme, Thomas Gare, William Ormeshead and Richard Scoles had their wool shipments in the earl of Warwick's ship when it was seized.[161] Three years later another of John Bedford's ships and its cargo worth 1,000 marks was stolen at Boston, and, in frustration, he became a licensed privateer in 1436.[162] York and Hull merchants complained of losing goods in 1432, 1436 and 1438 in the Sound. On the last occasion the Danes were the villains and goods said to be worth over £5,000 were taken, of which the Hull men claimed about £2,100.[163]

The veracity of these claims cannot be tested but merchants certainly felt justified in snatching back whatever they could whenever they could. Hugh Clitheroe and others of Hull captured a Danish ship in 1432 and simply shared out the cargo between themselves, thereby attracting the Crown's attention. In May 1436, John Bedford and Robert Holme of Hull got licences to fit out ships for war, and almost immediately attacked an Amsterdam ship, aided by Robert Shackles and three other ship-owners. They seized the ship and goods worth £200 under the pretence that they did not know it was Dutch and therefore no enemy of England. The Dutch ship set sail to escape but the 'Hullers' boarded him 'in manner of war'.[164]

A single year could be disastrous. In 1440 ten merchants had their goods seized in Denmark and William Crathorn's ship was detained for seventeen months. Richard Anson, Ralph Forne, John Henryson and John Thorn of Hull were captured *en route* for Denmark and compelled to serve aboard their own ship. When they finally reached Denmark, their licence to trade was out of date and they were out of pocket by at least £660. Two other Hull merchants and a York merchant were captured when they went ashore in Stralsund to deliver a cargo and had to pay £24 to be released.[165]

Hostile attacks continued. One of the more dramatic incidents of the Anglo-Hanseatic war involved the ambushing in 1468 of the earl of Northumberland's ship, the *Valentine*, while it lay at anchor in the Sound. According to eyewitnesses, 400 armed men from Hanse towns, in a Danish vessel and a 'blak shippe of Danske', drove off the crew and imprisoned them ashore. Thirty-one merchants had ventured capital in the cargo: eleven from Hull and twenty-one from York, eleven of whom were former mayors.[166] In the subsequent legal attack, the earl headed the

[161] *Urkundenbuch*, VII, p. 30; *CPR 1422–9*, p. 385. The other loss was incurred by Thomas Mayne and others of Beverley, who were granted the right to export 600 wool fells free of subsidy in compensation: *ibid.*, p. 349.   [162] PRO, C1/11/97; *CPR 1429–36*, p. 510.
[163] *CPR 1436–41*, pp. 294–5; *VCH Hull*, p. 62.   [164] *CPR 1429–36*, pp. 334, 357; *1436–41*, p. 87.
[165] *Hanserecesse, 1431–76*, II, pp. 542–5.
[166] *MB*, II, pp. xxii–xxiii; *VCH Hull*, p. 62; *VCH York*, p. 103; Power and Postan, *Studies in English Trade*, p. 138; *Urkundenbuch*, IX, no. 520.

petition for reparation. Personal safety was at stake in these encounters as well as lost profits. The English government never had the resources to combat piracy at sea, whether by denizens or foreigners, and could offer very little protection to English merchants travelling abroad. Overseas merchants had to be resilient and resourceful and Henry Mindram of Hull, for instance, made his own arrangements to be ransomed from French captivity in 1473: his brother collected the money together after Henry had signed a bond guaranteeing repayment on his return.[167]

The Treaty of Utrecht finally brought hostilities to an end, but as trade began to pick up once more, it became apparent that the old issue of equal trading concessions had not been resolved. Hull tried to ensure that Hanse business activities were confined to port, and away from the hinterland. Reciprocal constraints were imposed on the few Hull merchants who managed to get inside Prussia. Roger Bushell of Hull, for example, was attacked in Danzig and in 1499 itemised the large number of restrictions imposed on his trade by the easterlings.[168]

Merchants were drawn into warfare in other ways. They inevitably contributed cash in the form of 'loans', as individuals, as Calais Staplers[169] or as part of another group.[170] As often they were drawn into hostilities because the government ordered individuals to press men for service at sea, to arrest ships for naval service.[171] The Crown was heavily dependent on merchant shipping to provide transport for troops and to serve as warships, and requisitioned ships in times of war. The fleet of 700 ships in 1346 contained 217 from the east coast ports.[172] This was unavoidably inconvenient to their owners. Robert Bisset, a Hull merchant, complained on 26 July 1386 that his ship had been taken in the Thames for the king's service, had been captured, then recaptured and left in Sandwich for him to recover. No sooner had he retrieved his ship than it was blown off course onto the Danish coast where its cargo of herrings was stolen.[173] In *c.* 1379 a group of York and Hull merchants lost £9

---

[167] PRO, c1/48/408; sc8/26/1275; *CPR 1467–77*, p. 368. On arbitration, see C. Rawcliffe, '"That Kindliness Should be Cherished More, and Discord Driven Out": The Settlement of Commercial Disputes by Arbitration in Later Medieval England', in Kermode, *Enterprise and Individuals*, pp. 99–117. [168] *VCH Hull*, p. 63.

[169] E.g. £4,000 in 1407 and £2,000 in 1449–50. Repayment was through reduced customs and subsidies: *CPR 1405–9*, pp. 321, 415; *1446–52*, p. 323; *1452–61*, p. 211. See G. L. Harriss, 'The Struggle for Calais: An Aspect of the Rivalry between Lancaster and York', *EHR*, 75 (1960), pp. 35–8, 41–51.

[170] E.g. the money to pay for the 1388 embassy to Prussia was raised from each town seen to have an especial interest, on a town-by-town basis: *CPR 1385–9*, pp. 564–6.

[171] E.g. *CPR 1396–9*, p. 366; *1446–52*, pp. 88, 316; *1452–61*, pp. 172, 178, 220, 404, 554; *1467–77*, p. 20. In 1427 John Fitling was co-ordinating a levy on Humber shipping to pay for a beacon at Spurn Head: *CPR 1422–9*, p. 457. [172] Scammell, 'English Merchant Shipping', p. 339.

[173] *CCR 1385–9*, p. 167; *CPR 1381–5*, p. 505; *1385–9*, p. 167.

worth of wool when the Crown seized the ship which was carrying it for military purposes.[174]

Quite apart from these hazards, wars increased costs.[175] It was customary for large-scale investors to divide their cargoes between several ships, to spread the risk of losses,[176] but during declared hostilities merchants had to pay to sail in convoys and for hiring armed men for their ships. The wine trade was immediately affected by the introduction of fleets in the second half of the fourteenth century, organised to ensure the safe passage of royal wine. Costs rose. Some were met from subsidies imposed on wine: 1s per tun in February 1350, 3s 4d for one year from September that year, and 2s in 1360 and 1369. In the 1390s it was claimed that the former charge of 8s for the round trip to Bordeaux had risen to 24s or even 100s. These costs were passed on to the customer along with increased freight costs.[177] In 1372, the *George* of Hull increased its complement of men from twenty-six to forty-eight, with a comensurate increase in its wages bill. As late as 1486 the *Margaret Cely* carried the armed escort for the wool fleet: twenty-eight soldiers at 6s 8d per day, deductible from the customs and subsidies payable on each sarplar.[178] Merchants bought safe-conducts which were often ignored, even though to do so was treasonable after 1414. Bottomry, a form of insurance for vessels, was known in England, but no instance was recorded until 1442, when premiums of 12 to 15 per cent were charged on goods shipped from London to Pisa.[179] Losses could be incurred in other ways[180] and merchants had to seek what reparations they could from their own governments and from individuals and governments overseas.

Compensation and recovery

Merchants from every nation regarded themselves as defenders of their own country's interests and sometimes it is difficult to separate aggressive

---

[174] PRO, sc8/114/5653. See Vale, *English Gascony*, p. 17 for the numbers of ships involved in such seizures for English expeditions.　　[175] Salzman, *English Trade*, pp. 275–7.

[176] This was well established by the late thirteenth century: PRO, e122/55/5, 6. For the complex process undertaken by agents dispatching consignments in several ships, see Bradley, 'Datini Factors', p. 67.

[177] *Rot. Parl.* iii, p. 283; James, *Wine Trade*, pp. 24–7, 140–5. Edmund Fryde estimated the added costs for alum and woad to be 8 per cent, for wool 3.7–4.3 per cent, and less for cloth: 'Italian Maritime Trade', pp. 291–337 at pp. 318–19; Salzman, *English Trade*, p. 238.

[178] James, *Wine Trade*, p. 26; Hanham, *Celys and Their World*, p. 131.

[179] *Rot. Parl.* iv, 20; Salzman, *English Trade*, pp. 265–8.

[180] The practice of committing a wool clip in a long-term futures purchase could become hazardous when the seas were closed by physical hostilities. This was more likely in the earlier history of the wool trade when foreign merchants were buying up wool futures. Englishmen acting as their agents could find themselves bearing unanticipated losses when wool, having been held for the purchaser, deteriorated and lost its value. See Hall, *Select Cases*, ii, pp. 64, 70.

actions taken to compensate for losses suffered at the hands of foreigners from a general xenophobia. They had to accept liability for the acts of their fellow countrymen, and that goods in transit were legitimate prey for individuals seeking redress for fraud or defaulted debts, and vice versa. Every period of hostilities produced claims for compensation which had to be pressed through foreign courts. Some went on for years and years, often moving backwards and forwards between different jurisdictions.[181] Small wonder that many resorted to the most popular form of recovering compensation, namely seizing the goods of another merchant from the same country.[182]

Official records are full of claims for compensation, for the loss of goods in foreign markets and at sea, and, indeed, for the loss of ships at sea. Such claims could occupy a merchant or his agent for a considerable time, involving as they did an understanding of merchant law and the problem of deciding to which jurisdiction it was appropriate to submit a claim. The complications which could arise, when individuals resorted to the most popular form of recovering compensation, namely having the goods arrested of another merchant from the same country, is clearly illustrated by the case of Henry Damel of Hull. In 1308 his ship was attacked by a Frisian merchant while it was in Hamburg, and his cargo of ashes, flax, boards, pitch and tar worth £65 was stolen. In retaliation he had the goods of a Jacob de Fandermouth arrested, to the value of only £50, but Fandermouth claimed that as permission to make the arrest had been given by the bishop of Utrecht, and he was not under the bishop's jurisdiction, his goods should be released.[183] Damel had not made a very good choice. One gets the impression that the formal, legal machinery of each trading nation was solemnly processing claims of theft, piracy and so on, while individual merchants still continued direct action – attacking each other in ports and marketplaces.

CONCLUSION

Except in a few instances, insuperable problems remain for the historian in trying to calculate precisely the overheads and costs to estimate the final balance of a merchant's business.[184] Costs included so many regional

---

[181] Lloyd, *Alien Merchants*, pp. 143–4. For the problems involved in suing on the continent and the delays which occurred, see S. B. Chrimes, ed., *Fortescue's De Laudibus Legum Anglie* (Cambridge, 1942), pp. 131–3, 207–10.

[182] Bolton, *Medieval English Economy*, pp. 309–11; for Yorkshire examples, see *CCR 1337–9*, p. 327; *1392–6*, pp. 17, 300, 324; *Bronnen*, I, p. 472.

[183] *CCR 1307–13*, pp. 68–9, 211. See also Walter de Kelstern of Beverley adopting the same approach in 1310: *ibid.*, pp. 150, 228, 238, 247, 278.

[184] E. Power, 'The Wool Trade in the Fifteenth Century', in Power and Postan, *Studies in English*

and commodity variables, allowances to be made for likely hazards and unanticipated disasters, that it is difficult to comprehend how any individual negotiated transactions over a distance. For medieval merchants better regulated markets and developments in legal principle and process went some way towards reducing the costs in securing contracts, particularly at the regional level, but more ambitious trade required more sophisticated arrangements and an understanding of foreign legal systems. At home, experience and knowledge of local suppliers, prices and the creditworthiness of partners might determine success or failure, but for anyone investing in overseas trade, the most important factors lay beyond their localities. National regulation and international warfare affected every branch of long-distance trade and the consequent pressure on cash and credit as well as the increasing physical dangers raised all transaction costs.

Government fiscal policy speeded up the shift in English exports away from wool to cloth, bringing east coast merchants into direct conflict with their Baltic competitors. Geographical location was a key factor in determining differences between regions and the ultimate triumph of London. As warfare and diplomatic failure drove up costs for the east coast traders, Londoners overcame these obstacles because their overall transaction costs were lower. They enjoyed easier access to continental financial networks and could draw on the extensive commercial resources of the capital. The presence of the court guaranteed the largest consumer market in wine in England, and voyages to Calais and the Low Countries were shorter and less exposed to the depredations of North Sea pirates.[185] Ultimately, a combination of all these factors, explored more fully in chapter 8, undermined the merchants of York, Beverley and Hull so that by 1480 they had lost their early dominance in international trade.

Trade, pp. 70–1; A. Hanham, 'Foreign Exchange and the English Wool Merchant in the Late 15th Century', *BIHR*, 44 (1973), pp. 160–75, and 'Profits on English Wool Exports', pp. 139–47.

[185] James, *Wine Trade*, p. 6; P. Nightingale, 'The Growth of London in the Medieval Economy', in Britnell and Hatcher, *Progress and Problems in Medieval England*, pp. 103–4.

7

BUSINESS AND FINANCE

No-one can doubt the determination of the Yorkshire merchants who persisted in their efforts to trade during this turbulent period. They survived because they were prepared to seek profits throughout England and overseas in spite of the constantly changing political and economic environment at home and abroad. They took risks hoping for high returns: lost shiploads were claimed to be worth thousands of pounds and expectations of profits were commensurately high.[1] Every venture, whatever its prospects, required financial backing before a merchant could test his nerve and business acumen. The accident of birth favoured some: John Romondby inherited Romondby manor which he sold in 1368 to raise capital, whereas Thomas Brompton of Beverley raised credit from his successful father.[2]

All commercial dealing, whether local, regional or international, was conducted on a basis of exchange. This could be in the form of goods of an agreed equivalent value, cash in hand, direct and transferable credit, or some other secure asset. Working capital could be extended by various means, and this chapter will examine some of the ways merchants financed their ventures, what they used as assets, and how these were manipulated.

Merchant commerce was conducted against an international situation which was rarely conducive to steady trade. The competitive bullion policies of the English and Burgundian governments and the trade embargoes of the latter created obstacles which challenged any merchant whose business touched overseas trade. It is beyond the scope of this work to engage in the debates over the loss of specie from northern Europe, the fluctuations in the number of coins circulating within England and

---

[1] E.g. claims for a cargo worth £2,000 in 1313, *CCR 1313–18*, p. 7; for £1,000 in 1384, *CCR 1381–5*, pp. 366, 536; for £5,000 in the *Valentine* in 1468, *Urkundenbuch*, IX, p. 369. Cf. a 1350 claim for a cargo worth £4,000 plus £1,000 damages for a Dartmouth ship: Hall, *Select Cases*, II, pp. xxx–xxxi.   [2] *Yorks Deeds*, I, p. 146; Prob. Reg. III, f. 475.

Wales, or the shifting exchange rates which bedevilled foreign business transactions. But it is clear that merchants could not ignore either the intimate involvement of England's wool and cloth economy with that of its primary market, the Low Countries, or the repercussions of a government policy which used the Calais Staple and mint as its major bullion agency.[3] By the 1370s all international trade was touched by the exchange rates in Bruges, the 'banking and shopping centre of Europe'.[4] Broadly there is agreement that the shortage of bullion within Europe became severe from *c.* 1395 until *c.* 1415 and again in the 1440s, reaching acute proportions in the 1450s until the injection of 'new' silver began to increase the supply in the 1460s.[5] The details of the further debate about the relationship between the bullion famine, restrictive government policy and the use of credit to augment the money supply are also beyond this present study,[6] although some aspects of provincial practices will be discussed.

The environment in which merchants traded became more complicated, risky and dangerous the greater the distance away from their home base. The risks could be beyond the control of any individual, but merchants stretched their own financial resources and, in so doing, stimulated local government and central courts into providing the institutional means they required to secure their transactions. It is from those developing legal procedures that most records were generated but, unfortunately, few of the local civic court records have survived in Yorkshire. This discussion is therefore based mainly on central government and court records.

---

[3] See pp. 165–6, above; Bolton, *Medieval English Economy*, p. 298; Hanham, 'Foreign Exchange and the English Wool Merchant', pp. 160–75; Munro, *Wool, Cloth and Gold. passim*; P. Spufford, 'Calais and its Mint: Part 1', in N. J. Mayhew, ed., *Coinage in the Low Countries, 880–1500*, British Archaeological Reports, 54 (Oxford, 1979), pp. 171–83.

[4] Alison Hanham's description: *Celys and Their World*, p. 217. See D. M. Nicholas, 'The English Trade at Bruges in the Last Years of Edward III', *Jnl Med. Hist.*, 5 (1979), pp. 23–62.

[5] P. Spufford, *Money and its Use in Medieval Europe* (Cambridge, 1988), pp. 339–62; J. Day, 'The Great Bullion Famine of the Fifteenth Century', *Past & Present*, 79 (1978), pp. 3–45, and 'Crises and Trends in the Late Middle Ages', in his *The Medieval Market Economy* (Oxford, 1987), pp. 185–224; J. H. Munro, 'Monetary Contraction and Industrial Change in the Medieval Low Countries, 1335–1500', in Mayhew, *Coinage in the Low Countries*, pp. 95–137, and 'Bullion Flows and Monetary Contraction in Late-Medieval England and the Low Countries', in Richards, *Precious Metals*, pp. 97–158.

[6] J. I. Kermode, 'Money and Credit in the Fifteenth Century: Some Lessons from Yorkshire', *Business History Review*, 65 (1991), pp. 475–501, and 'Medieval Indebtedness: The Regions *versus* London', in N. Rogers, ed., *England in the Fifteenth Century*, Harlaxton Medieval Series, 4 (Stamford, 1994), pp. 72–88; J. H. Munro, 'Bullionism and the Bill of Exchange in England, 1272–1663: A Study in Monetary Management and Popular Prejudice', in *The Dawn of Modern Banking*, Center for Medieval and Renaissance Studies, University of California, Los Angeles (New Haven and London, 1979), pp. 169–240; P. Nightingale, 'Monetary Contraction and Mercantile Credit in Later Medieval England', *EcHR*, 2nd ser., 43 (1990), pp. 560–75, and *Medieval Mercantile Community*, pp. 351, 463, 527–8 and *passim*.

It is difficult to assemble a firm statistical overview of changes over time. The evidence is scattered through a wide range of local, national and overseas sources, and has been gleaned piecemeal. Only the Statute Staple Certificates have survived in a consistent series, sufficient to provide a relatively secure base for quantification[7] (see tables 7.1–3). The general picture is flawed though and what follows must be taken as an indication of a range of options.

From the fortuitous survival of Gilbert Maghfeld's ledger and of Richard and George Cely's papers and accounts,[8] several basic business principles can be identified which helped to secure English profits. Merchants faced increasing regulation and restrictions on the movement of coins and bullion from the mid-fourteenth century. They circumvented this, to an extent, by selling abroad on and for credit, generally paying one third in cash for purchases. However modest a merchant's investment, it was crucial that he sustained a connected and continuous flow of trade so that he could realise his profits, either at the Low Countries marts for goods or transferable credit, or for cash in England.[9] Successful merchants were those who were willing to deal flexibly and were reluctant to leave capital inactive. As we have seen, merchants were becoming less specialised in the later fourteenth century, diversifying into general merchandise. In the restrictive climate of more bullion control, coins were less mobile than instruments of credit and accounts were not settled in cash[10] if an alternative could be found. However, too many unpaid debts could undermine trade and astute merchants pursued their debtors vigorously.[11] Any assets could be mobilised to generate income or to secure credit, and might include land, rents, a share in a ship, an anticipated profit or even a merchant's personal business reputation or that of his compatriots. Fraud, shipwreck and piracy could wipe away profits so alert merchants used whatever formal and informal mechanisms

[7] For a comprehensive analysis of those issued in London, see E. Z. Bennett, 'Debt and Credit in the Urban Economy: London, 1380–1460' (Univ. of Harvard PhD thesis, 1989).

[8] James, 'A London Merchant', pp. 364–76; Hanham, *Celys and Their World*, and, ed., *The Cely Letters 1472–1488*, EETS (Oxford, 1975). The businesses of Thomas Betson and Thomas Paycocke cannot be reconstructed in as much detail: Power, *Medieval People*, pp. 120–73. There is some information about Sir William Stonor's wool dealings in C. L. Kingsford, ed., *The Stonor Letters and Papers, 1290–1483*, 2 vols., Camden Soc., 3rd ser., 29, 30 (1919) and Supplementary Stonor Letters and Papers, 1314–1482, *Camden Miscellany, XIII*, Camden Soc., 3rd ser., 34 (1924).

[9] On the key role of Bruges and the use of other Low Countries marts as a centre for brokers and financial services, see Nicholas, 'English Trade at Bruges', pp. 30, 43, 45; Hanham, *Celys and Their World*, pp. 16, 186–217.

[10] Even when buying a quarter of a boat and a cargo of fish from a Danzig merchant in 1439, John Denton of York and John Texton of Beverley paid for it in cloth and cash: *MB*, III, p. 122.

[11] A crucial factor behind the failure of Maghfeld's business was his failure to pursue debts: James, 'A London Merchant', pp. 369, 373–4.

there were to enforce contracts and to recover damages at home and over-seas.

There are no Yorkshire counterparts to the Maghfeld and Cely records, but it is possible to gain some impressions of the ways in which provincial merchants used their resources and tried to contain risks while effectively investing in overseas trade. Merchants were above all pragmatists, and however fierce the competition, they did work together to reduce their transaction costs by pooling resources.[12] Joint ventures had been common since at least the early fourteenth century and increased in sophistication to deal with the Crown during and after the 1337 monopoly.[13] Adam Pund and Alan Upsale of Hull were jointly licensed to ship wool to Flanders in 1349,[14] and Walter Frost, Geoffrey Hanby and Henry de Selby of Hull to export wool and to import wine in 1364. In 1384 William Tickhill, John Hoveden and Robert Talkan, all of York, shared a cargo of herrings,[15] and in 1394–5, William Sallay of York and Robert Crosse of Hull jointly imported figs from Algarve to Harfleur in Normandy.[16] In the early fifteenth century William Cockerham of Beverley was trading in Iceland with John Ricard of Hull, William Thorpe of Newcastle and William Abbot of Lynne, and William Brompton of Beverley and Thomas Alcock of Hull sought a licence to do so in 1455.[17] They were later collaborators in the Hull trading consortia.[18] Investment could also be shared amongst merchants from widely scattered home towns. In 1428 Richard Faxfleet of Hull, James Malpas of Chester, John Brand of Kingswear in Devon and three Normandy merchants bought 100 ells of cloth in Exeter. Together they were liable for defaulting on the payment of £53 3s 4d, but through what agency they had first met remains a mystery.[19]

Partnerships did not always work smoothly, and most of the evidence of their existence is derived from legal actions taken by one party against the other. It is rarely clear if these were *commenda* partnerships or contracts with all partners equally active. In *c.* 1440, for instance, Gilbert Bedenall of Beverley sued William Pakone, his

[12] In Exeter, 12 per cent of all imported cargoes were for partnerships: Kowaleski, *Medieval Exeter*, p. 209.   [13] Fryde, *Business Transactions of York Merchants.*
[14] *CPR 1349–54*, pp. 34, 59.   [15] *Ibid., 1361–4*, p. 491; *1381–5*, p. 505.
[16] *CCR 1382–6*, p. 324.   [17] *Bronnen*, II, p. 715; PRO, C76/149 m. 8.
[18] See above, p. 271.
[19] C. Gross, ed., *Select Cases Concerning the Law Merchant*, I, Selden Soc., 23 (1908), pp. 117–18. Another Hull merchant, John Grene, was indebted to a Londoner and two Chester merchants in 1463: *Cheshire Sheaf*, 22 (1925), p. 76.

partner for six years, for the profit accruing from their shared business, claiming that Pakone had kept it all for himself.[20] Indebtedness could result from joint ventures: Simon de Quixlay and John Hoveden of York owed Robert Garton £210 17s 2½d in 1398 and Francis Buk together with John Green of Hull owed Edmund Coppendale, also of Hull, £42 12s 4d in 1452.[21] Merchants of the three towns often collaborated: in 1441 Thomas Sanderson of Hull bound himself to John Bedale, John Calton and William Caterick, all of York, for 100 marks,[22] while at his death in 1421 Thomas Frost of Beverley was owed 105 marks by Thomas Skipwith, of Beverley, jointly with Richard Bedford of Hull.[23]

Given that men regularly exported and imported goods in the same ships, we might suppose that some close business relationships developed, but the evidence is ambiguous. Wool exporters in particular shipped together in the wool fleets, which sailed, with the seasonal shearings, to a single destination. The staplers usually divided their wool between several ships, especially at the beginning of the export season. On 4 October 1396, for example, William Bridd and John Topcliff of York, Thomas Caldbeck, William Rolleston and Richard Aglyon of Beverley, and Hugh Clitheroe and Geoffrey Upstall of Hull divided their wool amongst the same five ships.[24] Wine fleets offered the same opportunities for collaboration, but no clear pattern of combined shipping has emerged. In any event, when losses were threatened, each merchant looked after his own interests, as John Tutbury discovered in 1415 when Spanish pirates attacked the wine fleet and his ship was abandoned by the rest. However intimidating the obstacles or uncertain the outcome, business was business and Yorkshiremen even partnered their rivals in joint ventures. Henry Hyndelay shared a cargo, in the *Holyghost* of Hull, with a Danzig merchant in 1403; and forty years later, William Gaunt of York was shipping goods with a group of Prussians from London to Hull, when it was seized by a Newcastle ship.[25]

Commercial relations had to be based upon mutual confidence, but contracts were also bolstered by legal enforcement through local or national courts. All too often in practice, trust was misplaced and agreements broken, even between neighbours. William Todd sold a cargo of fish to fellow York merchant Richard York, before it was shipped from

[20] PRO, C1/9/382.   [21] *CCR 1396–9*, p. 416; Hull RO, BRB 1, f. 25.
[22] York RO, B/Y, f. 86.   [23] Arch. Reg. XVIII, ff. 384v.–5 (Frost).
[24] PRO, E122/52/26. See Hanham, *Celys and Their World*, pp. 129–30 for the London staplers' practice of loading an average of two sarplars per ship.
[25] *MB*, II, p. 10; *CPR 1452–61*, p. 174.

Iceland in 1487. The subsequent disagreement ended up before Chancery,[26] an example of an apparently straightforward sale requiring enforcement in a royal court.[27] This is typical of the evidence available for examining mercantile business and it is of negative events: of breaches of contract, fraud and indebtedness. Actions for debt were sometimes the last in a series of disputes which may have begun as an action of account, changed to detinue and finally to debt.[28] Even though burgesses were expected to sue fellow townsfolk in their own borough courts, long-distance trade disputes moved beyond local jurisdictions. Yorkshire merchants had to be prepared to take cases to the royal courts in London if necessary, and did so. John Humbrecolt of Beverley employed Robert Tirwhit as his attorney there in the 1380s, perhaps as much for commercial as for legal negotiations, since Humbrecolt stood as surety for one London woolmonger in 1389, with two others as co-sureties.[29] A dispute between William Bowes of York and a merchant from Epinal over a bond for £1,000 ended up in Chancery and was resolved out of court before arbitrators, who ordered Bowes to pay £254.[30] No doubt ways could be found to expedite matters more efficiently. A York mercer's bequest of a piece of silver to Peter Arden, 'chief baron of the Exchequer at Westminster'in 1450, intriguingly hints at some of those ways and previous favours.[31]

Overseas trading agreements further taxed an individual's resources in so far as he had to take his case into a foreign court. John de Waghen of Beverley, whose agreement with a Leiden merchant involving payment of 850½ nobles had been enrolled in Calais in 1396, was compelled to take out letters of marque to recover goods to the same value and had still not achieved a satisfactory settlement by 1415.[32] Calais was a convenient place for formalising deals and Robert Hadelsay of Hull enrolled his debt of £4 to a Bruges man there in 1400.[33] Intractable cases required strong

---

[26] PRO, c1/64/709.

[27] In addition to equity judgements, arbitration was frequently invoked. Carole Rawcliffe describes a great diversity of cases in London and elsewhere, usually of debt, detinue and account, in her essay, '"That Kindliness Should be Cherished More"', pp. 99–117 at p. 111–12. See also Hall, *Select Cases*, II, pp. 19, 21, 36–8, 148–50.

[28] S. F. C. Milsom has written extensively on this topic. See his 'Account Stated in the Action of Debt', *Law Quarterly Rev.*, 82 (1966), pp. 534–45; 'Sale of Goods in the Fifteenth Century', *ibid.*, 77 (1981), pp. 257–84; *Historical Foundations of the Common Law*, pp. 243–7, 250–5, 266, 275.

[29] *Cal. Plea & Mem. Rolls City of London, 1364–81*, p. 266; *CCR 1385–9*, p. 573. See also T. Twiss, ed., *The Black Book of the Admiralty*, 4 vols., Rolls Series (1871–6), for maritime disputes.

[30] *CCR 1441–7*, pp. 444–5; Rawcliffe, '"That Kindliness Should be Cherished More"', pp. 111–12. While in London in 1435, John Hanson of Hull witnessed a deed for fellow Hull merchant Richard de Holm: *CCR 1447–54*, p. 186.

[31] Robert Collinson, d. 1458: Prob. Reg. II, f. 379v.

[32] *Bronnen*, I, pp. 471–3, 575–6; *CPR 1408–13*, p. 328; *1413–16*, pp. 169, 189; *CCR 1413–19*, pp. 137, 140; PRO, sc8/212/10559.   [33] PRO, c1/7/71.

support from a higher level. In April 1309, a group of Beverley men, including Walter de Kelstern, entered into a deal in Bruges to change 2,200 great florins for 'good' silver money and petitioned Edward II for his assistance. Edward wrote four times to the Count of Flanders but in vain, and the following year gave the Beverley men permission to distrain the goods of Bruges merchants.[34] Ignorance of jurisdictions could also undermine a case. Wynand Morant of Beverley had an apparently secure claim for reparation against several Dutch merchants who owed him £272 in 1309. Edward II and his son wrote to the bishop of Utrecht on Morant's behalf, to no avail. Morant obtained writs to the bailiff of Hull to distrain the goods of some Groningen merchants, fellows of his debtors, but lost his claim before a jury of Dutch and Almain merchants, on the grounds that the emperor and not the bishop had temporal authority over Groningen.[35]

The simple solution to such unstable agreements would have been to employ a bill of exchange, an instrument of credit intended to facilitate international trade and currency exchanges. These were most effective when trade was flowing continuously. They were negotiable bills which could change hands many times before eventually being cashed. To guarantee their universal acceptability, merchants using them had to have access to notaries public, or to scriveners or an official empowered to enrol and seal bills, as well as to partners or investors who themselves had access to cash or secure resources. Both requirements could be affected by geographical location.[36]

Their use had spread to England by the fifteenth century in spite of discouraging legislation. The Celys were using them as a regular component of their business in the 1480s.[37] The English government, like its continental counterparts, legislated against the export of bullion and coins, but also saw the bill of exchange as a device to disguise the movement of coins overseas.[38] Amongst a long list of licences to draw up letters of exchange, granted to Ubertinus de Bardes, a Lombard living in London in 1425, was one for £10 payable 'in foreign parts' to Robert Holme, probably of York. The licence was granted 'provided no gold or

---

[34] *CCR 1307–13*, pp. 150, 228, 238, 247, 278. Royal support was solicited by Hugh Clitheroe of Hull and a group of Yorkshiremen suing for money owed in Holland in 1440: *Bronnen*, II, p. 732. His brother Richard was pursuing a debt owed to him in Danzig in 1436: *Urkundenbuch*, VII, p. 85.

[35] Hall, *Select Cases*, II, pp. liii, 81–3. See also p. 221 above.

[36] Postan, 'Credit in Medieval Trade', pp. 234–61, and his 'Private Financial Instruments', pp. 29–64, esp. p. 34; P. Spufford, *A Handbook of Medieval Exchange* (London, 1986), pp. xxxiii–xxxiv; *Cal. Plea & Mem. Rolls City of London, 1381–1412*, pp. xxxvi–xl.

[37] Hanham, *Celys and Their World*, pp. 188–92.

[38] Postan, 'Credit in Medieval Trade' and 'Private Financial Instruments', *passim*; Munro, 'Bullionism and the Bill of Exchange', pp. 169–215, esp. p. 198.

silver in the lump or in coin be sent over by colour of this command'.[39]

Yorkshire merchants did trade with bills of exchange as an ingredient of their international enterprises, but apparently only occasionally.[40] A bill for £100, the outcome of a deal agreed in Bruges between William Agland, servant to Roger Moreton of York, and Reyner Domenic of Florence, eventually appeared in London in 1373 as part of another arrangement, seemingly unconnected to the first.[41] There were notaries public in York,[42] qualified to draw up bills, but there is no way of knowing how many were drawn locally.[43] A decline in overseas transactions would in any case obviate the need for such instruments. Other forms of international credit, such as deposit banking and book money, were not available in England or, indeed, universally throughout Europe. In any case, as Peter Spufford has reminded us, the 'superstructure of international payments was only a superstructure and most transactions and monetary payments were extremely local in character'.[44]

RAISING FINANCE IN THE REGION

Overseas trade gave merchants access to an international commercial network, and even though few from Yorkshire appear to have engaged with Italian 'bankers',[45] the financial possibilities were sophisticated and extensive. Merchants had also to work at the more mundane local and regional level to generate the financial base for their businesses. More rudimentary than bills of exchange, deferred payments or sales credits

---

[39] *CCR 1429–35*, p. 369.

[40] E.g. *Bronnen*, II, pp. 1073–4. Cf. *Cal. Plea & Mem. Rolls City of London 1413–37*, pp. 11–12. Sealed royal tallies had the same status within England and were sold or exchanged like a banknote. A merchant from Lucca bought wool in Hull with tallies in 1397, but no Yorkshire merchant has been found using them: *ibid., 1381–1412*, pp. 130–1.

[41] *Cal. Plea & Mem. Rolls City of London, 1364–81*, p. 154. Exchange loan deals could degenerate into a network of taxing complexity. See the plight of Thomas Kesten: Hanham, *Celys and Their World*, pp. 91–103.

[42] York RO, E39, p. 110; Prob. Reg. I, f. 20 (will of Ann Durem); Postan, 'Private Financial Instruments', p. 34.

[43] All of the bills of exchange disputed in the London city courts between 1381 and 1412 had been issued by Italians: *Cal. Plea & Mem. Rolls City of London, 1381–1412*, p. xxxvii.

[44] P. Spufford, *Handbook*, pp. xxviii–xxix, and *Money and its Use*, pp. 256–8, 394–5. For a rural perspective, see E. Clark, 'Debt Litigation in a Late Medieval Vill', in J. A. Raftis, ed., *Pathways to Medieval Peasants* (Toronto, 1981), pp. 247–79; P. R. Schofield, 'Debt and Credit in the Medieval English Countryside', in M. Berthe and F. Brumont, eds., *Endettement et crédit dans les campagnes d'Europe au moyen âge et a l'époque moderne* (Toulouse, 1997).

[45] The Italians acted as brokers and as clearing houses for bills drawn in the Low Countries as well as throughout the Mediterranean commercial region. The focus of their English operations was London: Fryde, 'Italian Maritime Trade', pp. 322–8; Nicholas, 'English Trade at Bruges', pp. 25, 28; P. Spufford, *Handbook*, pp. xxix, xxxiv; R. de Roover, *Money, Banking and Credit in Medieval Bruges* (Cambridge MA, 1948), *passim*.

were commonly used between merchants. As has been said of eighteenth-century England: 'trade credit was crucial to the functioning of exchange . . . many firms had more of their assets tied up in credit than in capital'.[46] London merchant Gilbert Maghfeld's ledger confirms that sales credits were as fundamental three centuries earlier and he sold at least 75 per cent of his goods on sales credit in the 1380s and 1390s. Merchants with a long-standing business association rarely settled their accounts in cash, and if they did, it was for very small amounts. For a merchant such as Maghfeld, operating within domestic and overseas trade, it was easier to keep the situation fluid and to pay off one supplier of goods with the unpaid balance owed to him from another. The art of commercial survival was to keep ventures and credit in a state of constant motion, and Maghfeld used his credit abroad to satisfy domestic debts by transferring them to a third party, or indeed settling an overseas debt of one of his English creditors.[47]

Unfortunately the evidence which most frequently survives of credit operations is static and piecemeal: that of debts called in. Evidence of the importance of debts in the Yorkshire economy is quite extensive but not often detailed: we have no way of knowing if the debt in question had arisen from trade or private expenditure. It is rare to find an account of a debt settled. One recorded occasion was in 1391 when Richard Crull handed over a ship and cargo in payment of his debt to Thomas Holme of York.[48] Many wills recorded debts to be recovered or to be bequeathed but only in general terms. By custom, the payment of debts had priority in the execution of wills. By Edward IV's reign, debts of record took precedence over any others in the administration of a will[49] and it was quite common for testators to further instruct their executors to settle debts before disposing of the residue. Testators were aware that funds might prove inadequate for their needs. John Grantham of York left herrings to be sold to settle a debt in London in 1391. Robert Collinson of York, in 1456, instructed that a house be sold to meet debts. Others, like Edward Grenely of Hull, decided in 1492 that unspecified goods were to

---

[46] J. Hoppit, 'The Use and Abuse of Credit in Eighteenth-Century England', in N. McKendrick and R. B. Outhwaite, eds., *Business Life and Public Policy. Essays in Honour of D. C. Coleman* (London, 1986), pp. 64–6.

[47] James, 'A London Merchant', pp. 368–9. See also Hanham, *Celys and Their World*, pp. 109–255, 398–430; Postan, 'Credit in Medieval Trade', pp. 255–6 for the Celys and the London scrivener John Thorp's notebook; Wolff, 'English Cloth in Toulouse', p. 294.

[48] *CCR 1389–92*, p. 235.

[49] W. S. Holdsworth, *A History of English Law*, 4th edn (London, 1935), III, pp. 586–7. Such was the strength of the custom, that it prevailed over compassion in the London City court in 1396, when the payment of a debt took precedence over provision for two minors even though complex legal formalities had been completed to effect that provision. See *Cal. Plea & Mem. Rolls City of London 1381–1412*, p. 239.

be sold, whereas Richard Thuresby of York left £50 in 1402, £20 of which was to pay his debts.[50]

Some creditors arrived too late for satisfaction. In 1419 Robert Gaunt of York distrained in vain to recover £12 from the estate of John Rydding, a dyer: other creditors having beaten him to a settlement.[51] Executors could be pursued by the deceased's creditors, so that debts could become an issue between two parties (and their heirs), long after the initiating parties were dead.[52] The more actively and widely an individual had invested his money in lending in whatever form, the more difficult the resultant debts would be to collect.[53] The administration of the will of William Alcock, a Hull merchant, was given to a court-appointed executor in 1435, a man not named in Alcock's will, because of the 'multitude' of his debts. John Radclyffe of York anticipated unenthusiastic executors, and in 1444 left 20s to another merchant, William Langthorn, provided that he collected Radclyffe's debts. York merchant John Elwald realistically referred in his will of 1505 to all of his debts 'which can be recovered', and inventories regularly distinguished between *debita sperata* and *debita desperata*.[54]

Conversely, some creditors drawing up their wills charitably released their debtors. Not all did so wholeheartedly. Robert Louth and William Bedale, both of York, released those who could not pay, John Kelk of Beverley cancelled all debts under 40s, while Thomas Holme released those who could produce 'reasonable proof' that they could not pay![55] Some merchants took the opportunity of settling family obligations. Richard Wartre of York released his father-in-law John Moreton from a debt of £3 in 1458. John Kelk of Beverley was not so generous and in 1407 remitted his brother William only 63s 4d of a debt of 103s 4d.[56]

Debts were bequeathed like any other chattels. Thomas Preston of Hull (d. 1451) bequeathed an obligation for £24, which John Ricard of Hull owed him, to Joan Clitheroe; and to Thomas Bernard of Hedon he left an obligation from William Sage of Scarborough for £6 and a debt

---

[50] Prob. Reg. I, f. 45v. (Grantham); II, f. 110v. (Gare); III, f. 245 (Thuresby); V, f. 501 (Grenely); VI, f. 70 (Collinson).   [51] York RO, E39 p. 187.

[52] E.g. *CPR 1388–92*, p. 259; *1476–85*, p. 293; *MB*, I, p. 33; *Yorks Deeds*, II, p. 218; York RO, E39, pp. 266–7, 281; PRO, C1/15/193, 59/112, 64/1137, and for debts registered under Statute Staple C241/138/63, 72–3, 139/194.

[53] Robert Northwold, mercer of London, died *c.* 1374 leaving debts to be retrieved from Beverley, York, Ludlow, Oxford, Gloucester, Winchester and from a Lombard: *Cal. Plea & Mem. Rolls City of London, 1364–81*, pp. 168–9. A debt did not have to be large to be exploited. For example, a debt of £6 13s 4d was assigned to 'divers persons' in 1369: *ibid.*, pp. 111–12.

[54] Prob. Reg. II, f. 91 (Radclyff); III, f. 403 (Alcock); Dec. & Cap. II, f. 43 (Elwald); *Test. Ebor.* III, pp. 49–50, 104, 141.

[55] Prob. Reg. III, ff. 255–v. (Holme), 540 (Bedale), 263 (Kelk), 265–v. (Louth).

[56] Prob. Reg. III, f. 263 (Wartre); IV, ff. 115–17 (Bedale).

of £2 owed by Thomas Bernard's mother. John Brompton of Beverley left £202 of debts in several portions to his son Nicholas in 1444, which included two from the countess of Northumberland.[57] However stale or small, debts were still assets to be recovered and managed, whatever the inconvenience and cost.[58] Jordan Savage, one of the Dordrecht monopolists, died before he could repay a debt of £4 to William Gra of York. Gra recovered the debt in 1344 by exercising his right to repayment through reduced export duties.[59] Delays must have been detrimental; hence the offer of a discount for early settlement made by William Skyrwyth of York to a debtor in 1427. However difficult and discouraging the exercise, recovering debts was an essential part of business. Failure to do so could result in commercial disaster, as happened to Gilbert Maghfeld,[60] or the disappointment of legatees.

Debts mentioned in probate records could be the result of deferred payments for goods or services, not always made clear in wills,[61] though expressly stated in some inventories. For instance the inventory of Hugh Grantham, a mason of York, drawn up in 1410, itemised debts owed to him for the purchase of oats, barley and cloth, as well as debts owed through obligations, a total of £85 17s 10d outstanding to him. In turn he owed £58 13s 5d, mainly for deliveries of stone from his suppliers, and for loans through deferred payment or by negotiation.[62] The majority of debts mentioned in wills were probably either mutually acknowledged informal arrangements or formal legal instruments: recognisances, bonds and obligations. Recognisances could be enrolled in the borough courts of Hull and York but no court rolls as such are extant and enrolments survive in disappointingly small numbers in the memoranda books of York and bench books of Hull. A fragment of a sheriff's court roll and precedent book for mid-fifteenth century York and miscellaneous deeds comprise the rest of the known local sources.[63] These scarcely compare

---

[57] Prob. Reg. I, f. 50v. (Bridsall); II ff. 86v.–90v. (Brompton), 225 (Preston). See also III, f. 605 (Blackburn), for a bequest of debts to a third party who already had possession of the written obligations.

[58] In *c.* 1415 it cost John Talkan of York's executors £8 6s 8d to collect his debts and settle his estate: total value about £104. In 1451 Thomas Vicars' executors spent only £1. on tracing and collecting his debts, and a further £1 riding around to settle everything: *Test. Ebor.* III, pp. 87–9, 120–2. Cf. Bristol merchant Philip Vale, whose executors' expenses for settling debts and selling property in 1393 came to £7: *Cal. Plea & Mem. Rolls City of London 1381–1412*, pp. 208–15. See pp. 106–9 above, for problems in executing wills. [59] *CCR 1343–6*, p. 401.

[60] *MB*, II, p. 160; James, 'A London Merchant', pp. 369, 373–4. Perseverance was necessary. Agnes Brightwell of London lent her son-in-law £60 in 1406 and was eventually paid in a mixture of salt and cash in 1413: *Cal. Plea & Mem. Rolls City of London, 1413–37*, p. 10;

[61] E.g. Prob. Reg. II, ff. 21 (Stockton), 119v. (Shackles); III, ff. 415v.–16 (Blackburn); v, f. 29v. (Croule), 99 (Johnson), 167 (Ryddesdale). [62] *Test. Ebor.* III, pp. 49–50.

[63] Hull, RO BRG; BRE I, 2; BRB I; York RO, E25, 39; *Memorandum Books*, I, II and III; *Yorks Deeds* and *Yorks Fines*.

with the plentiful series of borough court rolls to match the London letter books, whose equivalents George Unwin envisaged piled temptingly high in provincial town halls, nor the 4,526 cases of debt heard in the mayor's court in Exeter between 1378 and 1388.[64] Substantial survivals of records in other towns imply that Yorkshire towns must once have had similarly extensive commercial transactions, and that the extant evidence represents a very small fragment of the original total.[65]

What has survived in formal enrolments is sufficient to indicate some of the characteristics of credit agreements. Some were designed to raise capital for a particular need and were explicitly loans. Thus, in June 1404, Richard Bawtre, a Scarborough merchant, and three York merchants enrolled a bond for a loan of £79 13s 4d to John Craven, also a York merchant, which was to be repaid the following June.[66] No interest was recorded, but as usury was illegal, this was scarcely surprising. Loans were usually made for a fictitious sum which included both principal and interest.[67] Very likely registering a bond of this kind was also a way of registering the financial basis of a short-term partnership, with John Craven in this instance as the active trader.

All the debts enrolled, including statutory bonds, set a date or dates for settlements, either in a single payment or in instalments.[68] The preference was for popular saints' days, Easter, Michaelmas, Pentecost, Martinmas, Christmas, the Purification of the Virgin, the Birth of John the Baptist and the feast of St Peter in Chains.[69] The choice of Pentecost, Martinmas and St Peter in Chains could have been of special significance in Yorkshire because there were fairs held in York at those feasts.[70] Debts were for every amount, but those enrolled under Statute Staple were generally for sums of between £15 and £40. There seems to have been no correlation between the size of a debt and its duration, nor between size and the time taken to initiate recovery[71] (see table 7.2.2). Sometimes

---

[64] 'London Tradesmen and Their Creditors', in Unwin, *Finance and Trade Under Edward III*, p. 19; Kowaleski, 'Commercial Dominance of a Medieval Provincial Oligarchy', p. 369.

[65] E.g. the 550 Pentice Court Rolls in Chester, 1298–1559. For a rare survival, see A. Beardwood, ed., *The Statute Merchant Roll of Coventry, 1392–1416*, Dugdale Soc., 17 (1939).

[66] *MB*, II, p. 98.

[67] R. H. Helmholz, 'Usury and the Medieval English Church Courts', *Speculum*, 61 (1986), p. 365; Postan, 'Private Financial Instruments', p. 31.

[68] In general the debt/loan was divided into equal portions and repaid at annual or six–monthly intervals. E.g. *MB*, II, p. 274; York RO, E39, pp. 106, 108, 267. For Statute Staple debts repayable in instalments as early as 1286, see Hall, *Select Cases*, III, p. 114.

[69] The analysis on which this is based was assisted by a grant from the ESRC, no. R000231782, and is fully discussed in Kermode, 'Medieval Indebtedness', pp. 72–88. The Birth of John the Baptist, St Michael Archangel, Easter, Christmas, Pentecost, the Purification and All Saints were dates on which the majority of London Staple debts fell due: E. Z. Bennett, 'Debt and Credit in London', p. 154. [70] *VCH York*, pp. 489–91.

[71] Kermode, 'Medieval Indebtedness', p. 83. The median Staple debt in Exeter was £37: Kowaleski, *Medieval Exeter*, p. 214.

one creditor would supply cash through several obligations to one person. Thus Cecily, widow of William Ferrour of Newcastle and daughter of a York painter, owed William Skyrwyth, a York clerk, six separate debts each of 40s to be repaid on 10 November in successive years from 1428.[72] Most of the recognisances enrolled in York and Hull dealt with rounded sums of money, suggesting that they may have been loans, as Postan argued, rather than settlements of commercial transactions involving exact costs.[73]

The entering into agreements for loans was a useful mechanism for raising capital and for making surplus capital work. The importance of keeping a record was obvious: John Stockdale of York had a debt book which was mentioned in his will in 1507, and others must have kept at least a loose file of bonds and deeds as Richard Wartre of York had done in the early fifteenth century. Possession of written instruments was always preferable, enabling a relatively uncomplicated closure of business or transmission of a legacy. For instance, Hugh Rose of London charged a York merchant, John Middleton, to deliver four bonds and an acquittance to Rose's servant Walter Randolph. Middleton discharged his duty in 1394, handing the documents over with 5s in coins, assorted mercery and 34lb of onion seed.[74] Lack of written evidence of a debt could prejudice its recovery, and could result in non-payment, even when the debt was recognised by the debtor.[75] If it was not, others might be summoned to the creation of the obligation: John Radclyffe of York lost a bond between Pavement and Coneystreet in 1420 but witnesses were called in to testify that Radclyffe had agreed to pay Thomas Farnlay £12 6s 8d.[76] Although a debt might be formally enrolled, the recovery of the acquittance or indeed of the record was not necessarily straightforward.

Enrolment did not guarantee repayment, though it must have been better than nothing, and many creditors had to take their case to the royal courts in London: King's Bench and Common Pleas in particular. The consequent legal trail left behind as much inferential evidence as the local enrolment of recognisances provides direct evidence. The Patent and Close Rolls regularly record writs *supersedeas* to local sheriffs, to prevent them implementing judgements of outlawry brought against the absent party in actions of debt and pardons to individuals for 'not appearing to answer' pleas of debt in the royal courts.[77] Usually these were bald statements that A owed B £x, but occasionally a surviving petition to the

---

[72] *MB*, II, p. 160. It may be that she was meeting obligations from her father's estate. For other examples, see *ibid.*, pp. 96, 114; York RO, E39, p. 267; and cf. *Cal. Plea & Mem. Rolls City of London, 1382–1412*, p. 239.   [73] Postan, 'Private Financial Instruments', p. 38.

[74] Prob. Reg. IV, f. 116 (Wartre); VI, f. 185 (Stockdale); *MB*, II, p. 13. Evidence material to the Bolton *v* Brandesby and Swan case, was contained in a ledger: see appendix 4.   [75] PRO, C1/289/10.

[76] *MB*, II, pp. 94–5.

[77] E.g. *CPR 1429–35*, p. 354; *1446–52*, p. 198; *1452–61*, pp. 384, 456; *1467–77*, pp. 9, 431.

Chancellor conveys the aggrieved feelings of the parties and the complexities of their transactions.

There are hints that local pressure sometimes operated powerfully in favour of local men in debt disputes and this may have been one reason for using the royal courts. In the middle of the fifteenth century a Nicholas Elerton was complaining that although he had brought a successful action for debt against John Northeby of Hull, he had been prevented from gaining satisfaction by 'subtle and strange means' and could get no remedy in Hull. However, Chancery judgements were not invincible either. John Spicer, possibly of Beverley, won an action against Thomas Etton of Hull, but when he went to Hull to deliver the writ, Etton took counter action against him in the local courts and had Spicer imprisoned. Eventually Spicer petitioned the Lord Chancellor for another writ to obtain his release.[78]

Religious institutions, as customers and as suppliers of wool, were well placed to provide cash loans or sales credit to merchants.[79] Sales credit could work both ways, with a merchant paying an instalment for wool ahead of the clip if market conditions warranted. Thomas and Richard Holme of Beverley, for example, bought 120 sacks of wool from Meaux Abbey in the 1350's for £240, but the abbey could only supply sixty-five sacks and was left owing the balance.[80] Large sums could be involved. In 1334 John de Womme of York, together with Bardi and Peruzzi merchants, owed Archbishop Melton £1,000, most likely sales credit on a wool purchase.[81]

Melton was also heavily involved as a lender to religious houses and to individual laypeople, exploiting the income from his temporalities.[82] Simon Swanland of Hull was his kinsman and banker, one of those unfortunately bankrupted in financing Edward III's war strategy.[83] But he was not the only money-lending cleric, although we know more about him than most. By their nature, religious bodies drew in the savings of the

---

[78] PRO, C1/17/95, 64/439.

[79] For the increasing indebtedness of London merchants to religious houses in the fourteenth century, see S. J. O'Connor, ed., *A Calendar of the Cartularies of John Pyel and Adam Fraunceys*, Camden Soc., 5th ser., 2 (London, 1993), p. 10.

[80] See p. 241 below for a fuller discussion; E. A. Bond, ed., *Chronica Monasterii de Melsa*, III, Rolls Ser. (1868), pp. 85, 144–5. In a sales agreement to his advantage he owed Durham Priory £174 10s in 1331: *Durham Acct Rolls*, II, p. 515. [81] *CCR 1333–7*, p. 315.

[82] His annual income was probably at least £2,500 during the 'lean' years of 1318–21. Between 1317 and 1340 he made at least 388 separate loans, roughly 70 per cent of which fell within the purview of his York receiver: L. H. Butler, 'Archbishop Melton, his Neighbours, and his Kinsmen, 1317–1340', *Jnl Eccl. Hist.*, 2 (1951), pp. 54–68 at pp. 55, 65.

[83] Borthwick Institute, R1/9, ff. 23v.–4, 35, 53v. Swanland and his brothers Nicholas and Thomas resided in London and served as the link between Melton and the Bardi and Peruzzi: Butler, 'Archbishop Melton', p. 67; J. L. Grassi, 'Royal Clerks from the Archdiocese of York in the 14th Century', *Northern History*, 5 (1970), pp. 12–33.

laity and must have enjoyed a level of cash liquidity, especially marked during bullion shortages. Irrespective of any direct commercial involvement, they were in a good position to finance individuals, and in York the Minster clergy certainly made small loans to craftsmen.[84] Melton loaned a York merchant, Henry de Belton, £100 in 1340, for three months on the security of a deposit of £120 worth of florins.[85] There is evidence from the Staple Certificates up to 1405 that the archbishop, the dean and chapter of the Minster, St Mary's Abbey and St Leonard's Hospital in York made loans, as did the bishop of Durham, the abbots of Meaux and Jervaulx, and the priors of Haltemprice, Kirkstall and Nostell.[86] We cannot tell whether or not these loans were made in their private or institutional capacity. Repayments could be in instalments: John de Beverley of York paid the final instalment in 1393 of a debt of £106 which he owed to the Carmelite Priory in York.[87]

Individual clerics were quite heavily engaged in financial dealing in the second half of the fourteenth century: notably those with substantial livings such as David Wooler, prebendary of Fridaythorpe in St Peter's, York, and Richard Thoresby, a canon of Beverley Minster. Thoresby and Richard de Ravenser, another regular Yorkshire creditor, both served as Keeper of the Hanaper.[88] Up to 1384 the evidence is quite clearly of loans, but thereafter, the actions pursued through Chancery were increasingly for the execution of recognisances and in such large sums, £20–1,000 marks (£666 13s 4d), as to suggest they were conditional bonds.[89] Such debts were not confined to the locality: Melton's loans had been to institutions and individuals throughout England, and in 1368 William Savage of York and three others owed the dean of St Stephen's, Westminster, £300. These instances were fewer after 1400 although there is evidence from the Close and Patent Rolls that clerics continued to lend and to pursue debtors well into the fifteenth century. Richard Louth of York owed £100 to the prebendary of Fridaythorpe in 1437.[90]

---

[84] Barrie Dobson refers to such a role, but it is a subject yet to be fully studied: Dobson, 'The Later Middle Ages', p. 61; J. Browne, ed., *Fabric Rolls and Documents of York Minster*, new edn (York, 1863), p. 129.

[85] Butler, 'Archbishop Melton', pp. 59–60. Five of Melton's clients were lent money after depositing silver plate at his York treasury, exceeding the loan in value.

[86] PRO, c241/151/139, archbishop; c241/158/62, 194/59, Minster; c241/149/67, 173/86, 184/34, 190/197, St Mary's Abbey; c241/144/19, 173/23, St Leonard's Hospital; c241/188/102, bishop of Durham; c241/155/36, 157/63 (debtor), Haltemprice; c241/140/66, Jervaulx; c241/151/48, Kirkstall; c241/143/97, Meaux; c241/157/179, Nostell.   [87] *Yorks Deeds*, I, p. 219.

[88] *CCR 1354–60*, p. 304; Grassi, 'Royal Clerks from the Archdiocese of York', pp. 25–6; A. Hamilton Thompson, 'Registers of the Archdeacons of Richmond', *Yorks Arch. Jnl*, 25 (1919), pp. 257–60; T. F. Tout, *Chapters in the Administrative History of Medieval England* (Manchester, 1928), III, p. 215.

[89] Kermode, 'Medieval Indebtedness', p. 78.   [90] *CPR 1364–8*, p. 467; *1436–41*, p. 102.

Quite apart from the universal problem of enforcing payment of a debt/loan, recognisances, bonds and bills of obligation were very difficult to transfer and this limited their usefulness. The appointment of an attorney was a legal requirement when the need arose to reassign an obligation effectively, and though fairly easy for the first transfer, reassigning a debt became increasingly difficult thereafter because a series of dependent documents became necessary.[91] The remedy was to register the debt/loan under Statute Merchant or Statute Staple. Under the Statute of Acton Burnel, 1283, the debtor practically signed a judgement against himself in the event of defaulting on payment and these provisions were strengthened by the Statute de Mercatoribus in 1285. In those towns such as York and Hull which were granted the right to hold the seal of Statute Merchant, there were supposed to be statutory registries wherein debts could be enrolled. After 1362, the Statute Staple extended to non-merchants the right to have debts registered in those towns where a mayor of the staple was appointed. Both York and Hull were granted that facility.[92]

Effectively this legislation had created a debt of record, statutory recognisances acceptable nationwide, relatively easily registered and recovered. Statute Merchant and Statute Staple bonds[93] had the strength of bills of exchange within England and should have offered an attractive alternative to the less formal arrangements already described. They were not impregnable however, since possession alone was sufficient title unless challenged. As autonomous documents they could be, and were, stolen. Another difficulty was the failure of the enrolling authority to cancel debts paid and the neglect of the debtor to recover the bond from the creditor. It was not until the reign of James II that creditors were obliged to cancel debts.[94]

What is difficult to establish is how popular these statutory recognisances were. They did not replace the traditional system of informal agreements enrolled in local courts,[95] and maybe that was adequate for

---

[91] *Cal. Plea & Mem. Rolls City of London, 1381–1412*, pp. xxxii–xxxiii; Postan, 'Private Financial Instruments', pp. 40–9.

[92] Hall, *Select Cases*, II, p. xi, *et seq.*; III, pp. xvi, xxviii, xxix; Plucknett, *The Legislation of Edward I*, p. 138; *CCR 1279–88*, p. 244. There is evidence to suggest that records were not kept efficiently. Chaos must have prompted the York council's decision in 1371 that the Statute Merchant Roll should be kept in the council chamber on Ousebridge, and that, as each mayor was responsible for the rolls of his year in office, his executors would inherit that responsibility after his death: *MB*, I, pp. 12–13.

[93] There were some differences. The most significant were that a debt enrolled under Statute Merchant carried the seal of the debtor as well as of the mayor and clerk, whereas Staple debts did not. Statute Merchant debts cost more to enrol: 1d in the pound (1½d at fairs), compared with Staple enrolments at ½d in the pound up to £100, and ¼d for larger amounts: Hall, *Select Cases*, III, p. lxxxv.   [94] *Cal. Plea & Mem. Rolls City of London, 1381–1412*, p. xxxv.

[95] There were about 6,000 cases brought under Statute Staple from 1390 to 1450 (E. Z. Bennett, 'Debt and Credit in London', p. 153), whereas the local courts in Exeter handled over 4,500 cases

Table 7.1. *Statute Staple Certificates, in percentages by decades*

Period	Total	London	York	Hull	Certificates[a]
1360–9	1,487	500 (33.6)	122 (8.2)	26 (1.7)	139–49
1370–9	1,461	699 (47.8)	81 (5.5)	12 (0.8)	150–62, 164
1380–9	1,404	581 (41.4)	40 (2.8)	9 (0.6)	163,5–177
1390–9	1,224	649 (53.0)	24 (2.0)	9 (0.7)	178–88
1400–9	954	484 (50.7)	31 (3.2)	7 (0.7)	189–200
1410–19	521	325 (62.4)	19 (3.6)	1 (0.2)	201–12
1420–9	492	216 (43.9) .	15 (3.0)	1 (0.2)	213–22
1430–9	365	232 (63.6)	10 (2.7)	4 (1.1)	223–8
1440–9	277	153 (55.2)	5 (1.8)	1 (0.4)	229–34
1450–9	281	199 (70.8)	7 (2.5)	3 (1.1)	235–42
1460–9	455	4 (0.8)	0		243–52
1470–9	380	10 (2.6)	0		253–60
1480–9	106	2 (1.9)	0		261–5
1490–9	347	4 (1.2)	0		266–8

Note:

( ) = Percentage of the total certificates.

[a] Reference numbers C214/139–268.

Source: Staple Certificates, PRO, C241. These were the orders sent out from Chancery to local sheriffs, in response to action taken against debtors defaulting on agreements which had been enrolled in local courts which possessed the seal of Statute Merchant or Statute Staple. With a few exceptions, the certificates record the names of the parties, size of debt, date and place where it was enrolled, the date it was due and the date the certificate was issued.

most debts, as Hubert Hall believed.[96] Research to date suggests that they were used more frequently in and around London. Of some 10,500 Staple Certificates, issued between 1360 and 1505 to recover unsettled debts, fewer than 600 emanated from Yorkshire or involved Yorkshire parties, and these declined steadily from 1370, to a mere trickle by 1415[97] (see tables 7.1–2). There is some patchy evidence of the use of the seal in York which suggests that statutory bonds met a particular need and were accepted as superior to other bonds. Statutory bonds seem to have been used for extra security in a particularly large or complex deal. For

between 1378 and 1388 and those at Colchester between 200 and 300 a year in the fifteenth century: Kowaleski, 'A Medieval Provincial Oligarchy', p. 369; Britnell, *Growth and Decline in Colchester*, p. 281.

[96] Hubert Hall thought that the volume of cases concerning enrolled obligations which were recorded in the Close and Plea Rolls, in the Miscellaneous Book of the Exchequer and in Kings and Commons Bench Plea Rolls, suggests that statutory recognisances did not supersede traditional enrolments for the repayment of trade debts and loans: *Select Cases*, III, p. xii.

[97] See Kowaleski, *Medieval Exeter*, p. 213 for a similar pattern.

Table 7.2. *Analysis of Yorkshire Staple Certificates: amounts, duration and action taken*

	7.2.1 Amount of credit							7.2.2 Length of credit (in months)						
	up to £5	£10	£25	£50	£75	£100	£100+	3	6	9	12	18	24+	total
1360–9	17	24	31	32	10	10	15	73	33	13	13	4	3	139
per cent	12	17	22	23	7	7	11	53	24	9	9	3	2	
1370–9	8	13	20	22	4	8	5	37	24	9	8	1	1	80
per cent	10	16	25	28	5	10	6	46	30	11	10	1	1	
1380–9	0	7	13	12	1	6	7	22	12	5	5	0	2	46
per cent	0	15	28	26	2	13	15	48	26	11	11	0	4	
1390–9	2	3	6	11	1	3	6	12	15	2	3	0	0	32
per cent	6	9	19	34	3	9	19	38	47	6	9	0	0	
1400–9	3	5	12	10	0	3	5	18	8	7	3	1	1	38
per cent	8	13	32	26	0	8	13	47	21	18	8	3	3	
1410–19	5	0	2	5	3	1	3	6	6	5	2	0	0	19
per cent	26	0	11	26	16	5	16	32	32	26	11	0	0	
1420–9	3	0	1	8	2	2	1	6	3	2	6	0	0	17
per cent	18	0	6	47	12	12	6	35	18	12	35	0	0	
1430–9	1	1	2	2	1	1	1	4	1	2	1	1	0	9
1440–9	0	2	0	0	2	0	1	0	3	1	0	0	1	5
1450–9	1	0	2	1	0	0	1	1	1	0	3	0	0	5
1460–9	0	0	1	1	0	1	0	1	1	1	0	0	0	3
1470–9	0	1	0	4	2	2	1	2	2	2	4	0	0	10
1480–9	[1 blank]	0	0	0	0	0	1	1	0	1	0	0	0	2
1490–9	0	0	0	2	0	1	1	2	2	0	0	0	0	4
1500–5	0	0	0	3	1	0	3	1	0	4	1	[1 blank]		7

7.2.3 Action taken within years as a percentage

	Duration (years)					
Period	0.5	1.5	3	4–5	6–10	10+
1360–9	26	19	14	2	11	28
1370–9	26	21	18	8	10	17
1380–9	33	15	12	18	13	9
1390–9	25	19	31	6	6	13
1400–9	16	15	18	23	13	15
1410–19	50	11	33	0	0	6
1420–19	6	6	24	18	18	28

Source: Staple Certificates, PRO, C241.

instance, one to the abbot of Furness in 1418 for £200 from Robert de Eare was enrolled in York; another in 1393 to the bishop of Durham for 200 marks from Adam Pund was enrolled in Hull, scarcely run-of-the-mill debts.[98]

Statutory bonds, like other bonds, could be used in property transactions to convert a fixed asset, land, into working capital. It must have been common practice to raise capital against the security of property: Londoners were doing so in the 1280s and, according to Sylvia Thrupp, a 'great many' fourteenth-century London merchants were raising loans against 'only small pieces of property, a few scattered holdings'.[99] The attachment of rents from property until a debt was settled was not new. As mentioned earlier, sometime between 1356 and 1367, Thomas Holme of Beverley and his son Richard contracted to buy 120 sacks from Meaux Abbey for £240, but Meaux could only supply sixty-five sacks. So the Holmes were granted Sutton Grange for forty years in lieu, but after four years of difficulties they handed it back. Some of the problems were no doubt due to labour shortages following the Black Death. The Holmes still required satisfaction, and instead of simply giving back the cash difference, Meaux agreed to pay Richard an annuity of 20 marks until the death of his son Richard, or the term of thirty-six years should Richard die before that. As it happened, Richard junior drowned in the Humber after twenty-two years. His father had predeceased him and the 20 marks was then being paid, according to Richard senior's arrangements, to his other son John and to Richard junior's wife, and only 5 marks to Richard junior. John naturally claimed the entire 20 marks following his brother's drowning, and the abbey agreed on a compromise payment of 17½ marks for the remaining fourteen years. By then the abbey must have been regretting not paying back the balance of £110, because it calculated that the Holme family eventually received £645, far more than their initial outlay of £240! Not all merchants were as astute, but the incident serves to demonstrate how profits could be gained: that it was during a period of depressed rents and wool prices is all the more remarkable.[100]

Using statutory bonds put mortgaging property onto a firmer footing, though some risks remained. Simon Grimsby of Hull, for instance, owned land in Hull worth 40 marks a year and he borrowed a further 40 marks from John Iwardby against the land, under Statute Staple. But Grimsby over-reached himself and enfeoffed a third party with the land,

[98] Hull RO, D248, 231; *CPR 1381–5*, p. 87; *CCR 1333–7*, p. 315. As early as 1286 the executors of a former archdeacon of York were pursuing a debt of 70 marks: Hall, *Select Cases*, III, p. 114.

[99] Thrupp, *London Merchant Class*, pp. 122–3.

[100] Bond, *Chronica Monasterii de Melsa*, III, pp. 144–5.

who subsequently refused to re-enfeof him, and Grimsby, under pressure to settle the debt to Iwardby, petitioned the Lord Chancellor for repossession. A charge on a property was no impediment to its sale. In 1358, for example, Gilbert Maunby sold a property in Thirsk with a charge of £80 under Statute Merchant still on it.[101]

FINANCIAL NETWORKS

Credit was essential but often uncertain and a variety of reciprocal arrangements developed to mitigate the risk. The most common was to use a third party as a guarantor, mainpernor, pledge or surety for the debt. When a loan was negotiated, the borrower had to find one or more men who stood as surety against payment. A wealthy and successful business-man, with the confidence of his creditor, might not always need pledges, but a relative newcomer or someone with neither property nor reputa-tion, or someone seeking an exceptionally large loan, would be dealt with according to the solvency of his pledges. In this way your choice of pledges could influence the size of the loan you could command, just as much as the viability of the venture did.[102] Yorkshire merchants often stood as pledges for each other and occasionally for merchants from distant parts of England and even from overseas: in 1319 William Barton, Richard de la Pole and John Rotenhering of Hull, and Nicholas Catton of York, acted as sureties for seven Lubeck merchants.[103]

Within the region loan arrangements reflected many political and social ties and patron–client relationships. Maryanne Kowaleski has been able to trace a credit network centred on Exeter in the late fourteenth century, which involved the civic elite standing as pledges for the local gentry in debt and land suits, and vice versa, as well as providing the same support for merchants from other Devon towns and for each other.[104] There is some evidence that similar networks operated in the north. For

---

[101] PRO, C1/44/89; *Yorks. Fines, 1347–77*, pp. 64, 72. Statute Merchant bonds were also used in prop-erty deals to ensure that seisin of a property was achieved: the bond becoming enforceable if the contract was not fulfilled, like the penalty clause in a modern conveyance. Thus when Hugh Swynflete conveyed a property in Hull to William Ripplingham, they entered a Statute Merchant bond, which was to lapse once 'delivery of possession of the property' had been completed: Hull RO, D301 and also D107; *MB*, II, p. 45.

[102] Postan, 'Private Financial Instruments', p. 31. When the case against Brandesby and Swan was moved from York to London, they had to find a new set of mainpernors since their original eight fellow burgesses could not meet the £489 6s 6d debt in the charge. Their new backers were two Yorkshire gentlemen: Hall, *Select Cases*, II, p. 109, III, p. xxix. See appendix 4.

[103] PRO, C1/289/10; York RO, E39, pp. 128, 172, 187, 205–7; *CCR 1318–22*, p. 170.

[104] Kowaleski, 'A Medieval Provincial Oligarchy', p. 366, and *Medieval Exeter*, p. 209. See late fourteenth-century Colchester where only 14.5 per cent of the pleas of debt heard before the borough courts were brought by outsiders, and there was no 'symbiosis' of the town and coun-tryside: Britnell, *Growth and Decline in Colchester*, pp. 107, 157.

instance, in May 1398 Thomas Holme had to find mainpernors to stand surety for £1,000, which was an unusually large sum required for no stated reason. Robert Gare of York was one of those who acted for Holme, and later in the same year he acted as co-pledge for 100 marks (£66 13s 4d), a more usual sum, for a John de Wallington.[105] In 1439[106] Hugh Clitheroe of Hull and John Paull of Holderness acted as joint sureties for £2,804 for a Richard Wastenes of Stowe.[107]

The Crown normally required sureties for its victuallers and for farmers of royal subsidies. Nicholas le Sauser of York was victualling for the Crown in 1316 and was also standing surety for several other York merchants who were similarly engaged. John Barden of York and Sir Thomas Clifford stood as sureties for the farmers of the cloth subsidy in Yorkshire, Cumberland, Westmorland and Northumberland in 1381–2; and Simon de Quixlay of York stood surety for John de Quixlay who was farming the cloth subsidy in 1384.[108] Robert Acastre of York, however, held the same farm from February 1363 until 1371 without surety because he was 'sufficient'.[109]

Mainperning was not without its risks. The pledges were legally liable for the loan and their goods could be distrained in the event of the debtor defaulting. In *c.* 1455, a Hull merchant, John Green, stood as surety for a York merchant, Thomas Ward, for £225 – the price of a cargo of wine purchased from four Bordeaux men. Payment was to be made only when the wine had been delivered to a third party, Richard Anson (a prominent Hull merchant), and the spoilt wine discounted. The wine duly arrived; seventeen tuns and one pipe were not good, but Green delivered the full £225 in a sealed packet to the common clerk of Hull to hold. When it was delivered to Ward, the wine was under the agreed amount by six tuns, and he paid only a percentage of the agreed price. The Bordeaux men sued for the full £225 against John Green in the court of Common Pleas, claiming that the obligation was made in London, not Hull, and Green counter-petitioned, claiming that the transaction had been completed in Hull and that no-one in London knew the whole truth of the matter![110]

From the pledge's point of view, a major advantage of registering a loan/debt under Statute Merchant was that the pledges were not liable if the debt could not be met from the debtor's goods and chattels. That

---

[105] *CCR 1396–9*, pp. 305, 398. William Savage of York and Thomas Frost of Beverley were co-pledges for Holme.   [106] *CPR 1436–41*, p. 429.
[107] For further examples of loans and pledging between the three towns, see *CCR 1392–6*, p. 133 (Santon of York); *1402–5*, p. 286 (Grimsby of Hull); York *MB*, I, p. 73 (Alkbarow of York); PRO, Treaty Roll 5 H VI m. 9 (Etton of Hull). For an example of rural gentry indebted to a York merchant, see *MB*, II, p. 274 (Neleson).   [108] *CCR 1313–17*, pp. 541–2; *1381–5*, pp. 94, 575.
[109] *Ibid.*, *1360–4*, p. 518; *1364–8*, p. 281; *1368–74*, p. 172.   [110] PRO, C1/16/163, 164.

alone should have encouraged greater use of statutory bonds, but maybe arrangements were not quite as simple as that, and there is evidence suggestive of merchants mortgaging their personal goods.[111] From time to time in the York borough records, there were enrolled gifts of goods from one individual to another, or to a small group of trustees. The terms always referred to all the grantor's goods but rarely mentioned a consideration.[112] This was a legal way of avoiding outlawry and evading distraint upon your goods for your own or someone else's debts.[113] In 1424 Peter Bukcy granted all his goods and the debts owing to him at home and abroad to his son John and another York merchant, Thomas Esingwold. Peter delivered 1d to John and Thomas in the name of seisin for greater security. Was he planning a journey overseas and wanting to settle his affairs quickly? Was the gift permanent? Peter did not die for another eight years. Similarly, Richard Auncell of Hull granted all his goods and chattels to a London merchant, Thomas Rikes, in 1453, but did not die until 1465.[114] Such gifts of goods may have been security against the repayment of a loan which, if repaid, meant that the goods never changed hands. Sometimes such grants were to other merchants, to act for the debtor in settling his debts. Thus John Bilton of Hull granted all his goods to two other Hull merchants, expressly for them to pay off his debts. Alternatively, he may have been winding up a partnership with them. Grants were sometimes a straight exchange for an agreed sum: John Doddington of York granted all his goods to Henry Percy and others in 1421, 'for a certain sum of money'. In 1432 William Hovingham, a York butcher, granted all his goods to John Edmondon and two clerics on 10 October, and on 13 December testified before the mayor that the grant had been without fraud or evil intent.[115] The implication that others might be dishonest was made explicit in a statute of 3 Henry VII, which claimed that such gifts were made 'to thentent to defraude ther creditors of their duties'.[116]

One positive advantage of these gifts was in gaining essential time before the bailiffs pounced: time for another deal to be completed, for a ship to come in,[117] or to recover other assets, even debts. Gaining a

---

[111] Pawning goods was another way of raising cash, and was common in Chester in the 1530s. Eventually the term 'mortgage' was used instead: Chester RO, Sheriffs' Book 7, ff. 7v., 31–2, 67.

[112] E.g. *MB*, I, pp. 187, 204, 215, 236, 245; II, pp. 34, 39, 112, 218; III, pp. 6, 7, 38, 52, 102.

[113] For a similar case, see Kowaleski, *Medieval Exeter*, p. 216, n.181.

[114] *MB*, III, p. 53; Prob. Reg. II, f. 612; *CCR 1447–54*, p. 465; Wedgwood, *Parliamentary Biographies*, p. 12.   [115] (Bilton) Hull RO, BRE 1, p. 263; *MB*, III, pp. 102, 105.

[116] *Statutes of the Realm*, II, p. 513. Quoted in *Cal. Plea & Mem. Rolls City of London, 1413–37*, p. xx.

[117] See, for example, the 1428 case of John Davy of Exeter who promised to settle a debt 'immediately after a certain ship . . . should chance to arrive at any port in England': Gross, *Select Cases*, I, p. 117. John Harrison of Hull made bequests in his will in 1526 contingent upon the arrival of the 'hulks out of Dansk': Prob. Reg. IX, f. 328.

Table 7.3. *Direction of debt/credit*

Period	YBH creditors to YBH debtors	YBH creditors to external debtors	Outside creditors to YBH debtors
1360–9	24 (17%)	55 (40%)	6 (4%)
1370–9	18 (22%)	23 (29%)	2 (3%)
1380–9	7 (15%)	17 (38%)	1 (2%)
1390–9	6 (16%)	11 (34%)	3 (9%)
1400–9	14 (56%)	13 (34%)	2 (5%)
1410–19	7 (37%)	8 (42%)	1 (5%)

Note:
( ) = The percentage of all the Yorkshire enrolled certificates.
Source: Staple Certificates, PRO, c241.

breathing space could be even more important for the heir of an entrepreneur's estate. Death was a time of reckoning when the flow of a business stopped and creditors and partners wanted settlement. Maybe this consideration lay behind Robert Louth of York's gift of all his goods to his son. Nicholas Louth was re-enfeoffed in 1439 after Robert's death, by the trustees chosen by his father: Guy Fairfax esq., Thomas Cleveland, clerk, and John Bolton and William Bowes, aldermen.[118] Even though his son would eventually have to accept liability for his father's debts as his executor, the delaying tactic would gain him time. A similar phenomenon was occurring in London, where increasing numbers of such gifts were enrolled in the mayor's court from 1413.[119] Was this a consequence of a shortage of bullion?

That individuals routinely had recourse to debts as a form of loan is clear. Given the propensity to register debts in some form and of the greater likelihood of negotiating pledges in a busy market, towns can be seen as a focus for financial services. The addition of international commerce as in York, Beverley and Hull enhanced that role and, in theory, when trade was bouyant credit should have flowed from urban purchaser to rural producer. The evidence of the enrolled Staple Certificates (see table 7.3) suggests that this was the pattern in the late fourteenth and early fifteenth centuries, when the majority of transactions were between the townsfolk of York, Beverley and Hull and outsiders. Loans from York accounted for the largest group. Debts/loans within each of the towns accounted for the next largest group.

[118] *MB*, III, pp. 121–2.
[119] *Cal. Plea & Mem. Rolls City of London, 1413–37*, pp. xix–xxiii; *1437–57*, pp. xxii–xxviii, 1; *1458–82*, pp. 147–79 for an appendix listing such gifts.

While many familiar Yorkshire merchants appear in the Staple Certificates, it is clear that people from a wide range of occupations and levels in society had recourse to credit. Between 1360 and 1379, twenty-four clerics, fifteen gentlemen and knights and 116 townsfolk were enrolled as creditors, compared with two clerics, twenty-six gentlemen and knights and thirty-eight townsfolk enrolled as debtors. Clergymen, gentlemen and craftsmen not normally associated with long-distance trade appear alongside mercers, merchants, victuallers, goldsmiths and bowyers. It is likely that there was an economic surplus from time to time, available for investment opportunities, and that other resources such as annuities, rents and land might provide sources of credit. The number of knights appearing as debtors and as creditors might reflect their dealings in wool, but the sums involved were not generally large, and although their numbers fell as the wool trade contracted, this was in line with a general fall in the number of debtors and creditors.

Few transactions involving debtors or creditors outside Yorkshire and North Lincolnshire were recorded in the Yorkshire enrolled certificates. The evidence, taken together with the probability that local fairs were used to set dates for loans, accordingly gives a clear indication of a pattern of regional finance strongly focused on York and, to a lesser extent, on Beverley and Hull.

Debts were also incurred outside the region by Yorkshire merchants, and most of these were with creditors in the south and London,[120] confirming suspicions that one of the reasons for the failure of provincial merchants to exploit their own region was that they were financially outflanked by Londoners. In a sample of debt cases brought before Common Pleas in London in 1384, 1403 and 1424, Yorkshiremen appeared twice as often as debtors as they did as plaintiffs.[121] It may be that collapsed partnerships were hidden in the increasingly frequent actions for debt brought by Londoners against Yorkshire merchants. Hindsight enables an appreciation of the long-term impact, but it is doubtful if William Savage,[122] who stood as a pledge for a Londoner, shipping wool from Hull to London in 1392, thought it bizarre. Merchants riding the tide of success would not understand that encouraging London merchants and credit north would eventually undermine local entrepreneurship, just as

---

[120] *CPR 1405–9*, p. 226; *1413–29*, p. 82; *1436–41*, p. 322; *CCR 1447–61*, p. 132; *1461–7*, p. 502; *1494–1509*, p. 3.

[121] I am grateful to the 'Markets Networks and the Metropolis *c.* 1400 Project' at the Centre for Metropolitan History for this information. The sample was for the Michaelmas term in each year.

[122] Arch. Reg. v, f. 419 (Frost); *CPR 1392–6*, p. 22; *1416–22*, p. 95. In the 1490s, Alan Staveley of Hull was buying wine from a London merchant to ship to Hull: PRO, c1/191/34.

they did not see that buying cloth from rural producers in the early fifteenth century would damage their fellow townsmen's textile industry.

CONCLUSION

In this chapter we have examined aspects of the commercial milieu in which merchants traded. It was a world wherein transactions of sometimes extraordinary complexity were negotiated, revealing how adroitly individuals had to move to recover profits from trade. The need to raise venture capital, whether as cash or credit, pushed merchants into partnerships and negotiations founded on trust which was sometimes misplaced. They relied on each other to act as agents and to share practical experience of trading procedures in foreign markets. Persistence and specialist knowledge were essential if they were to succeed in the marketplace and to recover some compensation when deals fell through. It is hard to imagine the continuous activity and uncertainties which characterised the long-distance merchant's life, although we can venture an assessment of the pattern of overseas trade conducted by merchants in the face of growing competition. It remains to be seen how effectively the merchants from York, Beverley and Hull met that challenge.

8

TRADE AND COMPETITION

In some respects, setting up in business was the least risky period in a merchant's career. Having completed his apprenticeship and raised his investment stake, all that remained was to keep ventures flowing and to sustain an edge over rivals. Competition came from many quarters: from partners and fellow townsmen as well as keen and often physically hostile traders from other regions and foreign countries. Once again, negotiating a successful path between what could be manipulated and what lay beyond all influence was part of the challenge and excitement of being a medieval entrepreneur.

FOREIGN COMPETITION

Without a doubt, the trade in which Yorkshire merchants faced the most direct and severe competition was that with Scandinavia and the Baltic. Unlike the French or Iberians, Hanse merchants came to trade in England, and especially along the east coast. Quite apart from direct confrontation with northern or southern Hanseatic traders, east coast merchants also found themselves entangled in North Sea diplomacy which generated its own shifting alliances. At different moments, they could be prey to Danish, Icelandic, Norwegian or Swedish hostility and were, of course, constantly under threat from their Scottish neighbours.

Competition focused particularly on access to the Baltic, via the Sound, and on the reluctance of the Hanseatic League to allow reciprocity of trading privileges to foreigners seeking business, in person, in Hanse towns. Baltic goods in most demand were fish, grain and timber.[1] Yorkshire merchants displayed considerable persistence in their pursuit of markets around the Baltic and Scandinavian coasts, in spite of an

---

[1] Grain was especially necessary during the dearths of 1417 and 1439, and timber was in such demand that it was sometimes imported in the form of Danzig-built ships: Postan, 'Relations of England and the Hanse', in Power and Postan, *Studies in English Trade*, p. 140.

extremely volatile political situation. These were areas geographically closer to northern merchants, less frequented by southerners, and offering an additional source of profit to the even more sharply contested cross-channel trade with Calais and the Low Countries. Their ventures were genuinely pioneering, taking them on often perilous journeys and into distant lands.

Early in the fourteenth century the Baltic and Scandinavian trade was dominated by aliens, although one or two Hull merchants had penetrated the Eastland as early as 1308, when Henry Damel had his ship laden with ashes, flax, tar and boards seized on his return voyage. Hanse merchants were certainly active in Hull by the 1310s when one complained of ill-treatment there and new regulations concerning prosecutions for debt in Hull were published in Stralsund and other Hanse towns in 1312.[2] *Kontore*, associations of Hanse merchants, were active in York and Hull in the fourteenth century, with the group in Hull predominant. Its complaint to the king in 1374, at the Hull council's imposition of the 'brocage' tax, earned exemption for the Hanse and a reprimand for the borough.[3] During the second half of the century, more Yorkshiremen ventured into the Hanse territory, and at first were not unwelcome.[4] In 1364 six Hull merchants obtained licences to export cloth to Prussia and Eastland, and in 1373 a York bowyer, Roger Swerd, was the earliest recorded Englishman to take up residence in Prussia. He shipped wine to Prussia in exchange for wheat and rye, and subsequently settled six of his men in Prussia to make bows and send them back to York.[5]

Tensions rose once the English began to claim reciprocal privileges in Hanseatic towns, and to open up retail businesses and rent property.[6] The Hanse were forbidden to ship goods in English vessels and by 1370 had almost entirely ousted the English from the Skania fairs. English insistence that the Hanse should pay tax on their imports and exports, coupled with an attack on German ships in 1385, provoked reprisals.[7] The goods of a contingent of English merchants were seized in Prussia: the majority, thirty-three, came from York, claiming goods worth £1,617;

---

[2] *CCR 1307–13*, pp. 68, 211; *VCH Hull*, p. 61.

[3] Dollinger, *Hansa*, pp. 105–6; Lloyd, *German Hanse*, p. 87; *VCH Hull*, p. 62.

[4] Dollinger, *Hansa*, p. 73.

[5] *VCH Hull*, p. 61; *CPR 1361–4*, pp. 497, 500, 517; *1364–7*, pp. 35, 92; *VCH York*, p. 102; Lloyd, *German Hanse*, p. 49.

[6] Several York merchants died in Danzig: John Helmesley in 1384, John Dunnock in 1389 and Thomas Fenton in 1395, and, more surprisingly, given the date, John Briscow in 1443. While this is not strong evidence for their residence, they were there long enough to make their wills! Moreover, fellow York men witnessed each will: two York dyers for Helmesley's, six York merchants for Thomas Fenton's, and John Ince, John Gaunt, Richard Scotton and Richard Bothe of York, for John Briscow's: Dec. & Cap. I, f. 76v. (Helmesley); Prob. Reg. I, ff. 2 (Dunnock), 89 (Fenton); II, f. 73 (Briscow). [7] Dollinger, *Hansa*, pp. 73–4.

twelve from Beverley claimed goods worth £306. Their claims were adjusted following negotiations: down to £1,151 for York but up to £324 6s 8d for Beverley. Only eleven Londoners and one Hull merchant, John Parker, also made claims. In a series of associated claims, several agents acting for Yorkshire merchants and resident in Prussia, submitted claims for assaults.[8]

The speed of Yorkshire penetration into Prussia is well evidenced by these figures, and, as a reflection of the importance of the region's interest, a York merchant, Thomas Gra, was one of the two English ambassadors sent to Marienburg to treat for peace in 1388.[9] In spite of diplomatic efforts, open hostilities flared between England and the Hanse, disrupting international trade between all the North Sea countries.

Imports from the Baltic remained an important component of Hull's inward trade: in 1398–9, excluding wine, the total value of imported goods was £3,350, of which £1,715 came from the Baltic. Herrings from the Skania fisheries accounted for £1,237, at least one half carried in local English ships.[10] Hanse exports from Hull, which had begun to contract in the 1370s, expanded again after the peace was signed in 1408. The recovery was short-lived however, and during the 1420s and 1430s, Hanse activity shrank to a mere trickle in some years. Exports through Hull fluctuated violently: thirty-eight cloths in 1434–5, none the following year, 803 in 1436–7, 507 in 1463–4.[11] As hostilities intensified in mid-century, the number of Baltic cargoes dwindled: four ships arrived in six months in 1452, three in six months in 1465, and none in two months in 1473. Denizens even lost opportunities in the carrying trade, as English ships were banned from Hanse ports.[12]

Following the signing of the Treaty of Utrecht in 1474, and concessions made to the Hanse merchants, especially in Hull, trade did pick up for the next decade. Cloth exports achieved the levels of the early fifteenth century and imports of wax rose sharply. Disputes inevitably re-emerged, as ever over the degree of reciprocity extended by each side. Hull attempted to confine the Hanseatic merchants to the port,[13] but could not prevent them from taking over parts of the region's trade. Overseas demand for lead stimulated a growth in production from a mid-century low,[14] and by 1471–2 constituted 74 per cent by value of all Hull

---

[8] *Urkundenbuch*, v, p. 409; *Hanserecesse, 1256–1430*, III, pp. 405–7, 412–14; Lloyd, *German Hanse*, p. 88.   [9] *CPR 1385–8*, p. 453; *MB*, II, pp. 1, 5.

[10] Lloyd, *German Hanse*, p. 89.

[11] Carus-Wilson and Coleman, *England's Export Trade*, pp. 94, 101.

[12] *VCH Hull*, p. 62; *VCH York*, p. 103; *Hanserecesse, 1431–76*, II, pp. 64–5.

[13] *VCH Hull*, p. 63.

[14] Pollard, *North-Eastern England*, pp. 74–5; Blanchard, 'Seigneurial Entrepreneurship', pp. 100–1.

exports excluding wool, cloth and hides. Joint ventures mounted by the Hull corporation accounted for most of the lead shipped in 1473, but by the 1490s the Hanse had come to dominate the trade. In 1492–3 they accounted for £585 of a total £1,342 of lead exported and in 1496–7 they shipped all £825.[15] The Baltic was to all practical intents and purposes closed to the English by the 1490s.

It has been argued that, for a government heavily dependent upon income from customs duties, to lose access to the major trading areas of the Baltic and, even more importantly, the Rhine, was incompetent folly. But the rivalry over the Baltic which initiated the hostility involved a relatively small number of merchants from the east coast ports: Hull, Lynn, Boston and Yarmouth. While the struggle with the Hanse raged, Londoners directed their energies towards the Low Countries, only supporting the war policy for a time.[16] In any case, those Hanseatic merchants still trading in England concentrated their efforts in London, not reappearing in the east coast ports in significant numbers again until after 1474.[17] By that date, the merchants of Yorkshire found themselves left with a diminishing share of the shrinking wool trade to Calais, intense competition for business in the Low Countries, and a rapidly disappearing trade in wine, woad and other commodities, collected in the Low Countries from France and Spain for transhipping to England.

Yorkshiremen did, however, venture further afield than continental Europe, seeking commercial opportunities in Iceland, but this was never a very large part of Hull's overseas trade. Icelandic fish had possibly been imported into Hull, via Norway, from the late fourteenth century, but by the 1420s there was a direct trade, with Yorkshire merchants carrying foodstuffs and manufactured goods to Iceland. After complaints about the behaviour of some Hull men in 1425, English merchants were banned from Iceland, and once more had to trade through Bergen. Worsening relations between Denmark and Norway in the 1430s inevitably affected trade.[18] York and Hull merchants complained of losing goods worth £5,000 in 1432, and, in 1436, one York and eleven Hull merchants had uncustomed goods on a Hull ship arrested on its way to Iceland; which suggests the prohibition was flouted. In 1439, William Cockerham of Beverley sought a massive £1,300 for a cargo of stockfish lost to Prussians, *en route* from Iceland.[19] Icelandic trade was controlled by licence by the 1440s, and at least eleven Hull merchants obtained them

[15] *VCH Hull*, p. 67; PRO, E122/62/7, 19.   [16] Bolton, *Medieval English Economy*, pp. 310–11.
[17] Dollinger, *Hansa*, p. 243.   [18] *VCH Hull*, p. 59; Carus-Wilson, 'Iceland Trade', pp. 163–7.
[19] This was probably tit-for-tat since he was accused of piracy to the value of £1,300 against a Danzig ship: *CPR 1436–41*, p. 270; *Bronnen*, II, pp. 714–15.

between 1442 and 1470.[20] During the 1460s and 1470s, at least one ship left Hull for Iceland each year, and sometimes more,[21] but as relations between England and Denmark deteriorated in the second half of the century, the risk of attack by the Hanse, now the allies of Denmark, increased.[22] By the end of the fifteenth century the Icelandic trade had seriously contracted.

Part of the response of English merchants to the accumulation of concessions by the Hanseatic merchants, and the need to concentrate their own negotiating powers, was to organise themselves, loosely at first, into an 'English nation'. By 1391, the 'nation' at Danzig was tightly organised, electing its own governor and acquiring privileges from the Grand Master of the Teutonic order, the Hanse. From such localised beginnings the company of merchant venturers evolved, and was paralleled by the establishment of individual mercers' and merchant adventurers' associations and companies in English towns in the early fifteenth century.[23] The York mercers and merchant adventurers were chartered in 1430, having developed from a religious fraternity whose objectives were ostensibly social and spiritual. The Company was empowered to buy land to relieve the poor members of their craft, a prescient aim,[24] and it seems likely that changes in the pattern of overseas trade had encouraged the mercantile group to formalise their association for their own protection. It was, however, to no avail in the long term.

LONDONERS

In addition to Hanse competition, Yorkshire merchants faced the threat of enterprising Londoners coming north and squeezing the local merchants out of the profitable trade in lead and cloth. A final straw was the Londoners' achievement of a monopolistic position in England's export trade by excluding Yorkshiremen from the government of the national company of merchant adventurers. Early in the fifteenth century the merchant adventurers of York and Newcastle took defensive measures against the London adventurers by keeping their stalls and everything to do with their cloth sales away from the 'southerners' at the foreign marts.[25] The merchants of York, Beverley, Hull, Scarborough and

---

[20] *CPR 1436–41*, pp. 294–5; Carus-Wilson, 'Iceland Trade', p. 169; Bartlett, 'Aspects of the Economy of York', pp. 113–14. See also PRO, CI/17/111.

[21] PRO, E122/62/7, 19.

[22] E.g. five Hull merchants were attacked by Hamburg ships as they sailed to Iceland. Carus-Wilson, 'Iceland Trade', pp. 177–82.

[23] Carus-Wilson, *Medieval Merchant Venturers*, pp. xx, xxix–xxxiii.   [24] *M&MA*, pp. v–x.

[25] E. M. Carus-Wilson, 'The Origins and Development of the Merchant Adventurers Organisation in London as shown in their own Medieval Records', *EcHR*, 4 (1933), pp. 169–70; *Feodora*, VIII, p. 464.

Whitby joined forces in 1478 to appeal to the Crown against the refusal of the Londoners to elect a northern governor of the Company as well as a southern governor. They claimed that the Londoners had the advantage over northerners just as they had at the cloth fairs, as a result of locating the northerners' stalls at the periphery of the market and so emphasising the poorer quality of northern cloth. The letter from the York Company is redolent of a sense of bitter injustice, especially as it pointed out that the governor of the English Company, John Pickering, accepted dues paid to him by all English merchants to act on their behalf.[26] Edward IV issued a proclamation ordering fairer treatment, but to no effect, and in 1495 the York merchants were trying to establish a maximum for the fees to be charged to them in Bruges, Antwerp, Barow and Middleburg. Two years later Yorkshire merchants may have collaborated with other non-Londoners in petitioning against charges imposed on them overseas by the London adventurers.[27] By then it was too late, and indeed it is doubtful if the provincial merchants would have gained any advantage from political pressure, however concerted.

Indications of decline and the eventual eclipse of Yorkshire merchants by Londoners were visible in the 1470s. Of all the estimates calculable, probably the most telling is the fact that in 1466–7 and 1471–2, 20 per cent of the wool trade and 52 per cent of the cloth trade through Hull were in the hands of merchants not from York, Beverley or Hull. The wool was shipped by other English merchants,[28] some of the cloth by the Hanse and other foreigners in 1466–7, but not the Hanse in 1471–2. Similarly, 60 per cent of the wine trade was in the hands of others in 1466–7, but this had shrunk to 25 per cent in 1471–2 (see tables 5.1, 5.2 and 5.4 on pp. 167, 172 and 178). Ultimately, nothing could counter the purchasing power of the largest wine consumer in the realm – the royal household. Its more or less continuous presence in London guaranteed a level of imports and a concentration of specialised market and associated services difficult to rival elsewhere. Moreover, London merchants found it almost as cheap to ship wine along the east coast as they did to transport it overland to the Home Counties, and many included the east coast customers as a regular part of their business. The wine was shipped north, coal south, and the wine debts collected later by land.[29]

[26] *M&MA*, pp. 65, 74–80; *YCR*, I, pp. 66, 133–4, III, pp. 22–4; *VCH York*, pp. 103–4, 130; Heaton, *Yorks Woollen and Worsted Industries*, p. 155; Salzman, *English Trade*, p. 333.

[27] *M&MA*, p. 87; N. J. M. Kerling, *Commercial Relations of Holland and Zeeland with England from the Late Thirteenth Century to the Close of the Middle Ages* (Leiden, 1954), p. 155.

[28] Hanham, *Celys and Their World*, pp. 243–5, points out that the London wool trade was also shrinking by the 1480s. In 1488 only nine merchants, 4.3 per cent of London shippers, exported over 200 sacks each. [29] James, *Wine Trade*, pp. 176–87, 189–90.

THE CHANGING SCALE OF OVERSEAS TRADE IN YORK, BEVERLEY AND HULL

So far, much of the discussion has drawn on anecdotal evidence which serves to establish an impression of the competition faced by merchants from the three towns and their fight to gain and keep a place in overseas markets. As a way of moving behind general trends to gain a sharper understanding of the varied range of mercantile businesses, this study tries to establish a trading history for each merchant identifiable as an overseas investor and as a York, Beverley or Hull man: 695 to date.[30] Individual profiles based on estimates of the annual values of the goods they traded and the scale of their commercial enterprises immediately create an awareness of differences and similarities within the merchant class. These are inevitably limited profiles, not as multi-dimensional and 'fleshed out' as the characters Eileen Power reconstructed for Thomas Betson or Thomas Paycocke,[31] since the focus here is on only one aspect of their life: earning a living. However, this form of analysis graphically exposes the great variety amongst the men investing in overseas trade, lets in the small-scale trader, and qualifies the impression created by biographies of outstanding individuals.

Another advantage of this prosopographical approach is that it becomes possible to examine comparatively, in aggregate, merchants by town groups to suggest differences in the ways each town experienced the transformation of overseas trade in the fourteenth and fifteenth centuries. As we shall see, the fortunes of York, Beverley and Hull followed very different courses.

The quantification of much historical data is often a fraught endeavour and regarded with scepticism. There are many methodological hurdles to overcome in such an ambitious project: some arising from the sources used and others from the criteria employed to categorise individuals. In this study, neither the sources nor the methodology is without flaws and the conclusions must remain speculative. It is not claimed that all the merchants from those three towns have been traced: identifying Hull and Beverley merchants can be especially difficult, given the absence of a complete series of freemen's rolls. However, by using contextual links

---

[30] The analysis presented in my paper, 'Merchants, Overseas Trade, and Urban Decline: York, Beverley, and Hull *c.* 1380–1500', *Northern History*, 23 (1987), pp. 51–73, was based on customs accounts only. Here, I have added in all those identified in printed sources whose overseas trading activities fell strictly within the defined periods, even though others, known to have been alive at the time, were active outside those periods. Although the numbers involved differ slightly, as anticipated, the relationship between the groups does not.

[31] Kermode, 'Merchants of York, Beverley and Hull', appendix 4 contains biographies for 1,400 individuals; Power, *Medieval People*, pp. 120–51, 153–73.

it seems possible to identify the majority of very active merchants from the three towns. Any merchants overlooked are most likely those trading on a small scale and shipping infrequently. The existence of merchants in all three towns with the same surname generated some confusion. Merchants named Broun, Ferriby, Frost, Holme, Kelstern, Upsale and Waghen, for instance, appeared in York, Beverley and Hull at one time or another and sometimes contemporaneously, while William de Burton must have been one of the most common names in later medieval England. It is possible that a handful of individuals, such as Walter Kelstern and Thomas Holme, were in fact freemen of all three towns and so were variously described as of York, of Beverley or of Hull. In compiling the individual biographies on which this analysis is based, care has been taken to identify each of them as separate individuals. The implications of counting one man twice have been minimal for this level of statistical analysis.

Sources

In addition to printed English calendars of royal chancery documents and collections of Hanse documents,[32] the main records used here are those of the national customs systems:[33] all of those extant for Hull, as well as several for Scarborough and Ravenser[34] when they were not included in the Hull rolls, and a sample for Newcastle and Grimsby between 1298–9 and 1508–9. There are four main categories of customs records: collectors and controllers account rolls; searchers accounts; writs and receipts; and miscellaneous items.[35] The account rolls are the most substantial source. As a consequence of the different customs and subsidies levied, each commodity was recorded differently and in separate sections of the roll. Exported wool and woolfells and hides were listed by quantity; cloth by type and quality or value; lead by quantity and value; miscellaneous exports by type and value. Miscellaneous imports were listed by type, value and quantity, wine by quantity and/or value.

   The consolidation of customs and subsidies and their collection by one collector[36] meant that a merchant exporting cloth and wool could be paying four rates at once on two different bases. His wool was assessed by quantity for the ancient custom and *ad valorem*, by the sack, for the sub-

[32] *Bronnen*; *Urkundenbuch*; *Hanseakten*; *Hanserecesse*.
[33] E. Carson, 'Customs Records as a Source for Historical Research', *Archive*, 58 (1977).
[34] Hull's outports were busier at the very beginning of the fourteenth century and less so in the fifteenth: Childs, *Hull Customs Accounts*, p. xx.
[35] PRO, E122: King's Remembrancer Particular Customs Accounts.
[36] For details, see Gras, *Early English Customs*, pp. 61, 66–7, 74–5, 79–85.

sidies. In the petty custom accounts, his cloth was assessed only for the 1347 custom, so the cloth was recorded by type and quantity, the number of pieces or occasionally a continuous strip measured in ells. In the custom and subsidy roll, cloth was assessed at the same customs rate together with the poundage subsidy,[37] and so the value of the cloth was recorded but not the quantity nor the specific type. This means that in a customs and subsidy roll, the value has to be estimated from average values calculated from a contemporaneous petty customs account or other source. Sometimes, all the goods being exported were lumped together so that it is not possible to isolate the value of different commodities.[38] However, it is always possible to differentiate between petty customs and customs and subsidy rolls by the form of entry and the amounts paid. Not all rolls cover a complete year or contain accounts of imports and exports,[39] but in this analysis, complete rolls have been used whenever possible as a leading indicator. What cannot be established is the degree of underrecording by officials, but that is a constant factor.

There is the possibility that a merchant fails to appear in some account rolls because the roll is incomplete. However, part-year rolls became less common from the mid-fourteenth century, and since a characteristic of the successful merchant was the frequency of his trading ventures, it is unlikely that his activities would be lost altogether. The most likely category of merchant to fall through the gaps in the rolls was therefore the small-scale merchant, and the numbers in this category are certain to be underestimated.

Once the home town of each individual had been established, some means of aggregating and comparing trade was required. Annual turnover, reinforced by shipping frequencies, provided an effective basis for dividing individuals into four broad groups. The value of goods rather than volume has been used to make possible comparisons between the fluctuating values of shipments of wool, cloth, wine and miscellaneous goods in the three periods chosen: 1306–1336, 1378–1408 and 1460–1500. The choice of periods was dictated by the survival of the Particular Customs Rolls. The first, 1306–1336, covers the years when wool accounted for the bulk of England's exports and denizens were replacing alien merchants in handling the trade. The second period, 1378–1408, covers the years when cloth was poised to overtake wool as the major commodity exported and straddles the boom years of the late

---

[37] 12d in the pound in 1433: *ibid.*, p. 83.

[38] E.g. on 1 June 1467 Nicholas Elys and others shipped goods to the value of £480 which included 80 lasts of barley meal, 70 lasts of beer, 200 ells of linen cloth: PRO, E122/60/10.

[39] E.g. PRO, E122/60/2 which runs from Easter 1401 until 7 July the same year for the collection of a subsidy of 2s per tun of wine and 8d in the pound.

fourteenth century and the onset of recession in the early fifteenth century. The third, 1460–1500, encompasses the final phase of the depression and the improving conditions which succeeded the signing of the Treaty of Utrecht in 1474.

Each merchant's wool trade has been estimated by using the regional average prices listed by T. H. Lloyd. This may mean that shipments through Hull have been overvalued, since northern wool was generally cheaper.[40] Following Carus-Wilson and Coleman, the 364 lb sack has been taken as the measure throughout, and not the lighter (315 lb) Calais sack.[41] Where woolfells have been converted, it has been done at the rate of 240 per sack, as established in 1368.[42] Calculations before that date might be underestimates. Cloth values, given in the Hull customs rolls, were generally about £1 10s for a single cloth, *sine grano*, although they were £1 13s in 1383–4. These values compare with a national average value of £1 15s between 1421 and 1461. Unless a specific value was recorded, the value of an individual's cloth trade has been estimated using £1 10s as the average price in the fifteenth century.[43]

Wine was sold retail in York at about £5 per tun during the fifteenth century, rising to £8 during a period of scarcity in 1458–9, following the loss of Bordeaux. Margery James suggested an average price of £5 per tun of red wine in the 1430s, but both she and Wendy Childs price French and Spanish wine at £4 a tun in the 1490s, whereas Hull prices remained at between £5 and £5 0s 9d.[44] There are dangers in using a single value over such a long time-span, but a rough multiplier for individual merchants' wine imports of £5 per tun has been used. Undervaluation, where it has occurred, would affect merchants importing wine in the mid-1370s and in 1380–1.[45] The value of miscellaneous imports and of exported lead and foodstuffs was recorded in the customs accounts, and requires no adjustment.

The parameters of the categories were designed to reflect the clustering of merchants once ranked, as well as the wide range of different levels of trading activity both within and between groups. Individuals were

---

[40] Lloyd, *Movement of Wool Prices*, pp. 40–4. For Yorkshire wool prices, see above, pp. 200–1.

[41] Carus-Wilson and Coleman, *England's Export Trade*, p. 13. It is clear that this measure, the 'English sack', was used in Edward III's 1337 wool monopoly transactions, in spite of regional variations as to the size and number of stones comprising a sack: Lloyd, *English Wool Trade*, p. 149; Hanham, *Celys and Their World*, p. 133; D. Postles, 'Fleece Weights and Wool Supply, *c.* 1250– *c.* 1350', *Textile History*, 12 (1981), pp. 96–103 at p. 97.

[42] Carus-Wilson and Coleman, *England's Export Trade*, p. 194; *Rot. Parl.* II, p. 295.

[43] PRO, E122/58/9, 66/2; Bolton, *Medieval English Economy*, p. 292. Unusually, specifically white cloths were valued in 1430–1 at £1, those without grain at £1 6s 8d: E122/61/32; Bartlett, 'Aspects of the Economy of York', pp. 71–8, 345.

[44] Bartlett, 'Aspects of the Economy of York', pp. 66, 67, 69; Childs, *Anglo-Castilian Trade*, p. 63.

[45] James, *Wine Trade*, pp. 27–8.

allocated to broad bands as follows: A includes those merchants with a regular annual turnover in excess of £100, B those with a turnover of £50–£100, C those with a turnover of £25–£50, and D those with a turnover of less than £25. Group D also includes 'ghosts', those who appeared only once in the records. The absence of import figures for early fourteenth-century merchants means that individual businesses may have been undervalued. Further division into more categories was rejected because it did not refine a fairly basic analysis.

The individuals under observation here are those actively involved in overseas trade, even though they may have been described elsewhere as mariners or drapers or even as apothecaries, as in the case of Laurence Swattock of Hull. Three widows – Elena Box and Alice Day of Hull, and Marion Kent of York – have also been included since they continued to trade after their respective husbands' deaths. Marion Kent indeed, traded for three years from her husband's death in 1470, and she invested in at least sixteen ventures mainly exporting lead and cloth.[46]

Individuals have been placed into categories on the basis of the predominant pattern of two factors: the frequency of their shipments and their average annual investment. A minority did not obviously fit comfortably. The most problematic were those whose first and solitary appearance in the records came at the end of the period under observation and who displayed some of the characteristics of a very active investor.[47] Category A has been reserved for merchants observable over several years and who regularly invested over £100 on average in multiple shipments. Examples of men in each category will be discussed later.

Even though a numerical analysis has been attempted here, it must be borne in mind that calculations were made primarily to test impressions, for without some quantification of individual trading patterns and of the numbers of traceable active merchants, any discussion remains anecdotal and impressionistic. If any individuals have eluded the net, they would most likely be the less active and smaller-scale merchants whose appearance in the customs rolls was infrequent anyway. These omissions would not significantly qualify any conclusions about the changes in the relationship between the different categories, since the lesser merchants always constituted the largest group. Only those whose trading activities were recorded within the defined periods have been included here, and therefore some merchants alive during each period have been omitted from this statistical analysis. Robert de Yarom of York and Thomas

---

[46] PRO, E122/62/12, 13, 16, 19.
[47] John de Brompton of Beverley and William Fysshe of Hull were examples of this. Both appeared once only in 1332–3, with two and three shipments respectively, worth £95 and £80: E122/58/2. They were put in group B.

Table 8.1. *The merchants of York, Beverley and Hull and overseas trade in the fourteenth and fifteenth centuries*

1306–36					1378–1408					1460–1500				
A	B	C	D	Total	A	B	C	D	Total	A	B	C	D	Total
No. of merchants in each category														
35	40	30	52	157	44	60	65	142	311	16	24	43	144	227
Same as %														
22	26	19	33	100	14	19	21	46	100	7	11	19	63	100

Notes:
A includes those merchants with an annual turnover worth £100+.
B includes those merchants with an annual turnover worth £50–£100.
C includes those merchants with an annual turnover worth £25–£50.
D includes those merchants with an annual turnover worth £0–£25.

Kirkham, for instance, became freemen in 1389 and 1402 respectively, but the only record of them trading was in 1430–1, outside the periods of analysis, and so they have not been included here.[48]

A clear sense of the ebbs and flows of individuals investing and prospering in overseas trade emerges from estimating the numbers of merchants in each category, active in each period. Table 8.1 shows how striking the movement was between the four categories relative to each other over two centuries. In real and in relative terms the number of large-scale merchants diminished from 22 per cent (35) in 1306–36 to 7 per cent (16) in 1460–1500 as the less active merchants doubled in number from 33 per cent (52) to 63 per cent (144). Within each category, the composition of cargoes and pattern of trade changed from the early narrow specialised dealings of wool merchants to the diversified trade of the general merchant.

Merchants were naturally very different from one another in the scale and value of their trade, and a wide range of ventures is revealed within each category.[49] Those classed as D merchants operated on a relatively limited scale. Richard Brigenhall of York sent one shipment of wool each year for four separate years between 1320 and 1333, with an average value of £20, but other wool shipments were surprisingly small: William Birkyn of Hull shipped wool worth £2 10s in 1311–12 and £3 in 1320–1. John Humbrecolt of Beverley was typical of those merchants operating

[48] PRO, E122/61/32.   [49] See appendix 3 for profiles of merchants.

on a more ambitious scale in category C, and the value of his wool exports ranged from £35 to £50 spread between two or three separate shipments each year. John de Kelstern of York exported in only two years: wool worth £28 in 1320–1 and £12 in 1332–3, each in a single shipment. The average annual value of a merchant's business sometimes obscured an occasional boom year, so that although Thomas Holme of Beverley exported wool in seven separate years with an average annual value of £30, in 1306–7 he sent seven shipments of wool with a total value of £200. Thereafter his exports never again exceeded £40 in a single year.

The larger an individual's turnover, the greater the frequency and scale of shipments. Typical of the B group was Thomas Waghen of Beverley, a regular exporter between 1306 and 1326, usually sending several shipments each year with annual values ranging from £25 to £130. Occasionally, insights can be gained into the fluctuations of one man's business. Thomas Redenesse of York expanded his investment between 1298 and 1313. Prior to 1306 his annual trade in wool did not exceed an average £50, but in that year his exports increased to £105, and remained high. In his last appearance, in the accounts of 1313, that year's trade was worth about £80. In contrast, John de Thornton of York's annual business gradually declined from £140 in 1308–9 to £24 in 1320–1.

The really large merchant businesses are easily distinguished in category A. William de la Pole is probably the most eminent and best-known example of a successful fourteenth-century merchant,[50] and although no other Yorkshire merchant has been discovered who could rival de la Pole, several others built up impressive export businesses. William Kelstern of Beverley exported wool regularly between 1312 and 1333, and in only three years sent fewer than five shipments. The average annual value of his exports was between £200 and £400, with annual figures ranging from as high as £639 in 1321–2 to as low as £42 in the following year. Walter de Kelstern, also of Beverley,[51] possibly William's cousin or brother, had his best years between 1306 and 1325 when he only once exported wool worth less than £350 in eighteen years of trade. In 1308–9 his exports were worth £1,160, but after 1323 his business tailed off, although he was active in the 1337–8 wool collection. Other examples of major exporters were Richard Allerton and Henry de Belton of York, and Richard Tirwhit of Beverley.

As already noticed, hardly any cloth was exported in the early fourteenth century, but by the 1370s the situation had changed. Cloth had

---

[50] See Fryde, *Wool Accounts of William de la Pole* and *William de la Pole. Merchant and King's Banker*.

[51] It is difficult to disentangle him after 1312 from William due to the way in which their names were recorded: PRO, E122/6/11.

supplanted wool as the major export commodity, Hanseatic trade had taken off and the Baltic had become a major market for English cloth, supplying a variety of goods in return. Following the Black Death, north European commerce was enjoying boom conditions, and in Yorkshire itself, as textile production and the volume of trade expanded, so the number of active merchants multiplied. The smaller investors, group D, had almost trebled in number and constituted 46 per cent of all merchants, and though the number of merchants in group B had increased by one third, they constituted a slightly smaller proportion: 19 per cent of all merchants. Similarly, although group A had increased in numbers, it constituted only 14 per cent compared with 22 per cent in the early fourteenth century (see table 8.1).

In addition to the dramatic increase in active merchants, the other striking feature of late fourteenth-century trade, as we have seen, was the amazing variety of commodities imported back to England from the Low Countries in particular. Merchants in every category could be found importing, including those in group D who rarely exceeded one export and import shipment a year. Henry de Preston of York sent one shipment of cloth worth £16 in 1395–6 and imported one of miscellaneous goods worth £11 1s 4d. In 1401–2 he again had one export and one import shipment worth £15 and £11 13s 4d respectively. However, John Carleton of Beverley exported and imported regularly between 1387 and 1397, but in only one year did he have both outgoing and incoming shipments.

Merchants in groups B and C, usually invested in both exports and imports, sending and receiving several shipments each year. Robert Louth of York was typical of group B. He traded regularly between 1383 and 1401, generally exporting two or three shipments of cloth each year and importing two or more shipments of mixed goods. Imports and exports in any single year rarely balanced. In 1395–6 he exported cloth worth £39 and imported goods worth £28. The difference was larger in 1398–9 when his cloth exports were worth £43 1s 4d and his imports only £7 11s 8d. Although cloth had replaced wool as the major export commodity, it is interesting that most of the wool still exported was by merchants in groups A and B, and generally comprised the most valuable part of their trade. In this respect there was no difference between wool-exporting staplers and other merchants; one or two like Thomas Gra of York traded entirely in wool, but most wool exporters engaged in the cloth export trade as well, and in importing wine and miscellaneous goods. John Topcliff of York, for example, exported both cloth and wool, as did many of his contemporaries in group B (such as William Pound of Hull). He also imported herrings, wine and miscellaneous goods. His wool shipments were always more valuable than his cloth shipments: in 1390–1 he exported cloth worth £15 and wool worth £107; in 1391–2 he exported cloth worth £22 and wool and fells worth about £168. His imports were generally small and in 1391–2 his one shipment of mixed goods was worth £2 1s, but his more specialised shipment that year contained herrings and wine worth about £95.

The most active merchants, comprising group A, in the late fourteenth century are once again easily identified by the value of their trade and the frequency of their shipments. Although some merchants sent all their cloth in one big shipment (Robert Holme of York, for example, sent one shipment worth £83 in 1390–1), most merchants in this group spread the risk over several shipments each year. As in group B, wool usually constituted the most valuable part of their trade. The value of Richard Aglyon of Beverley's cloth exports, worth £310 0s 4d in 1383–4, was exceptional even for him: his cloth exports were usually worth £50 or less, whereas his wool exports were only once less than £100. A small number of merchants exported only one commodity. Thomas Gra of York apparently concentrated on exporting wool between 1378 and 1390, unlike William Terry of Hull who exported only cloth between 1383 and 1401. The same William Terry was something of a specialist importer also, and the most valuable part of his imports was wine. In 1389–90 he imported miscellaneous goods worth £3 6s 8d together with fifty-six tuns of wine, and in 1398–9 he imported herrings worth £4 6s 8d and twenty-two tuns one pipe of wine. John Liversege was another Hull specialist wine importer, though on a smaller scale, and they exemplify the Hull merchants' dominance of the wine trade through Hull at this time.

Generally speaking, the value of goods imported was less than that of goods exported and this also applied to the trade of individual merchants, excepting those who imported wine on any scale. None the less, some annual imports of mixed goods were very considerable. Robert Holme, of either York or Beverley, imported £724 worth of goods in 1383–4 and Robert Ward of York brought in £339 worth of imports in the same year. Compared to their predecessors of the early fourteenth century, the most active merchants were impressive: investing more and handling more complex enterpises. John Gisburn exported over £1,000 worth of wool and a little cloth in 1378–9, and £782 worth of wool in the following year. Simon de Quixlay, his protagonist in the contested election of 1381,[52] never matched such a massive turnover in one year, but for six out of eight years between 1378 and 1392 the annual value of his trade

---

[52] *VCH York*, pp. 81–2.

Table 8.2. *The trade of Robert Ward of York, 1383–1402*

	Shipments	Total value
1383–4	19	£556 and 10 pipes wine
1389–90	11	£289
1391–2	32	£1,118
1395–6	7	£92
1398–9	10	£74 and 1 pipe wine
1401–2	12	£334

Source: PRO, E122 59/1, 2, 5, 7, 8, 14–16, 19, 22–6; 60/2, 5; 159/11; 160/1.

never fell below £222. The major difference between the two was that Quixlay exported mainly wool and had an active import trade, whereas Gisburn exported cloth as well as wool but infrequently invested in imports. Robert Holme of York's activities have been described elsewhere,[53] but must be treated with caution as a contemporaneous Robert Holme of Beverley was also active in trade and the records rarely differentiate between them.

Robert Ward of York provides a more reliable example of an outstandingly active merchant of the period. He traded regularly between 1378 and 1401, exporting cloth and wool and importing mixed goods, particularly woad. For the six years for which both import and export figures have survived, the annual value of his trade was as shown in table 8.2.

In addition, the annual value of his exports in five other years never fell below £360. Other, although less remarkable, enterprise was achieved by his brother Thomas as well as Nicholas Blackburn snr, and John Hoveden of York, Richard Aglyon and William Rolleston of Beverley.[54]

As the fifteenth century opened, it was already apparent that the commercial boom was coming to an end and England was caught up in a wider recession.[55] The overall value of Hull's export trade began to decline from £400,000 between 1407 and 1417, falling dramatically in the decade 1427–37 to £270,000 and reaching its lowest value of £100,000 in the decade 1457–67. Hull's trade between 1467 and 1487 was worth only about £120,000 and the value of exports remained fairly constant thereafter, rising temporarily to £200,000 in 1497–1507. In the course of the fifteenth century, trade through Hull declined by an estimated 75 per cent.[56]

---

[53] J. N. Bartlett, 'Robert Holme Citizen and Merchant of York', *Jnl Bradford Textile Soc.*, 98 (1952–3).
[54] See appendix 3.
[55] Miskimin, *Early Renaissance Europe*, p. 96; Bolton, *Medieval English Economy*, pp. 294, 299.
[56] Bartlett, 'Expansion and Decline', p. 28; *VCH York*, p. 105.

Not surprisingly, the number of indigenous merchants trading through Hull had fallen by the late fifteenth century: those identified from York, Beverley and Hull by about 37 per cent to 227. With the exception of group D, each group had shrunk in number, and although their relative relationships had not changed, the degree of difference between them had changed. Of all the merchants traced, 63 per cent were the least active, group D; 11 per cent were in group B and 7 per cent in group A. Far fewer merchants were able to maintain a high annual investment and certainly fewer merchants achieved the scale of business of Robert Ward.

The nature of merchant businesses had altered in response to changes in the international situation: access to the Baltic had all but closed and the loss of Burgundy to the French had seriously undermined the French wine trade. The most immediate differences were the increasing degree of diversification amongst the larger-scale businesses and the contraction of investment in wool.

Among the merchants in groups C and D the same characteristics were evident as in the earlier periods: goods were sent in one or occasionally two shipments a year and the merchants in the group concentrated on the export of cloth and import of miscellaneous goods. A handful dealt in more specialist commodities: Robert Bennington of Hull exported lead regularly between 1461 and 1472, and imported more wine and stockfish than mixed goods. The quantities were usually very small: a typical year was 1466–7 when he exported lead worth £1 13s 4d and imported stock-fish worth £8. A small number of group C and D merchants exported wool, even though it was no longer a major export commodity. John Dalton of Hull was one of the more active merchants in this trade and shipped wool worth £10 in 1469–70, £26 in 1471–2 and £32 in 1473. More merchants in group D were importing wine than had previously been the case and about 25 per cent imported some wine, albeit in such small quantities as one pipe. This increased diversification among the smaller merchants was a useful strategy in reacting to alien competition.

Compared with the figures for the late fourteenth century, the number of merchants in group B was reduced by almost two thirds. Again, with the exception of a few merchants who exported wool only, the story is one of diversification. There was less dependence on the export of cloth and on exports generally. Exports included more lead and foodstuffs, and less cloth. No member of the group exported cloth only and even William Todd of York, a relatively big cloth exporter, regularly exported quantities of lead. In 1464, for example, he exported twelve undyed cloths and lead worth £16 13s 4d; twenty-one undyed cloths and lead worth £26 13s 4d in 1471–2. Henry Williamson of York exported eight and a half undyed cloths, together with beer and victuals worth £6 8s 4d, in 1461; leather worth £6 and twenty-nine undyed cloths in 1471–2. Such mixed exports suggest that merchants in group B could no longer depend on cloth as their staple export. Increasingly their imports were exceeding their exports and they were apparently settling more into the role of general goods importers than of primarily exporters. For instance, Thomas Neleson of York, a regular trader, exported cloth, lead and wool worth £210 and imported goods worth £364 and six tuns of wine, between 1460 and 1472.

Very few merchants relied heavily on wool: Thomas Lokton of York was one, exporting only wool between 1466 and 1471, shipping over £200 worth in three years. Others in group A, John Marshall and John Thirsk of York, as well as John Swan of Hull, were also wool-only exporters. The evidence suggests that if a merchant could ship wool in sufficient quantities, his export business could survive on wool alone, whereas even the biggest cloth exporters had to export other goods. It must be remembered, however, that each of these staplers had a significant investment in imports, even though (on customs evidence at least) their trade was balanced in favour of their wool exports. Were their unimported profits financing the import trade of others in the region?

The number of merchants in group A had diminished dramatically to sixteen. They were also diversifying their export cargoes and investing more in imports. John Kent of York exported goods worth approximately £289 between 1460 and 1467 but his imports were worth £533 and twenty-five tuns of wine. The biggest shipments of the group tended to be of imports rather than big wool exports as in the two earlier periods. John Wood of Hull, for example, imported miscellaneous goods worth £313 6s 8d in three shipments in 1470–1. Moreover, while each of them regularly had an annual turnover in excess of £100, no individual reached the scale of trade that had been a characteristic of the largest investors in the late fourteenth century. The nearest was probably Thomas Beverley of York, whose average annual trade was worth just over £250 for three separate years between 1460 and 1473. None of the group depended solely on cloth exports, and John Gaunt, who exported 150 undyed cloths and only £7 6s 8d worth of lead and leather in four years between 1464 and 1473, was unusual.[57]

SEPARATE TOWNS, SEPARATE FORTUNES

It may be misleading to attempt to locate every merchant within a particular town, since mobility was one of the characteristics of a trader.

---

[57] Marion Kent, in group C, was more typical of the big cloth merchants in exporting lead of approximately the same value as her cloth exports: PRO, E122/62/12, 13, 16, 19.

Table 8.3. *The merchants of York, Beverley and Hull and overseas trade by town group*

	1306–36					1378–1408					1460–1500				
	A	B	C	D	Total	A	B	C	D	Total	A	B	C	D	Total
York															
No. of merchants in each category:															
	9	12	15	23	59	24	37	48	95	204	9	11	20	55	95
Same as %:															
	15	20	25	40	100	12	18	23	47	100	9	12	21	58	100
Beverley															
No. of merchants in each category:															
	24	22+	10★	21	77	7★	10	4	22	43	1	2	2	19	24
Same as %:															
	31	29	13	27	100	16	23	10	51	100	4	8	8	80	100
Hull															
No. of merchants in each category:															
	2	6	5	8	21	13★	13	13★	25	64	6	11	21	70	108
Same as %:															
	9	29	24	38	100	20	20	20	40	100	6	10	19	65	100

Notes:

A includes those merchants with an annual turnover worth over £100.
B includes those merchants with an annual turnover worth £50–£100.
C includes those merchants with an annual turnover worth £25–£50.
D includes those merchants with an annual turnover worth £0–£25.

★ includes one Beverley/Hull merchant.
+ includes one Beverley/York merchant.

Moreover, there was a certain amount of coming and going between York, Beverley and Hull, creating a fairly fluid situation. Tirwhits and Kelsterns, for example, can be found trading from both Beverley and York in the 1330s, Frosts in Beverley and Hull around 1400, Fishers from Beverley and Hull, and Ferribys in York and Hull in the 1460s, while in 1469 a Beverley mercer owned a ship in Hull.[58]

However, the majority traded under one flag as it were, and by aggregating their commerce town by town, a sharper profile of each town's group of overseas merchants can be constructed for the periods under discussion. Their experiences were significantly different. The evidence collated in table 8.3 reveals that Beverley men were most active in trade

[58] See Kermode, 'Merchants of York, Beverley and Hull', appendix 4; Wm Hewitt, Prob. Reg. IV, f. 137.

in the early fourteenth century when, taking advantage of their proximity to the Wolds, they began to challenge the dominant Italians. In three customs rolls between 1306 and 1311, Beverley merchants outnumbered those of York, and in 1306–7 Beverley merchants exported more wool than those of York.[59] Wool exports by the York merchants, on the other hand, exceeded those of the Beverley men by thirty-seven sacks in 1311–12, and this small margin was maintained, certainly until 1325–6.[60] However, a document of 1338 acknowledging royal debts to Yorkshire merchants after the 1337 monopoly and granting repayment against the subsidy on wool exports, shows Beverley still to be the dominant trading town. It lists thirty-eight merchants from Beverley, eleven from York and one from Hull. The Beverley men were responsible for loans totalling £7,661 4s 1d; the York men for £3,556 15s 3d; and the solitary Hull man, William de la Pole, was responsible for £4,362 11s 1d.[61]

In turn, the Beverley men were losing ground to local rivals by the 1360s, in so far as levels of wool purchasing were reflected in the numbers prosecuted for buying wool at measures below the statute weight in 1361. Of those charged, the largest group of twenty-seven, including a butcher, came from York and had been buying mainly in the North and East Ridings. Only six men from Beverley and one from Hull were prosecuted, and their purchases had been confined to the East Riding. A handful of others, from Malton, Rydale, Pocklington, Sutton and Stockton-on-the-Moor, also appeared.[62] Perhaps the Beverley merchants were more circumspect, or, as seems likely, their investments in wool were beginning to shrink. Some continued, though in closer partnership with competitors than was perhaps wise: John Humbrecolt of Beverley was dealing with London woolmongers in 1389.[63] By the 1370s, producers were finding it more difficult to sell their wool, especially in the north-east of England. More fells were exported, perhaps in response to increasing demand from the Dutch textile workers around Leiden.[64]

The reasons why Beverley's merchants lost ground, just as textile production and overseas trade were booming, can only be surmised. Maybe the Black Death had decimated their ranks beyond recovery and the greater attractions of York diverted immigrants away. Hull was growing fast and active merchants basing themselves in the port included some from Beverley families: Alcocks, Holmes, Hadelsays and Bromptons. It

---

[59] PRO, E122/55/22 (1306–7); 56/8 (1308–9); 56/13 (1310–11).
[60] PRO, E122/56/15 (1311–12); 6/11; 56/16, 17, 19, 20, 23, 26; 57/3, 5–8, 10–12, 21, 27; 58/18; 157/6 (1312–26).   [61] PRO, E122/177/33.   [62] Putnam, *Yorks Sessions*, pp. 13–15, 84–5.
[63] *CCR 1385–9*, p. 573. Several Beverley Humbrecolts had exported wool earlier in the century: Kermode, 'Merchants of York, Beverley and Hull', Appendix 4.
[64] Lloyd, *English Wool Trade*, pp. 310–12; Kerling, *Commercial Relations with England*, pp. 65–6.

may well have been that York's larger textile industry was beginning to attract more wool, as well as more immigrant craftsmen. Certainly the numbers of new freemen rose rapidly between 1351 and 1361, especially in the crafts associated with textile production, and although much of that immigration was triggered by the Black Death, it is significant that York proved to have the greater pull.

Compared to Beverley, York was prospering and the city enjoyed boom conditions during the second and third quarters of the fourteenth century, directly related to its increased textile production and rising investment in international trade. As a group, the overseas merchants based in the city achieved considerable prosperity.[65] Their numbers seem to have quadrupled and in 1398–9 York merchants may have been responsible for a turnover of at least £10,387 out of a total trade turnover through Hull that year of some £25,000. At times they outnumbered those from any other English town trading in Prussia.[66]

By the late fourteenth century the number of Beverley merchants had almost halved whereas those from York and Hull had more than trebled. York's dominance was clear, although Hull's share of overseas trade was expanding rapidly. Few Hull men had been involved in Edward III's monopoly, and only one was charged with buying underweight wool in 1361.[67] However, a Hull merchant had been trading in Hamburg in 1308 and others had been licensed to purvey victuals in 1319, 1321 and 1322, and were active in the coastal trade. John Bedford, for example, was shipping goods worth £60 to Newcastle in 1316 when his ship was blown off course onto the Norwegian coast.[68] In 1347–8 Durham Priory had eight tuns of wine, purchased in Hull, sent by sea to Newcastle, and was using the same route in 1504–5.[69] Hull men were also increasingly engaged in direct trade with Europe, especially in exporting grain and peas. Walter Helleward and Roger Swerd shipped wheat, peas and beans, 400 qts in all, to Gascony in 1336; John Helleward and John de Barton, wheat and corn in 1347. Adam Pund and Richard Santon of Hull shipped grain to Portugal in the same year.[70] By the 1380s and 1390s, the number of Hull merchants active in overseas trade had trebled since a generation earlier.

It is possible to create a series of comparisons of the relative values of specific commodity trades between each town by refining this analysis further. Tables 8.4 and 8.5 are statements of the differences between each

[65] Bartlett, 'Expansion and Decline', pp. 20, 22.   [66] See above, note 8.
[67] Adam Pund; see Putnam, *Yorks Sessions*, pp. 13–15, 84–5.
[68] Henry Damel, *CCR 1307–13*, pp. 68–9, 211; *1313–18*, p. 326.
[69] *Durham Acct Rolls*, II, p. 545; III, p. 658.
[70] *CPR 1334–8*, p. 345; *1345–8*, pp. 216, 281, 282; *CCR 1349–54*, pp. 34, 59.

Table 8.4. *Comparative trade figures,*
fourteenth century

8.4.1 1391–2 wool and cloth exports

	Wool (by quantity)	Cloth (by value)
York	1,515 sacks	£2,387
Hull	16 sacks + 2,758 fells	£317
Beverley	156 sacks + 2,033 fells	£297

Source: PRO, E122 59/23, 24.

8.4.2 1398–9 cloth exports and imports

	Cloth (by value)	Wine (non-sweet, in tuns)	Miscellaneous imports (by value)
York	£986	432	£764
Hull	£144	200	£112
Beverley	£97	16	£120

Source: PRO, E122/159/11. This is a tonnage and poundage ledger and therefore does not include wool.

town's merchant investment at five points: 1391–2, 1398–9, 1430–1, 1466–7 and 1471–2.[71] They are derived by aggregating the information available for each identified merchant on a town-by-town basis. This is not an entirely satisfactory method, since prominent individuals may be missed fortuitously by the choice of year. However, it does give rather more precise views of the trends which developed between 1376 and 1500.

Table 8.4 confirms the relative position of the three towns in the late fourteenth century, notably the pre-eminence of York in every branch of trade. Most remarkable is the evidence of Beverley's failure to move into the cloth trade to compensate for a shrinking wool trade. It may have

---

[71] These years have relatively full records and were chosen to match Dr Bartlett's assessment for York's trade in the same years. He claimed a number of Beverley and Hull men as York merchants. The error is quite understandable, since there is no reason to suppose that there might be more than one branch of a family with the same surname, nor indeed several men with exactly the same name as in the case of the possible five Robert Holmes! The misidentification may be mine of course, and if some merchants were freemen of all three towns, then there may have been one man and not five. Most of the wrong ascriptions, though, were not names which appeared several times in all three towns: Bartlett, 'Expansion and Decline', p. 25; 'Aspects of the Economy of York', pp. 353–78.

been that the magnetic pull of York at its zenith, or even the attraction of an expanding Hull within the relative openness of the cloth trade, was too tempting, so that Beverley drifted into an economic backwater. The broadening base of cloth merchants evident in York and Hull was absent in Beverley, where most of the bigger merchants were still investing in wool. Even more significantly, investment in the wine trade was minimal. Low investment in the cloth and wine trades persisted into the next century.

In table 8.5, Beverley's withdrawal from international trade by 1466–7 is starkly revealed, although a comparison with 1471–2 suggests 1466–7 might have been an unusually unsuccessful year. Only one merchant had an annual turnover in excess of £100 and another two had trade worth over £50 (see table 8.3). Beverley's strength was still in the wool trade, but there were merchants investing in cloth exports in 1471–2 and several had doubled the value of their miscellaneous imports. No traceable Beverley merchant exported lead, foodstuffs or general commodities, and the almost complete absence of wine in Beverley cargoes is notable. This contraction was almost certainly the inevitable result of being squeezed between two geographically advantaged neighbours. Moreover, Beverley's physical location, which had once served the wool-producing Wolds so well, had now isolated the town from the increasingly lucrative trade in Pennine lead.

It was the lead trade, as well as early and collective investment in general exports, which marked Hull out from its neighbours and accounted for the increase in the number of its merchants. The river system which bypassed Beverley brought Derbyshire and Yorkshire lead via the Trent, Aire, Ure, Nidd, Wharfe and Ouse straight to Hull's quays. In 1465–6 fourteen Hull merchants exported lead worth £612 and six York merchants lead worth £296. Although the value of lead exports had fallen in 1466–7, the trend was well established, and Hull's superiority in lead exports was maintained into the 1470s, until eventually Hanse merchants, advantaged by the Treaty of Utrecht in 1474, wrested the trade away.[72]

Other features of Hull's trade during the late fifteenth century are worth observing. One was the tendency of its burgess mariners[73] and shipmasters, with easy access to ships, overseas ports and buyers, to venture small sums in trade on their own behalf: men like William Bank and Robert Bennington, Henry Stable and Robert Stevenson. Many remained small-scale, very occasional investors, but some did build up a

---

[72] *VCH Hull*, p. 67; Bartlett, 'Expansion and Decline', p. 19.

[73] It was customary for part of a mariner's wages to be paid by allowing him to ship goods free: Salzman, *English Trade*, pp. 238–9; Twiss, *Black Book of the Admiralty*, III, p. 197.

respectable business. Robert Michelson was one such fortunate man. In 1449 a man of that name (his father ?) had had a share in the *Margaret* of Hull. Robert became a burgess of Hull as a mariner in 1463, and imported about £12 worth of wine and goods the following year. In 1466–7 and 1470–1 his turnover was about £15–£20 and in 1471 he received a £5 annuity from the Hull customs for his service to Edward IV, which was increased to £10 for life in 1485. Michelson was still active as the master of the *Peter* of Hull in 1489–90, with a share in a consortium exporting fourteen cloths and goods worth £16.[74]

Another notable difference in Hull's commercial fortunes was a surge of collective enterprise in the 1460s and 1470s. In 1463 Hull was granted £40 a year from the customs in the form of free trade for its burgesses.[75] This could have been a strong stimulus for the mayor and corporation to sponsor seven shipments worth £721 in 1465: generally made up of barley, honey, butter, and items such as hats, kettles and so forth destined for Iceland.[76] Several private consortia were formed, mainly by the more active merchants in groups A and B, and that trade alone accounted for exports worth £480 in 1466–7. The consortia, following the council's short-lived example, also concentrated on exporting general merchandise, with an occasional return cargo of wine. In 1466–7, Edmund Coppendale, William Eland, Nicholas Ellis and Thomas Etton jointly exported £480 worth of victuals; in 1469–70, Robert Alcock, William Brompton and John Whitfield imported thirty-two tuns; in 1470–1, Brompton, Whitfield, Robert Bennington and Thomas Patrington collaborated in exporting £200 worth of beer, barley, butter, linen, bonnets and other items; and Brompton, Robert Alcock, Roger Bushell and John Ricard exported a similar cargo worth £240 in the following year.

Collaborative ventures effectively spread the risk and seemed a popular form of investment for some. Three consortia in 1469–70 exported £60, £80 and £240 worth of goods. Thomas Alcock belonged to two of them, to two more importing wine in the same year, and to another exporting £48 worth of victuals in 1470–1. His brother Robert belonged to exporting consortia in 1469–70, Brompton's in 1471–2 and to two wine importing consortia in 1469–70.[77]

There is no sign of equivalent collective investment in either York or Beverley in this period, even though it was possible through the York Merchant Adventurers' Company. One or two Beverley and York men joined consortia ventures in 1489–90 when Lawrence Swattock, Ralph Langton, Henry Mindram and other Hull merchants, plus Richard York of York, jointly exported twenty-nine cloths and goods worth £80 10s;

---

[74] Hull RO, BRB 1/11; PRO, E122/62/5, 63/8.   [75] *CPR 1461–7*, p. 289.
[76] PRO, E122/62/7.   [77] PRO, E122/62/9, 10, 12–16.

Table 8.5. *Comparative trade figures, fifteenth century*

8.5.1 1430–1 cloth exports

	value
York	£1,869
Hull	£140
Beverley	£9 10s

Source: PRO, E122/51/32.

8.5.2 1466–7 exports and imports (by value and bulk)

	Exports				Imports	
	Cloth	Wool	Lead	Misc.	Wine	Misc.
York	212 v. £318 (57%)	282 sacks (31%)	£2	£42	79 tuns (26%)	£1,105
Hull	50 v. £75 (24%)	111 sacks (12%) + 4,232 fells	£225	£788	39 tuns (13%)	£83
Beverley		43 sacks (5%) + 6,000 fells			9 tuns (3%)	£32

Note:
The percentages are of the total quantity of a given commodity shipped by all merchants, denizen and alien.

1466–7 total wool exported = 896.5 sacks + 22,957 fells (95.5 sacks)
      total cloth exported = 374 cloths without grain
      total wine imported = 300 tuns 1 pipe
      total miscellaneous goods = £3,495
Source: PRO, E122/52/9, 10.

fourteen cloths and goods worth £16; and without Richard York exported fifteen cloths and goods worth £66; while a second group of John Armstrong of Beverley, Edward Baron of Hull and others exported nine cloths and goods worth £18.[78]

What of York's late-fifteenth-century trends? Table 8.5 attests to a continuing dominance in both the cloth and wool trades, as well as in wine and miscellaneous imports. Indeed wine imports by York merchants almost quadrupled between 1466–7 and 1471–2, from 79 tuns to 302 tuns. York merchants were slower than their Hull neighbours to move into lead as an alternative export commodity to cloth, but by 1471–2

[78] *M&MA*, pp. 40, 68, 72–3, 195; *CPR 1476–85*, p. 455; *VCH Hull*, p. 42; PRO, E122/63/8.

8.5.3 1471–2 exports and imports (by value and bulk)

	Exports				Imports	
	Cloth	Wool	Lead	Misc.	Wine	Misc.
York	395 v. £593 (47%)	145 sacks (36%)	£371	0	302 tuns (48%)	£1,161
Hull	228 v. £342 (27%)	55 sacks (14%) + 5,576 fells	£489	£329	168 tuns (27%)	£256
Beverley	51 v. £76 (6%)	51 sacks (13%)	0	0	1 pipe	£65

Note:
The percentages are of the total quantity of a given commodity shipped by all merchants, denizen and alien.

1471–2 total wool exported = 402 sacks + 48,993 fells (204 sacks)
      total cloth exported = 840 cloths without grain
      total wine imported = 631 tuns 1 pipe
      total miscallenous goods = £3,781 10s
Source: PRO, E122/62/16, 17.

were beginning to catch up, only to be overtaken like every other denizen by the resurgent Hanse in the 1480s. Unlike Hull merchants, men from York never did invest heavily in the Icelandic trade or mixed export cargoes. The apparent upturn in York's fortunes was short-lived and by 1525 the value of its trade was £2,502.[79]

The overall pattern of change in overseas trade as it affected the merchant groups of each of the three towns is fairly clear, but how did it affect relations between them? While the merchants from each town may have been united in their opposition to the infiltration of southern and alien merchants into northern markets, there was still antagonism between them. As commercial competition became more intense so did inter-town hostility. It was particularly apparent in Hull's insistence on treating merchants from York and Beverley as it would any other foreigners. In 1448, for example, Beverley and Hull were disputing the claim of Beverley merchants to the right of toll-free passage for their goods through the haven of Hull into the Humber.[80] This particular dispute was

---

[79] Bartlett, 'Expansion and Decline', p. 31.
[80] Both York and Hull, along with other commercial centres, passed regulations, particularly hosting orders, to control the activities of aliens residing or trading in their midst. Attention to these intensified as commerce contracted. See *VCH York*, p. 105; *VCH Hull*, pp. 50–2; A. A. Ruddock, 'Alien Hosting in Southampton in the 15th Century', *EcHR*, 16 (1946), pp. 30–7.

settled amicably; but in 1487 regulations passed by the Hull council to protect the employment of Hull men servicing ships in the port were specifically directed against Beverley men.[81]

The hostility between York and Hull merchants was more difficult to appease since they were competing for the same business, whereas Beverley merchants were slowly being pushed out of international trade. Merchants from both York and Hull sought an alternative to the Baltic in trade with Iceland. It was conducted under licence and in the late fifteenth century York men were complaining that Hull merchants were engaged in illegal trade with Iceland, to the detriment of the York men.[82] In 1463, York city council was concerned at its loss of control over its own merchants, accusing its Hull counterpart of allowing York merchants to complete transactions with foreign importers in Hull. By 1508, the fear grew that Hull was refusing to allow York men to deal directly with foreigners and was imposing extra heavy local duties on York merchandise.[83]

CONCLUSION

Observing what was a fluid and changing situation, recorded in incomplete records has exposed the differences between York, Beverley and Hull sharply. Isolating three periods for closer study has made it possible to describe the shifting involvement of the three towns in overseas trade, rising to a peak in the later fourteenth century as more men invested in cloth exports, and contracting again under the impact of Hanse hostility and deepening international recession. By the mid-fifteenth century, and possibly earlier, there was little that the Yorkshire merchants could do to prevent their share in overseas trade from dwindling. Some continued to export cloth, wool, lead and foodstuffs, and to import a range of raw materials and manufactured goods, but they no longer dominated the export of the region's cloth, nor indeed the supply of northern beef to the southern counties. In both they had been supplanted by others, mainly Londoners, whose access to superior financial resources and predominance in the Low Countries enabled them to undermine the long-distance trading enterprise from much of provincial England.

To a considerable extent, each town's group of merchants was equally vulnerable to the collapse of the wool trade, exclusion from the Baltic

---

[81] W. Brown, ed., *Yorkshire Star Chamber Proceedings*, I, YAS Rec. Ser., 41 (1909), p. 151; Bartlett, 'Aspects of the Economy of York', p. 68.

[82] *VCH York*, pp. 104–5; J. Tickhill, *A History of the Town and County of Kingston-upon-Hull* (Hull, 1878), p. 107.

[83] PRO, C1/17/111; Carus-Wilson, 'Iceland Trade', p. 169; *VCH Hull*, p. 51; *M&MA*, pp. 119–20.

markets and consequent downgrading of their financial resources. They all suffered from the loss of Burgundy and the growth of the port of London in every branch of trade, but the pace and timing of their losses differed. York's contraction was perhaps the most dramatic, given that city's earlier confident presence in international markets.

By locating individuals within a collective assessment of each town's merchant group, interesting perspectives emerge. In each period there was a core of conspicuously successful individuals, full-time merchants, augmented by less active traders. These smaller scale traders were always more numerous, suggesting that a variety of individuals occasionally invested in a single shipment as the opportunity presented itself. This raises questions over the exclusivity of occupational ascriptions and the dangers of relying on those alone. Striking anomalies emerge. Even as the fortunes of the Beverley and York groups foundered, there were some outstandingly successful traders. In late fourteenth-century Beverley, Richard Aglyon, William Brid and Roger Ruyston each had a high annual turnover in wool. As York's share of overseas markets contracted, John Gaunt, father and son, sustained a profitable business as general merchants between 1462 and 1473. Other flourishing York traders were John Ince, between 1437 and 1472, and Thomas Neleson, between 1440 and 1475 or later. This suggests that individual entrepeneurship could make a difference even within the wider context of regional disadvantages.

9

MERCANTILE ESTATES

Wealth was a key determinant of status in medieval society, except perhaps in the case of butchers, a group rarely represented in elite urban circles. Townsfolk equated social position and political power with the economically successful: invariably the highest skilled craftsmen but more commonly merchants. Although a disposable income and comfortable lifestyle were the most obvious manifestations of commercial profit, savings were invested less visibly in land and property in all its forms: houses, rents and leases. It is possible to posit the size of mercantile estates in terms of accumulated cash and property at will-making, but more difficult to assess the management of assets during a person's life.

Entrepreneurs could not detach real estate revenue from the rest of the business cycle of trade and credit since each had an impact upon the other. This was demonstrated in north-east England, when tumbling property values deepened the major economic recession of the 1430s.[1] The role of real property and especially of rents in capital formation remains uncertain.[2] An investment in rents has been likened to the advantages of deposit banking with similar long-term attractions in a stable or expanding land market. However, the fall in rural land values after the Black Death, followed by a decline in urban rents from the 1420s,[3] would extend the period of return and probably discouraged large-scale investment in property.

ACCUMULATED WEALTH: REAL ESTATE

The fundamental importance of real property in the evolution and persistence of a landed social and political hierarchy and in the development

---

[1] Pollard, *North-Eastern England*, pp. 48–51.

[2] R. H. Hilton, 'Rent and Capital Formation in Feudal Society', in *Second International Conference of Economic History, Aix–en-Provence, 1962* (Paris, 1965), pp. 66–7. See O'Connor, *Cartularies of Pyel and Fraunceys*, pp. 37–75, for a discussion of two fourteenth-century Londoners' real estate investment in and around London.

[3] Hatcher, 'The Great Slump', pp. 247, 259–61; Keene, *Survey of Winchester*, I, pp. 100, 243–8.

of English law, encourages historians to accept a simple socio-political perspective. Territorial possession carried and symbolised jurisdictional and political authority at the personal and national level, but the role of land-ownership in the medieval economy was complex as men and institutions acquired property by various means and for many reasons. Property generated income through rents and, in the countryside, through direct demesne farming. Both fluctuations in revenue and crop yields have been favoured by historians seeking explanations for long-term economic trends in agriculture. Traditionally then, most discussions of land in the economy have concentrated on the management of rural estates, especially those of major religious institutions such as Durham and Canterbury Cathedral Priories.[4] However, lay property holding in towns has scarcely been discussed.

Urban estates are harder to identify, even though religious houses invested heavily in towns: six religious institutions owned over 1,000 properties in York, but only the Vicars' Choral estate can be readily described.[5] Lay urban estates are even more elusive.[6] Few merchants accumulated large urban holdings, certainly not as permanent estates, and where it has been possible to calculate, their income from urban rents was rarely very high.[7] Even taking rural property into account, few Yorkshire merchants acquired large estates outright and the majority held scattered parcels of land, assorted tenements and rent charges, that is, limited assignments in rents.[8]

Some impression of how economically significant as a group merchants[9] were, ranked against other property owners, is suggested by the

[4] Dobson, *Durham Priory*; C. Dyer, *Lords and Peasants in a Changing Society. The Estates of the Bishopric of Worcester, 680–1540* (Cambridge, 1980); B. Harvey, *Westminster Abbey and its Estates in the Middle Ages* (Oxford, 1977); M. Mate, 'The Estates of Canterbury Cathedral Priory before the Black Death', *Studies in Medieval and Renaissance History*, 8 (1987), pp. 3–31, and 'Agrarian Economy after the Black Death: The Manors of Canterbury Cathedral Priory, 1348–91', *EcHR*, 2nd ser., 37 (1984), pp. 341–54.

[5] S. R. Rees Jones, 'Some Aspects of the Topography and Economy of Medieval York' (Univ. of York D.Phil thesis, 1987), pp. 199–200, 278–82. The Vicars' Choral estate is described in F. Harrison, *Life in a Medieval College: The Story of the Vicars Choral of York Minster* (London, 1952).

[6] One example is the Catesby estate in Coventry which may have yielded just over £36 in 1360, £25 in 1457, and £16 in 1484: N. W. Alcock, 'The Catesbys in Coventry: A Medieval Estate and its Archives', *Midland History*, 15 (1990), pp. 1–36 at p. 15.

[7] W. G. Hoskins, 'English Provincial Towns in the Sixteenth Century', in his *Provincial England* (London, 1963), pp. 77–8; R. H. Hilton, 'Some Problems of Urban Real Property in the Middle Ages', in C. H. Feinstein, ed., *Socialism, Capitalism and Economic Growth: Essays Presented to Maurice Dobb* (Oxford, 1967), p. 331; Langton, 'Late Medieval Gloucester', p. 271.

[8] London merchants achieved a similar pattern of land-holding: O'Connor, *Cartularies of Pyel and Fraunceys*, pp. 52–4; Thrupp, *London Merchant Class*, pp. 119, 122.

[9] Compared with Londoners, the average Yorkshire merchant was not wealthy in terms of either cash or landed income. The 1436 Lay Subsidy for London reveals that 145 merchants comprised 73 per cent of all the citizens assessed at over £10. Of those merchants, 84 (84 per cent) were assessed at over £20 and five merchant aldermen at over £100: PRO, E179/238/90. See Thrupp,

lay subsidies which were assessed on income from real estate in town and country. In the 1412 subsidy returns, only three merchants were assessed at £20 in York, whereas in Beverley, merchants accounted for four out of the six so assessed and in Hull, merchants accounted for three out of five taxed landowners.[10] In York by 1436, the twenty-five merchants were the second largest group assessed (23 per cent), after the forty-two chaplains (39 per cent). Merchants comprised 18 per cent of those with incomes from land assessed at £5 per annum; 18 per cent of those assessed at £6–£10; 47 per cent of those assessed at £11–£20; and 33 per cent of those assessed at £21 and over. John Bolton was quite exceptional, being assessed at £62.[11] If he made a will it has not survived, so we cannot describe the scale, type or distribution of his holdings. By contemporary standards though, his income from property was considerable, closely matching his high investment in wool exports.[12] Other stray references suggest that he was not an isolated example. By the late fifteenth century, William Neleson and John Gilyot were said to derive over £40 a year from their property, and Richard York's manor of Sledmore was said to be worth £30 a year.[13]

These were exceptional and, perhaps, inspiring examples. Few others accumulated such propertied wealth. None the less merchants continued to acquire property in all its forms: as free- and lease-hold, rents, rent-charges and annuities;[14] by outright purchase, through reversionary interests and defaulted debts.[15] Real property was a more versatile asset than has perhaps been supposed, and could be employed in many ways for commercial and legal, as well as personal, purposes. Undoubtedly an over-riding motive for many was to ensure spiritual security for themselves, by investing in prayers and charity, and to provide temporal security for their children.[16] Others, with more worldly aspirations, may even have tried to build up rural estates to satisfy social ambitions and to ease their transition into the gentry.[17] But even in those instances, capital tied up in land had to play some part in the overall enterprise of the individual merchant.

London Merchant Class, p. 126; M. Albertson, 'London Merchants and Their Landed Property During the Reigns of the Yorkists' (Univ. of Bryn Mawr PhD thesis, 1932), pp. 63–4.

[10] In York, thirty-seven individuals were assessed at £20, sixteen were of the gentry and nobility: *Feudal Aids*, VI (HMSO, 1921), pp. 544–6.   [11] PRO, E179/217/42.

[12] See biography in appendix 3.

[13] *VCH York*, p. 113; *Cal. Inq. Post Mortem HVII*, II (HMSO, 1915), pp. 95–6.

[14] Investment in rent-charges or annuities was more common on the continent. Hilton, 'Some Problems of Urban Real Property', pp. 336–7; H-P. Baum, 'Annuities in Late Medieval Hanse Towns', *Business History Review*, 59 (1985), pp. 24–48.

[15] See Horrox, *The de la Poles of Hull*, p. 26; O'Connor, *Cartularies of Pyel and Fraunceys*, pp. 55, 73, for a similar process in London.   [16] Cf. Thrupp, *London Merchant Class*, pp. 122–3.

[17] *Ibid.*, pp. 272, 279–87. See late sixteenth-century Exeter where few could afford to purchase enough land to make the social jump: McCaffrey, *Exeter 1540–1640*, p. 261.

The evidence for mercantile property interests is mainly of two kinds. The first is contained in testamentary records and is problematic because of the particular and additional problems associated with real estate. Burgage property was freely devised in York, Beverley and Hull, and was treated as though it were a piece of moveable property, as were leases and rents.[18] In wills the nature of a tenancy cannot always be established, even though, by the late fourteenth century, wills often dealt with real estate subject to feudal custom. In addition, the nature of the testator's interest was not always made clear.[19] In any case, real estate was not always disposed of in the *ultima voluntas* and may have been dealt with in a separate document. Eldest sons could have received title to the main estate already, obviating the need for its inclusion in the will. This may explain why Nicholas Blackburn snr noted only his house in North Street plus rents in the Shambles and Needlergate in his 1435 will, but the following year his son was assessed as having land worth £15 per annum.[20]

Other sources make it clear that property was not always mentioned in probate records. There was no reference to a garden in John Gyll of Hull's will, but eleven years after his death his widow sold one to pay for his obits. (She may have acquired it subsequently of course.) The expected per annum income from lands assigned to endow a chantry suggests an individual did own some property even when none was specified. Sale values of properties were rarely given, although the value of rents sometimes was. John Fitling's estimate that his twelve messuages and gardens in Hull were worth £30 in 1434 was unusual.[21] The portmanteau term 'all my lands and tenements in York, Beverley, Hull' might have described a single plot or extensive holdings. Inevitably therefore, the historian is assessing a possibly partial statement of uncertain economic values at a random point in an individual's career.

The second type of evidence is even more difficult to assess, since it is that of separate deeds, charters, final concords and bonds which have randomly survived, usually as isolated documents.[22] These are evidence of *inter vivos* transactions and cannot be used to estimate the size of an individual's estate at a given time. They can be used to survey the type of property merchants had, the location, approximate amount (one as

---

[18] *MB*, II, p. 253; *CChR 1257–1300*, pp. 475–6.

[19] The *testamentum* strictly dealt with personal property, chattels, money and debts. The *ultima voluntas* dealt with real estate and had come to be regarded as a means of conveying instructions to feoffees in the fifteenth century. By the fourteenth century, both sections were usually contained in one document: Pollock and Maitland, *English Law*, II, p. 331, and pp. xix–xxi for this development in the Prerogative Court of Canterbury.

[20] Prob. Reg. II, f. 605; PRO, E179/217/42.

[21] Prob. Reg. III, ff. 384v.–5 (Fitling); VI, f. 175 (Gyll); Hull RO, D561.

[22] *Early Yorkshire Charters*; *Yorks Deeds*; *Yorks Fines*; *York Memorandum Book*.

opposed to ten tenements) and sometimes the transmission of property within or outside the family. Lastly, they may explain how property was used as security in raising credit, as a dynamic rather than a fixed asset which allowed the financial exploitation of property beyond the obvious and final cash realised in selling.

Characteristics of mercantile estates

From the scattered locations and different types of property, rents and leases, gardens, assorted tenements and undeveloped plots, we must conclude that merchants were interested in whatever property came their way, although, with the exception of rural manors, mercantile estates were generally not consolidated units, but comprised a piecemeal assortment. Many merchants mentioned no property in their wills and of those who did, most referred to the house they lived in, the capital messuage, and perhaps one or two additional properties. For instance, John Fribois of York, who died in 1362, left his capital tenement, with its shop in Petergate, another tenement in the city and a croft near Monkbar.[23] In Beverley, Thomas Frost left his house plus a garden and orchard in Newbiggin in 1421, while Robert Preston of Hull left one tenement and six cellars there in addition to a house on the outskirts at Southferry in 1347.[24]

Cellars were a common feature of houses in Hull and, to be worthy of mention, were probably particularly large cellars for storing wine. Another feature in Hull was the availability of undeveloped plots in the mid-fourteenth century, either reflecting the slow development of Edward I's new town, or an extensive sub-division of burgages.[25] It was not uncommon for merchants to use them. Gilbert de Bedford was renting six plots from the Crown in 1357, in addition to owning two shops and land in the town fields.[26]

Orchards and gardens were common enough in all three towns, but in Beverley merchants invested in a form of urban farming not practised as extensively by their fellows in either York or Hull, even though both towns had common fields. Beverley retained its common grazing and open fields and many Beverley merchants had selions and crofts in the town fields. Thus Geoffrey Humbrecolt and his wife acquired twenty acres of land and five acres of meadow in Beverley in 1330, and Edmund Portington held a close and several ridges in 1463.[27] The keepers never

[23] York RO, B/Y, f. 110.
[24] Arch. Reg. X, ff. 322–v. (Preston); XIV, f. 18v. (Gervays); XVIII, ff. 384v.–5 (Frost).
[25] Horrox, *Selected Rentals*, p. 10.   [26] Hull RO, BRE I, pp. 23, 132, 138.
[27] *Yorks Fines, 1327–47*, p. 29; Prob. Reg. II, f. 595.

had any difficulty in leasing out the town's grazing, often to themselves, and it would appear that several Beverley merchants were still active in agriculture, albeit in a small way.[28] One indication of the continuing importance of their livestock was William Holme's fight against Wartre Priory for Beverley's rights of common in Saintgilescroft. He won his case in 1412.[29] Farming properties outside the town were small and mainly in East Riding villages close to the town or a little further away, in places like Bainton, Bilton, Sigglesthorne or Wallington. Nicholas Ryse, for example, left two bovates in Wallington, and a part of Speeton Manor.[30]

Merchants often lived in houses which incorporated a shop, as John Fribois did, but it is not clear if any used retail outlets themselves. Some acquired shops which they leased out. Ralph Horneby's twenty-six shops in York were exceptional, certainly when compared to the three shops which William Selby left to the city in 1427, or Robert Holtby's half shop which he devised in his will in 1438.[31] In Beverley and Hull the councils invested in commercial property, building shops as speculative ventures. The Dyngs was purpose built by the Beverley keepers, with shops in front of domestic quarters, and either section could be let. Thus Robert Jackson was renting six shops in the Dyngs from the council for £2 18s 8d in 1449 and Robert White two shops there for 13s 4d in 1494.[32] Four of Robert Crosse's Hull properties included shops, and there is evidence that Hull merchants had shops incorporated into their houses and rented out shops more often than their York or Beverley counterparts. The council was the largest shop rentier in Hull and, for example, leased ten in Kirklane to Walter Helleward in 1351, and two shops and one cellar to Peter Stellar in 1384. Simon Grimsby was renting a tenement and shop from the earl of Suffolk in 1390.[33] The more frequent occurrence of shops and cellars in property dealing amongst Hull merchants perhaps indicates an interest in retail as well as wholesale trade in the late fourteenth century. It was a more cosmopolitan town and could expect numbers of temporary shopkeepers. It is interesting though that in the fifteenth century, investment in shops by Hull and Beverley merchants was not common and only a handful of references have been found: John Carleton owned two in Beckside in 1401.[34]

Merchants took whatever opportunities presented themselves to invest in every conceivable form of property to generate income. One or two

---

[28] Humberside RO, BC II/6/1–15, *passim*.   [29] *Yorks Deeds*, VII, pp. 22–3.
[30] *Ibid*., p. 79; IX, p. 163. See also Arch. Reg. XVI, f. 141 (Carleton); Prob. Reg. II, ff. 86–90v. (Brompton); VI, f. 117 (Armstrong).
[31] Dec. & Cap. I, ff. 227–9 (Selby); Prob. Reg. II, ff. 220–2v. (Horneby); III, f. 542v. (Holtby).
[32] Humberside RO, BC II/6/12, 15.   [33] Hull RO, BRE I, pp. 144, 163; CQ I, f. 5.
[34] Arch. Reg. XVI, f. 141.

Beverley merchants owned or leased mills: William de Wilton a mill on the Beck in 1400 and Thomas Manby a horse-mill in 1402.[35] In Hull, Thomas Ferlay and John Whitfield owned mills in 1463 and 1479 respectively, and John Harrison left both his oil mill and a supply of seed when he died in 1526.[36] Ralph Langton of Hull, who leased the salt-house in High Street from the city council, left twenty weys of salt in 1501.[37] One York merchant, Thomas Holme, acquired a regionally important source of raw material, Stapleton quarry, leaving the remaining years of his lease on it to his nephew in 1406.[38]

They also owned houses and shops in other towns, most often in other market centres in the region. For York merchant testators, Hull, Beverley and Ripon were the most usual locations, followed by Malton, Pontefract, Richmond, Scarborough, Selby and Whitby. Property of York merchants was also to be found further afield in Berwick, Newcastle, Yarm, Preston, Newark and London.[39] Such properties may have been used as much as trading bases as an investment for rents, and individuals rarely owned more than one or two. Oliver Middleton, who owned four tenements in Ripon, was exceptional, and in any case had probably migrated from there.[40] Few Beverley merchants invested in other towns in the fourteenth century: more did so in the fifteenth.[41] Hull was the most common location, maybe because water access from Beverley to the port was worsening. William Hewitt, who died in 1468, found it useful to have a shop there.[42] Hull merchants' investments in other towns were generally limited to a single rent or tenement in Beverley or York.[43] Robert Crosse had a property in Scarborough.[44]

In addition to their investment in property in England, several merchants owned and leased houses and other premises overseas. Most were in Calais and in the Low Countries. Some overseas property was a legacy of migration, just as some rural English property was. Thus Peter Upstall of York still owned property in Harsyll and Brabant in 1430, although a naturalised Englishman.[45]

---

[35] Prob. Reg. III, ff. 74v.–5 (Manby); Arch. Reg. XVI, f. 141 (Carleton's will).

[36] Prob. Reg. II, f. 479v. (Ferlay); V, f. 148v. (Whitfield); IX, f. 328 (Harrison).

[37] Hull RO, BRB 1, f. 177; Prob. Reg. VI, f. 22v.

[38] Prob. Reg. III, f. 225v. See Thrupp, *London Merchant Class*, p. 128 for a similar interest.

[39] William Chimney is the only York merchant discovered with references to London property in his will: Prob. Reg. VIII, f. 3.   [40] Prob. Reg. VI, f. 130.

[41] See, for example, Prob. Reg. III, f. 263 (John Kelk); V, f. 99 (Jackson); Arch. Reg. XVIII, f. 15 (William Kelk).

[42] See also Prob. Reg. II, ff. 86–90v. (John Brompton); III, f. 475 (Thomas Brompton); IV, f. 37 (Hewitt).

[43] Hull RO, D126 (Pund), a 4s rent in Coneystreet, York. See also Prob. Reg. I, f. 98 (Stellar); II, f. 489 (Spencer); IV, f. 79 (Day); VI, f. 22v.(Langton).

[44] Prob. Reg. II, f. 418; Hull RO, D 179.   [45] Prob. Reg. II, f. 633v. (Upstall).

Migrants into medieval towns were as likely to move from a secure base as from poverty. Many left property behind in their place of birth which they used in different ways. Some retained an interest even after long years away.[46] Robert Savage still owned a house in his native Tynemouth at his death in 1398, and at least three other York merchants left property in the north: John Asseby, shops and houses in Richmond; Richard Bagot, the house in Yarm in which his father still lived in 1476; and Sir Richard York, property in his native Berwick in 1498. Ralph Langton of Hull retained extensive property in Northumberland at his death in 1502 and John Thompson of Beverley left property at the opposite end of the country in Dunstable in 1505.[47]

An alternative was to realise the immediate potential of one's patrimony by selling it and transferring funds into an urban business. This was quite a common practice in fourteenth-century York: John Romondby sold Romondby manor in 1368 to raise capital during a time of expanding trading opportunities. Sometimes sales involved property acquired through marriage: in 1354 John Gisburn and his wife sold off her land in Sharrowe, and the next year a fellow York merchant, John de Acastre, and his wife sold her property in Over Catton.[48] The majority of merchants' rural estates comprised small and dispersed holdings, unlikely to provide an independent livelihood.[49] It is impossible to evaluate such estates, beyond assuming that town dwellers probably required the services of a steward to collect rents, negotiate leases or supervise any farming. Most merchants simply listed their property generally by location unless a manor was involved, so that although the list of localities might in itself be extensive, the acreage held may not have been. Robert Collinson of York, for example, held unidentified properties in twenty different rural localities at his death in 1458 without attaching a value or size.[50]

Owning a manor suggests a manageable entity, and one viable as a rural estate.[51] Manors were more numerous among the estates of York and Hull merchants in the fourteenth century, perhaps a consequence of the weak land market following the Black Death. In Hull, Walter Box bought Ackton manor (W.R.) in 1366; Walter Frost, one half of Little Smeaton

---

[46] Many London merchants held small properties throughout England as a result of inheritance: Thrupp, *London Merchant Class*, p. 128.

[47] Prob. Reg. II, ff. 396v.–7v. (Asseby); III, f. 17 (Savage); VI, ff. 22v. (Langton), 146 (Thompson); Dec. & Cap. I, f. 332 (Bagot); PRO Prob. 11/11, f. 36 (York).

[48] *Yorks Deeds*, I, p. 146; *Yorks Fines, 1347–77*, pp. 44, 48.

[49] See, for example, Prob. Reg. V, ff. 215v.–16v. (Thornton snr), 116v. (Thornton jnr); Hull RO, BRE I, p. 87 (Bedford); *Test. Ebor.* I, p. 119 (Ferriby).

[50] Prob. Reg. II, ff. 378–80 (Collinson).

[51] In fourteenth-century London, merchants paid large cash sums for manors, especially those located within easy reach of the city: Thrupp, *London Merchant Class*, p. 120.

manor (W.R.) in 1374; and John Dimelton a share in the lease of Myton manor, including 1,700 sheep and lambs, in 1382.[52] Each transaction was to achieve a different goal. Henry Scoreby, for example, acquired a life interest in Estanfield manor in 1338, probably in resolution of an inheritance.[53] On the other hand, John de Acastre, who had extremely large urban holdings, bought the manor of Asthorpe, Lincolnshire, in 1371 with a partner, from fellow York merchant William Sallay. Acastre continued to live in York, and further evidence of land purchases with Sallay the following year suggests he was a property speculator.[54] In 1381 John Barden of York took a thirty-nine-year lease on Hedelay manor from Holy Trinity Priory, one of his many purchases of rural property. He had bought two mills and land in Aberford in 1374, and when he died in 1396, he left, in addition, property around York and Leeds and the manor of Kydall.[55]

Rural rents had begun to recover by the later fifteenth century, offering a reasonably attractive return to investors. However, the level of Beverley and Hull mercantile investment in country properties apparently remained stable: still on a small scale and invariably within a ten-mile radius. There is some evidence of an increased investment in rural property among York merchants in the later fifteenth century,[56] but only two have been found with manorial interests. Alan Staveley was leasing Acomb manor from the Minster,[57] and Sir Richard York bought Sledmere manor in 1489 and had also acquired the rectory of Ryle in Lincolnshire by his death in 1498.[58] It was uncommon for merchants to own manors before the 1530s.[59] Perhaps the relatively buoyant land market made sizeable rural estates expensive.

Land did convey status but it is difficult to gauge the extent to which merchants aspired to the status of gentlemen or were able to amass sufficient property to live independently of trade. Some entered urban trade with a ready-made country estate. Ralph Langton migrated from Northumberland to Hull, and in 1501 left a house in York, properties in Hull, land in Orde, Unthank, Norhamshire and Hallamshire, and fishing

[52] *Yorks Fines, 1347–77*, pp. 119, 165. 183. See also Hull RO, D150 (Dimelton).

[53] *Yorks Fines, 1327–47*, p. 127.   [54] *Yorks Fines, 1347–77*, pp. 159, 230.

[55] Prob. Reg. I, ff. 95v., 100; *Yorks Deeds*, I, p. 3; *Yorks Fines 1347–77*, p. 175; *CPR 1381–5*, pp. 56, 318. John Gisburn was leasing Raskelf (North Riding): *Cat. Ancient Deeds*, I (HMSO, 1890), A517; *VCH York*, p. 112.

[56] For a fuller discussion see Kermode, 'Merchants of York, Beverley and Hull', chapter 4 and appendix 4.   [57] *Test. Ebor.* IV, p. 295.

[58] *Yorks Deeds*, VII, p. 3; PRO, Prob. 11/11, f. 36 (York).

[59] Palliser, *Tudor York*, p. 204. No manors have been traced to fifteenth-century Hull merchants. However, sixteenth-century Exeter merchants could expect to hold the lordship of one or two manors and to possess farms in half a dozen parishes: Hoskins, 'Merchants of Exeter', p. 176. None the less, according to McCaffrey, few achieved gentry status: *Exeter 1540–1640*, p. 261.

rights in the river Tweed. When his son John died in 1542, the estate was more or less unchanged, including the fishing rights in the Tweed.[60] A century earlier, Ralph Horneby of York more self-consciously purchased property to create an estate in his birthplace, in an apparent display of new wealth aspiring to landed status.[61]

Horneby, a York draper active in overseas trade, died *c.* 1379. He was probably a first-generation immigrant (free in 1351), who built up a sizeable estate in his native Hornby-in-Cleveland through purchases in 1359 and 1368. Nine houses and twenty-six shops were assigned to his chantry in St Helen's, Stonegate in 1379, and in 1428 it was said that at his death he owned thirty-four houses in York, a 6s rent and the advowson of the perpetual chantry of St Michael in St Helen's.[62] By regional standards, his accumulated estate was extensive. Adam Tutbury of Hull's dealings were as interesting for the variety they included. Adam acquired at least sixteen properties in Hull between 1366 and 1390, ranging from empty land near the river Hull, to the lease of a brewhouse and the acquisition of another merchant's entire holdings in Beverley Street, in three separate portions over two years.[63] In addition he acquired rents worth £12 6s 3d.[64] Examples of large-scale property investors were less common among Beverley's merchants, but there were one or two like John Sleford, who left twenty properties in 1449, in addition to his house in Barliholme: fifteen were in the Beckside area and one was outside West Bar.[65]

Sizeable urban estates can be described in all three towns throughout the fifteenth century[66] but, from the available evidence, the most typical merchant holdings comprised three to eight different properties.[67] The pattern of property interests confirms the impression of individuals moving easily between the three towns: acquiring a house or rents in lieu of cash or purchasing with a view to gaining an entree into another town. After all, York burgesses also became freemen of Hull.[68]

[60] Prob. Reg. VI, f. 22v. (Ralph); XI, f. 600 (John).

[61] See p. 283 above. William de Custon, a London mercer, built up an estate in Edmonton between 1307 and 1356, and Pyel was acquiring land for social as well as economic reasons: O'Connor, *Cartularies of Pyel and Fraunceys*, pp. 46–8, 52–4.

[62] *Yorks Deeds*, II, p. 276; *Yorks Fines, 1347–77*, pp. 73, 129; *CPR 1377–81*, p. 375; *CCR 1422–9*, pp. 420–1.   [63] Hull RO, D123, 124, 127, 128A, 128B, 133A.

[64] Hull RO, D121, 122, 128A, 131, 136, 160. See also Robert Crosse who left at least eighteen properties in Hull in addition to extensive rural holdings and shops and houses in several other towns including London and Scarborough in 1395: Hull RO, D179.

[65] Prob. Reg. II, f. 184 (Sleford). See also *ibid.* VI, f. 117 (Armstrong).

[66] William Holbeck was a fifteenth-century equivalent of Ralph Horneby, owning twenty-nine properties, including the Crowned Lion in Micklegate, at his death in 1477: Prob. Reg. V, ff. 122v.–3 (Holbeck). See also *ibid.*, ff. 212–13 (Neleson); VIII, f. 117 (Kirke).

[67] See, for example: Prob. Reg. II, ff. 220–2v. (Bedford), 605 (Blackburn); III, f. 580 (Bowes); IV, f. 235 (Green); V, ff. 483v.–5 (Dalton).

[68] E.g. John Percy and John Raghton: Hull RO, BRE I, pp. 244, 246.

Real estate as assets

An investment in property could be short or long term. It could form part of an ambition to accumulate a landed estate for direct exploitation, to enjoy flexible returns as a rentier, or to establish a dynasty. This was not an ambition which emerges from contemporary sources and it is only occasionally possible to state with certainty that estates were passed on intact. The York Thomas del Gares, father and son, provide an interesting example. Thomas snr granted property in Coneystreet, Little Shambles, Nether and Over Ousegate to his son in 1427, in return for a life pension of 20 marks. When Thomas jnr died in 1445, he left property in Coneystreet, Shambles and Nether Ousegate, but had added more in Goodramgate, Patrick Pool and an empty plot in Calais.[69] In 1413, John Sanderson of Hull left a house in Hull Street, thirteen other properties in Hull and two gardens outside. The bulk of his estate remained intact until his son Thomas sold ten messuages in 1448, probably to meet a liquidity crisis.[70]

In trying to set an overall balance of an individual's enterprises, some assets are not always visible to the modern historian and, indeed, may not always have been to the merchant himself. It was difficult to anticipate the benefits of being a residuary legatee so acquiring wealth which may not have actually been received for several generations or so. Thomas del Gare snr of York, for instance, inherited six selions of land in Newland in 1426, from three generations back.[71] The ubiquitous ascription 'cousin' must have rendered such claims confusing without a strongly persistent family tradition.

So far, most of the evidence examined has been illustrative of a static, single moment in time, and yet it is clear that an individual could receive a life-interest in a property, inherit outright, buy and sell, lease short, medium or long term several times during his lifetime and leave no sign of the frequency or scale of such transactions in his will. The survival of an excellent collection of deeds in Hull[72] demonstrates just how active a property market[73] there was there, and may have been in our other two towns. Again, it is impossible to produce a balanced account for any individual, but Adam Tutbury was engaged in a large number of property

---

[69] Prob. Reg. II, ff. 110v.–11v. (Thomas jnr); Dec. & Cap. II, f. 47 (Thomas snr). See also the Kelk estate, Prob. Reg. III, f. 263 (John); Arch. Reg. XVIII, f. 15 (William); and Langtons, Prob. Reg. VI, f. 22v. (Ralph); XI, f. 600 (John).   [70] Prob. Reg. III, ff. 608–9; Hull RO, D369, 382.

[71] *Yorks Deeds*, IX, p. 129. See also *Yorks Fines, 1347–77*, p. 129; PRO, C1/14/25, 15/86.

[72] L. M. Stanewell, *Calendar of the Ancient Deeds, Letters, Miscellaneous Old Documents etc., in the Archives of the Corporation* (Hull, 1951); R. Horrox, *The Changing Plan of Hull 1290–1650* (Hull, 1978).

[73] In London, property transactions generated enough business for brokerage to be profitable: Thrupp, *London Merchant Class*, p. 128.

deals during his lifetime both in his own right as well as acting as trustee for friends. In Tutbury's case, his will of 1397 revealed nothing of the scale of his activities in property; it referred merely to 'property in Hull', and a messuage and garden which he left to the Corpus Christi Guild. As it happened, he had granted 'all his property in Hull' to a group of trustees, including his son and heir Lawrence.[74] Almost any sort of interest in real estate was valuable, however piecemeal, small and insignificant an individual tenement or rent might seem. That they played a significant part in urban incomes is confirmed by the keen pursuit of small sums of rent arrears: in late fourteenth-century Exeter these comprised 12 per cent of all debt cases.[75] It is likely that many investments were for a short term only.[76] In London, certainly, there were examples of the same property being bought and sold repeatedly within the merchant class.[77]

If investments in property were made to gain a source of immediate income, what level of income might be expected? Where it has been possible to calculate outside London,[78] income from urban rents was rarely high[79] but there were exceptions. Thomas Strykhill of York disposed of rents worth £25 in 1394. However, it is not clear if this was from his own property or if these were rents he had been assigned. Thomas del Gare, also of York, anticipated an annual income of at least £10 from five tenements in York plus 'lands and rents in Calais' in 1438.[80] When John de Ake of Beverley endowed his maisondieu in 1398, he allocated two messuages, two plots and a tenement in the centre of Beverley.[81] A single property might sustain a high rent. In 1444, John Brompton of Beverley expected the rent from a single house in Hull to be a significant contribution to the education of his son Thomas, and in 1458, William Rolleston, also of Beverley, was the recipient of an annual pension of £2 derived from one property in Eastgate. By 1509, John Gilyot jnr of York hoped that an investment of £400 in rural properties would generate an annual income of £7 to pay his chantry priest.[82]

The rate of return on property investment depended on many factors but we lack relevant information for Yorkshire merchants. Sylvia Thrupp, working from fuller records, cites Ralph Honilane, a London vintner, as

---

[74] Prob. Reg. III, ff. 39v.–40; Hull RO, D176 and see Hull biographies in Kermode, 'Merchants of York, Beverley and Hull', appendix 4.   [75] Kowaleski, *Medieval Exeter*, p. 207.

[76] *VCH York*, pp. 112–13.   [77] Thrupp, *London Merchant Class*, p. 128.

[78] In London, some merchants' income from rent was considerable – as high as £80–150 – and a return of 6–8 per cent might have been expected in the fourteenth century, 5 per cent from rural property in the fifteenth century: Thrupp, *London Merchant Class*, pp. 119–30.

[79] Hilton, 'Rent and Capital Formation in Feudal Society', p. 66, and 'Some Problems of Urban Real Property', p. 331; Langton, 'Late Medieval Gloucester', p. 271.

[80] Prob. Reg. I, f. 70 (Strykhill); II, ff. 110v.–11v. (Gare).   [81] *Yorks Deeds*, VII, pp. 26–32.

[82] Prob. Reg. II, ff. 86–90v. (Brompton); 370–v. (Rolleston). For Gilyot, see *ibid.* v, f. 213 (Gilyot); PRO, C142/25/113. I am grateful to David Palliser for this reference.

typical of fourteenth-century merchants. He held two messuages worth £18 from which was diverted an annual rent of £5 to another citizen, 20s to St Giles hospital, 16 per cent was allowed for repairs and he derived a clear £10. Other properties he held, two cellars and two shops, were depreciating at a rate of 6 per cent: a possibly artificially high rate set as a defence against creditors. Taking such aspects as depreciation as well as fluctuating property prices into account, Sylvia Thrupp estimated that when conditions were 'favourable', a return of 6–8 per cent might be expected, falling to 5 per cent in the fifteenth century when rural land values began to rise. Thomas Bataill, for example, left 100 marks in 1445 to purchase a rent charge of 4 marks per annum.[83]

On the basis of testamentary evidence some general trends may be tentatively suggested. There is little evidence of many merchants accumulating sufficient land or rents to achieve 'gentrification'.[84] The majority of investments in land, urban and rural, were short rather than long term.[85] Although there was a noticeable increase in the number of York merchants owning rural estates after the middle of the fifteenth century, this was not a pattern found amongst Beverley or Hull merchants. Leasing selions in their town fields met their domestic needs, in addition to a scatter of small properties in their immediate hinterland.

Large urban estates at death were also unusual amongst Beverley and Hull merchants, although one or two did amass considerable holdings. For the rest it may have been that speculative investment during their lifetimes was simply not reflected in testamentary records. There is enough evidence in York, however, to suggest that investment in urban property was still seen as profitable in the fifteenth century, in spite of falling rents,[86] and that some merchants certainly put some of their surplus into houses, tenements and rents in the city. The possibility that such an action reflected a conscious alternative to investment in contracting overseas trade will be discussed in the conclusion.

Alternatively, merchants acquired property in the routine cycle of business, by accepting leases or rents as security against a deferred payment or as collateral for loans: employing property as another element in a complex arrangement of cash, credit and investment. Even small

[83] Thrupp, *London Merchant Class*, pp. 119, 122–3.
[84] The combining of inherited land and commercial wealth through the marriage of the wealthy John Bolton's daughter Margaret into two county families favoured the gentry side. Margaret inherited three manors from her first husband, Roger Salvayn, in 1420, and her inheritance was ultimately of benefit to the family of her second husband, Henry Gascoigne: Prob. Reg. II, ff. 212–13; v, f. 398–9. [85] *VCH York*, pp. 112–13.
[86] The city could still easily find tenants for centrally located properties in Petergate and Stonegate in the fifteenth century: Rees Jones, 'Aspects of York Topography', pp. 258–61.

properties could be used in such an arrangement.[87] In 1323 Thomas Durant, a York merchant, leased a rent of £1 3s 3d in Marketshire (Pavement) from John Esingwold. John entered a bond to pay Thomas three sacks of good wool worth £20 within four years or to allow Thomas the rent for fifteen years. In addition, if the present tenant Walter Cottingwith died, Thomas was to have first option on any future disposal of the property. On the face of it, this was not an immediately profitable deal, but on the same day that he entered the lease, Thomas let the property to a fourth party for £1 7s. Thomas was seeking advantage where he could, and in 1324 acquired another release from Cottingwith, of a life-interest in a second Pavement property.[88]

In a different sort of transaction merchants accepted property as security against a cash loan. For instance, a York draper, Thomas de Kilburn, did just that in 1382 when he accepted land in Little Ribstan from John Blome against Blome's payment of 10 marks within ten years. The defaulting debtor eventually forfeited the land.[89] The attachment of rents until a debt was settled was a common outcome of legal actions, and was also employed in wills to ensure debts were paid *post mortem*.[90] It is clear that this was anticipated by Thomas Gare of York who specified which properties' rents were to be used. The more famous Richard Cely enfeoffed land to the use of his in-laws until his debts to them were satisfied, and his widow Anne was instructed to sell land in Oxfordshire and Northamptonshire to meet debts.[91] Others effected such settlements during their lifetime. Henry de Belton paid off his debts to a fellow York merchant by transferring a messuage in Coupmanthorpe to him in 1341.[92]

Juggling land and money could create a complex series of negotiations. A fourteenth-century Beverley merchant, William Lyndelowe, provides an excellent example. He had established interests in the village of Escrick when he bought the manor there in June 1341 for £36 13s 8d. Three years later, in May 1344, he assigned an annual rent of £40 derived from all his lands in Escrick to a John Bentlay. Presumably because he became

---

[87] Londoners also raised mortgages on very small acreages of land: O'Connor, *Cartularies of Pyel and Fraunceys*, p. 53.   [88] *Yorks Deeds*, VIII, pp. 175–6.

[89] *Yorks Deeds*, X, pp. 139–40. A better-documented example was that of a London mercer, William Causton, who acquired considerable rural property in the fifteenth century as a consequence of lending money to country folk on the security of their land: Thrupp, *London Merchant Class*, p. 121; see also Gilyot, PRO, C142/25/113.

[90] *Yorkshire Fines 1347–77*, p. 64; *Yorks Deeds*, IX, p. 67; Hull RO, D126. Cf. *Cal. Plea & Mem. Rolls City of London 1413–37*, p. 142; *Cal. London Letter Books*, C, pp. 245–8.

[91] Hanham, *Celys and Their World*, pp. 412, 414.

[92] *Yorks Deeds*, VI, p. 175. John Gudale of York acquired eight tenements in Coliergate from Henry Warwick of Beverley in the same way. See Prob. Reg. II, f. 442. John Barden specified which of his properties were to be sold to meet his debts: *ibid.*, I, ff. 95v., 100.

indebted to Bentlay, Lyndelowe granted all his Escrick property to Bentlay the following year but the grant was to be void if certain conditions were fulfilled. Lyndelowe was to pay Bentlay's debt to Nicholas Trank of Northampton: £40 plus an indemnity of £80, as agreed in a Statute Merchant bond registered in London. He also had to pay an unspecified indemnity to Thomas de Ketryngham and John Randworth. By January 1347 a John de Neuton had acquired the estate and Bentlay and Lyndelowe were releasing all their rights to him.[93] Such a tale raises more questions than can be answered: had Lyndelowe overreached himself in buying the manor? Had he bought it for cash or on credit? Had Bentlay been over-ambitious in his turn? To be as indebted as he became suggests he had large-scale ventures underway. It was not the final balance of either party's profits and losses which was important to their business but rather the shorter term advantages which investing in land brought them.

Such evidence suggests that land was used as an asset in commercial enterprise, 'the mobilisation and de-mobilisation of capital', as Professor Postan once described it.[94] There were other considerations which should not be forgotten. For many medieval people purchasing rent-charges was a way of securing an annuity, and merchant wills confirm that this was an important consideration. How else might an individual ensure an income for his dependants after his death? The clearest example of how a person regarded his real estate in terms of both outright ownership and long-term income is the dispositions made by Thomas Gare. He apparently hoped to arrange his affairs so that his widow Elizabeth would have a life-interest in his property in York, plus £20 from his Calais property if she remained unmarried. Otherwise she was to have one third of 'these lands'. After her death the property was to descend through the male line. At the same time, he wanted to ensure that his two daughters should have 100 marks each for their dowries, and so £10 a year was to be earmarked from the rents and farms on his property in York, the county and Calais, and was to be in the custody of his widow, presumably during the twelve years or so it would take for the dowries to accumulate. He was, in effect, making his property work like an annuity. Richard Hebson of Beverley employed another way of unlocking capital when he left his land to fellow merchant William Rolleston in 1399, on condition that Rolleston paid Hebson's widow and son £3.[95]

The best-documented area of mercantile exploitation of real estate is of its use as security against cash loans or credit. It was common practice

---

[93] *Yorks Deeds*, IX, pp. 65–7.   [94] Postan, 'Credit in Medieval Trade', pp. 248–9.
[95] Prob. Reg. II, ff. 210v.–11v. (Gare); III, f. 24 (Hebson). See also Thrupp, *London Merchant Class*, p. 119.

to raise capital against the security of property: Londoners were doing it in the 1280s, and it was a way to utilise capital which was otherwise trapped. Moreover, it did not seem to matter that the property involved was a scatter of small-holdings, and as we have seen with Thomas Durant, a variety of manipulations of different levels of interest were possible. According to Sylvia Thrupp, 'a great many' fourteenth-century London merchants were raising loans against 'only small pieces of property, a few scattered holdings'.[96] Although the lack of comparable records for Yorkshire is frustrating, there is plenty of indirect evidence that land and/or rents were important elements in merchants' financial operations, confirmed by the number of small properties disposed of in wills as well as the high levels of speculative dealing *inter vivos*.[97]

Engaging with a group outside the 'feudal' structure, and adopting a more pragmatic attitude, closer perhaps to the attitude of merchants themselves, has exposed an interest in real property that had little directly to do with political status. It is difficult to identify many merchants at this time for whom the accumulation of property was an end in itself, or who experienced a Buddenbrook cycle concluding with landed gentry status. Rather, real estate in all its forms was accepted as an asset to be exploited as effectively as possible, within the context of fluctuating land values. The Black Death precipitated a fall in rural rents, and by the 1420s urban rents were falling. Undoubtedly some merchants capitalised on these opportunities to increase their investment. Equally, however, some must have suffered reverses as their credit capacity fell with falling rents. The evidence from Hull suggests a continual movement of investors and property within the town, perhaps similar to the situation in London where there was such an active land market that it supported property brokers, and indeed led to some properties being resold repeatedly amongst merchants, purely as a form of speculative investment.[98]

Yorkshire merchants, then, can be seen as active speculators in the land market comparable with London merchants. The evidence, while inconclusive, suggests that property was a useful asset in their primary trading activities, rather than an end in itself.

ACCUMULATED WEALTH: MONEY

The most obvious measure in trying to assess and rank individual merchants is by estimating the size of cash estates at death recorded in probate

---

[96] Thrupp, *London Merchant Class*, pp. 122, 126; G. Unwin, 'London Tradesmen and their Creditors', in *Finance and Trade Under Edward III*, p. 32.

[97] Kermode, 'Merchants of York, Beverley and Hull', appendix 4.

[98] Thrupp, *London Merchant Class*, pp. 127–8.

records. There are, however, several important observations which should be borne in mind. The first is to consider what the will is evidence of. It presents a frozen statement of account, but at what point in a person's career was it drawn up? Was it at the outset, before a young merchant had had the time to establish his business; in the middle when the expenses of rearing a family were perhaps still high, but profits were accumulating; in old age, when significant provision for children had already dispersed assets, but capital was diminishing without being replaced; or at some other intermediate stage? Fortunately, the majority of the wills in this study had been proved within four months of being written, almost all within one year, so there is not the additional problem of evaluating a document rendered irrelevant by intervening years.[99] For this reason the year of probate has been used as the year of death in describing cash estates.

Probate records can never be claimed as a comprehensive statement of a *post mortem* estate. Older children might have been omitted from a will because they had already received an *inter vivos* settlement[100] and could legally claim no more from the estate.[101] Some property might not be included in a will,[102] and property acquired after the will was drawn up would have to be dealt with in a codicil. However, they are virtually our only source and the absence of detailed inventories[103] means that we must rely upon each merchant's assessment of his worth. A cash total has been suggested by the simple mechanics of aggregating every sum bequeathed. Adding up the cash bequests in a will can rarely be more than an approximate estimate since bequests of '1d to each prisoner in the Kidcote in York' or to 'each leper' can never be multiplied accurately. Silver and gold items were rarely given a value and few merchants were as precise as John Brompton of Beverley, who noted the exact weight in ounces of each gold and silver item he bequeathed in 1444.[104] Nevertheless, silver spoons, goblets, bowls, servers, gold rings and bracelets and so forth were valuable and negotiable assets even though we cannot measure their worth.

---

[99] E. F. Jacob found that Canterbury wills were proved within two months on average: *The Register of Henry Chichele*, II, Canterbury and York Soc., 42 (1937), p. xxv.

[100] For example, Thomas Gare of York gave his son all his property in 1427 in return for a life pension. Thomas was dead by 1435: York RO, B/Y, f. 47; *Corpus Christi Guild*, p. 248. John Gregg of Hull made a settlement of cash, silver spoons and a lease on a house on his daughter in 1431. No mention is made of her in his will of 1437: Hull RO, BRE I, p. 263. For missing eldest sons, see G. A. Williams, *Medieval London: From Commune to Capital* (London, 1963), p. 316.

[101] G. D. Lamb, ed., *Testamenta Leodiensia*, Thoresby Soc., 19 (1913), p. vii.

[102] Dobson, 'Residentiary Canons of York', p. 169.

[103] John Talkan of York's estate was one of the few inventoried in the early fifteenth century. His household goods were worth £118 16s 3d and his debts £22 9s 3d: *Test. Ebor.* III, pp. 87–9. A Bristol merchant's inventory reveals that Philip Vale's real estate was sold for £322 8s 4d in 1393; his total estate, including debts, was approximately £757: *Plea & Mem. Rolls City of London, 1381–1412*, pp. 213–15. [104] Prob. Reg. II, f. 86v.

In the northern province of the church, as in London,[105] wills were subject to the custom of legitim, whereby personal property was divided into three parts, giving the wife and children two thirds of the testators' estate, one third to the wife, the other third equally divided between the children. If either children or wife were sole survivors, then the estate was divided into two parts.[106] The custom did not extend to real estate and had evolved through ecclesiastical encouragement to testators to make provision for their souls and for their dependants. The custom of legitim raises problems.[107] Should it be assumed that in his will, the married male testator was disposing of only his third, the 'dead's part'? There is some evidence to suggest that such indeed was the case. William Marshall of York spoke of portions in his will of 1492 as following 'the custom of the city of York', and Thomas Gra of York left his wife Alice an extra £10 out of his part, as well as 'the ascertained portion belonging to her by right'.[108] On the other hand, Robert Flinton of Hull (d. 1491) asked that all his property (with the exception of 2s 2d and some clothing) should be divided into two portions, one each for his wife and son,[109] as though such a division would not automatically be made. It is impossible to resolve this ambiguity in most wills and so the figures given in this study are simple totals of the cash recorded in each will.

Cash bequests in medieval wills were made on the understanding that debts would have to be recovered by legatees,[110] and although it must be a somewhat rough approximation, it has been possible to calculate the proportion of debt to available cash in a few instances. For the majority of these, debts accounted for between one and two thirds of their cash estates, close to the 25–50 per cent range proposed for the estates of sixteenth-century Exeter merchants.[111] In 1421 Thomas Frost of Hull left about £76, of which about £70 were debts owed to him. Among the wealthier testators, Robert Preston, also of Hull, left about £210, of which only £30 were debts owed to him.[112] It would be dangerous to

---

[105] Pollock and Maitland, *English Law*, II, p. 351.

[106] T. F. T. Plucknett, *A Concise History of the Common Law*, 5th edn (London, 1956), pp. 743–5; Holdsworth, *History of English Law*, III, p. 434.

[107] Real estate was not the subject of legitim. See S. J. Bailey, *The Law of Wills*, 7th edn (London, 1973), pp. 12, 21.

[108] Prob. Reg. v, ff. 424–5v.; III, f. 235. Thomas Aldestonemore of York, d. 1435, and John Dalton jnr, of Hull, d. 1496, both specified bequests to be made from their own portions: *ibid.*, III, f. 413; v, f. 484. Margaret Blackburn, widow of Nicholas jnr, in 1435 asked for her portion to be used to supplement one of the bequests in her husband's will if necessary: *ibid.*, III, f. 417.

[109] *Ibid.*, v, f. 401.

[110] E.g. Thomas Frost of Beverley left his daughter Margaret £40, of which £30 had to be recovered in debts: Prob. Reg. v, f. 271v.

[111] Hoskins, 'Merchants of Exeter', pp. 173–4.

[112] See also Brompton, 1444, *c.* £600, debts £200; Barley, 1468, £74, debts £53; Fisher, 1476, £13, debts £10. Prob. Reg. II, ff. 86–90v. (Brompton), 225 (Preston); IV, f. 60 (Barley); v, f. 8v. (Fisher); Arch. Reg. XVIII, ff. 384v.–5 (Frost).

assume that such negative assets were automatically realised: 40 per cent of Richard Toky of London's assets were debts none of which could be recovered.[113]

Depending on circumstances, some real estate would have to be sold to meet the provisions of a will. John Barden of York made arrangements in his will in 1396 that if property had to be sold to meet the provisions of the will, his manor of Kydall should be sold and his future son-in-law, John Moreton, should have the first option on buying it. William Ormeshead, also of York, made provision in his will dated 1437 for the sale of his property to be supervised, and William Burgh of Hull explicitly stated in his will in 1460 that property was to be sold to clear his debts.[114] This sort of provision could mean that in discussing cash bequests in isolation from real estate, a false distinction is being made. However, most of those wills which listed real estate made it quite clear that individual properties were being bequeathed in addition to cash bequests.

If it is assumed that the testator's belief that his estate could satisfy the provisions of his will was justified, then cash bequests can be used as an indicator of relative wealth. The merchant may, of course, have lost all sense of proportion in trying to ensure his salvation with grandiose funeral arrangements beyond his means, but this seems unlikely considering the care which the average merchant showed in settling his affairs and the generally modest provisions specified.

Other assets such as iron, cloth, mercery, livestock, as well as ships pose further difficulties. Ship-ownership has been discussed above, and although it clearly reflected an accumulation of capital, once the investment was made, the real value of owning a ship was the steady income derived. The capital value cannot be estimated. The value of a merchant's stock in trade, or the return expected on an investment, are equally impossible to estimate. Several merchants did refer to ventures as they were drawing up a will. Richard Bille of Hull left two lasts of stockfish owed to him in Iceland in 1451, and John Aldestonemore of York left 300 bales of wool in Calais. In both cases the goods were to be sold by executors.[115] Some of John Henryson of Hull's bequests had to wait for the arrival of the 'hulks out of Dansk'. Other merchants left capital tied up in commodities at home. John Kent of York left seventeen ells of cloth, a useful legacy for his wife Marion, who carried on the business after his death.[116] Richard Sawer, a York mercer, bequeathed a lot of

---

[113] Thrupp, *London Merchant Class*, p. 109.
[114] Prob. Reg. I, f. 100 (Barden); II, f. 423v. (Burgh); III, ff. 503–4v. (Ormeshead).
[115] Prob. Reg. II, f. 233v. (Bille); PRO, C1/10/296.
[116] Prob. Reg. IX, f. 328 (Henryson); IV, f. 53 (Kent).

mercery, including bonnets, in his shop in 1477. John Petty, a glazier and merchant of York, left some Normandy glass;[117] John Tutbury of Hull left iron and timber; Ralph Langton of Hull left salt;[118] Thomas Wood of Hull left iron and cloth of gold; Guy Malyerd of Beverley left timber; and William Hewitt of Beverley left several lead cisterns.[119] All the commodities listed above were valuable and could either be sold outright or kept within a business.

More complicated was the arrangement made by John Henryson of Hull in 1526. He left cisterns of lead, horses and an oil mill to his son John. His widow Agnes was to receive half the oil produced from the seed Harrison left, but she was also to pay half the milling costs.[120] We need more details before determining whose was the greatest benefit.

We do not know what determined the incidence of will-making, although generally wills survive in increasing numbers from the late four-teenth century, and that was certainly the pattern in the York diocese. The collection of wills preserved in the York Diocesan Probate Registers begins in 1387 and contains the copies of those wills proved before the Diocesan Exchequer Court.[121] There is no evidence of an earlier probate register, but at least some wills had previously been enrolled in the general registers of the archbishop, possibly when probate had been administered by him in person, or following a visitation by himself or his official. Such wills continued to be enrolled in the registers after 1389, and several of the Beverley and Hull wills are of this kind. The other probate court, the peculiar court of the Dean and Chapter of York Minster, kept a separate register.[122] The majority (90 per cent) of the wills consulted for this study, all copies, were proved before the Diocesan Exchequer Court, the remainder proved before the archbishop in person or before the peculiar court of the Dean and Chapter of York Minster. Local losses have left us with virtually no wills registered in York between 1409 and 1425, none for 1470, and a few other years provide only partial registration.[123] Burgesses were encouraged to enrol their wills in the borough courts, which explains the relatively high incidence of early fourteenth-century wills in Hull.

[117] *Ibid.*, v, f. 190 (Sawer); Dec. & Cap. II, f. 76v. (Petty).

[118] Prob. Reg. III, ff. 371v.–2v. (Tutbury); VI, f. 22v. (Langton).

[119] *Ibid.*, v, ff. 402v.–3v. (Wood); 309v. (Malyerd); IV, f. 137 (Hewitt).   [120] *Ibid.*, IX, f. 328.

[121] See C. I. A. Richie, *The Ecclesiastical Courts of York* (Arbroath, 1956), for a fuller discussion of this court.

[122] The Probate Registers and the Archbishops' Registers are in the Borthwick Institute of Historical Research, York, and the Dean and Chapters' collection of wills are in the Minster Library, York. Printed indexes have been published by the Yorkshire Archaeological Society, Record Series: *Wills in the York Registry, 1389–1514*, 6 (1889); *Dean and Chapter Wills, 1321–1636*, 38 (1907); *Wills in the Registers of the Archbishops of York, 1316–1822*, 92 (1936).

[123] *Wills in York Registry 1389–1514*, pp. 199–202.

Bearing in mind the inconclusive nature of the evidence, some sort of analysis of testamentary estates must still be attempted. Table 9.1 suggests a broad pattern of the distribution of wealth using cash bequests as an indicator. The testamentary evidence of merchants' wives and widows has not been used, except to note those who left silver or gold items. The 425 wills analysed in table 9.1 are those which included any cash bequests, but we cannot confidently assume that testators who specified none had none to leave.

As the number of wills increased up to 1460, the balance between each category remained stable, with wills over £50 accounting for about 34 per cent and those for less than £50 accounting for about 65 per cent of all those containing cash bequests. After 1460 the distribution changed, with fewer large cash estates: 17 per cent over £50 and 83 per cent under £50. Most wills fell within the lower category: some wills made the most basic provision and in many instances prior arrangements must have been made. It is clear, though, that the smallness of an estate did not deter testators for whom the major motivation was to observe religious conventions and to establish legitimate heirs. Small amounts of cash were involved, for example the 2s left by Nicholas Thornton of York in 1478. An 'average' will at this level was that of Thomas Diconson of Hull who died in 1447 and left £1 12s 6d, of which 2s 6d was for a friend and the rest was divided between his parish priest and other religious institutions.[124] Where ages can be estimated, the majority of testators under thirty made no specific provisions or left very little cash.[125]

In the context of capital accumulation, it is the largest estates which attract our attention (see table 9.2). Several sizeable fortunes were left in the late fourteenth century, the largest belonging to York staplers: Robert Louth (£482), John Gisburn (£300), William Vescy (£300) and Robert Holme snr a staggering £2,418. Holme's fortune was unsurpassed.[126] The remaining estates of over £100 left in York belonged to general merchants, but one of £390 came from a draper, Henry de Yarom. In Beverley, only two wills left sums close to the higher York levels: those of a stapler, John Kelk (£511), and Thomas Rolleston (£272), a merchant's son. The 1347 will of Robert Preston of Hull merits comment because there is so little testamentary evidence for this early period. He left over £120 in cash and, although a self-styled draper, much of his wealth came from investments in wool exports. By the late fourteenth

---

[124] Prob. Reg. II, f. 258 (Dickinson); v, f. 116 (Thornton).

[125] The evidence of wills in early Tudor Colchester suggests a similar pattern. Ward, 'Wealth and Family in Early Sixteenth Century Colchester', pp. 110–7 at p. 111.

[126] Prob. Reg. I, ff. 15v.–16 (Gisburn), 100v.–3v. (Holme); III, ff. 265 (Louth), 266v.–8v. (Vescy).

Table 9.1. *Estimated cash estates in merchant wills*

	York	Beverley	Hull	Total
Before 1370				
Silver/gold	0			
	[1 wife]			
£100+	1		1	2
£50+	2		1	3
£20+	1	1	1	3
-£20	1	1	10	12
Total with cash	**5**	**2**	**13**	**20**
	(5)	(2)	(16)	(23)
1370–1420				
Silver/gold	8	2		10
£100+	16	2	1	19
	[4 × £300+]			
£50+	14	2	1	17
£20+	18	2	4	24
<£20	27	9	5	41
Total with cash	**75**	**15**	**11**	**101**
	(88)	(15)	(11)	(114)
1420–60				
Silver/gold	12	1	6	19
	[+4 wives]			
£100+	18	2	6	26
	[1430s 5 × £300+]			
£50+	12	6	5	23
£20+	19	5	1	25
<£20	48	7	19	74
Total with cash	**97**	**20**	**31**	**148**
	(107)	(22)	(32)	(161)
1460–1500				
Silver/gold	2	4	6	12
£100+	8	1	2	11
£50+	7		3	10
£20+	8	3	4	15
<£20	38	12	33	83
Total with cash	**61**	**16**	**42**	**119**
	(66)	(16)	(45)	(127)

Total of wills analysed: 425

Note:
( ) = All wills excluding letters of administration.
Sources: York Probate Registers and Archbishops' Registers, Borthwick Institute, York; Probate Registers of the Dean and Chapter, Minster Library, York; Prerogative Court Canterbury, PRO London; BC III, Humberside RO; Hull Bench Books and Deeds, Hull RO; York Memorandum Books, York RO.

Table 9.2. *The scale of merchants' investments compared: land, cash and trade*

9.2.1 York

	1st date	Dead	Occup.	Land	Cash	Trade	Age
1370–1420							
Acastre J de f.W	1358	1379	merch.	A		A	42+
Barden J de	1368	1396	merch.	A	£25	dom	49+
S Bolton J snr	1374	1395	mercer		£4	A	42
Cottesbroke Edm	1400	1405	merch.	A	£141		
Craven J de	1376	1415	merch.	A	£87	dom	60+
Fysshe W	1367	1392	merch.	C	£97		46+
S Gare T del f.W	1385*		merch.	B		A	60+
S Gisburn J de	1347*	1390	mercer		£300	A	64
Hamerton Alan	1375*	1406	merch.	B?	£108		52
S Holme Rob de snr	1347*	1396	mercer	A+	£2,148	A	. 70
S Holme Rob jnr	1390*	1406	mercer		£137	A	37
S Holme T br.R snr	1354*	1406	mercer	A	£60	A	73
Ireby W de	1357*	?1393	merch.	B	£110		
S Louth Rob jnr	1386*	1407	merch.		£482	B	42
More J de	1382*	1398	mercer	D	£138		37
Ruyston T f.T	1396	1407	merch.	D	£111		31+
Sallay W	1383	1408	merch.	A	£2.5	D	46+
Santon J de	1344*	1394	draper	D	£96		71
S Savage Rob f. W	1364*	1399	merch.	C	£107	A	56
Talkan J ?f.R	1415	1415	merch.		£119		
S Vescy W	1376*	1407	mercer	D	£300	A	52
Yarom H de	1365*	1391	draper	D	£390	dom	47
1420–60							
S Aldestonemore J	1412*	1435	merch. •	A	£359	B	44
Bedale W f.J	1403*	1438	merch.	A	£92	D+dom	56
S Blackburn N snr	1396*	1432	merch.	C	£644	A	57
S Bolton J jnr f.J	1410*	1445	mercer	A	£26	A	56
S Bowes W	1391	1439	merch.	B	£180	B	69+
Bracebridge T	1393*	1437	weaver		£119	dom	65
Carre T	1406*	1444	draper		£336	dom	59
Collinson Rob	1425	1458	mercer	D	£142	dom	54
Fauconer Rob	1415*	1435	merch.		£130	A	41
S Gare T jnr f.T	1418*	1445		A	£133	A	48
Girlington W	1405*	1444	draper	D	£108	dom	60
Holme Rob f.Rob	1395*	1433		A	£80	B	59
Kirkham T	1402	1437	mercer	D	£188	D	56+
Market Henry	1412*	1443	merch.		£198		52
Moreton J f.Rog	1398*	1434		A	£69	B	57
S Northeby J	1402*	1432	merch.	A	£724	B	51
S Ormeshead W	1404*	1437	merch.	A	£120	D	54
Radclyffe J	1411*	1444	merch.		£178		54
S Russell Ric	1396*	1435	merch.	A+	£756	B	60

9.2.1 **York** (*cont.*)

	1st date	Dead	Occup.	Land	Cash	Trade	Age
S Selby W	1378	1427	merch.	A	£52	B	49+
Wranby W	1410★	1432	vintner		£184	D	43
Yarom W f.Rob	1412	1436	mercer	C	£115	D	45+
1460–1500							
Beverley T f.J	1440★	1480	merch.	D	£100	A	61
S Carre J f.T	1434★	1488	merch.	D	£145		75
Ferriby J	1447★	1491	merch.	A	£66	C	65
Gaunt J	?1450★	1488	merch.		£17	A	59+
Gaunt J jnr	?1456★		merch.			A	36+
Gaunt J jnr	1471		merch.			A	
Gilyot J snr f.W	1439★	1484	mercer	A	£155	B	66
Gilyot J Sir f.J	1481★	1510	merch.	A+	£722	B	50
Holbeck W	1425★	1477	mercer	A	£6	D	73
Ince J f.J	1448★	1487	mercer		£137	A	60
Kent J snr	1438★	1468	merch.	A	£95	A	51
Kirk G f.W esq.	1475★	1514	merch.	A+	£66	D	60
S Marshall J	1445★	1487	mercer		£67	A	63
S Neleson T	1433★	1484	merch.	A+	£250	B	72
Nelson W f.T	1488★	1525	merch.	A	£27	58	
S Thirsk J	1427★	1473	merch.			A	67
Thornton N f.Ric	1441★	1478	mercer	A	2s		58
Thornton Ric	1441	1474	walker	A	£3		54+
Thornton R f.N	1481★	1507	grocer	A	£31		47
Todd W	1462★	1503	merch.	A	£7	A	62
S Wartre Ric f.W	1416★	1466	goldsmith (merch. in will)		£755		71
S York Ric	1457★	1498	merch.	A++	£124	B	62

9.2.2 **Beverley**

	1st date	Dead	Occup.	Land	Cash	Trade	Age
1370–1420							
S Kelk J f.T	1380	1407	merch.	A	£511	B	48+
Rolleston T f.W	1415	1415			£272		
1420–60							
S Brompton J	1391	1444	merch.	B	£600+	B	74+
S Brompton T f.J	1436	1436	merch.	A	£500		
Sleford J	1416	1449		A	£19		54+
1460–1500							
S Middleton J	1448	1475	merch.	C	£155	A	48+

9.2.3 Hull

	1st date	Dead	Occup.	Land	Cash	Trade	Age
Before 1370							
Preston Rob	1321	1347	draper	A	£110	B	47+
1370–1420							
Crosse Rob del	1360	1395		A	£202	B	65+
Ferriby Ric	1378	1381		A	£17		40+
Pund Adam	1344	1369		A	£61	D	36+
Pund W f.A	1387					A	46+
Sanderson J	1418	1418	merch.	A	£37		
Stellar P	1377	1396	merch.	B	£38	A	40+
1420–60							
Bedford J	1412	1451		A	£9	C	60+
Bille Ric	1447	1451	merch.		£97		26+
Crosse Rob	1438			A		D	
Fitling J	1392★	1434	merch.	A	£8	B	63
Garton J	1442	1456		D	£412		44+
S Gregg J	1398★	1437		A	£191	A	60
Hanson J	1421★	1459	mariner (merch. in will)	A	£69	B	59
S Holme Rob	1415★	1449	merch.		£775	B	55
Preston T	1430	1451	merch.	C	£9	D	42+
Shackles Rob	1395★	1446		C	£88	A	72+
Tutbury J	1378	1433		B	£140	A	76+
1460–1500							
S Alcock R f.W	1454★	1484	merch.	D	£122	B	51
S Auncell Rob	1437★	1465					49
S Coppendale Edm	1450★	1490	merch.		£4	A	61
S Day J	1454★	1472	merch.	A	£24	B	39
Eland W	1453	1488	merch.+lawyer	A	£11	C	56
S Goodknappe W	1488★	1504		D	£299	C	37
Langton Ralph	1461★	1502		A	£125	B	62
S Swan J	1440★	1476			£164	A	56
Whitfield J	1451★	1479		A	£61	A	49

Notes:

       f = Son of.

       S = Wool stapler.

       ★ = Date of entry as burgess.

1st Date = Earliest reference if no date of entry as a burgess.

  Dead = Generally the date of probate.

 Occup. = Occupation (merch.= merchant).

   Land = A rough estimate of the scale of activities:

       A = 20+ properties; B = 10–20; C = 5–10; D = <5.

Notes to Table 9.2.3 (*cont.*)

> Cash = Unadjusted total of cash disposed of in each will.
> Trade = A rough estimate of the scale of activities. See p. 258 above for a full
> discussion of the methodology.
> dom = Domestic trade only.
> Age = Age at death based on assumed age of twenty-one years at entry as burgess
> or evidence from other sources (+ indicates estimated minimum age at
> death).

century, it was a general trader, Robert Crosse, who left the sole large cash estate (£202).[127]

Between 1420 and 1460 the number of large estates at death increased slightly, but with a concentration amongst York testators in the 1430s. One hesitates to make too much of these figures, but it may be that the mortality crisis of the 1430s carried off a larger than average number of merchants in their commercial prime. Twelve York testators died in the 1430s leaving over £100, four of whom left over £300: John Aldestonemore, Nicholas Blackburn snr, John Northeby and Richard Russell. All four were staplers and Blackburn's widow, Margaret, left over £500 within three years of his death.

In Hull five of the wealthiest merchants and their wives died in the 1430s.[128] There is no evidence for a similar occurrence in Beverley where only two estates over £100 were recorded: those of the Bromptons, father and son, both staplers. Thomas predeceased his father John in 1436 and left about £500. John Brompton died in 1444 leaving £800, including £202 in debts, a three-quarters share of a ship and an exceptionally large amount of precisely weighed gold and silver items.[129] Hull had six merchants who left over £100 after 1420, but none of them matched the Bromptons' estates. The largest belonged to staplers: John Gregg (£174), whose widow Joan died a year after her husband leaving £240, and Robert Holme (£775).[130] In the second half of the fifteenth century fewer merchants left cash estates of over £50. Seven York merchants left large estates, four of whom were staplers: John Carre (£145), Thomas Neleson (£250), Richard Wartre (£755) and Richard York (£124);[131] and three were general merchants: Thomas Beverley snr (£100), John

[127] *Ibid.*, I, f. 48v. (Yarom); II, ff. 83v.–5 (Crosse); III, f. 263 (Kelk); Arch. Reg. X, f. 322 (Preston); XVIII, f. 34v. (Rolleston). For Preston's trade see PRO, E122/56/20–22, 57/12, 58/5.

[128] Prob. Reg. II, ff. 605 (Nicholas Blackburn), 619–20 (Northeby); III, ff. 415v.–16 (Margaret Blackburn), 439–41 (Russell).

[129] *Ibid.*, II, ff. 86–90v. (John Brompton); III, f. 475 (Thomas Brompton).

[130] *Ibid.*, II, ff. 211–12 (Holme); III, ff. 507v.–8 (John Gregg), 555v.–556v. (Joan Gregg).

[131] *Ibid.*, IV, ff. 115–17 (Wartre); V, ff. 212–13 (Neleson), 327–9 (Carre); PRO Prob. 11/11, f. 36 (York).

Gilyot snr (£155) and John Ince (£137).[132] Beverley's wife died within two years of her husband and left £137. Staplers also left the large cash estates in Beverley and Hull: John Middleton in Beverley (£155), and John Swan (£164) and William Goodknappe (£275) in Hull.[133]

CONCLUSION

A number of general conclusions can be suggested. First, age was an important factor in cash accumulation, with at least 60 per cent of estates over £100 belonging to men over fifty. However, it is difficult to assess the significance of age regarding investments in real property. Second, although most of the large cash estates were left by international merchants, involvement in overseas trade did not automatically generate sizeable cash savings (see table 9.2). Indeed it could have been the necessity of keeping commerce flowing which ensured that capital did not always accumulate as disposable income. A direct correlation between active trading and cash accumulation cannot easily be measured because of the varied length of merchants' business lives. There was a lag between entrepreneurial prosperity at the end of the fourteenth century and the deaths of that cohort of merchants whose careers had begun in the 1380s and 1390s and ended during the early fifteenth-century recession. The loss of wills from 1409–25 and a corresponding loss of customs records are complicating factors, but a number of merchants who died during the 1430s had been active traders earlier: Blackburn, Bowes, Bracebridge, Holme, Moreton, Russell and Selby of York, Gregg, Shackles and Tutbury of Hull, all began to trade in the late fourteenth century. Not only were merchants dying wealthy in the 1430s, but large fortunes were being amassed.

Second, the testamentary evidence suggests that fortunes could also be created from domestic trade. In Hull, for instance, one of the largest cash estates, the £412 of John Garton (1456), belonged to a man who may not have been a merchant, and another of £360 to Thomas Preston (1451), who dealt with overseas merchants without apparently trading himself.[134] In York, several drapers became extremely prosperous: John de Santon and Henry de Yarom in the late fourteenth century, Thomas Carr and William Girlington in the 1430s and 1440s. Carr left over £336 in 1444, supplied cloth wholesale to Durham Priory and apparently made his fortune as a middleman in textiles.[135] John Radclyffe, a merchant who died in the same year leaving £178, has not been traced in any records

---

[132] *Ibid.*, v, ff. 184 (Beverley), 237 (Gilyot), 308 (Ince).

[133] *Ibid.*, IV, f. 96v. (Middleton); V, ff. 7 (Swan), 28–9 (Beverley); VI, f. 107 (Goodknappe).

[134] *Ibid.*, II, ff. 225 (Preston), 327v. (Garton); BRE I, p. 252.

[135] Prob. Reg. I, ff. 71–2 (Santon), 57v. (Yarum); II, ff. 83–4 (Girlington), 79v. (Carr); *Durham Acct Rolls*, II, p. 616.

as active in any branch of trade, though he left debts to be recovered.[136]

Third, the speed with which fortunes were dispersed in cash bequests had a dramatic impact which was intensified at times of high mortality. When John Aldestonemore died in February 1435, aged about forty-four, he left most of his estate to his daughter, brother and other close relatives in large cash bequests of £10, £20 and £40. His cash estate amounted to some £369, of which £42 was to be spent on his soul. The rest was divided between his daughter Agnes Holbeck, his brother Thomas and nephew John. Thomas was about fifty-five when he died within three months of his brother, leaving £46. We know nothing of the other heirs.[137] The bulk of Nicholas and Margaret Blackburn's bequests were dispersed amongst close relatives, particularly grandchildren, and religious institutions. Nicholas died in 1432, aged about fifty-seven, leaving £644, almost half of that for his soul. Margaret inherited a life-interest in his property, and when she died in 1435, left about £520, £42 of which was intended for spiritual provision. The bulk of her cash was distributed in numerous small sums: eighteen for 10 marks and six for £10. Margaret also claimed, as 'part of her portion', a bond for £400, owed to her late husband by their son-in-law John Bolton and Alice his wife. Margaret left it with Bolton 'ad mercandizand' for the two years following her death, after which he was to pay her heirs the £400. No more is heard of this bond, and her son and heir Nicholas benefited very little (according to the testamentary evidence). When he died in 1448, sixteen years after his father, he left only £19, and his grandson Richard left only £9 in 1513. John Northeby's two sons each received £200 in 1432 and the rest of his £724 went to friends and charity. When his son John died in 1438, six years after his father, he left only £31.[138]

Fourth, few merchant dynasties emerged in these three Yorkshire towns. The custom of legitim guaranteed division, and the poor survival rate of male heirs ensured the wide dispersal of accumulated wealth. Richard Russell of York died aged about sixty in 1435, five months after his wife Petronella. Their estate was divided between their daughter Ellen, wife of York stapler John Thirsk, Russell's sister and the families of his two brothers. His estate was over £756 and he disposed of over £216 for his soul and the remainder in numerous cash bequests, ranging from 6s 8d to £40. Most of his land was eventually alienated for a perpetual chantry and all that his daughter inherited was a silver piece and 20s.[139]

---

[136] Prob. Reg. II, f. 91.   [137] *Ibid.*, III, ff. 406–8 (John), 413 (Thomas).

[138] *Ibid.*, II, ff. 123 (Northeby jnr), 168v.–9 (Nicholas jnr), 605 (Nicholas snr); 619–20 (Northeby snr); III, ff. 415v.–16v. (Margaret); VIII, f. 105 (Richard).

[139] *Ibid.*, III, ff. 439–40 (Russell). Petronella left £47 in small sums. *Ibid.*, III, f. 425v. See also III, f. 244v. (Hamerton).

Piety could claim a large percentage of disposable income: as much as 76 per cent in the case of William Wranby of York, who left £140 out of total bequests of £184 to religious projects.[140] The examples of the Blackburns, cited earlier, demonstrate all these tendencies. Few widows continued to make their husband's capital work in commerce. Of the handful who might have, Elena Box, Margaret Bushell and Alice Day of Hull, and Marion Kent of York, only the latter continued to trade for any length of time.[141] However, intermarriage and the remarriage of widows undoubtedly kept inherited capital within the merchant class, if not within individual families.

Finally, there does seem to have been a decline after 1460 in the numbers of the very wealthy: those men leaving exceptionally large cash estates. This may have been due to the bullion famine, at its worst between 1450 and 1465, which perhaps diverted more cash into commercial ventures. Alternatively, it may have been that merchants were adopting a long-term policy by investing more heavily in land, although the evidence is inconclusive. Perhaps the simplest explanation is that with diminishing ranks of Yorkshire staplers, fewer had the opportunities the wool trade presented for large cash savings.[142]

---

[140] Prob. Reg. III, f. 344. See also Richard Wartre of York who spent £469 out of £755 on religious bequests: *ibid.*, IV, ff. 115–17.   [141] See appendix 3.

[142] *VCH York*, p. 85; Bartlett, 'Expansion and Decline', pp. 28–30. See Nightingale, *Medieval Mercantile Community*, pp. 442–3 on an increase in property interests amongst grocers in the 1430s aftermath of the Bullion Ordinances, but a continued need for liquidity amongst others.

PROFITS AND LOSSES: A CONCLUSION TO PART II

General assumptions about the positive correlation between overseas trade and capital accumulation in cash or real estate are difficult to sustain because they are difficult to establish. The fate of the two late medieval English enterprises for which fairly complete evidence does survive, Gilbert Maghfeld's and the Celys', should perhaps be taken as the norm.[1] Merchants invested in most projects from which they could hope to make a profit, but even the most financially agile and astute could come to grief. As Alison Hanham has observed, 'a high proportion of the people amongst the Celys' business and family connections died in debt and poverty'.[2] The fortunes of leading merchants could be ephemeral even for those who retained some of the bounty of their life's work, while smaller merchants may have had little to show at the end of a lifetime beyond a capacity to support themselves and a family.

It is difficult to draw up a final balance of activities and profit for individual merchants, to measure the value of different investments and their interaction, or to assess overall success or failure. Late-fourteenth-century Colchester clothiers made profits of some 10 per cent. In the fifteenth century, estimates range from profits of 10 per cent for London grocers to an average 20 per cent for wool staplers later in the century. Annual incomes of £100 or more could be achieved,[3] but on the evidence of trade-turnover, lower incomes were more common amongst Yorkshire merchants.

In Yorkshire, impressions of trade and, to some extent, investments in real estate, derive from the records of active and perhaps unfinished enter-

---

[1] James, 'A London Merchant', pp. 364–76; Hanham, *Celys and Their World*, pp. 17, 306, 405 *et seq.*

[2] Hanham, *Celys and Their World*, p. 203. Sales credit had become such a common feature of European trade that newcomers needed letters of introduction to establish their credit.

[3] C. Dyer, *Standards of Living in the Later Middle Ages. Social Change in England c. 1250–1520* (Cambridge, 1989), pp. 193–4. These estimates are based on the Celys, a Winchester vintner, Mark le Fayre, Londoners Maghfeld and Whittington, and fourteenth-century Colchester clothiers.

prises over several years if not a whole lifetime. By contrast, wills give only a fleeting insight into death-bed intentions. All are partial and incomplete and render conclusions uncertain. There can be no general rule applicable to all merchants' preferences regarding savings and investment choices, and it must remain a matter for conjecture which factors were the most influential. Theoretically, a bullion shortage could encourage liquidity, as amongst London grocers in the 1430s, and depressed markets could divert investment away from trade and into real property.[4] Merchants like William Bedale and William Ormeshead of York and Robert Crosse of Hull, who died in 1437–8, left extensive real estate, cash and plate, and appear not to have been very active overseas traders. With only a scatter of customs records extant for the years 1408–40 it is difficult to be sure. Conversely there were others who died after periods of expansion and depression, who were highly successful in international trade and left large cash estates, but little, if any, traceable land.[5] Thomas de Beverley (1480), Nicholas Blackburn snr (1432), John Carre (1488) and William Vescy of York (1407), and John Swan of Hull (1476), were significantly all wool staplers. Uneven investment of this sort was not at all uncommon among merchants elsewhere.[6] Simon Eyre, for instance, left over £4,700 at his death in 1464, most of it invested in his business, but his real property yielded only £10 per year and he lived in a rented house.[7] Fortunes could be amassed in any branch of trade but wool staplers figured disproportionately amongst those accumulating outstanding sums of cash.

Testamentary evidence can only be evaluated properly against the age of the testator: estimated for some 330 Yorkshire merchants on the assumption that men became burgesses at twenty-one. Ages have been included in table 9.2, which represents an attempt to identify the most successful, those who traded at the highest level or amassed sizeable estates, and for whom we have some evidence of other activities. It is apparent that most of those merchants who were successful in every way, – who bequeathed large cash estates, had high trade profiles, and left sizeable investments in property – were men over fifty. Several were possibly over seventy when they died, for example Robert and Thomas Holme and Thomas Neleson of York, and John Tutbury of Hull. But not all old

---

[4] Nightingale, *Medieval Mercantile Community*, p. 442

[5] See appendix 3. York's John Bolton, amongst the wealthiest taxpayers in 1436, was a large investor in the wool trade and in land, but without a will we cannot make any assumptions about the cash he accumulated.

[6] In sixteenth-century Exeter, W. G. Hoskins estimated real estate comprised only a small proportion of mercantile estates: 'Merchants of Exeter', p. 172.

[7] Thrupp, *London Merchant Class*, p. 127. Richard Whittington opted for liquidity and left maybe £5,500 in cash as well as jewels and plate: Barron, 'Richard Whittington', pp. 228–9.

men died wealthy. A merchant may have been successful in midlife, but relatively impoverished in old age when perhaps the depredations of family settlements and his own unproductive demands on his estate left very little to dispose of after his death or even for his own maintenance. A former Master of the Merchant Adventurers' Company, Robert de Yarom of York, had to seek its support in 1444 in the form of a weekly pension of 9d and a place in its almshouse. The Company spent 8s 9d on his funeral the following year.[8]

Living too long could accordingly prejudice a merchant's chances of transmitting a fortune or thriving business to the succeeding generation. In addition, the extremely poor rate of survival of male heirs further reduced the opportunities for mercantile dynasties to emerge. Thomas Holme of York died in 1406, aged over seventy, and left £60 plus extensive investments in property in Calais, Newark, Pontefract and elsewhere. He had no surviving children of his own, and made bequests to his nephews, Robert, son of the outstandingly wealthy Robert Holme, and Thomas, son of the not so successful John Holme. The bulk of his considerable estate was to be sold after his widow's death to provide for the hospital founded by his brother Robert.[9] As we have seen, the fortunes of younger men could be diverted away from commerce and dispersed rapidly too.

However, some of the very wealthy did successfully transmit their life's profits directly to a second male generation. Thomas del Gare of York, for instance, engaged heavily in overseas trade, but also invested extensively in real estate in the late fourteenth century. His son Thomas, dying in 1445 aged forty-eight, had emulated his father's international business expertise but probably owned more real estate. He left two sons who have been traced no further.[10] Another example is Thomas Carre, a York draper, who died in 1444 aged fifty-nine, leaving £336. His 31-year-old son John survived him and was already well established, possibly in partnership with his father. Thomas left him £20, and to his grandchildren he left £50 to his namesake Thomas and £20 to each of his three granddaughters. Such generous bequests removed major financial responsibilities from John; and when he died in 1488, aged at least seventy-five, he left an estate of £145 and property in York. None of his children appear to have survived him, or else they were too well provided for to attract bequests from their father. There are other examples of the second generation inheriting large estates: Thomas Beverley, Nicholas Blackburn, John Bolton, John Gilyot, Thomas Neleson, John Northeby,

[8] *M&MA*, p. 45; *Corpus Christi Guild*, p. 25. Thomas Gray, York's mayor in 1497, was allowed to resign his alderman's gown in 1514 and given an annual pension of £4: *ibid.*, p. 80 n.; York RO, House Book IX, pp. 34, 77. [9] Prob. Reg. III, f. 255. [10] *Ibid.*, II, ff. 110v.–11v.

Richard Thornton and Richard York, all of York, and John Brompton of Beverley.[11] These, however, were probably the exception.

Death with no male heir could terminate a business, but different complications could arise if a merchant left several sons and/or daughters. His estate would be broken up as the custom of legitim demanded a tripartite division of the moveable estate. A long-lived widow could exhaust assets before they were returned to the next generation at her death. Her remarriage was therefore preferable as a means of keeping assets active in commerce, even though some widows continued their husband's export trade.[12] Intermarriage compensated to some extent, by helping to keep cash, land, expertise and reputation within the merchant group as a whole: as evidenced by the fate of John Aldestonemore's estate, much of which was absorbed into another merchant's business through his daughter's marriage. It was as a social group rather than in individual dynasties that merchants survived.

The fortunes of the merchants from our three towns were directly affected by external factors, notably competition from fellow Englishmen and the loss of the Baltic trade. Londoners' tentacles were long and spreading. Their presence in the north was not new; after all Fountains Abbey was selling wool futures through its London agent in 1274,[13] and in the fourteenth century there were Londoners buying Yorkshire wool and cloth and shipping it out through Hull.[14] Yorkshiremen collaborated with Londoners from time to time: for instance a Hull merchant, John Fitling, and William Holgryn, fishmonger of London, were partners in a deal in 1417, and in 1425 a London grocer, William Burton, witnessed Walter Frost of Hull's will.[15]

Londoners were becoming much more visible from the mid-fifteenth century. While the east coast ports foundered during the prolonged hostilities with the Hanseatic League, London was tightening its grip on the cloth trade with the Low Countries. In 1420–1, for instance, Hanse merchants were exporting York coverlets through London.[16] Earlier

---

[11] See appendix 3.

[12] For active widows see Barron and Sutton, *Medieval London Widows*. In London the custom of free bench was extended to life to encourage widows to continue their husband's business: *ibid.*, pp. xxviii.

[13] H. E. Wroot, 'Yorkshire Abbeys and the Wool Trade', *Miscellanea*, Thoresby Soc., 33 (1935), pp. 14–15.

[14] E.g. Reginald Aleyn in 1391–3: *CPR 1391–6*, p. 398. Hostilities between the Hanse and the east coast ports, in particular, probably accelerated the carriage of Yorkshire cloth via London. In 1420–1, for instance, Hanse merchants were exporting York coverlets through London: Gras, *Early English Customs*, pp. 120, 459, 469. See also PRO, CP40, Michaelmas 1403, m. 342 for a London woolmonger in debt to a Beverley merchant. I am grateful to the Market Networks and Metropolis Project for these and later CP40 references.

[15] *CPR 1416–22*, p. 95; Arch. Reg. V, f. 419.   [16] Gras, *Early English Customs*, pp. 120, 459, 469.

references had hinted at a growing mercantile presence in the region.[17] London goods were in York shops by the mid-fifteenth century and probably earlier. The inventory of a chapman, Thomas Gryssop, drawn up in 1446, lists a variety of goods – many obvious imports, but also London purses, coffers, belts and glasses. Gryssop's debts included £1 10s 6d to a London spicer and 40s to a London capmaker.[18] The importing of similar small manufactured items through Hull suggests that local craftsmen could not compete in terms of price or perhaps fashion. One Beverley mercer left a cloak of London russet in 1469: brought back from a visit or purchased locally?[19] Gryssop was only one of a number of northerners indebted to London merchants: two grocers in particular, Thomas Phillips and Robert Mildenhall,[20] had nearly £400 of debts owed by York dyers, merchants and spicers enrolled in York in 1444–5. A further £84 was owed to other Londoners, including sums owed by merchants from Hull and Doncaster and chapmen from Durham and Lancashire.[21] Recent research points to a decline in the activity of London grocers in provincial markets, but their place may have been taken by others less formally organised.[22]

Even in interregional trade, the merchants from York, Beverley and Hull were losing ground to southerners. By 1505, butchers from London and the Home Counties began to appear alongside London grocers, haberdashers and occasional craftsmen in the lists of felons claiming sanctuary in Beverley Minster, most of them pursued for debt.[23] Londoners began to acquire other investments in Yorkshire. In 1404 Thomas de Leycester, a London grocer, hired two York men to collect his rents in York. Robert Kelam, another Londoner, hired a rent-collector and agent

---

[17] PRO, CP40, Michaelmas 1403, m. 73d.; 1424 mm. 22d., 75d., 91, 337d., 403, 532d.

[18] *Test. Ebor.* III, pp. 101–5.

[19] Prob. Reg. IV, f. 137 (Hewitt). Lawrence Tutbury of Hull was probably buying from a Southwark saddler in 1424: PRO, CP40, Michaelmas 1424, m. 189d.

[20] Mildenhall and Phillips were not in the London Grocers' Company livery but were probably acting as agents of John Phillips who joined the livery in 1437–9. Phillips may have migrated from York and used local contacts to draw York dyers and traders into a commercial network based in London. He left cash to a friend, expressly to be given to the poor people of York with whom he used to buy and sell: *CCR 1441–7*, p. 47; Nightingale, *Medieval Mercantile Community*, pp. 448–9.

[21] York RO, E39, ff. 278, 284–5, 288, 295. In 1453 Phillips was pursuing Thomas Helmesley for debt: PRO, C1/21/25.

[22] After the mid-century, London grocers found it cheaper to attend Stourbridge Fair than to bear the direct costs of up-country trading: Nightingale, *Medieval Mercantile Community*, pp. 448–9. For the argument that the grocers continued to be major agents in provincial trade, see Thrupp, 'The Grocers of London', pp. 252–3, 270, 273–6.

[23] BL, Harl. MS 560; J. Raine, ed., *Sanctuarium Dunelmense et Sanctuarium Beverlacense*, Surtees Soc., 5 (1837), pp. 114, 118, 122, 170–81. For the growth of London's demand for meat from the fourteenth century, see G. Rosser, 'London and Westminster: The Suburb in the Urban Economy in the Late Middle Ages', in Thomson, *Towns and Townspeople*, p. 52.

to look after property acquired by his marriage to a York merchant's widow.[24] Income was draining out of the region in other ways as Yorkshiremen setting up in business in London used their northern inheritance as security to raise working capital in the south.[25] Given the decline of Beverley and York and the opportunities for the adventurer in London, the decision to migrate was rational.

Faced with discouraging obstacles to trade in the Baltic region, the Yorkshire merchants' share of England's overseas trade steadily shrank. A handful of individuals managed to sustain a competitive position but the growing ascendancy of London was hard to resist. To an extent, this was due to the interplay between the three elements we have been discussing: cash, credit and land. These were the basis of locally generated finance and, although there was a range of credit options actively pursued by provincial merchants, they tended to be small-scale, local, and too exposed to personal vagaries to supply adequate resources to compete with Londoners during much of the fifteenth century. Dependent as they were on personal rather than on the institutional resources of banking or finance houses, provincial credit was especially vulnerable. The regional contraction in those resources which secured credit was therefore critical. That contraction was most likely the result of several apparently short-term processes, which combined into a spiral of decline.

The first was the reduced involvement in international trade by Yorkshire merchants in the early fifteenth century. The flow of trade was interrupted, jeopardizing overseas credit arrangements. Most particularly, the decline in wool exports through Hull, and the Yorkshire merchants' diminishing share of a nationally shrinking trade, closed off important financial resources to all but a few. They lost access to the Calais Staple which played a central role as a foreign currency exchange and credit agency for wool merchants. According to Professor Postan, 'most had something in the nature of a current account with the [Calais] mint'. Warrants of payment and bills of mint were issued to merchants, either as part of the process of repaying loans to the Crown, or to allow merchants to draw credit abroad against their compulsorily deposited bullion and coin in the Staple. These Staple documents circulated between merchants in Calais and in other European centres like 'modern negotiable paper'.[26] As exports of wool through Hull plummeted from 4,250 sacks per year in the decade 1419–29, to 1,609 sacks per year in the following decade, so the trade to fuel the Calais Staple shrank and opportunities to

---

[24] *MB*, II, pp. 9–10, 169.
[25] E.g. William Bracebridge of York (*Yorks Deeds*, IV, p. 161); William Brompton of Hull (Hull RO, D533, 534). Richard Blackburn moved to London but returned before he died: *MB*, II, p. 160; Prob. Reg. VIII, f. 105.   [26] Postan, 'Private Financial Instruments', pp. 49–51.

employ Staple credit were no longer available.[27] When the mint closed in 1442, merchants lending to the Crown via the Staple received Staple 'debentures' or 'obligations of Staple', which changed hands like any other asset and could be used routinely to offset customs payments.[28]

Local alternatives such as rents and mortgages were affected by the demographic consequences of successive visitations of plague and famine-related epidemics in the region. There were mortality crises in the diocese of York in 1391, 1429, 1436, 1438 and 1458–9.[29] Rural and urban rents and land values were falling, most sharply in the 1420s and 1430s.[30] The harvest failure in the region in 1438–9 undermined demographic recovery. The 1438–40 crisis had a massive effect on the northern economy, and in parts of Durham and North Yorkshire rents fell still further.[31] Thus rents as a source of cash income and as security for credit were contracting, and even the large institutions such as Fountains Abbey were affected. In the 1450s Fountains was settling debts with merchants by paying them in kind, either in lead or wool, as well as operating its customary system of delayed payment of 'old' debts.[32]

Another, more specific, demographic factor was the high mortality amongst the merchant class of York, at least in the 1430s.[33] It is harder to measure mortality rates for Hull, but five of the wealthier merchants and their wives died in the 1430s. Their deaths dispersed accumulated capital, interrupted the commercial flow, froze the debt and credit cycle of indi-

---

[27] Hanham, 'Foreign Exchange and the English Wool Merchant', pp. 160–75; Carus-Wilson and Coleman, *England's Export Trade*, pp. 57–60.

[28] Hanham, *Celys and Their World*, pp. 224–5, 231, 235.

[29] P. J. P. Goldberg, 'Mortality and Economic Change in the Diocese of York, 1390–1514', *Northern History*, 24 (1988), pp. 41–2.

[30] Bartlett, 'Expansion and Decline', pp. 28–30; J. M. W. Bean, *The Estates of the Percy Family 1416–1537* (London 1958), pp. 17, 36, 37, 41; Dyer, *Lords and Peasants*, pp. 167–71, 374.

[31] Goldberg, 'Mortality and Economic Change', pp. 45, 49; A. J. Pollard, 'The North-Eastern Economy and the Agrarian Crisis of 1438–40', *Northern History*, 25 (1989), pp. 88–105, and *North-Eastern England*, pp. 44–52.   [32] *Mem. Fountains*, III, pp. 33, 76.

[33] Merchant deaths in York from the probate registers:

1401–10	31
1411–20	2
1421–30	20
1431–40	55*
1441–50	26
1451–60	23
1461–70	10
1471–80	17
1481–90	28
1491–1500	10
1501–10	19
1511–20	12

* Not all active traders were identified as merchants in their wills and, if they are included, sixty-three merchants died in the 1430s.

vidual concerns and also brought to account a circle of financial partners, all at an unfortunate time when international trade was struggling through a serious depression.

A depleted group of Yorkshire merchants did survive the catastrophe of their exclusion from Baltic markets, but the accumulated impact of demographic crises on provincial credit arrangements in the region must have been as severe a setback. All English merchants faced increasingly difficult conditions as exchange rates adjusted. The Celys had to raise loans in the city of London as the falling rate of Flemish money against sterling in the mid-1480s made it harder to 'make over' sums to English merchants in the Low Countries. By then, the accelerating volume of trade going through London and its deeper pool of traders carried the capital over that temporary crisis.[34] No such growth bailed out the merchant groups of York, Beverley and Hull. Their golden century of trading was over.

---

[34] Hanham, *Celys and Their World*, p. 400; M. E. Bratchel, 'Italian Merchant Organisation and Business Relationships in Early Tudor London', *Jnl European Econ. Hist.*, 7 no. 1 (1978), pp. 26–7.

10

CONCLUSION

The opportunities to accumulate capital from trade, and the commercial exploitation of land and credit, gave merchants an occupational sophistication of an identifiable kind. To a greater extent than any other urban group, they were directly and rapidly affected by fluctuations in international trade. The shift from wool exports to cloth, and rising domestic consumption, transformed merchants into a class at the apex of urban society: differentiated by their mode of dress, lifestyle, economic and political expectations. No others could claim as much, and it has been argued that this easy recognition of a mercantile mentality gave craftsmen their identity as an artisan class.[1]

Their activities energised towns and the contribution of their particular skills, as well as the dispersal of accumulated profits through their spending as consumers and as employers, and death-bed charity, was to the benefit of many citizens beyond their immediate households. Collectively, they brought European commerce to their fellows, opened up distant markets for locally produced textiles and met the demand for imports. On the debit side, they undermined the livelihood of some fellow citizens by buying wherever prices were most advantageous and by importing manufactured items which competed with local manufactures. Their entrepreneurial and financial skills, in particular, made them important agents between town and countryside. Inevitably, as traders, they directly influenced the growth of towns as regional or local market centres, but they also acted as financial channels, transforming rural wealth into workable capital. Their need for cash and credit, far more than any social ambition, developed a capitalist attitude to land as an exploitable resource, and they did not hesitate to use it for their urban-based trade. Towns which lost those specialist entrepreneurial skills drifted back into local obscurity.

---

[1] Swanson, *Medieval Artisans*, pp. 172–3.

The half century from the early 1350s was an expansive time for international and domestic trade, and, indeed, for some towns. Investment opportunities in cloth production gave more people access to international trade beyond the monopoly of the wool staplers, increasing the number of active overseas merchants. The catastrophe of the Black Death had a mixed impact, creating opportunities in one town or hastening decline in another. Not many urban populations recovered their pre-plague levels, and regionally specific conditions determined their fates.[2] In York, and probably in Hull, the numbers becoming freemen rose in the second half of the fourteenth century, while in the surrounding region, textile production and other manufacturing was buoyant and the consumption of imported basics and luxuries was increasing.[3]

Commercial contraction from the turn of the fifteenth century mirrored the triumphs of the late fourteenth and merchants were forced to adapt their ventures accordingly. Fewer traded in wool. Yorkshire cloth was increasingly exported through London and northern merchants extended their investments into general imports, exporting more foodstuffs and lead. The number of men actively engaged in international commerce fell, as did the proportion of the very successful. By the end of the fifteenth century, to all intents and purposes, York and Beverley had been left high and dry by international commerce. Hull's continued involvement was almost entirely due to the use of its harbour facilities and not to the activities of its merchants.

How can one calculate the economic contribution of these overseas traders and regional merchants to their own towns? International trade had been part of Yorkshire's economy for centuries, connecting local producers with overseas markets and enhancing financial resources. The entrepreneurial failure of the region's overseas merchants had repercussions, not the least upon their own towns. Hull survived as a port, marginal to European trade, but took over as the commercial centre of east Yorkshire, relegating Beverley to the role of a minor market centre, a process well under way by the late fourteenth century.[4]

Dr Swanson has argued recently that merchants undermined urban craftsmen by their determination to retain control over the trade in key commodities. Given that imported raw materials such as alum, flax, pitch, tar and timber were crucial to specific industries, whether in small or large quantities, overseas merchants could dictate commercial terms to dependent craftsmen.[5] This became critical as York (and Beverley) textile

---

[2] R. H. Britnell, 'The Black Death in English Towns', *Urban History*, 21 (1994), pp. 200–1, 206–9, and *Commercialisation*, p. 170; Hatcher, *Plague, Population and the English Economy*, pp. 34, 49–50.

[3] Bartlett, 'Expansion and Decline', pp. 22–3; *VCH York*, pp. 114–16.

[4] *VCH Beverley*, p. 56.   [5] Swanson, *Medieval Artisans*, pp. 131, 149.

workers faced growing competition from rural producers at least from the late 1370s.[6] Merchants worked against the city's craft interests, Swanson argues, because they invested in lead rather than local cloth and discouraged the development of small-scale entrepreneurship and of a putting-out system. Moreover, York's costly civic pomp increased borough taxes and raised the costs of setting up in business. Indeed, such expenses were more likely to deter investment by outsiders than monopolistic guild regulations were.[7]

The general thesis that merchants were better placed to manipulate a town's commercial regulations cannot be challenged, though there is some evidence to suggest that merchant oligarchs were capable of seeing beyond their own interests.[8] Undoubtedly merchants did control the mechanics of supply and distribution, but some artisans invested in regional trade, handling grain and lead, and occasionally can be found importing from overseas.[9] Such a blurring of occupational activities confirms that artisans could be as single minded as merchants when it came to profit.

There were, however, more complex reasons for the decline in York's textile production, specifically of broadcloths, than simply mercantile exploitation. The growing demand for cloth at home and abroad in the later fourteenth century put clothworkers under considerable pressure to increase production. It is likely that York and Beverley cloth was expensive to make because production was under-mechanised. Following the loss of labour in the Black Death, productivity rose in some areas due to increased mechanisation: water-powered fulling mills initially, and gig mills by the fifteenth century.[10] The swifter flow of water in the Pennine region clearly lent itself to such developments, but there is no technical reason why the flow on the slower lowland rivers could not have been increased.[11] There were watermills in York, but they were used for grinding corn, and although there was at least one watermill and several horse-

---

[6] 'Tolls of the Collectors in the West Riding of the Lay Subsidy in Richard II', *Yorks Arch. Jnl* 5 (1879); 6 (1881); 7 (1882).   [7] Swanson, *Medieval Artisans*, p. 149.

[8] The council supported city guilds fighting rural competition. See e.g. bowyers, founders, weavers in the 1390s: *MB*, I, pp. 53, 84; *CPR 1396–9*, p. 506; *VCH York*, pp. 88–9; girdlers in 1417, fullers in 1425 and 1470s: *MB*, I, pp. 181–4; II, p. 159; *YCR*, I, p. 20; Heaton, *Yorks Woollen and Worsted Industries*, pp. 34–7, 44, 50–2. In 1406, in response to complaints, the council prohibited the practice of some merchants who were selling 'foreign' cloth and wool in York as their own and evading the proper tolls to the detriment of the city: *MB*, II, pp. 204–5.

[9] Swanson, *Medieval Artisans*, pp. 132–41.

[10] Bridbury, *Medieval English Clothmaking*, p. 65; Kerridge, 'Wool Growing and Wool Textiles', p. 22.

[11] For instance, a weir was constructed at Chester, on the River Dee, to increase its flow to power watermills: B. Harris, *Chester*, Bartholemew City Guides (Chester, 1979), p. 135.

mills in and around Beverley, archaeological opinion discounts their use in fulling.[12]

In York, the evidence of the freemen's rolls suggests that increased production depended on an increase in manpower, since the rate of entry of new fullers was strikingly higher than for any other group of textile workers, including weavers. Between 1341 and 1351, only two fullers became freemen compared to the fifteen between 1351 and 1361, a sevenfold increase; whereas twenty weavers became freemen between 1341 and 1351, and forty-four between 1351 and 1361, just over twice as many.[13] York made up much of its losses of skilled labour in the decades following the Black Death, but successive visitations of plague or other epidemic diseases probably kept the supply of labour low well into the fifteenth century in spite of a flurry of freemen admissions following crisis years. One consequence was an expansion in employment opportunities for women, well recorded from the 1370s, suggesting that skilled men were scarce.[14] A reliance on manpower instead of on mechanical fulling[15] partly explains the higher unit cost of urban cloth compared to rural cloth.[16]

While trade was buoyant in the late fourteenth century, production throughout the region expanded,[17] the price of wool was down and most cloth seemed to find a ready market. Once the recession began to bite early in the fifteenth century, cheaper cloths had the advantage in the mass market overseas, and clothworkers in York and Beverley were undermined by their rural competitors.[18] Putting-out and piece-working probably contributed to the process.[19] Few merchants risked capital by investing it in equipment and, like the wealthier artisans, exploited the independent craftsmen by leaving that burden to them. A few, like Robert Holme in the late fourteenth century, and Thomas Clynt and Thomas Carre of York in the 1430s and '40s, directly employed rural out-

---

[12] *VCH York*, pp. 506–8; *RCHMSS Beverley*, p. 33.

[13] Bartlett, 'Expansion and Decline', p. 22.

[14] Goldberg, 'Female Labour, Service, and Marriage', pp. 19, 28–32, and 'Mortality and Economic Change', pp. 41–2, 45–6, 51–2.

[15] Cf. Colchester, where mechanical fulling has been credited with the successful expansion of the town's textile production in the second half of the fourteenth century: Britnell, *Growth and Decline in Colchester*, pp. 67–8.

[16] E.g. there were fulling mills and dye vats (at Tenter Hill) in Leeds in 1438–9: J. W. Kirby, ed., *The Manor and Borough of Leeds, 1425–1662: An Edition of Documents*, Thoresby Soc., 57 (1981), pp. 4–5. More generally on Yorkshire, see Bridbury, *Medieval English Clothmaking*, p. 114; Heaton, *Yorks Woollen and Worsted Industries*, pp. 47–79.

[17] Heaton, *Yorks Woollen and Worsted Industries*, pp. 60, 75; Goldberg, 'Mortality and Economic Change', p. 50.

[18] Perhaps in quality as well as quantity. There were complaints that Beverley weavers were producing shoddy goods in 1437: *Bev. Town Docs.*, p. 33.

[19] Swanson, *Medieval Artisans*, pp. 34, 114; Bridbury, *Medieval English Clothmaking*, pp. 2, 6, 11, 55.

workers,[20] undeterred by wider considerations of the urban common weal to which they undoubtedly paid lip-service.

By 1473, West Riding production surpassed that of York (see table 5.3 on p. 176). The city was not alone in losing ground, and fulling mills in north Yorkshire began closing down in the 1470s.[21] York tapiters and linen-weavers made something of a comeback later in the fifteenth century, supplying the luxury end of the market, and it is possible that dyeing and other finishing processes retained a regional importance. It is not clear what role local merchants played.[22]

Merchants bought cloth wherever they could, producers sold it to whoever had the cash or secure credit.[23] The accumulation of resources following the Black Death had turned some rural survivors into small-scale entrepreneurs,[24] vital to the industrial expansion of the West Riding. Their ability to establish a distribution network independent of urban merchants presaged the contraction of York's textile manufacturing base and ultimately the failure of her merchants. Once it became possible to retain marketing control within an expanding and unregulated production area, that would be preferred simply because it kept costs down: particularly compared to urban costs such as guild charges and borough taxes.[25]

The suggestion that York merchants deserted local cloth in favour of investments in lead is difficult to sustain. It was not as important an item for them as was cloth until the 1470s (see table 8.5 on p. 273), well past the onset of the city's textile decline. Moreover, the process of marketing cloth did not give the overseas merchants the monopolistic control ascribed to them, even within the confines of urban regulation. All sorts of people sold cloth, and merchants from our three towns had to compete

---

[20] See above, p. 205.

[21] Heaton, *Yorks Woollen and Worsted Industries*, pp. 70–5; Pollard, *North-Eastern England*, p. 73.

[22] Bartlett, 'Aspects of the Economy of York', pp. 66–9; *VCH York*, p. 89. In Colchester, merchants promoted the manufacture of a higher quality cloth to replace russets: Britnell, *Commercialisation*, p. 176

[23] At this point in the acceleration of the trade in cloth, sale credits probably became as important as cash as the volume of transactions rose and there was a shortage of bullion. Certainly London grocers were struggling to activate sufficient credit to finance the demand for cloth: Nightingale, *Medieval Mercantile Community*, pp. 327–30; Postan, 'Credit in Medieval Trade', p. 261.

[24] This may have occurred earlier than elsewhere: E. M. Carus-Wilson, 'Evidence of Industrial Growth on some Fifteenth Century Manors', *EcHR* 2nd ser., 12 (1959), pp. 193–6 (mid-fifteenth century), pp. 198–200, 202 (by 1409); C. Dyer, 'A Small Landowner in the Fifteenth Century', *Midland History*, 1 (1972), pp. 1–14.

[25] Mercers and general merchants were listed in the 1379 Poll Tax: R. B. Dobson, 'Yorkshire Towns in the Late Fourteenth Century', *Miscellany*, Thoresby Soc., 18 (1983), pp. 1–21; Lister, *Early Yorks Woollen Trade*, pp. 35–100; Swanson, *Medieval Artisans*, p. 144. See also Bridbury, *Medieval English Clothmaking*, p. 63; D. C. Coleman, 'Proto-Industrialisation: A Concept Too Many', *EcHR* 2nd ser., 36 (1983), p. 440.

with each other and with Hanseatic and London traders. Indeed, it could be argued that it was the failure of the broadcloth industry in York and Beverley to adjust costs to match rural competition which contributed to the collapse of overseas trade and drove merchants to export lead instead, to initiate a two-way trade.[26]

The investment by urban merchants in rural industry is one element in this model; another and perhaps the most influential, was the re-routing of Hanse purchasing, away from the east coast ports and towns, and out of the region through London.[27] A further consideration was the impact of demographic events and of market forces external to Yorkshire, which resulted in London merchants pushing into the lead in the nation's overseas trade.[28] Further challenges came from the expanding group of York-based chapmen whose number grew as the number of York's textile workers diminished, suggesting that they were taking an increasing share of the region's trade at the expense of the large-scale operators.[29]

The shrunken merchant class of mid- to late-fifteenth-century York was a pale reflection of its predecessors. Capital resources were consider-ably diminished and, in spite of a handful of wealthy individuals, there was no longer a sizeable group with middling to large investments in trade. To paint them as the villains in urban decline, because of their potential to dominate all aspects of the market, and their failure to con-tinue to generate long-distance trade, is to ignore important external factors. In any case, investment in York by outsiders was not deterred, as the activities of London grocers confirm, but whatever profits accrued from their investments were syphoned away to the south-east.[30]

Access to opportunities did not automatically lead to success. While some merchants prospered exceedingly, others barely survived. As Sylvia Thrupp observed, 'there were men who had to struggle to keep their heads above water and died without materially increasing the small prop-erty with which they had started their business'.[31] Even when massive mercantile fortunes could be acquired in the late fourteenth and early fif-teenth centuries, the merchant class perforce included men barely dis-tinguishable from hawkers. This is an important point to emphasise since it is easy to use the term merchants to imply a homogeneous wealthy elite. While it is argued that more opportunities to accumulate capital

---

[26] Swanson, *Medieval Artisans*, pp. 141–2, and see p. 204 above.

[27] Gras, *Early English Customs*, pp. 120, 459, 469.

[28] Kermode, 'Merchants, Overseas Trade and Urban Decline', pp. 51–73.

[29] *VCH York*, pp. 114–16. Braudel argues that these peripatetic traders emerged during recessions, when economic conditions favoured low-cost enterprises: F. Braudel, *Civilisation and Capitalism, 15th–18th Century, II: The Wheels of Commerce*, translated by S. Reynolds (London, 1982–3), pp. 75–80. I am grateful to Pamela Nightingale for this reference.

[30] York RO, E39, pp. 278, 284–5, 288, 295.   [31] Thrupp, *London Merchant Class*, p. 110.

were available to merchants, other townsmen also waxed rich. In terms of accumulated landed wealth, the position of merchants *vis-à-vis* other townsmen could vary markedly. In York, merchants comprised a minority amongst a galaxy of earls and knights owning land valued at over £20, whereas in smaller Beverley and Hull, merchants were the largest landowners.[32] By London standards, of course, the average Yorkshire merchant was not wealthy in terms of cash or landed income. In 1436, 145 London merchants were assessed at over £10, that is 73 per cent of all citizens assessed at that level. Of these, eighty-four were assessed at over £20 and five aldermen at over £100.[33]

The biographies of the small merchants suggest that many ended up with little disposable income and few assets. Yet they were an important penumbra, a transitional stratum, through which immigrants and a small percentage of occupationally mobile craftsmen moved.[34] In contrast, others moved straight into the middle or even top ranks of the merchant class by virtue of wealth or influential connections.[35] Inevitably it was the commercially and politically successful who gave the merchant class its high profile in urban affairs. The implications of short-lived merchant families and of the greater importance of class, as opposed to individual family survival, were especially marked in local government. In each of the three boroughs, merchants were the politically advantaged group. In the absence of dynastic dominion in York, the continuity of government was sustained by a system of self-perpetuating oligarchies, and their construction of a corporate ethic. In smaller Beverley and Hull, continuity was sustained by a core group, reinforced by effective institutions.

Like many of their fellow townsfolk, not all merchants subscribed to the oligarchs' perception or chose actively to propagate it.[36] For all their apparent self-confidence, public display and efforts to legitimise their government in the eyes of their fellow townsmen, the myth of able government was vulnerable. In Beverley, economic decline was met with attempts to tighten oligarchic control. As a minor centre, the town escaped the worst ravages of the Lancastrian and Yorkist struggle, though it did contribute men and money.[37] In contrast, York experienced a quarter of a century of turmoil as its economy slid further into recession. In the 1470s, '80s and '90s, the merchant rulers were under severe

---

[32] Swanson, *Medieval Artisans*, pp. 158–9, and see p. 278 above.

[33] Thrupp, *London Merchant Class*, p. 126; PRO, E179/238/90.

[34] Dr Swanson has calculated that only 7 per cent of the 806 *per patrem* artisan entrants between 1387 and 1534 moved into mercantile occupations: *Medieval Artisans*, p. 165.

[35] Brian Conyers of York, for example, was well connected, but said to be poor: Kermode, 'Merchants of York, Beverley and Hull', appendix 4.

[36] Thomas Scotton of York, for instance, was fined for refusing to become an alderman in 1490: *YCR*, I, p. 37; York RO, House Book VII, ff. 2v., 4.   [37] *VCH Beverley*, p. 34.

pressure as the city's economy contracted and townsmen challenged guild and council authority.[38] At the same time, the factional politics of the Wars of the Roses and their aftermath spilled over, confusing an already disturbed situation.[39] Whatever the injustice inherent in mercantile domination of civic government, it is to the credit of the rulers of York that complete anarchy did not occur, although at times the council was close to losing its grip.

Unlike York, Hull did not have to accommodate members of each faction, although the council did distribute largesse to both Yorkists and Lancastrians. As in York, there is evidence of divided loyalties but not of the riotous outbursts which exercised the York council. The Lancastrian mayor of Hull, merchant Richard Anson, was killed at the battle of Towton. Other individuals pursued their own partisan politics, whatever the attempts of the council to placate the new king, and in May 1461, thirty-two men were expelled from the city for 'misrule' and three more imprisoned soon after. Hull diligently courted the favour of Richard of Gloucester, but showed little sign of continued loyalty to him after Bosworth.[40] Hull councillors have left an impression of careful detachment, of a desire to minimise the town's involvement in national politics, and certainly of less grandiose pretensions than their counterparts in York.

The perception by others of the merchant class was probably mixed, but in some important respects merchants were at one with their fellows. The evidence for the three towns suggests that although new associations did develop the family retained its key role in mercantile society, even though consideration was given in *post mortem* provision not just to immediate kin, but to a wider network of responsibilities. Wealthy merchants could afford material benevolence to circles of friends and acquaintances, both to influential citizens and servants, thereby acknowledging public association as well as personal affection. Mutual interdependence, especially amongst the middling to top-ranking merchants, is well illustrated by their reliance upon each other to act as guardians to children, advisors to widows and executors of wills. Dynasties were rare and families generally short-lived, but often with a complex intermingling of step- and half-siblings. For merchants at least, the family remained a significant social and economic unit but was complemented

---

[38] *VCH York*, pp. 82–4.

[39] *Ibid.*, pp. 59–65; M. Hicks, 'The Yorkshire Rebellion of 1489 Reconsidered', *Northern History*, 22 (1986) pp. 39–62.

[40] Demands for men, ships and money depleted Hull's resources to such an extent that the city had an enormous deficit in 1461 which continued to burden it for the rest of the century, in spite of royal compensation: *VCH Hull*, pp. 23–6; A. E. Goodman, *The Wars of the Roses* (London, 1981), pp. 218–20; E. Gillett and K. MacMahon, *A History of Hull* (Oxford, 1980), pp. 63–9.

by other associations which extended into the wider context of neighbourhood, town and region. Some of these came from business transactions and others were the outcome of political and social aspirations. Marriage played a key role in reinforcing political connections and retaining wealth and commercial expertise within the merchant class.

By following the religious conventions and philanthropic fashions of their day, merchants shared more common ground with other townsfolk. Affirming family identity through several generations was clearly important for those who could afford to pay for prayers. Most of their religious provision was directed towards parish churches, their chosen place of burial, although the mendicant orders and monastic houses within the region were often recipients. Even so, conspicuous spending marked out merchant benefactors, making death an opportunity for reinforcing differences of status in funereal and charitable display. Names prominent on windows and liturgical robes monogrammed with the donor's initials kept the memory of wealthy merchants alive before the congregation's gaze. Membership of an elitist association such as the Corpus Christi Guild ensured social equals were in attendance at funerals, as well as the paupers waiting for doles.

In an age when rank was determined by riches, merchants were at the centre of the stage and dominated urban society through their wealth, their marriage networks and political power. Understandably, their achievements often frustrated the aspirations of others, creating considerable tension. Theirs was the occupation *par excellence*, which held out the promise of advancement, but which also held on to what it had achieved by a combination of formal and informal institutions. Local religious fraternities might have been open to and have attracted merchant support alongside others, but entry to the York or Hull Corpus Christi Guilds was socially exclusive and artisans were not encouraged.[41]

The York Mercers and Merchant Adventurers' Company had a distinctive character quite unlike that of the local craft guilds and closer to that of a London company.[42] Although in its early days all sorts of men, including countryfolk, had been allowed to join, it soon became an exclusive association of traders. Individuals could choose to borrow venture capital or to take shares in a collective enterprise. To a remarkable extent, its records replicated municipal accounts of council proceedings and official business. There are details of commercial disputes, letters between the York company and the national adventurers' company, documents relating to the company's own hospital of St

[41] See above, chapter 1.
[42] See Unwin, *Gilds and Companies of London, passim*; Thrupp, 'The Grocers of London', pp. 247–62, 284–8.

Thomas, registers of new members including merchants' wives, accounts of quarterage payments, of arrears and so forth.[43] The company hall must have resembled a corporation headquarters and its importance was consolidated by the steady stream of masters of the company into the mayoralty.[44]

However, merchants did not monopolise the top of the civic ladder for long. Their political demise inexorably followed their commercial failure and civic office became accessible to nearly all occupational groups. By the middle of the sixteenth century merchants were just one of several economically important groups, and in York and Beverley erstwhile inferior occupations were moving in to share power.[45] In Hull, however, merchants retained their authority well into the seventeenth century.[46] In the three towns, the legacy of mercantile domination was far-reaching. The political and social culture which had emerged during their struggle for, and enjoyment of, power became synonymous with urban living itself.

[43] *M&MA*, pp. 40, 68, 72–3, 195 and *passim*.
[44] For the list of masters/governors, see *ibid.*, pp. 322–8. Only two of the thirty-seven men who served as master did not also serve as mayor or sheriff.
[45] Palliser, *TudorYork*, pp. 106–7; *VCH Beverley*, p. 66.
[46] *VCH Hull*, pp. 121–2. Merchants hung on to power in Exeter and Bristol also: W. G. Hoskins, *Old Devon* (Newton Abbot, 1966), p. 76; D. H. Sacks, *Trade, Society and Politics in Bristol*, 2 vols. (New York, 1985), II, pp. 694–8.

Appendix 1

OFFICES AND ELECTION PROCEDURES

We know enough about York and Hull to identify key stages in their election systems, whereas election to Beverley's single tier of government remains obscure.

YORK

The central figure in York's government was the mayor. By 1343, he was elected annually on 15 January to serve from 3 February. From 1392, and possibly earlier, the retiring mayor nominated two or three aldermen from whom the commonalty elected one and witnessed his oath-taking. A regulation agreed in 1372, banning anyone who had held office within the preceding eight years from election, had not been observed, and from 1392, no-one was to be elected for a further term until all of the aldermen had served.[1]

Following riots at election time in 1464, Edward IV ordered a change in the procedure. The retiring mayor was to summon the searchers of each craft on 14 January to order them to ensure that their members should attend at the Guildhall on 15 January. The craftsmen were to nominate two aldermen (three in 1489), neither of whom had been mayor twice nor had served during the five preceding years (six in 1489). The nominations were to be handed to the mayor and council, which included the recorder and common clerk, for them to vote in a secret ballot. Non-voting officials acted as tellers. (In 1516 the mayor claimed two votes but it is unclear if this was or had been customary.) The candidate with the highest vote was declared on 3 February.[2]

Further unrest led to further changes in 1473 so that the crafts chose one alderman to serve as mayor.[3] In 1489, perhaps as a consequence of a rising by the commons of the rural areas which evoked a response in York and led to the occupation of the city by the country rebels, the council petitioned the king to have the 1464 procedure restored. Henry VII agreed in December 1489[4] in time for that year's election, and confirmed the procedure in 1492.[5] In 1494 the

---

[1] York RO, c/y, ff. 4, 9v.; *MB*, I, p. 116; II, p. 255.   [2] *CPR 1461–7*, p. 366; *YCR*, III, p. 52.
[3] *CPR 1467–77*, p. 416.   [4] *CPR 1485–94*, p. 297.
[5] *YCR*, II, pp. 50, 54–5, 104; York RO, House Book VII, f. 22v.

searchers of every craft 'and other citizens' met and wrote down three names. Further election riots occurred in 1504, moving the archbishop to advise the council to direct the guild searchers to ask the craftsmen what complaints they had and to present them in writing![6] However, there was no change in the election procedure until 1517, ironically as a consequence of jealousies amongst the aldermen. Thereafter an election committee, composed of craft representatives and twenty-eight senior searchers, was to nominate the mayoral candidates.[7]

The full text of the 1489 regulation discloses a number of other features such as physical arrangements and the solemn binding of the burgesses to the outcome of the election:

Grant to the mayor and citizens of the city of York, on surrender of their letters patent dated 20 December, 13 Edward IV, and to put an end to dissensions, that the election of a mayor shall be made in form following: – The existing mayor shall on the eve of St Maur, viz. 14 January, summon all the searchers of every mistery to warn all the artificers of their mistery to appear personally in the Gildhall on the next day for the election of a mayor. The artificers so met shall elect three aldermen, no one of whom has been twice mayor or once mayor within six years. These three names shall be presented in writing by the sheriffs and the common clerk of the city or any two of them, to the mayor, aldermen and council of the mayor's chamber, which done, the said sheriffs and clerk, or two of them, shall go to a fit spot to be appointed by the mayor, aldermen and council, and the mayor and every alderman and every other member of the council shall say secretly to the said sheriffs and clerk or two of them which of the then nominated aldermen he wishes to have as mayor, and the common clerk, in view of the sheriffs or one of them, shall make pricks or marks over the names as the electors give their votes; and he over whose name are the greatest number of pricks or marks shall be declared by the sheriffs and clerk or two of them to be mayor from the feast of St Blaise following for one year. If the votes are equal the mayor shall select the one he wishes to have. If the mayor so elected die or leave or be dismissed from office, then the second of the three aldermen elected as aforesaid shall be elected mayor for the rest of the year, or the other one at the discretion of the twelve aldermen and council. The mayor so elected shall remain in authority until the feast of St Blaise following, and on that day at about ten o'clock before mid-day in the Gildhall, he who is newly declared and elected to be mayor shall take the usual oath before all the citizens then present and that done, shall be mayor. Afterwards the said aldermen and citizens (concives) there present shall swear to be aiding and supporting to him during his mayoralty in all that pertains to his office concerning the honour and utility or prosperity of the city. If any citizen attempt anything by word or deed against the form of this election he shall forfeit by that all his liberties and franchises in the said city, and further be punished at the discretion of the mayor and pay £10 for the common utility of the city, if his goods and means permit, if not, then according to his means as estimated at the discretion of the mayor, aldermen and council.

The mayor was assisted by three bailiffs up to 1396, elected to serve from 29 September to coincide with the Exchequer's financial year.[8] At least from 1357 they chose their own successors, who had to have two pledges each as sureties and, once elected, were presented to the mayor and commonalty for approval.

[6] *YCR*, III, pp. 4–5.   [7] *VCH York*, p. 137.   [8] *VCH York*, pp. 71–2; York RO c/y, f. 313.

The bailiffs chose their subordinate officials themselves.[9] After 1396, when York acquired county status, the three bailiffs were replaced by two sheriffs,[10] elected on 21 September for the 29th. They were elected by those 'to whom the election pertained', members of the council who deliberated in the inner chamber of the Guildhall while the mayor and commonalty waited outside to be told of the choice.[11] At least from 1418 the sheriffs became ex officio members of the twenty-four and remained as members after their year in office was ended. In 1494 it was made compulsory for sheriffs to have served previously as a chamberlain.[12] Their election was the key to the mayoralty since new aldermen were chosen exclusively from the twenty-four, and in 1504 some members of the commonalty asked for the nomination of shrieval candidates but were refused. In 1499 the mayor had to be reminded not to select new aldermen on his own.[13]

The last important annually filled office was that of chamberlain.[14] In 1376 the chamberlains' election was moved from 29 September to 3 February to coincide with the mayoral election. They were chosen by the new mayor and council on that day, and after 1475 election to the office was restricted to those men who had previously served as a bridgemaster.[15]

The mayor and council were assisted by a number of non-elected officials, appointed by the council, of whom the most most important were the common clerk and recorder.[16] Of the officials noted above only the mayor, common clerk and recorder received an annual fee. In 1385 the mayor's fee was raised from £20 to £40 and to £50 in 1388. As part of the 1392 reforms, it was decided that his fee should not exceed £50, but the commons considered the fee to be excessive in 1490 when they asked for it to be reduced.[17]

The twelve became known as aldermen after 1396 and in the fifteenth century

---

[9] *MB*, II, p. 259.   [10] *Ibid.*; *VCH York*, p. 72.   [11] *MB*, II, pp. 52, 74–5; House Book IX, f. 50.

[12] House Book VII, f. 109. See Kermode, 'Urban Decline?', pp. 179–98.

[13] *MB*, II, p. 75; *YCR*, II, p. 141; III, p. 8; York RO, House Book IX, f. 19v.

[14] There were usually three chamberlains, four in 1483, six in 1487, and three again in 1500. The numbers fluctuated in an effort to share the load. Chamberlains carried an invidious responsibility. They had no control over the collection of revenue, but were expected to balance the accounts at the end of their year in office and to be available at all times, and after 1379 they were fined if they refused to sit with the mayor to conduct business in the council chamber. There was usually a current deficit and the chamberlains had to meet day-to-day expenses out of their own pockets in anticipation of future incoming revenue. From 1484, outgoing chamberlains were to be paid £140 in three instalments by their successors, as recompense for personal losses, while the incoming chamberlains were to assume the debt themselves, reimbursing their predecessors as a matter of course. It was hoped that the problem of former chamberlains constantly petitioning the council for redress would be resolved. In 1487 two aldermen, two of the twenty-four and four honest commoners were set up as an auditing committee to examine the chamberlains' accounts retrospectively from the 1470s. *MB*, I, pp. 33–4; *YCR*, I, pp. 89–90; House Book V, ff. 6v., 17v.–18v.; VI, f. 92. For a comprehensive description of their duties, see Dobson, *York City Chamberlains' Account Rolls*, pp. xxi–xxxi.   [15] *MB*, I, p. 16; II, pp. 246, 257.

[16] *MB*, I, p. 40; House Book IX, f. 46v.; *VCH York*, p. 74. For a discussion of the important part played by recorders in civic affairs, see Horrox, 'Urban Patronage', p. 160.

[17] The common clerk was receiving £7 13s 4d in 1445/6 but could also expect to receive a pension after his term of office was ended. The recorder was receiving £1 6s 8d in 1445/6, and in 1490 it was agreed, on the request of the commonalty, to reduce his annual fee to 20d. *VCH York*, p. 70; *YCR*, II, p. 54; York RO Acct. Roll, 1445–6. The chamberlains received a fee from time to time: e.g. 3s 8d each in 1445/6, York RO Acct. Roll, 1445–6.

two aldermen were associated with each of the six wards in the city. Aldermen served until they died or were too old or ill to attend meetings, and vacancies were filled by the remaining aldermen choosing a replacement from the twenty-four within four days. The twenty-four were, of course, excluded from these deliberations.[18] After 1418 membership was limited to ex-sheriffs. It seems unlikely that the twenty-four often had twenty-four members, as entry was via the office of sheriff, and numbers fluctuated above and below twenty-four depending on the supply of ex-sheriffs willing to attend.[19]

HULL

The structure of Hull's government was similar to that of York.[20] The mayor was being elected annually from the 1330s and, by 1434, by a secret ballot on 30 September. The full procedure was recorded for the first time in 1443. The aldermen nominated two of their number, one of whom was chosen by the burgesses as mayor.[21] From 1379, no senior official was to be re-elected within three years of each term in office, [22] but this restriction was either ignored or was impossible to implement with regard to the mayoralty, and from 1440 was amended so that no-one was to serve for two successive years. Two bailiffs assisted the mayor, elected annually on the same day as the mayor at least from 1434.[23] When Hull acquired county status in 1440, they were replaced with one sheriff. According to the charter of 1440, those who had previously served as a bailiff were excluded from the shrievalty, [24] but one of the bailiffs in 1439–40, William Spencer, became the first sheriff. The sheriff was to be elected by the burgesses from among themselves, but by 1443 the nomination of two candidates was in the hands of the aldermen, and one candidate was chosen by the burgesses.

The town's financial affairs were the responsibility of two chamberlains, elected annually after 1443 from four nominees of the aldermen.[25] They were supervised by four auditors annually appointed by 1452.[26] The mayor and council were assisted by a number of non-elected officials, appointed by the council, of whom the most important were the common clerk and the recorder.[27] As in York, only the mayor, common clerk and recorder and some

[18] *YCR*, II, pp. 258, 261; House Book VII, f. 37v.; IX, f. 27v.
[19] *MB*, II, pp. 75, 259–60; House Book VIII, f. 37v.; IX, f. 27v.; Attreed, *York House Books*, I, p. xxix, n. 41.
[20] Before Edward I transformed Wyke-on-Hull into a borough in 1299, it had been governed by the abbey's bailiffs. Between 1299 and 1331, six royal wardens ruled, all regular Crown servants: *VCH Hull*, p. 29.   [21] Hull RO, BRE I, pp. 98, 117, 164 *et seq.*; *CPR 1441–6*, pp. 180–1.
[22] Hull RO, BRE I, p. 210.
[23] *CPR 1441–1516*, pp. 180–1; Hull RO, BRE I, p. 164; BRG I, f. 12.
[24] *VCH Hull*, pp. 32–3; *CChR 1427–1516*, pp. 8–11.
[25] *VCH Hull*, pp. 31–3; *CChR 1427–1516*, pp. 8–11; *CPR 1441–6*, pp. 180–1.
[26] Hull RO, BRE I, p. 173; BRB I, f. 23; BRG I, f. 14.
[27] These included three or four common serjeants, one coroner (two after 1447), common attorneys, a schoolmaster, ferrymen, minstrels and a bellman. *VCH Hull*, pp. 30, 32, 34; Hull RO, BRE I, p. 206; BRE 2, ff. 13, 21–2v.; BRG I, f. 14v.; BRB I, ff. 24v., 56; M479 *passim*.

of the minor officials received a regular fee. In 1356 the mayor's fee was set at £13 6s 8d and was to be supplemented by the profits of the assizes of bread and wine. The sum fluctuated, however, and in 1409 it was £20; £33 6s 8d in 1448; and £20 again in 1451.[28] The sheriff was granted certain issues in lieu of a fee.[29] The chamberlains received no income for their services and indeed, from 1434, were expected to contribute £20 for the town's benefit within eight days of their election.[30] The chamberlains and sheriff filled another office, that of bailiff of the Tripett.[31]

The mayor was advised by a council which had existed informally since the mid-fourteenth century.[32] In 1351, for example, the mayor and bailiffs were assisted by nineteen named burgesses in approving craft legislation, and in 1356 the chamberlains were ordered not to make any payments or gifts without the assent of the mayor and six of the better burgesses. In 1379, eight burgesses were to be elected annually 'd'asser ove le maier' and bailiffs. These were not a random selection. Of the eight elected that year, three were former mayors, one a former bailiff, one later served as mayor, and one, Thomas Swynfleet, was married to the niece of a former mayor, Geoffrey Hanby. Thereafter no official was to be re-elected within three years.[33]

In 1440 the 'best burgesses' were given formal status as a council of twelve aldermen, who served for life. From 1443 vacancies were to be filled by the burgesses choosing one of the two candidates nominated by the remaining aldermen.[34] There was no formal outer council in Hull but an informal group was summoned from time to time, composed of those who had served as sheriff and as chamberlains, and those who were 'likely to serve' as chamberlains.[35] Craft guilds were slow to emerge in Hull and apparently played no formal role in elections, but 'worthy' burgesses, chosen by their fellows, assisted the common clerk in taking votes. In 1458–9, the candidates themselves chose men to 'go with the book' amongst the voters. The ballot was said to be secret in Hull and in 1451 burgesses had to be reminded to vote once only.[36]

Two other offices in Hull should be noted, although they were not separate full-time appointments. Four auditors were appointed annually, at least from the mid-1450s, and from 1454, four bailiffs of the Tripett, an area to the north of

---

[28] The common clerk was paid very little in comparison: £1 6s 8d until 1444 and £3 6s 8d thereafter. The recorder received even less: 13s 4d in 1440, rising to £2 13s. 4d in 1458. Hull RO, M479/1/1, 6, 2/22, 25, 27; BRE 1, pp. 173, 205; BRB 1, f. 65.

[29] In 1442 the sheriff shared the profits of the assizes of bread and wine with the mayor, collected money from the prisoners in the town gaol, and received payment for serving in other capacities, such as a justice of the sewers. Hull RO, BRE 2, f. 23v.; BRB 1, f. 81v.

[30] Hull RO, BRE 1, p. 164. From 1440 the £20 was paid directly to the mayor, BRE 2, f. 14v. The chamberlains had to meet current expenses out of their own pockets, and retiring chamberlains regularly faced difficulties in persuading their successors to reimburse them. See, for example, BRB 1, ff. 17, 36, 81.   [31] See below, note 37.

[32] The earliest mention discovered refers to *probi homines* witnessing a quitclaim in 1339: BRE 1, p. 90.   [33] *Ibid.*, pp. 90, 170, 173, 210, 271.

[34] *CPR 1441–6*, pp. 180–1; Hull RO, BRE 1, p. 13, BRG 1, f. 13v.

[35] Hull RO, BRB 1, ff. 67, 77v., 81.

[36] *VCH Hull*, p. 36; BRE 1, p. 164; BRE 2, ff. 93(i), (ii); BRB 1, f. 55v.

Hull in which the city had been granted certain privileges by the Charterhouse.[37] The auditors had all previously served as sheriff, or were respected men, past and future mayors. It is not clear how burdensome their duties were, but some men acquired a great deal of experience as auditors. Edmund Coppendale, for example, was an auditor at least ten times, and first served one year after his term as sheriff.[38] Thomas Etton was another willing auditor and served at least eleven times.[39]

The four bailiffs of the Tripett comprised the sheriff, the current chamberlains or those of the previous year, and one other. A man could serve several times as a Tripett bailiff: first as a chamberlain and then as sheriff. Thus Roger Bushell was chamberlain and a bailiff of the Tripett in 1458–9, sheriff and a bailiff in 1461, and again in 1462.[40] This was a common pattern and some men also acted as a bailiff in between their terms as a chamberlain and sheriff.

BEVERLEY

The structure of Beverley's government was quite different from the hierarchies of York and Hull. By 1306 Beverley had its own common seal and was governed by a council of twelve keepers, under its seigneur, the archbishop of York.[41] The bailiff of the archbishop's liberty in Beverley was appointed yearly to act as the archbishop's agent.[42] During the fourteenth century there were often two bailiffs acting for the archbishop in Beverley, and they received all royal letters and mandates which were addressed to 'the bailiffs and men of Beverley'.[43] Bailiffs were often drawn from the same families as the keepers and they enlisted the bailiff's help, and from time to time accounts of payments made to him were recorded as were payments made to the archbishop's receiver.[44]

The twelve keepers, later known as governors, ran the town under the arch-

---

[37] *VCH Hull*, pp. 33–4; Hull RO, BRB I, ff. 32, 37. 119v.

[38] BRB I, ff. 46, 59, 80, 95v., 107, 110v., 114v., 118v., 127v., 132.

[39] *Ibid.* and ff. 65v., 72v., 113, 116, 120v., 129v., 142.

[40] BRB I, ff. 65v., 80, 82v.   [41] Humberside RO, BC II/3, f. 6.

[42] A. H. Thompson ed., *Archbishop Greenfield's Register*, I, Surtees Soc., 145 (1931), pp. xxv–xxvi, 169, 218, 232. He acted as supervisor to the reeve, who was responsible for dispatching supplies for the archbishop's use and for certain rents and farms, such as those for the water-houses in the bailiwick: *ibid.*, I, p. 172; IV, Surtees Soc., 152 (1938), p. 277; V, Surtees Soc., 153 (1940), p. 41. The bailiff was assisted by a clerk of the toll and a collector of rents in the vill of Beverley. There was also a receiver appointed by the archbishop and the bailiff audited his accounts before they were sent to the general receiver's office at York: *ibid.*, I, p. 195; V, pp. 37, 41.

[43] E.g. *Rotuli Scotiae*, I, pp. 217, 330, 350, 461; F. Grose, *Military Antiquities* (London, 1786), I, pp. 10, 125; Humberside RO, BC II/2, f. 2.

[44] E.g. Humberside RO, BC II/6/3, 5, 9. The bailiff did not only act in a supervisory capacity. In 1307 he collected the monies due to the collectors of the one thirtieth subsidy, and three years later he was ordered to relax distraints he had made against Sir Hubert Fitzjohn for homages and reliefs due to the archbishop. In the course of the archbishop's dispute with the men of Hull, the Beverley bailiff was called upon to denounce as excommunicate all those infringing the archbishop's liberty in the water of the River Hull. Occasionally the bailiff received petitions on the archbishop's behalf and answered them as advised by his lord. Thompson, *Archbishop Greenfield's Register*, I, pp. 173–4, 196, 224, 265; V, p. 41.

bishop's bailiff. By 1345, the keepers were elected annually on 25 April by the burgesses with the assent of the retiring keepers and with the archbishop's representative present.[45] In 1359 the keepers changed the procedure in the 'Magna Carta' which they issued, perhaps as a result of election riots in 1356.[46] The power to nominate was limited to the retiring keepers who chose eighteen of the 'more sufficient men' of Beverley, excluding those who had served as keepers within the preceding three years, and the burgesses elected twelve.[47] By 1498, when the pool of nominees was reduced from thirty back to eighteen, as desired by 'the whole town', there had obviously been some slight modifications to the procedure which were largely ineffective.[48] The concept of collective responsibility applied to the other duties of the keepers as they shared out the most important functions between themselves, and were assisted by such minor paid officials as a common serjeant, a common clerk, a bellman, a town raker, sheep- and swine-herds.[49] No fees were paid to the keepers but their expenses for specific duties were met, and those paying borough accounts out of their own pockets were reimbursed.[50]

---

[45] Humberside RO, BC II/2, f. 31; BC II/3, ff. 15v., 27.   [46] BC II/2, f. 16; *Beverlac*, pp. 126–8.

[47] 6d for an absence, 40s for refusing office. BC II/2, ff. 6, 16.

[48] By 1498, a new council comprised of former keepers, the thirty-six, chose twelve, the retiring keepers and certain burgesses 'assisting in the Guildhall' chose a further twelve. None of these twenty-four nominees were to have served in the preceding two years. A further six worshipful men who had not previously held office completed the list of thirty candidates from whom the burgesses elected twelve. The number was reduced to eighteen in 1498 by excluding the twelve candidates with previous experience who were not members of the thirty-six. BC II/3, ff. 7v., 21, 26.   [49] BC II/3, ff. 9, 15v.; BC II/7/1, ff. 19v., 29, 30, 57v., 147, 152.

[50] BC II/6/1–15.

YORKSHIRE MERCHANTS IN THE 1337 WOOL MONOPOLY

York merchants	1338	allowed interim	1343
John de Acomb★	£139 9s 4d	£12 0s ½d	£127 9s 3½d
Ric de Allerton snr	£186 7s 8d	£45 12s 4d	£140 15s 4d
Henry de Belton	£1,667 19s 8d		
Ric Brigenhall	£389 15s 1d	£41 6s 11¾d	£347 9s 1¾d
Wm de Estrington★ & Rob de Skelton	£216 0s 3d	£16 0s 0d	£200 0s 3d
Wm de Friston	£94 4s 9d	£49 10s 9½d	£44 13s 11½d
Henry Goldbeter★ & John de Luterington	£400 9s 3d		
Henry Goldbeter	£414 9s 3d+	£30 4s 7½d	£384 4s 7½d
Wm de Grafton★	£90 1s 2d		
Wm de Grantham★ & Wm de Selby★	£312 8s 11d	£82 7s 8d	£230 1s 2½d to Selby's executors inc. Grantham
John Hansard★	£166 15s 6d	£66 0s 3½d	£100 15s 2½d
Walter Kelstern★	£432 4s 8d		
John de Luterington	£432 4s 8d+	£77 5s 6¾d	£354 19s 1¼d
Wm de Luterington★	£101 9s 2d	£22 13s 1¼d	£78 16s ¼d
John Randman	£269 2s 0d	£46 7s ½d	£222 4s 11½d
Wm Rigton★	£88 3s 8d		
Jordan Savage	£54 0s 9d		
Henry de Scoreby	£592 4s 1d	£34 11s 0d	£557 13s 11½d
Wm de Sutton★	£49 5s 2d		
Henry Goldbeter, Walter Kelstern, Wm de Luterington, John Randman, John de Luterington	owed £1,402 13s 4d		£467 11s 1d
Hull merchants			
Rob de Denton	£76 18s 5d	£33 6s 8d	£13 12s 2d+
Rob de Denton	£46 18s 5d+		£30 0s 0d

York merchants	1338	allowed interim	1343
John de Eshton	£182 8s 5d	£80 7s ¼d	£102 1s 4¾d
Wm de la Pole	£2,039 12s 7d	£1,006 18s ½d	£1,032 14s 6½d
			£180 7s 6d
Beverley merchants			
Peter de Besewyk★	£84 14s 4d	£6 10s 0d	£78 4s 4d
Thos de Bifford★	£22 17s 9d		
Rob de Brunne	£45 0s 1d	£6 17s 8¾d	£38 2s 4¼d
John de Thornton	£455 3s 10d		£71 19s 10¾d
Coppendale			(1344)
Wm de Coppendale jnr	£104 15s 10d	£11 0s 0d	£93 15s 10d
Thos de Frismersk	£101 4s 3d	£26 15s 6¾d	£74 11s 8¼d
Walter Frost & Thos Ryse	£97 0s 4d		
Walter Frost & Thos Ryse	£527 15s 10d	£130 6s 4d	£397 9s 6d
Thos Haral	£227 11s 11d	£64 10s 1¾d	£163 11s 9¼d
Thos de Holme	£415 12s 7d	£415 12s 7d	
Geof de Humbrecolt	£459 11s 9d	£60 18s 7d	£398 13s 2d
			to his executors inc.
			wife Mabel
Rob Jolyf	£339 2s 0d		
John Jurdan	£201 4s 0d	£48 17s 1¼d	£152 7s 4¾d
Wm de Kelstern	£421 2s 1d	£88 6s 3¾d	£332 15s 9¼d
	through Boston		
Ric Lesset★	£80 3s 0d	£73 7s 1¼d	£6 15s 10¾d
Thos de Lokington★	£46 6s 2d	£14 19s 2¾d	£31 6s 11¼d
Alice Lumbard★	£97 19s 4d	£30 9s 5d	£67 9s 11d
Wm Lyndelowe★	£94 8s 9d	£67 18s 7½d	£26 10s 1½d
John de Manby	£303 6s 3d	£535 0s 6¾d	£250 0s 8¼d
Amand de Routh	£44 5s 6d	£11 17s 8¾d	£32 7s 9¼d
John de Silesthorne	£66 4s 2d	£9 0s 0d	£57 4s 2d
Nich Spicer★	£49 11s 0d	£32 12s 5d	£16 18s 7d
John de Thorneton★	£267 5s 1d	£4 1s 6½d	£94 13s 9½d
John de Thorneton★	£98 15s 3d+		
Adam Tirwhit snr	£348 7s 8d	£68 4s 9¼d	£280 2s 10¾d
Adam Tirwhit jnr	£176 9s 11d	£16 12s 5d	£159 17s 6d
Hugh Tirwhit	£61 7s 3d	£6 14s 8¼d	£54 12s 6¾d
Joan widow of Ric Tirwhit	£185 3s 10d	£131 18s 7¾d	£53 5s 2¼d
Thos de Waghen	£86 4s 10d	£10 10s ¾d	£75 14s 9¼d
Henry de Wyghton★	£119 5s 6d	£30 4s 6¾d	£75 19s 11¼d

Notes:
May 1338 grant of repayment by allowance of 20s off the 40s wool subsidy per sack
shipped via Hull unless otherwise stated, *CCR 1337–9*, pp. 424–34. July 1343 the same
allowance, *ibid.*, *1343–6*, pp. 145–9, 159; January 1344, *ibid.*, p. 399.
★ = Those with no previous recorded exports.
+ = Sum recorded in 1343 *for* 1338.

SOME MERCHANT BIOGRAPHIES

This is a selection taken from J. I. Kermode, 'The Merchants of York, Beverley and Hull in the 14th and 15th Centuries', Univ. of Sheffield PhD thesis, 1990, appendix 4. For documentary references to service as MP and in civic office, see *ibid.* (to be published as *Yorkshire Merchant Biographies:An Exercise in Reconstitution* (Liverpool, forthcoming)).

Occupations as given at entry as burgess or in will. a = auditor; b = bailiff; c = chamberlain; db = dead by date (usually from will unless stated otherwise); fr = entry as burgess; k = keeper; m = mayor; MP = member of parliament; s = sheriff; tuns = wine; w = wife; wid = widow. Total cargoes = all the separate shipments recorded in the extant customs records, but these cannot be taken as the complete trading career of an individual. *EWT* = J. Lister, ed., *The Early Yorkshire Woollen Trade*. For other abbreviations see p. xiv.

William AGLAND, of York: mercer, fr 1371; b 1381. 1378–90 exported 145+ sacks / cloth v £90 13s 4d; imported misc v £53 16s 4d / 19 tuns: total 27 cargoes (E122/59/2, 5, 7, 8, 15). Resident in Bruges, *c.* 1373, as servant to Rog de Moreton of Y (Thomas, *Cal Plea & Mem Rolls City of London, 1364–81*, 154).

Richard AGLYON, of Beverley: k 1392, 1405, 1410. 1378–1401 exported 168 sacks + 222 fells / 64½ cloths + cloth v £522; imported misc v £306; total 59 cargoes (E122/58/14; 59/7, 8, 14, 22–6; 60/2; 159/11; 160/1). Paid aulnage on 29 cloths in 1378–9 (*EWT*, 36). Exporting 400 qts grain to Middelburgh, 1388 w Jn Burgoyn & Wm Rolleston of B (*CPR 1385–9*, 566). Involved w Adam Coppendale in 1381 riots (*CCR 1381–5*, 113, 146).

Thomas le AGUILER snr, of York: c 1303, b 1311, MP 1311. 1295–1312 exported 390 sacks + 1,105 fells / 864 hides in 38 cargoes (E122/55/3, 5, 8, 10, 14, 21, 22; 56/5, 8, 11, 13).

Robert ALCOCK, of Hull: son of Wm and bro of Jn bishop of Ely, fr 1454 *per patrem* (BRG I, f. 21v.), db 1484; c 1465, s 1471, m 1480, MP 1478. 1452–73 exported 59½ sacks + 2,020 fells / 28 cloths / lead v £72 6s 8d / misc v £6 2s 6d + share in £240 cargo of beer & barley w Wm Brompton, Rog Bushell & Jn Ricard of H; imported misc v £81 / stockfish v £118 10s / 8 tuns + share in 62 tuns w Thos Alcock, Wm Brompton, Jn Whitfield of H: total 46 cargoes (E122/61/71, 74; 62/1, 4, 5, 7–13, 16, 19). Bought *La Calanta* from the Crown for 200 marks in 1471 (*CPR 1467–77*, 267). Survived by wid, son Rob, dau Katherine, w of John Dalton, bro Jn, nephew Jn (see fig. 3 on p. 89). Left a house & oratory; £122 cash bequests, inc £106 of debts due, ¼ of the *George*. Beq of £69 to Jn Dalton, promised on his marriage to Katherine, conditional on him enfeoffing her of any property Dalton might purchase. The £69 made up of £20 debt from Rob Chapman of H; £26 debt from Jn Alcock, bishop of Ely, and £23 at executors' discretion. Debt of £60 from Hen Johnson to pay for a priest for 12 years. Goods in Calais to be sold for 'greatest profit' by Dalton (Prob. Reg. v, 229v.; *Test. Ebor.* III, 295–6).

John ALDESTONEMORE, of York: merchant, fr 1412, db Feb 1435; c 1419, s 1421, m 1427, MP 1425, 1429; 1416 w wife member Corpus Xti Guild (*CCG*, 18); 1410 smuggling 40 sacks out of Newcastle w Nicholas Blackburn of Richmond (*Bronnen*, I, 543); 1430–1 exported 39 cloths (E122/61/32); survived by bro Thomas, sis Katherine, dau Agnes w of Wm Holbeck, mo Agnes. Left 300 sarplars of wool in Calais, property in Bishophill, Carrgate, Coneyst, Dringhouses, Mickelgate, Northst, Skeldergate. Execs inc bro Thos, Wm Holbeck & Wm Stokton, all of Y: cash bequests £359 (Prob. Reg. III, 406–8). Mo died 1438, left £3 4s (*ibid.*, 554).

Thomas ALDESTONEMORE, of York: bro of Jn, mercer, fr 1401, db May 1435; c 1432; 1424 member Corpus Xti Guild (*CCG*, 24). Survived by wid Katherine, son Jn, mo Agnes, exec Thos Gare of Y: cash bequests £46 + £13 6s 8d from bro Jn's estate for a 10 yr chantry. To be buried next to Jn Gare if dies in Calais (Prob. Reg. III, 413v.–14).

Richard ALLERTON, of York: mercer, fr 1291. 1306–33 exported 330 sacks + 1,637 fells / 9 lasts 4 dickers 5 hides; total 62 cargoes (E122/55, 22; 56/8, 11, 15–8, 20–2, 26; 57/6, 7, 13; 58/2). Selling corn to, and buying wool from, Bolton Priory, 1320–5 (Kershaw, *Bolton Priory*, 93). In EIII's wool monopoly (*CCR 1337–9*, 429; *1343–6*, 146).

Robert AMYAS, of York: merchant, fr 1463, db 1486; c 1468, s 1469, m 1481, MP 1478: 1462 member M&MA (*M&MA*, 66) and Corpus Xti Guild (*CCG*, 91). 1466–7 exported 7 cloths (E122/62/9) and other goods to Prussia (*Urkundenbuch*, IX, 369–70); survived by wid Katherine, unnamed children, bro Ralph. Left cash bequests 13s 4d (Prob. Reg. V, 279).

John de APPLETON jnr, of York: mercer, fr 1374, db 1406; c 1383. 1381–1401 exported 16 sacks, cloth v £212, misc (inc cloth & hides) v £131 19s 2d; imported goods v £106 10s / 1 tun (E122/59/7, 8, 15, 19, 22, 24; 159/11; 60/2); buying wool from Durham Priory 1394–8 and selling wine 1395–6 back (Morimoto, 'Durham Wine Trade', 125–6).

John de BARDEN, of York: merchant (*Yorks Deeds*, IX, 487), db 1396; c 1368, b 1372, m 1378, MP 1379, 1381, keeper king's fish pond in the Foss for life (*CPR*

1374–7, 173). 1377–93 apptd to 12 royal commissions (*CPR 1377–81*, 37, 354; *1385–8*, 81, 254, 471; *1388–92*, 524; *1391–6*, 199, 214; *CCR 1377–81*, 503, 518; *1392–6*, 84). 1394–5 paid ulnage on 6 cloths (*EWT*, 46). 1374, bought 2 mills + 2 acres at Aberford (*Yorks Fines*, II, 277; *Yorks Deeds*, I, 3, 4). 1381 took up 30 yr lease of Hedelay manor from Holy Trinity Priory, Y (*CPR 1381–5*, 56). Survived by wid Alice, dau Alice w of Henry Wyman of Y, dau Ellen w of Sir Jn Dawney of Escrick (*Yorks Deeds*, IX, 72), and Margaret, betrothed to Jn, son of Roger Moreton of Y. Left property in Aberford, Burton Leonard, Earswick, Huntington, Leeds Woodhouse, Shadwell (London?), Towthorpe, Rydal manor, and 2 houses on Pavement in Y: cash bequests £25 (Prob. Reg. I, 95, 100). 1407 chantry est in St Crux for Barden and wife by Henry Wyman, with 3 messuages in Fossgate (*CPR 1405–8*, 312).

William BEDALE, of York: son of Jn (*CCG*, 22), fr 1403, db 1438; c 1425, s 1423, m 1437, MP 1435; 1423 member Corpus Xti Guild (*CCG*, 22); 1432, 1434, master of M&MA (*M&MA*, 322). 1413 lost shipment at sea, 1422 importing from Danzig (*CPR 1413–16*, 19; *Hanserecesse 1431–76*, II, 65). Debts due: 1427, £2 13s 4d from York dyer, and 1436, £2 from a carrier of Carnforth, Lancs (*CPR 1422–9*, 366; *1429–36*, 167). Property assessed at £18, 1436 (E179/217/42). Survived by merchant sons Jn & Nich, dau Agnes. Left £92 cash, property in Carrgate, Northst and unspecified in York (Prob. Reg. II, 123; III, 540). Wife Agnes db 1437 (survived by sons Roger, Wm, dau Joan; left property outside Mickelgate: cash bequests £25 14s, *ibid.*, III, 495). Dau Joan db 1447, buried nxt to father in St Martin's, left £1 15s (*ibid.*, II, 155).

Henry de BELTON, of York: db 1340 (*Yorks Deeds*, VI, 176); b 1329, m 1334–7, MP 1326. 1309–5 exported 426 sacks in 48 cargoes (E122/56/11, 18, 20–22; 57/7, 11, 13; 58/2; 155/42); monopolist 1337–44 (E356/8 m. 30; *CPR 1334–8*, 480; *CCR 1337–9*, 430; *1343–6*, 402); purveyor to royal household (*CPR 1324–7*, 148; *1321–4*, 342). Debts inc £80 from master Rich de Hovering, 1322; £4 from Rob lord of Flamborough, 1332; and £40 by Jn Hanbury (*CCR 1318–23*, 687; *1330–3*, 611, 616). Debts owed inc £387 to canon of St Peter's, 1333; £400 to Henry Percy snr, 1335 (*CCR 1333–7*, 84, 521); 1340 borrowed £100 from Archbp Melton on security of florins v £120 (Melton's Register, 65). His tenement 'Le Cokerowe' in Coneyst, newly acquired in 1340, sold after his death to pay his debts (*Yorks Deeds*, VI, 576). 1336 bought a shop in Y (*Yorks Fines*, I, 101). 1337 licensed to build a chantry chapel in cemetery of All Saints, Ousegate (*CPR 1334–8*, 385; *Yorks Chantry Survey*, II, 556). His wid Margaret married his exec Jn de Jarum by July 1341 (*Yorks Deeds*, VI, 175).

Robert BENNINGTON, of Hull: merchant, fr 1445 as mariner (BRG I, 20), db 1472. 1460–72 exported 1½ cloths / lead v £30 / misc v £39 + share in misc v £240 w Rob & Thos Alcock & Jn Whitfield of H / share in misc v £200 w Wm Brompton, Thos Patrington & Jn Whitfield of H; imported stockfish v £24 / 10 tuns; total 12 cargoes (E122/62/1, 9, 11, 12, 13, 15, 16). Survived by wid Emmota (Prob. Reg. IV, 181).

Thomas BEVERLEY, of York: merchant, son of Jn, fr 1440, db 1480; c 1447, s 1450, m 1460, MP 1459; 1461 Master of M&MA, wife a member (*M&MA*, 67, 322); w wife Alice member of Corpus Xti Guild 1453 (*CCG*, 52). 1452–74 exported 111 sacks + 1,020 fells / 88 cloths / lead v £342 10s; imported misc v £731 (inc iron v £135) / 22 tuns; total 76 cargoes (E122/61/7, 74, 75; 62/1–7, 9–13, 16, 20). Married Henry Market's dau, Alice. Survived by wid Alice (db 1482, Prob. Reg. v, 28–9), sons Nich, Rich, Jn (married Ann, dau of Jn Ferriby, merchant mayor of Y). Left property and £100 (Prob. Reg. v, 184). Son Thos, fr as merch in 1471, db 1472 and left £145 cash. Debts still not recovered in 1482 (Prob. Reg. IV, 176; *CPR 1476–85*, 293).

William BIRKYN, of Hull: 1303–22 exported 12 sacks + 60 fells / 4 dicker 2 hides; total 6 cargoes (E122/55, 10, 13; 56/5, 11, 15, 18).

Nicholas BLACKBURN snr, of York: merchant, fr 1396 (of Richmond), db 1432; admiral north of Thames (*CPR 1405–8*, 171), m 1412; 1414 w wife member Corpus Xti Guild (*CCG*, 16). 1395–1431 exported via Newcastle, 128 sacks + 22 fells / 40+ sacks w Jn Aldestonemore, Jn Sampson & 86+ sacks w Thos Gare, Rich Russell; coal v £1 via Scarborough / 61½ cloths + 31 coverlets; imported iron v £6 13s 4d (E122/5/35, 106/26, 134/7, 61/32; *Bronnen*, I, 503, 543). Victualling Berwick 1405 + king's household 1416 (*CPR 1405–8*, 30, 1416–22, 52). Loaned £100 + £46 13s 4d to Henry V (Bartlett, 'Aspects of the Economy of York', 399); £67 13s 4d to archbp Bowet (*Test. Ebor.* III, 82). Est chantry in St Agnes' Chapel, Fossgate in 1424 (*Yorks Chantry Survey*, I, 61). Survived by wid Margaret (db 1435, Prob. Reg. III, 415v.–16), sons Nich, Chris, Wm, daus Agnes, Alice, Isabella (see fig. 1 on p. 83). Left cash bequests £644 (£310 on soul), £40 to city of Y towards royal tax, property in North St & Shambles. Window in his name in All Saints, North St (Prob. Reg. II, 605).

John de BOLTON jnr, of York: mercer, fr 1410 *per patrem* w bro Wm; c 1416, s 1420, m 1431, MP 1427?; 1430 w wife member Corpus Xti Guild, dau Agnes member 1441 (*CCG*, 30, 38). 1426 lost cargo of 5+ sacks wool (*CCR 1422–9*, 349). Property assessed at £62, 1436, poss inc manors of Hersewell, Holme-in-Spaldingmore, Thorpe-le-Street, and land in Holderness (*Yorks Deeds*, I, 83–4; E179/217/42). Married Alice, dau Nich Blackburn snr, their dau Margaret married Sir Roger Salvayn and Henry Gascoigne, son judge Sir Wm of Gawthorpe (*CCG*, 38n.). Son Rob predeceased father in 1428 (Prob. Reg. III, 463v.). Survived by wid. Left cash bequests £26 (Prob. Reg. II, 107).

Elene BOX, of Hull: wid of Walter Box, vintner of H. 1383–4 she imported misc. v £29 6s 8d / 16 tuns; total 3 cargoes (E122/59/8). Walter m 1351, 1367, date of death unknown.

William BRID/BIRD snr, of Beverley: k 1404; warden of St Mary's 1392; in riots of 1381 (*CPR 1381–5*, 146; *1392–6*, 150). 1379–1401, exported 290 sacks / 21½ cloths + cloth v £182 5s; imported misc v £205 / 5 tuns 1 pipe; total 50 cargoes (E122/58/14; 59/14, 16, 23–6; 60/2; 160/1–2). Same Wm Brid? as of H db 1407 (Prob. Reg. III, 270).

Richard BRIGENHALL, of York: c 1329, b 1330, MP 1334, 1336, 1337; assessor & collector of the tenth in Y (*CPR 1334–8*, 40). 1321–32 exported 16 sacks; total 5 cargoes (E122/56/18, 21, 22, 26; 58/2). In EIII's wool monopoly, buying wool in Durham (*CPR 1334–8*, 482, 485). 1336 goods v £140 stolen from a Barton ship in Flanders (*CCR 1337–9*, 327).

John BROMPTON, of Beverley: merchant, db 1444; k 1407, 1416, 1425, 1428, 1432, 1436, 1440. 1391–1401 exported 74+ sacks / cloth v £17; imported soap v 13s 6d / canvas v £7 13s 10d; total 18 cargoes (E122/59/24–6; 60/2; 159/11; 160/1). Predeceased by w Elene, sis to Margaret, w of Ad Baker merchant keeper (db 1436, Prob. Reg. III, 71v.) Survived by son Nich & children of his dead son Thos (db 1436), 4 sons, inc bastard Thos. Left £600+ cash, woolhouse in Calais (Prob. Reg. III, 475). Left 8 properties in B & H; £800 cash inc £200 in debts owed by son Thos; gold items weighing 214 ounces and others unweighed, ¾ the *Bartholemew*. Bequests to Thos Brompton, husbandman of Langetoft & his 3 chapmen sons (Prob. Reg. II, 86–90v.; *Test. Ebor.* II, 96–105).

Margaret BUSHELL, of Hull: wid of imp general merchant Roger snr (db 1483, survived by wid, son Rog, daus Eliz, Marg, Joan, w of Rich Beverley. Left £46 cash and property in H; Prob. Reg. V, 87v.) Margaret licensed to trade at Bordeaux in 1483 (BL Harl. MS 1433, 78d.), no traces in customs rolls.

John CARLETON jnr, of Beverley: spicer, db 1401. Difficult to disentangle from his brother Jn (db 1391, Prob. Reg. I, 38v.). Probably jnr exported, 1383–97, cloth v £34+; imported misc v £31 15s (inc spices); total 9 cargoes (E122/59/8, 14, 22, 23, 25, 26, 28). Survived by wid Alice; left £17 + 5 properties + farmland and rents (Arch. Reg. XVI, 141).

John CARRE, of York: son of Thos, draper; fr 1434, db 1488; c 1438, s 1440, m 1448, 1456, MP 1449; member of M&MA (*M&MA*, 68). Shared in the Staplers' loan of £2, 000 to Crown in 1450 w Yorks group inc Nich Bedford of H, Wm Bracebridge, Wm Stokton & Jn Thirsk of Y (*CPR 1446–52*, 316). Left £145 cash bequests, property in Finkelst, H (Prob. Reg. V, 327). Chantry est for self and parents, Jn & Joan, in 1489 in St Sampson's, Y (*CPR 1485–8*, 265).

Hugh CLITHEROE II, of Hull: merchant, fr 1421 (BRE 1, 254), db 1463 (BRB 1, 88v.); c 1426, b 1428, m 1442, 1446, 1448, 1457, MP 1435, 1436, 1444/5, 1448/9, a 1453, 1456, coroner 1458 (BRB 1, 33, 55, 62); 1st commissioner of Admiralty Ct of H, 1447 (BRE 2, 24v.–6v.) On 6 royal commissions 1446–58 (*CPR 1446–52*, 88, 316; *1452–61*, 172, 220, 404, 436, 440). Exported 30 cloths, 2 cargoes 1430–1; imported woad v £37 10s, 2 cargoes 1452–3 (E122/61/32, 71). Accused of piracy v Danzig ship in 1434, sueing Dutch merchants in Holland in 1440 (*CPR 1429–36*, 357; *Bronnen*, II, 732). Shared in the Staplers' loans to Crown: e.g. £2, 000 in 1450 w Yorks group inc Nich Bedford of H, Wm Bracebridge, Wm Stokton & Jn Thirsk of Y (*CPR 1446–52*, 323; *1452–61*, 211). One of 3 sureties for Rich Wastenes, of Stowe, Lincs, in £2, 806 15s 6¾d (*CPR 1436–41*, 429). Registered 3 apprentices in 1436, 1451, 1454 (BRE 1, 266; BRG 1, 21). Married Joan, dau Rob Holme of H. He left Clitheroe's children, Rob, Hugh, Anne, land in Hedon + £40 each (1449, Prob. Reg. II, 211).

Adam COPPENDALE, of Beverley: db 1336 (murdered, *CCR 1333–7*, 582); 1330 collector of custs in H (*CFR 1327–37*, 211). 1305–34 exported 184 sacks + 746 fells; total 29 cargoes (E122/55/21; 56/5, 8, 15, 22; 57/6, 11; 58/2; 6/11; 155/42). Share in ship + cargo wax, oats, cloth etc. v £2,000, pirated at Gt Yarmouth *en route* from Middelburgh in 1320, partners Alan de Appleby of Y, Amand de Routh of B, Wm Shirwood of Ripon (*Bronnen*, I, 175–6). 1335 loan of 50 marks to EIII for Scottish expedition (*CPR 1334–8*, 153). Accused of murder in 1319. Murdered by Thos Manby & Rob Seton, clerks of B in 1336 (*CPR 1317–21*, 375; *1334–8*, 272, 278). Several generations of Coppendales traded from and held office in Beverley into the late 15th century (see Kermode, 'Merchants of York, Beverley and Hull', appendix 4; *VCH Beverley*, 198–200).

Edmund COPPENDALE, of Hull: merchant and probably bro of Adam Coppendale of B. fr 1450 (BRG I, 20v.), db 1490; c 1451, s 1453, m 1459, MP 1472, a 1455, 1458, coroner 1455, 1460 (BRB I, 46, 62, 72v.) Pardoned w the Lancastrians 1455, 1462 (Wedgwood, *Parliamentary Biographies*, II, 220). 1452–90 exported 33+ sacks for customs allowance against loan of £321 to Crown w Wm Bracebridge / 23 cloths + share in 85 cloths w Hen Mindram & Jn Beverley of H/ lead v £4 / beer v £11 / share in £240 of beer, barley, linen etc. w Wm Eland, Nich Ellis, Thos Etton of H / share in £80 of same misc w Nich Ellis & Jn Whitfield; imported misc v £28 / stockfish v £71 / Bay salt v £6 / 21 tuns 1 hoggeshead wine; total 25 cargoes (E122/61/68; 61/1, 3–9, 11–13, 16, 17, 19; 62/2, 8). Attorney for Rob Holme of H? in 1431 (*CCR 1429–35*, 112). 1483 licensed to trade at Bordeaux (BL Harl. MS 1433, 78d.). Registered 3 apprentices (BRG I, 24, 26). Survived by wid Janet. Left a house, £3 10s cash inc £1 for 'forgotten tithes' (Prob. Reg. V, 383v.)

Robert del CROSSE, of Hull: db 1395; b 1360, m 1373, 1376, 1382; on 3 royal commissions 1370–80; collector of 1377 lay sub in H; 1386, 1389 controller of customs in Grimsby, Hull, Scarborough (*CPR 1364–70*, 425; *1374–7*, 502; *1377–81*, 37, 515; *1385–9*, 247; *1389–92*, 50; E179/206/45). 1383–92 exported cloth v £13 10s; imported misc v £83 15s / 23 tuns; total 12 cargoes (E122/59/8, 14, 19, 23). Shipping figs from Algarve to Harfleet / wheat from Danzig to Bordeaux in 1394–5 (*CCR 1392–6*, 17, 324; PRO C1/19/43). Survived by wid Isabel, sons Wm & Jn; left bible & missal; £202 cash and at least 18 properties + 2 rents. Bequests to Scarboro ch, silver chalices to Lincoln cathedral & abbot of Thornton, cash to friaries in B, Lincoln, Pontefract, Scarboro, Y + priories of Burnham, Gisburgh, Pickering, Swyn, Werkeham & Wilberfoss; £20 for windows in Holy Trinity, H (Prob. Reg. II, 83v.–5).

John DALTON, of Hull: merchant, fr 1475 appr to Jn Swan, stapler of H (BRG I, 25v.), db 1496; c 1478, s 1482, m 1488, MP 1485/6. 1469–73 exported 22+ sacks + 600 fells; total 8 cargoes (E122/62/12, 16, 19). Survived by wid Katherine, 6 sons, dau Eliz, mo, bro Thos, sis Eliz (see fig. 3 on p. 89); left £25 10s + 3 houses (Prob. Reg. V, 483v.–5; *Test. Ebor.* IV, 21–6).

Alice DAY, of Hull: wid Jn Day, stapler of H (db 1472, left £20 + 8 properties; Prob. Reg. IV, 79). Alice exported 4 cloths in 1473–4 (E122/62/19).

John GAUNT, of York: merchant, fr 1450, db 1488. Member M&MA 1472 (*M&MA*, 67). 1462–72 exported 172 cloths / lead + hides v £16 13s 4d; imported misc v £83 10s / 56 tuns; total 26 cargoes (E122/62/3, 5, 9, 11, 13, 16, 17, 19). Survived by wid Isabelle, son Jn (by 1st w Elene), dau Agnes. Left £17 cash bequests (Prob. Reg. v, 336).

Sir John GILYOT, of York: merchant, fr 1481 (son of Jn snr), db 1510; c 1482, s 1484, m 1490, 1503; MP 1487, 1489, knighted 1503: 1481 w wife member Corpus Xti Guild (*CCG*, 109); Master M&MA 1485, 1486, 1500, 1501 (*M&MA*, 323). 1489–90 exported 26 cloths / lead v £46 13s 4d; imported misc v £49; total 3 cargoes (E122/63/8). 1504 invested 13s 4d for 2 voyages w M&MA (*M&MA*, 113). Married Katherine (db 1488), Maud, dau of Sir Henry Vavasour of Haslewood. Survived by Lawrence, Wm, Peter, Maud, Margaret (latter 3 minors). Peter married dau of Peter Jackson m 1526, Margaret married Jn Hogeson m 1533, Maud married Peter Robinson m 1544. Son Peter to become patron of St Thomas chantry in All Saints, Pavement. Bequests inc extensive property throughout Y, £722 cash (£400 to purchase land to endow a chantry). 1513 son Wm est chantry in St Saviour's for Jn (Prob. Reg. VIII, 32–4; *Test. Ebor.* v, 12–15; *Yorks Chantry Survey*, I, 67). His father, a mercer, fr 1429, db 1484; c 1451, s 1452, m 1464, 1474, master M&MA 1459, 1460, 1476 (*M&MA*, 322). Exported cloth + lead, imported misc goods. Survived by wid Joan (dau Jn Lancaster), dau Agnes, son Jn; £154 cash and property in Y, Sherburn, Towthorpe (Prob. Reg. v, 237).

Peter GILYOT, of York: merchant, fr 1522 (son of Sir Jn), db 1525; c 1524. Survived by wid Alice; daus Matilda & Alice: cash bequests £25, houses in Y (Prob. Reg. IX, 324–5).

John GISBURN, of York: mercer, fr 1347, db 1390; b 1357 (election overthrown by m Jn Langton (York RO C/Y, 313v.), m 1371, 1372, 1380, MP 1360, 1361, 1373; appointed to 8 royal commissions (*CPR 1370–4*, 111; *1374–7*, 490; *1377–81*, 45, 471, 515, 572, 631); alder of Calais (*VCH York*, 102). Prominent in the Peasants' Revolt (Dobson, 'The Risings', 120). 1371–90 exported 416 sacks / cloth v £91+; imported goods v £128 6s 8d / 28 tuns; total 38 cargoes (E122/59/1, 2, 5, 8, 14, 15, 28); 1358 buying wool & hides in Scotland (*CPR 1358–61*, 87); 1381 supplied lead to New College, Oxford (*CPR 1381–5, 50*). Leased manor of Raskelf (ER) for life (*Cat. Ancient Deeds*, I, A417). 1st wife Beatrice. Survived by wid Elene (db 1408, left £142 cash, inc debt of £40 from Wm Frost to Jn Gisburn, Prob. Reg. III, 283), daus Alice, w of Sir Wm Plumton, & Isabella w of Wm Frost of Y. Left cash bequests £300 inc religious houses in the north + cash for road and bridge repairs (Prob. Reg. I, 15v.–16). 1390, with his opponent of 1381, Sim de Quixlay, executor of fellow merchant Richard Wardeby's will (*MB*, II, 33). 1392 chantry est in St Martin's (*CPR 1391–6*, 145).

Thomas GRA, of York: son of Wm; m 1375, 1398, MP x 11, 1376–96; 1388, one of 3 ambassadors to negotiate treaty w Hanseatic League (*CPR 1385–9*, 453), and on royal comm into York castle gaol (*C. Inq. Misc., 1387–93*, 417). 1378–90 exported 384 sacks; total 28 cargoes (E122/59/2, 5, 7, 15).

John GREGG, of Hull: fr 1398 (BRE I, 241), db 1437; m 1421, MP 1425, 1426, 1432. 1391–1401 exported 38+ sacks / 518 fells / 26½ cloths; imported misc v £30 3s 10d / wax v £8; total 13 cargoes (E122/59/22, 23; 60/2; 160/1). Registered 7 apprentices (BRE I, 246, 252, 254, 256, 258). Survived by wid Joan. Left £191 cash, silverware v £14, property in Hull & Myton. Rent from 4 crofts to pay for masses from 4 orders of friars in Y and 2 in H. Elaborate religious provision inc bequests to 8 religious guilds in H + guild of St Mary in St Bridget's, Fleet Street, London; weekly doles to poor in B & H; £4 for window in Brantigham ch; £19 for region's roads (Prob. Reg. III, 507v.). Estate comprising 12 tenements + 1 messuage to endow his chantry, founded in 1445 (Hull RO, D315, 317, 350, 352), and support the almshouse, prob built by his w Joan, in Old Kirklane, chantry & almshouse to be maintained by H corporation (*VCH Hull*, 343). Joan, db 1438, left £240 cash, silverware, a thirty-second share in the *George*. Property to support her almshouse, cash to same guilds & roads as Jn; £20 towards a conduit for water into H; elaborate funeral provision inc cloth & cash doles for poor: total £106 13s 4d (Prob. Reg. III, 555v.–6v.).

Thomas HOLME, of York: mercer, br of Robert snr, fr 1354, db 1406; b 1366, m 1374, MP 1385, 1387, appointed to 5 royal commissions 1379–91 (*CCR 1374–7*, 545; *1389–92*, 37, 192; *CPR 1392–6*, 84; *C. Inq. Misc. 1387–93*, 127). 1378–1400 exported 348 sacks / cloth v £25+; imported misc v £125 12s 8d; total 32 cargoes (E122/59/2, 5, 7, 8, 15, 16, 22–6; 159/11; 160/1). Paid ulnage on 88 cloths in 1384–5, on 23½ cloths in 1398–9 (*EWT*, 61, 73–4, 101). Debts inc dyers from Kingston-on-Thames, Knaresborough, a London merchant (*CCR 1377–81*, 523; *1385–9*, 111; *CPR 1388–92*, 396). Est chantry, 1377, in St Mary, Castlegate (*VCH York*, 393). Survived by wid Katherine, dau of Wm Frost of Y, nephews Rob & Thos. Left £60 cash bequests, share in Stapleton quarry, property in Ackworth, Catshelf?, Featherstone, Newark, Northwood, Pontefract, Preston, Y and Calais. Benefactor of Trinity Hospital, Fossgate (Prob. Reg. III, 245v.–55v.)

Robert de HOLME snr, of York: mercer, fr 1347, db 1396; c 1352, b 1353, m 1368, MP 1365, 1372; collector of subsidy in WR 1389 (*CCR 1385–9*, 555). Caught up in 1381 revolt (*CCR 1377–81*, 524). 1378–96 exported 1,567 sacks / 70 cloths + 2 coverlets + cloth v £219; imported misc v £903 / 13 tuns 1 pipe; total 119 cargoes (E122/59/2, 5, 7, 8, 14–16, 23–5). There may be a slight overlap w Rob Holme of B, or there was perhaps only one merchant of that name. 1361 est chantry in Holy Trinity, Goodramgate (*Yorks Chantry Survey*, I, 52). Survived by son Rob, bastard son Rob, children of bro Jn, of Thos de Holme of B. Left property in central Y: at least £2,148 (£963 for spiritual provision). Cash to parishes where purchased wool, to repair roads, £86 for poor; books for Holy Trinity; 200 lb wax for candles throughout Y (Prob. Reg. I, 100v.–3v.).

Thomas de HOLME, of Beverley: Assaulted in Bev in 1324 when deputed to raise a royal levy in Holderness (*CPR 1321–4*, 454). 1302–23 exported 209 sacks + 5,475 fells / 10 hides; total 41 cargoes (E122/55/8–10, 13, 14, 21, 22; 56/13, 15, 21, 22; 57/6; 6/11). With 6 others was paid 28 sacks for 60 tuns wine by EII in 1312 (*CCR 1307–13*, 395). Resident in Bruges in 1332 (*CCR 1330–3*, 446); part of EIII's wool monopoly (*CCR 1337–9*, 426; *1343–6*, 155; *1349–54*, 343). Nich Marini of the Bardi acting as agent for Thos Holme before 1346 (*CPR 1345–8*, 193). Owed £174 10s in 1329/30 by Durham Priory (*Durham Acct Rolls*, II, 515); £42 by prior of Malton in 1336 (*CCR 1333–7*, 728); buying wool from Malton and from Meaux Abbey (*ibid*, 518; *Chronica Melsa*, III, 85, 144–5; see above, p. 241).

John HOVEDEN, of York: b 1374, m 1386, MP 1384, 1387, 1388, 1391. 1379–92 exported 256 sacks + 312 fells / 400 small cloths + cloth v £12; imported misc v £63 17s; total 18 cargoes (E122/59/5, 7, 8, 15, 23, 24). Shipping herrings from Denmark, 1384 (*CPR 1381–5*, 505). Paid aulnage on 8 cloths (*EWT*, 52, 86).

Geffrey HUMBRECOLT snr, of Beverley: db 1349 (*CPR 1343–6*, 149). 1302–41 exported 690 sacks + 2,055 fells; total 115 cargoes (E122/55/8, 10; 56/5, 11, 13, 16, 18, 20; 57/11–13; 58/2; 6/11; 155/42). In EIII's wool monopoly (*CCR 1337–9*, 426; *1343–6*, 149).

John INCE, of York: mercer, fr 1436; c 1448, s 1455; member M&MA & involved in company shipping (*M&MA*, 48, 60, 62). 1560–72 exported 16 cloths; imported misc v £78 5s; total 6 cargoes (E122/62/1, 3, 6, 9, 16).

William KELSTERN, of Beverley: k 1345; 1309–41 exported 637 sacks + 768 fells / 3 lasts 5 dicker 2 hides; total 79 cargoes (E122/56/11, 16–18, 20–22; 57/11, 12; 58/2; 6/11; 155/42). In EIII's wool monopoly (*CCR 1337–9*, 428; *1341–3*, 47; *1343–6*, 145; *CPR 1340–3*, 266; PRO E356/8, 30–1).

John KENT, of York: merchant, fr 1438 (appr to Thos Kirkham), db 1468; c 1456, s 1460, m 1466; 1463 Master M&MA (*M&MA*, 322); w wife Marion, member Corpus Xti Guild (*CCG*, 49). 1459–67 exported 115 cloths / lead v £212 13s 4d / misc v £12; imported misc v £706 / 31 tuns; total 43 cargoes (E122/61/75; 62/1–7, 9, 10). Survived by wid Marion, 3 sons (unnamed); left £95, 17 ells cloth, property in Acomb, Bishopthorpe, Kirkby-on-Wharfe, Staxton (Prob. Reg. IV, 53).

Marion KENT, of York: wid John, db 1500; member M&MA 1472, member of its ruling mistery, 1474 (*M&MA*, 64, 67). 1469–73 exported 56 cloths / lead v £45; imported misc v £65 10s; total 15 cargoes (E122/62/12, 13, 16, 19). Owed lead v £8 by Miles Radclyff of Rilston, 1478 (*CPR 1476–85*, 84). 1493 bought land in Bishopsthorpe (*Yorks Fines*, I, 7). 1468 licence for oratory in her house (*CCG*, 49). Son Rob, clerk, died 1486 (Prob. Reg. v, 288). Her will made in 1488, when anticipated leaving £30 to son Henry and his children (Prob. Reg. III, 320–1).

John LIVERSEGE, of Hull: m 1394, 1396, 1399, 1403, 1406, 1407, MP 1407?. 1388–1402 exported 148 sacks + 120 fells / 20+ cloths; imported misc v £68 / 17 tuns; total 29 cargoes (E122/59/14, 23–5; 158/2; 159/11; 160/1).

Thomas LOKTON, of York: merchant. 1466–71 exported 85 sacks + 1,853 fells; imported stockfish v £6 13s 4d; total 11 cargoes (E122/9, 10, 12, 13).

Robert LOUTH, of York: merchant, fr 1386, db 1407; c 1387, b 1389. 1383–1401 exported 26 sacks / cloth v £167; imported misc v £188; total 27 cargoes (E122/59/8, 14, 22, 23, 25, 26; 60/2; 159/11). 1385, 1388 goods arrested in Prussia (*Hansetage*, III, 405, 412). Survived by wid Joan (dau of Nich Lokton, db 1436; Prob. Reg. III, 450–1), son Jn. Left £482 inc gifts to nuns of Clementhorpe, Monkton, Keldholme, Rosedale, Thykland, Wilberfoss (Prob. Reg. III, 265).

Henry MARKET, of York: merchant, fr 1412, db 1443. German naturalized in 1430 (*CPR 1429–36*, 43); c 1437, s 1442; 1428 w wife Matilda member of Corpus Xti Guild (*CCG*, 27); 1433 steward of M&MA (*M&MA*, 39). Survived by wid Matilda (db 1447, Prob. Reg. II, 168), dau Alice, w of Thos Beverley of Y; cash bequests £198 inc prayers for 1st w Mary, Nich Blackburn & w, fellow German Henry Wyman & w. Honoured 2 bequests made by 1st wife (Prob. Reg. II, 69–70).

John MARSHALL, of York: mercer, fr 1445, db 1487; c 1455, s 1457, m 1467, 1480, MP 1467; member Corpus Xti Guild 1470 (*CCG*, 76). 1452–73 exported 158 sacks + 3,107 fells; imported misc v £262 / 6 tuns; total 24 cargoes (E122/61/71; 62/1, 3, 8, 10, 12, 16, 17, 19). Sold cloth to Durham Priory 1449–50, 1457–8 (*Durham Acct Rolls*, III, 632, 636). Shared in Staplers' loans to Crown, e.g. of 3, 000 marks in 1449 w Jn Thirsk *et al.* (*CPR 1446–52*, 316). Survived by son Wm; left £67 + property. Paid for masses for self, w Joan & Rich & Joan Bukden (Prob. Reg. v, 311).

John MIDDLETON, merchant of Beverley: db 1475; k 1448, 1452, 1465, 1469. 1459–73 exported 169 sacks + 10, 629 fells / 18 cloths / lead v £30; imported misc v £110; total 40 cargoes (E122/61/75; 62/3–5, 7–10, 12, 13, 16, 17, 19). Survived by wid Agnes, sons Jn & Edw, daus Alice, Dionesia, w of Wm Brigham, Eliz, w of Ralph Langton of H, & sis Agnes, w of Edm Brackenburgh B merchant. Left £155 cash, house, gdn, orchard in Lairgate, B (Prob. Reg. IV, 96v.). Exec of Jn Day of H and of Edm Brackenburgh (Prob. Reg. II, 237; IV, 79).

Henry MINDRAM, of Hull: mercer, db 1508; c 1482, s 1489, m 1496, 1505–6, MP 1497, coroner 1497, a 1498 (BRB I, 154v., 155v.). 1489–90 exported share in 90 cloths w Jn Beverley, Edm Coppendale *et al.* of H, Wm Todd of Y / share in 44 cloths + misc v £146 10s w Ralph Langton, Laur Swattock, apothecary, *et al.* of H, Wm Todd & Rich York of Y; imported stockfish v £5 6s 8d / 17 tuns wine; total 5 cargoes (E122/62/13, 16; 63/1, 8). With Jn Mathewe & other H merchants, imprisoned in France 1473. Mathewe's brother raised the ransom on Mindram's bond (PRO C1/48/204). Survived by wid Margaret, sons Rich, Edm, Rob, dau Ellinor. Left £3 cash + several houses in H. To be buried next to his former master Jn Whitfield, also inc in his obit (Prob. Reg., VII, 24–5v.).

Thomas NELESON, of York: fr 1433, db 1484; c 1442, s 1447, m 1454, 1465, MP 1453; member M&MA w wife Katherine 1437 (*M&MA*, 48). 1452–72 exported 23+ sacks / 45 cloths / lead v £48; imported misc v £387 / 12 tuns; total 28 cargoes (E122/61/71, 75; 62/1, 3–5, 7, 9–13, 16). 1440 claimed goods seized in Danzig, a share of the goods v £5,000 seized in earl of Northumberland's *Valentine* in 1468 (*Hanserecesse 1431–76*, II, 542; *Urkundenbuch*, IX, 369). Owed small debts by men in Bolton-on-Dearne, Hedon, Hunmanby, Snaith, Whitby, 1459–74; £60 by 5 husbandmen in 1481 (*CPR 1446–52*, 198; *1452–61*, 384, 456; *1465–77*, 9, 431; *MB*, II, 274). Survived by sons Thos (db 1489) & Wm (db 1525), son Chris described as 'gentleman' (*CCG*, 168), dau Agnes; left £250 + silverware, house by the city crane + 4 in Thursdaymarket; property in Bolton-on-Dearne, Brantingham, Cottingham, Doncaster, Fenton, Halifax, East & West Lutton, Poppleton, Ricall, Shirburn; £10 for road repairs (Prob. Reg. V, 212v.–13v.). Dau Eliz married to Brian Conyers by 1473 (*Yorks Deeds*, X, 127).

William ORMESHEAD, of York: merchant, fr 1404 (of Richmond), db 1437; c 1411, s 1415, m 1425, 1433, MP 1421, 1425, 1430; w wife member of Corpus Xti Guild (*CCG*, 16). Exported 11+ sacks in 1426 / 10½ cloths in 1430 (E122/61/32; *CPR 1422–9*, 385). Property in Y and country assessed at £18 in 1436 (E179/217/42). Debts from a Penrith baker (*CPR 1441–6*, 7). Licensed to have a portable altar in 1430 (*C. Papal Reg. 1427–47, Letters*, 188), thrice married. Survived by wid Elene, daus Isabelle & Joan. Left cash bequests £120, inc to Richmond parish and to relatives Alice, w of Jn Bolton, Joan W of Nich Wispington; friends Elene, w of Thomas Gare, Katherine wid Thos Aldestonemore, children of all above and of Nich Blackburn. Left 12 properties in Y. Codicil asked Wispington to take his place as one of Nich Blackburn's executors (Prob. Reg. III, 503–4v.)

Henry PRESTON, of York: mercer, fr 1381, db 1441; c 1400, s 1404, m 1422, MP 1420. 1391–1401 exported cloth v £56 10s; imported misc v £22 13s 4d (inc wainscotting + bowstaves); total 7 cargoes (E122/59/23, 25; 60/2). Paid aulnage on 30 cloths, 1394–9 (*EWT*, 72, 102). W Emma db 1401 left £38, son Thos (married to Katherine, dau of Rob Holme), dau Agnes (Prob. Reg. III, 60v.–1; York RO B/Y, 45). Henry survived by son Rob, mercer fr 1433 (Prob. Reg. II, 19v.)

Simon de QUIXLAY, of York: fr 1366, db 1400 (*CPR 1399–1401*, 312); b 1375, constable of the walls from Mickelgate to Tofts 1380 (*MB*, I, 152), m 1381–3, MP 1384. Leader of a faction in Peasants' Revolt (Dobson, 'The Risings', 121–3). 1378–92 exported 382 sacks / cloth v £33 13s 4d; imported misc v £260 15s (inc woad v £45); total 45 cargoes (E122/59/2, 5, 7, 8, 14–16, 23, 24, 28). Leased cloth subsidy in northern counties @ £40 pa for 6 years (*CCR 1381–5*, 575). In 1398 w Jn Hoveden of Y, in debt to Rob Galton for £201 12s 2½d and to the Crown for £403 14s 5d. Crown debt still unpaid on Simon's death (*CCR 1396–9*, 416; *CPR 1396–9*, 368; *1399–1401*, 312). Co-executor of Richard Wateby's will with Jn Gisburn, his 'opponent' in 1381 revolt (*MB*, II, 33).

Thomas REDNESSE, of York: fr 1305; c 1309, b 1319, m 1318, MP 1312, 1322, 1323, 1327. 1298–1313 exported 43 sacks + 265 fells; total 8 cargoes (E122/55/5, 14, 22; 6/11). 1322 licensed to bring victuals north to Y & Newcastle (*CPR 1321–4*, 110). Owed £100 by Roger Ughtred *et al.*, 1319; w 3 clerics owed £200 to Thos de Keteringham *et al.* (*CCR 1318–23*, 206; *1333–7*, 90, 128).

William de ROLLESTON, of Beverley: mercer; k 1399, 1405, 1409; 1387 agent for archbp of Y in Hull and several ER villages w Jn Liversege of H (*C. Inq. Misc. 1392–9*, 199); 1410 w Ad Tirwhit & Rich de Beverley negotiated purchase of Saint Gilescroft from prior of Wartre in 1413 for the town of B (*Yorks Deeds*, VII, 23–4). 1378–1401 exported 245 sacks + 2,033 fells / 36 cloths + cloth v £56 13s 4d / grain v £14 13s 4d; imported misc v £94 10s + woad v £67 10s / 9 tuns; total 58 cargoes (E122/59/2, 5, 7, 8, 14–16, 19, 22–24; 159/11; 160/1–2). Paid aulnage on 30 cloths in 1378–9 (*EWT*, 36). With Steph Coppendale lent king £100 for 'Scottish expenses' in 1400 (*CPR 1399–1401*, 355). Lands assessed at £38 in 1412 (*Feudal Aids*, VI, 545). Kinsman? of Sir Roger Rolleston, who gave Wm a pension of £2 pa (Prob. Reg. II, 370). Married Elene, sister of Margaret, w of Ad Baker, merchant & keeper (Prob. Reg. III, 71v.) Son Thos db 1415 (survived his w Eliz, sis of Richard Holm of B. Left £293 cash, Arch. Reg. XVIII, 34v.).

Richard RUSSELL, of York: merchant, fr 1396, db Dec 1435; c 1409, s 1412, m 1421, 1430, MP 1422, 1425; m 1425 of Calais Staple (*MB*, II, 159); w wife Petronella member Corpus Xti Guild (*CCG*, 25). Educated by the monks at Durham 1391–1431 (Dobson, *Durham Priory*, 60 n. 1). Exported 86 sacks (w Nich Blackburn) / cloth v £26 / 100 calf skins; imported misc v £2 13s 4d / 6 tuns; total 5 cargoes (E122/59/22; 106/26; 159/11; 60/2; 61/32). Shared in Staplers' loans, e.g. of £4, 000 to Crown in 1407 w Richard Whittington, Wm Bowes of Y *et al.* (*CPR 1405–8*, 321). Property assessed at £6 in Jan 1436 (E179/217/42). Sis Alice, w of Pet Upstall, db 1431. Wife Petronella db July 1435, left £47 + cloth (Prob. Reg. II, 640; III, 425). Rich db Dec 1435. Survived by dau Ellen, wife of Jn Thirsk, sister Joan, bro Henry, nephews and nieces. Left 13+ properties in Y; £756 + cash bequests inc: £30 to nephew Rob to attend Oxford; 20s to wool suppliers in Wolds; £10 to same in Lyndsey; 20 marks to repair bridges and causeways within 10 leagues of Y. Money to St John's, Hungate for windows & belfry and his books + altar cloths; 10 marks to Durham. Provision for 4 chantries: perpetual, 30 yr, 10 yr, 3 yr. Land v 11–12 marks pa to be bought to endow the perpetual chantry (Prob. Reg. II, 439–41; *Test. Ebor.* II, 53–6). 1460 chantry est for Jn & Petronella Russell, Jn & Petronella Thirsk, by Jn Thirsk, Guy Fairfax, Jn Shirwood. Thirsk est 2nd chantry for same plus his wives Ellen, Agnes, Alice (*CPR 1452–61*, 632; *1461–7*, 541).

Roger RUYSTON, of Beverley: 1390–6 exported 113 sacks (some via Newcastle) / cloth v £26 6s 8d; total 16 cargoes (E122/59/16, 19, 24; 106/26).

John SWAN, of Hull: from Felton, Northumberland, stapler, fr 1440 as appr (BRG I, 18v.), db 1476; c 1450, s 1455, m 1465, 1474. 1452–73 exported 175 sacks + 11,962 fells / share in £160 misc w Ralph Langton, Jn Ricard, Jn Stubbs / share in £60 misc w Langton, Jn Whitfield & Ralph Garton; imported misc v £60 / fish v £39 / 15 tuns; total 34 cargoes (E122/61/1, 71, 75; 62/3, 5, 7, 9–13, 16, 19, 20). Registered 2 appr: Jn Scott & Jn Dalton (BRG I, 23, 25v.) Married Agnes dau Jn Bedford. Survived by wid Joan, dau Joan, wid's sons Rob & Jn Ripplingham; left £164, silverware. Bequests to Felton ch, window for Holy Trinity, bells for St Mary's (Prob. Reg. v, 7).

Thomas SWANLAND, of Beverley: draper; k 1408, 1418, 1421, 1433, 1437. Churchwdn of St Mary's in 1400 (*Bev. Town Docs.*, 23). 1388–1401 exported cloth v £67 10s; imported misc v £33 4s 10d / Spanish iron v £3 6s 8d; total 5 cargoes (E122/59/14; 60/2; 159/11).

William TERRY, of Hull: m 1397, 1401, MP 1307, 1399; 1398 on royal comm to assemble sea patrol v pirates (*CPR 1396–9*, 366). 1383–1402 exported cloth v £267; imported misc v £9 6s 8d / iron v £41 / salt v £7 / herrings v £4 16s 8d / 154 tuns wine; total 38 cargoes (E122/59/8, 14, 23, 25; 60/2; 158/2; 159/11). Paid aulnage on 9 cloths in 1378–9 (*EWT*, 35). Owned the *Janet* & the *George* in 1402 (*CPR 1401–5*, 55). Heavily involved in licensed privateering w Jn Tutbury of H, which led to disputes w Hanse merchants, the seizure of goods, claims & counter-claims of piracy between 1387–1409 (*Hanseakten*, 189–90; *Urkundenbuch*, v, 323, 483; *CPR 1385–9*, 339; *1399–1401*, 352; *1401–5*, 55; *1405–8*, 302; *CCR 1399–1402*, 533; *1402–5*, 1–2, 42, 56, 256; *1405–9*, 60). Wife Elene db 1407, survived by Wm, 2 sons & Wm's dau Alice Terry. Left £2 6s 8d (Arch. Reg. x, 318).

John THIRSK, of York: merchant, fr 1427, db Oct 1473 (Wedgwood, *Parliamentary Biographies*, I, 845); c 1433, s 1435, m 1442, 1462, MP 1445, 1449, 1450, 1467; 1456–73 m of Calais Staple, and treasurer 1467–73 (Wedgwood, *Parliamentary Biographies*, I, 845–6). Exempted for life from civic office (*CPR 1441–6*, 395); custodian of the King's Staith in Y (*CPR 1467–77*, 455). 1452–71 exported 117 sacks + 52 fells / lead v £8; imported misc v £55 / woad v £184+ / iron v £33 6s 8d / corn v £8 / 1 tun; total 21 cargoes (E122/61/71; 62/1, 5, 7, 9–11, 16). Shared in Staplers' loans to Crown: e.g. of £2,020 in 1449 and £843 6s 8d in 1458 (cost of embassy to Philip of Burgundy) (*CPR 1446–52*, 316; *1452–61*, 211–12, 423). Est chantries for self and Richard Russell (*qv*); 1458 co-founded religious guild in Y w Wm Holbeck (*CPR 1452–61*, 465).

Richard TIRWHIT, of Beverley: 1302–22 exported 1,066 sacks + 12,431 fells / 2 last 5 dicker hides; total 126 cargoes (E122/55/8–10, 13–14, 21–2; 56/5, 8, 11, 15–16, 18; 57/6–7; 6/11).

William TODD, of York: merchant, fr 1462, db 1503; c 1471, s 1476, m 1487, MP 1489; Master of M&MA, 1472 (*M&MA*, 322); with w Agnes, member Corpus Xti Guild 1464 (*CCG*, 65); knighted in 1487, granted annuity of £20 from Hull customs (*CPR 1485–94*, 256–7; *CCR 1485–1500*, 97). A disputatious man: refused to serve as alderman until threatened w a fine, squabbled w Jn Harper about precedence, and accused of fraudulent business practice (*YCR*, I, 37–9, 153, 155, 170; *MB*, II, 288–9). Resigned through sickness & old age in 1501 (House Book, IX, 9v.). 1462–90 exported 1,475 cloths / lead v £108 / share in 85 cloths w Edm Coppendale, Hen Mindram *et al.* of H / share in misc v £66 w Mindram, Jn Spicer *et al.* / share in 90 cloths w Edm Coppendale, Hen Mindram *et al.* of H / share in 44 cloths + misc v £146 10s w Ralph Langton *et al.* of H, & Rich York of Y; imported misc v £294 / 64 tuns; total 54 cargoes (E122/62/2, 5, 7, 9–13, 16, 19–20; 63/1–2, 8). 1466, accused of receiving stolen goods; 1487, breaking the law in Iceland (PRO C1/64/709; 478/31). Survived by 3rd w Eliz Eland of H, daus Isabel, Jane, Marion, Matilda & nephews; left £7, property in Fulford, Naburn, Ripon, Scarborough, Stillington, a salthouse in Whitby. 2nd wife Marg, wid of Thos Eckisill of Scarboro (Prob. Reg. V, 199; VI, 59).

John TOPCLIFF, of York: merchant, fr 1385; c 1388, b 1390. 1381–99 exported 132 sacks + 60 fells / cloth v £72; imported misc v £16 / herrings v £39 6s 8d / 14 tuns; total 36 cargoes (E122/59/7–8, 14, 16, 19, 23–6; 159/11). Paid aulnage on 26½ cloths 1394–9 (*EWT*, 52, 92, 101). 1407 in debt to abbot of Jervaulx (*CCR 1405–9*, 271).

William VESCY, of York: chapman, fr 1376, db 1407. 1383–92 exported 196 sacks; imported misc v £73; total 19 cargoes (E122/59/8, 14, 16, 23–4). Goods arrested in Prussia (*Hansetage*, III, 405, 412). 1st w Emma db 1393 (Prob. Reg. I, 60v.). Survived by 2nd w Emma; left £300 + silverware; house in Mickelgate + lease in Walmgate. Cash for proxy pilgrims, for a wake, and to 14 priories in Yorks. His servant Jn Northeby licensed to est chantry for Wm & Marion Vescy in All Saints, Northst, 1410 (Prob. Reg. III, 266v.–8v.; *CPR 1408–13*, 162).

Thomas WAGHEN, of Beverley: 1302–22 exported 124 sacks + 1,390 fells / 3 lasts 3 dicker hides; total 37 cargoes (E122/55/8–9, 13–4, 21–2; 56/5, 8, 11, 15–16, 18; 57/6–8; 6/11). In EIII's wool monopoly (*CCR 1337–9*, 427; *1343–6*, 146). Victualling Y & Newcastle, 1322 (*CPR 1321–4*, 109).

Robert WARD, of York: fr 1368 as serv of Rob Holme, db 1405; c 1377, b 1380, MP 1402, 1380 keeper of Monkgate keys (*MB*, I, 154). 1378–1402 exported 776 sacks + 8,278 fells / 1,445½ cloths & cloth v £395 / calfskins v £10 15s; imported misc v £600 (inc woad v £66) / 11 pipes wine; total 146 cargoes (E122/59/1, 2, 5, 7, 8, 14–16, 19, 22–6; 60/2, 5; 159/11; 160/1). Paid aulnage on 125 cloths & 13½ kerseys in 1394–5, on 7 cloths in 1399 (*EWT*, 52, 75–6, 88, 91, 102). Goods seized in Prussia in 1385, 1388 (*Hansetage*, III, 405, 412); at least 2 cargoes shipwrecked (*CPR 1391–6*, 233; *CCR 1396–9*, 38). Debts to him of £8 in 1392 & 1395 from Rob Dockwra and Ad Wariner of Kirkby in Kendal (*CPR 1391–6*, 253, 677). Survived by son Jn (fr 1403) (Prob. Reg. III, 234).

Henry WILLIAMSON, of York: merchant, fr 1446, db 1499? (House Book, VIII, 47); c 1472, s 1474; member M&MA mistery 1474 (*M&MA*, 64, 66).

1452–73 exported 77½ cloths / lead v £11 13s 4d / misc v £15; imported misc v £27 / 84 tuns; total 23 cargoes (E122/61/71; 62/1, 5, 9–10, 13, 15–16, 19).

Thomas WRANGWISH, of York: merchant, fr 1453, db 1491 (*MB*, II, 242); c 1463, s 1466, m 1476, 1484, MP 1472, 1483, 1484; Master M&MA 1471, 1472; wife a member 1472 (*M&MA*, 66, 322); w wife member Corpus Xti Guild (*CCG*, 63). 1462–72 exported 44 cloths; imported misc v £160 10s (inc 160 lb almonds) / 5 tuns Sp wine; total 18 cargoes (E122/62/3–5, 7, 9, 11–13, 16). Cargo seized in the Sound of Denmark *en route* for Prussia (*Urkundenbuch*, IX, 369–70). Famous supporter of Richard of Gloucester: attended king's council in 1480, commanded York city's forces fighting for Richard in 1481 & 1483 and named as Richard's man in tavern gossip in 1483 mayoral elections (*YCR*, I, 30, 38, 48–52, 68–9, 83). Granted life annuity of 20 marks from the issues of Sheriff Hutton for services to Richard (*CPR 1476–85*, 450).

Henry WYMAN, of York: fr 1387, naturalised German 1388 (*CPR 1385–9*, 463, 518), db 1411 (tombstone in St Crux, *CCG*, 239); b 1388, m 1407, 1408, 1409. 1378–1401 exported 135+ sacks / 288 cloths + cloth v £474; imported misc v £321 10s / 40+ tuns; total 55 cargoes (E122/59/1 as an alien; 58/14; 59/7, 8, 14, 16, 23, 25, 26; 60/2; 159/11). In 1385 discharged from liability to have his goods seized in reprisals on grounds he was a Hanseatic merchant (*CCR 1383–9*, 2). W John Bolton, cargo shipwrecked in 1392 (*CPR 1391–6*, 233). Paid ulnage on 41½ cloths in 1394–5 (*EWT*, 75, 80); 1395 pardoned infringements against statutes re buying wool (*CPR 1391–6*, 630). Owned a house in H (BRE I, 50). Married Jn Barden's dau Agnes, and their dau Joan married Sir Wm Gascoigne of Gawthorpe, eldest son of the Lord Chief Justice (Prob. Reg. I, 95v.; *CCG*, 239). 1407 est chantry for Jn Barden (*CPR 1405–8*, 312).

Richard YORK, of York: merchant from Berwick-on-Tweed, db 1498; c 1460, s 1465, m 1469, 1482, MP 1472, 1474, 1475, 1483, 1485, 1489; m of Calais Staple 1466 (Wedgwood, *Parliamentary Biographies*, I, 979); 1475 Master M&MA (*M&MA*, 322); knighted in 1487; an ambassador to the Hanse in 1491 (Wedgwood, *Parliamentary Biographies*). Granted annuity of £20 in 1488 from H customs, for loyalty during Simnel's rebellion (*CPR 1485–96*, 256). 1463–90 exported 73 sacks / 98 cloths / linen v 30s / misc v £5+; imported misc v £104 / iron v £80 / woad & madder v £40 / 20+ tuns; total 28 cargoes, 1 exp jointly w H merchant Henry Mindram *et al.* (E122/62/4, 5, 9, 10, 13, 16, 17; 63/8). 1482 licensed to trade in Bordeaux (BL Harl. MS 1433, 78d.) One of trustees for Miles Metcalfe's heirs in Sledmere manor in 1489 (*Yorks Fines*, I, 2). Married Joan, wid of Jn Whitfield, m of Hull (see fig. 3 on p. 89). Survived by wid Joan & 7 sons. Left property in Barneby-on-the-Moor, Berwick, Bishopthorpe, Bowden, Dringhouses, Donnington, Flaxby, Heslington, Holtby, Hull, Morton, Poppleton, Newcastle, Normanby, Sledmere, York and a separate endowment of property to est a chantry in St John's, Hungate. Cash bequests £124 + 20 ells velvet, inc cost of memorial in St Katherine's chapel, Berwick; repairs to St John's choir roof. Left rights in church of Ryle, Lincs, to son Chris. Confirmed agreement w prioress of Clementhorpe to est an almshouse 'of the Trinity'. In case of disputes between sons, the bishop of Carlisle and Reginald Bray to act as executors. Will made in the Doctors Commons in London (PRO Prob. 11/11, 36). Son Thomas held civic office as c 1501, gdson Bartholomew, fr as merchant in 1526, c in 1533. Richard's chantry est in St John's, Ousebridgend (*Yorks Chantry Survey*, I, 78).

Appendix 4

THE CASE OF JOHN BOLTON AGAINST
JOHN BRANDESBY AND
SIMON SWAN OF YORK, 1445

PRO Exchequer Plea Roll E13/143, mm. 40–2. There is an edited transcription in H. Hall, *Select Cases Concerning the Law Merchant*, II, Selden Soc. 46 (1930), pp. 106–9, 156–9. I am grateful to Simon Corcoran for his help with this document.

PLEAS BEFORE THE BARONS OF THE EXCHEQUER AT WESTMINSTER EASTER TERM 23 HENRY SIXTH (1445).

Be it remembered that the sheriffs of the city of York, namely William Clyff and Richard Claybruke, have returned here now in one month of Easter Day, a certain writ of the now lord King under his Great Seal, directed to them, of which writ, indeed, the tenor follows in these words:

Henry by the Grace of God, King of England and France and Lord of Ireland, to the Sheriffs of the city of York, greeting. On behalf of Simon Swan of York and John Brandesby of York (taken and detained in our prison of the city aforesaid, for arrears of their account, in which John Bolton, citizen and merchant of York, asserts that they are bound to him for the time when they were receivers of the moneys of the same John Bolton) it is shown to us that the auditors of the account aforesaid, deputed for this, have aggrieved them, Simon and John Brandesby, unduly upon the same account; by charging them with receipts which they have not received and by not allowing to them expenses and reasonable payments, to the no small loss and grievance of them, Simon and John Brandesby. And because we are unwilling that the same Simon and John Brandesby should be injured in this respect we order you that if the aforesaid Simon and John Brandesby shall have been delivered up to you by the testimony of the auditors of the account aforesaid and shall have found you sufficient sureties who will mainpern them, to have them before our Treasurer and Barons of the Exchequer in one month of Easter Day to render to the aforesaid John Bolton his account aforesaid, according to the form of the Statute provided herein by the common council of our realm, then you shall cause them, Simon and John Brandesby, to be delivered from our prison in the meantime by the mainprise aforesaid, if they are detained in the same for that cause and none

348

other. And you shall make known to the aforesaid John Bolton that he is then to be here with the rolls and tallies by which the same Simon and John Brandesby previously rendered their account, to do and receive what of right and according to the form of the Statute aforesaid shall remain to be done in the premises. And you are to have there the names of these mainpernors and this writ. Witness myself at Westminster, the 27th day of February in the twenty-third year of our reign.

[The mainpernors were Thomas Cotes, John Littester, John Middleton, Robert Preston, Thomas Selby, William Southerd, William Vescy and Thomas Warde, citizens of York.]

And the writ aforesaid is indorsed thus: The answer of William Clyff and Richard Claybruke, sheriffs of the city of York, appears in the writing below and in a certain schedule annexed to this writ.

And the testimony of these auditors appears in a certain schedule annexed to this writ (see below, p. 351), and the tenor of the same schedule follows in these words: This indenture made at York on the last day of January in the twenty-third year of the reign of King Henry, sixth after the Conquest, witnesses that John Brandesby and Simon Swan, servants and receivers of the moneys of John Bolton, citizen and merchant of York, owe clearly to the same John Bolton at the end of their account rendered and terminated at York the day and year aforesaid before Henry Gascoigne and Richard Burton, auditors of the account of the aforesaid John Brandesby and Simon as appears in the same account; all things being reckoned and allowed with the exception of the moneys respited to them in the same account, £489 6s 6d; (for which sum, indeed, the aforesaid John Brandesby and Simon were arrested by the auditors aforesaid and delivered to William Clyff of York, merchant, and to Richard Claybruke of York, chapman, sheriffs of the city of York, to be kept and guarded safely and securely in the gaol of the same city under their custody); as reckoning and statement of the account exact and require according to the force, form and effect of the Statute provided for that purpose, under the penalty incurred thereby. In witness of which they as well as the aforesaid Henry and Richard Burton, auditors of the account aforesaid, as the before-mentioned William and Richard Claybruke, sheriffs of the said city, have affixed their seals to the respective parts of this indenture: These are witnesses, Thomas Danby, William [of] Aberford, merchants, Robert Colynson, mercer, William Shefeld of York, skinner, Adam Fell, and others. Dated in the day, place and year above said.

And now at the month aforesaid came here the aforesaid Simon and John Brandesby in their proper persons. And hereupon the aforesaid John Bolton came here by William Essex and John Byspryham, his attorneys, and proffered and showed to the court here a certain roll of account previously rendered by them, Simon and John; besides a certain book of paper, containing twenty-eight leaves, by which the aforesaid Simon and John Brandesby previously accounted; and he asks that the aforesaid Simon and John Brandesby may be committed to the lord King's prison of the Fleet for arrears of the account aforesaid, there to remain until, etc. And hereupon the aforesaid Simon and John Brandesby are committed to the said lord King's prison of the Fleet; and incontinently the said roll with the book of paper are delivered to Robert Mildenhale, clerk of the Pleas of this Exchequer, here, etc., to be safely kept, etc.

And hereupon John Somer and Richard Bedford, two Auditors of this Exchequer, are assigned by the Barons for hearing a recital of the account aforesaid within the Octaves of the Holy Trinity next to come; and incontinently the aforesaid roll and book are delivered by the above-mentioned Robert Mildenhale to the before-mentioned John Somers and Richard Bedford, Auditors of this Exchequer, by precept of this court, to hear the recital of the same account, etc.

And hereupon the aforesaid Simon and John Brandesby found mainpernors, namely Peter Bukton of Bukton, knight; Thomas Cotes of York, gentleman; Christopher Millom of Scarborough, gentleman; William Langdale of Malton in Rydale, gentleman.

At which day the parties aforesaid came here, namely the said John Bolton by his attorneys and the aforesaid Simon and John Brandesby in their proper persons. And the aforesaid Auditors of this Exchequer delivered here the said roll of account with the aforesaid book of paper previously delivered to them, together with a certain roll of Articles of Complaints of them, Simon and John Brandesby, as well of divers sums of money unjustly charged upon them in the account aforesaid by the Auditors aforesaid appointed by the before-mentioned John Bolton, as of divers expenses and payments likewise unjustly disallowed to them and placed in respite. And this roll and book remain in fact in the custody of the before-mentioned Robert Mildenhale, clerk of the Pleas of this Exchequer; and the tenor of that roll of Articles follows in these words.

And hereupon the aforesaid John Bolton, called upon to answer the Articles aforesaid, says that he at present is not advised to answer the same Articles, and he craves a day for arguing on them, till the Octaves of S. Michael within which, etc., and this is granted to him by the court. And the same day is given to the before-mentioned Simon and John Brandesby, here, etc. And because the mainpernors aforesaid of the said Simon and John Brandesby are not fully able to make a solution of the arrears specified in the account aforesaid, namely £489 6s 6d (in the case where those arrears may happen to be adjudged as due to the before-mentioned John Bolton), as the court is credibly informed, therefore it is said by the court to the before-mentioned Simon and John Brandesby that they are to find other sufficient mainpernors who are willing to mainpern them with the other mainpernors abovesaid, in manner and form above recognized by the same mainpernors.

And hereupon Robert Hynkershill of Rotherham in the county of York, gentleman, and John Wylcock of Over Hoyland, in the same county, gentleman, came before the Barons of this Exchequer on the fourteenth day of July in the twenty-third year of the said now lord King, in their proper persons, and mainperned to have the bodies of the aforesaid Simon and John Brandesby here, etc., in the Octaves of S. Michael next to come, and so from day to day and term to term until there has been a discussion of the premises, or else that they have

acknowledged that they and each of them owe to the before-mentioned John
Bolton the arrears in the account aforesaid, namely £489 6s. 6d., which they
have granted and each of them by himself has granted to be levied from his lands
and chattels to the use of the said John Bolton, in case that they shall not have
here the said Simon and John Brandesby at the Octaves of S. Michael aforesaid,
and so from day to day and term to term until there has been discussion of the
premises in the form aforesaid, etc.

SUMMARY OF THE AUDITORS' REVIEW

All the receipts, payments and expenses made by John Brandesby and Simon
Swan, as merchants and receivers of moneys for John Bolton, from 10th May,
1443 to 18th January, 1445: one whole year and 36 weeks.

1. First, whereas in the same account under the heading 'John Brandesby' there
   is a statement of arrears £25 4s 9d, the same John says that he is charged by
   the auditors with this sum unjustly ('minus juste') for that no such statement
   was ever rendered by him as supposed in the above account; and this he is
   prepared to aver; whereof he craves judgment, and that he may be exonerated in respect of the same £25 4s 9d.
2. Also, whereas in the said account under the head of 'Moneys received by
   the said Simon' is contained a debit of £97 10s 6d lent (*ex mutuo ad usum*)
   for the purchase of wool by the said Simon, who deposes that no such loan
   was ever made to him.
3. Also in respect of receipts for sales of wool amounting to £3,286 8s 2d,
   being the price of 113 sarplers and 6 pokes of wool from the store of John
   Bolton, sold by the aforesaid John and Simon to certain persons by indenture of sale as between Simon Swan and John Bolton. The plaintiffs deny
   responsibility for this transaction, suggesting that the wool was sold by
   Bolton himself, *per advisamentum ipsius Simonis*: without that any such
   expenditure should be allowed to them in consideration of their payments
   and expenses entered in a paper book produced to the auditors.
4. The complainants explain that the 4 casks 1 pipe of woad charged to them
   for £49 15s were wrecked in the 'Busse de Cales' at Dover, by misfortune
   and a stormy sea: without that they were lost by Simon's default.
5. The sum of £25 4s 1d debited in the account as the price of 1 sarpler of
   wool sold, was included in the sum of £3,828 6s 3d, being the price of 130
   sarplers 7 pokes of wool sold at Calais in two parcels, one by John Bolton
   before Simon Swan's arrival at Calais; the other by John Bolton and Simon
   Swan together; without that any of this wool was wanting or deficient.
6. Among the expenses incurred for payment of customs duties occurs the
   item of 70s paid for the expenses of Philip of Cassel, labouring for John
   Brandesby to be delivered from prison at Dunkirk, as on folio 14 of the
   paper book. This item was disallowed by the auditors, unjustly, because long
   before, at York, John Bolton made John Brandesby his factor and receiver
   of 1,331 sarplers 6 pokes of wool, parcel of the wool aforesaid, which were

to be sold and the money accruing therefrom to be expended to the use and profit of the said John Bolton as should seem best to John Brandesby and all such other things to be done and executed in the name and on behalf of the same John Bolton as ought and are accustomed to be done and executed by such factor and attorney, according to the law and the use of merchants. And the same John Brandesby being bound by a writing obligatory to certain Lombard and Picard merchants in the sum of £67 10s, to be paid at Candlemas 1443, in default of payment was detained in prison till payment should be made, so that he was prevented from attending to business to the loss of John Bolton himself and the no slight scandal and lessening of his state, name and honour among merchants of his acquaintance; moreover to the manifest peril of the loss of many of his wares. Wherefore (forasmuch as the aforesaid John Bolton had beforetime sufficiently and lawfully given his full authority and power, according to the law merchant, to the same John Brandesby as his factor and attorney for doing and executing all manner of things as well in payments and receipts of moneys as in sales, purchases, exchanges, barters, chevances, and governances of merchandises and things whatsoever, as well of the same John Bolton as for the same John) the same John Brandesby on behalf of the same John Bolton, to avoid such loss, scandal, disparagement and peril engaged the aforesaid Philip (of Cassel) to labour for his deliverance from prison, who pledged 20 casks of his own woad as security for the payment of £67 10s on behalf of John Bolton, as is supposed in the account; and this he is ready to aver, etc., and he craves allowance of the 70s aforesaid.

Simon Swan has not to account for this item and therefore does not crave allowance hereof.

7. Under the heading 'Paid to John Bolton by the aforesaid John Brandesby' is the entry of the proceeds of one sarpler of wool sold to a merchant of Louvain with pledges taken for payment at Easter 1445. This item was disallowed by the auditors, unjustly, because the wool was parcel of the 113 sarplers previously referred to.

Also John Brandesby claims allowance for 1 poke of 'medyll wolle vocata reffuse', part of the same 113 sarplers, and which the same John Brandesby as factor and attorney of John Bolton, in his name and behalf, and by the authority and power aforesaid, according to the law merchant sold to Colyn Landusse at Bruggemart for £11 12s 2d.

8. As to three pieces of linen cloth bought in exchange for two sarplers, one poke of the wool of John Bolton, in respect of which the sum of £55 12s 11d was not allowed to the complainants, but was placed 'in respite' at the foot of their account, this refers to 30 pieces of Holland cloth, charged in the account with the sum of £3,286 8s 2d; which cloth was delivered to John Bolton, at York, as the defendants are ready to aver, etc.

9. Objection was taken by the auditors to the payment of 30s to the friars of Calais for a house in Friar Street in addition to £6 13s 4d previously paid. Also to payments made by the accountants to John Huson, 'makelere' of

wool at Bruges, and to others, for the advantage (*melioracione*) of wool sold, called 'Betterynges'. These payments were not allowed by the auditors but were respited. Brandesby declares that it concerned Bolton's honour and profit to pay these sums: that it was important to get possession of the house in question, in which merchandise could be stored and exposed for sale (*vendicioni demonstrare*). The dealings in wool referred to four sarplers of Scarsdale wool of John Bolton sold by John Brandesby as his factor and attorney, on his behalf and in his name, by warrant, for the 'bettering' of 12 sarplers of Scarsdale wool.

10. With respect to the objection to allowance of certain bills payable at the Mint in Calais, long before bills for £30 4s were taken to that mint by John and Simon, it was ordained in the Staple of Calais that on the sale of every sarpler of wool of Lindsey worth 14 marks, or more, a bill should be brought into the mint to the value of £6; and so for Yorkshire wool of the Wold and Scarsdale, of more than 12 and less than 14 marks value, a like bill of £5 was required: and for middle wool £4. And Brandesby, as Bolton's factor, not having bills or money ready to comply with the ordinance, namely for one third of the true value of the wool, became indebted to men of Flanders for certain exchanges amounting to £32 17s 1d, which the Bolton's auditors have disallowed, though this transaction was duly entered in the paper book (produced for audit) and was authorized by letters in the hands of the accountants.

    Another item of 46s 8d paid for herring bought at Calais by Brandesby and paid for on Brandesby's security was disallowed or held over because Bolton had made arrangements for the money to be paid by one of his servants without Brandesby's knowledge.

11. The auditors also disallow the sum of £32 17s 1d paid by John Brandesby and Simon Swan to divers men of Flanders and Calais for wares bought and for differences in exchange of moneys.

12. The auditors disallow £617 4s 3½d paid in London to the customers of Kingstown-on-Hull for wools shipped for John Bolton by John Brandesby as his factor and attorney, including the sum of £259 14s 2d due to the Crown on a bond given by Brandesby for the advantage and honour (*pro commodo et honore*) of John Bolton.

13. Certain payments made by Brandesby and disallowed by the auditors are said to have been authorized by a ledger book, but the pages have been sewn together.

14. Finally John Brandesby claimed payment of his fee of £13 6s 8d yearly, for four years, but this claim was disallowed, John Bolton having asserted that two years before the date of this account he retained John Brandesby at York as his factor and attorney for two years at an inclusive fee of £6 13s 4d, and 2 cloaks and 2 hoods price 40s: but did not pay him. Brandesby claims to be allowed the 40s in lieu of the above livery.

SELECT BIBLIOGRAPHY

MANUSCRIPT SOURCES

LONDON: BRITISH LIBRARY

Additional, Harleian and Landsdowne manuscripts

LONDON: PUBLIC RECORD OFFICE

C1   Early Chancery Proceedings
C47   Chancery Miscellanea
C142 Inquisitions Post Mortem
C76   Treaty Rolls
CP40 Court of Common Pleas
E122 King's Remembrancer Customs Rolls
E179 Lay Subsidy Rolls
E356 Customs Accounts of the Exchequer
KB25 King's Bench: Coram Rege Rolls
SC8   Ancient Petitions

YORK: BORTHWICK INSTITUTE OF HISTORICAL RESEARCH

Dean and Chapter original wills and inventories (fourteenth to sixteenth centuries)
    L2/5a (Dean and Chapter Probate Register 2)
    Probate Registers 1–9 (Probate Registers of the Exchequer and Prerogative Court of
      the Archbishop)
    Archbishops' Registers

YORK CITY ARCHIVES

B1–9   House books
C59   Murage Rolls, 1442–3, 1445–6
C80–5–80.10 Accounts of the Bridgemasters of Fossbridge, 1445–89
C82.10–87.1 Accounts of the Bridgemasters of Ousebridge, 1440–1522
C99.3–100.3 Accounts of the Corpus Christi Guild

Select bibliography

CCI, CCIa Chamberlains' Account Books 1446–50, 1448–58, 1480–3
E20, 20A (lettered A/Y, B/Y etc) York Memorandum Books
E39 Sheriffs' Court Book

YORK MINSTER LIBRARY

L2/4 (Dean and Chapter Probate Register 1)

HUMBERSIDE RECORD OFFICE

BC II/2   Town Cartulary
BC II/3   Great Gild Book
BC II/7/1   Governors' Minute Book
BC II/6/1–15 Account Rolls
BC III   Charters and Deeds

HULL CITY RECORD OFFICE

BRG 1 Bench Book 1
BRE 1 Bench Book 2
BRE 2 Bench Book 3
BRB 1 Bench Book 3A
M479 Chamberlains' Account Rolls
D   Deeds

PRINTED SOURCES

Unless otherwise stated, the place of publication is London.

Calendar of Charter Rolls preserved in the Public Record Office, 1257–1516 (1906–27)
Calendar of Close Rolls preserved in the Public Record Office, 1272–1509 (1900–63)
Calendar of Fine Rolls preserved in the Public Record Office, 1272–1509 (1911–63)
Rotuli litterarum patentium in turri Londinensi: I. Record Commission (1835)
Calendar of the Patent Rolls preserved in the Public Record Office, 1272–1509 (1901–16)
Calendars of Inquisitions Miscellaneous preserved in the Public Record Office, Henry III–Henry V (1916–69)
Lords' Report on the Dignity of Peers, 5 vols. (1820–9)
The Return of the Name of Every Member of the Lower House, 1213–1702 (1878)
Anon 'The Rolls of the Collectors in the West Riding of the Lay Subsidy (Poll Tax) 2 Richard II', Yorks Arch. Jnl 5 (1879); 6 (1881); 7 (1882)
Attreed, L. C. ed. York House Books 1461–90, 2 vols. (Stroud, 1991)
Baildon, W. P. ed. Feet of Fines for the County of York, 1327–47, YAS Rec. Ser., 42 (1910); 1347–77, 52 (1915)
Barnum, P. H. ed. Dives and Pauper, I, EETS, OS, 275 (1976)
Bartlett, J. N. ed. 'The 1381 Lay Poll Tax Return for the City of York', Trans. East Riding Antiq. Soc., 30 (n.d.)
Bateson, M. ed. Borough Customs, I–II. Selden Soc., 18 (1904), 21 (1906)
Beardwood, A. ed. The Statute Merchant Roll of Coventry, 1392–1416, Dugdale Soc., 17 (1939)

Bell, J. V. and Bell, H. C. *Lyndwood's Provinciale* (1929)

Bond, E. A. ed. *Chronica Monasterii de Melsa*, I–III, Rolls Series (1866–8)

Brown, W., Clay, C. T., Hebditch, M. J. and Price, M. J. S. eds. *Yorkshire Deeds*, I–X, YAS Rec. Ser., 39 (1909); 50 (1914); 63 (1922); 65 (1924); 69 (1926); 83 (1932); 102 (1940); 109 (1948), 120 (1955)

Brown, W. ed. *Yorkshire Star Chamber Proceedings*, I, YAS Rec. Ser., 41 (1909)

Caley, J., Illingworth, W. and McPherson, D. eds. *Rotuli Scotiae in turri Londinensi*, I–II, Rec. Com. (1814–19)

Charlesworth, J. and Hudson, A. eds. *Index of Wills and Administrations entered in the Registers of the Archbishops at York, 1316–1822*, YAS Rec. Ser., 93 (1937)

Childs, W. R. ed. *The Customs Accounts of Hull 1453–1490*, YAS Rec. Ser., 144 (1986)

Collins, F. ed. *Index of Wills in the York Registry, 1389–1514, 1514–53*, YAS Rec. Ser., 6 (1889); 11 (1891)

Index of the Freemen of the City of York, I, Surtees Soc., 96 (1896)

Index of Wills from the Dean and Chapter's Court at York, 1321–1636, YAS Rec. Ser., 38 (1907)

Cox, J. C. 'A Poll Tax Return of the East Riding [1379]', *Trans. East Riding Antiq. Soc.* 15 (1908)

Dendy, F. W. and Blair, C. H. eds. *Visitations of the North*, I–III, Surtees Soc., 122 (1912); 133 (1921); 144 (1930)

Farrer, W. ed. *Early Yorkshire Charters*, I–III, YAS Rec. Soc., extra series, 1 (1914–16)

Fowler, J. T. ed. *Extracts from the Account Rolls of the Abbey of Durham*, I–III, Surtees Soc., 99 (1898); 100 (1899); 103 (1901)

Memorials of the Abbey of St Mary of Fountains, III, Surtees Soc., 130 (1918)

Gross, C. ed. *Select Cases Concerning the Law Merchant*, I, Selden Soc., 23 (1908)

Hall, H. ed. *Select Cases Concerning Law Merchant*, II–III, Selden Soc., 46 (1930); 49 (1932)

Hohlbaum, K., Kunze, K., and Stein, W. eds. *Hansisches Urkundenbuch*, 10 vols., Halle and Leipzig (1876–1907)

Horrox, R. ed. *Selected Rentals and Accounts of Medieval Hull, 1293–1528*, YAS Rec. Ser., 141 (1983).

Kingsford, C. L. ed. *The Stonor Letters and Papers, 1290–1483*, 2 vols., Camden Soc., 3rd ser., 29, 30 (1919) and Supplementary Stonor Letters and Papers, 1314–1482, *Camden Miscellany, XIII*, Camden Soc., 3rd ser., 34 (1924)

Kirby, J. W. ed. *The Manor and Borough of Leeds, 1425–1662: An edition of Documents*, Thoresby Soc., 57 (1981)

The Plumpton Letters and Papers, Camden Soc., 5th ser., 8 (Cambridge, 1996)

Kitchin, G. W. ed. *The Records of the Northern Convocation*, Surtees Soc., 113 (1907)

Koppman, C., von der Ropp, G. F. and Schafer, D. eds., *Die Recesse und and ere Akten der Hansetage, 1256–1530*, 17 vols. (Leipzig, 1870–97)

Kunze, K. ed. *Hanseakten aus England, 1275–1412* (Halle, 1891)

Lamb, G. D. ed. *Testamenta Leodiensia*, Thoresby Soc., 19 (1913)

Leach, A. F. ed. *Memorials of Beverley Minster, The Chapter Act Book*, I–II, Surtees Soc., 98 (1898); 108 (1903)

Early Yorkshire Schools, I, YAS Rec. Ser., 27 (1899)

Beverley Town Documents, Selden Soc., 14 (1900)

Report on the Manuscripts of the Corporation of Beverley, Royal Commission on Historical Manuscripts (1900)

Leggett, J. I. 'The 1377 Lay Poll Tax Return for the City of York', *Yorks Arch. Jnl*, 43 (1971)

Select bibliography

Lister, J. ed. *The Early Yorkshire Woollen Trade*, YAS Rec. Ser., 64 (1924)

Malden, H. E. ed. *The Cely Papers*, Camden Soc., 3rd ser., l (1900)

Marsden, R. G. ed. *Select Pleas in the Court of the Admiralty*, I, Selden Soc., 6 (1892)

O'Connor, S. J. ed. *A Calendar of the Cartularies of John Pyel and Adam Fraunceys*, Camden Soc., 5th ser., 2 (1993)

Percy J. W. ed. *York Memorandum Book B/Y*, III, Surtees Soc., 186 (1973)

Poulson, G. *Beverlac, or the Antiquities and History of the Town of Beverley* (1892)

Putnam, B. H. ed. *Yorkshire Sessions of the Peace, 1361–4*, YAS Rec. Ser., 100 (1939)

Raine, A. ed. *York Civic Records*, I–III, YAS Rec. Ser., 98 (1939); 103 (1941); 106 (1942)

Raine, J. ed. *Sanctuarium Dunelmense et Sanctuarium Beverlacense*, Surtees Soc., 5 (1837)

Raine, J. snr and jnr eds. *Testamenta Eboracensia*, I–IV, Surtees Soc., 4 (1836); 30 (1855) 45 (1865); 53 (1869)

Sellers, M. ed. *York Memorandum Book*, I–II, Surtees Soc., 120 (1911); 125 (1914)
 The York Mercers and Merchant Adventurers Company, Surtees Soc., 129 (1918)

Severen, G. van ed. *Cartulaire de l'ancienne estaple de Bruges*, 4 ed. vols. (Bruges, 1904–6).

Skaife, R. H. ed. *The Register of the Guild of Corpus Christi in the City of York*, Surtees Soc., 57 (1872)

Smit, H. J. ed. *Bronnen tot de Geschiedenis van den Handel met Engeland, Schotland, en Ierland, 1150–1485*, 2 vols. (The Hague, 1928)

Stanewell, L. M. *Calendar of the Ancient Deeds, Letters, Miscellaneous Old Documents etc. in the Archives of the Corporation* (Hull, 1951)

Thomas, A. H. *et al.* eds. *Calendar of the Plea and Memoranda Rolls of the City of London, 1323–1482*, 6 vols. (Cambridge, 1926–61)

Thompson, A. H. ed. *Archbishop Greenfield's Register*, I–V, Surtees Soc., 145 (1931); 149 (1934); 151 (1936); 152 (1938); 153 (1940)

Toulmin-Smith, L. ed. *English Guilds*, EETS, OS, 40 (1870).
 The Itinerary of John Leyland in or about the Years 1535–1543 (1907)

Turner, G. J. ed. *Year Book 4 Edward II*, Selden Soc., 26 (1911)

Twiss, T. ed. *The Black Book of the Admiralty*, 4 vols., Rolls Series (1871–6)

Unger, W. S. ed. *Bronnen tot de Geschiedenis van Middelburg in den landsheerlikjen Tijt*, 2 vols. (The Hague, 1923–6)

Walbran, J. R. ed. *Memorials of the Abbey of St Mary of Fountains*, I–II pt 1, Surtees Soc., 42 (1863); 67 (1878)

Warner, G. ed. *The Libelle of Englyshe Polycye* (Oxford, 1926).

Wood-Legh, K. L. ed. *Kentish Visitations of Archbishop William Warham and his Deputies, 1511–1512*, Kent Records, 24 (1984)

SECONDARY WORKS

Addyman, P. V. and Black, V. E. eds. *Archaeological Papers Presented to M. W. Barley* (York, 1984)

Albertson, M. 'London Merchants and Their Landed Property During the Reigns of the Yorkists' (Univ. of Bryn Mawr PhD thesis, 1932)

Alcock, N. W. 'The Catesbys in Coventry: A Medieval Estate and its Archives', *Midland History*, 15 (1990)

Allison, K. J. ed. *Victoria History of the County of York. East Riding*, I (1969)
 Victoria History of the County of York. East Riding, VI (1989)

Atchley, E. G. C. F. 'Some More Bristol Inventories', *Trans. of the St Paul's Ecclesiological Society*, 9 (1922–8)

Atkinson, T. *Elizabethan Winchester* (1963)

Attreed, L. C. 'The King's Interest: York's Fee Farm and the Central Government 1482–92', *Northern History*, 17 (1981)

'Preparation for Death in Sixteenth-Century Northern England', *The Sixteenth-Century Journal*, 13 (1982)

'Medieval Bureaucracy in Fifteenth-Century York', *York Historian*, 6 (1985)

'Arbitration and the Growth of Urban Liberties in Late Medieval England', *Jnl British Studies*, 31 (1992)

'The Politics of Welcome: Ceremonies and Constitutional Development in Later Medieval English Towns', in Hanawalt and Reyerson, *City and Spectacle*

Bailey, S. J. *The Law of Wills*, 7th edn (1973)

Ballard, A. and Tait, J. *British Borough Charters, 1216–1307* (Cambridge, 1923)

Barron, C. M. 'Richard Whittington: The Man Behind the Myth', in A. E. J. Hollaender and W. Kellaway, eds., *Studies in London History Presented to Philip Edmund Jones* (1969)

The Medieval Guildhall of London (1974)

'The Parish Fraternities of Medieval London', in Barron and Harper-Bill, *The Church in Pre-Reformation Society*

Barron, C. M. and Du Boulay, F. R. H., eds. *The Reign of Richard II: Essays in Honour of May McKisack* (1971)

Barron, C. M. and Harper-Bill, C. eds. *The Church in Pre-Reformation Society. Essays in Honour of F. R. H. Du Boulay* (1985)

Barron, C. M. & Sutton, A. F. eds. *Medieval London Widows, 1300–1500* (1994)

Bartlett, J. N. 'Robert Holme, Citizen and Merchant of York', *Jnl Bradford Textile Soc.*, 98 (1952–3)

'Some Aspects of the Economy of York in the Later Middle Ages, 1300–1550' (Univ. of London PhD thesis, 1958)

'The Expansion and Decline of York in the Later Middle Ages', *EcHR*, 2nd ser., 12 (1959–60)

Baum, H-P. 'Annuities in Late Medieval Hanse Towns', *Business History Review*, 59 (1985)

Bean, J. M. W. *The Estates of the Percy Family 1416–1537* (1958)

Beauroy, J. 'Family Patterns and Relations of Bishop's Lynn Will-makers in the Fourteenth Century', in L. Bonfield *et al.*, eds., *The World We Have Gained. Histories of Population and Social Structure* (1986)

Bennett, E. Z. 'Debt and Credit in the Urban Economy: London, 1380–1460' (Univ. of Harvard PhD thesis, 1989)

Bennett, J. M. 'Spouses, Siblings and Surnames: Reconstructing Families from Medieval Village Court Rolls', *Jnl Brit. Stud.*, 23 (1983)

Women in the Medieval English Countryside. Gender and Household in Brigstock Before the Plague (Oxford, 1987)

Bird, R. *The Turbulent London of Richard II* (1949)

Bittle, W. G. & Lane, R.T. 'Inflation and Philanthropy in England: A Reassessment of W. K. Jordan's Data', *EcHR*, 2nd ser., 29 (1976)

Blake, J. B. 'Medieval Smuggling in the North East', *Arch. Aeliana*, 4th ser., 43 (1965)

Blanchard, I. S. W. 'Seigneurial Entrepreneurship and the Bishops of Durham and the Weardale Iron Industry, 1406–1529', *Business History*, 15 (1973)

Bolton, J. L. *The Medieval English Economy 1150–1500* (1980)

Select bibliography

Bonney, M. *Lordship and the Urban Community. Durham and its Overlords, 1250–1540* (Cambridge, 1990)

Bossy, J. *Christianity in the West 1400–1700* (Oxford, 1985)

Boulton, J. *Neighbourhood and Society. A London Suburb in the Seventeenth Century* (Cambridge, 1987)

Boutruche, R. *La crue d'une société: seigneurs et paysans de Bordelais pendant la guerre de cent ans* (Paris, 1947)

Bowden, P .J. *The Wool Trade in Tudor and Stuart England* (1962)

Bradley, H. 'The Datini Factors in London, 1380–1410', in Clayton *et al.*, *Trade, Devotion and Governance*

Bratchel, M. E. 'Italian Merchant Organisation and Business Relationships in Early Tudor London', *Jnl European Econ. Hist.*, 7 no. 1 (1978)

Braudel, F. *Civilisation and Capitalism, 15th–18th Century*, 3 vols., translated by S. Reynolds (1982–3)

Bridbury, A. R. *England and the Salt Trade in the Later Middle Ages* (Oxford, 1955)
Medieval English Clothmaking. An Economic Survey (1982)

Brigden, S. *London and the Reformation* (Oxford, 1989)

Britnell, R. H. 'Colchester Courts and Court Records, 1310–1525', *Trans. Essex Archl. Hist. Soc.*, 3rd ser., 17 (1986)
Growth and Decline in Colchester, 1300–1525 (Cambridge, 1986)
The Commercialisation of English Society, 1000–1500 (Cambridge, 1993)
'The Black Death in English Towns', *Urban History*, 21 (1994)

Britnell, R. H. and Hatcher, J. eds. *Progress and Problems in Medieval England* (Cambridge, 1996)

Brown, A. D. *Popular Piety in Late Medieval England. The Diocese of Salisbury 1250–1550* (Oxford, 1993)

Brown, A. N., Greville, J. C. and Turner, R. C. *Watergate Street. The Rows Research Project*, Chester City Council (1987)

Brown, E. A. R. 'Death and the Human Body in the Later Middle Ages: The Legislation of Boniface VIII on the Division of the Corpse', *Viator*, 12 (1981)

Burgess, C. R. '"For the Increase of Divine Service": Chantries in the Parish in Late Medieval Bristol', *Jnl Eccl. Hist.*, 36 (1985)
'"By Quick and by Dead": Wills and Pious Provision in Late Medieval Bristol', *EHR*, 102 (1987)
'A Service for the Dead: The Anniversary in Late Medieval Bristol', *Trans. Bristol & Glos. Arch. Soc.*, 105 (1987)
'"A Fond Thing Vainly Invented": An Essay on Purgatory and Pious Motive in Later Medieval England', in S. J. Wright, ed., *Parish Church and People* (1988)
'Late Medieval Wills and Pious Convention: Testamentary Evidence Reconsidered', in M. A. Hicks, ed., *Profit, Piety and the Professions in Later Medieval England* (Gloucester, 1990)

Butcher, A. F. 'The Origins of Romney Freemen, 1433–1523', *EcHR*, 2nd ser., 27 (1974)
'Freemen Admissions and Urban Occupations', unpublished paper, Urban History Conference, Canterbury (1983)

Butler, L. H. 'Archbishop Melton, his Neighbours, and his Kinsmen, 1317–1340', *Jnl Eccl. Hist.*, 2 (1951)

Cameron, Euan *The European Reformation* (Oxford, 1991)

Campbell, J. 'Norwich', in Lobel, *The Atlas of Historic Towns*

Carlton, C. *The Court of Orphans* (Leicester, 1974)

Carpenter, C. 'The Religion of the Gentry of Fifteenth-Century England', in D. Williams, ed., *England in the Fifteenth Century. The Proceedings of the 1986 Harlaxton Symposium* (Woodbridge, 1987)

Carr, D. R. 'The Problem of Urban Patriciates: Office Holders in Fifteenth-Century Salisbury', *Wilts Arch. & Natural Hist. Magazine*, 83 (1990)

Carrington, P. *English Heritage. Book of Chester* (1995)

Carson, E. 'Customs Records as a Source for Historical Research', *Archive*, 58 (1977)

Carus-Wilson, E. M. 'The Merchant Adventurers of Bristol in the Fifteenth Century', *TRHS*, 4th ser., 11 (1928)

'Iceland Trade', in Power and Postan, *Studies in English Trade*

'The Origins and Development of the Merchant Adventurers Organisation in London as shown in their own Medieval Records', *EcHR*, 4 (1933)

'Evidence of Industrial Growth on some Fifteenth Century Manors', *EcHR*, 2nd ser., 12 (1959)

Medieval Merchant Venturers (paperback edn. 1967)

'Bristol', in Lobel, *The Atlas of Historic Towns*

Carus-Wilson, E. M. and Coleman, O. *England's Export Trade 1275–1547* (Oxford, 1963).

Charles, L. and Duffin, L. eds. *Women and Work in Pre-Industrial England* (1985)

Chiffoleau, J. 'Les testaments provençaux et comtadins à la fin du moyen âge: richesse documentaire et problèmes d'exploitation', in P. Brezzi and E. Lee, eds., *Sources of Social History: Private Acts of the Late Middle Ages*, (Toronto, 1984)

Childs, W. R. *Anglo-Castilian Trade in the Middle Ages* (Manchester, 1978)

'England's Iron Trade in the Fifteenth Century', *EcHR*, 2nd ser., 34 (1981)

'To Oure Losse and Hindrance', in J. I. Kermode, ed., *Enterprise and Individuals in Fifteenth-Century England* (Stroud, 1991)

'England's Icelandic Trade in the Fifteenth Century: The Role of the Port of Hull', *Northern Seas Yearbook*, 5 (1995)

'The English Export Trade in Cloth in the Fourteenth Century', in Britnell and Hatcher, *Progress and Problems*

Chorley, P. 'English Cloth Exports During the Thirteenth and Early Fourteenth Centuries: The Continental Evidence', *Hist. Research*, 61 (1988)

Clark, E. 'Debt Litigation in a Late Medieval Vill', in J. A. Raftis, ed., *Pathways to Medieval Peasants* (Toronto, 1981)

Clark P. and Slack, P. *English Towns in Transition 1500–1700* (Oxford, 1976)

Clarke, E. 'City Orphans and Custody Law in Medieval England', *Am. Jnl Legal Hist.*, 34 (1990)

Clayton, D. J., Davies, R. G. and McNiven, P. eds. *Trade, Devotion and Governance* (Stroud, 1994)

Coleman, D. C. 'Proto-Industrialisation: A Concept Too Many', *EcHR*, 2nd ser., 36 (1983)

Coleman, O. 'Trade and Prosperity in the Fifteenth Century: Some Aspects of the Trade of Southampton', *EcHR*, 2nd ser., 16 (1963–4)

Cooper, T. P. 'The Medieval Highways, Streets, Open Ditches and Sanitary Conditions of the City of York', *Yorks Arch. Jnl*, 28 (1913)

Cressy, D. 'Kinship and Kin Interaction in Early Modern England', *Past & Present*, 113 (1986)

Cullum, P. H. '"For Pore People Harberles": What was the Function of the Maisonsdieu?', in Clayton *et al.*, *Trade, Devotion and Governance*

Cullum, P. H. and Goldberg, P. J. P. 'Charitable Provision in Late Medieval York: "To the Praise of God and the Use of the Poor"', *Northern History*, 29 (1993)

Cuming, G. J. ed. *Studies in Church History*, IV (Leiden, 1967)

Davies W. K. D. & Herbert, D. T. *Communities Within Cities. An Urban Social Geography* (1993)

Day, J. 'The Great Bullion Famine of the Fifteenth Century', *Past & Present*, 79 (1978)
The Medieval Market Economy (Oxford, 1987)

Dickens, A. G. 'A Municipal Dissolution of Chantries at York, 1536', *Yorks Arch. Jnl*, 36 (1944–7)

Dinn, R. 'Baptism, Spiritual Kinship, and Popular Religion in Late Medieval Bury St Edmunds', *Bull. John Rylands Library*, 72 (1990)
'Death and Rebirth in Late Medieval Bury St Edmunds', in S. Bassett, ed., *Death in Towns. Urban Responses to the Dying and the Dead, 100–1600* (Leicester, 1992)
'"Monuments Answerable to Men's Worth": Burial Patterns, Social Status and Gender in Late Medieval Bury St Edmunds', *Jnl Eccl. Hist.*, 46 (1996)

Dobson, R. B. 'The Foundation of Perpetual Chantries by the Citizens of Medieval York', in Cuming, *Studies in Church History*.
'Admissions to the Freedom of the City of York in the Later Middle Ages', *EcHR*, 2nd ser., 26 (1973)
Durham Priory 1400–1450 (Cambridge, 1973)
'The Later Middle Ages, 1215–1500', in G. E. Aylmer and R. Cant, eds., *A History of York Minster* (Oxford, 1977)
'The Residentiary Canons of York in the Fifteenth Century', *Jnl Eccl. Hist.*, 30 (1979)
'Yorkshire Towns in the Late Fourteenth Century', *Miscellany*, Thoresby Soc., 18 (1983)
'Mendicant Ideal and Practice in Late Medieval York', in Addyman and Black, *Archaeological Papers Presented to M. W. Barley*
'The Risings in York, Beverley and Scarborough, 1380–1381', in Hilton and Aston, *The English Rising of 1381* (1984)
'Urban Decline in Late Medieval England', in Holt and Rosser, *The Medieval Town*
'Citizens and Chantries in Late Medieval York', in D. Abulafia, M. Franklin and M. Rubin, eds., *Church and City 1000–1500* (Cambridge, 1992)

Dobson, R. B. ed. *York City Chamberlains' Account Rolls 1396–1500*, Surtees Soc., 192 (1980)

Dollinger, P. *The German Hansa* (1964, translated 1970).

Dorrell, M. 'The Mayor of York and the Coronation Pageant', *Leeds Studies in English*, NS, 5 (1971)

Dorrell, M. and Johnston, F. 'The Domesday Pageant of the York Mercers', *Leeds Studies in English*, NS, 5 (1971)

Duffy, E. *The Stripping of the Altars. Traditional Religion in England 1400–1580* (New Haven and London, 1992).

Dyer, C. 'A Small Landowner in the Fifteenth Century', *Midland History*, 1 (1972)
Lords and Peasants in a Changing Society. The Estates of the Bishopric of Worcester, 680–1540 (Cambridge, 1980)
'Small-Town Conflict in the Later Middle Ages: Events at Shipston-on-Stour', *Urban History*, 19 (1992)

Edwards, K. *The English Secular Cathedrals in the Middle Ages* (2nd edn, Manchester, 1967)

Finucane, R. C. *Miracles and Pilgrims. Popular Beliefs in Medieval England* (1977)

'Sacred Corpse, Profane Carrion: Social Ideals and Death Rituals in the Late Middle Ages', in J. Whalley, ed., *Mirrors of Mortality. Studies in the Social History of Death* (1981)

Fleming, P. W. 'Charity, Faith and the Gentry of Kent, 1422–1529', in A. J. Pollard, ed., *Property and Politics. Essays in Later Medieval English History* (Gloucester, 1984)

Flower, C. T. 'The Beverley Town Riots, 1381–2', *TRHS*, NS, 19 (1905)

Foster, F. F. *The Politics of Stability: A Portrait of Rulers in Elizabethan London* (1977)

Fryde, E. B. 'Edward III's Wool Monopoly of 1337', *History*, NS, 37 (1952)

The Wool Accounts of William de la Pole, Borthwick Paper No. 25 (York, 1964)

Some Business Transactions of York Merchants: John Goldbeter, William Acastre and Partners, 1336–1349, Borthwick Paper No. 29 (York, 1966)

'Italian Maritime Trade with Medieval England (c. 1270–c. 1530)', *Recueils de la Société Jean Bodin*, 32 (1974)

William de la Pole. Merchant and King's Banker (1988)

Studies in Medieval Trade and Finance (1993)

Gee, E. A. 'The Architecture of York', in A. Stacpoole *et al.*, eds., *The Noble City of York* (York, 1972)

Gillett, E. and MacMahon, K. A. *A History of Hull* (Oxford, 1980)

Gittings, C. *Death, Burial and the Individual in Early Modern England* (1984)

Given-Wilson, C. J. 'Purveyance for the Royal Household, 1362–1413', *BIHR*, 56 (1983)

The Nobility of Later Medieval England: The Fourteenth-Century Political Community (1988)

Goldberg, P. J. P. 'Female Labour, Service, and Marriage in Northern Towns during the Later Middle Ages', *Northern History*, 22 (1986)

'Marriage, Migration, Servanthood and Life-cycle in Yorkshire Towns in the Later Middle Ages: Some York Cause Paper Evidence', *Continuity and Change*, 1 (1986).

'Mortality and Economic Change in the Diocese of York, 1390–1514', *Northern History*, 24 (1988)

'Women in Fifteenth-Century Town Life', in Thomson, *Towns and Townspeople*

'Urban Identity and the Poll Taxes of 1377, 1379, and 1381', *EcHR*, 2nd ser., 43 (1990)

Women, Work, and Life Cycle in a Medieval Economy. Women in York and Yorkshire c. 1300–1520 (Oxford, 1992)

Goodman, A. E. 'Responses to Requests in Yorkshire for Military Service under Henry V', *Northern History*, 17 (1981)

Gottfried, R. S. *Bury St Edmunds and the Urban Crisis 1290–1539* (Princeton, 1982)

Gras, N. S. B. *The Early English Customs* (Cambridge MA, 1918)

Business and Capitalism (Harvard, 1939)

Grassi, J. L. 'Royal Clerks from the Archdiocese of York in the 14th Century', *Northern History*, 5 (1970)

Gross, C. *The Gild Merchant. A Contribution to British Municipal History*, 2 vols. (Oxford, 1890)

Haigh, C. ed. *The English Reformation Revised* (Cambridge, 1987)

Hammer, C. J. 'Anatomy of an Oligarchy: The Oxford Town Council in the Fifteenth and Sixteenth Centuries', *Jnl British Studies*, 18 (1979)

Hanawalt, B. A. 'Keepers of the Lights: Late Medieval English Parish Gilds', *Jnl Med. & Ren. Studies*, 14 (1984)

'Re-marriage as an Option for Urban and Rural Widows in Late Medieval England', in S. S. Walker, ed., *Wife and Widow in Medieval England* (Ann Arbor, 1993)

Hanawalt, B. A. and Reyerson, K. L. eds. *City and Spectacle in Medieval Europe* (Minnesota, 1994)

Hanham, A. 'Foreign Exchange and the English Wool Merchant in the Late 15th Century', *BIHR*, 44 (1973)

'Profits on English Wool Exports, 1472–1544', *BIHR*, 55 (1982)

The Celys and Their World. An English Merchant Family of the Fifteenth Century (Cambridge 1985).

Hanham, A. ed. *The Cely Letters 1472–1488*, EETS (Oxford, 1975)

Harding, V. 'Burial Choice and Burial Location in Later Medieval London', in S. Bassett, ed., *Death in Towns: Urban Responses to the Dying and the Dead, 100–1600* (Leicester, 1992)

Harris, B. *Chester*, Bartholomew City Guides (Chester, 1979)

Harrison, F. *Life in a Medieval College: The Story of the Vicars-Choral of York Minster* (1952)

Harriss, G. L. 'The Struggle for Calais: An Aspect of the Rivalry between Lancaster and York', *EHR*, 75 (1960)

Harvey, B. *Westminster Abbey and its Estates in the Middle Ages* (Oxford, 1977)

Harvey, J. H. 'Richard II and York', in Barron and Du Boulay, *Reign of Richard II*

Hastings, M. *The Court of Common Pleas in the Fifteenth Century* (Ithaca, 1947)

Hatcher, J. *Plague, Population and the English Economy 1348–1530* (1977)

'The Great Slump of the Mid-Fifteenth Century', in Britnell and Hatcher, *Progress and Problems*

Heath, P. 'Urban Piety in the Later Middle Ages: The Evidence of Hull Wills', in R. B. Dobson, ed., *The Church, Politics and Patronage in the Fifteenth Century* (Gloucester, 1984)

Heaton, H. *The Yorkshire Woollen and Worsted Industries* (2nd. edn, Oxford, 1965)

Helmholz, R. H. 'Roman Law and Guardianship, 1300–1600', *Tulane Law Rev.*, 52 (1978)

'Usury and the Medieval English Church Courts', *Speculum*, 61 (1986)

Henratta, J. A. 'Social History as Lived and Written', an *AHR* forum, *Am. Hist. Rev.*, 84 (1979)

Herlihy, D. and Klapisch-Zuber, C. *Tuscans and Their Families: A Study of the Florentine Catasto of 1427* (New Haven, 1985)

Hey, D. *Yorkshire from AD 1000* (1986)

Hicks, M. A. 'Dynastic Change and Northern Society: The Career of the 4th Earl of Northumberland', *Northern History*, 14 (1978)

'Chantries, Obits and Almshouses: The Hungerford Foundations, 1325–1478', in Barron and Harper-Bill, eds., *Church in Pre-Reformation Society*

Hilton, R.H. 'Rent and Capital Formation in Feudal Society', in *Second International Conference of Economic History, Aix-en-Provence, 1962* (Paris, 1965)

'Some Problems of Urban Real Property in the Middle Ages', in C. H. Feinstein, ed., *Socialism, Capitalism and Economic Growth: Essays Presented to Maurice Dobb* (Oxford, 1967)

'The Small Town as Part of Peasant Society', in his *The English Peasantry in the Later Middle Ages* (Oxford, 1975)

'Medieval Market Towns and Simple Commodity Production', *Past & Present*, 109 (1985)

'Popular Movements in England at the End of the Fourteenth Century', in his *Class Conflict and the Crisis of Feudalism* (1985)

Hilton, R. H. and Aston, T. S. *The English Rising of 1381* (Cambridge, 1984)

363

Hodgson, P. '*Ignorantia Sacerdotum*: A Fifteenth Century Discourse on the Lambeth Constitutions', *R. of English Studies*, 24 (1948)

Hohenberg, P. M. and Lees, L. H. *The Making of Urban Europe 1000–1950* (Cambridge, MA, 1985).

Holdsworth, W. S. *A History of English Law*, 17 vols. (4th edn, 1935)

Holt, R. and Rosser, G. *The Medieval Town. A Reader in English Urban History 1200–1540* (1990)

Hoppit, J. 'The Use and Abuse of Credit in Eighteenth-Century England', in N. McKendrick and R. B. Outhwaite, eds., *Business Life and Public Policy. Essays in Honour of D. C. Coleman* (1986)

Horrox, R. *The Changing Plan of Hull 1290–1650* (Hull, 1978)
  'Urban Patronage and Patrons in the Fifteenth Century', in R. A. Griffiths, ed., *Patronage, the Crown, and the Provinces in Later Medieval England* (Gloucester, 1981)
  The de la Poles of Hull, East Yorkshire Local History Series, no. 38 (Hull, 1983)
  Richard III and the North (Hull, 1986)

Hoskins, W. G. 'The Elizabethan Merchants of Exeter', in S. T. Bindoff, J. Hurstfield and C. H. Williams, eds., *Elizabethan Government and Society* (1961)
  'English Provincial Towns in the Sixteenth Century', in his *Provincial England* (1963)
  The Age of Plunder (1976)

Howell, C. *Land, Family and Inheritance in Transition: Kibworth Harcourt, 1280–1700* (Cambridge, 1983)

Hulton, M. '"Company and Fellowship," The Medieval Weavers of Coventry', Dugdale Soc. Occasional Papers, No. 31 (1987)

Hutton, D. 'Women in Fourteenth Century Shrewsbury', in Charles and Duffin, *Women and Work*

Imray, J. M. '"Les bones gentes de la mercerye de Londres": A Study of the Membership of the Medieval Mercers' Company', in A. E. J. Hollaender and W. Kellaway, eds., *Studies in London History Presented to Philip Edmund Jones* (1969)

Jalland, P. 'Revolution in Northern Borough Representation', *Northern History*, 11 (1976)

James, M. K. 'A London Merchant in the Fourteenth Century', *EcHR*, 2nd ser., 8 (1955–6)
  Studies in the Medieval Wine Trade (1971)

James, M. R. 'Ritual, Drama, and Social Body in the Late Medieval English Town', *Past & Present*, 98 (1983)

Jennings, J. M. 'The Distribution of Landed Wealth in the Wills of London Merchants 1400–1450', *Medieval Studies*, 39 (1977)

Jewell, H. M. 'The Bringing up of Children in Good Learning and Manners: A Survey of the Secular Educational Provision in the North of England, *c.* 1350–1550', *Northern History*, 18 (1982)

Johnston A. F. and Rogerson, M. eds. *Records of Early English Drama: York*, 2 vols. (Toronto and London, 1979)

Jones, W. R. 'English Religious Brotherhoods and Medieval Lay Piety: The Inquiry of 1388–9', *The Historian: A Journal of History*, 36 (1974)

Jordan, W. K. *The Charities of London, 1480–1660* (1960)

Kaye, W. J. 'Yorkshiremen who Declined to take up their Knighthood', *Yorks Arch. Jnl*, 31 (1932–4)

Keen, M. *English Society in the Later Middle Ages 1348–1500* (1990)

Keene, D. *A Survey of Medieval Winchester*, 2 vols. (Oxford, 1985)

Kermode, J. I. 'The Merchants of Three Northern English Towns', in C. H. Clough, ed., *Profession, Vocation and Culture in Later Medieval England* (Liverpool, 1982)

'Urban Decline? The Flight from Office in Late Medieval York', *EcHR*, 2nd ser., 35 (1982)

'Merchants, Overseas Trade, and Urban Decline: York, Beverley, and Hull *c.* 1380–1500', *Northern History*, 23 (1987)

'Obvious Observations on Oligarchies in Late Medieval English Towns', in Thomson, *Towns and Townspeople*

'The Merchants of York, Beverley and Hull in the 14th and 15th Centuries' (Univ. of Sheffield PhD thesis, 1990)

'Money and Credit in the Fifteenth Century: Some Lessons from Yorkshire', *Business History Review*, 65 (1991)

'Medieval Indebtedness: The Regions *versus* London', in N. Rogers, ed., *England in the Fifteenth Century* (Stamford, 1994)

Kerridge, E. 'Wool Growing and Wool Textiles in Medieval and Early Modern Times', in J. G. Jenkins, ed., *The Wool Textile Industry in Britain* (1962)

Kershaw, I. *Bolton Priory. The Economy of a Northern Monastery, 1286–1325* (Oxford, 1973)

Kettle, A. J. '"My Wife Shall Have It": Marriage and Property in the Wills and Testaments of Later Medieval England', in E. M. Craik, ed., *Marriage and Property* (Aberdeen, 1984)

Kightly, C. and Semlyen, R. *Lords of the City. The Lord Mayors of York and their Mansion House* (York, 1980)

Knowles, D. and Hadcock, N. eds. *Medieval Religious Houses in England and Wales* (1953)

Kowaleski, M. 'The Commercial Dominance of a Medieval Provincial Oligarchy: Exeter in the Late Fourteenth Century', *Medieval Studies*, 46 (1984)

'Women's Work in a Market Town: Exeter in the late Fourteenth Century', in B. A. Hanawalt, ed., *Women and Work in Pre-Industrial England* (Bloomington, 1986)

'The History of Urban Families in Medieval England', *Jnl Med. Hist.*, 14 (1988)

'Port Towns in Fourteenth-Century Devon', in M. Duffy, B. Greenhill, S. Fisher and J. Youings, eds., *A New Maritime History of Devon*, 1 (1992)

Local Markets and Regional Trade in Medieval Exeter (Cambridge, 1995)

Kowaleski, M. and Bennett, J. M. 'Crafts, Gilds and Women in the Middle Ages', *Signs*, 14, no. 2 (1989)

Krause, J. T. 'The Medieval Household – Large or Small?', *EcHR*, 2nd ser., 9 (1956–7)

Kreider, A. *English Chantries, the Road to Dissolution* (Cambridge MA, 1979)

Lacey, K. 'Women and Work in 14th and 15th-Century London', in Charles and Duffin, *Women and Work*

Lamb, G. D. and Plucknett, T. F. T. *A Concise History of the Common Law* (5th edn, 1956)

Lamb, H. H. *Climate, Past, Present and Future*, 2 vols. (1977)

Langton, J. 'Late Medieval Gloucester: Some Data from a Rental of 1455', *Trans. Institute British Geographers*, NS, 2 (1977)

Laslett, P. and Wall, R. eds. *Household and Family in Past Time* (Cambridge, 1972)

Le Goff, J. *The Birth of Purgatory* (translated in 1984 from the French 1981 edition)

Lipson, E. *A Short History of Wool and its Manufacture* (1953)

Lloyd, T. H. *The Movement of Wool Prices in Medieval England*, *EcHR*, Supplement No. 6 (1973)

The English Wool Trade in the Middle Ages (Cambridge, 1977)

Alien Merchants in England in the High Middle Ages (Brighton, 1983)

Select bibliography

England and the German Hanse 1157–1611 (Cambridge, 1991)

Lobel, M. D. *The Atlas of Historic Towns*, 2 vols. (1969, 1975)

MacKie, P. 'Chaplains in the Diocese of York, 1480–1530: The Testamentary Evidence', *Yorks Arch. Jnl*, 58 (1986)

Masschaele, J. 'Transport Costs in Medieval England', *EcHR*, 2nd ser., 46 (1993)

Mate, M. 'Agrarian Economy after the Black Death: The Manors of Canterbury Cathedral Priory, 1348–91', *EcHR*, 2nd ser., 37 (1984)

'The Estates of Canterbury Cathedral Priory before the Black Death', *Studies in Medieval and Renaissance History*, 8 (1987)

McCaffrey, W. T. *Exeter 1540–1640: The Growth of an English Town* (1958)

McGrath, P. V. 'The Wills of Bristol Merchants in the Great Orphan Books', *Trans. Bristol & Glos. Arch. Soc.*, 68 (1951)

McHardy, A. K. 'Some Late-Medieval Eton College Wills', *Jnl Eccl. Hist.*, 27 (1977)

McKisack, M. *The Parliamentary Representation of English Boroughs during the Middle Ages* (Oxford, 1932)

McLure, P. 'Patterns of Migration in the Late Middle Ages: The Evidence of English Place-Name Surnames', *EcHR*, 2nd ser., 32 (1979)

McRee, B. R. 'Religious Gilds and the Regulation of Behavior in Late Medieval Towns', in J. Rosenthal and C. Richmond, eds., *People, Politics and Community in the Later Middle Ages* (1987)

'Religious Gilds and Civic Order: The Case of Norwich in the Late Middle Ages', *Speculum*, 67 (1992)

'Charity and Gild Solidarity in Late Medieval England', *Jnl British Studies*, 32 (1993)

'Unity or Division? The Social Meaning of Guild Ceremony in Urban Communities', in Hanawalt and Reyerson, *City and Spectacle in Medieval Europe*

Michel, F. *Histoire du commerce et de la navigation à Bordeaux*, 1 (Bordeaux, 1867)

Miller, E. 'The Fortunes of the English Textile Industry in the Thirteenth Century', *EcHR*, 2nd ser., 18 (1965)

Miller, E. and Hatcher, J. *Medieval England Towns, Commerce and Crafts 1086–1348* (1995)

Mills, David. 'Chester Ceremonial: Re-creation and Recreation in the English "Medieval" town', *UHY* (1991)

Milsom, S. F. C. 'Account Stated in the Action of Debt', *Law Quarterly Rev.*, 82 (1966)

Historical Foundations of the Common Law (2nd edn, 1981)

'Sale of Goods in the Fifteenth Century', *Law Quarterly Rev.*, 77 (1981)

Miskimin, H. *The Economy of Early Renaissance Europe, 1300–1460* (Cambridge, 1975)

Mollat, M. *Le commerce maritime normand à la fin du moyen âge* (Paris, 1952)

Moran, J. *Education and Learning in the City of York, 1300–1560*, Borthwick Paper No. 55 (York, 1979)

Morimoto, N. 'The English Wine Trade and Durham Cathedral Priory in the Fourteenth Century', *Nagoya Gakuin University Review*, 10 (1973)

Munro, J. H. 'Monetary Contraction and Industrial Change in the Medieval Low Countries, 1335–1500', in N. J. Mayhew, *Coinage in the Low Countries 880–1550* British Archaeological Reports, 54 (Oxford, 1979)

'An Economic Aspect of the Collapse of the Anglo-Burgundian Alliance, 1428–1442', *EHR*, 85 (1970)

Wool, Cloth, and Gold. The Struggle for Bullion in Anglo-Burgundian Trade 1340–1478 (Toronto, 1972)

'Wool-Price Schedules and the Qualities of English Wools in the Later Middle Ages c. 1270–1499', *Textile History*, 9 (1978)

'Bullionism and the Bill of Exchange in England, 1272–1663: A Study in Monetary Management and Popular Prejudice', in *The Dawn of Modern Banking*, Center for Medieval and Renaissance Studies, University of California, Los Angeles (New Haven and London, 1979)

'The 1357 Wool-Price Schedule and the Decline of Yorkshire Wool Values', *Textile History*, 10 (1979)

'Bullion Flows and Monetary Contraction in Late-Medieval England and the Low Countries', in Richards, *Precious Metals*

'The Medieval Scarlet and the Economics of Sartorial Splendour', in N. B. Harte and K. G. Ponting, eds., *Cloth and Clothing in Medieval Europe* (1983)

'Patterns of Trade, Money, and Credit', in T. A. Brady, H. A. Oberman and J. D. Tracy, eds., *Handbook of European History 1400–1600: Late Middle Ages, Renaissance and Reformation*, 1 (Leiden, New York, 1994)

Murray, J. 'Kinship and Friendship: The Perception of Family by Clergy and Laity in Late Medieval London', *Albion*, 20 (1988)

Myers, A. R. 'The Wealth of Richard Lyons', in T. A. Sandquist and M. R. Powicke, eds., *Essays in Medieval History Presented to Bertie Wilkinson* (Toronto, 1969)

Nelson, A. H. *The Medieval English Stage: Corpus Christi Pageants and Plays* (Chicago, 1974)

Nicholas, D. M. 'The English Trade at Bruges in the Last Years of Edward III', *Jnl Med. Hist.*, 5 (1979)

The Domestic Life of a Medieval City. Women, Children, and the Family in Fourteenth-Century Ghent (Lincoln NE, 1985)

Nicholson, G. H. 'Bristol Merchants and their Wills in the Later Middle Ages' (Univ. of Birmingham MA thesis, 1970)

Nightingale, P. 'Capitalists, Crafts and Constitutional Change in Late Fourteenth-Century London', *Past & Present*, 124 (1989)

'Monetary Contraction and Mercantile Credit in Later Medieval England', *EcHR*, 2nd ser., 43 (1990)

A Medieval Mercantile Community. The Grocers' Company and the Politics and Trade of London, 1000–1485 (Yale, 1995)

'The Growth of London in the Medieval Economy', in Britnell and Hatcher, *Progress and Problems*

North, D. C. 'Transaction Costs in History', *Jnl European Econ. Hist.*, 14 (1985)

O'Connor, S. J. 'Adam Fraunceys and John Pyel: Perceptions of Status Among Merchants in Fourteenth-Century London', in D. J. Clayton, R. G. Davies and P. McNiven, eds., *Trade, Devotion and Governance. Papers in Later Medieval History* (Stroud, 1994)

'Finance, Diplomacy and Politics: Royal Service by two London Merchants in the Reign of Edward III', *BIHR*, 68 (1994)

Palliser, D. M. 'Some Aspects of the Social and Economic History of York in the Sixteenth Century' (Univ. of Oxford DPhil thesis, 1968)

The Reformation in York, 1534–53, Borthwick Paper No. 40 (York, 1971)

'The Union of Parishes at York, 1547–86', *Yorks Arch. Jnl*, 46 (1974)

Tudor York (Oxford, 1979)

'Richard III and York', in Horrox, *Richard III and the North*

'A Regional Capital as Magnet: Immigrants to York, 1477–1566', *Yorks Arch. Jnl*, 57 (1985)

'Urban Society', in R. Horrox, ed., *Fifteenth-Century Attitudes. Perceptions of Society in Late Medieval England* (Cambridge, 1994)

Palmer, R. C. *English Law in the Age of the Black Death* (Chapel Hill, 1993)

Pantin, W. A. 'The Merchants' Houses and Warehouses of King's Lynn', and 'Medieval English Town-House Plans', *Med. Arch.*, 6–7 (1962–3)

Pelham, R. A. 'Medieval Foreign Trade, Eastern Ports', in H. C. Darby, ed., *An Historical Geography of England Before 1800 AD* (Cambridge, 1936)

Pevsner, N. *The Buildings of England. Yorkshire: York and the East Riding* (1972)

Phythian-Adams, C. 'Ceremony and the Citizen: The Communal Year at Coventry 1450–1550', in P. Clark and P. Slack, eds., *Crisis and Order in English Towns 1500–1700* (1972)

    Desolation of a City. Coventry and the Urban Crisis of the Late Middle Ages (Cambridge, 1979)

    'Coventry and the Problem of Urban Decay in the Late Middle Ages', unpublished paper, Urban History Conference, London, 1977

Platt, C. *Medieval Southampton: The Port and Trading Community, AD 1000–1600* (1973)

    The English Medieval Town (1976)

Plucknett, T. F. T. *The Legislation of Edward I* (1949)

    A Concise History of the Common Law (5th edn, 1956)

Pollard, A. J. 'The Tyranny of Richard III', *Jnl Med. Stud.*, 3 (1977)

    The Wars of the Roses (1988)

    'The North-Eastern Economy and the Agrarian Crisis of 1438–40', *Northern History*, 25 (1989)

    North-Eastern England During the Wars of the Roses. Lay Society, War, and Politics 1450–1500 (Oxford, 1990)

Pollock, F. and Maitland. F. W. *The History of English Law Before the Time of Edward I* (2nd edn, 1911)

Postan, M. M. 'Credit in Medieval Trade', *EcHR*, 1 (1927–8)

    'Private Financial Instruments in Medieval England', in his *Medieval Trade and Finance* (Cambridge, 1933)

Postles, D. 'Fleece Weights and Wool Supply, *c.* 1250–*c.* 1350', *Textile History*, 12 (1981)

Pounds, N. G. *An Economic History of Medieval Europe* (2nd edn, 1994)

Power, E. 'Thomas Betson, a Merchant of the Staple in the Fifteenth Century', and 'Thomas Paycocke of Coggeshall, an Essex Clothier in the Days of Henry VII', in her *Medieval People* (1924)

    The Wool Trade in English Medieval History (Oxford, 1941)

    'The Wool Trade in the Reign of Edward IV', *Camb. Hist. Jnl*, 1 (1926–8)

Power, E. and Postan, M. M. *Studies in English Trade in the Fifteenth Century* (Cambridge, 1933)

Raban, S. 'Mortmain in England', *Past & Present*, 62 (1974)

Ramsay, G. D. *English Overseas Trade during the Centuries of Emergence* (1957)

Rappaport, S. *Worlds within Worlds: Structures of Life in Sixteenth-Century London* (Cambridge, 1989)

Rawcliffe, C. '"That Kindliness Should be Cherished More, and Discord Driven Out": The Settlement of Commercial Disputes by Arbitration in Later Medieval England', in J. I. Kermode, ed., *Enterprise and Individuals in Fifteenth-Century England* (Stroud, 1991).

RCHM *Beverley. An Archaeological and Architectural Study*, Supplementary Series, 4 (1982)

    City of York, III, South-west of the Ouse (1972)

Reed, C. G. 'Transaction Costs and Differential Growth in Seventeenth Century Western Europe', *Jnl Econ. Hist.*, 32 (1973)

Rees-Jones, S. R. 'Some Aspects of the Topography and Economy of Medieval York' (Univ. of York DPhil thesis, 1987)

Rees-Jones, S. R. ed. *York 600: The Government of Medieval York. Essays in Commemoration of the 1396 Royal Charter*, Borthwick Studies in History, 3 (York, 1997)

Reid, R. R. *The King's Council in the North* (1921)

Renouard, Y. ed. *Bordeaux sous les rois d'Angleterre* (Bordeaux, 1965)

Reynolds, S. *An Introduction to the History of English Medieval Towns* (Oxford, 1977)

'Medieval Urban History and the History of Political Thought', *UHY* (1982)

'Social Mentalities and the Case of Medieval Scepticism', *TRHS*, 6th ser., 1 (1990)

Richards, J. F. ed. *Precious Metals in the Later Medieval and Early Modern Worlds* (North Carolina, 1983)

Richie, C. I. A. *The Ecclesiastical Courts of York* (Arbroath, 1956)

Richmond, C. F. 'English Naval Power in the Fifteenth Century', *History*, 52 (1967)

'The War at Sea', in K. Fowler, ed., *The Hundred Years War* (1971)

'Religion and the Fifteenth-Century Gentleman', in R. B. Dobson, ed., *The Church, Politics and Patronage in the Fifteenth Century* (1984)

'The English Gentry and Religion *c.* 1500', in C. Harper-Bill, ed., *Religious Belief and Ecclesiastical Careers in Late Medieval England* (Woodbridge, 1991)

Rigby, S. H. 'Urban "Oligarchy" in Late Medieval England', in Thomson, *Towns and Townspeople*

Medieval Grimsby: Growth and Decline (Hull, 1993)

English Society in the Later Middle Ages. Class, Status and Gender (1995)

'Power and Authority', in D. M. Palliser, ed., *The Cambridge Urban History of Britain*, I, (Cambridge, forthcoming)

Rogers, A. 'Late Medieval Stamford: A Study of the Town Council, 1465–92', in A. Everitt, ed., *Perspectives in English Urban History* (1973)

Roover, R. de *Money, Banking and Credit in Medieval Bruges* (Cambridge MA, 1948)

Rosenthal, J. T. *The Purchase of Paradise* (1972)

'Aristocratic Widows in Fifteenth-Century England', in B. J. Harris and J. K. McNamara, eds., *Women and the Structure of Society* (Durham NC, 1984)

'Heirs' Ages and Family Succession in Yorkshire, 1399–1422', *Yorks Arch. Jnl*, 56 (1984)

Roskell, J. S. *The History of Parliament. The House of Commons 1386–1421*, 4 vols. (Stroud, 1992)

Rosser, G. 'The Essence of Medieval Urban Communities: The Vill of Westminster, 1200–1540', *TRHS*, 5th ser., 34 (1984)

'Communities of Parish and Guild in the Late Middle Ages', in S. J. Wright, ed., *Parish, Church and People. Local Studies in Lay Religion 1350–1750* (1988)

'London and Westminster: The Suburb in the Urban Economy in the Late Middle Ages', in Thomson, *Towns and Townspeople*

Medieval Westminster 1200–1540 (Oxford, 1989)

'Parochial Conformity and Voluntary Religion in Late-Medieval England', *T.R.H.S.*, 6th ser. 1 (1991).

'Going to the Fraternity Feast: Commensality and Social Relations in Late Medieval England', *Jnl British Studies*, 33 (1994)

Rotz, R. A. 'Investigating Urban Uprisings with Examples from Hanseatic Towns, 1374–1416', in W. J. Jordan, B. McNab and T. F. Ruiz, eds., *Order and Innovation in the Middle Ages. Essays in Honor of Joseph R. Strayer* (Princeton, 1976)

Routh, P. E. S. 'A Gift and its Giver: John Walker and the East Window of Holy Trinity Goodramgate, York', *Yorks Arch. Jnl*, 58 (1986)

Rubin, M. *Charity and Community in Medieval Cambridge* (Cambridge, 1987)
 Corpus Christi: The Eucharist in Late Medieval Culture (Cambridge, 1991)

Ruddock, A. 'Alien Hosting in Southampton in the 15th Century', *EcHR*, 16 (1946)
 'London Capitalists and the Decline of Southampton in the Early Tudor Period', *EcHR*, 2nd ser., 2 (1950)

Ruiz, T. F. 'The Transformation of the Castilian Municipalities: The Case of Burgos 1248–1350', *Past & Present*, 77 (1977)

Sabine, E. L. 'City Cleaning in Medieval London', *Speculum*, 12 (1937)

Sacks, D. H. *The Widening Gate. Bristol and the Atlantic Economy 1450–1700* (Berkeley and London, 1991)

Salzman, L. F. *English Trade in the Later Middle Ages* (Oxford, 1931)

Saul, N. 'The Religious Sympathies of the Gentry in Gloucestershire, 1200–1500', *Trans. Bristol & Glos. Arch. Soc.*, 98 (1980)

Sayles, G. 'The Dissolution of a Guild at York in 1306', *EHR*, 55 (1940)

Scammell, G. V. 'English Merchant Shipping at the End of the Middle Ages: Some East Coast Evidence', *EcHR*, 2nd ser., 13 (1961)

Scarisbrick, J. J. *The Reformation and the English People* (Oxford, 1984)

Schofield, P. R. 'Debt and Credit in the Medieval English Countryside', in M. Berthe and F. Brumont, eds., *Endettement et credit dans les campagnes d'Europe au Moyen Age et a l'Epoque Moderne* (Toulouse, 1997)

Shaw, D. G. *The Creation of a Community. The City of Wells in the Middle Ages* (Oxford, 1993)

Sheehan, M. M. *The Medieval Will* (Toronto, 1963)

Simpson, A. W. B. *An Introduction to the History of the Land Law* (Oxford, 1961)
 A History of the Common Law of Contract. The Rise of the Action of Assumpsit (Oxford, 1987)

Smith, A. H. 'A York Pageant, 1486', *London Medieval Studies* (1939)

Spufford, M. 'The Scribes of Villagers' Wills in the Sixteenth and Seventeenth Centuries', *Local Population Studies*, No. 7 (autumn 1971)

Spufford, P. 'Calais and its Mint: Part 1', in N. J. Mayhew, ed., *Coinage in the Low Countries, 880–1500*, British Archaeological Reports, 54 (Oxford, 1979)
 A Handbook of Medieval Exchange (1986)
 Money and its Use in Medieval Europe (Cambridge, 1988)

Stacey, M. 'The Myth of Community Studies', *British Jnl of Sociology*, 20 (1969)

Stephenson, M. J. 'Wool Yields in the Medieval Economy', *EcHR*, 2nd ser., 41 (1988)

Stevenson, A. W. K. 'Trade Between Scotland and the Low Countries in the Later Middle Ages' (Univ. of Aberdeen PhD thesis, 1982)

Sumption, J. *Pilgrimages. An Image of Medieval Religion* (1975)

Sutton, A. 'William Shore, Merchant of London and Derby', *Derbys Arch. Jnl*, 106 (1986)
 'Alice Claver, Silkwoman', in Barron and Sutton, *Medieval London Widows*

Swanson, H. 'The Illusion of Economic Structure: Craft Guilds in Late Medieval English Towns', *Past & Present*, 121 (1988)
 Medieval Artisans. An Urban Class in Late Medieval England (Oxford, 1989)

Swanson, R. N. *Church and Society in Late Medieval England* (Oxford, 1989)

Tanner, N. 'Popular Religion in Norwich with Special Reference to the Evidence of Wills, 1370–1552' (Univ. of Oxford DPhil thesis, 1973)
 The Church in Late Medieval Norwich 1370–1532 (Toronto, 1984)

Taylor, M. *Community, Anarchy and Liberty* (Cambridge, 1982)

Thompson, A. Hamilton 'Registers of the Archdeacons of Richmond', *Yorks Arch. Jnl*, 25 (1919)

Thomson, J. A. F. 'Clergy and Laity in London, 1376–1531' (Univ. of Oxford DPhil thesis, 1960)

'Piety and Charity in Late Medieval London', *Jnl Eccl. Hist.*, 16 (1965)

Towns and Townspeople in the Fifteenth Century (Gloucester, 1988)

'Wealth, Poverty and Mercantile Ethics in Late Medieval London', in J-P. Genet and N. Bulst, eds., *La ville, la bourgeoisies et la genèse de l'état moderne (xiiᵉ–xviiiᵉ siècles)* (Paris, 1988)

The Early Tudor Church and Society (1993)

Thrupp, S. L. 'The Grocers of London, a Study of Distributive Trade', in Power and Postan, *Studies in English Trade*

The Merchant Class of Medieval London (Ann Arbor, 1948)

'The Problem of Replacement Rates in the Late Medieval English Population', *EcHR*, 2nd ser., 18 (1965)

Tickhill, J. *A History of the Town and County of Kingston-upon-Hull* (Hull, 1878)

Tillot, P. M. ed. *Victoria History of the County of York. City of York* (1961)

Todd, B. J. 'The Remarrying Widow: A Stereotype Reconsidered', in M. Prior, ed., *Women in English Society 1500–1800* (1985)

Tonnies, F. *Community and Society*, translated by C. P. Loomis (2nd edn, New Brunswick, 1988)

Unwin, G. *The Gilds and Companies of London* (1908)

Unwin, G. ed. *Finance and Trade under Edward III* (1918)

Vale, M. G. A. *English Gascony 1399–1453* (Oxford, 1970)

Piety, Charity and Literacy Among the Yorkshire Gentry, 1370–1480, Borthwick Paper No. 50 (York, 1976)

Vann, R. T. 'Wills and the Family in an English Town: Banbury, 1550–1800', *Jnl Family Hist.*, 4 (1979)

Ward, J. C. 'Wealth and Family in Early Sixteenth Century Colchester', *Essex Archaeology and History*, 21 (1990)

Wedgwood, J. C. and Holt, A. D. *Histories of Parliament. Biographies of the Members of the Commons House 1430–1509* (1936)

Westlake, H. F. *The Parish Gilds of Medieval England* (1919)

White, E. *The St Christopher and St George Guild of York*, Borthwick Papers, no. 72 (York, 1987)

Wilkinson, B. *The Medieval Council of Exeter*, History of Exeter Research Group, Monograph No. 4 (Manchester, n.d.)

Williams, G.A. *Medieval London: From Commune to capital* (1963)

Winkelmann, J. ed. *Wirtschaft und Gesellschaft* (Tubingen, 1972), cited in J-P. Genet and N. Bulst, eds., *La ville, la bourgeoisie et la genèse de l'état moderne (xiiᵉ–xviiiᵉ siècles)* (Paris, 1988)

Wolff, P. 'English Cloth in Toulouse, 1380–1450', *EcHR* 2nd ser., 2 (1950)

Wood, R. A. 'London and Bury St Edmunds: A comparative Study of Urban Piety *c.* 1380–*c.* 1415', unpublished paper circulated to the Fifteenth-Century Colloquium at Winchester in 1987

Wood-Legh, K. *Perpetual Chantries in Britain* (1965)

Wroot, H. E. 'Yorkshire Abbeys and the Wool Trade', *Miscellanea*, Thoresby Soc., 33 (1935)

Zell, M. L. 'The Use of Religious Preambles as a Measure of Religious Belief in the Sixteenth Century', *BIHR*, 50 (1977)

INDEX

and see appendices

Cambridge Studies in Medieval Life and Thought
Fourth series

Titles in series

★ Also published as a paperback